# Constructivism
*in Practice*

# Constructivism
## in Practice

## Methods and Challenges

*Cynthia Franklin and Paula S. Nurius*

Families International, Inc., Milwaukee, Wisconsin

Copyright 1998 Families International, Inc.
Publishing in association with Family Service America
11700 West Lake Park Drive
Milwaukee, WI 53224

Library of Congress Cataloging–in–Publication Data

Constructivism in practice : methods and challenges / edited by Cynthia Franklin
 and Paula S. Nurius.
    p.    cm.
  Includes bibliographical references.
  ISBN 0–87304–303–0
  1. Social service—Psychological aspects. 2. Constructivism (Psychology)
3. Social perception.  I. Franklin, Cynthia. II. Nurius, Paula S.
HV40.C663  1997
361.3'2—dc21                                 97–36573

Printed in the United States of America

*To our most recent and beloved constructions*

*Anova Francesca Nurius*
*and*
*Christina Mae Franklin*

# Table of Contents

# About the Editors

**Cynthia Franklin** is associate professor in the School of Social Work at the University of Texas at Austin, where she teaches courses on clinical practice and research. Dr. Franklin has published widely on clinical assessment, practice theory, research methods, and child and family practice. She is the co-author, with Dr. Catheleen Jordan, of *Clinical Assessment for Social Workers: Quantitative and Qualitative Methods* and *Family Practice: Brief Systems Methods for Social Work*. Dr. Franklin maintains a part-time clinical practice specializing in marriage and family therapy.

**Paula S. Nurius** is professor and director of the doctoral program in the School of Social Work at the University of Washington. Dr. Nurius has focused her scholarship primarily on cognitive analyses of the self-concept and its function in self-management as well as perception and decision making under conditions of stress or uncertainty. Her current research focuses on factors that influence women's appraisals of and coping with counterintuitive and complex threats such as harm from partners or acquaintances as well as from health and social conditions. She is the co-author of *Social Cognition and Individual Change* and *Human Services Practice, Evaluation, and Computers* and co-editor of *Controversial Issues in Social Work Research and Education* and *Research for Empowerment Practice*.

# Contributors

Ruth Anderson
Senior Lecturer, Massey University, Palmerston, North New Zealand

Insoo Kim Berg
Director, Brief Family Therapy Center, Milwaukee, Wisconsin

Sharon B. Berlin
Professor, School of Social Service Administration, University of Chicago

Joan L. Biever
Associate Professor, Department of Psychology, Our Lady of the Lake University

Aaron M. Brower
Associate Professor and Harold C. Bradley Faculty Fellow, Social Work and Integrated Liberal Studies, University of Wisconsin–Madison

Peter De Jong
Director of Social Work, Calvin College

John W. Gibson
Executive Director, Institute for Successful Aging, Seattle, Washington

Roberto Cortéz González
Associate Professor, Department of Educational Psychology and Special Services, College of Education, University of Texas at El Paso

Donald K. Granvold
Professor, School of Social Work, University of Texas at Arlington

Lorraine M. Gutiérrez
Associate Professor, School of Social Work, University of Michigan

Chad L. Hagans
Doctoral student, Department of Psychology, University of Florida

Catheleen Jordan
Professor, School of Social Work, University of Texas at Arlington

Joan Laird
Professor Emerita, Smith College School for Social Work

Charles Lord
Doctoral student, Social Work and Anthropology, University of Michigan

Michael J. Mahoney
Professor, Department of Psychology, University of North Texas

Jack Martin
Professor, Faculty of Education, Simon Fraser University

Greg J. Neimeyer
Professor, Department of Psychology, University of Florida

Robert A. Neimeyer
Professor, Department of Psychology, University of Memphis

Dennis Saleebey
Professor, School of Social Welfare, University of Kansas

Wes Shera
Dean, Faculty of Social Work, University of Toronto

Alan E. Stewart
Assistant Professor, Department of Psychology, University of Florida

Tracy Todd
President, Brief Therapy Institute of Denver, Inc., Westminster, Colorado

# Foreword

Franklin and Nurius have produced a timely and scholarly book. *Constructivism in Practice: Methods and Challenges* addresses an important new perspective in social work, one that has engendered considerable debate among scholars and practitioners. Defining and illustrating the methodology and practice of constructive theories is indeed a daunting task. Franklin and Nurius use their thorough grounding in the tradition of the profession and their considerable analytical skills to select authors and topics that uncover truths about human behaviors and relationships.

This book charts an intriguing possible path for social work in the 21st century. The various chapter authors do not shrink from the challenges inherent in constructivist theory and practice. The book goes farther than earlier works by developing important conceptual content and descriptive practical applications of constructivism, and by showing constructivism's ability to foster a greater understanding of client behaviors and other dynamics bearing upon the helping process.

The book is impressive in its breadth, covering a range of issues confronting the profession today, with content on current trends, assessment, and practice with individuals, groups, families, communities, and organizations. Franklin and Nurius have assembled an impressive array of contributors whose multiple areas of expertise are in full evidence. The profession's best intellectual leadership provides thoughtful analysis on the application and related challenges of constructivism.

*Constructivism in Practice* is the most current and comprehensive book on this topic in the literature. Scholars, students, and practitioners will find it a useful resource for many facets of social work research and practice.

*Paula Allen-Meares*
*Dean and Professor*
*School of Social Work*
*University of Michigan*

# Preface

## Constructivist Practice for Social Workers: New Directions in Social-Cognitive Theory

Therapies based on constructivist and social constructionist metatheory are proliferating within social work and allied professions (Brower & Nurius, 1993; Chapter 3). Diverse therapies are being grouped and defined under terms such as strengths perspective, constructivist, social constructionist, narrative, and postmodernist practice, and varying therapeutic approaches have influenced authors to develop schemes that define the differing constructivist and constructionist perspectives (Gonçalves, 1995; Lyddon, 1995; Martin & Sugarman, 1996; also see Chapter 3). R. A. Neimeyer and Mahoney (1995) identified these practice perspectives as representing the influence of constructivism in psychotherapy. Because of the diversity of theoretical models used in constructivist practice, neither constructivism nor social constructionism can be defined in simple terms. Diverse practice perspectives exemplify the proliferation of constructive (term implying the use of constructivist and constructionist perspectives) perspectives within psychotherapy: Kelly's personal construct theory (G. J. Neimeyer & Neimeyer, 1990); cognitive behavioral practice models (Mahoney, 1991; Mahoney & Lyddon, 1988); constructivist and constructionist family therapies influenced by cybernetic systems theories, and postmodernist/poststructuralist social theories (Gergen & McKaye, 1992; Keeney, 1983; White & Epston, 1990); structural developmental cognitive theories (Ivey & Gonçalves, 1988); and narrative psychology consistent with hermeneutic perspectives on social sciences (Polkinghorne, 1988).

Although theoretically distinct, practice perspectives from diverse constructive theories share common assumptions about human behavior (DiGiuseppe & Linscott, 1993; Mahoney, 1988a, 1988b; R. A. Neimeyer, 1993a, 1993b). In general, practices based on constructive theories have common metatheoretical assumptions. One such assumption is that humans actively participate in the construction of the reality in which they respond. In cognitive constructivist traditions such as those found in cognitive therapy, humans are viewed as proactive beings with higher cortical structures who are capable of using generative, "feed-forward" mechanisms in storing sensory perceptions and memories and using anticipation, goals, and expectations to motivate and self-regulate their behavior. Social constructionists, borrowing more from sociological theory, believe that humans participate interactively in language communities in which they generate their own social realities.

Constructive theories posit that humans cannot know (perceive) objective reality absolutely and that their own constructions must be considered. Cognitive constructivists believe that one's cognitive and emotional schema (matrix of meanings that prompt attention, memory, and interpretations of environmental stimuli) come into play. Social constructionists focus on the social embeddedness of culture, language, and community and on how cognitive constructions are formed and maintained. In this sense humans create their own realities. Constructive views, however, differ from solipsism (belief that the self is the only reality) because most constructive practice perspectives do not deny the existence of an objective, ontologically based reality beyond the self. Constructivists and constructionists have a range of views concerning the role of direct perception and the influence of objective reality on human cognitive perceptions, structures, and behaviors (see Chapter 3).

In addition, social constructionists and constructivists believe that human cognition, affect, and behavior form an interactive system and that they cannot be clearly separated from one another. Cognitive constructivists focus on psychosocial narratives, including narratives about the self, personal construct systems, and core ordering processes. Social constructionists focus on the socially embedded nature of cognitions and how social and political processes cannot be separated from the stories people tell in a community and the language games they play with one another. Life-span development and changes in organisms in the course of time are also important to the cognitive constructivists, whereas social context and meaning are the main focus of the social constructionists. Behavior is best understood by an analysis of systemic, complex, and reciprocal aspects of causality. Such analysis must include the interpersonal, cultural, and social basis for behavior. For cognitive constructivists, internal cognitive (including affective) structures, such as core ordering processes, deep structures, meaning systems, and narratives (life stories), are important in maintaining and changing behavior. Social constructionists do not accept implied psychological constructs but do focus on social and political narratives about the self in practice applications (Franklin & Jordan, 1996).

Some have argued that increased interest in constructive metatheory points to a significant intellectual movement that is part of a broadly based paradigmatic shift within the social sciences and services (Mahoney, 1995; R. A. Neimeyer, 1993a, 1993b). Others have argued that this movement functions at the level of epistemology and ideology and that little in the way of practical utility or demonstrated benefit to clients has been proffered (Held, 1995). Our inspiration for this volume indeed arose from this tension. In our view, it is time to move beyond abstract discussions and to begin to describe demonstration, evaluation, and inwardly focused critical analysis of practice issues. As editors, we challenged the authors to focus on different aspects or foci of constructivist practice, first articulating a brief theoretical rationale that undergirds their prescriptions, then identifying how practice methods stem from theory. What would a practitioner do or not do differently as a result of incorporating these concepts (e.g., in assessment, relationship building, working with a client to formulate goals, implementing and adjusting change efforts)?

Constructive theories often lack operational details concerning their procedures, techniques, and evaluation of their effectiveness. A few notable exceptions are evident in the techniques of personal construct psychology (see chapters 5 and 7), such as repertory grids, for which research studies have been performed (G. J. Neimeyer & Neimeyer, 1990). On the other hand, practice approaches, such as the solution-focused therapy presented by Berg and De Jong (see Chapter 11) are rich in thick descriptions of procedures and techniques but have not been systematically evaluated with regard to effectiveness. Authors were asked to embed their prescriptions for constructivist and constructionist practice within the context of contemporary practice settings. This requires attention to how one can assess the impact of constructivist concepts or methods (e.g., assessment tools, reasonable evaluation approaches) as well as attention to the environmental pressures and constraints that shape service providers' professional lives.

This edited volume represents a continuation of our effort to define and illustrate the practice methods of constructive theories. We first began this project with a special issue of *Families in Society* in June 1996. In this book, we include the manuscripts from that special issue as well as offer a comprehensive set of chapters that demonstrate practice methods, illuminate theoretical and developmental issues, and raise important challenges for constructive practice. This volume, for example, provides chapters on the empirical basis of constructivism from the cognitive sciences, readings that trace earlier developments and distinctions between constructivist and social constructionist theory, and discussions concerning a broad array of practice applications across multiple levels—individuals, families, groups, organizations, and communities. Because most of the literature on constructive practice emphasizes individual and family interventions, the examination of applications to include communities and organizational practice is a valuable addition to the field.

What is so special about constructivist and constructionist theories that we should attempt to define and illustrate practice methods from these perspectives? We believe that constructivism and social constructionism have an empirical basis in the psychological and sociopsychological sciences and that the basic research that undergirds these perspectives may provide an important contribution to applied practice fields such as social work and allied disciplines. From this vantage point, looking at practice methods from the theoretical basis of constructive theories offers important opportunities to apply new understandings from basic research to practice applications. We realize, however, that not all practitioners from diverse traditions of constructive practice have drawn directly from the basic sociopsychological sciences. Rather, we believe that the underlying basis for a practitioner's reliance on the "root metaphor" of constructive theory and many of the emerging practice methods may be grounded in research-based perspectives when practitioners and researchers learn to connect these perspectives (see Chapter 1; Goldfried, 1995). That is, constructive practice may be grounded in newer sociocognitive theories (Brower & Nurius, 1993). We further believe that the integrated theories presented in this volume on constructivism and social constructionism represent an advance in cognitive theory for social work practice and should be understood as the possible beginning of new innovations in cognitive practice methods. However, we wish to make our position clear: Regardless of the practice traditions of the various constructivists and social constructionists (e.g., family therapy, cognitive–behavioral practice, social work), the practice methods emerging from constructive metatheories are distinctly cognitive or sociocognitive in their orientation to changing human behavior. The sociocognitive orientation can be seen in the self-reflexive methods of the cognitive constructivists; the imaging, meaning-generating, and interpretive methods of solution-oriented and narrative therapists; and in the strengths-enhancing, empowering, and competency-based assessments of social work practitioners.

The research basis for the constructive theory to which we refer is found primarily within the psychological sciences (see Chapter 1). Research into cognitive and social structures and processes provide support for many of the tenets discussed in constructivist therapies: social cognition and memory functioning (Fiske & Taylor, 1991; Nurius, 1994; Nurius & Berlin, 1995); evolutionary epistemology (how humans construct knowledge; Mahoney, 1991); ecological psychology (Greenberg & Pascual-Leone, 1995); narrative psychology (Van den Broek & Thurlow, 1991); new social cognitive, applied developmental, and learning theories (Aldridge, 1993; Bandura, 1989; Prawat, 1993); and complexity systems theory (Mahoney, 1995; Warren, Franklin, & Streeter, in press). Brower and Nurius (1993) review empirical research from cognitive, personality, social, and ecological psychology and describe the importance of constructivist and constructionist perspectives.

Martin (1989) further describes the socially embedded nature of cognition and the fact that all acts in a social context lend themselves to multiple interpretations and differing outcomes. Studies by Martin, Cummings, and Hallberg (1992) and Martin, Martin, and Slemon (1989) support the constructive nature of social situations and cognition. From the standpoint of cognitive mediation (and constructivist theory), the meanings and consequences of social acts are uncertain unless one has full knowledge of the intentions and cognitive operations of the actors, knowledge that is never completely attainable (Martin, 1989). Both social context and one's cognitive constructions are therefore intertwined, following a dynamic, constructive, and socially constructed interplay of meanings, behaviors, and consequences. Because of the constructive nature of cognition and social interactions, cognitive and behavioral effects may yield patterned but unpredictable outcomes in the sense that one-to-one correspondence between stimuli and consequences can never be predicted (Martin, 1989; Warren et al., in press).

Both the theoretical and the research basis for constructivism are discussed at length by Mahoney (Chapter 1) and Nurius (Chapter 2). Franklin (Chapter 3) further grapples with the theoretical and research distinctions between constructivism and social constructionism, offering an analysis of how these distinct theoretical perspectives carry through in practice applications.

Assessing and understanding the interplay of cognitive (including affective responses) and social processes and using this information to collaborate with clients in their reconstruction of meanings (cognitive changes) about social situations and changes in their consequent behaviors are at the heart of most constructivist and constructionist approaches to psychotherapy. G. J. Neimeyer, Hagans, and Anderson offer a review of constructivist clinical assessment and illustrate how constructivist assessment is used in practice with a female client (Chapter 5). Franklin and Jordan

(Chapter 4) further discuss the qualitative and interpretive research underpinnings of several constructivist assessment methods and review how these assessment approaches have been used in social work practice. These authors also highlight some of the potential limitations of these methods.

Several illustrations of constructive theory to diverse practice applications across multiple levels—individuals, families, groups, organizations, and communities—are included in the volume. Constructivism is a central theoretical construct for contemporary cognitive therapies, having become a guiding principle for theorists as diverse as Mahoney (1991), Meichenbaum and Fitzpatrick (1993), and Ellis (1990). A noticeable gap exists, however, between the guiding constructs from constructivist theory and demonstrations of the constructivist methods for cognitive change. Granvold (Chapter 6) presents a summary of current constructivist theory within cognitive–behavioral therapy and demonstrates constructivist methods and how they complement traditional cognitive practice. R. A. Neimeyer and Stewart (Chapter 7) capture the essence of the reconstructive process in their narrative description of the changes in a client suffering from post-traumatic stress disorder. Brower (Chapter 9) describes the constructive process as it unfolds in group work. Nurius and Gibson (Chapter 8) illustrate ways that, as an intrinsic part of human reasoning, constructivism affects practitioners, often unwittingly, in their helping services with clients.

Laird (Chapter 10) discusses the use of social constructionism in family therapy and the importance of this cultural, narrative perspective for family practice. Berg and De Jong (Chapter 11) illustrate solution-focused therapy and how a client whose children have been removed from her home owns resources in the form of cognitive affirmations, coping responses, and existing effective behaviors that may be used to amplify and solidify changes. Biever and Franklin (Chapter 12) focus on social constructionism in action by demonstrating the processes of reflecting teams and their outcomes in practice with an African American family seeking help for an adolescent member.

Gutiérrez and Lord (Chapter 13) discuss the theoretical basis of social constructionism in community practice and how a constructionist approach can enhance and complement more traditional community approaches in social work. Saleebey (Chapter 14) also illustrates the uses of social constructionism in economically distressed communities. Shera (Chapter 15) shows how constructive theory may be used within organizations. Todd (Chapter 16) shows how business relationships within managed behavioral health care may be developed and maintained through using constructive practice principles. Gonzáles (Chapter 17) illustrates constructivist practice with multicultural clients by blending various constructivist and constructionist traditions from the different perspectives discussed in this volume.

The theoretical and research mechanisms for understanding constructive processes are also examined by Martin (Chapter 18) and further illustrated by Berlin (Chapter 19), who sets forth a constructivist theoretical perspective for social work practice. Finally, Nurius and Franklin (Afterword) offer some concluding remarks and analysis concerning the progress of constructivist practice.

Practitioners increasingly are being exposed to constructive theories and practice applications, and some are aligning themselves with one or more of these perspectives. Many discussions about constructivism and constructionism are extremely abstract and are framed as arguments against more traditional practice and research methods. Within a developmental perspective, much of this discussion has been useful in distilling alternatives and honing distinctions. Now, however, we are ready to tackle questions regarding how we implement and teach constructivist practice. How do we know that constructivist therapies contribute to better practice? How do we retain a critically reflective capacity to guide judicious application of theory and ideology and that alerts us to limitations and caveats? These next steps will require considerable effort on the part of theorists, researchers, and practitioners. We believe that this volume contributes to this challenging endeavor.

*Cynthia Franklin*
*Paula S. Nurius*

# References

Aldridge, J. (1993). Constructivism, contextualism, and applied developmental psychology. *Perceptual and Motor Skills, 76*, 1242.

Bandura, A. (1989). Human agency in social cognitive theory. *American Psychologist, 44*, 1175–1184.

Brower, A. M., & Nurius, P. S. (1993). *Social cognition and individual change: Current theory and counseling guidelines*. Newbury Park, CA: Sage.

DiGiuseppe, R., & Linscott, J. (1993). Philosophical differences among cognitive–behavioral therapists: Rationalism, constructivism, or both? *Journal of Cognitive Psychotherapy, 7*, 117–130.

Ellis, A. (1990). Is rational-emotive therapy (RET) "rationalist" or "constructivist?" *Journal of Rational-Emotive & Cognitive Behavior Therapy, 8*(3), 169–193.

Fiske, S. T., & Taylor, S. T. (1991). *Social cognition* (2nd ed.). New York: McGraw-Hill.

Franklin, C., & Jordan, C. (1996) Does constructivist therapy offer anything new to social work practice? In B. A. Thyer (Ed.), *Controversial issues in social work practice* (pp. 16–28). Boston: Allyn and Bacon.

Gergen, K. J., & McKaye, S. (1992). Beyond narrative in the negotiation of therapeutic meaning. In S. McNamee & K. J. Gergen (Eds.), *Therapy as social construction* (pp. 166–185). Newbury Park, CA: Sage.

Goldfried, M. (1995). *From cognitive–behavior therapy to psychotherapy integration*. New York: Springer.

Gonçalves, O. F. (1995). Cognitive narrative psychotherapy: Hermeneutic construction of alternative meanings. In M. J. Mahoney (Ed.), *Cognitive and constructive psychotherapies: Theory, research and practice* (pp. 139–162). New York: Springer.

Greenberg, L., & Pascual-Leone, J. (1995). A dialectical constructivist approach to experiential change. In R. A. Neimeyer & M. J. Mahoney (Eds.), *Constructivism in psychotherapy* (pp. 169–191). Washington, DC: American Psychological Association.

Held, B. S. (1995). The real meaning of constructivism. *Journal of Constructivist Psychology, 8*, 305–315.

Ivey, A. E., & Gonçalves, O. F. (1988). Developmental therapy: Integrating developmental processes into clinical practice. *Journal of Counseling and Development, 66*, 406–412.

Keeney, B. P. (1983). *Aesthetics of change*. New York: Guilford.

Lyddon, W. J. (1995). Forms and facets of constructivist psychology. In R. A. Neimeyer & M. J.

Mahoney (Eds.), *Constructivism in psychotherapy* (pp. 69–92). Washington, DC: American Psychological Association.

Mahoney, M. J. (1988a). Constructive meta-theory: Basic features and historical foundations. *International Journal of Personal Construct Psychology, 1*, 1–35.

Mahoney, M. J. (1988b). Constructive meta-theory: II. Implications for psychotherapy. *International Journal of Personal Construct Psychology, 1*, 299–315.

Mahoney, M. J. (1991). *Human change processes*. New York: Basic Books.

Mahoney, M. J. (1995). Continuing evolution of the cognitive sciences and psychotherapies. In R. A. Neimeyer & M. J. Mahoney (Eds.), *Constructivism in psychotherapy* (pp. 39–68). Washington, DC: American Psychological Association.

Mahoney, M. J., & Lyddon, W. J. (1988). Recent developments in cognitive approaches to counseling and psychotherapy. *Counseling Psychologist, 16*, 190–234.

Martin, J. (1989). A rationale and proposal for cognitive–mediational research on counseling and psychotherapy. *Counseling Psychologist, 17*, 111–135.

Martin, J., Cummings, A. L., & Hallberg, E. T. (1992). Therapists' intentional use of metaphor: Memorability, clinical impact, and possible epistemic/motivational functions. *Journal of Consulting and Clinical Psychology, 60*, 143–145.

Martin, J., Martin, W., & Slemon, A. G. (1989). Cognitive–mediational models of action–act sequences in counseling. *Journal of Counseling Psychology, 36*, 8–16.

Martin, J., & Sugarman, J. (1996). Bridging social constructionism and cognitive constructivism: A psychology of human possibility and constraint. *Journal of Mind and Behavior, 17*, 291–320.

Meichenbaum, D. K., & Fitzpatrick, D. (1993). A constructionist, narrative perspective on stress and coping: Stress inoculation applications. In L. Goldberger & S. Bresnitz (Eds.), *Handbook of stress: Theoretical and clinical aspects* (2nd ed., pp. 61–87). New York: Free Press.

Neimeyer, G. J., & Neimeyer, R. A. (Eds.). (1990). *Advances in personal construct psychology*. Greenwich, CT: JAI Press.

Neimeyer, R. A. (1993a). An appraisal of the constructivist psychotherapies. *Journal of Consulting and Clinical Psychology, 61*, 221–234.

Neimeyer, R. A.(1993b). Constructivism and cognitive psychotherapies: Some conceptual and strategic contrasts. *Journal of Cognitive Psychotherapy, 7*, 159–172.

Neimeyer, R. A., & Mahoney, M. J. (1995). *Constructivism in psychotherapy*. Washington, DC: American Psychological Association.

Nurius, P. (1994). Assessing and changing self-concept. Guidelines from the memory system. *Social Work, 39*, 221–229.

Nurius, P. S., & Berlin, S. B. (1995). Cognition and social cognitive theory. In *Encyclopedia of Social Work* (19th ed., pp. 513–524). Washington, DC: NASW Press.

Polkinghorne, D. (1988). *Narrative knowing and the human sciences*. Albany, NY: State University of New York Press.

Prawat, R. S. (1993). The value of ideas: Problems versus possibilities in learning. *Educational Researcher, 22*(6), 5–16.

Van den Broek, P., & Thurlow, R. (1991). The role and structures of personal narratives. *Journal of Cognitive Psychotherapy, 5*, 257–274.

Warren, K., Franklin, C., & Streeter, C. L. (in press). New directions in systems theory: Chaos and complexity. *Social Work*.

White, M., & Epston, D. (1990). *Narrative means to therapeutic ends*. New York: W. W. Norton.

# Acknowledgments

In every creative venture, various people provide service and inspiration toward the completion of the work. We offer special thanks to all those who contributed to the development of this book. We especially want to thank the contributors for commiting themselves without compensation to this work. A special thanks is extended to Robert Nordstrom and Ralph Burant, who realized the significance of this project and offered ample editorial guidance and advice. I, Cynthia Franklin, would like to thank the faculty in the Department of Psychology at Our Lady of the Lake University, especially Joan Biever, for the opportunities they provided me in their clinic, both to observe and to practice constructive therapies.

We thank the following publishers for permission to reprint materials: "Assessing and Changing Self-Concept: Guidelines from the Memory System," P. S. Nurius (copyright 1994, National Association of Social Workers, Inc., *Social Work, 39*, 221–229); "Clinical Observation, Inference, Reasoning, and Judgment in Social Work: An Update," P. S. Nurius and J. W. Gibson (copyright 1990, National Association of Social Workers, Inc., *Social Work Research and Abstracts, 26*(2), 18–25); "Human Memory: A Basis for Better Understanding the Elusive Self-Concept," P. S. Nurius (copyright 1993, The University of Chicago Press, *Social Service Review, 67*, 262–278); "Continuing Evolution of the Cognitive Sciences and Psychotherapies," M. J. Mahoney (copyright 1995, American Psychological Association, *Constructivism in Psychotherapy*, pp. 39–67).

# Part 1:

◙ **Current Trends in Constructivist Practice** ◙

# 1

# Continuing Evolution of the Cognitive Sciences and Psychotherapies

*Michael J. Mahoney*

In an era of heightened self-consciousness about the limits of historiography (the writing of history) and the fallible basis on which many historical interpretations are based, it is perhaps foolish to venture a narrative on the evolution of the cognitive sciences and their applied (service-focused) counterparts (the cognitive psychotherapies). It is clear, nevertheless, that these two related developments have captured the imagination and hopes of a whole generation of educators, psychologists, psychiatrists, social workers, and researchers who view the cognitive approaches as the latest and most promising contenders in a multicentury competition for the most adequate models of human experience and the most effective methods for servicing pathologies and problems in human adjustment (Dobson, 1988; Sperry, 1993). This chapter is intended to offer a necessarily personal synopsis of three related discussions: (a) developments in the cognitive sciences (and cognitive psychology) during the twentieth century, (b) the emergence and differentiation of the cognitive psychotherapies, and (c) a brief discussion of issues likely to challenge future developments in both areas in the twenty-first century.

In each of these three major topics of discussion, I propose that constructivism reflects some of the most exciting and viable developments in psychology and psychotherapy. As will be elaborated, I consider constructivism to be a multifaceted expression of a philosophical tradition that recognizes the individual as an active, anticipatory, and developing participant in his or her own life-span experience. This tradition, which has influenced a number of approaches to psychotherapy, seems uniquely suited to further evolution, and its clinical promise is gaining the interest of increasing numbers of health service providers in and beyond psychology. The premises and promise of constructivist theory in psychotherapy may be best understood in the context of the three discussions mentioned above.

# Twentieth-Century Developments in the Cognitive Sciences

Future historians may find it interesting and challenging to identify a single individual, date, or event by which to mark the beginning of the so-called cognitive revolution (whether in psychology or in the sciences in general). That such a revolution took place in the second half of the twentieth century is undisputed. Where and when it started, how it was first expressed, and by whom it was inaugurated are matters that historiographers (writers of history) are already disputing. Consider, for example, the possible candidates for pioneers and pioneering contributions to the cognitive sciences from 1860 to 1970, which are summarized in the Appendix. The works listed also predate some of the important developments associated with postmodernism and postrationalism (Gergen, 1991; Guidano, 1991; Kvale, 1992; Madison, 1988; Mahoney, 1991a; Tarnas, 1991). Postmodernism and postrationalism are themselves reflections of developments that transcend philosophy and the academic disciplines; they are reflections of planetary life in the past decade of the twentieth century. Therefore, they are also reflections of the complexities and apparent paradoxes that challenge imminent developments in psychology and psychotherapy. The list in the Appendix is hardly exhaustive, of course, but it does render a sense of the wide range, diversity, and, in some cases, simultaneity of contributions that probably contributed to what modern observers consider the cognitive era in psychology, psychiatry, and many allied sciences.

## *Cybernetics and Information Processing*

Although there were many precursors to the emergence of the cognitive revolution within and beyond psychology, historians of the cognitive sciences have suggested that these developments achieved critical mass and momentum sometime around midcentury. Bruner and Postman (1947a, 1947b) introduced the "new look" in perception in 1947, and Norbert Wiener's (1948) *Cybernetics* was published the next year (see Appendix). It was also in 1948 that the Hixon Symposium on Cerebral Mechanisms in Behavior provided a forum for such pioneers as John von Neumann, Warren McCulloch, and Herbert Simon to lay the foundations of information theory and to consider the promise of modeling theories of brain functioning by using computer analogies. Information processing soon became a respected field of research and development. Throughout much of the literature of the 1950s and 1960s, the terms *cognitive psychology* and *information processing* were often used synonymously. *Artificial intelligence*, in those decades, was a term and focus more radical and imaginative than was felt tolerable by mainstream gatekeepers in cognitive research.

There were, as always, personal and paradigmatic politics, the details and dynamics of which have barely been touched on in the most popular historiographies of the cognitive sciences (Baars, 1986; Gardner, 1985; Hirst, 1988). There were biases of method and traditions of metaphors that are now, historically, apparent. Gardner (1985), for example, asserted that the first three key features of cognitive science were its reliance on mental representation, its reliance on computation, and its "de-emphasis of such murky concepts as affect, context, culture, and history" (p. 42). All three of these so-called key features are topics of considerable controversy in the cognitive sciences of 1994, where metaphors of representation are under reappraisal; the limits of solely computational programs are increasingly recognized; and culture, affect, history, and context are among the most interesting topics in human knowing and experience (M. Johnson, 1987; Mahoney, 1991a; Merleau-Ponty, 1962, 1963; Miró, 1989; Salthe, 1985; Shanon, 1988; Tarnas, 1991; P. P. Wiener, 1974).

One must beware, however, of the tendency toward dichotomies in acceptance and rejection processes. These earliest efforts to develop more and more of a science of mind were themselves the engines of understanding and the generators of new ideas about human knowing. It will probably be centuries before their contributions to our inquiries are adequately appreciated. To be sure, the models and theories of these first decades of "black box" research tended to accentuate contrasts over continuities, states over processes, and physical metaphors over abstract orders. The black-box metaphor had been introduced to emphasize behaviorists' neglect of the inside story of experience. As long as functional relations could be demonstrated between stimulus and response, intervening processes were deemed irrelevant. In these early cognitive models, the mind was said to be a central way station—a relatively passive and usually consistent transducer of energy input (stimulation) and energy output (response). The Gallilean-Cartesian dream of certain and objective knowledge may have been fundamental to the development of psychology as a discipline separate from philosophy and experimental physiology in the eighteenth and nineteenth centuries. However, the more the pioneers in cybernetics and information processing began to look into and model the so-called black boxes of their experimental subjects (and, no doubt, themselves), the more complex were their impressions of human perception, learning, and memory, and the more pervasive became views of "opponent process" (essential tensions) and complex dynamics in motivation and learning (see below).

For all of their flaws and limitations, the cybernetic and information-processing traditions in the cognitive sciences served, and continue to serve, as an invaluable reference point and source of technological development. They are not yet history, and their presence is apparent in all other recognized perspectives in the cognitive sciences (Mazlish, 1993). Moreover, researchers associated with these traditions have continued to respond creatively to the challenges of increasing complexities in models and theories of the human mind. For this alone, the high regard of these traditions in the cognitive sciences is amply warranted.

## Connectionism and Computational Neuroscience

Since the emergence and elaboration of modern cognitive sciences in the third quarter of the twentieth century, there have been significant and palpable evolutions within that successful revolution. One of these developments has been the emergence of a perspective called *connectionism*, which is a movement spanning the cognitive sciences, computer sciences, and neurosciences. Briefly put, connectionism is an approach to learning, memory, and development that relies on the computational capacities of supercomputers, which are essentially systems of systems with capacities for "massively distributed parallel processing" of information.

Like other such events, this evolution had at least some of its origins in events that occurred decades earlier. It is, for example, more than coincidental that modern connectionism shares its core metaphor with the turn-of-the-century learning theory of E. L. Thorndike (1898; also called *connectionism*). Then, in 1932, Tolman staggered the behaviorist majority with his book titled *Purposive Behavior in Animals and Men*. In 1943, Warren McCulloch and Walter Pitts published the seminal paper "Logical Calculus of the Ideas Immanent in Nervous Activity." It was an incredible idea itself. And in 1948, Norbert Wiener published *Cybernetics*, a book on the cybernetic modeling of purposive behavior—the conceptual prototype later elaborated by Miller, Galanter, and Pribram (1960) as the TOTE (Test, Operate, Test, Exit). The TOTE was the essence of cybernetic logic: Test the current value of a variable, begin adjustment operations if necessary, test the variable again, and repeat this process until its values are acceptable.

In 1949, Donald O. Hebb published his classic theory of the organization of behavior, and the foundation for what is now known as connectionism was firmly in place. An unspoken rivalry began to develop between those drawn toward computer science metaphors and those drawn toward the organic processes of self-organization. The rivalry became a conscious skirmish after the 1962 publication of Frank Rosenblatt's *Principles of Neurodynamics,* a pathbreaking move toward the modeling of neuronlike learning systems. Rosenblatt's ideas were harshly criticized by "computophiles" Marvin Minsky and Seymour Papert (Minsky & Papert, 1969) and were functionally ignored by mainstream information scientists for more than a decade. But the ideas and technologies that would come to characterize connectionism continued to be elaborated. And they at least shared the following features: (a) a shift in emphasis from the computer to the living nervous system as the primary source of information about the structures and functions of human knowing; (b) a creative use of continuing developments in computer technology to refine models simulating human learning; and (c) a recognition that computational processes cannot adequately deal with a complexity of "subsymbolic processes" that operate pervasively in all human experience.

As its constituents have formed productive collaborations with leading neuroscientists—creating the sub-subspecialization of "computational neuroscience" (Sejnoski, Koch, & Churchland, 1988)—connectionists have become increasingly confident in the promise that the directions they are taking are leading toward truly revolutionary views of brain function and learning processes. Connectionism has become a movement of major proportions in late-twentieth-century cognitive science. It has both staunch defenders and harsh detractors (Feldman & Ballard, 1982; Fodor & Pylyshyn, 1988; Schneider, 1987; Seidenberg, 1993). And, perhaps most important, it has considerable interest as a theme of dialogue in contemporary cognitive science.

To reiterate, connectionism in its modern form is a mature and sophisticated type of stimulus–response associationism. It presumes that some form of computation is basic to learning and memory. With its concessions to "subsymbolic processes" and to the lessons of studying knowing systems in operation, connectionism may also represent a conceptual bridge from the centuries-old doctrine of associationism to the recent rise of constructivist and evolutionary theories of learning.

## Constructivism and Evolutionary Epistemology

At about the same time that connectionism was coming together as a contemporary identity within cognitive science, another set of developments was taking place that would lead to an important differentiation within the cognitive sciences. These developments appeared to be relatively independent of a parallel set of developments in the cognitive psychotherapies in the period between 1950 and 1975.

At some point in all of this complexity, a coherent and viable perspective began to emerge. In 1952, the University of Chicago Press published a book that was initially ignored and yet remains in press more than four decades later. It was subtitled *Reflections on the Foundations of Theoretical Psychology*, and it was authored not by a psychologist, but by an economist. His name was Friedrich Hayek, and his book was *The Sensory Order* (1952). It was (and is) a masterpiece and classic expression of the modern transition from objectivist–naive and rationalist–passive-sensory metatheories of the human mind to more projectivist, postrationalist, and active motor-evolutionary perspectives. In his dense little volume, Hayek pushed the empiricist program to (and well beyond) its limits. In doing so, he demonstrated that the contents of experience— all frequencies, intensities, magnitudes, and diverse nuances—must be, neurologically and otherwise, the products of higher order categorization or classification processes that, with lessons from experience, participate in creating "the sensory order." The theoretical significance of Hayek's work has yet to be fully appreciated (Hamowy, 1987; Hayek, 1964; Mahoney & Weimer, 1994), but the power of its practical implications has already begun to be explored (Burrell, 1987; Ford, 1987; Mahoney, 1991a).

Constructivism is a tradition in the cognitive sciences that has been traced back at least as far as the writings of Vico, Kant, and Vaihinger in Western civilization, and its expressions in the literatures of Asiatic philosophies and religions are indisputable (Mahoney, 1988a, 1988b, 1991a). Essentially, constructivism is a family of theories and therapies that emphasize at least three interrelated principles of human experience: (a) that humans are proactive (and not passively reactive) participants in their own experience—that is, in all perception, memory, and knowing; (b) that the vast majority of the ordering processes organizing human lives operate at tacit (un- or superconscious) levels of awareness; and (c) that human experience and personal psychological development reflect the ongoing operation of individualized, self-organizing processes that tend to favor the maintenance (over the modification) of experiential patterns. Although uniquely individual, these organizing processes always reflect and influence social systems. Pioneering expressions of constructivism can be found in the writings of Wilhelm Wundt (1896), Pierre Janet (1898), Charles Sherrington (1906), William James (1890), Jean Piaget (1926), and Frederic Bartlett (1932), to name some of the most familiar.

After midcentury, expressions of constructivist perspectives began to be elaborated. Berger and Luckmann's (1966) classic, *The Social Construction of Reality*, ushered in a wave of writings on the social construction of everyday life and social processes in science (Gergen, 1985, 1991; Tarnas, 1991). Meanwhile, the beginnings of evolutionary epistemology—the study of developments in knowing systems— were established by Donald Campbell and others (Callebaut & Pinxten, 1987; Campbell, 1974; Dell & Goolishian, 1981; Radnitzky & Bartley, 1987). Because I have dwelt elsewhere on historical details and more recent expressions of constructivism and evolutionary epistemology within the cognitive sciences (Mahoney, 1988a, 1991a), I shall not reiterate them here. As the title and focus of this volume reflect, however, I remain appreciative of the past and future contributions of these metatheories to both the mind sciences and health services.

## Hermeneutics and Narrative

In reflecting on the early days of the cognitive revolution, Jerome Bruner (1990) noted the following:

> It would make an absorbing essay in the intellectual history of the last quarter-century to trace what happened to the originating impulse of the cognitive revolution. ... Very early on, for example, emphasis began shifting from "meaning" to "information," from the construction of meaning to the processing of information. These are profoundly different matters. The key factor in the shift was the introduction of computation as the ruling metaphor and of computability as a necessary criterion of a good theoretical model. (p. 4)

After introducing (with Postman) the "New Look in Perception" in 1947, Bruner went on to explore a "new look in knowing" as well. That look involved an acknowledgment that narrative processes are pervasive in human knowing. This view is now a popular and growing element in (and beyond) the cognitive therapies, as is its companion field of hermeneutics.

*Hermeneutics* is one of those terms that began to gain respect in the social and health sciences in the 1990s. It comes from the Greek *hermeneutikos,* meaning "interpretation," and it is associated with the Greek god Hermes (synonymous with the Roman god Mercury), whose task was to serve as messenger of the gods. Not surprisingly, perhaps, the first formal appearance of hermeneutics as a specialization was in theology, where the interpretation of sacred scripture was of central importance. Through a tapestry of historical developments too intricate to trace here, however, hermeneutics became secularized in the twentieth century. It also began to cross-fertilize with linguistics, semiotics (theory of signs), analytic philosophy, literary criticism, psychoanalysis, and evolutionary epistemology (Carr, 1986; Dilthey, 1976; Freeman, 1993; Gadamer, 1975, 1976, 1988; Heidegger, 1927/1962, 1959/1971; Madison, 1988; Messer, Sass, & Woolfolk, 1988; Palmer, 1969; Stent, 1985; Wachterhauser, 1986).

Interestingly, one of the formative debates in hermeneutics was about validity and the objectivity of interpretations. Those championing objectivism argued that the meaning of a text literally resided within it; that is, the meaning was lying there waiting to be discovered and understood from an adequate reading of the text. Those championing other positions have ranged from relativists to radicals, and they have participated in a conceptual transformation of unprecedented proportions. They challenge, for example, traditional boundaries between subject and object, not to mention the presumed boundaries among author, text, and reader. Indeed, the postmodern reader is said to be "in the text" as an active and individualizing context for its "languaging" (which is a much more active and complex verb than "reading"; Fischer, 1987; Iser, 1978).

One can now see the striking parallels between narrative psychology and hermeneutics. Both have to do with stories and meanings that are personally interpreted. Both involve active generative processes and equally active reflective processes—"acts of meaning," as Bruner (1990) has called them. Both are reflections of the continuing human quest to understand—to experience and possibly express some of the order within the chaos. Narrative and hermeneutic approaches, in my opinion, have just begun to be appreciated for their possible contributions to psychotherapy. It will be interesting to observe their evolution in the coming decades.

## Complex Systems Approaches

The last theme that I address as a development in twentieth-century cognitive science is the rise of the sciences of complexity and their contemporary cross-fertilization. Like other themes in the cognitive sciences, complexity can be traced to writers and works that long predated the recent surge of popularity in the term (Bonner, 1988; Hamowy, 1987; Hayek, 1964; Lewin, 1992; Waldrop, 1992; Weimer, 1982). In recent decades, the appreciation for complexity and complex systems analyses has been stimulated by development in the field of chaos. Although there have been varying interpretations about the boundaries of that field (Glass & Mackey, 1988; Gleick, 1987), chaos is a subspecialization within the broader context of studying complex systems. Chaos researchers and theorists have been primarily interested in the influence of initial conditions on subsequent system parameters—hence their affinity for the so-called butterfly effect, in which the minuscule air turbulence created by a butterfly in one hemisphere can—through the amplifications afforded by "strange attractors"—eventually influence the formation of a hurricane or tornado in another hemisphere. Complexity specialists are interested in the phenomena and processes of chaos, but their questions and emphases are much more diverse. They have been relatively more occupied, for example, with emergent properties, developing methods for modeling nonlinear dynamics (e.g., Morrison, 1991), and the essential tension between disequilibrium (disorganizing) and self-organizing processes in the development of open systems (e.g., Bienenstock, 1985; Bienenstock, Soulié, & Weisbuch, 1986; Hager, 1992).

Much of the early work in complex systems was authored by evolutionary biologists, organic chemists, thermodynamicists, and social systems experts (e.g., Campbell, Eccles, Eigen, Hayek, Jantsch, Pattee, Popper, Prigogine, Waddington, and Zeleny). The discovery of the self-replicating hypercycle and the demonstration of clear "dissipative" (self-organizing) structures in both living and nonliving systems led to conceptual leaps that are still in process (Depew & Weber, 1995; Jantsch, 1980, 1981; Mahoney, 1991b; Salthe, 1993; Varela, 1979; Weimer, 1987; Zeleny, 1980, 1981). In the last two decades, there have been exciting developments in this area, not the least of which are those formulated by Vittorio Guidano, Humberto Maturana, and Francisco Varela. As I elaborate toward the end of the next section, the evolution of constructivist psychotherapies from and toward the sciences of complexity is a trend worthy of note. (For contemporary expressions of the relationship between the sciences of complexity and the cognitive and computer sciences, see Glass and Mackey, 1988; M. H. Johnson, 1993; Kauffman, 1993; Lewin, 1992; Searle, 1992; and Waldrop, 1992.) It seems increasingly clear that future models of human experience (and hence, both education and psychotherapy) will be intimately linked with metaphors and models found useful in the study of adaptation and learning in other complex systems.

## Twentieth-Century Developments in Cognitive Psychotherapies

Like the foregoing narrative about developments in the cognitive sciences, this discussion on cognitive therapies is a limited and linear attempt to construct an order from which to view the history and current events of the cognitive psychotherapies. Having been a participant–observer of developments since the 1960s, I am sure that my reflections, recollections, and integration of developments in the cognitive psychotherapies have been shaped by my experiences with them and their representatives over the last quarter century.

### *The Mind Cure Movement*

Contemporary cognitive psychotherapy owes at least part of its practical legacy to the "psychology of healthy mindedness" and the so-called mind cure movement that swept through parts of western Europe and North America in the late nineteenth and early twentieth centuries (James, 1958; Mahoney, 1993; Meyer, 1965; Parker, 1973). It was out of that movement, for example, that Pierre Janet's (1898) "fixed ideas"—thought to be involved in neurotic disorders—were challenged by what would later come to be called "the power of positive thinking" (Peale, 1960). Active rituals of self-talk and healthy thinking were practiced, as were other health regimens. These practices were often packaged as part of a program for success and self-development that was aimed at Christian audiences.

Whatever their aim, the books on how to be healthy minded were a financial success. It takes only a casual stroll through an average bookstore almost anywhere on the planet to realize that the lay public has come to virtually equate psychology with self-help or self-improvement. Positive thinking and the psychology of optimism remain popular themes in the trade literature, and "feeling good" is now commonly associated with thinking right. This association is particularly apparent, I believe, in the literature devoted to rational emotive therapy.

## Rational–Emotive Therapy

Albert Ellis developed one of the most popular and influential forms of cognitive psychotherapy with his 1962 book, *Reason and Emotion in Psychotherapy*, the "big book" founding rational–emotive therapy. In it, he integrated the Stoic philosophy of Epictetus with a practical guide for identifying and eliminating a list of basic irrational ideas said to be responsible for a wide range of unnecessary human suffering. Ellis (with whom I have had the honor of working and the pleasure of friendship) soon became the nucleus of a worldwide network of centers and practitioners of rational emotive therapy. Thousands of his personal workshops have drawn large audiences on five continents. Shocking to some, "Al" is quite direct and often provocative. He has not been a reticent participant in twentieth-century culture. He has inspired many to explore the relations between philosophy and psychotherapy and between thinking and feeling, as well as the meaning of living a theory. Because this chapter is meant to be a historiography of the cognitive therapies, I shall not venture into an evaluative review of rational–emotive therapy (Mahoney, Lyddon, & Alford, 1989). More important for the present volume is the acknowledgment that Albert Ellis and rational–emotive therapy have been and continue to be major and navigational elements in the continuing evolution of the cognitive psychotherapies.

## Personal Construct Psychology

Another, even earlier, classic in cognitive therapy was George Kelly's (1955) two-volume masterpiece, *The Psychology of Personal Constructs*. Kelly did not call it "cognitive," however, and he was equally intentional in emphasizing that his system could not be adequately classified by any of the modern "isms" in psychology. Kelly was a master at metatheory—that is, conjectures at the level of superordinate processes (as contrasted, e.g., with the concrete particulars of "ordinary" experience). He was in the good company of his contemporary, Charles Osgood, in appreciating that the dimensions of human experience are carved from polar contrasts and that the measurement of meaning is fundamentally the measurement of personal dimensions of differences. This was but one of George Kelly's insights, however, and I shall resist elaborating themes here that may be quite familiar to readers of this volume. The contributions of Kelly and subsequent personal construct theorists have been elaborated by Neimeyer (1985) and are discussed in a number of other chapters in this volume.

## Cognitive–Behavior Modification

The approach called *cognitive–behavior modification* is more difficult to describe than others, in part because it has continued to evolve over the decades since the 1970s. In my personal reconstruction of events, however, cognitive–behavior modification seemed to appear on the heels of two earlier developments in behaviorism and behavior therapy. The first was the emergence of the conceptual and practical mutant known as *covert conditioning,* and the second was the surge of interest and activity in what was then called *behavioral self-management.* Covert conditioning was inaugurated by Lloyd Homme (1965). A student of Skinner, Homme proposed that human thoughts could be treated as "covert operants"—unobserved, internal responses "operating" on the environment—or "coverants," obeying the same principles of behavior and, therefore, susceptible to contingency management and thought-control strategies. My first interactions with Skinner were over Homme's proposal, about which he was skeptical. Skinner was, however, quite enthusiastic about behavioral self-control, to which he had devoted an entire chapter in his 1953 book.

Joseph Cautela (1966) published a more Pavlovian idea about thought control, proposing that images and words could be conditioned by other images and words, thereby permitting much of behavior therapy to be practiced in and with the client's imagination. Cautela believed that, rather than presenting painful stimuli in vivo, therapists could achieve comparable results by appropriately pairing imaginary stimuli and responses. Early research on the prospects and procedures of covert sensitization yielded ambiguous answers (Mahoney, 1974), and other perspectives and procedures began to receive increasing attention. Among these were the contributions of Donald H. Meichenbaum (1969, 1974, 1977), a University of Illinois graduate who, in his dissertation, had investigated thought patterns and their modification in hospitalized schizophrenics. Inspired by readings of Luria and Vygotsky, among others, Meichenbaum elaborated practical procedures for studying and possibly modifying the private, ongoing "self-statements" that lie beneath or behind people's behavioral and emotional difficulties. As his interests and activities have continued to diversify over the ensuing decades, Meichenbaum (1995) has contributed to health psychology, psychotherapy, and literatures in areas ranging from the unconscious to human narrative.

The book *Cognition and Behavior Modification* (Mahoney, 1974) was the result of several forces in my life. I had been working on the idea behind it since the late 1960s. The topic I proposed for my first term paper in graduate school was "an information processing analysis of behavior modification"; it was declined as lacking sufficient literature for a term paper. In 1973, as a young assistant professor at Pennsylvania State University, I spent a summer teaching in Brazil. That same year, at the annual convention of the American Psychological Association, in Montreal, I met B. F. Skinner for dinner. I was moved by the certainty with which Skinner pronounced cognitive psychology a regression to mysticism and an obstacle to scientific psychology. At the end of the evening, I paid my respects and expressed my appreciation to "Fred" for our conversation. I said that I disagreed about cognitive science, but that I would have to take a closer look at its models and the research on their practical value. He shook my hand warmly and said with a smile, "I think you'll be wasting your time, but I wish you well in the research."

Our interpretations of the results of that research were, of course, quite different. I concluded that the early cognitive sciences and therapies warranted some cautious optimism about their promise. Skinner and others called cognitive–behavior modification an oxymoron (self-contradiction), and there began a long-standing tension between cognitive and behavioral emphases in postmodern (liberalized, or relativized) behavior therapy. The literatures of the 1970s and 1980s are scattered with skirmishes among various cognitivists and behaviorists. One of those skirmishes took place between Fred Skinner and myself. In 1987, he challenged psychology to come back to its identity as a science of behavior and to recognize the three major obstacles to the foundations and future of psychology as a science— namely, cognitive psychology, psychotherapy, and humanistic psychology. I responded with a candid criticism of what I experienced as an arrogance and elitism that seemed prevalent in "scientistic" and radical "objectivist" traditions in psychology (Mahoney, 1989). Some of Skinner's friends and admirers were incensed by my words, and—with encouragement and feedback from Skinner—Charles Catania (1991) wrote a response. Skinner, in the advanced stages of leukemia, worked to prepare the article that he presented with dignity just weeks before he died (1990). In it, he compared cognitive psychology to creationism and himself to Charles Darwin facing the conservative clergy of the previous century. It was a fitting and touching final narrative from the author of *Walden Two* (1948) and *Beyond Freedom and Dignity* (1971).

I was present at Skinner's last public appearance, and my admiration for him as a pioneering scientist was even further augmented. Even though I disagreed with his well-elaborated theory of learning and life, I admired his dignity and determination in the final hours of his exceptional life. It is no coincidence, I believe, that the last word uttered by Fred Skinner was "marvelous!" It was his response to a final drink of water. It might also express our collective gratitude to a human being who dared to challenge the mentalist tradition. After his death, I organized a tribute to Skinner by humanists, psychotherapists, and cognitive scientists (Mahoney, 1991b). I would like to think that the death of such an ideological giant might also signal an opportunity for the passing of animosities. Given the activity emphasis of contemporary cognitive science, I believe that the possibilities for a dialectical synthesis are substantial. In 1992, members of the European Association for Behavior Therapy voted to change the name of their organization to the European Association for Behavioral and Cognitive Therapies. Thus, there are promising signs that the behaviorist–cognitivist dichotomies are undergoing some kind of dialectical synthesis that preserves and elaborates the wisdom and praxis of both traditions.

## Aaron T. Beck's Cognitive Therapy

One of the most visible representatives of the cognitive psychotherapies has been Aaron Timkin Beck, a Yale-trained psychiatrist whose theories, research, and practice wrought much of what came to be called "the cognitive revolution" in psychiatry, psychopathology, and psychotherapy. Originally trained as a psychoanalyst, Beck was interested in the dreams of depressed clients, and he soon began to study cognitive distortions in the thinking of his patients (Beck, 1963). After years of work and creative ideation, Beck published his classic (1967) treatise on depression and was soon thereafter outlining the basics of his cognitive therapy. More than a quarter of a century later, Beck's cognitive therapy—now applied to anxiety and personality disorders as well as to depressive disorders—is among the most popular and highly respected approaches in the world. Moreover, its potential applications continue to be explored in ways that promise to expand its domain of relevance.

I have known and respected Tim Beck for more than two decades now, and I continue to marvel at his enthusiasm for new research and theoretical developments. My favorite personal memory with him occurred in November of 1974. We had met less than a year before and had become fast friends. When my book *Cognition and Behavior Modification* (1974) came out in October, I made plans to visit Tim to personally deliver a copy. When I arrived at his office, he was surveying the partly finished chapters of his own forthcoming book, *Cognitive Therapy and the Emotional Disorders* (Beck, 1976). He was excited to see his project taking its final form after years of thinking and writing, and he showed me chapter headings devoted to belief systems, cognitive processes, and the like. I suddenly felt a sinking sensation in my stomach as I (erroneously, it turned out) imagined that I had unintentionally "scooped" the master. Tim noticed my face paling and asked what was wrong. I awkwardly explained that I felt like the young Alfred Russell Wallace in that moment in 1858 when he realized his impetuous synchrony with Charles Darwin. Tim looked at me warmly as I handed him my book, and he said, "How very generous of you to compare me with Charles Darwin!"

## *Constructivist and Complex Systems Therapies*

Constructivism and motor-evolutionary developments in psychotherapy were almost totally independent of those taking place in the cognitive sciences until the last two decades. Prior to 1955, the main works on constructivist approaches were in the realm of theory, cognitive science, and psychobiology. Then, George Kelly (1955) published his brilliant principles of experiential construction, the basis for his book titled *The Psychology of Personal Constructs.* Kelly's ideas were not immediately noticed, let alone welcomed, by either theoretical or applied psychologists. Indeed, the current popularity of his ideas is more apparent internationally than in North America (Neimeyer, 1985; Neimeyer, Baker, & Neimeyer, 1990).

Besides the system outlined by G. A. Kelly (1955) and elaborated by his followers, constructivist psychotherapies have been proposed by logotherapist Viktor Frankl and by an international collection of scholars and practitioners (e.g., Luis Joyce-Moniz and Óscar Gonçalves of Portugal; Guillem Feixas, Mayte Miró, and Manuel Villegas of Spain; Giampiero Arciero, Vittorio Guidano, Gianni Liotti, and Mario Reda of Italy; Juan Balbi and Héctor Férnandez-Alvarez of Argentina; Humberto Maturana, Roberto Opazo, Alfredo Ruiz, and Tito Zagmutt of Chile; Hubert Hermans of the Netherlands; and, from North America, individuals like Jerome Bruner, Mary Baird Carlsen, Mark Burrell, Paul Dell, Don Ford, Harry Goolishian, Leslie Greenberg, Lynn Hoffman, Bradford Keeney, Hazel Markus, Juan Pascual-Leone, myself, Eleanor Rosch, Hugh Rosen, Jeremy Safran, Esther Thelen, and Paul Watzlawick). Needless to say, I have my biases about constructivism and complex systems psychotherapies. As a conceptual base camp, they provide what I personally find to be an accommodating and viable perspective from which to observe, understand, and, at times, facilitate human experience and the life-span dynamics of psychological development.

There are, however, problems with constructivism that deserve consideration. To begin with, there is the variety of meanings for the terms *constructive* and *construction*. Relatedly, there is the differentiation between the so-called radical and critical constructivists (Mahoney, 1991a; Maturana, 1970; Maturana & Varela, 1980, 1987; Mittenthal & Baskin, 1992; von Foerster, 1984; von Glasersfeld, 1984; Watzlawick, 1984). The radical constructivists contend that all experience is personal construction, and they reject not only objectivism but also all forms of realism. Critical constructivists admit to being hypothetical realists, but they deny that we can ever develop a metric of correspondence between ontological reality (the nature of things in themselves) and epistemological reification (the process of acting as if there were some orderly relation between the furniture of the universe and the architectural designs of our knowing processes).

There is also the disputed difference between constructivist and rationalist cognitive psychotherapies. For me, this apparent difference began to emerge in the context of dialogues with John Bowlby, Donald Campbell, Vittorio Guidano, Friedrich Hayek, Mario Reda, and Walter Weimer in the early and mid-1980s. It seemed increasingly clear that the model of human learning and psychopathology adopted by rationality-emphasizing cognitive psychotherapists was fundamentally different from that expressed in those cognitive therapies emphasizing epistemological, evolutionary, and self-organizing processes. When I wrote about my early impressions of this differentiation, however, I was surprised to learn that virtually every cognitive therapist I knew considered himself or herself to be constructivist rather than rationalist in preference (e.g., Ellis, 1988). Of course, if there are no rationalists to create such a contrast, then the proposed distinction between rationalist and constructivist cognitive therapies may have limited usefulness. This matter—the meaning and practical connotations of being a constructivist therapist—is likely to be one that will persist into the twenty-first century.

I close with a very brief glance toward the future. Will constructivism persist to shape and reflect future models of human experience? Yes, I think so. But I am not so sure that the label itself will survive. To the extent that everyone claims to be a constructivist, the label will serve little purpose. It is, perhaps, because of this terminological and conceptual ambiguity that I welcome the larger expanses of complex systems terminology in the continuing evolution of cognitive and constructivist psychotherapies (e.g., Pattee, 1973, 1977, 1978; Prigogine, 1980; Prigogine & Stengers, 1984; Salthe, 1993). Even though a parallel development is likely—that is, that increasing numbers of psychotherapists (cognitive and otherwise) will identify themselves as complex (vs. simple) systems specialists—I believe that the terrain and language of discourse in the sciences of complexity may be less cluttered with excess historical baggage than most (if not all) contemporary systems of theoretical psychology and psychotherapy.

# Future Directions and Challenges

My personal hopes and fears about the future of constructivism as a force in psychotherapy cannot be separated from related reflections on the future of psychology and psychotherapy in general (Mahoney, 1993, 1994, 1995a, 1995b). To summarize those reflections, I welcome the diversity and dialogue that are being encouraged by the decline in the North American hegemony (domination and unchallenged leadership) and the emergence of both culturally contextualized and transcultural perspectives on psychotherapy (Feixas & Villegas, 1990; Férnandez-Alvarez, 1992; Fisher, 1989; Gonçalves, 1989; Guidano, 1987, 1991; Joyce-Moniz, 1985; Maturana, 1970; Merleau-Ponty, 1963; Miró, 1989; Moghaddam, 1987; Opazo, 1992; Reda, 1986; Rosenzweig, 1992). Beyond the differentiation of rationalist and constructivist cognitive therapies (a distinction that I continue to find useful in my attempts to understand the field), I (imperfectly, of course) anticipate the following developments.

1. I believe there will be an increasing appreciation of the role or roles of emotionality and emotional knowing processes in the facilitation of enduring psychological change (e.g., Greenberg & Safran, 1987).

2. Beyond a simple acceptance, the tacit (unconscious) organizing processes of knowing and feeling will be increasingly appreciated, with the practical implication that, like our clients, we therapists know more than can be described in symbols (Ellenberger, 1970; Polanyi, 1958, 1966; Shevrin & Dickman, 1980).

3. Issues of embodiment—the bodily context that affords all forms of experiencing—will become increasingly central to therapeutic relevance; that is, embodied therapies will fare better than those therapies that are relatively disembodied (as in "talking heads" therapies; Berman, 1989; M. Johnson, 1987; Mahoney, in press-b; Montagu, 1978).

4. There will be an increasing appreciation of the centrality of personal identity (self) in real-life and everyday experience, with at least two corollary implications: (a) that all acts of counseling, education, parenting, and psychotherapy are necessarily acts of participation in individual "selving" processes (Guidano, 1987, 1991), and (b) that the psychological development of the self is most powerfully constrained and shaped—for better and for worse—by the intimate relationships that have had the most emotional power for the individual (Bowlby, 1988; Sroufe, 1979; Stolorow & Atwood, 1992).

5. There will be increasingly active involvement in explorations regarding eclecticism and the "psychotherapy integration" movement, in part because these explorations offer new opportunities for a diverse and rapidly changing world (Férnandez-Alvarez, 1992; Norcross & Goldfried, 1992; Opazo, 1992; Stricker & Gold, 1993).

6. The authoritarian (justificationist, objectivist, or positivist) domination of the social sciences will be superseded by alternatives that encourage active exploration and dynamic metrics of evaluation (Bernstein, 1983; Dell, 1982a, 1982b; Hermans, 1988, 1989; Mahoney, 1976).

7. Distinctions among the cognitive, behavioral, and affective approaches will recede, with an increasing acknowledgment of holism (wholeness) as an individuating factor in all cases of assessment, diagnosis, and therapy.

8. The "cerebral primacy" and "rationalist supremacy" traditions of past decades will bow to somatopsychic and otherwise embodied expressions of holism (M. Johnson, 1987; Lakoff & Johnson, 1980; Leder, 1990).

9. Issues of value—good-bad, right-wrong, and sacred–profane—will become increasingly central in psychotherapy, with the dimensions of religiosity and spirituality taking on new meanings in psychological assessment (T. A. Kelly & Strupp, 1992; Payne, Bergin, & Loftus, 1992; Sperry, 1988; Tarnas, 1991; Vaughan, 1991).

10. The fundamental promise and power of the child will be further documented in research and theory illustrating the continuity between early, intermediate, and later life experiences (Belsky & Nezworksi, 1987; Mahoney, in press-a).

All of the above are speculations, of course, and I cannot honestly separate what I expect to happen from what I hope will happen. My sense is that this disability is not unusual.

## Concluding Remarks

There is little doubt in my mind that the cognitive sciences and cognitive psychotherapies have evolved quite rapidly in the last half century. They are evolving as I write and you read these words. Models and theories of knowing, as well as therapies that are phenomenological in their epistemologies, are developing in leaps and bounds that are impossible to deny. The complexity, I believe, is much greater than that of contemporary meteorology, because changes in weather are substantially more accurate as the time interval increases (e.g., from seconds to seasons). This reflects the fact that contemporary cognitive sciences and the cognitive psychotherapies—which have historically been independent entities—are just now beginning to dialogue in ways that are stimulating changes in all parties involved. These changes require a considerable degree of resilience, flexibility, and openness on the part of the scientist and practitioner associated with these specializations. Being, as they are, in process, such changes also make it difficult to symbolically describe or survey those fields with any degree of finality. In this chapter I have ventured a brief historiography of the cognitive sciences and cognitive psychotherapies. In both of these domains, I have concluded that some of the most promising developments in both theory and practice have emerged from the tradition known as constructivism. The warrant for that conclusion and illustrations of constructivism in psychotherapy are elaborated in the other chapters of this volume.

# References

Baars, B. J. (Ed.). (1986). *The cognitive revolution in psychology.* New York: Guilford.

Bartlett, F. C. (1932). *Remembering.* Cambridge, England: Cambridge University Press.

Beck, A. T. (1963). Thinking and depression: 1. Idiosyncratic content and cognitive distortion. *Archives of General Psychiatry, 9,* 324–333.

Beck, A. T. (1967). *Depression.* New York: Hoeber.

Beck, A. T. (1976). *Cognitive therapy and the emotional disorders.* New York: International Universities Press.

Belsky, J., & Nezworksi, M. T. (Eds.). (1987). *Clinical implications of attachment.* Hillsdale, NJ: Erlbaum.

Berger, P. L., & Luckmann, T. (1966). *The social construction of reality.* Garden City, NY: Anchor Press.

Berman, M. (1989). *Coming to our senses.* New York: Simon & Schuster.

Bernstein, R. J. (1983). *Beyond objectivism and relativism.* Philadelphia: University of Pennsylvania Press.

Bienenstock, E. (1985). Dynamics of the central nervous system. In J. P. Aubin, D. Saari, & K. Sigmund (Eds.), *Dynamics of macrosystems* (pp. 3–20). New York: Springer-Verlag.

Bienenstock, E., Soulié, F. F., & Weisbuch, G. (Eds.). (1986). *Disordered systems and biological organization.* New York: Springer-Verlag.

Bonner, J. T. (1988). *The evolution of complexity by means of natural selection.* Princeton, NJ: Princeton University Press.

Bowlby, J. (1988). *A secure base.* New York: Basic Books.

Bruner, J. (1990). *Acts of meaning.* Cambridge, MA: Harvard University Press.

Bruner, J., & Postman, L. (1947a). Emotional selectivity in perception and reaction. *Journal of Personality, 16,* 69–77.

Bruner, J., & Postman, L. (1947b). Tension and tension-release as organizing factors in perception. *Journal of Personality, 15,* 300–308.

Burrell, M. J. (1987). Cognitive psychology, epistemology, and psychotherapy: A motor-evolutionary perspective. *Psychotherapy, 24,* 225–232.

Callebaut, W., & Pinxten, R. (1987). *Evolutionary epistemology: A multiparadigm program.* Boston: Reidel.

Campbell, D. T. (1974). Evolutionary epistemology. In P. A. Schilpp (Ed.), *The philosophy of Karl Popper* (Vol. 14, pp. 413–563). Peru, IL: Open Court.

Carr, D. (1986). *Time, narrative, and history.* Bloomington: University of Indiana Press.

Catania, A. C. (1991). The gifts of culture and of eloquence: An open letter to Michael J. Mahoney in reply to his article "Scientific psychology and radical behaviorism." *Behavior Analyst, 14,* 61–72.

Cautela, J. R. (1966). The treatment of compulsive behavior by covert sensitization. *Psychological Record, 16,* 33–41.

Dell, P. F. (1982a). Beyond homeostasis: Toward a concept of coherence. *Family Process, 21,* 21–41.

Dell, P. F. (1982b). In search of truth: On the way to clinical epistemology. *Family Process, 21,* 407–414.

Dell, P. F., & Goolishian, H. A. (1981). Order through fluctuation: An evolutionary epistemology for human systems. *Australian Journal of Family Therapy, 2,* 175–184.

Depew, D. J., & Weber, B. H. (1995). *Darwinism evolving: System dynamics and the genealogy of natural selection.* Cambridge, MA: MIT Press.

Dilthey, W. (1976). *Selected writings.* Cambridge, England: Cambridge University Press.

Dobson, K. S. (Ed.). (1988). *Handbook of cognitive behavioral therapies.* New York: Guilford.

Ellenberger, H. F. (1970). *The discovery of the unconscious.* New York: Basic Books.

Ellis, A. (1962). *Reason and emotion in psychotherapy.* New York: Lyle Stuart.

Ellis, A. (1988). Are there "rationalist" and "constructivist" camps of the cognitive therapies? A response to Michael Mahoney. *Cognitive Behaviorist, 10*(2), 13–17.

Feixas, G., & Villegas, M. (1990). *Constructivismo y psicoterápia* [Constructivism and psychotherapy].

Barcelona, Spain: Promociónes y Publicaciónes Universitarias.

Feldman, J. A., & Ballard, D. H. (1982). Connectionist models and their properties. *Cognitive Science, 6,* 205–254.

Férnandez-Alvarez, H. (1992). *Fundamentos de un modelo integrativo en psicoterápia [Fundamentals of an integrative model of psychotherapy].* Buenos Aires, Argentina: Paidos.

Fischer, R. (1987). On fact and fiction—The structures of stories that the brain tells to itself about itself. *Journal of Social and Biological Structures, 10,* 343–351.

Fisher, D. (1989). Boundary work: A model of the relation between power and knowledge. *Knowledge: Creation, Diffusion, Utilization, 10,* 156–176.

Fodor, J. A., & Pylyshyn, Z. W. (1988). Connectionism and cognitive architecture: A critical analysis. *Cognition, 28,* 3–71.

Ford, D. H. (1987). *Humans as self-constructing living systems: A developmental perspective on behavior and personality.* Hillsdale, NJ: Erlbaum.

Freeman, M. (1993). *Rewriting the self: History, memory, narrative.* New York: Routledge, Chapman & Hall.

Gadamer, H. G. (1975). Hermeneutics and social sciences. *Cultural Hermeneutics, 2,* 307–352.

Gadamer, H. G. (1976). *Philosophical hermeneutics.* Berkeley: University of California Press.

Gadamer, H. G. (1988). *Truth and method.* New York: Crossroad.

Gardner, H. (1985). *The mind's new science: A history of the cognitive revolution.* New York: Basic Books.

Gergen, K. J. (1985). The social constructionist movement in modern psychology. *American Psychologist, 40,* 266–275.

Gergen, K. J. (1991). *The saturated self: Dilemmas of identity in contemporary life .* New York: Basic Books.

Glass, L., & Mackey, M. C. (1988). *From clocks to chaos: The rhythms of life.* Princeton, NJ: Princeton University Press.

Gleick, J. (1987). *Chaos: Making a new science.* New York: Viking Press.

Gonçalves, Ó. F. (Ed.). (1989). *Advances in the cognitive therapies: The constructivist–developmental approach.* Lisbon, Portugal: APPORT.

Greenberg, L. S., & Safran, J. D. (1987). *Emotion in psychotherapy.* New York: Guilford.

Guidano, V. F. (1987) . *Complexity of the self: A developmental approach to psychopathology and therapy.* New York: Guilford.

Guidano, V. F. (1991). *The self in process: Toward a post-rationalist cognitive therapy.* New York: Guilford.

Hager, D. (1992). Chaos and growth. *Psychotherapy, 29,* 378–384.

Hamowy, R. (1987). *The Scottish Enlightenment and the theory of spontaneous order.* Carbondale: Southern Illinois University Press.

Hayek, F. A. (1952). *The sensory order.* Chicago: University of Chicago Press.

Hayek, F. A. (1964). The theory of complex phenomena. In M. Bunge (Ed.), *The critical approach to science and philosophy: Essays in honor of K. R. Popper* (pp. 332–349). New York: Free Press.

Hebb, D. O. (1949). *The organization of behavior.* New York: Wiley.

Heidegger, M. (1962). *Being and time.* New York: Harper & Row (Original work published 1927).

Heidegger, M. (1971). *On the way to language.* New York: Harper & Row (Original work published 1959).

Hermans, H. J. M. (1988). On the integration of nomothetic and idiographic research methods in the study of personal meaning. *Journal of Personality, 56,* 785–812.

Hermans, H. J. M. (1989). The meaning of life as an organized process. *Psychotherapy, 26,* 11–22.

Hirst, W. (Ed.). (1988). *The making of cognitive science.* Cambridge, England: Cambridge University Press.

Homme, L. E. (1965). Perspectives in psychology: XXIV. Control of coverants, the operants of the mind. *Psychological Record, 15,* 501–511.

Iser, W. (1978). *The act of reading: A theory of aesthetic response.* Baltimore: Johns Hopkins University Press.

James, W. (1890). *Principles of psychology.* New York: Henry Holt.

James, W. (1958). *The varieties of religious experience.* New York: New American Library (Original work published 1902).

Janet, P. (1898). *Neurosis and fixed ideas.* Paris: Alcan.

Jantsch, E. (1980). *The self-organizing universe: Scientific and human implications of the emerging paradigm of evolution.* New York: Pergamon.

Jantsch, E. (Ed.). (1981). *The evolutionary vision: Toward a unifying paradigm of physical, biological, and sociocultural evolution.* Boulder, CO: Westview Press.

Johnson, M. (1987). *The body* in *the mind: The bodily basis of meaning, imagination, and reason.* Chicago: University of Chicago Press.

Johnson, M. H. (Ed.). (1993). *Brain development and cognition.* Oxford, England: Oxford University Press.

Joyce-Moniz, L. (1985). Epistemological therapy and constructivism. In M. J. Mahoney & A. Freeman (Eds.), *Cognition and psychotherapy* (pp.143–179). New York: Plenum.

Kauffman, S. A. (1993). *The origins of order: Self-organization and selection in evolution.* Oxford, England: Oxford University Press.

Kelly, G. A. (1955). *The psychology of personal constructs* (2 vols.). New York: Norton.

Kelly, T. A., & Strupp, H. H. (1992). Patient and therapist values in psychotherapy: Perceived changes, assimilation, similarity, and outcome. *Journal of Consulting and Clinical Psychology, 60,* 3–40.

Kvale, S. (Ed.). (1992). *Psychology and postmodernism.* Newbury Park, CA: Sage.

Lakoff, G., & Johnson, M. (1980). *Metaphors we live by.* Chicago: University of Chicago Press.

Leder, D. (1990). *The absent body.* Chicago: University of Chicago Press.

Lewin, R. (1992). *Complexity: Life at the edge of chaos.* New York: Macmillan.

Madison, G. B. (1988). *The hermeneutics of postmodernity.* Bloomington: Indiana University Press.

Mahoney, M. J. (1974). Cognition and behavior modification. Cambridge, MA: Ballinger.

Mahoney, M. J. (1976). *Scientist as subject.* Cambridge, MA: Ballinger.

Mahoney, M. J. (1988a). Constructive metatheory: I. Basic features and historical foundations. International *Journal of Personal Construct Psychology, 1,* 1–35.

Mahoney, M. J. (1988b). Constructive metatheory: II. Implications for psychotherapy. *International Journal of Personal Construct Psychology, I,* 299–315.

Mahoney, M. J. (1989). Scientific psychology and radical behaviorism: Important distinctions based in scientism and objectivism. *American Psychologist, 44,* 1372–1377.

Mahoney, M. J. (1991a). *Human change processes: The scientific foundations of psychotherapy.* New York: Basic Books.

Mahoney, M. J. (1991b). B. F. Skinner: A collective tribute. *Canadian Psychology, 32,* 628–635.

Mahoney, M. J. (1993). Theoretical developments in the cognitive psychotherapies. *Journal of Consulting and Clinical Psychology, 63,* 187–193.

Mahoney, M. J. (1994). Developments and directions in psychology. *Boletín de Psicología, 43,* 7–23.

Mahoney, M. J. (Ed.). (1995a). *The cognitive and constructive psychotherapies.* New York: Springer.

Mahoney, M. J. (1995b). The modern psychotherapist and the future of psychotherapy. In B. Bongar & L. E. Beutler (Eds.), *Comprehensive textbook of psychotherapy: Theory and practice.* (pp. 474–488). Oxford, England: Oxford University Press.

Mahoney, M. J. (in press-a). *Constructive psychotherapy.* New York: Guilford.

Mahoney, M. J. (in press-b). *Embodying the mind: Constructive health psychology.* New York: Guilford.

Mahoney, M. J., Lyddon, W. J., & Alford, D. J. (1989). The rational-emotive theory of psychotherapy. In M. E. Bernard & R. DiGuisepe (Eds.), *Inside rational-emotive therapy* (pp. 69–94). San Diego, CA: Academic Press.

Mahoney, M. J., & Weimer, W. B. (1994). Friedrich A. Hayek, 1899–1992. *American Psychologist, 49,* 63.

Maturana, H. R. (1970). *Biology of cognition* (Biological Computer Laboratory Report 9.0). Urbana: University of Illinois.

Maturana, H. R., & Varela, F. J. (1980). *Autopoeisis and cognition: The realization of the living.* Boston:

Reidel.

Maturana, H. R., & Varela, F. J. (1987). *The tree of knowledge: The biological roots of human understanding*. Boston: Shambhala Publications.

Mazlish, B. (1993). *The fourth discontinuity: The co-evolution of humans and machines*. New Haven: CT: Yale University Press.

McCulloch, W. S., & Pitts, W. (1943). A logical calculus of the ideas immanent in nervous activity. *Bulletin of Mathematical Biophysics, 5,* 115–133.

Meichenbaum, D. (1969). The effects of instructions and reinforcement on thinking and language behaviors of schizophrenics. *Behavior Research and Therapy, 7,* 101–114.

Meichenbaum, D. (1974). *Cognitive behavior modification*. Morristown, NJ: General Learning Press.

Meichenbaum, D. (1977). *Cognitive behavior modification*. New York: Plenum.

Meichenbaum, D. (1995). Changing conceptions of cognitive behavior modification: Retrospect and prospect. In M. J. Mahoney (Ed.), *Cognitive and constructive psychotherapies* (pp. 20–26). New York: Springer.

Merleau-Ponty, M. (1962). *Phenomenology of perception* (C. Smith, Trans.). London: Routledge & Kegan Paul.

Merleau-Ponty, M. (1963). *The structure of behavior* (A. L. Fisher, Trans.). Boston: Beacon Press.

Messer, S. B., Sass, L. A., & Woolfolk, R. L. (Eds.). (1988). *Hermeneutics and psychological theory: Interpretive perspectives on personality, psychotherapy, and psychopathology*. New Brunswick, NJ: Rutgers University Press.

Meyer, D. (1965). *The positive thinkers*. Garden City, NY: Doubleday.

Miller, G. A., Galanter, E., & Pribram, K. H. (1960). *Plans and the structure of behavior*. New York: Holt.

Minsky, M. L., & Papert, S. A. (1969). *Perceptrons*. Cambridge, MA: MIT Press.

Miró, M. (1989). Knowledge and society: An evolutionary outline. In Ó. F. Gonçalves (Ed.), *Advances in the cognitive therapies: The constructive–developmental approach* (pp. 111–128). Lisbon, Portugal: APPORT.

Mittenthal, J. E., & Baskin, A. B. (Eds.). (1992). *The principles of organization in organisms*. Reading, MA: Addison-Wesley.

Moghaddam, F. M. (1987). Psychology in three worlds. *American Psychologist, 42,* 912–920.

Montagu, A. (1978). *Touching: The human significance of the skin* (2nd ed.). New York: Harper & Row.

Morrison, F. (1991). *The art of modeling dynamic systems: Forecasting for chaos, randomness, and determinism*. New York: Wiley Interscience.

Neimeyer, R. A. (1985). *The development of personal construct psychology*. Lincoln: University of Nebraska Press.

Neimeyer, R. A., Baker, K. D., & Neimeyer, G. J. (1990). The current status of personal construct theory. In R. A. Neimeyer & G. J. Neimeyer (Eds.), *Advances in personal construct theory* (Vol. 1, pp. 3–22). Greenwich, CT: JAI Press.

Norcross, J. C., & Goldfried, M. R. (Eds.). (1992). *Handbook of psychotherapy integration*. New York: Basic Books.

Opazo, R. (Ed.). (1992). *Integración en psicoterápia* [Integration in psychotherapy]. Santiago, Chile: Centro Científico de Desarrollo Psicológico.

Palmer, R. E. (1969). *Hermeneutics: Interpretation theory in Schleiermacher, Dilthey, Heidegger, and Gadamer*. Evanston, IL: Northwestern University Press.

Parker, G. T. (1973). *Mind cure in New England*. Hanover, NH: University Press of New England.

Pattee, H. H. (1973). *Hierarchy theory: The challenge of complex systems*. New York: George Braziller.

Pattee, H. H. (1977). Dynamic and linguistic modes of complex systems. *International Journal of General Systems, 3,* 259–266.

Pattee, H. H. (1978). The complementarity principle in biological and social structures. *Journal of Biological and Social Structures, I,* 191–200.

Payne, I. R., Bergin, A. E., & Loftus, P. E. (1992). A review of attempts to integrate spiritual and standard psychotherapy techniques. *Journal of Psychotherapy Integration, 2,* 171–192.

Peale, N. V. (1960). *The power of positive thinking.* Englewood Cliffs, NJ: Prentice Hall.

Piaget, J. (1926). *The language and thought of the child.* New York: Harcourt Brace.

Polanyi, M. (1958). *Personal knowledge: Towards a post-critical philosophy.* Chicago: University of Chicago Press.

Polanyi, M. (1966). *The tacit dimension.* Garden City, NY: Doubleday.

Prigogine, I. (1980). *From being to becoming: Time and complexity in the physical sciences.* New York: Freeman.

Prigogine, I., & Stengers, I. (1984). *Order out of chaos: Man's new dialogue with nature.* New York: Bantam Books.

Radnitzky, G., & Bartley, W. W. (Eds.). (1987). *Evolutionary epistemology, theory of rationality, and the sociology of knowledge.* Peru, IL: Open Court.

Reda, M. A. (1986). Sistemi cognitivi complessi e psicoterápia [Complex cognitive systems and psychotherapy]. Rome: Nuova Italia Scientifica.

Rosenblatt, F. (1962). *Principles of neurodynamics.* New York: Spartan Books.

Rosenzweig, M. R. (1992). Psychological science around the world. *American Psychologist, 47,* 718–722.

Salthe, S. N. (1985). *Evolving hierarchical systems.* New York: Columbia University Press.

Salthe, S. N. (1993). *Development and evolution: Complexity and change in biology.* Cambridge, MA: MIT Press.

Schneider, W. (1987). Connectionism: Is it a paradigm shift for psychology? *Behavior Research Methods, Instruments, and Computers, 19,* 73–83.

Searle, J. R. (1992). *The rediscovery of the mind.* Cambridge, MA: MIT Press.

Seidenberg, M. S. (1993). Connectionist models and cognitive theory. *Psychological Science, 4,* 228–235.

Sejnoski, T. J., Koch, C., & Churchland, P. S. (1988). Computational neuroscience. *Science, 241,* 1299–1306.

Shanon, B. (1988). Semantic representation of meaning: A critique. *Psychological Bulletin, 104,* 70–83.

Sherrington, C. S. (1906). *The integrative action of the nervous system.* New Haven, CT: Yale University Press.

Shevrin, H., & Dickman, S. (1980). The psychological unconscious: A necessary assumption for all psychological theory? *American Psychologist, 35,* 421–434.

Skinner, B. F. (1948). *Walden Two.* New York: Macmillan.

Skinner, B. F. (1953). *Science and human behavior.* New York: Macmillan.

Skinner, B. F. (1971). *Beyond freedom and dignity.* New York: Knopf.

Skinner, B. F. (1987). What ever became of psychology as the science of behavior? *American Psychologist, 42,* 786–789.

Skinner, B. F. (1990). Can psychology be a science of mind? *American Psychologist, 45,* 1206–1210.

Sperry, R. W. (1988). Psychology's mentalist paradigm and the religion science tension. *American Psychologist, 43,* 607–613.

Sperry, R. W. (1993). The impact and promise of the cognitive revolution. *American Psychologist, 48,* 878–885.

Sroufe, L. A. (1979). The coherence of individual development: Early care, attachment, and subsequent developmental issues. *American Psychologist, 34,* 834–841.

Stent, E. S. (1985). Hermeneutics and the analysis of complex biological systems. In D. J. Depew & B. H. Weber (Eds.), *Evolution at a crossroads* (pp. 209–225). Cambridge, MA: MIT Press.

Stolorow, R. D., & Atwood, G. E. (1992). *Contexts of being: The intersubjective foundations of psychological life.* Hillsdale, NJ: Analytic Press.

Stricker, G., & Gold, J. (Eds.). (1993). *Comprehensive handbook of psychotherapy integration.* New York: Plenum.

Tarnas, R. (1991). *The passion of the Western mind.* New York: Ballantine Books.

Thorndike, E. L. (1898). Animal intelligence: An experimental study of the associative processes in animals [Monograph]. *Psychological Review, 2*(8).

Tolman, E. C. (1932). *Purposive behavior in animals and men.* New York: Appleton-Century-Crofts.

Varela, F. J. (1979). *Principles of biological autonomy.* New York: Elsevier North-Holland.

Vaughan, F. (1991). Spiritual issues in psychotherapy. *Journal of Transpersonal Psychology, 23,* 105–119.

von Foerster, H. (1984). On constructing a reality. In P. Watzlawick (Ed.), *The invented reality: Contributions to constructivism* (pp. 41–61). New York: Norton.

von Glasersfeld, E. (1984). An introduction to radical constructivism. In P. Watzlawick (Ed.), *The invented reality: Contributions to constructivism* (pp. 18–40). New York: Norton.

Wachterhauser, B. R. (Ed.). (1986). *Hermeneutics and modern philosophy.* Albany: State University of New York Press.

Waldrop, M. M. (1992). *Complexity: The emerging science at the edge of order and chaos.* New York: Simon & Schuster.

Watzlawick, P. (Ed.). (1984). *The invented reality: Contributions to constructivism.* New York: Norton.

Weimer, W. B. (1982). Hayek's approach to the problems of complex phenomena: An introduction to the theoretical psychology of *The Sensory Order.* In W. B. Weimer & D. S. Palermo (Eds.), *Cognition and the symbolic processes* (Vol. 2, pp. 267–311). Hillsdale, NJ: Erlbaum.

Weimer, W. B. (1987). Spontaneously ordered complex phenomena and the unity of the moral sciences. In G. Radnitzky (Ed.), *Centripetal forces in the sciences* (pp. 257–296). New York: Paragon House.

Wiener, N. (1948). *Cybernetics.* New York: Wiley.

Wiener, P. P. (Ed.). (1974). *Dictionary of the history of ideas: Studies of selected pivotal ideas.* New York: Scribner.

Wundt, W. (1896). *Outlines of psychology.* Leipzig: Engelmann.

Zeleny, M. (1980). *Autopoiesis, dissipative structures, and spontaneous social orders.* Washington, DC: Association for the Advancement of Science.

Zeleny, M. (1981). *Autopoiesis: A theory of living organization.* New York: Elsevier North-Holland.

# Appendix

SELECTED INDIVIDUALS AND EVENTS IN COGNITIVE SCIENCE, 1860–1970

1860 Fechner published the first quantitative rule regarding the relationship between physical stimulation and psychological experience.

1874 Brentano inaugurated "act psychology," with an emphasis on psychological processes (in contrast with formerly popular structures).

1880 Galton published the first study of naturalistic memory ("what one had for breakfast").

1885 Ebbinghaus published his famous self-studies on memory.

1890 William James's *Principles of Psychology* anticipated many themes later central to cognitive science.

1896 Dewey published his famous critique of the reflex-arc concept.

1907 Poincaré demonstrated the phenomenon of incubation in problem solving.

1912 Wertheimer published his early work on the phi phenomenon.

1916 de Saussure founded modern linguistics.

1926 Piaget's *The Language and Thought of the Child.*

1929 Cassirer's *Philosophy of Symbolic Forms*; Korzybski's Institute for General Semantics is founded.

1931 Lewin's field theory and topological psychology.

1932 Tolman's *Purposive Behavior in Animals and Men*; Bartlett's *Remembering.*

1934 Vygotsky's *Thought and Language.*

1940 von Bertalanffy's general systems theory.

1943 Hull's *Principles of Behavior.*

1946 Heider introduces balance (consistency) theory.

1947 Bruner & Postman announce the "new look" in perception (with emphasis on perceptual set).

1948 Hixon Symposium on Cerebral Mechanisms in Behavior.

1949 Hebb's *The Organization of Behavior*; Shannon & Weaver's *Mathematical Theory of Communication.*

1952 Hayek's *The Sensory Order*; Osgood's introduction of the semantic differential technique for measuring personal meaning.

1955 Cambridge Conference on Cognition; Kelly's *The Psychology of Personal Constructs.*

1956 Dartmouth Conference on Artificial Intelligence; Massachusetts Institute of Technology Conference on Cognition (including Austin, Chomsky, Miller, Newell, & Simon); Bruner, Goodnow, & Austin's *A Study of Thinking;* Miller's "The Magical Number Seven"; Whorf's *Language, Thought, and Reality;* Newell & Simon's "The Logic Theory Machine."

1957 Chomsky's *Syntactic Structures;* Festinger's theory of cognitive dissonance.

1958 Broadbent's funnel (filter) theory of attention; Rosenblatt's perception theory.

1959 Frankl's logotherapy.

1960 Miller, Galanter, & Pribram's *Plans and the Structure of Behavior.*

1961 Luria's *The Role of Speech in the Regulation of Normal and Abnormal Behavior.*

1962 Harvard established its Center for Cognitive Studies; Rosenblatt's *Principles of Neurodynamics;* Ellis's *Reason and Emotion in Psychotherapy;* Merleau-Ponty's *Phenomenology of Perception.*

1963 Bandura & Walters's *Social Learning and Personality Development.*

1966 J. J. Gibson's *The Senses Considered as Perceptual Systems;* Spielberger and colleagues demonstrated awareness in learning.

1967 Neisser's *Cognitive Psychology;* Beck's *Depression.*

1968 Atkinson & Shiffrin's model of information processing; Bever, Fodor, and Garrett's attack on associationism.

1969 Bandura's *Principles of Behavior Modification;* Minsky & Papert's critique of *Perceptrons;* Norman's *Memory and Attention.*

1970 Bower's work on imagery in memory; founding of the journal *Cognitive Psychology.*

# 2

**∎**
**∎**
**∎**
**∎**

# Memory and Constructivism

*Paula S. Nurius*

Memory in many ways reflects the story of our life. Humans are intrinsically and compellingly meaning-making creatures. We do not approach each moment or circumstance of our life with a blank slate. Rather, we arrive as a complex amalgamation of life experiences. How do these experiences assume form and structure? How do they fit into our lives? How are we to understand the interplay among attention, interpretation, emotion, memory, and action?

Questions like these motivated my work on the two articles reprinted in this chapter. Many people picture memory as a kind of storage bin. Perhaps a big and complicated bin, but nevertheless a container in which our memories can be filed and stored for retrieval. Today, however, memory is understood as a complex and dynamic process. Different forms of memory exist. This chapter outlines some of these distinctions.

A broad distinction can be made between explicit and implicit memory. Explicit memory can be thought of as intentional recollection of previous experiences (Basic Behavioral Science Task Force, 1996, see suggested reading list). We are able consciously to recollect these memories and exert control over them. Implicit memory refers to the ways in which people's experiences influence their perceptions, judgments, and behaviors without their being aware of that influence. Research suggests that implicit and explicit memories are relatively independent and that different types of implicit and explicit memories exist. Moreover, information is represented in memory and later retrieved in different ways (Carlston & Smith, 1996, see suggested reading list). Memory can fail or be distorted or damaged in various ways, for example, through illness, accidents, or psychological trauma. Learning about the architecture and systematic functioning of memory holds tremendous potential for guiding intervention, whether it be for amnesia from brain injury; memory failures related to aging or aging-related illnesses; memory problems associated with depression, anxiety, and trauma; or helping people to make life changes.

This chapter provides a foundation on how people construct meaning, link these lessons and experiences across a lifespan, and bring memory into play. Understanding how these critical processes involving memory work helps us operationalize some of the "hows" of cognitive constructivism and social constructionism. This understanding, in turn, serves to guide our practice activities. The two articles in this chapter complement each other. The first provides a conceptual overview and the second focuses on specific implications for practice (e.g., how an understanding of memory functioning can guide a practitioner's assessment and intervention efforts to help make changes in a client's self-concept). Content of memory varies considerably, depending on contextual differences among people and their life circumstances. However, the basic mechanisms and processes are believed to function in relatively comparable or universal ways, taking into account, of course, factors such as age and developmental stage, impairment, and impoverishment (e.g., deficiencies in nutrition, stimulation, or feedback). Thus, although the focus in these articles is on self-concept, understanding basic memory mechanisms and processes can help guide constructivist practice assessment and change efforts across a range of life problems.

The mechanisms of meaning construction, retention, and use are complex and interconnected. Higgins and Kruglanski (1996, see suggested reading list) illustrate this point through their multilevel analysis of factors affecting meaning—from the biological to the cultural—and their discussion of basic principles that underlie social behavior and social psychological phenomena. Knowledge development with respect to memory and its involvement in constructivism is one example of the benefit of contributions across multiple disciplines and areas of study. The relations between the biological, cognitive, personal motivational, interpersonal, group, and cultural levels are interconnected. Together, they shed light on our social nature and our constructivist endeavors.

The following two articles do not provide a comprehensive overview of memory. The topic is too vast. The following list of articles and books are suggested, however, for readers who wish to pursue the topic more fully.

## Suggested Reading List

Basic Behavioral Science Task Force. (1996). Basic research for mental health: Perception, attention, learning, and memory. *American Psychologist, 51,* 133–142.

Carlston, D. E., & Smith, E. R. (1996). Principles of mental representation. In E. T. Higgins & A. W. Kruglanski (Eds.), *Social psychology: Handbook of basic principles* (pp. 184–210). New York: Guilford.

Higgins, E. T., & Kruglanski, A. W. (Eds.). (1996). *Social psychology: Handbook of basic principles.* New York: Guilford.

Nurius, P. S., & Berlin, S. (1995). Cognition and social cognitive theory. In R. L.

Edwards & J. G. Hopps (Eds.), *Encyclopedia of social work* (19th ed. pp. 513–524). Washington, DC: NASW Press.

Nurius, P. S., & Berlin, S. (1994). Treatment of negative self-concept and depression. In D. K. Granvold (Ed.), *Cognitive and behavioral treatment: Methods and applications* (pp. 249–271). Pacific Grove, CA: Brooks/Cole.

Pennebaker, J. W., & Memon, A. (1996). Recovered memories in context: Thoughts and elaborations on Bowers and Farvolden. *Psychological Bulletin, 11,* 381–385.

Schwarz, N., & Clore, G. L. (1996). Feelings and phenomenal experiences. In E. T. Higgins & A. W. Kruglanski (Eds.), *Social psychology: Handbook of basic principles* (pp. 433–465). New York: Guilford.

# Human Memory: A Basis for Better Understanding the Elusive Self-Concept

There has been a long-standing recognition of the influential role the self-concept plays in an individual's life. Our sense of personal identity is a thread running through our historical and social past and serves as a pivotal anchor in constructing an understanding of reality and our place in it. Yet for such an important phenomenon we find surprisingly little specificity in the social work literature regarding what the self-concept is and how it goes about exerting its influence.

In part, this dearth is due to the extraordinary difficulty in defining, measuring, and studying this vital, yet amorphous, factor. However, recent research on human memory has afforded new approaches to addressing some of the questions and ambiguities that have surrounded the self-concept. Thus, the goal in this article is to help link this growing knowledge base to the work of social work practitioners, educators, and researchers.

Specifically, I will present a visual and narrative picture of the major components of human memory and the processes that connect them. Although self-concept is the clinical focal point of this article, many of the links between human memory and social functioning can be generalized to a broad spectrum of other problem areas, such as difficulties in problem solving, coping, and relapse prevention. This is partly because the self-concept is involved in so many aspects of social functioning, but also because the same components and processes that bear on self-defining memories bear in a parallel fashion on other memories.

## The Architecture of Memory

Typically, when we encounter a complex or baffling phenomenon, we rely on metaphors and experience to provide an image and set of references to use in talking about the phenomenon. One common metaphor for memory is that of an audio or video recorder. We speak of "old tapes" and of "replaying scenes" of our lives. This metaphor also reveals our implicit notion that memory is laid out as a chronological catalogue of our lives and, to the extent we can recall it, reflects a true recording of what we observed and experienced. We are now finding, however, that this somewhat passive recorder analogy is misleading and overly static. Rather, memory exerts considerable license in directing and editing and is composed of component parts that differ in important ways.

One of the most comprehensive memory models to have emerged that speaks directly to social-psychological functioning is the Adaptive Control of Thought, or ACT*, model (Anderson, 1983). Drawing on this model and elaborations on human information processing, I depict the major components of memory in Figure 1 (Ashcraft, 1989; Kihlstrom et al., 1988; Smith, 1984). One essential distinction is between long-term and short-term memory, the latter often referred to as "active," or "working," memory. Within long-term memory we see distinctions between declarative memory and procedural memory. The sensory perceptual system that links these memory systems to the outside world also has memory properties. However, for purposes of this discussion, the central functions of the sensory perceptual system are those concerned with attending, encoding (registering and interpreting input), and cuing (activating other memory components).

We begin to see from Figure 1 how multifaceted and interactive the phenomenon of memory is. Terms such as "activation" reflect the notion that memories are held in a dormant state and need to be stimulated or activated to be used. Differences in the types of long-term memory and in the nature of their interaction with active or working memory suggest important variations in how we go about recording different aspects of our lives and views of ourselves and the world. The relation of working memory to our sensory perceptual system suggests that there are limits to what we can, quite literally, work with in our memory at any one point in time. Finally, a notion of an "executive controller" is introduced as a way to talk about means of directing attention and mental resources important to self-concept functioning. Let us now look more closely at these components.

### Sensory Perceptual System

By far, the majority of our perception and attention is performed automatically. We rely greatly on our sensory perceptual system to continuously scan our environment and to "bring to our attention" only that information that requires more purposeful attention. For example, we might believe we are not listening to the cacophony of background sounds in a crowded railway station as we talk with a friend. Yet

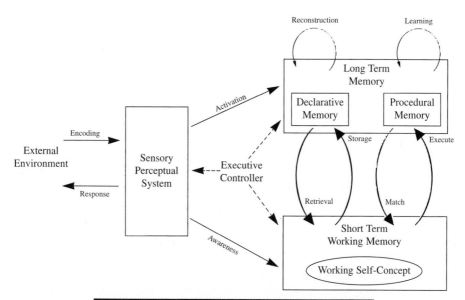

**FIG. 1.** *Elaborated architecture of memory functioning.*

our name spoken amid the rabble is piercingly noticeable, and we can hardly resist turning around to more fully attend to the source.

Apparently, we look and listen continuously. But we must be parsimonious about what we "see" and "hear" in a more conscious sense or risk being quickly overwhelmed by the flood of inputs. (The same is true for feeling, tasting, and smelling, although these have been considerably less studied.) As the above example of hearing one's name amid competing sounds illustrates, environmental input related to our self-concept is sensed and perceived as important and thus has a privileged status among inputs. Yet this is also a highly selective process. As part of our filtering process, we tend to search for information that is consistent with what we "know" and what we expect and to neglect information for which we have no experience or that is contradictory to our beliefs and expectations.

Even at this initial level, we can begin to see how our memory and information processing system serves to sustain our conception of self by biasing that which we notice in the direction of that which we expect and know how to interpret (Swann, 1985). We can also begin to see how this phenomenon has different consequences depending on the nature of these a priori beliefs and expectations. For example, the depressed person who "knows" he or she is worthless and shunned by others will anticipate, notice, and interpret events consistent with these preexisting beliefs in essentially the same fashion as the well-adjusted person who "knows" he or she has good friends and a happy life will send and receive cues consistent with his or her preexisting beliefs. In later sections I will show how this process of selective attention and perception reverberates in the memory system through other processes and in the physical form that memory structures take.

### *Long-Term Memory—Declarative Versus Procedural*

One way to understand the difference between declarative and procedural memory is to distinguish between "knowing about" and "knowing how." For example, as a child we may first gain semantic information about what the word "church" means—what a church looks like, why people go to church, what things do and do not take place in a church, and so forth. Over time we may add to this abstract knowledge our own memories of going to church as we experience its sights and sounds, thus developing increasingly complex memories. For example, we elaborate our general church images with recordings of ourselves and people in our lives, with whether our experiences were positive or negative, and with other constructs and meaning as we become more capable of understanding the sermon. Through our experiences, we further develop procedural knowledge about how one is supposed to behave, and we become increasingly more sophisticated in our own capacity to participate (e.g., in prayers, songs, and rituals).

Although these different types of memory are obviously interrelated and derive from some of the same sources, there are important distinctions in how they develop and in what their effects are. For example, a child may hear about churches and store this information in memory, but unless he or she experiences churchgoing, the child will attain little self-referent memory relative to churches and churchgoing and will develop limited procedural knowledge about how to interpret this context and behave effectively within it. We can, of course, use our imaginations to *construct* images about people, places, and events that we do not actually experience, including an understanding of how to read cues and respond appropriately. Yet, through the process of experience—particularly if the experience is repeated and personally relevant— memory structures become more detailed, more complexly organized and related to other structures, more easily accessed, and more powerful. These effects are particularly important toward transforming generic and rudimentary procedural knowledge rules (if this, then that) into more effective guides for context-specific behavior (Klein & Kihlstrom, 1986; Linville & Clark, 1989). I will consider the implications of these distinctions for intervention, but let us first more fully examine their differences.

## *Long-Term Declarative Memory*

This component of long-term memory contains what is referred to as "semantic memory" (general concepts about oneself, other people, how the world works) as well as "episodic memory" (memory of events and experiences in one's life). Semantic memory has been likened to a dictionary or encyclopedia. Episodic memory tends to be organized temporally and to include introspective knowledge of our subjective experiences (our thoughts, feelings, and bodily sensations)—thus the analogy to a movie projector within our heads. Episodic memories of unique events draw on general semantic knowledge to translate and infer meaning of the events, and semantic memories develop through the accumulation and abstraction of information obtained from episodic events. Thus, the two types interact constantly and combine to form knowledge structures in memory and, with increasing experience and complexity, organized clusters and networks of information in memory.

Thus arises the notion of "schemata," or schemas, for the structures that organize and store information, information in the form of memories of actual events and of abstractions that we generate. A schema is a system of registering information and action in an organized form (an indexing or classification system) and a guide for interpreting subsequent information and action (a schematic diagram or map). For example, a schema for the construct of independence would facilitate our noticing, retrieving, and storing information related to our independence as well as provide us with information about how to elicit and manifest what we conceive independence to be. Moreover, schemata tend to be stored in terms of their interrelatedness, such that activating one of the elements in a network or cluster of schemata should increase the accessibility of neighboring elements (Kihlstrom & Cantor, 1984; Taylor & Crocker, 1981).

The idea of mental structures as schemata through which we concretely manifest and use memory is a crucially important idea for the practitioner. Otherwise, the notion of memories remains on a relatively ethereal level and provides little guidance regarding how memories may function to influence the individual's present thought, feeling, and action. For example, the ordering of schemata in interrelated memory networks helps us both anticipate and explain how activation of one construct (e.g., incompetent) can spread to other related constructs (e.g., dumb, unemployed, poor, abandoned, loser), resulting in a negative experience of self, and how that activation has specific and intrusive influences on subsequent information processing, including serving as a nucleus around which new knowledge is achieved and stored (Greenwald & Banaji, 1989; Guidano & Liotti, 1983; Segal, 1988).

In addition to the fact that what we already know (e.g., have memory structures for) exerts a strong influence on what we take in and remember, our "recall" of a memory can be significantly influenced by experiences after storing that memory. In short, memory is a constantly integrative, reconstructive process. Eyewitness memory research has found, for example, that not only can memories of observed events be easily revised, but, because the observer is unable to discriminate between the new and original information, revised memories may actually appear to be the original memory (Johnson & Sherman, 1990; Loftus, 1979). Consider the implications for practice of this natural editing aspect of memory functioning.

Because episodic memory tends to be more private, self-referential, idiosyncratic, and subjective, it is particularly vulnerable to unbeknownst revision and distortion, unlike semantic memory, which is often based on commonly shared information. Clients' reporting of personal histories reflects less recall, in the sense of backing up a video recorder, than a current construction of that history and its meaning. This gives us insight into why individuals who shared the same experience may later have considerably different recollections of it. In memory, our past is not maintained as a historical record but undergoes change—to a greater or lesser extent as we do.

## Long-Term Procedural Memory

Procedural memory consists of rules, skills, and strategies through which declarative knowledge can be manipulated and used. Referred to as "production memory" by John Anderson, this is the component of memory that organizes and stores means-ends knowledge of how to do things, of "procedures" (Anderson, 1983). Whereas declarative knowledge is represented by concepts and propositions such as "social support helps people under stress," procedural knowledge would take the form of an if–then clause linking conditions and actions in general (*if* under stress, *then* talk with a supportive person) or specific form (*if* under stress, *then* decide what type of support is desired, consider which person would be most appropriate, find his or her phone number, give him or her a call, and let him or her know what you need). In addition to developing procedural rules for behavioral reactions, we also develop procedural rules for thought and feeling reactions (e.g., *if* I see $X$ type of facial expression, *then* I will infer $Y$ type of meaning and feel $Y$ related emotions).

Procedural memory is engaged through a process of matching an if–then rule to the relevant conditions. When a rule is selected (or "fired") its "then" action is deposited in active working memory, providing needed means–ends guidance for what to do. Whether that action is actually undertaken by the individual is contingent on a number of factors, not the least of which include environmental facilitators and constraints. Finally, procedural memory has a self-monitoring learning mechanism through which new if–then rules are acquired and existing rules are modified. Through this learning function we see one aspect of how the individual's interactions are integrated into memory and how the same memory processes can contribute to both positive and negative effects, depending on the nature of these interactions (e.g., whether feedback is consistent or inconsistent, enhancing or injurious, clear or ambiguous).

Procedural knowledge generally begins as conscious, declarative knowledge about how, theoretically, one would go about performing some covert or overt action. In this fashion, production rules provide the needed connection between one's declarative knowledge (e.g., about a trait) and one's ability to actually think, feel, or behave in ways that actualize that trait and to recognize conditions for which the trait in question is understood to be appropriate. With actual use and practice, procedural knowledge becomes more complex and habitual, but in the process it also becomes more unconscious and more difficult to articulate. Whereas declarative knowledge is generally available to conscious introspection, procedural knowledge tends to be much less so. The notions of if–then clauses, rules, and productions speak to mechanisms through which we develop cognitive skills and construct a sense of order (of contingencies between situations and actions) rather than an internal dialogue per se. Although in early stages of learning, we may say or think to ourselves, "In this situation, if . . . , then . . . ," we soon lose awareness of the discrete steps as our mastery is consolidated (Mandler, 1985). Consider how many times you have found it is far easier to show someone how to do something than to explain how it is done, even something as simple as tying a shoelace.

Some production rules are very general (applying to a variety of situations), whereas other are domain or situation specific (applying only under specific conditions). In the process of learning and grappling with novel situations, people apply general production rules (*if* people feel anxious, *then* they should seek a solution to their problems) to domain-specific declarative knowledge to interpret the situation and determine a response. With repetition, the learning mechanisms of ACT* build on the memory of prior efforts to incrementally develop domain- or situation-specific production rules (*if* I feel anxious about handling an unreasonable request, *then* I should pay attention to the specifics of the circumstances, explicitly reflect on my preferences, remind myself of times I have handled similar situations satisfactorily, rehearse my response to this situation before trying it out, and repeat this process, seeking alternatives if the first solution is blocked).

This learning process is predicated on knowledge compilation, which consists of two mechanisms—composition and proceduralization—that work together in developing new productions. Proceduralization is the process of integrating domain-specific declarative knowledge that has been activated in a situation and interpreted by general productions into new productions that incorporate the outcomes of that situation. In this way, domain-general productions are translated into domain-specific productions. When sets of productions are repeatedly used together to guide a response, they can be collapsed or "chunked" together into a new single, consolidated production. This process is called "composition." Because the resultant new production contains all the information formerly in several separate productions yet takes up one "unit" of cognitive space, it is far more efficient and, with use, gains considerable strength (Anderson, 1983; Linville & Clark, 1989; Smith, 1984). Knowledge compilation permits us to know and do many more things at once and to undertake complex interpretations and responses more easily. Yet, it also complicates efforts to challenge and change highly patterned knowledge, a point I will address later regarding self-concept change.

Inherent in procedural memory are several sources of vulnerability for the self-concept and for self-concept change. For example, if self-conceptions are left at the abstract level in declarative knowledge ("I am a worthy person," "I am not a failure"), there will be little "how-to" knowledge to enable one to manifest that quality. This lack of self-referential enactment detail, in turn, increases the risk of unsatisfactory outcomes, which are then fed back into memory, undermining the original declarative knowledge. Although the declarative memory structure may nevertheless continue to reflect and even reinforce the importance of not being a failure or of being a person of worth, without procedural guidance, a discrepancy between the construct and feedback is likely to result, leading to confusion or a sense of inauthenticity.

Note that one of the prior examples was in a not-me, negating form ("I am *not* a failure"). When one is dissatisfied with some current or possible future aspect of one's life, it is common to initially frame goals in negative terms ("I don't want to be so shy"; "I will not become the angry, bitter person my mother became"). Self-conceptions defined in this manner contain memories of states from which to move away but provide little if any positive declarative knowledge on which to begin to build models to move toward. Procedural knowledge building then rests on escape, minimization, or avoidance strategies relative to the disliked or feared attribute. The person with a negative schema of being or appearing shy is likely to avoid social situations that might activate his or her shy-self memories, a response style likely to further exacerbate the problem. Although a strong negative schema will tend to carry considerable emotional fuel for action, a clear, assertive, or socially skilled self-schema is needed to help provide the means–end guidance (production rules) for actually *being* "not shy."

An extension of this dilemma is the problem that arises if procedural definitions are begun but left at a shallow level. For example, if the if–then production rules for new selves are infrequently activated and practiced, they will have insufficient strength to compete with contradictory self-schemata ("I am a total social zero" or "I always embarrass myself in these situations") that encompass a wealth of autobiographical memory and production rules amassed over time. This is in part because the very process of frequent activation of schemata renders them more accessible (easier to activate) and the production rules more likely to be automatically fired, particularly when high arousal (anxiety, anger, fear) inhibits access to weaker and less elaborated memory structures (Linville & Clark, 1989).

## Working Memory

The numerous terms applied to this aspect of memory provide clues to its nature—active memory, short-term memory, temporary memory, working memory. Metaphors used to explain its function are that of a workbench or mental work space where conscious mental effort is applied. It is a continuously shifting composite of new information and of existing memory structures that have been activated or "brought on line" to meet the information processing needs of the moment. Because we do not have access to total memory at once, working memory refers to that portion that we automatically or purposefully make use of at any given moment.

Particularly given its importance, working memory is a surprisingly limited work space, permitting approximately seven (plus or minus two) cognitive units to be active at any one time (Miller, 1956). Of course, the more complex these units are (e.g., the more organized or interconnected declarative memory nodes are, the more compiled production rules are), the more actual information can be sustained, a point I will return to later in the article. Because of its capacity limitations, working memory is the bottleneck of information processing, constraining the two-way transfer of information between the sensory perception system and the vastly more expansive long-term memory.

Memory structures about the self are constrained in the same ways that are other memory structures. Therefore, only a limited portion of our total self-concept knowledge stored in long-term memory is accessible to us at any given moment. Parallel to the notion of a working memory, we have a working self-concept—that is, a continuously shifting composite of self-schemata that have been activated in response to situational cues and events (Markus & Nurius, 1986). Thus, in terms of memory functioning and subsequent information processing, it is our working self-concept that functions as our most immediate source of information about the self as we interact with the outside world (Markus & Kunda, 1986; Nurius & Markus, 1990).

Thus, following a public embarrassment, schemata that depict the self as inadequate, foolish, hurt, and rejected may be active, whereas a competent, creative, proud, and admired self would emerge following a public honor. We also encounter circumstances in which our working self-concepts contain a discrepant set of active schemata, which can generate a sense of confusion, inauthenticity, and reticence in responding. For example, when caring for aging parents, both caretaker and child schemata may be present. Both accomplishment and fraudulence schemata may be active if an individual receiving an award sees her- or himself as an imposter. Particularly under these latter circumstances the nature of the memories (e.g., how elaborated the declarative knowledge is, how routine the firing of if–then production rules has become) becomes very important in determining which schemata will dominate.

The self-concept is a product of person–environment interactions. Self-schemata arise from social experiences and messages (stored as episodic and semantic memory) and incrementally take how-to form in procedural memory as roles, relations, and attributes are incorporated and played out, all collectively contributing to a fund of self-memories in long-term memory. Who we are in a moment-to-moment sense is also a function of responsiveness to the prevailing situation. Rather than a single "true self," our self-concept is a product of ongoing competitions among a variety of personal realities and of subprocesses that make each of these more or less accessible to us in the moment (Mahoney, 1990; Nurius & Berlin, 1994). It is to some of these processes that I turn next.

## *Executive Controller*

The notion of an executive controller is a metaphor used to describe a number of exchange and communication functions among components of the overall memory system (see Figure 1). The executive controller can be imagined as a set of processes that serve to parcel out and direct attention and information among the different components, in much the same way a conductor cues and directs the rising and waning of various instruments in an orchestra (Ashcraft, 1989). When trying to memorize a phone number, for example, the executive controller summons a verbal rehearsal process and allocates attention to that memorization task. In contrast, when trying to remember how you know a familiar face at a party, an associative network of memories would be primed, initiating the search with most likely starting points (e.g., other social functions you have attended similar to this one).

A complete discussion of memory processes is beyond the scope of this article (see cited works for further reading on memory: Anderson, 1983; Ashcraft, 1989; Langer, 1989; Loftus, 1980; Mandler, 1985; Neisser, 1976, 1982). One major feature, previously noted, is that activation of memory structures is not random but tends to spread across memories that are meaningfully related in the individual's mind and have been stored in memory in an interrelated fashion (e.g., clusters, lists, or networks with interconnecting pathways). The basis of these interrelations can take many forms (e.g., according to categories and concepts, life domains and roles, events and chronology).

Thus, the qualitative nature and meaning of information influences what external information is noticed, what memories are drawn into working memory, and what information is stored, both in general and with respect to the self-concept. One influential factor is mood-congruence. For instance, when one feels anxiety, other self-schemata that have been distinctly encoded with anxiety become part of an associative network of memories and are far more likely to be activated than memories that have no relation to anxiety (Bower, 1981; Clark & Isen, 1982). Thus, we can see how memory processes underlie vicious cycles, such as anxiety about a possible negative outcome drawing into the working self-concept the very self-schemata associated with past failures that, in turn, augment the feeling of anxiety and of ineptitude and make access to competing self-conceptions difficult. Conversely, we can see how the same basic processes work toward more satisfactory outcomes for people who are accustomed to optimistic, confident moods and to positive messages from the social environment, all of which tend to draw into the working self-concept self-schemata consistent with and facilitative of optimism and competence (Taylor & Brown, 1988).

Other features predispose activation of some memories over others. One of these is self-reference, as was illustrated earlier by the sound of one's name commanding attention amid other noise. The more vivid (positively or negatively) a memory is, the easier it is to recall, and the more distinctive a feature is, the more likely it will be active (e.g., being the only female in a science class will make female-related memory structures more salient than in a setting where gender is balanced or reversed). One particularly important feature involves the strength of a structure. A number of factors contribute to strength, including the frequency with which a memory is activated, how well developed it is (elaborated), how many associative pathways it has (organized), and how successful use of that memory has been in the past (Klein & Kihlstrom, 1986).

In short, memories are neither created nor applied equally. Those that are not highly developed or are not often used and those that are not highly distinctive or salient will tend to be remote and not compete well. For example, being a person with two able legs will not likely function as a core, well-elaborated schema for an able-bodied individual (this will be tacit information that is simply assumed or taken as a given). But the reverse would be expected for an individual with a spinal injury. By and large, these biasing forces in memory and information processing are enormously useful. We are inherently biased toward self-enhancement and self-confirmation, and, so long as interaction with our social environments is relatively positive, clear, and consistent, these biases serve us well. However, they are conservative in nature and thus pose considerable challenge for self-concept *change*, as I will discuss more fully in the following section.

In the foregoing, I have laid out a graphic and narrative depiction of the human memory system and the roles it plays in self-concept development and functioning. In the following section I turn to modes of memory functioning, both conscious and unconscious, and how these relate to self-concept development, functioning, and change.

## Mindlessness and Unconscious Processing of the Self

In dissecting and detailing the various components of human memory, one could get the impression of a highly rational system. Quite the contrary, part of what is both exquisite and challenging about human memory is how implicitly and automatically it functions, how rife it is with enormous inferential leaps and presumptions, how capable it is of essentially rewriting history, and how utterly factual we experience our "recollections" as being. Most of the time we are not even aware our memory is actively at work, and that is both a blessing and a bane.

Memory functions in both conscious and automatic modes of processing. Innate reflexes aside, most mental processes likely begin at the conscious level with many shifting to unconscious processing once they become highly familiar (whether walking, talking, or making inferences about oneself). That is, concentration and introspection are an inherent part of the learning process. But they wane with familiarity, practice, and a sense that something is known. Contrast the novice who is extremely vigilant, attentive to detail, and "mindful" of each component part in a task to the expert who seems to sweep up great amounts of information at a glance, fills in information gaps from her or his store of concepts and experiences, and can tolerate interruptions and simultaneous tasks during this efficiently "mindless" mode (Chi, Glaser, & Rees, 1982).

Mindfulness and mindlessness are terms not intended in the colloquial sense. Rather, they distinguish the degree of attentiveness to details in a situation, of reliance on past construals of the situation stored in memory, and of consideration of alternatives to the production rules most easily activated (Langer, 1989). Both modes of processing are important, even essential. If we attempted to be truly "mindful" of each expectation, observation, recollection, and so forth, we would very quickly become overwhelmed with minutiae and paralyzed with the enormity of the task. Because automatically processed memories do not require the attention resources (awareness) of working memory, automatic processing permits us to take on more numerous and complex tasks without getting bogged down when information is incomplete or unclear since we can fill in with details from memory.

Even though experts are far more efficient and more sophisticated in the scope of information they can retrieve and process at one time, evidence suggests their analyses and judgments are not consistently more accurate or valid (Dawes, Meehl, & Faust, 1989). With repeated exposure and practice, certain semantic, episodic, and procedural memories become so frequently activated, so aggregated in larger chunks, and so interrelated in the associative networks that their functioning becomes automatic, rapid, and extraordinarily difficult both to articulate and to change. A key to accuracy in expertise is the validity of the underlying constructs held in memory. If that knowledge is inaccurate, incomplete, biased, or obsolete (e.g., the rules of the game change, and what once was true may no longer be so), then the advantages of an efficient processing structure actually become hindrances to rendering accurate judgments.

One begins to see how the dilemma of expertise relates to the self-concept (of which each of us is the premiere expert—accurate or not). Part of what makes self-concept change so difficult is that a great deal of the processing of self-related information and memories is mindless. What is more familiar to us than ourselves? In what realm could we claim more unique knowledge? Given the myriad inputs through social messages, personal experience, introspection, and trial and error, we develop highly complex schemata—more elaborated, interassociated, and procedurally "chunked." This permits many extant memories and theories about the self to be active at one time, even given the seven or so unit constraints of working memory. But the price is that much of that information comes in "predigested" form that is difficult to "de-chunk," to have an awareness of the many assumptions we are building on and to disentangle the separate elements. When the schema for "shy" is activated, for example, we may also activate a string of negative memory associations (anxiety, images of painful embarrassment or rejection, admonishments for not being outgoing like one's sister, shame for this apparent weakness) and productions that have compiled inferential, emotional, and behavioral rules into a veritable expertise in shyness.

As with expertise in other domains, we require just the slightest cue to trigger information about the self. From that point, we often do not even attend to our sensory perceptual processing (i.e., our source of data from the external environment). Instead, we rely on our internal data source (e.g., our richly constructed memories, theories, and evaluations) that have come to feel like facts. Moreover, because we feel we *know* something, we cannot help but see it (e.g., signs of our failings or unworthiness; signs of our goodness and success—depending on the nature of the prevailing schemata), even if that seeing involves a great inferential leap (Hollon & Garber, 1988; Segal, 1988).

# A Developmental Framework for Self-Concept Change

Normally, the memory system related to the self-concept is distinctly biased toward promoting a positive image of and expectations for the self (Rosenberg, 1979; Taylor, 1983; Taylor & Brown, 1988). However, even when negative self-schemata are dominant in active memory, the "totalitarian ego" is apparent, for example, screening out information that challenges the status quo, soliciting input from environmental sources likely to confirm the prevailing working self-concept (Greenwald, 1980). A balance between data-driven processing (attention to specifics of the current situation) and concept-driven processing (reliance on historical experiences and assumptions stored in schemata) is important. Yet self-concept change requires reorienting what was formerly mindless to become mindful (neglected environmental inputs—habitual patterns of activating some schemata rather than others) and what is presently mindful to become mindless (for energy-intensive efforts in activating, practicing, and elaborating new, preferred selves to become more automatic and feel more natural).

These features of self-concept lay the groundwork for a developmental framework of change. Part of this framework is founded in recognition that knowledge about oneself is acquired through learning just as any other knowledge is acquired, and this learning is a highly social process. This is easy to see in the formative years of childhood and adolescence, when the influence of significant others is so evident and growth in individuals' repertoires of self-conceptions is so rapid. Yet we now understand the process of self-concept development to be ongoing across the life span and that it is through repeated interactions that new self-conceptions take form (i.e., become elaborated, organized, compiled), that certain working self-concepts become habitual responses to certain situations, and that self-conceptions undergo change (e.g., memories are edited, contradictory cognitive structures gain strength and replace others in working memory) (Cross & Markus, 1991; Ogilvie, 1987).

In prior sections, I spoke about various forms of depth of development in each of the memory subsystems. Terms such as depth of processing, levels of representation, tacit versus explicit knowledge, and deep versus shallow structures have been used in distinguishing levels of construct development (Greenwald, 1988; Guidano, 1987; Klein & Kihlstrom, 1986; Rogers, Kuiper, & Kirker, 1977). Rather than "deleting" undesired elements of the self-concept per se, the process of change involves working to strengthen preferred schemata to render them more competitive, working to make what has become mindless more explicit so that more volitional action can be taken with it (such as searching for and encoding input that contradicts prior assumptions— purposefully activating more adaptive schemata), and assisting clients in understanding how their experiences of the self have become organized and how they can translate this understanding into managing their own self-concept change. Thus, given the persistence of self-related processes, attention to adequate depth of development of preferred structures and processes is important to establishing desirable change.

This conservatism of the memory system, particularly with regard to self-concept, has led to the lay impression that the self-concept is virtually immutable. That is not the case, but significant and enduring self-concept change requires focused effort and considerable time and repetition. Given the cost, time, and accessibility limitations of clinical services in many social agencies today, this work can be productively begun but will often need to extend beyond formal intervention. Realistically, it will also need to involve purposeful and consistent involvement by significant others in the client's social niche to help invoke preferred schemata and to provide elaborative and rein-forcing feedback (Brower & Nurius, 1993; see following article).

Moreover, crafting changes in one's sense of self and of future possibilities, of one's very identity, is a profoundly unsettling undertaking. The very tenacity that sustains memory structures and thus protects the integrity of the self-concept (posi-tive or negative) will naturally arise as an inherent resistance to challenge, even toward desired goals. An educational approach with an eye to the need for long-term change efforts is important to positively motivate clients to persevere and to aid them in understanding these otherwise perplexing impediments. More specifically, one must adopt the perspective of intervention as a training opportunity to aid clients in transferring and extending the self-change work they begin in formal intervention. One resource to support clients' awareness and ongoing management of their change efforts is metamemory.

## Metamemory as Self-Concept Change Aid

Metamemory refers to knowledge about one's memory, how it works, and how it fails to work. Metamemory is a subset of the more familiar term "metacognition," which refers to knowledge about and awareness of the functioning of one's cognitive system (Ashcraft, 1989; Flavell & Wellman, 1977). Because the workings of the self-concept are so often shrouded in an air of mysticism beyond one's control, provid-ing a client with a basic understanding of the human memory system and how it works will serve to demystify self-concept change and make it seem more achiev-able. Moreover, metamemory skills will be essential to the client, who will need to carry forward for months and years self-concept change and maintenance goals begun in treatment.

A tool for moving from general self-concept awareness to more specific, situa-tional awareness is self-monitoring. This technique helps the client gain some objec-tivity concerning one's memory habits and inclinations. Given that much of the pro-cessing about the self-concept is highly automatic, self-monitoring is a difficult skill to acquire. Aids include use of mnemonics to help encapsulate and simplify complex sequences, recording systems to monitor patterns over time, and techniques such as "think aloud" and knowledge "mining" that help the client to articulate more of the associative and procedural knowledge that he or she draws on but has difficulty artic-ulating (Goldberg & Shaw, 1989; Nurius & Nicoll, 1992).

In part because of the difficulty of self-concept change, it is best to begin with narrowly focused goals and specific circumstances that appear particularly trouble-some. Although broad-scale, abstract revisions in self-concept may be an ultimate goal, the steps toward that goal must be very focused for the client to develop metamemory skills, to accomplish enduring change in self-schemata and schematic processing, and to avoid becoming overwhelmed and discouraged. Changes in every aspect of memory functioning will be needed: changes in what the sensory perceptual system attends to and encodes, changes in which cognitive structures are activated into working memory, changes in the pool of declarative and procedural knowledge available to draw on and the relative development of new knowledge, and changes in the habits of activity in each subsystem. In this regard, one can view strategic self-concept development as a skill, and, like all skills, it is best undertaken in a delimited, incremental, progressive fashion.

It has become clear that insight into the nature of our self-schemata, their origin, or how they currently influence us is insufficient to generate change. The process of self-concept change may *begin* with an ardent commitment to change, salient representations of what not to be, an understanding of the social cognitive factors that shape self-concept functioning, and even an image of an ultimate preferred possible self. However, fundamentally, significant and durable self-concept change is predicated on changed and new memories, which are in turn predicated on changed and new experiences, which are generally predicated on changed or new conditions. Deliberate strategies for learning and practicing alternatives are essential. To "de-automate" routines and to make new ones successfully competitive, extensive deliberate rehearsal is needed. Initial focus on specific change goals will increase the likelihood of observable change and will facilitate clients' ability to self-monitor their incremental change process (Brower & Nurius, 1993; Guidano, 1987; Hollon & Garber, 1988; Nurius & Berlin, 1994; see following article).

## Conclusion

I have argued that recent advances in understanding human memory provide an important key to the self-concept. Through a better understanding of the memory-based building blocks and processes that govern self-concept, the practitioner can better integrate human behavior theory with practice techniques and thus strengthen assessment, intervention, and client self-management efforts.

The principal goal of this article has been to make recent advances in human memory research more accessible to the social work practitioner, educator, and researcher. Building on this and related foundations, subsequent work is needed to specify and test the utility of assessment and intervention methods for work with the self-concept and other aspects of social-psychological functioning.

## References

Anderson, J. R. (1983). *The architecture of cognition.* Cambridge, MA: Harvard University Press.
Ashcraft, M. H. (1989). *Human memory and cognition.* Glenview, IL: Scott, Foresman.
Bower, G. H. (1981). Mood and memory. *American Psychologist, 36,* 129–148.

Brower, A. M., & Nurius, P. S. (1993). *Social cognition and individual change: Current theories and counseling guidelines.* Beverly Hills, CA: Sage.

Chi, M. T. H., Glaser, R., & Rees, E. (1982). Expertise in problem solving. In R. J. Sternberg (Ed.), *Advances in psychology of human intelligence* (pp. 7–75). Hillsdale, NJ: Erlbaum.

Clark, M. S., & Isen, A. M. (1982). Toward understanding the relationship between feeling states and social behavior. In A. Hastorf & A. M. Isen (Eds.), *Cognitive social psychology.* New York: Elsevier-North Holland.

Cross, S., & Markus, H. (1991). Possible selves across the life span. *Human Development, 34,* 230–255.

Dawes, R. M., Meehl, P. E., & Faust, D. (1989). Clinical versus actuarial judgment. *Science, 243,* 1668–1673.

Flavell, J. H., & Wellman, H. M. (1977). Metamemory. In H. W. Reese & L. P. Lipsett (Eds.), *Perspectives on the development of memory and cognition.* Hillsdale, NJ: Erlbaum.

Goldberg, J. O., & Shaw, B. F. (1989). The measurement of cognition in psychopathology: Clinical and research applications. In A. Freeman, K. M. Simon, L. E. Beutler, & H. Arkowitz (Eds.), *Comprehensive handbook of cognitive therapy* (pp. 37–59). New York: Plenum.

Greenwald, A. G. (1980). The totalitarian ego: Fabrication and revision of personal history. *American Psychologist, 35,* 603–618.

Greenwald, A. G. (1988). Self-knowledge and self-deception. In J. S. Lockard & D. L. Paulhus (Eds.), *Self-deception: An adaptive mechanism?* (pp. 113–131). Englewood Cliffs, NJ: Prentice-Hall.

Greenwald, A. G., & Banaji, M. R. (1989). The self as a memory system: Powerful, but ordinary. *Journal of Personality and Social Psychology, 57,* 41–54.

Guidano, V. F. (1987). *Complexity of the self: A developmental approach to psychopathology and therapy.* New York: Guilford.

Guidano, V. F., & Liotti, G. (1983). *Cognitive processes and emotional disorders.* New York: Guilford.

Hollon, S. D., & Garber, J. (1988). Cognitive therapy. In L. Y. Abramson (Ed.), *Social cognition and clinical psychology: A synthesis* (pp. 209–216). New York: Guilford.

Johnson, M. K., & Sherman, S. J. (1990). Constructing and reconstructing the past and future in the present. In E. J. Higgins & R. M. Sorrentino (Eds.), *Handbook of motivation and cognition: Foundations of social behavior* (pp. 482–526). New York: Guilford.

Kihlstrom, J. F., & Cantor, N. (1984). Mental representations of the self. In L. Berkowitz (Ed.), *Advances in experimental social psychology* (Vol. 17). New York: Academic Press.

Kihlstrom, J. F., Cantor, N., Albright, J. S., Chew, B. R., Klein, S. B., & Niedenthal, P. M. (1988). Information processing and the study of the self. *Advances in Experimental Social Psychology, 21,* 145–178.

Klein, S. B., & Kihlstrom, J. F. (1986). Elaboration, organization, and the self-reference effect in memory. *Journal of Experimental Psychology: General, 115,* 26–38.

Langer, E. J. (1989). *Mindfulness.* Reading, MA: Addison-Wesley.

Linville, P. W., & Clark, L. F. (1989). Can production systems cope with coping? *Social Cognition, 7,* 195–236.

Loftus, E. F. (1979). *Eyewitness testimony.* Cambridge, MA: Harvard University Press.

Loftus, E. F. (1980). *Memory.* Reading, MA: Addison-Wesley.

Mahoney, M. J. (1990). *Human change processes.* New York: Basic Books.

Mandler, G. (1985). *Cognitive psychology.* Hillsdale, NJ: Erlbaum.

Markus, H., & Kunda, Z. (1986). Stability and malleability of the self-concept. *Journal of Personality and Social Psychology, 51,* 858–866.

Markus, H., & Nurius, P. S. (1986). Possible selves. *American Psychologist, 41,* 954–969.

Miller, G. A. (1956). The magical number seven, plus or minus two: Some limits on our capacity for processing information. *Psychological Review, 63,* 81–97.

Neisser, U. (1976). *Cognition and reality.* San Francisco: Freeman.

Neisser, U. (1982). *Memory observed: Remembering in natural contexts.* San Francisco: Freeman.

Nurius, P. S., & Berlin, S. B. (1994). Negative self-concept and depression. In D. Granvold (Ed.), *Cognitive and behavioral treatment.* Pacific Grove, CA: Brooks/Cole.

Nurius, P. S., & Markus, H. (1990). Situational variability in the self-concept: Appraisals, expectancies, and asymmetries. *Journal of Social and Clinical Psychology, 9,* 316–333.

Nurius, P. S., & Nicoll, A. E. (1992). Capturing clinical expertise: An analysis of knowledge "mining" through expert system development. *Clinical Psychology Review, 12,* 705–717.

Ogilvie, D. (1987). The undesired self: A neglected variable in personality research. *Journal of Personality and Social Psychology, 52,* 379–385.

Rogers, T. B., Kuiper, N. A., & Kirker, W. S. (1977). Self-reference and the encoding of personal information. *Journal of Personality and Social Psychology, 35,* 677–688.

Rosenberg, M. (1979). *Conceiving the self.* New York: Basic Books.

Segal, Z. V. (1988). Appraisal of the self-schema construct in cognitive models of depression. *Psychological Bulletin, 103,* 147–162.

Smith, E. R. (1984). Model of social inference processes. *Psychological Review, 91,* 392–413.

Swann, W. B., Jr. (1985). The self as architect of social reality. In B. R. Schlenker (Ed.), *The self and social life* (pp. 100–126). New York: McGraw-Hill.

Taylor, S. E. (1983). Adjustment to threatening events: A theory of cognitive adaptation. *American Psychologist, 38,* 1161–1173.

Taylor, S. E., & Brown, J. D. (1988). Illusion and well-being: A social psychological perspective on mental health. *Psychological Bulletin, 103,* 193–210.

Taylor, S. E., & Crocker, J. (1981). Schematic bases of social information processing. In E. T. Higgins, C. P. Herman, & M. P. Zanna (Eds.), *Social cognition* (pp. 89–134). Hillsdale, NJ: Erlbaum.

*The author thanks Mary Lou Balassone, Walter Hudson, and reviewers for comments on an earlier version of this article.*

# Assessing and Changing Self-Concept: Guidelines from the Memory System

*[Regarding the self-concept:] What began as an apparently singular, static, lump-like entity has become a multi-dimensional, multi-faceted dynamic structure that is systematically implicated in all aspects of social information processing. (H. Markus & E. Wurf, 1987)*

Adding to a long-standing appreciation of the enormously influential role of the self-concept in our individual constructions of reality, the epigraph reflects significant changes in our understanding of the forms that role takes. Earlier work has discussed the difficulties in concretely grounding and operationalizing the elusive self-concept as well as the limitations imposed when such a central feature of social functioning remains vaguely defined (Nurius, 1989, see preceding article). Recent advances in allied fields regarding understanding of the human memory system provide promising approaches to better understanding the self-concept.

This article extends prior work by focusing on implications for self-concept change and interventions designed to facilitate therapeutic self-concept change goals. Although the clinical focus of this article is the self-concept, the linkages described here generalize to many other clinical foci as well. Memory structures and processes related to self-identity information function in essentially the same fashion as do memory structures and processes related to other types of information about the person or about his or her social world. Thus, change goals that involve developing substantially new memory structures or working differently with memory structures, such as enhancing problem-solving, coping, and relapse prevention patterns, can apply to many of the recommendations offered here.

## Architecture of Memory

As seen in Figure 1, human memory is a highly interactive system. Long-term memory is what most people think of when we speak of memory, and two types are distinguished: declarative and procedural. Declarative memory consists of general knowledge about oneself and the world (semantic memory), which has a great deal of overlap with other people's general knowledge, and very specific autobiographical memories gleaned from one's own experiences and subjective introspection (episodic memory). In contrast to the "knowing about" type of declarative knowledge, procedural memory consists of "knowing how" knowledge—the skills, rules, and strategies for doing things. The physical form that memory structures take is referred to as schemas or schemata. Short-term memory is often referred to as active or working memory to denote that it is the portion of our total memory store that has been activated and is presently dominant in our awareness and cognitive "work space." Because we do not have simultaneous access to all of our memories related to our sense of self,

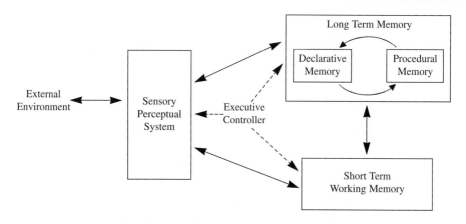

**FIG. 1.** *Basic architecture of memory functioning.*

our concept of the moment derives largely from that subset of self-schemata currently salient in working memory, that is, our working self-concept. The sensory perceptual system serves as the conduit for our memory system to the outside world and works closely with the "executive controller," which is actually a metaphor for the numerous communication and interchange processes among the memory components.

We tend to develop habits with respect to which of these processes we rely on and how we use them. Memory functioning that has become highly patterned and automatic is referred to as mindless or unconscious processing. Under such conditions we tend to overlook, ignore, or discount data in our environment, and memory functioning becomes highly concept driven (that is, we use our memories to fill in the information gaps, to make inferences and predictions). It is beyond the scope of this article to provide a detailed discussion of consciousness, including distinctions among preconscious, unconscious, and mindless information access and processing. A more apt, although more cumbersome, term for "mindlessness" may be "awarelessness," that is, a relatively low degree of mental alertness and attentiveness to the stimuli at hand. The interested reader is referred to Fiske and Taylor (1991), Kihlstrom (1987), Loftus (1992), and Uleman and Bargh (1989) for more in-depth discussion. For more detail regarding memory components and functioning, refer to specialized sources (Anderson, 1983; Ashcraft, 1989; Brower & Nurius, 1993; Langer, 1989; Loftus, 1980; Ross, 1989; see preceding article).

## Key Assessment Questions

The preceding provides a descriptive overview on which the practice guidelines presented in this article can build. However, the goal here is not simply to ask the reader to adopt a set of techniques or recommendations. Rather, the goal is to aid the reader in conceptualizing self-concept functioning and self-concept change in terms of the underlying architecture that houses and governs it, and thereby to be better able to make creative, judicious use of recommendations offered here and elsewhere. This is by no means to argue that memory functioning is a complete framework. Instead, it serves as an overlay, providing complementary knowledge about what the self-concept consists of and how it operates.

As with any problem area, we must undertake a kind of translation or mapping to link the specific nature of the client's problem gleaned through assessment with the underlying apparatus to plot an appropriate intervention plan. With respect to desired self-concept change, a number of assessment questions related to the memory system are indicated. Consider a woman who sees herself as weak, ineffectual, and not very bright and who would like to change that self-view. The process of clarifying what this means to her, what she bases her self-perception on, and what her change goals look like provides the opportunity to address certain questions.

Does she appear to lack a reasonably clear picture of what alternative self-concept goals would look like? If so she may have impoverished semantic knowledge about what being strong, capable, and bright literally look like. If she has some general capacity to define and envision these alternatives but cannot see herself being or doing them, she likely has impoverished episodic or autobiographical knowledge. These are signals that, among other things, her long-term declarative memory is lacking in the types of memory structures it needs to build an alternative self-concept.

Does she appear to have memory structures about these alternatives (both general semantic knowledge and specific episodic knowledge) but reports that these seem remote to her, that it has been a long time since she recalled earlier memories of herself in that way? This suggests that self-schemata resources are available in long-term memory but that they are weak and are not being recruited into working memory for active use.

Does she report a sense of inauthenticity and confusion about herself, that the ways she sees herself seem at times very contradictory? This occurs when discrepant self-schemata are recruited simultaneously into working memory. For example, when she finds she is able to recall vivid memories of herself both as capable and ineffectual, as both intelligent and hopelessly befuddled, it is difficult to ascertain at that moment what is "real" about the self, and this can be very disturbing (Higgins, Bond, Klein, & Strauman, 1986).

Does she appear able to recruit memories of these alternative selves into working memory but cannot provide much detail about how to go about manifesting them—in this case, of behaving in ways that actualize images of strong, capable, and bright? This would suggest that although she has some degree of declarative memory, she is significantly lacking in procedural memory. That is, these memory structures have not progressed sufficiently in their development to get beyond a relatively abstract, general level, leaving her with relatively primitive how-to knowledge and habits of actualizing these desired end states.

Does she seem to pay only minimal attention to the information in her environment with respect to her self-concept perceptions? That is, does she appear to presume that others are viewing her as weak, ineffectual, and not very bright, and does she tend to automatically and frequently interpret outcomes and feedback as alluding to these qualities in her? This signals that she has shifted into a mindless or automatic mode of functioning from being data driven (paying close attention to the information in her environment) to being concept driven (being memory driven and inattentive to environmental specifics) in how she uses her sensory perceptual system to encode information from her external environment.

Does she appear to be relatively unaware of her own memory functioning and have little understanding of how it works and how it fails to work? Does she appear to experience her recollections and situational self-perceptions as being beyond her influence? This is true for many of us and reflects an untapped potential for meta-memory. We all have considerably greater potential than we tend to make purposeful use of for shaping what we otherwise experience as being an automatic set of memory-related processes.

## Targeting Change in the Memory System

The preceding examples illustrate means of translating understanding of memory functions into assessment questions about new and different components that may be related to the presenting problem. At this point let us consider more specific intervention targets and approaches that take this understanding into account. The goal here is to identify various guidelines related to self-concept change that appear most promising on the basis of memory functioning as it is presently understood. Thus, rather than an exhaustive or unique list, these guidelines serve to modify and extend existing intervention approaches and are organized according to major components and processes of the memory system and how they relate to change.

### *Enriching One's Fund of Knowledge: Declarative Memory*

Declarative memory is essentially the storehouse of memories that an individual has amassed over time and draws from. We have distinguished between episodic memory (the idiosyncratic, introspective knowledge about the person's thoughts and experiences) and semantic memory (general knowledge about concepts, attributes, and language) as different types of mental representations about the self encoded in memory alongside representations of other objects and phenomena in the world. These two types of memories form the fund of knowledge that individuals draw from to make sense out of what they encounter, to identify options for responding, and to experiment with efforts to manifest or do what is desired and to avoid or guard against what is undesirable. Because memories are available (have been encoded and stored) does not mean that they are necessarily accessible (easily retrievable into working memory) nor that they exist in a well-developed or easily applied form. Enriching the fund of knowledge, then, involves introducing needed knowledge structures and making efforts to elaborate them and flesh them out.

With respect to self-concept one key assessment issue is precisely this distinction: whether the preferred self-schemata are absent from declarative memory or whether they exist but there is difficulty retrieving them. If the sample client has had few models or experiences related to what a preferred self (for example, being a capable woman) means and looks like, she will need to develop these basic memory structures through the process of learning.

Semantic and episodic memories interact and thereby serve to more fully flesh out or elaborate a memory structure in multiple forms (for example, language, symbols, images, and other sensory traces). Thus, learning efforts should include explicit attention to general world knowledge (for example, in what different ways can attributes of capable, strong, and intelligent be defined, and what are prototypical examples of them?) as well as attention to experiential, self-referential knowledge.

Degree and form of elaboration are barometers of how influential a schema will be once activated. Thus, the more numerous and vivid the episodic memories of being or doing what the schema entails, and the more detailed and interassociated the semantic memories about what the attributes consist of, the more retrievable and powerful (and, therefore, more competitive) these new self-schemata will be in working memory.

The primary mechanism through which new information gets transferred or "copied" to long-term memory is through rehearsal (recycling and practicing the contents of working memory; the greater the frequency, the stronger the transfer; Hasher & Zacks, 1984). The mere exposure afforded by traditional one-hour-a-week treatment schedules is by no means sufficient. Moreover, relevant rehearsal appears to be the key versus simple repetition (as when trying to commit a phone number to memory).

Examples of ways to enhance relevance in rehearsal include replicating as much as possible in rehearsal the conditions that characterize retrieval (that is, the target situations under which the preferred self-schemata are most needed), making explicit efforts to rehearse reflectively (for example, to draw meaningful associations and emotional responses), and using imagery to form sensory-rich representations (for example, visualization, modeling). Rehearsal that is irrelevant, in these terms, for the desired conditions (for example, when the client feels threatened or is at risk of self-denigration) appears to result in shallow processing and be of limited benefit.

Efforts designed to elaborate schemata (for example, imagery, focused reflection, and rehearsal) are unlikely to be effective unless they explicitly include visualization of and reference to oneself. Individuals often have abstract schemata for attributes and phenomena or have memory structures related to other people (for example, "my sister is the smart one"). If the desired attribute has not been encoded as self-schemata, then it does not function as self-schemata.

A corollary to adding desired knowledge structures is getting rid of structures that are undesired. Existing self-schemata, however, cannot readily be deleted or purged from memory per se. Rather, efforts should be directed toward reducing their retrievability and strength and to simultaneously enhancing that of preferred schemata. Two methods of reducing the influence of undesired self-schemata are (1) to purposefully revise them (for example, through cognitive reframing and reconstruction) and (2) to reduce the frequency with which they are activated, thus weakening the retrieval pathway.

Emotion is a strong element in memory. Thus, elaboration efforts should include attention to mood congruence in the moment (that is, explicitly invoking a positive mood in the process of learning and rehearsing). When anxious, for example, anxiety-coded memory structures tend to be primed and readily activated. Conversely, purposefully activated schemata that are confidence coded will help bring that information with them to working memory.

Prompting and feedback from the environment are important to increasing frequency of activation and to elaborating the memory structure. However, feedback is often so subtle and vague that it can be readily overlooked or discounted. Thus, highly visible, specific, and frequent feedback is optimal.

## Translating "Knowing About" into "Knowing How": Procedural Memory

Procedural knowledge of how to go about being a given attribute or achieving a given goal is highly interactive with declarative knowledge about what those attributes and goals involve. For example, intervention efforts to promote procedural knowledge, such as engaging clients in training and practice, become a source of autobiographical memory that further elaborates declarative memory at the same time that hands-on practice is being obtained. However, because procedural knowledge is an essential and often overlooked component of self-concept change, guidelines specific to its development and functioning follow.

An important assessment distinction is whether there is a deficit of production rules (that is, if–then knowledge about how to actualize an attribute or accomplish an act) germane to the self-concept goal in question; whether appropriate production rules exist in long-term memory but are not being activated; or whether these rules are activated but are presently overwhelmed by the influence of competing, maladaptive rules made salient at very nearly the same time.

An additional assessment distinction involves whether the production rule may not be inherently inappropriate but is contextually so. For example, a rule such as "If I feel threatened, then withdraw from the situation" may be quite appropriate for some circumstances, such as the risk of violence. However, if the rule has become matched with circumstances that are generating a vicious cycle (such as repeatedly calling in sick at work to avoid anxiety-producing tasks), it will serve to strengthen a self-schemata of oneself as weak and ineffectual and thus to strengthen the likelihood of these schemata being activated the next time the client feels anxious. Assessment of situational appropriateness is therefore important.

Procedural memory is more inclined to activate specific rather than abstract or broad rules in particular situations. Thus, new production rules to accompany self-concept change will be most effective if they begin as task- or domain-specific rules and are limited in scope. For example, rather than "If I feel threatened, then be assertive," a rule such as "If I feel anxious about a work task, then use that feeling as a reminder to reflect on my change goals and visualize myself performing satisfactorily with the task and rehearse what I would say and do and contact a trusted friend to help me feel positive and confident" will be more likely to be recalled and to provide more useful means–ends information.

One aid to bypassing resistance to changing long-standing views of self is to focus on possible selves (for example, "I just can't see myself as very competent or together now, but I can accept that I might be able to reach that point in the future"). The steps of elaborating declarative and procedural knowledge for possible selves are the same as with any memory structure. By framing means–ends connections of how one would go about being or accomplishing a hoped-for possible self or avoiding a feared possible self, knowledge structures may be developed in memory with a less-felt sense of threat or cognitive dissonance (Markus & Nurius, 1986; Nurius & Berlin, 1994).

"Why" explanations are useful in developing semantic knowledge to elaborate preferred self-schemata. However, "how-to-do-it" instruction is more effective for developing procedural knowledge. The single most significant factor in this type of instruction is to make alternative production rules competitive with currently dominant ones in extensive practice, preferably under conditions that approximate those in which the rule is needed (Linville & Clark, 1989). In memory, procedural knowledge tends to function more unconsciously relative to declarative knowledge. Therefore, early practice efforts should emphasize reflectiveness and mindfulness to help ensure that desired rule sequences are being encoded and routinized.

The shift from use of relatively slow, general problem-solving production rules to more direct, domain-specific rules relies on routinization and composition. Routinization is most directly increased through repetition. Composition involves collapsing a sequence of rules used in problem solving into a single, more complex, specialized, and individualized rule that has the same effect. Thus, therapeutic practice will be enhanced if the desired rule for a preferred self-schema (for example, how one goes about actualizing the attribute of strength or accomplishing the goal of competence in a particular domain) is introduced in specific incremental steps that can be consolidated as the client gains expertise.

Because self-schemata derive largely from experience, mental representations of being a new attribute will often lag behind behavioral approximations toward this goal. Thus, clients need to be encouraged to persist in developing procedural knowledge toward their change goal even though it may feel artificial and unfamiliar to them initially and even when they feel they have made true attitude change. It is through significant, incremental changes in the response habits of the individual and in the response of the social environment to the individual that revisions in the self-concept become phenomenologically and durably incorporated.

Too often, feedback from the environment is subtle, vague, or distant in time. As with declarative knowledge, specific and immediate feedback from the environment will facilitate the development and routinization of goal-specific procedural memory, making this memory component of new self-schemata more fine-tuned to the individual more quickly.

Although humans learn automatically, the ability to purposefully manage one's memory system toward specific change goals involves acquired skill. Because enduring self-concept change typically involves considerable time and repeated effort, it is important for clients to develop skills in constructing production rules on their own and with the supports of their natural environment as they encounter situations that challenge new self-schemata.

## Getting It When It Is Needed: Working Memory and the Executive Controller

In many respects, working memory is the hub of self-concept change efforts. It is the most conscious and readily accessed memory component and is most closely tied to interaction with the environment. Although people know more than they can draw from in any given moment, working memory is the main vehicle for actually tapping what is needed when it is needed. In this section guidelines focus on what is needed to more mindfully and effectively bias working memory toward desired memory subsets. Because the executive controller is a set of memory processes associated with working memory, intervention guidelines for both are discussed here.

In terms of assessment, it is important to ascertain the composition of self-schemata active within the working self-concepts of target situations. For example, when the previously described client is considering returning to finish school to get a better job, what is the qualitative nature of the self-conceptions she is able to describe? Are they completely negative, or are some positive self-conceptions salient as well (for example, "I'm a hard worker")? Are they predominantly in the form of not-me conceptions ("I'm not smart," "I'm not good at meeting people")? Are they predominantly affective, or is some concrete means–ends information salient (for example, perhaps in addition to conceptions of herself as anxious, the worst student in the class, and being derided by others, she also has an image of herself as a cutup with clear means–ends information about how to use her humor to cope). These qualitative distinctions in how the dominant self-schemata have been encoded provide directions for what is needed to fill in gaps (for example, to work more on shifting the balance from not-me to me frameworks and from predominantly affective to more means–ends conceptions).

Recruitment of memory structures into active working memory is heavily dependent on the retrieval cues salient in the moment. Thus, it is important to recreate as fully as possible the conditions associated with targeted situations to aid assessment, intervention, and progress monitoring. Evoking mood states typical of those circumstances is one mechanism for activating the self-schemata typical within them (for example, through imagery or various forms of experiential role play and enactment).

Because the mind is constantly active, the targeted working self-concept will tend to wane in working memory as other thoughts and recollections compete for dominance. Therefore, it is necessary to continually prompt and reactivate the memory structures of interest during monitoring and intervention efforts.

One important aid to both a durable record in memory and to fast, self-generated retrieval from memory is use of mnemonic devices (strategic memory cues such as images, acronyms, and rhymes). Thus, one way to assist clients is to devise mnemonic tags to help them block automatic patterns and to activate the self-schemata they prefer. Examples might include using mnemonic devices such as

SODA (Slow down the process, Observe self and situation, Draw in preferred self-images, Act in ways consistent with these) or "I am CRISP" (Calm, Resourceful, Intelligent, Sturdy, and Proud of myself), or pairing surges of anxiety or self-denigration with an encouraging or coping image, such as that of a white-hatted cavalry riding in to drive out the troublesome black-hatted schemata.

One powerful retrieval or activation cue is emotion. Because maladaptive self-schemata are often strongly mood encoded (for example, memories of embarrassment or failure are primed by acute anxiety), it is very difficult to prevent their activation at the times one most seeks alternatives (when feeling anxious). Thus, part of client preparation to self-activate preferred self-schemata may include interventions such as affect management techniques and use of negative mood to signal the onset of active coping.

Motor and kinesthetic aspects of schema representation should not be overlooked. For example, if certain postures, actions, or expressions have been explicitly associated with preferred self-schemata, then use of them will strengthen activation efforts (for example, smiling and erect posture being visually and bodily associated with self-conceptions of competence).

To develop alternative memory structures and to significantly increase their dominance (their likelihood of activation and their relative strength once activated) requires incorporation of intervention into everyday life. Thus, clients need to be trained both to detect maladaptive working self-concept composites and to purposefully activate preferred self-schemata related to new goals. This training involves use of metamemory, a topic discussed in the next section.

Because the way memory structures become influential in any given moment is through activation, it is best not to rely completely on the environment to fortuitously provide desired retrieval cues. Rather, clients should proactively seek assistance from their natural environment toward retrieving and reinforcing preferred schemata. This assistance could include notes and visible prompts to oneself as well as involvement of family and friends.

## Paying Attention in More Helpful Ways:
## Sensory Perceptual System

Although the sensory perceptual system has vast capabilities, discussion here is restricted to its attention and encoding properties. The sensory perceptual system is the prime conduit between the memory system and the outside world. Many of the following guidelines are also related to working memory to the degree they involve active awareness. However, the sensory perceptual system offers a distinctive "point of entry" regarding self-concept change and thus will be considered separately.

By nature, the memory system is conservative, inclined to resist contradiction and to seek confirmation. Thus, it is best to prepare the client for the task of encoding new information that disconfirms his or her present sense of self and of reality. For example, inform the client of the natural tendency to resist unfamiliar and seemingly disconfirmatory input and of the importance of using felt resistance as a signal to mindfully attend to new input (Goldfried & Robins, 1983).

Educate clients that natural retrieval tendencies tend to work against change, particularly within the stressful contexts that self-concept change is most often desired. For example, the memories that are most easily retrieved are those that have been most frequently activated in the past, those that are very imaginably or effectively vivid, and those that are congruent with the mood of the moment. All of these memories are more likely to involve old self-schemata than new ones. Particularly given this tendency, clients need to label intrusive maladaptive schemata as memories rather than as facts about themselves.

Initially assist the client to become more data driven than concept driven. This involves mindfully attending to details and feedback in the environment rather than relying on automatic inferences, which tend to reflect the negative things the client "knows" to be true. Such action will involve slowing down the automatic observation-activation-interpretation-response sequence, a goal that mnemonic aids (like SODA) will assist with.

Microanalysis of a sample situation can help uncover information that may be useful for disconfirming maladaptive schemata and as future retrieval cues for new schemata. The sample client, for example, may have literally lost sight of environmental cues confirming her capability because she stopped attending to external data as she has come increasingly to rely on her memory-based presumptions for what information exists in the environment. Efforts to promote dissonance regarding undesired or maladaptive schemata go hand-in-hand with efforts to promote more mindful memory processing.

One specific client aid in becoming more data driven is to practice encoding data in behavioral rather than inferential and evaluative terms. For example, rather than automatically interpreting a smile in response to a suggestion as barely suppressed derisive laughter, observe the range of observable information. Is this coworker also affirmatively shaking his head? What verbal feedback did he offer? Can the client detect herself feeling anxious? If so, this is one source of data suggesting that negatively biased memory priming and subsequent interpretations are likely.

Changes in the working self-concept are not necessarily symmetrical. That is, increased recruitment of new, preferred self-schemata does not ensure that negative schemata have not also been activated (particularly because more habitual structures often literally require less cognitive space relative to those that are newer and less consolidated). Thus, it is best, at least initially, to search for environmental data and reinforcement that disconfirm negative self-schemata as well as data that confirm more adaptive ones.

An important source of data often overlooked or discounted by clients is their own changes over time. Thus, clients need to be aided in discriminating between past and present with respect to incremental shifts in their working self-concepts. The qualitative profile of self-conceptions salient during targeted situations is one example of a baseline aid against which clients can contrast later profiles.

# Conclusion

The principal goal of this article has been to serve a bridging and translation function. Specifically, the objective has been to encapsulate recent findings regarding human memory functioning and to identify implications these research findings hold for practice targets and methods. Readers will find that some points are familiar, these having been incorporated over the past decade into treatment strategies related to self-concept and self-appraisal change (Arnkoff & Glass, 1992; Guidano & Liotti, 1983; Lazarus & Folkman, 1984; Mahoney & Freeman, 1985; Segal & Blatt, 1993; Winfrey & Goldfried, 1986). The recommendations offered here are intended to extend this process with the objective of enhancing the likelihood of effecting durable self-concept changes and of more fully illuminating potential resources and impediments inherent in the architecture and operation of human memory.

In any in-depth discussion of cognitive factors, there is always the danger of "staying all in the head" and underrecognizing the multiplicity of factors that influence development and change. Although already noted, the enormous roles of socialization and many forms of environmental constraint and support in shaping self-concept development bear repeating. In addition, the need for self-concept change arises in widely varied problem areas and domains of practice. There clearly are additional and differing elements that will need to be considered in change efforts in each of these areas (for example, in working with chemical addiction versus family violence versus eating disorders).

Regardless of practice domain or theoretical orientation, better understanding of human memory provides the opportunity to better anticipate inherent barriers to change and to pursue change efforts most compatible with innate functioning. Self-concept change is rarely an easily done deed. It may best be thought of as a relatively long-term undertaking that is given a good start through formal intervention efforts. Thus, self-help preparation is essential for clients to learn methods of plotting their own courses of self-concept change in what has remained for so long mysterious waters.

# References

Anderson, J. R. (1983). *The architecture of cognition.* Cambridge, MA: Harvard University Press.

Arnkoff, D. B., & Glass, C. R. (1992). Cognitive therapy and psychotherapy integration. In D. K. Freedheim (Ed.), *History of psychotherapy* (pp. 657–694). Washington, DC: American Psychological Association.

Ashcraft, M. H. (1989). *Human memory and cognition.* Glenview, IL: Scott, Foresman.

Brower, A. M., & Nurius, P. S. (1993). *Social cognition and individual change: Current theory and counseling guidelines.* Newbury Park, CA: Sage.

Fiske, S. T., & Taylor, S. E. (1991). *Social cognition* (2nd ed.). New York: McGraw-Hill.

Goldfried, M. R., & Robins, C. (1983). Self-schema, cognitive bias, and the processing of therapeutic experiences. In P. C. Kendall (Ed.), *Advances of cognitive–behavioral research and therapy* (Vol. 2, pp. 33–80). New York: Academic Press.

Guidano, V. F., & Liotti, G. (1983). *Cognitive processes and emotional disorders.* New York: Guilford Press.

Hasher, L., & Zacks, R. T. (1984). Automatic processing of fundamental information: The case of frequency of occurrence. *American Psychologist, 39,* 1372–1388.

Higgins, E. T., Bond, R. N., Klein, R., & Strauman, T. (1986). Self-discrepancies and emotional vulnerability: How magnitude, accessibility, and type of discrepancy influence affect. *Journal of Personality and Social Psychology, 51,* 5–15.

Kihlstrom, J. F. (1987). The cognitive unconscious. *Science, 237,* 1145–1152.

Langer, E. J. (1989). *Mindfulness.* Reading, MA: Addison-Wesley.

Lazarus, R. S., & Folkman, S. (1984). *Stress, appraisal, and coping.* New York: Springer.

Linville, P. W., & Clark, L. F. (1989). Can production systems cope with coping? *Social Cognition, 7,* 195–236.

Loftus, E. F. (1980). *Memory.* Reading, MA: Addison-Wesley.

Loftus, E. F. (Ed.). (1992). Special issue on the unconscious. *American Psychologist, 47*(6).

Mahoney, M. J., & Freeman, A. (Eds.). (1985). *Cognition and psychotherapy.* New York: Plenum.

Markus, H., & Nurius, P. S. (1986). Possible selves. *American Psychologist, 41,* 954–969.

Markus, H., & Wurf, E. (1987). The dynamic self-concept: A social psychological perspective. *Annual Review of Psychology, 38,* 299–337.

Nurius, P. S. (1989). Form and function of the self-concept: A social-cognitive update. *Social Casework, 70,* 285–294.

Nurius, P. S., & Berlin, S. B. (1994). Negative self-concept and depression. In D. K. Granvold (Ed.), *Cognitive and behavioral treatment: Methods and applications* (pp. 247–271). Pacific Grove, CA: Brooks/Cole.

Ross, M. (1989). Relation of implicit theories to the construction of personal histories. *Psychological Review, 96,* 341–357.

Segal, Z. V., & Blatt, S. J. (Eds.). (1993). *The self in emotional distress: Cognitive and psychodynamic perspectives.* New York: Guilford Press.

Uleman, J. S., & Bargh, J. A. (Eds.). (1989). *Unintended thought.* New York: Guilford Press.

Winfrey, P. L., & Goldfried, M. R. (1986). Information processing and the human change process. In R. E. Ingram (Ed.), *Information processing approaches to clinical psychology* (pp. 241–258). New York: Academic Press.

*The author thanks Mary Lou Balassone, Walter Hudson, and anonymous reviewers for their feedback on an earlier version of this article.*

**3** □
□
□

□

# Distinctions Between Social Constructionism And Cognitive Constructivism: Practice Applications

*Cynthia Franklin*

In this chapter, I expand upon Atherton's (1993) discussion and my earlier reply to that article (Franklin, 1995) concerning the epistemological debates over social constructionism and cognitive constructivism by drawing distinctions between different types of social constructionism and constructivism and discussing their relationships to both research and practice. As I pointed out in my earlier article, epistemological debates within social work and allied disciplines are related to competing research paradigms, but the more recent wave of debates within the social sciences is connected to the social critique of science and a changing world view that has implications for both research and practice. The purpose of this chapter is to illustrate how the theoretical perspectives of social constructionism and constructivism are being used to formulate clinical practice models and to point out some of the differences between these theories and their implications for practice. I also discuss research methods, describing the epistemological and methodological preferences of each perspective.

## Social Science Debates About Research Methodologies: Parallel Processes

Social constructionism and constructivism have been debated in social work education as part of a metadebate regarding science (objectivity versus subjectivity) and the appropriateness of differing research methods. Quantitative and qualitative methods are usually discussed within social work. Quantitative methods rely primarily on deduction in theory building, prediction, measurement in data collection, and statistical methods for building evidence for one's observations. (See Grinnell, 1993, and Rubin and Babbie, 1989, for research from an objectivist perspective.) Qualitative methods rely primarily on induction in theory building; understanding narrative forms of data collection such as interviewing, participant observations, and case records; and interpretive processes such as grounded theory, narrative analysis, dimension analysis, and other methods that allow the discovery of empirically derived categories by systematically comparing multiple sources of data. (See Berg, 1989; Gilgun, 1993; Gilgun, Daly, and Handel, 1992; and Miles and Huberman, 1994, for discussion of these methods; see Anastas and MacDonald, 1994, for an integrative perspective; see Chapter 4 for an explanation of how these methods have been transported into practice.)

Quantitative and qualitative methods have rich histories within the social science disciplines (Epstein, 1985; Feagin, Orum, & Sjoberg, 1991; Hamel, Dufour, & Fortin, 1993; Jacob, 1987; Lancy, 1993). In the social sciences, qualitative researchers did not object to using statistics in their studies, and quantitative methodologists have noted the importance and place of qualitative research. In a review of the implications of chaos theory for the social sciences, Gregersen and Sailer (1993) concluded that if social scientists are going to take the social phenomena of chaotic patterns seriously, then the importance of qualitative research becomes apparent.

Both qualitative and quantitative approaches to research have evolved together in a continuing struggle over which research approach is more appropriate for the human sciences (Diesing, 1991). Acceptance of research methods varies according to the social science discipline, time period, and attention given to differing theoretical or epistemological views. For example, qualitative field methods have always been used and esteemed within anthropology. Qualitative methods were dominant in American sociology while the Chicago school controlled the profession until the 1940s. But they were later dismissed by those who gained control of the profession and who favored quantitative methods (Hamel et al., 1993). Though qualitative research has continued to be a favorite method used by many sociologists and social psychologists, quantitative methods have dominated American psychology for most of this century (Gholson, Shadish, Neimeyer, & Houts, 1989). Psychology, however, has its own history of qualitative research rooted in ecological psychology, cognitive studies, and human ethnology (Lancy, 1993), and psychological writers have increasingly advocated for more diverse methodologies (Polkinghorne, 1983, 1984, 1991; Strong, 1991). To summarize, both quantitative and qualitative research methods have long histories in the social sciences, and diverse disciplines have been involved in ongoing dialectical discourses concerning which approach to research is more appropriate for the human sciences. Some researchers favor quantitative approaches and others favor qualitative approaches. A third group suggests that both approaches to research should be used. Certainly, the debates within social work closely parallel this history.

## Epistemological Debates and the New Understandings of Science

During the 1980s, critics politicized, deconstructed, and redefined science. Challenges to science were based on epistemological arguments and changing world views that challenged the acceptance of objectivity, established hierarchies, and privileged particular truths. Postmodernism and poststructural philosophies, feminist writers, multiculturalism, critical theory, and advocates of strict constructionism have led attacks on the objectivistic roots of science and belief in a stable and knowable objective reality. Postmodernism, in particular, has been influential in creating a new world view (Anderson, 1990; Katovich & Reese, 1993; Rosenau, 1992; Sarup, 1993). Postmodernism is associated with a philosophical movement begun in the 1960s. According to Anderson (1990), the postmodern individual is constantly reminded that different peoples have entirely different concepts of the world. Social institutions are human creations; personal identity may change from context to context, and all beliefs are just that—beliefs. Mass communication and vast information networks contribute to the postmodern condition (Gergen, 1991).

In response to these changing views, a general call has been made for a more reflexive human science that considers one's epistemic views, values, and assumptions. Both qualitative and quantitative research traditions have been criticized by those who call for a new reflexivity in science. Though qualitative research traditions have often accepted a phenomenological or more constructivist epistemology, studies have not been conducted with a subjectivist or reflexive orientation. Pollner (1991) states that even reflexive methodologies such as ethnomethodology have become mainstream in sociology and have lost their previous radical reflexivity. Recent writings by qualitative methodologists present criticisms of qualitative research, including the fact that qualitative researchers such as ethnographers traditionally believed that their analyses were objective and that they are not exempt from the same epistemological criticisms as those confronting quantitative researchers (Clifford, 1988; Clifford & Marcus, 1986; Denzin, 1992; Eisner, 1985; Geertz, 1983, 1988; Hammersley, 1992). In response, many contemporary ethnographers no longer consider their research interpretations to be objective truths, but rather a form of fiction.

Science is changing and gaining new understandings. These changing views accompany the resurgence of interest in phenomenological perspectives such as those represented by social constructionism and constructivism. As discussed by renowned psychologist and research methodologist Donald Campbell (1989), logical positivism and logical empiricism are uniformly rejected by contemporary epistemologists and philosophers of science and referred to as naive empiricism by many across various disciplines. Postpositivist epistemologies such as critical realism, hypothetical realism, fallibilistic realism, and transcendental realism have replaced earlier positivist views, reflecting a more reflexive and modified objectivism (Bhakaskar, 1989; Mahoney, 1988a; Manicas & Secord, 1982; Phillips, 1990). Modified objectivism accepts the postpositivist view that it is impossible to remove completely the influences of the subject from the object of analysis and that objective reality cannot be absolutely known. The Duhem-Quine (a natural epistemologist and philosopher of science) thesis holds that an experiment cannot test a theoretical prediction in any final way, because the test itself depends on the validity of the various theories that support the experiment (Anderson, 1990, p. 77). Practitioners in both research and clinical practice are seeking theories and methods for practice that reflect these newer sentiments concerning one's interpretations. New and more sophisticated quantitative methods such as structural equation modeling help researchers with this dilemma. Such methods assume that it is necessary in statistical models to test the assumptions of the researcher and the measurement instruments (Loehlin, 1992). Both recursive and nonrecursive variables may be used in the models. At the same time, some clinical practitioners return to interpretive theories and reflexive methods of client change.

## Distinctions Between Social Constructionism and Constructivism

Social constructionism and constructivism are distinct metatheories, but the terms have been used interchangeably within social work, family therapy, and other practice professions. Recently authors have drawn comparisons or contrasts between social constructionism and constructivism in an attempt to either integrate or delineate distinctions between the two (Dean, 1993; Franklin, 1993; Hoffman, 1990; Lyddon, 1995; Martin & Sugarman, 1996; McNamee & Gergen, 1992; Real, 1990). Dean (1993), for example, does a good job defining the theoretical differences between the larger concepts of social constructionism and constructivism but chooses to collapse the two perspectives, using the term constructivism in her subsequent discussion on constructivist clinical practice methods. The goal of this chapter is to further the comparisons and distinctions between the two metatheories and provide some examples of how these approaches are used in practice. Both social constructionism and constructivism are similar in that they emphasize human agency (or the participatory role of humans) and assert that reality is socially or psychologically constructed. They propose an interactional view of human behavior that assumes that persons and social environments are intricately connected and that the interpersonal, social, and psychological are intertwined. A common belief between social constructionism and constructivism is the rejection of the received view or correspondence theory of reality, which assumes that one makes objective contact with reality through sensory perceptions imprinted on the mind like an image on film. Rather, social constructionists and constructivists believe that it is impossible to receive an exact replica of objective reality in the mind without structuring it according to one's cognitive structures, subjective or linguistic meanings, and unique social experiences (Mahoney, 1988a).

Thus, it is said that social constructionists and constructivists do not believe in an objective reality. This statement is often mistaken to mean that they do not believe in an objective physical or social reality. Speed (1991) and Held (1990) provide good examples of this type of criticism. Most social constructionists and constructivists, however, do not take an "all-is-in-the-head" view of reality. Nor do they reject the existence of a structured physical or social reality, although some radical constructivists believe that it is impossible to know anything except one's own mind. But this does not mean that they have totally rejected the idea that something exists outside themselves. For example, a few radical constructivist biologists, such as Maturana

(1988) and Varela (1989), whose cybernetic systems theories have been influential in family therapy, purported that we are blind to the world and that all we can experience is perturbations bouncing against whatever might be out there that register with us as neural feedback loops within a closed central nervous system. Watzlawick (1984) and Keeney (1983) present discussions of how this type of radical constructivism has been applied as the foundation of practice models such as the brief therapy approaches of the Mental Research Institute. Social constructionists and constructivists to a greater or lesser degree do believe that the structures that exist beyond oneself cannot be objectively known. But they hold a range of views on how our constructions interface with structured realities to produce meaningful feedback regarding the viability of perceptions. However, the basic view of both social constructionism and constructivism is that the operations of human cognitive structures and processes and the nature of language and social processes, in particular, make it impossible for us to know an objective reality completely. This view is consistent with genetic epistemology and the social constructivist cognitive and developmental theories of Piaget and Kegan (Doise, 1989).

Social constructionists and constructivists differ in their respective views on the significance of cognitive structures and developmental processes versus the importance of language, culture, and social processes in the formulation of one's constructions. Constructivists emphasize cognitive structures such as core ordering processes (organizing principles), deep structures (i.e., schemas about the self), neural feedback and feedforward mechanisms, and the processes of human development. In contrast, social constructionists emphasize language, narratives, and sociohistorical and cultural processes as primary factors in understanding one's constructions (Dean, 1993; Franklin, 1993; Lyddon, 1990; R. A. Neimeyer, 1993a; Real, 1990). Constructivists elicit deep or second-order changes through the use of clinical methods such as the exploratory Socratic method and presuppositional questioning (asking questions that solicit solutions), reframing, paradox, experiential homework assignments, hypnosis, and restructuring cognitive meanings (including emotions) and systemic processes.

Social constructionist practitioners focus on sociocontextual issues such as the formulation of the stories the client tells, the meaning of a problem within a client's social networks, and the sociopolitical processes involved in labeling a problem a problem. This includes the analysis of political discourse and social oppression. One clinical technique used by social constructionists—externalizing the problem—changes the way clients and their social networks view a problem by redefining its meaning and helping them view the problem as external to them. For example, a therapist might say, "How long has bulimia been ruining your life?" This method is also used to help clients recognize oppressive internalized discourses. For example, if a client told a gender-biased story concerning the role of women, the therapist might ask directly, "Where did you get that idea?" or say something like, "I am wondering if you will be willing to explore certain myths that you hold?" Another method used by social constructionists—the reflecting team—purposefully solicits the views and social interactions of everyone involved in a problem scenario and introduces multiple explanations for the problem aimed at shifting the meanings and social interactions around a socially constructed problem. Examples of therapeutic techniques and models used by social constructionist and constructivist practitioners are described below.

## Social Constructionist Metatheory

Social constructionism developed in the 1960s within the discipline of sociology with the publication of Berger and Luckmann's (1966) classic book on the sociology of knowledge, *The Social Construction of Reality*. Though a fairly young theory, the essence of social constructionism can be traced to earlier sociological theories. Social constructionism is remarkably similar to Schutz's (1962) phenomenological sociology, a branch of sociology in which subjectivity is paramount and the researcher focuses on how social experiences are made meaningful. Garfinkle's (1967) radical approach to research, ethnomethodology, which studies how people create, sustain, and manage their sense of everyday reality, is also similar to social constructionism. Similarities between these approaches should come as no surprise, however, in that Berger and Garfinkle were students of Schutz (Wallace & Wolf, 1991).

Gergen (1985) describes social constructionism as concerned with the social processes by which people come to describe, explain, and account for their world. Meanings are believed to arise in particular settings or traditions. Cultures, communities, and institutions influence the way we see the world. Both personality and identity are social constructions that may change from situation to situation. Social constructionist theory also recasts social problems as being social constructions— products of claims making, labeling, and other constitutive definitional processes (Kituse & Spector, 1973; Miller & Holstein, 1993; Spector & Kituse, 1974, 1977). The theory was first introduced in social-problems theory within sociology in the 1970s and has become a major approach to understanding social problems. It was adapted into social psychology, where it is used to deconstruct common understandings of human development, anger, gender, and other social psychological phenomena (Gergen, 1982; McNamee & Gergen, 1992). Objectivists have expressed concerns about social constructionism because of its relativistic views, but recent criticisms have also come from within its own ranks (Best, 1993; Rafter, 1992; Woolgar & Pawluch, 1985). The main criticism addresses social constructionism's inconsistency, in that social constructionism relies on objectivist notions in analyzing social problems. When social constructionism tries to remain theoretically and methodologically consistent, it is believed to slip into hopeless relativism and extreme subjectivity. Held (1990) provides a similar critique, pointing out that it is impossible for therapists who use the social constructionist or constructivist theories to maintain a relativistic stance apart from objective reality when treating client problems.

Social constructionist theory may be viewed as struggling with a postmodern dilemma, because it rejects the one-absolute-truth criterion of objectivism in favor of multiple constructed realities. But it has not yet established clear methods other than social consensus or the values embedded in social responsibility for decision making or evaluating one claim over another. Critics contend that social constructionists take an anything-goes approach, which is not the case. Social consensus alone, however, is not adequate for clinical decision making or evaluating a research study. The analytical criteria used in making differential decisions regarding issues such as right and wrong behavior for family members, distribution of social resources, or the specific merits of a study, and, perhaps more important, determining whose criteria will prevail are important issues for social constructionists to address. In this regard, Best (1993) argues for a more objectivist approach to social constructionist analysis and states that objectivism can be found in the original writings about the theory. Woolfolk (1992) suggests that hermeneutics may be a useful approach for clinicians to use in resolving this dilemma. My reading of the early social constructionist writings is that objectivist criteria were assumed, and I believe that hermeneutics or another criterion must be established if social constructionist metatheory is to reach its full potential for social work practice.

## Social Constructionist Research

Three types of social constructionist research were described by Best (1989). First, strict social constructionist researchers argue that one should not make assumptions about objective reality. Such researchers examine the perspectives of those who are making claims or are socially constructing social problems. Strict social constructionist researchers believe that actual social conditions are irrelevant to the analysis of problems. Rather, they believe that it is important to study what individuals say about the problems. Researchers do not try to check out the accuracy of the claims. Objective facts such as statistical reports that might add validity to the statements are viewed as social constructions that do not add anything to the analysis. This approach is consistent with the extreme epistemological subjectivist view.

A second type of social constructionist research assumes an objectivist position very compatible with empiricist research approaches. According to Pollner (1993), objectivist social constructionist research presupposes a determinate, objective order in which people differentially perceive, define, and make claims about objective conditions. Both social constructions of a problem and the objective conditions of the problem are presumed to be equally important in understanding social problems. Objectivist social constructionist research ranges from debunking—showing that individuals' claims about social problems are not consistent with other facts—to including diverse methods such as documented sources and statistics to establish claims.

Contextual social constructionism is the third type of research approach. Most social constructionist research falls in this camp. Researchers using contextual approaches stay focused primarily on the claims-making process or the social constructions of those talking about problems, but they also make some assumptions about objective social conditions. Contextual researchers believe that attending to social conditions helps locate a problem within its social context. These researchers argue that any claim can be evaluated by using various sorts of evidence and that it is important to do so. Like the strict constructionists, contextualists acknowledge that sources are socially constructed but believe that they can still use them.

## *Social Constructionist Practice Applications*

Postmodernism and social constructionism have been so influential in family therapy that writers have referred to it as a movement denoting a paradigm shift in practice. Several authors have also presented social constructionism as an important theory for social work practice (Goldstein, 1990; Laird, 1993; Payne, 1991; Witkin, 1990). I agree with Dean (1993) that many aspects of the practice applications of social constructionism are not new to social work. Sociocultural, sociopolitical, and contextual analysis of client problems are embedded in the practice foundations of the profession. It should come as no surprise, therefore, that social constructionism has recently emerged within the theoretical perspectives of several practice models. Saleebey (1992) uses social constructionism in his strengths perspective model, and social constructionism is a core theme in Brower and Nurius's (1993) newly formulated practice approach called the cognitive ecological model. White and Epston's (1990) solution-oriented, narrative practice model uses a social constructionist perspective. As mentioned previously, adherents of social constructionist theory have also formed a major movement within the field of marriage and family therapy (Sprenkle & Bischof, 1994).

The three approaches to social constructionist research described above also have significance for the constructionist metatheories underlying different approaches to clinical practice. For example, the cognitive ecological model developed by Brower and Nurius (1993) clearly relies on a more objectivist constructionism. One chapter, for example, is devoted to helping practitioners objectively evaluate their clinical judgments. The model was developed by using empirical research from social and personality psychology as well as ecological practice perspectives. Social constructionism, however, is one of the core themes of the model. To understand a client's problem, the authors contend that it is necessary to comprehend his or her cognitive construction of reality or how an individual makes sense or meaning out of the world. Selective perceptions, life stories, and the processes of memory are believed to play a significant role in social realities. At the same time, it is equally important to evaluate people within their niche, the portion of the social environment in which they have routine contact and become interdependent. The model uses cognitive and behavioral methods and offers guidelines for moving clients through the change process using the concepts of mindfulness and the necessity of making changes within the self-system and the niche.

Other practice models hold more strictly to the tenets of strict social constructionism. For example, family therapy approaches based on second-order cybernetics, that is, observing systems or language systems, such as post-Milan therapy or collaborative language systems, are theoretically consistent with strict constructionism. As discussed by Real (1990), these models have at their core "the eradication of the idea of objectivity. Human beings are closed systems. Information is not representational. We do not discover reality; we construct it through social discourse, through language" (p. 257).

Practice methods are conversational and include such diverse techniques as circular questioning, opening a space for conversation, and narrative reconstruction, which therapeutically alters the client's story about a problem.

## Social Constructionist Therapy

Despite its recent popularity in clinical practice, social constructionism is not a clinical practice model but was historically adopted into social work, and more recently into family therapy, as a metaframework for practice (cf. Hoffman, 1990; Richan & Mendelsohn, 1973; Saleebey, 1992; Witkin, 1991). Since social constructionism was used as a guiding framework for social-problems theory, it was integrated into social work practice in accordance with this view. Many social work scholars, however, rejected social constructionism, and it has been a point of contentious debate for the profession for the past 15 years (Atherton, 1993). Berger and Luckmann's (1966) original work on social constructionism criticized both psychology and psychotherapies for serving "social control" and "legitimizing" functions. A social constructionist framework for practice provides an approach that will deconstruct therapies and provide an alternative framework for conducting clinical practice—a framework that constructionists believe will subsequently be able to deconstruct client problems. The title of McNamee and Gergen's (1992) edited text, *Therapy as Social Construction*, indicates this orientation. In the text, several diverse practice methods, including those associated with narrative reconstruction, collaborative language systems, second-order cybernetics, and solution-oriented methods, are all loosely connected under the social constructionist umbrella.

Therapists within the social constructionist perspective challenge the basic premises and social functions of therapy and other institutions with an intent to change their practices (Hoffman, 1992). Social constructionists, for example, believe in using alternative methods to those they view as being mainstream therapy. For example, constructionists describe themselves as: (a) collaborative rather than directive, (b) conversational instead of technical, (c) rejecting the deficit model and instead affirming client strengths, (d) questioning "metaphors" and "truths" such as the medical model, (e) taking a nonexpert position, and (f) viewing change as coming from the client instead of the therapist. The sociocultural and contextual focus of social constructionism also places sociopolitical and moral discourses as relevant issues for therapy (Gergen & Kaye, 1992; Hoffman, 1990; Saleebey, 1992; Witkin, 1991).

Sociocultural discourses may be defined as tacit belief systems that people adopt because of their experiences within a culture. Discourses are those unspoken assumptions that we hold as irrefutable and on which we base our lifestyle. For example, in our culture such values as individuality, autonomy, and the importance of power and wealth are interwoven into the fabric of our beliefs about ourselves and others. These narratives are acted out in the problems that bring people to therapy, for example, intrafamily conflicts focusing on job and family, narratives about loneliness and lack of meaning, and aggression for the purpose of obtaining power and material possessions. Therapists practicing from a social constructionist perspective focus on the analysis and deconstruction of client narratives that have significant sociocultural themes, such as the importance of power and money to one's individual success, the overarching influence of patriarchy, and the deficits of families that have experienced divorce. To deconstruct narratives, therapists ask reflexive questions aimed at exposing the connections among clients' beliefs, cultural narratives, and presenting problems. After these connections are acknowledged, clients are provided the opportunity to explore and deconstruct these cultural discourses with the intent of freeing themselves from their influence (see Freedman & Combs, 1996).

**Examples of Social Constructionist Practice Approaches**. Writers contributing to the social constructionist movement in clinical practice include Hoffman (1990), White and Epston (1990), Anderson and Goolishian (1988), Andersen (1991), Berg (1994), de Shazer (1991, 1994), and Freedman and Combs (1996), among others. To describe all the ideas of these authors is beyond the scope of this chapter, but I will summarize the practice approaches known as narrative practice developed by White and colleagues and solution-focused therapy developed by de Shazer and Berg (1992). (See Chapters 11, 12, and 14 in this volume for further discussions of practice applications.)

Both the narrative and solution-focused models share some similar assumptions about practice:

■ Practitioners are suspicious of the search for absolue truths in the client's story or narrative accounts. History and personal accounts are viewed in a reconstructive manner, and all descriptions are conceived of as being perspectival.

■ Meanings are developed through social interaction and social consensus. All social and psychological realities are socially constructed.

■ The intermingling of ideas and meanings in our conversation with one another is emphasized. In this manner we can influence another person but can never predict exactly how this encounter will end.

■ Meanings are transitory, and there is no absolute truth or single way to understand a problem. The ways in which we understand problems are more or less useful or oppressive. The practitioner guides clients toward understandings that work better for their lives or free them from the results of social oppression.

■ Value is placed on the adoption of the "not knowing" approach to understanding human problems. This means the practitioner becomes client centered and focuses on the meanings the client makes in the sessions.

■ Practice is a creative process rather than a discovery process. Therapists and practitioners co-construct problem definitions and solutions in an interactive process through their conversations.

■ Practitioners use the generative and co-constructive approach, whereby clients' descriptions of themselves and problems are believed to be tentative and changing from moment to moment.

■ Practitioners use narratives (stories the client tells) and a sociocultural framework as a basis for conducting therapy.

Working with language and the reconstruction of meanings is the main way of generating change in clients, although both solution-focused therapy and the narrative approach have particular methods for creating behavior change. Narrative practice emphasizes the "landscape of action," an idea borrowed from Bruner (1986), whereby the practitioner asks questions about the behaviors and steps a client has taken or will take as a means of focusing on behavior change. Solution-focused therapy also emphasizes envisioning and practicing specific behavioral changes as a basis for cognitive and meaning reconstruction.

Michael White, a social worker and family therapist from Australia, is one of the most influential narrative family therapists. White claims to borrow directly from Foucault and has encapsulated in his clinical theory an approach to social justice that has little to do with Foucault but is consistent with historical social work practice. Lupenitz (1992) had a similar, yet more radical, reflection during her review of White's constructionist applications of Foucault's work to family therapy. Lupenitz suggests that White's practice methods are not a good match with Foucault's theory. Rather, a better application of Foucault's ideas would be to research the ways in which "the writings and methods of nineteenth-century social workers and community activists were subjugated in order to generate family therapy's creation myth, according to which the field was conceived by brave white male psychiatrists in the 1950s" (p. 283).

White's (1988) therapy technique emphasizes storytelling followed by a series of purposeful questioning techniques, reflections, and probing aimed at introducing new ideas and elucidating parts of the client's story not previously emphasized (called a counterplot). White's (1993, 1994) interpretive approach to practice theory is clearly seen in the assumptions he makes about human behavior. White and Epston (1990) make this clear in their book on narrative practice. White's assumptions about human behavior, based on his writings and workshops, are as follows:

■ Human beings are interpretive beings. We are all active in the interpretation of and in giving meaning to our experience as we live our lives. An act of meaning interpretation is an achievement in human functioning.

■ It is impossible for us to interpret our experience in a vacuum. A frame of intelligibility, usually of a cultural nature, is necessary for interpreting any lived experience.

■ Such frames provide a context for our experience and make the attribution of meaning possible.

■ The meanings we derive in the process of interpretation have real effects on the shape of our lives and on the steps we take in life. Thus, such meanings are not neutral in their effects on our lives.

■ The personal story or self-narrative provides the principal frame of reality for our lived experience.

■ The personal story or self-narrative is not radically invented inside our heads. Rather, it is something negotiated and distributed within various communities of persons and in the institutions of our culture.

■ The personal story or self-narrative structures our experience. It determines what aspects of our stock of lived experience are selected for expression.

■ The personal story or self-narrative determines the shape of the expression or particular aspects of our lived experience.

■ The stories we have about our lives actually shape or constitute our lives.

■ Our lives are multistoried. No single story of life can be free of ambiguity and contradiction. No single personal story or self-narrative can handle all of the contingencies of life.

■ The act of living requires that we be engaged in the meditation of the dominant stories and substories of our lives.

■ Narratives follow a sequence of events across time and have a plot.

■ A storied life is multiverse, with many stories that have not been told. Life is richly complex. Counterplots can always be found and new stories developed.

According to White (1994), the context of clinical practice does not have a privileged location outside the culture at large. The practice context is not exempt from the structures and from the ideology of the dominant culture, and this includes issues of social justice such as racism, gender bias, heterosexism, and other forms of privileged discourse. The practice context, therefore, is not exempt from the politics of gender, class, race, and culture. Nor is practice free from the politics associated with the hierarchies of knowledge and the politics of marginalization. By marginalization White takes the position that some individuals assert benefits and power over others and that society often creates narratives and social constructions not helpful to some people. Marginalized people internalize these oppressive representations of themselves. White borrows from Foucault's ideas here. He believes that clients are in marginalized positions and must be helped to develop new narratives that counter their oppressive socially constructed stories. White and followers (e.g., Freedman & Combs, 1996) contend that it is impossible, perhaps even unethical, for a therapist to ignore the political realities of client's lives that the broader society imposes on clients. It is therefore important for practitioners to expose these political realities as part of therapy.

Within White's approach is encased a true sociocultural view of therapy and a political orientation that demand the therapist take a position of client advocacy and proactive social change. White's views that the therapist should take a political stance in therapy is a point of increasing contention among social constructionist therapists. Some social constructionists contend that the therapist should not take political positions in therapy because doing so could possibly mean imposing a value system on clients. Instead therapists should join and support the individual belief systems of the client. This is believed to be consistent with social constructionism's "respect for diversity" and "multiple interpretations of reality" (Biever, de las Feuentes, Cashion, & Franklin, in press). A nonpolitical approach to therapy, for example, is advocated by solution-focused therapists such as de Shazer and Berg. Solution-focused therapists approach social change by helping clients find their own solutions that will empower them toward social change. Solution-focused therapies are described in more detail below.

White believes that when people visit a practitioner's agency or office, they walk into a context structured by politics and bring with them the politics of their relationships. To White, whether we bring politics into our practice is not an issue; whether we are prepared to acknowledge the existence of these politics or to what degree we are prepared to be "complicit" (a term White uses frequently to describe tacit processes of cultural reproduction) in the reproduction of these politics is an issue. The unquestioned acceptance of the assumption that social work practice has some privileged location outside the broader oppressive culture guarantees that the practice of social workers will be aligned with the dominant culture.

For White, the unquestioned acceptance of our objectivity ensures a parallel process whereby we unwittingly reproduce the very context that is constitutive of many of the problems for which people seek our help. We become synonymous with those in power, using privileged discourse to oppress rather than heal. We feed into the oppressive stories that keep our clients down. We must, therefore, use self-awareness to acknowledge that as practitioners serving a cultural elite, we may inevitably play a role in the reproduction of the dominant culture.

Narrative therapy addresses questions of culture, power, and social influence and focuses practitioners' attention on complex value issues through the following methods (White, 1993, 1994):

■ Creating in the therapeutic context awareness of the politics of relationship. This includes the appropriate ways for us to acknowledge the imbalance of power inherent in the therapeutic relationship.

■ Insisting that we deal with the sociopolitical dilemmas raised in our work. White, for example, directly challenges dominant gender discourses.

■ Focusing us on not being wholly complicit in the reproduction of the dominant social order and instead creating conditions in therapy sensitive to the politics of gender inequities, heterosexual dominance, race discrimination, and issues of culture and class.

■ Working with clients in ways that assist them to identify, embrace, and honor their resistance to the oppression of dominant knowledge and practices of power embedded in this modern culture. For example, a woman who has been labeled with anorexia nervosa might be asked to expound on the times that she defied anorexia and didn't give in to the cultural prescriptions for female thinness.

■ Subverting the hierarchies of knowledge that give privilege to professional knowledge claims and opening up new possibilities for clients to behave. For example, a practitioner may challenge a diagnosis given to a woman client who has marital problems by saying, "So, the psychiatrist says that you are very depressed. Now, how would you know the difference between being depressed and being mad at your husband?"

■ Being open to alternative knowledge and the knowledge of those persons who seek our help. Clients are the real experts on their lives.

■ Focusing on how we might successfully confront ourselves with the moral and ethical responsibilities we have for the real consequences of our interactions with those persons who seek our help. This includes establishing structures that make our work accountable to those persons who seek our help and that expose the real and the potential abuses in the practice of therapy.

### *Therapeutic Roles of Social Construction/Narrative Therapy*

The following therapeutic roles are either discussed by White or implied in his writings:

■ White views the therapist as a learner, someone who must put aside his or her own power and expertise in favor of the expertise of the client.

■ The multistoried nature of the social constructionist theory puts therapists in roles in which they must entertain multiple ideas about a client. All ideas should be held as hypotheses, and a practitioner should not be too wedded to any single story about a client or hypothesis about what is wrong. Therapists' understandings are tentative and evolve through time. Ideas are held only as possibilities.

■ Curiosity is a third role that practitioners practicing from a narrative or social constructionist stance assume. Effective therapists remain curious about a client's story and continue a "not knowing" approach.

■ Narrative practitioners are collaborative in their approach to solution building.

■ Practitioners maintain a focus on solving the client's presenting problem. History is used only to deconstruct or re-story the presenting situation in a way that works better for clients.

■ Finally, practitioners focus on the beliefs that are restraining clients from acting in more appropriate ways. Invitations to responsibility are given as a means of helping clients behave in ways that free them from socially oppressive roles.

**Techniques of narrative/social constructionist practitioners.** Freedman and Combs (1996) discuss the following clinical techniques used by narrative therapists:

■ *Deconstructing meanings and behavioral practices.* Deconstructive listening means listening for other possible meanings, and deconstructive questioning helps therapists and clients see stories from different perspectives. Deconstructive questioning helps clients see that stories are constructed and how they are constructed. For example, a practitioner might ask, "Thinking back, who first had the idea that you were an angry person?" Narrative practitioners also help clients question their assumptions and beliefs, bringing forth problematic beliefs, practices, feelings, and attitudes. For example, a practitioner might ask, "What is your relationship with the belief, practice, attitude, or feeling?" "What are the effects of the belief?" "How does the belief get you to act in a certain way?" (Freedman & Combs, 1996).

■ *Building on strengths.* Narrative practitioners often interview clients about exceptions to their problems instead of the occurrence of the problem itself. They are very interested in times when people are doing well or their lives are better. They listen for tiny victories they can build on and help them acknowledge their coping abilities and strengths. For example, a narrative therapist might say to an incest survivor who claims to be a failure, "You say you are a failure but you just graduated from college. How did you ever get into college? Tell me how you did that."

■ *Understanding internalized conversations.* Narrative practitioners understand that clients participate in internalized conversations that are the internalized versions of the dominant sociocultural discourses that oppress their lives. Practitioners seek to help clients find new stories that are more empowering. For example, a practitioner working with a new immigrant who presents a story of isolation from the family and fear of disappointing the children may say something like, "You are very brave to come here to America. Your family must be very proud of you. How did you develop such a noble heritage? Have other members of your family been such pioneers?" After listening to the client, the practitioner might add:

*You are starting a new legacy of freedom from poverty and government oppression to pass on to your children. What do you think your family back home might be saying about your bravery? Do you think that they know how much you are like your grandfather?*

In this way the practitioner seeks to help the client tell a new story about immigration, a story that reframes the client's experiences into a positive light that compliments the family instead of detracts from it.

■ *Externalizing the problem.* Practitioners use this technique to increase the personal agency of clients and help them see that problems exist separate from the self. Problems invade the lives of people from the outside. They are not the person. People's lives are more than the problem-saturated stories that dominate their "landscape of consciousness." Mapping the influence of the problem is an externalization technique the practitioner uses to help clients see how a problem has influenced their lives. Mapping the influence of relationships to problems is another externalization technique; it is used to show clients how a problem has affected their relationships and how they have been able to influence problems.

■ *Constructing unique outcomes.* Practitioners question clients' unique outcomes such as the absence of problems or times when the problems do not occur in their story.

■ *Naming the plot.* Clients are asked to put a name on their experiences for the purpose of exploration and understanding, for example, labeling their anger as the "fire within."

■ *Tracking contextual influences of the problem.* This technique helps clients see how social relationships and other contextual influences facilitate and maintain their problems. Questions asked include, "What feeds the problem or starves it?" "Who supports certain problems?" "Who benefits from this way of doing things?"

## Brief Solution-Focused Models in Family Therapy

Franklin and Moore (in press) describe the basic tenets of solution-focused therapy. Solution-focused therapy is a strengths-based therapy model developed at the Brief Family Therapy Center in Milwaukee, Wisconsin, by de Shazer and colleagues (de Shazer, 1985, 1988, 1991, 1994; de Shazer et al., 1986) and Berg and associates (Chapter 11; Berg, 1994; Berg & Miller, 1992), as well as others (e.g., Miller, Hubble, & Duncan, 1996; Walter & Peller, 1992) during the past 15 years. Recently, solution-focused therapy has aligned itself with social constructionist theory and emphasized how language is used to construct reality. This model is being applied to a wide variety of clinical problems and fields of practice such as inpatient psychiatric disorders (Webster, Vaughn, & Martinez, 1994), alcohol abuse (Berg & Miller, 1992), school-related behavior problems (Metcalf, 1995), crisis-oriented youth services (Franklin, Corcoran, Streeter, & Nowicki, 1997; Franklin, Nowicki, Trapp, Schwab, & Petersen, 1993), sexual abuse (Dolan, 1991), and spouse abuse (Sirles, Lipchik, & Kowalski, 1993). Assumptions of solution-focused therapies include the following:

■ Focus is on the strengths and competencies of the client.
■ Insight and awareness are not needed to produce change.
■ Personality and other individual characteristics are not static.

- The cause, function, or meaning of the complaint (unless organic in nature) does not need to be known.
- The practitioner's responsibility in treatment is to create an atmosphere in which change can occur.
- Behavior change outside the session is most important.
- Past experiences do not limit present or future behavior.
- Clients have resources that can be enhanced or used in solution building. If the practitioner listens closely to the client, he or she will know how to use those resources (O'Hanlon & Weiner-Davis, 1989).

**Strategies and relationship roles in solution-focused therapy.** Solution-focused therapists, like narrative therapists, use a "not knowing" approach to relationships with clients. The practitioner is client centered, and the client is treated as the expert. Solution-focused practitioners also build expectancy and seek to establish a future orientation. They ask questions to determine the extent to which clients identify with problem roles and to which clients are invested in their own explanations. They specifically assess how motivated a client is to change. Like narrative therapists, solution-focused therapists also examine previous problem-solving successes and are more interested in exceptions to problems than the occurrence of the problems themselves (Franklin & Moore, in press). The role of the therapist is to facilitate flexibility and provide multiple explanations to problems. Solution-focused therapists believe that goals can be achieved in various ways and that change is inevitable. They seek to build on changes in a way that helps clients accomplish their goals.

**Techniques of solution-focused therapy.** Solution-focused therapy is a strengths-based therapy model that is behavioral and goal directed. For example, solution-focused therapists use a set of behaviorally and cognitively oriented therapy techniques to amplify positive behaviors and reinforce the use of effective coping strategies. Solution-focused therapy differentiates itself from prescriptive approaches by its emphasis on process and its focus on future behaviors that will help clients accomplish their goals and get the rewards they want from the environment. For this reason, solution-focused therapists do not spend very much time exploring problems but instead are more interested in working with clients to construct a set of behavioral tasks that lead to a rapid solution. Consistent with the social constructionist theory, they also address how the client talks about the problem and interacts with other people around the problem. For this reason, solution-focused therapists seek to shift conversations, meanings, and relationship patterns into a state of solution so that all people involved will believe and act as if the problem is solved (Franklin & Moore, in press).

Strategies of the solution-focused therapist include the following:

- Tracking solution behaviors (e.g., times when the problem does not occur, effective coping responses).
- Increasing motivation toward a new set of behaviors by reinforcing times when the problem is absent and constantly complimenting and attending to small differences in behavioral change.

■ Taking a client-centered orientation, whereby the therapist starts from the cognitive frame of the client and works with those meanings to construct solutions that will help the client accomplish goals.

■ Focusing on the future instead of the present or the past.

■ Using presuppositional language aimed at helping clients restructure meanings about themselves and their problems, for example, *when* you start doing better instead of *if*. Or 25% of the time you get sent to the principal's office, but I am amazed that 75% of the time you don't. Let's just pretend that you do know what to do to get along with your teacher (Franklin & Biever, 1996).

Solution-focused therapists use Socratic questioning techniques:

■ Exception questions (e.g., When does the problem not occur? How did you get that to happen? How come the problem is not worse? What was different about those times when things were better between you and your teacher?).

■ Relationship questions, which have a powerful way of focusing on social constructions (e.g., What would your teacher say about your grades? What would your mother say? If you were to do something that made your teacher very happy what would that be? Who would be most surprised that you did really well on the test? What would that person say about the fact that you are doing so well?).

■ Scaling questions, which help anchor the reality of the client and help move forward (e.g., On a scale of 1 to 10, with 1 being that you are getting in trouble every day in the class, picking on Johnny and Suzy, getting out of your seat, and being scolded by your teacher, and 10 being that instead of fighting with Johnny and Suzy you are doing your work, you ask permission to get out of your seat, and your teacher says something nice to you, where would you be on that scale now?) (Franklin & Biever, 1996).

Franklin and Moore (in press) describe several other uses of the scaling technique in the therapy process: asking questions about where the client is on the scale in relation to solving the problem, using the scaling experience to find exceptions to the problems, and employing scales to construct "miracles" or to identify solution behaviors. For example, the therapist asks where on the scale (with 1 representing low and 10 representing high) the client is and how he or she will get from, say, 1 to a 3. Or the therapist may ask how clients managed to move from 4 to 5. What new behaviors did they implement? What was different in their lives? Solution-focused therapists may also express surprise that the problem is not worse on the scale as a way of complimenting the client's coping behavior or as a way to use language to change the client's perception of the intractable nature of their problem. Or the therapist may use the scale along with the "miracle question" by asking the client, "If a miracle occurred during the night and you could get to a 9 or 10 on the scale, what would be the first thing you would notice different?" Solution behaviors described by the client through the use of the scaling technique are often used as specific tasks or homework assignments that are prescribed and discussed in future sessions. Coping and motivation questions are other methods the solution-focused therapist might use (e.g., On a scale of 1 to 10, how well are you coping with the problems? How much do you want this problem to change?). The therapist might use the miracle question (e.g., Let's suppose that an overnight miracle happened and the problem you are having with your teacher disappeared. But you were sleeping and did not know it. When you came to school the next day what would be the first thing you would notice?). The therapist helps the client envision a new way of behaving and how things could be different. Detail is elicited to help develop a set of solution behaviors that are concrete and behaviorally specific. Compliments are used frequently, and the therapist develops as many compliments as possible aimed at amplifying positive behaviors. Homework assignments are given as specific tasks, and behavioral prescriptions focus the client on developing different behaviors. Similar to narrative practice, externalizing questions are a set of questioning techniques aimed at separating the problem from the self and increasing a person's self-agency over the problem behaviors (e.g., When ADHD tries to get you in trouble with your teacher, what does it make you do? When the fears are trying to scare you, what do they whisper in your ears? Are there times that you stand up to ADHD and don't let it push you around?). See Table 1 for a description of several solution-focused therapy techniques.

## Constructivist Metatheory

Constructivism represents a family of related theories that challenge objectivist world views and their approaches to practice and research. I have already discussed the general views of constructivists and the epistemological views of radical constructivists in particular. Another popular epistemological view, critical constructivism, is essentially the same as that of a critical realist (Mahoney, 1988a). Critical constructivists are often associated with information science and the cognitive therapies (Adams-Webber, 1989; Agnew & Brown, 1989; Ellis, 1989; Mahoney, 1989). These researchers view the perception of external reality as a hypothesis for which we constantly seek evidence. Although we may never make objective contact with external reality, we may through our repeated interactions discover an adaptive or good-enough fit to approximate a contact.

Several different types of constructivist practice theories have emerged, including those developed within psychoanalytic, cognitive, and family practice models (Guidano, 1991; Lyddon, 1990; Mahoney, 1991; Spence, 1982; Varela, 1989). Cognitive science and cognitive therapies are the most influential contemporary perspectives, thrusting constructivist metatheories to the forefront. In particular, constructivism has been used widely as a theoretical framework for cognitive-behavior therapies. Constructivism theory is being applied by such diverse cognitive-behaviorists as Mahoney (1991), Meichenbaum and Fitzpatrick (1993), and Ellis (1989)—cited in Franklin and Nurius (1996). In a recent commentary the cognitive theorist Albert Ellis (1996) says,

> I myself, though one of the early phenomenologists in the field of therapy ... , was indeed a logical positivist up to the mid 1970s. But Bartley ... , Mahoney ... , and Popper ... showed me that I was wrong, and therefore I have been a nonpositivist, a constructionist, and even a postmodernist since then... . So many other clinical psychologists have

**TABLE 1.** *Techniques used in solution-focused therapy.*

Joining: informal conversation to build rapport and make the client feel understood and comfortable.

Soliciting a brief description of the problem: "What has changed since we last talked?"

Behaviorally specific questions to search for exceptions to the problems by tracking and identifying times, occurrences, and contexts in which the problems did not occur.

■ What is different about the times when the problem is not happening?

■ How do you get that to happen? What do you do differently? What do other people do differently?

■ How is your day different when the problem is not occurring? How do you respond to other people differently when the problem is not happening? How do others respond differently when the problem is not happening?

■ Who else noticed that the problem was not happening? How could you tell that others were affected by the problem not occurring? How do you feel when the problem is not occurring?

■ How did you get him (or her) to stop the problem behavior? How did you get the fight to end?

■ How did you handle the situation differently from the way you might have handled it before? Did you inform him (or her) that you felt different because the problem did not occur?

■ How can you use what you know to solve the problem?

■ When you had this difficulty in the past, how did you work it out? What would you need to do now to work it out again?

Scaling techniques (from 1–10) to help the client anchor the problem and identify changes. For example, your problem is at 6 now; how will you move it to 8?

Normalizing and depathologizing the problem.

■ Can be communicated indirectly by remaining calm and unmoved by client's concerns.

■ Use normalizing comments: "sounds normal," "naturally," "of course," "I've known a lot of people who have experienced that," "so what else is new?"

■ Tell anecdotes or stories to place client's situation in normal context.

■ Interrupt client's description of situation and finish for him or her. Or ask, "Does he ever do this?"

■ Use indirect approach. "I'm a bit confused. How can you tell the difference between your problem and a situation in which the problem is not occurring?"

■ Normalizing compliments: "On the basis of everything that happened in the last few months, I'm surprised you're doing as well as you are."

Offering compliments, positive feedback, and positive connotation.

Homework assignments that ask clients to track exceptions to problem behavior or to practice solution behaviors to reinforce changes.

Asking presuppositional and future-oriented ("fast-forward") questions that assume the situation is already changing and that ask the client to describe the changes.

■ Presuppositional questions and statements use language in a way that communicates to the client that change is inevitable. For example, "When you start communicating better what will you be saying?"

■ Miracle question: "Let's suppose you went to sleep and while you were sleeping the problem was solved, but you did not know that it had been solved. What will be the first thing you notice when you

**TABLE 1.** *continued*

awake? What will be different?" Or "If I pulled out a magic wand and were able to perform magic on your situation, what would be different from before?" The mere act of constructing a vision of the solution acts as a catalyst for bringing out change.

■ Assume the problem has been resolved and ask about all the changes that will have occurred as a result: "How will your life be different?" "Who will be the first to notice?" "What will he do or say?" "How will you respond?"

Use videotalk or concrete behavioral descriptions to translate vague labels and stories about behavior into observable behaviors like those that can be seen or heard on a video. "Give me a recent example." Track sequence of events: "What happened?" "And then . . . ?" "Who is present when the problem occurs?" "What does each person say or do?" "And then what happens?" Track the context of the problem: "Where does the problem occur most frequently?" "Where is it least likely to occur?" "Is there a particular time (of day, month, year) when the problem is likely or unlikely to occur?" Track the relational aspects of the problem: "How is it a problem for you or someone else?" "If your wife were here now, what would she say about your conversation?"

Introduce pattern interventions that help clients change routine and repetitive behaviors.

Use rituals and symbols that will help clients resolve unfinished business relating to anger, loss, and bereavement.

Develop well-formulated goals.

■ Salient to the client

■ Small goals

■ Concrete, specific, behavioral goals

■ Focus on the presence rather than absence of something

■ Emphasize a beginning rather than an end

■ Realistic and achievable goals within the context of the client's life

■ Perceived as "hard work"

Adapted from Berg & Miller (1992), Hudson & O'Hanlon (1991), Kiser, Piercy, & Lipchik (1993), and O'Hanlon & Weiner-Davis (1989).

> *now followed Kelly ... in taking a constructivist position in their theory and practice that quite a long list of them could easily now be compiled. (p. 18)*

It may be surprising that even staunch behavior therapists who subscribe to behavioral analysis, a type of behavioral practice that originated with B. F. Skinner, are interested in social constructionism and hermeneutics. Behavioral analysis was once thought to be the bastion of empiricism, but some recent authors have been writing about the importance of social constructionism and hermeneutics and their usefulness in behavior analysis (e.g., Dougher, 1993). Again, Ellis (1996) states,

> *Indeed, for clients social reality largely does exist in intersubjective communication and in their relationships to practical problems. Virtually all counselors, including radical behaviorists like Jacobson ... and Hayes ... , now acknowledge this existence, because they see that people have interpersonal and social problems and other problems. (p. 23)*

Many criticisms of the applications of constructivist theories are similar to those regarding social constructionism. Authors have also lamented the fact that constructivism seems to be long on theory but short on distinct clinical methodologies. For example, despite the philosophical differences between rationalist (objectivist) and constructivist cognitive therapies, the methods of the two overlap. A full explication of the different metatheories of constructivism are beyond the scope of this chapter, but I will discuss some of the major ideas undergirding cognitive constructivist approaches. See R. A. Neimeyer and Mahoney (1995) for a fuller explication of emerging constructivist approaches to practice within psychology.

## Constructivist Research

Constructivist research paradigms are emerging within education and psychology and are developing new perspectives on how to conduct research (Guba, 1990). In particular, constructivist research relies on the viability of knowledge instead of its validity. Notions of pragmatic fit, coherence, and credibility are emphasized over standard notions of validity and reliability. Constructivists in general do not accept the tenets of logical positivism and look for new types of scientific methods to verify and make decisions about their observations. Many constructivists, however, do not hesitate to use statistics as analytical tools in their research and use qualitative methodologies together with quantitative methods.

Constructivists have developed different methods for measuring client characteristics. These methods measure the internal structures of a client's meaning system and processes of change. (See G. J. Neimeyer, 1993, and Chapter 5 in this volume for a review of assessment and measurement methods.) Although constructivists do not accept the principles of verification, critical constructivists would likely accept Popper's postpositivist method of falsification. Other more radical constructivists, however, would not accept these methods (R. A. Neimeyer, 1993a).

## Cognitive Constructivist Practice Applications

Constructivist clinical practice applications can be traced to four traditions in psychotherapy: (a) personal construct theory, (b) structural developmental approaches, (c) narrative psychology, and (d) family therapy (R. A. Neimeyer, 1993b). Radical constructivism, for example, has a tremendous influence on family therapy practice. Constructivist approaches are also a growing influence in contemporary psychological practice. For example, using scientometrics, the use of quantifiable indicators to measure rate and dynamics of scientific growth, R. A. Neimeyer, Baker, and Neimeyer (1990) demonstrated that the number of studies about personal construct theory doubled in the past 10 years (more than 1,700 studies). Especially notable is the fact that more than 20 cognitive therapies exist, and these therapies have been split according to the classifications of constructivist versus rationalist approaches (Mahoney & Lyddon, 1988). Recent empirical research also supports this classification (DiGiuseppe & Linscott, 1993) but emphasizes the fact that cognitive therapists may use both constructivist and rationalist methods in their practice. A second interesting trend within psychology is the fact that the social constructivist developmental theories of Piaget and other developmentalists are being used to build new practice models (Guidano, 1991; Ivey & Gonçalves, 1988). See R. A. Neimeyer (1993a) for a more comprehensive review of the constructivist psychotherapies.

Social workers have not been as interested in constructivism as they are in other practice-based disciplines, although their interest appears to be increasing (Dean & Fleck-Henderson, 1992). Fisher (1991) recently published a book on constructivism for social workers, but this work primarily introduces the use of personal-construct theory of the American psychologist George Kelly in work with clients. Practice methods in Fisher's book are very creative, but the author makes errors concerning the pragmatic constructivism of Kelly, for example, confusing the critical constructivist views of Kelly with radical constructivism. Dean (1993) and Laird (1994, Chapter 10) also recently illustrated practice methods for constructivist and social constructionist social workers. Methods described are consistent with family and psychodynamic models. In this chapter I focus on practice methods from cognitive constructivist therapies.

## Cognitive Constructivist Therapies

Mahoney (1988a) identified three "broad and overlapping themes" that he believed epitomized the basic features of cognitive constructivism: (a) proactive cognition, (b) morphogenic nuclear structure, and (c) self-organizing development. Proactive cognition means that humans are "co-creators of the realities in which they respond" (p. 2). Morphogenic nuclear structure refers to the belief that human systems are organized so that their central or core processes are in charge of more peripheral processes. Cognitive constructivists differentiate between deep structures and surface structures. The implication is that "core themes of reality such as identity, power, and values are among the most difficult to alter, with or without professional assistance" (Mahoney, 1988a, p. 8). Self-organizing development means that human systems organize themselves in order to protect and perpetuate their internal coherence. From this viewpoint, cognitive constructivists believe that psychological realities are private phenomena even when shared with others. It also means that people will resist change to these core ordering mechanisms. The main target for change, however, exists in the core psychological processes of the self. Lyddon (1990) compares the change focus of constructivism to the idea of second-order change as described in the systemic therapies. Making a bona fide change requires totally restructuring and reorganizing the self. In keeping with self-organizing development and complexity systems theory it is also believed that human beings are in constant spontaneous development toward this end. In this way the real problems come when people get stuck and cannot self-organize. Therapists can assist clients as they move toward self-organizations as a part of these developmental processes.

Constructivists operate from theories of personality and cognition, which differentiates them from psychodynamic schools. In general, constructivists view humans as capable of change and believe that other humans may be instrumental in promoting these changes through relationships. They reject the notion that the clinician's experience is far removed from that of the client's. Like the social constructionists, constructivists prefer the collaborative approach in therapy and do not assume a posture of an all-knowing authority. Constructivists view human development as dynamic and include developmental contexts and history in their clinical work. Developmental history, however, is viewed quite differently from how it is viewed in traditional psychoanalytical practice. It is not seen as an objective recounting of past history leading to a diagnosis and cure, but rather a subjective reconstruction of one's personal constructions and experiential meanings. Instead of viewing problems as psychological dysfunctions, constructivists take a strengths perspective, viewing a client's problems as a discrepancy between adaptive capacities and current demands of the social environment. For example, they view problems within the context of clients' best but faulty efforts to deal with life situations.

Constructivism also takes a much different view of emotions from the way many psychotherapy theories view them. Emotions, thinking, and behavior are seen as parts of an interactive system. Distressing emotions are not viewed as pathological but are instead viewed in systemic terms, that is, as powerful and primitive knowing processes. The disorganizing influence of distressing emotions is believed to represent a normal stage in reconstructing oneself to meet the demands of one's own development and the social environment. This process is referred to in systemic terms as self-organizing or autopoietic development (Granvold, 1994; Mahoney, 1988b).

Because constructivists differentiate between deep and surface cognitive structures, they focus on individual client change at three different levels. The first level is the presenting-problem level, which, as with behavioral therapies, involves focusing on recent episodes of the problem. Second is the pattern level, focusing on recurrent regularities and themes in the problems across episodes. Finally, constructivists focus on the process level, which emphasizes generative patterns and cognitive constructions that continue the patterns. Constructivists prefer to make changes at the process level and believe that by doing so the other two levels will be affected. They think about changes in social systems in much the same way, differentiating between first-order and second-order changes (Lyddon, 1990; Mahoney, 1988b). As noted by R. A. Neimeyer (1993a), at the "core of constructivist theory is a view of human beings as active agents, who, individually and collectively, co-constitute the meaning of their experiential world" (p. 222). In contrast with traditional cognitive therapies, constructivists are described as viewing "cognitions, emotions, and behavior as interactive within a social/environmental context" (Granvold, 1994, p. 12). Constructivists, as mentioned, also emphasize life-span development, the importance of language and meanings, attachment relationships, and the intersubjective nature of reality. "Knowing oneself and the world is always in relationship to others" (R. A. Neimeyer, 1993a, p. 223).

Concerning therapeutic interventions, R. A. Neimeyer (1993a) notes that cognitive constructivists are stylistically less technical and directive than traditional cognitive-behaviorists. Constructivist therapists tend to be "reflective, elaborative, and intensely personal" (p. 224). Clients are also believed to always "know themselves in relationship to others" (R. A. Neimeyer, 1993a, p. 223), which highlights the intensely interpersonal nature of therapeutic interventions. For this reason, therapists may seek to have an impact on the family and interpersonal environments, which they believe reinforce cognitive constructions (Alexander, 1988; Russell, 1991; Van den Broek & Thurlow, 1991). Therapists make use of metaphor, narrative reconstructions, and emotional self-explorations, as well as more traditional cognitive therapy, as methods for change. Since constructivists view cognitions, affects, behaviors, and interpersonal relationships as an interactive system, they believe that change in any system may affect other systems. For example, changing cognitions may influence behaviors, and changing behaviors may change cognitions. Furthermore, changing interpersonal interactions may change behaviors and cognitions and vice versa.

Constructivists, however, believe that it is especially important to promote second-order changes in the core ordering processes concerning the self, such as organizing principles, deep structures, and self-schemas. Treatments focus on client history and unconscious processes, intentionality, the search for meaning, and the need for integrity. Clinical practice is characterized by an emphasis on intervening with emotions, helping clients find new meanings, and using the therapeutic relationship in ways that establish a safe and caring environment in which clients can explore beliefs. Constructivists emphasize, for example, the use of "hot cognitions," affect-laden ideas that therapists may use to help clients access important cognitive schemas that need to change (Dobson & Craig, 1996).

Some leading cognitive constructivist therapists include Mahoney (1988a, 1988b, 1991), Meichenbaum (1993, 1996), R. A. Neimeyer (1993a, 1993b), G. J. Neimeyer (1993), Guidano (1991), Martin (1984, 1985, 1994), Lyddon (1990, 1995), and Gonçalves (1995), among others. Mahoney's and Meichenbaum's approaches are described below. See Chapter 7 (R. A. Neimeyer), Chapter 5 (G. J. Neimeyer), and Chapter 18 (Martin) for further examples.

**Mahoney's constructivist developmental psychotherapy.** Mahoney (1991) describes the basic principles of human helping and change and some specific techniques for initiating psychological developmental change in clients. He suggests that therapists follow humanistic values that include encouragement of self-caring and social responsibility, respect and protection of human rights, and respect for individual choice. Much of Mahoney's constructivist therapy model is consistent with the work of Bowlby (1969a, 1969b, 1969c) and emphasizes the importance of interpersonal relationships and early attachment relationships in forming self-identity. Therapeutic change is seen as an interpersonal process that is highly individualized from person to person. The person is viewed as embedded in interpersonal and social experiences, and, to be effective, the therapist must work within this context. It is of utmost importance for a practitioner to be able to experience, accept, and understand an individual's phenomenology. However, this empathic understanding is not viewed as sufficient to bring forth change. In order for clients to change, they must experience a reorganization of their core selves. Practitioners can facilitate this change, but to do so they must provide safety, consistency, and patience. The pace of change is different for each person and is dictated by core ordering processes.

Practitioners can model psychological health and resiliency to help clients discover ways to change. Practitioners working from the constructivist perspective are willing to share their own humanness by revealing aspects of themselves through stories and shared reflections. They are also willing to seek help when it is needed. To bring forth change, the practitioner helps the client engage and process emotions. However, constructivist developmentalists generally move with the resistance of the client instead of working against it. In this way, they join the belief systems of client as a method of penetration and change. Reflexive questions and "soul searching" exercises are used to help clients loosen self-protective processes and begin to explore different ways of being. Practitioners use the individualized experiences of clients, such as their unique gender and cultural experiences, to empower them toward change. This also includes religious and spiritual issues and experiences that may also be transformative. Rituals, such as those involving compassion, love, and forgiveness, are encouraged. The power and resilience of the human spirit are honored. Table 2 outlines the steps of developmental psychotherapy.

Mahoney (1991) discusses some major psychotherapeutic techniques used to bring forth change. Borrowing from James Joyce, Mahoney defines techniques as "ritualized methods of human relatedness and communication … stylized languages for expressing and exploring the ongoing narrative of a life in process" (p. 287). Most techniques discussed by Mahoney require the client to self-reflect and engage in ongoing introspection aimed at accessing feelings and bringing forth psychological change. Techniques described here share these goals. None of the techniques are new to psychotherapy but are borrowed from earlier psychological literature. Four techniques used by Mahoney are described below.

■ *Correspondence and narrative writing* help clients express their feelings and are especially encouraged in the constructivist developmental approach. Mahoney shares with White and Epston (1990) the view that writing can be therapeutic to clients. In one exercise recommended by Mahoney, clients are asked to write three unsent letters both to and from someone by whom they feel wronged. In the first letter, the client writes a letter to the person, sharing his or her most intense feelings. In the second letter, the client is asked to write an unsent letter back from the person to whom he or she wrote the letter. The client is to pretend that he or she is that person and has just received the first letter. According to Mahoney, usually clients will write back an angry and defensive letter. Finally, the client is asked to write a third letter, again from the other person, which expresses what the client would like to hear the person say in response to the first letter. Other types of writing are also encouraged, such as poetry, short stories, informal musings, and a personal-development journal.

■ *Life review* is used as a technique. Mahoney suggests the following method for making a life portfolio. The clients fill in each year of their lives on separate note cards, beginning with the year before birth. Attachments such as photos and other memory-enhancing items may accompany the cards. Personal research is encouraged. Clients are further encouraged to make their own interpretations of the meanings and insights that may emerge from this project.

**TABLE 2.** *Therapeutic steps for constructivist developmental psychotherapy.*

| Interval or stage | General focus and areas of activity |
| --- | --- |
| Intake | Identification of primary and other presenting concerns/problems |
| | Risk and urgency appraisal |
| | Basics about current life situation (e.g., significant others, employment, health, and brief medical history) |
| | Brief life history and basics about family of origin |
| | Initial assessment of therapeutic "fit" (compatibility, mutual regard, relevant professional expertise, and so on); referral if appropriate |
| | Assessment of client expectations for psychotherapy (e.g., prior therapy experience, goals, fears, etc.) |
| | Initial global appraisal and, when appropriate, assurance (e.g., warrant for hope, wisdom of having sought help) |
| | Agreement on a "therapeutic contract" (e.g., goals, roles, the process of active inquiry and exploration, and agreement to review progress and reappraise goals at specified interval) |
| | Review of client rights and therapist responsibilities; signing of informed consent |
| Assessment | Basic psychometrics of choice, with special attention to core issues (identity, reality, power, and values) |
| | Basic health assessment (including diet, sleep, exercise, chemical use and abuse, and medical history) |
| | Self-system assessment and appraisal of current developmental level |
| Leveling | Discussion of possible choices of focus; selection of a domain of present focus (specific problem or problems, recurrent patterns, coping skills, or experience-generating processes) |
| | Agreement on a general preliminary strategy for addressing that level |
| Early work | Deepening development of working alliance (via authentic caring, affirmation, and encouragement) |
| | Active behavioral homework exercises; encouragement of self-exploratory activities (if appropriate, initiation of personal journal work, life-review project, meditation, or physical activity) |
| | More detailed exploration of current life situation and primary and secondary concerns |
| | More intensive and extensive exploration of life history, family of origin, and identity development |
| Intermediate work | Except in cases of borderline functioning, extreme emotional instability, or if acute self-focus might be risky, introduction of exercises aimed at amplifying (a) self-awareness, and (b) positive self-relationships (e.g., stream of consciousness work, mirror time, dream and fantasy work, and so on) |
| | In-session exercises emphasizing exploration, novelty, and empowerment (e.g., dialectical dialogues, psychodrama) |
| | Homework assignments aimed at self-caring rituals, internalization/exploration of novel "real world" adaptations, and emotional/conceptual/behavioral edging |
| | If appropriate, encourage involvement of willing family members and significant |

**TABLE 2.** *continued*

| Interval or stage | General focus and areas of activity |
| --- | --- |
| | others; involve co-therapists and other relevant professionals as they are needed |
| | Acknowledgment of, respect for, and work with (rather than against) resistance |
| | Emphasis on pacing and respect for cycles of progress and regress |
| Review and choice | Review of general goals |
| | Review of work to date |
| | Global appraisal of progress |
| | Assess client satisfaction and motivation for or merit of continued therapy<br>a. if agreement is to discontinue, proceed to stages below<br>b. if agreement is to continue, return to "leveling" stage and proceed with selective adaptations and elaborations of exploratory exercises |
| Assessment | Repeated as outlined above with additions or deletions suggested by work to date |
| Exit | Assess client attributions of responsibility for progress and sensed autonomy; if disempowering beliefs are expressed, suggest a graduated schedule of separation |
| | Affirm client's uniqueness and strengths as an individual |
| | Affirm client's past pursuit of personal development (intent, effort, activity) |
| | Encourage future openness to professional counsel |
| | Discuss possible expressions and experiences of the separation process |
| | Develop an individualized separation ritual that includes a symbolic exchange and an explicit farewell |
| | If it is appropriate to do so, encourage follow-up contacts at graduated intervals |

■ *Stream of consciousness* is a technique similar to free association. In this exercise, clients are invited to tune in to their inner experience and report images, thoughts, and musings. Clients' privacy is protected by encouraging them not to report thoughts they wish to keep private. This directive makes the technique different from free association.

■ Finally, *mirror time* is a technique used specifically to promote self-study through having the clients view themselves in a mirror. Mahoney uses this technique with clients to promote self-change. He even keeps a mirror in his office on the back of the door and gives instructions to clients to study themselves in the mirror to develop self-consciousness, which, according to Lacan (1978), may be an important step to self-change.

**Meichenbaum's constructivist cognitive-behavioral model.** Meichenbaum (1996) contrasts the constructivist approach to cognitive therapy with that of standard cognitive-behavior therapy. Constructivist therapists "place greater emphasis on the developmental history; target deeper core beliefs and processes; explore the behavioral impact, emotional toll, and personal price of the client's holding certain root metaphors; and engage the client in a discovery oriented process" (p. 18). Therapists using constructivist theory help clients discover how they create their realities and the consequences that follow their personal beliefs and constructions. They help clients tell their stories about their strengths as well as about their problems and irrationalities. Meichenbaum refers to the focus on client strengths as being the "rest of the story."

Meichenbaum (1993) emphasizes the use of the constructive narrative in cognitive-behavior therapy. He is very adamant that his constructive approach to therapy represents an evolution in cognitive-behavior therapy and not some other brand of psychotherapy. Describing the evolution of cognitive-behavioral therapies toward constructivist/narrative perspectives, Meichenbaum (1993) examines the three guiding metaphors that have affected the development of cognitive-behavior therapies. First, with *conditioning* as a metaphor, cognitions are viewed as covert behaviors subject to the same laws of learning as overt behavior in the conditioning paradigm. Second, with *information processing* as a metaphor, mind as computer is the guiding metaphor in the language of information processing and social learning theory (e.g., decoding, encoding, retrieval, attributional bias, cognitive structure, schemata, belief systems, cognitive distortion, and cognitive errors). Finally, with the metaphor of the *constructive narrative*, cognitive phenomenology is emphasized along with personal meanings, multiple realities, and consequences of cognitive constructions. The therapist acts as co-constructor, helping clients alter their narratives and life stories. The therapist helps clients reframe stressful life experiences and emotions as normal. The focus is on strengths, resources, coping abilities, and narrative reconstruction (Meichenbaum, 1993).

According to Meichenbaum, the tasks of the constructivist cognitive-behavioral therapist include the following:

▪ *Developing a therapeutic alliance and helping clients tell their stories.* A collaborative working alliance between client and practitioner are encouraged. Therapists use the art of questioning to help clients first to tell the story about their troubles and then to tell the story about their coping abilities and strengths.

▪ *Educating clients about their clinical problems.* Meichenbaum believes that education is in every form of therapy. Constructivists use a Socratic approach to educating clients, and this process takes place in the course of therapy.

▪ *Helping clients reconceptualize their "problems" in a more helpful fashion.* Clients are encouraged to take vague problems and define them in concrete ways that can be solved.

▪ *Ensuring that the client has coping skills.* The focus of treatment must be not only on reframing problems but also on teaching clients intrapersonal and interpersonal coping skills for managing their lives. Skills such as self-monitoring, relaxation, self-instruction training, imaginal rehearsal, cognitive restructuring, assertiveness training, and relapse prevention, among other standard cognitive-behavioral skills training approaches, are used to increase client coping.

▪ *Encouraging clients to perform personal experiments.* The therapist encourages clients to practice coping skills and new behaviors in vivo, in the real world, in the form of personal experiments. The goal is to increase the self-efficacy of clients.

▪ *Ensuring that clients take credit for the changes they have brought about.* The therapist helps clients take credit for the changes they make and helps them develop personal explanations that account for the changes.

■ *Conducting relapse prevention.* The therapist helps the client anticipate and prepare for relapses in an attempt to establish generalization and maintenance of changes.

Some therapeutic techniques used by Meichenbaum include the following:

■ *Attending to and having clients elaborate on hot cognitions* (affect-laden, emotionally driven cognitions). Reflect affective words back to client and communicate a curious orientation to know more about this feeling or reaction. The goal is to increase metacognitive awareness.

■ *Normalizing and validating client experiences.* With this method the therapist helps clients develop their stories. They focus on narrative structure and meanings (schemas). Therapists further listen for themes, variations (counterplots), and inactive or emerging schemas (possible selves).

■ *Using client metaphors.* The therapist uses the language of the metaphor as a definition of experience and speaks to clients about their experiences using the metaphorical description. For example, "What will be different in your life when the 'ball and chain' are removed?" Meichenbaum further encourages therapists to elicit or elaborate on behavioral, cognitive, and affective aspects of metaphor.

■ *Expanding the context by exploring other situations* in which clients feel the same way or have certain experiences. "In what other situations do you feel this way and with whom?" Ask circular questions. Search for triggers of maladaptive schemas or reinforcing cognitions and behaviors (e.g., avoidance, overcompensation).

■ *Obtaining developmental history.* In the past, when and in what situations did clients experience these cognitions, emotions, or behaviors? Where did they get these ideas? How do they explain the origins of their responses? By getting the developmental history, therapists are able to identify important cognitive schemas that underlie current problems.

■ *Eliciting social constructions* that may be involved in the maintenance of difficulties: "What would your husband say or do? How might your friends relate to you differently when you change? Who might object? How can your husband help you change? Who will support your new self?"

■ *Exploring consequences.* What are the consequences of their beliefs and actions? Is this working in the present? Use the client's own language and metaphors. Emphasize that it is not working. What is the price that they pay? Emphasize where it is working and what coping responses work. Amplify effective responses.

■ *Exploring positive aspects of difficulties* to help them see any reinforcing aspects of cognitions, behaviors, and emotions.

■ *Collaborating with client to set therapeutic goals for change.*

■ *Giving homework* to keep track of clients' experiences or to keep track of when they do not have the experience but think, feel, or behave in the way they want. This assignment is usually completed in the first session and is similar to keeping track of the exceptions to the problem or the first-formula task as used in the solution-focused therapy. Subsequently, homework assignments are aimed at increasing effortful metacognitive awareness and processing (e.g., journaling), cognitive and behavioral rehearsal and reconstruction, and rearranging the social environment to elicit positive feedback and reinforcement for new ways of being.

# Implications for Social Work Practice

In this chapter, I described both constructivism and social constructionism and illustrated practice approaches from each perspective. In addition, I described their metatheories and their research perspectives. In concluding this chapter, I offer further reflections on distinctions between the two metatheories of social constructionism and cognitive constructivism as they are applied in clinical practice.

Constructivism and social constructionism are developing in very different contexts, and these contexts are influential in defining differences in their clinical-practice models. Constructivism is developing in the context of mainstream psychology within cognitive-behavior therapies. It is a respected psychological theory that incorporates psychological knowledge from the cognitive sciences and current conceptualizations in the philosophy of science. Constructivism qualifies as a bona fide clinical-practice model that provides its own set of methods for assessment and intervention. Methods are predominantly psychological or interpersonal and include approaches such as the study of past history, uses of the therapeutic relationship, narrative reconstruction of meaning, and changing interpersonal environments that obstruct changes in core constructs or meanings. It is historically rooted and continues to evolve within the formal discourses of psychology and psychotherapy.

In contrast, social constructionism developed within sociology in the context of analysis, social criticism, and social action. It is the "grand of grand theories," having evolved from the historical, sociological tradition of developing explanatory social theories. Social constructionism was transplanted into social psychology and other psychological fields as part of a critical discourse about logical-positivist science and the development of psychological and social knowledge. It continues its tradition of social criticism and has found new fertile soil in postmodernism. It is currently serving as a metaframework for deconstructing family therapies and developing new interactional approaches to practice. The new practice approaches it redresses tend to be self-reflexive, critical, and progressive. They challenge time-honored "metaphors" of therapy, such as families as systems and the power of the therapist, emphasizing instead (a) collaboration and conversation within broader relational networks (i.e., community systems or anyone in conversation about the problem), (b) creating distinctions in language and cognitions as a way to deconstruct client problems, (c) emphasis on solutions instead of problems, and (d) awareness and concern for broader sociopolitical "realities" that maintain problems (i.e., gender inequities, cultural differences, institutional discrimination). Social constructionism invites a multiple and metadisciplinary critical discourse about psychotherapies and family therapies in particular. All sociocultural discourses and client narratives are deconstructed for the purpose of increasing client agency, responsibility, and self-determination.

Obvious metatheoretical distinctions between constructivism and social constructionism are their micro versus macro perspectives, interpersonal versus interactional focus, and individual versus relational emphasis. Although constructivism emphasizes social interactions in the constructions of subjective human experience and asserts the impetus of language, narratives, meanings, human agency, and social contexts, its lenses conform to the contour of the individual and his or her social environment. This individual focus can be seen in cognitive constructivism's emphasis on human development and the necessity of change in the core ordering processes. It can further be seen in constructivist views of narrative reconstruction and focus on changes in the personal meaning systems and the self.

In contrast, social constructionism emphasizes language, narratives, meanings, and social contexts but views the individual as being intricately and inseparably a part of their sociocultural and relational networks. From the view of social constructionism, the self does not exist except in relationship to others—in the collectivity of narratives, meanings, and social contexts. Thus, the idea of internal structures, such as deep structures that resist change or core ordering processes, are viewed as just other social constructions. The only core ordering processes are the social structures that we construct and maintain in language among ourselves. If changes are to occur, they must be socially transacted and legitimated in distinctions we make in conversation with others. Of course, this includes the distinctions we learn to make between our desires and aspirations and those cultural narratives.

This chapter has emphasized distinctions in metatheories, but compatibilities between constructivism and social constructionism are evident as well. Though integrations between the two would likely be difficult at the metatheoretical level, similarities between their constructivist epistemologies are strengths that may aid their integrations. These approaches appear to be most congruent at the level of their practice methods. Many points of convergence are evident (i.e., narrative reconstruction, use of metaphors, conversations, and relationships). I view constructivism and social constructionism as complementary approaches and believe that clinical practice fields may benefit from an exploration of both.

Clinical practice in a social constructionist and constructivist framework is described as new and postmodern. But this orientation and the values and philosophical discourses that have historically undergirded social work practice are comparable in many ways. By social work practice, I refer to professional social workers and not those who are employed by social services agencies but are not trained as professional social workers. Social workers, for example, share common ideological beliefs with the social constructionist framework. Consistent ideologies between social work and social constructionist and constructivist frameworks include (a) supremacy of the social environment or person-in-environment metaphor; (b) the strengths perspective; (c) collaborative, client-centered orientation; (d) disinclination to subscribe to the medical model and other types of labeling of the client; (e) belief in client self-determination or that people have the right to direct their own lives, including their therapy; (f) belief that problems are contextual and may be resolved through a mutual understanding and coordinated actions among those involved, an idea that has been explained in social work literature as including the "observing systems" of the social worker and other systems in which he or she works (however, social workers have not used the language or metaphors of postmodernism to explain this view); (g) use of empowerment as a guiding metaphor; (h) respect for diversity, including multiple meanings and perspectives of clients; and (j) commitment to social action (Compton & Galaway, 1989; Hepworth & Larsen, 1993; Pincus & Minahan, 1973; Smalley, 1967).

Of course, all social work authors or practitioners do not reflect these ideological commitments, but the point is that these ideological beliefs are an integral part of the values orientation and indigenous practice perspectives taught and used within the social work profession. Weick (1987), for example, identified three core beliefs in the philosophy of social work practice: (a) the inherent capacity of human beings to transform themselves, (b) the complexity and interdependence of human relationships and processes, and (c) the role of the professional relationship in the processes of change. Hepworth and Larsen (1993) state,

> Basic social work values embody the beliefs that clients have the capacity to grow and change and to see and develop solutions to their difficulties, as well as the right and capacity to exercise free choice responsibly. ... The type of relationship that affirms self-determination and fosters growth is a partnership wherein practitioner and client (whether individual, couple or group) are joined in mutual effort to search for solutions to problems and promote growth. ... Although these facilitative functions often prove invaluable to clients, the ultimate determinant of outcome of the shared ventures resides, as it should, with the client. (pp. 71–72)

## Conclusion

In practice-based professions such as social work, debates over research epistemologies are not usually in the forefront of the minds of practitioners. I doubt that many practitioners would even give a passing thought to such issues unless confronted with these discussions in the context of their clinical education and training. Debates about metatheories and epistemologies emerge in the form of new practice theories and models such as those developing through the influence of social constructionism in family therapy and cognitive constructivism in cognitive–behavioral therapies. It is impossible, for example, to receive training in the popular narrative therapies or solution-oriented approaches to family practice without entertaining discussions about the social constructionist or constructivist metatheories that undergird the models (de Shazer & Berg, 1992; O'Hanlon & Weiner-Davis, 1989; White & Epston, 1990). As discussed in this chapter, social constructionist and constructivist practice models are emerging in the context of epistemological debates within the social sciences. At the center of these debates are the changing world views of postmodernism and a new philosophy of science. Certainly, it would be a grave mistake to ignore these trends or to pass them off as being inconsequential. Conservatively, these trends may be seen as a passing fad or temporary illusion. Less conservatively, these developments may be viewed as a significant shift in metatheories for clinical practice. Regardless of where one fits on this continuum of views, it's hard to deny that social constructionism and constructivism are part of a broader intellectual movement that is having a profound effect on both research and practice.

# References

Adams-Webber, J. (1989). Kelly's pragmatic constructivism. *Canadian Psychology, 30*(2), 190–193.

Agnew, N., & Brown, J. (1989). The rhythms of reality: Entrainment theory. *Canadian Psychology, 30*(2), 193–201.

Alexander, P. C. (1988). The therapeutic implications of family cognitions and constructs. *Journal of Cognitive Psychotherapy, 2,* 219–236.

Anastas, J. W., & MacDonald, M. L. (1994). *Research design for social work and the human services.* New York: Lexington Books.

Andersen, T. (1991). Guidelines for practice. In T. Andersen (Ed.), *The reflecting team: Dialogues and dialogues about dialogues* (pp. 24–41). New York: W. W. Norton.

Anderson, H., & Goolishian, H. (1988). Human systems as linguistic systems: Preliminary and evolving ideas about the implications for clinical theory. *Family Process, 27,* 371–393.

Anderson, W. T. (1990). *Reality isn't what it used to be.* San Francisco: Harper & Row.

Atherton, C. R. (1993). Empiricists versus social constructionists: Time for a cease fire. *Families in Society, 74,* 617–624.

Berg, B. L. (1989). *Qualitative research methods for the social sciences.* Needham Heights, MA: Allyn and Bacon.

Berg, I. K. (1994). *Family based services: A solution-focused approach.* New York: W. W. Norton.

Berg, I. K., & Miller, S. D. (1992). *Working with the problem drinker: A solution-focused approach.* New York: W. W. Norton.

Berger, P., & Luckmann, T. (1966). *The social construction of reality.* Garden City, NY: Doubleday.

Best, J. (1989). Extending the constructionist perspective: A conclusion and introduction. In J. Best (Ed.), *Images of issues: Typifying contemporary social problems* (pp. 243–252). Hawthorne, NY: Aldine de Gruyter.

Best, J. (1993). But seriously folks: The limitations of the strict constructionist interpretation of social problems. In G. Miller & J. A. Holstein (Eds.), *Constructionist controversies: Issues in social problems theory* (pp. 109–130). Hawthorne, NY: Aldine de Gruyter.

Bhakaskar, R. (1989). *Reclaiming reality: A critical introduction to contemporary philosophy.* London: Verso.

Biever, J. L., de las Feuentes, C., Cashion, C., & Franklin, C. (in press). The social construction of gender: A comparison of feminist and post-modern approaches. *British Journal of Counseling Psychology.*

Bowlby, J. (1969a). *Attachment and loss, volume 1, attachment.* New York: Basic Books.

Bowlby, J. (1969b). *Attachment and loss, volume 2, separation, anxiety and anger.* New York: Basic Books.

Bowlby, J. (1969c). *Attachment and loss, volume 3, sadness and depression.* London: Hogarth Books.

Brower, A. M., & Nurius, P. S. (1993). *Social cognition and individual change: Current theory and counseling guidelines.* Newbury Park, CA: Sage.

Bruner, J. S. (1986). *Actual minds, possible worlds.* Cambridge, MA: Harvard University Press.

Campbell, D. T. (1989). Fragments of the fragile history of psychological epistemology and theory of science. In B. Gholson, W. R. Shadish, R. A. Neimeyer, & A. C. Houts (Eds.), *Psychology of science: Contributions to metascience* (pp. 21–46.). New York: Cambridge University Press.

Clifford, J. (1988). *The predicament of culture: Twentieth century ethnography, literature, and art.* Cambridge, MA: Harvard University Press.

Clifford, J., & Marcus, G. E. (1986). *Writing culture: The poetics and politics of ethnography.* Berkeley, CA: University of California Press.

Compton, B. R., & Galaway, B. (1989). *Social work processes* (4th ed.). Belmont, CA: Wadsworth.

Dean, R. (1993). Constructivism: An approach to clinical practice. *Smith College Studies in Social Work, 63,* 127–146.

Dean, R., & Fleck-Henderson, A. (1992). Teaching clinical theory and practice through a constructivist lens. *Journal of Teaching in Social Work, 6*(1), 3–20.

Denzin, N. K. (1992). Whose Cornerville is it, anyway? *Journal of Contemporary Ethnography, 21,* 120–132.

de Shazer, S. (1985). *Keys to solution in brief therapy.* New York: W. W. Norton.

de Shazer, S. (1988). *Clues: Investigating solutions in brief therapy.* New York: W. W. Norton.

de Shazer, S. (1991). *Putting difference to work.* New York: W. W. Norton.

de Shazer, S. (1994). *Words were originally magic.* New York: W. W. Norton.

de Shazer, S., & Berg, I. K. (1992). Doing therapy: A poststructural re-vision. *Journal of Marital and Family Therapy, 18,* 71–81.

de Shazer, S., Berg, I. K., Lipchik, J., Nunnally, E., Molnar, A., Gingerich, W., & Weiner-Davis, M. (1986). Brief therapy: Focused solution development. *Family Process, 25,* 207–222.

Diesing, P. (1991). *How does social science work: Reflections on practice.* Pittsburgh, PA: University of Pittsburgh Press.

DiGiuseppe, R., & Linscott, J. (1993). Philosophical differences among cognitive–behavioral therapists: Rationalism, constructivism, or both? *Journal of Cognitive Psychotherapy, 7,* 117–130.

Dobson, K. S., & Craig, K. D. (1996). *Advances in cognitive–behavioral therapy.* Thousand Oaks, CA: Sage.

Doise, W. (1989). Constructivism in social psychology. *European Journal of Social Psychology, 19,* 389–400.

Dolan, Y. M. (1991). *Resolving sexual abuse: Solution-focused therapy and Ericksonian hypnosis for adult survivors.* New York: W. W. Norton.

Dougher, M. (1993). Interpretive and hermeneutic research methods in the contextualistic analysis of verbal behavior. In S. Hayes, L. Hayes, H. Reese, & T. Sarbin (Eds.), *Varieties of scientific contextualism* (pp. 211–221). Reno, NV: Context Press.

Eisner, E. (Ed.). (1985). *The art of educational evaluation: A personal view.* Englewood Cliffs, NJ: Prentice Hall.

Ellis, A. (1989). Is rational emotive therapy (RET) rationalist or constructivist? In W. Dryden (Ed.), *The essential Albert Ellis* (pp. 199–233). New York: Springer.

Ellis, A. (1996). A social constructionist position for mental health counseling: A reply to Jeffrey T. Guterman. *Journal of Mental Health Counseling, 18,* 16–28.

Epstein, I. (1985). Quantitative and qualitative methods. In R. M. Grinnell (Ed.), *Social work research and evaluation* (pp. 263–274). Itasca, IL: F. E. Peacock.

Feagin, J. R., Orum, A. M., & Sjoberg, G. (1991). *A case for case study.* Chapel Hill, NC: University of North Carolina Press.

Fisher, D. D. (1991). *An introduction to constructivism for social workers.* New York: Praeger.

Franklin, C. (1993). *In search of metatheories: Distinctions between cognitive constructivism and social constructionism.* Unpublished manuscript, School of Social Work, University of Texas at Austin.

Franklin, C. (1995). Expanding the vision of the social constructionist debates: Creating relevance for practitioners. *Families in Society, 76,* 395–407.

Franklin, C., & Biever, J. (1996). *Evaluating the effectiveness of solution-focused therapy with learning-challenged students using single-case designs.* Unpublished manuscript, School of Social Work, University of Texas at Austin.

Franklin, C., Corcoran, J., Streeter, C. L., & Nowicki, J. (1997). Using client self-anchored scales to measure outcomes in solution-focused therapy. *Journal of Systemic Therapies, 16,* 246–265.

Franklin, C., Nowicki, J., Trapp, J., Schwab, A. J., & Petersen, J. (1993). A computerized assessment system for brief, crisis-oriented youth services. *Families in Society, 74,* 602–616.

Franklin, C., & Moore, K. C. (in press). Solution-focused, brief therapy for families. In C. Franklin & C. Jordan (Eds.), *Family practice: Brief systems methods for social work.* Pacific Grove, CA:

Brooks/Cole.

Franklin, C., & Nurius, P. (1996). Constructivist therapy: New directions in social work practice. *Families in Society, 77,* 323–325.

Freedman, J., & Combs, G. (1996). *Narrative therapy: The social construction of preferred realities.* New York: W. W. Norton.

Garfinkle, H. (1967). *Studies in ethnomethodology.* Englewood Cliffs, NJ: Prentice Hall.

Geertz, C. (1983). *Local knowledge: Further essays in interpretive anthropology.* New York: Basic Books.

Geertz, C. (1988). *Works and lives: The anthropologist as author.* Stanford, CA: University of California Press.

Gergen, K. J. (1982). *Toward a transformation in social knowledge.* New York: Springer-Verlag.

Gergen, K. J. (1985). The social constructionist movement in modern psychology. *American Psychologist, 40,* 266–275.

Gergen, K. J. (1991). *The saturated self: Dilemmas of identity in contemporary life.* New York: Basic Books.

Gergen, K. J., & Kaye, J. (1992). Beyond narrative in the negotiation of therapeutic meaning. In S. McNamee & K. J. Gergen (Eds.), *Therapy as social construction* (pp. 166–185). Newbury Park, CA: Sage.

Gholson, B., Shadish, W. R., Neimeyer, R. A., & Houts, A. C. (Eds.). (1989). *Psychology of science.* Cambridge, MA: Cambridge University Press.

Gilgun, J. F. (1993). *Dimension analysis and grounded theory: Interviews with Leonard Shatzman.* Minneapolis, MN: School of Social Work, University of Minnesota.

Gilgun, J. F., Daly, K., & Handel, G. (1992). *Qualitative methods in family research.* Newbury Park, CA: Sage.

Goldstein, H. (1990). The knowledge base of social work practice: Wisdom, analogue, or art. *Families in Society, 71,* 32–43.

Gonçalves, Ó. F. (1995). Cognitive narrative psychotherapy: Hermeneutic construction of alternative meanings. In M. J. Mahoney (Ed.), *Cognitive and constructive psychotherapies: Theory, research and practice* (pp. 139–162). New York: Springer.

Granvold, D. K. (1994). Concepts and methods of cognitive treatment. In D. K. Granvold (Ed.), *Cognitive and behavioral treatment: Methods and applications* (pp. 3–26). Pacific Grove, CA: Brooks/Cole.

Gregersen, H., & Sailer, L. (1993). Chaos theory and its implications for social science research. *Human Relations, 46,* 777–802.

Grinnell, R. M. (1993). *Social work research and evaluation* (4th ed.). Itasca, IL: F. E. Peacock.

Guba, E. G. (1990). *The paradigm dialog.* Newbury Park, CA: Sage.

Guidano, V. F. (1991). *The self in process.* New York: Guilford.

Hamel, J., Dufour, S., & Fortin, D. (1993). *Case study methods.* Newbury Park, CA: Sage.

Hammersley, M. (1992). *What's wrong with ethnography? Methodological explorations.* London: Routledge.

Held, B. S. (1990). What's in a name? Some confusions and concerns about constructivism. *Journal of Marital and Family Therapy, 16,* 179–186.

Hepworth, D. H., & Larsen, J. A. (1993). *Direct social work practice: Theory and skills* (4th ed.). Belmont, CA: Brooks/Cole.

Hoffman, L. (1990). Constructing realities: An art of lenses. *Family Process, 29,* 1–12.

Hoffman, L. (1992). A reflexive stance for family therapy (pp. 166–185). In S. McNamee & K. J. Gergen (Eds.), *Therapy as social construction.* Newbury Park, CA: Sage.

Hudson, P. O., & O'Hanlon, W. H. (1991). *Rewriting love stories: Brief marital therapy.* New York: W. W. Norton.

Ivey, A. E., & Gonçalves, Ó. F. (1988). Developmental therapy: Integrating developmental processes into clinical practice. *Journal of Counseling and Development, 66,* 406–412.

Jacob, E. (1987). Qualitative research traditions: A review. *Review of Educational Research, 57,* 1–50.

Katovich, M. A., & Reese, W. A. (1993). Postmodern thought in symbolic interaction: Reconstructing social inquiry in light of late-modern concerns. *Sociological Quarterly, 34,* 391–411.

Keeney, B. P. (1983). *Aesthetics of change.* New York: Guilford.

Kiser, D. J., Piercy, F. P., & Lipchik, E. (1993). The integration of emotion in solution-focused therapy. *Journal of Marital and Family Therapy, 19,* 235–244.

Kituse, J. I., & Spector, M. (1973). Toward a sociology of social problems: Social conditions, value judgements and social problems. *Social Problems, 20,* 407–419.

Lacan, J. (1978). *The four fundamental concepts of psychoanalysis.* Trans. A. Sheridan. New York: W. W. Norton.

Laird, J. (1993). Family-centered practice: Cultural and constructionist reflections. *Journal of Teaching in Social Work, 8,* 77–110.

Laird, J. (1994). Thick description revisited: Family therapist as anthropologist–constructivist. In E. Sherman & W. J. Reid (Eds.), *Qualitative research in social work* (pp. 175–189). New York: Columbia University Press.

Lancy, D. E. (1993). *Qualitative research in education.* New York: Longman.

Loehlin, J. C. (1992). *Latent variable models: An introduction to factor, path, and structural analysis* (2nd ed.). Hillsdale, NJ: Lawrence Erlbaum.

Lupenitz, D. A. (1992). Nothing in common but their first names: The case of Foucault and White. *Journal of Family Therapy, 14,* 281–284.

Lyddon, W. J. (1990). First- and second-order change: Implications for rationalist and constructivist cognitive therapies. *Journal of Counseling and Development, 69,* 122–127.

Lyddon, W. J. (1995). Forms and facets of constructivist psychology. In R. A. Neimeyer & M. J. Mahoney (Eds.), *Constructivism in psychotherapy* (pp. 69–92). Washington, DC: American Psychological Association.

Mahoney, M. J. (1988a). Constructive metatheory: Basic features and historical foundations. *International Journal of Personal Construct Psychology, 1,* 1–35.

Mahoney, M. J. (1988b). Constructive metatheory: II. Implications for psychotherapy. *International Journal of Personal Construct Psychology, 1,* 299–315.

Mahoney, M. J. (1989). Holy epistemology: Construing the constructions of the constructivists. *Canadian Psychology, 30,* 187–189.

Mahoney, M. J. (1991). *Human change processes.* New York: Basic Books.

Mahoney, M. J., & Lyddon, W. J. (1988). Recent developments in cognitive approaches to counseling and psychotherapy. *Counseling Psychologist, 16,* 190–234.

Manicas, P. T., & Secord, P. F. (1982). Implications for psychology of the new philosophy of science. *American Psychologist, 38,* 390–413.

Martin, J. (1984). The cognitive mediational paradigm for research on counseling. *Journal of Counseling Psychology, 31,* 558–571.

Martin, J. (1985). Measuring clients' cognitive competence in research on counseling. *Journal of Counseling and Development, 63,* 556–560.

Martin, J. (1994). *The construction and understanding of psychotherapeutic change.* New York: Teachers College Press.

Martin, J., & Sugarman, J. (1996). Bridging social constructionism and cognitive constructivism: A psychology of human possibility and restraint. *Journal of Mind and Behavior, 17,* 291–319.

Maturana, H. R. (1988). Reality: The search for objectivity or the quest for a compelling argument. *Irish Journal of Psychology, 9,* 25–82.

McNamee, S., & Gergen, K. J. (1992). Introduction. In S. McNamee & K. J. Gergen (Eds.), *Therapy as social construction* (pp. 1–6). Newbury Park, CA: Sage.

Meichenbaum, D. K. (1993). Changing conceptions of cognitive-behavior modification: Retrospect and prospect. *Journal of Consulting and Clinical Psychology, 61,* 202–204.

Meichenbaum, D. K. (1996). *Mixed anxiety and depression: A cognitive–behavioral approach* [A viewers manual]. New York: Newbridge Professional Programs.

Meichenbaum, D. K., & Fitzpatrick, D. (1993). A constructionist, narrative perspective on stress and coping: Stress inoculation applications. In L. Goldberger & S. Bresnitz (Eds.), *Handbook of stress: Theoretical and clinical aspects* (2nd ed., pp. 63–82). New York: Free Press.

Metcalf, L. (1995). *Counseling toward solutions: A practical solution-focused program for working with students, teachers, and parents.* Englewood Cliffs, NJ: Prentice Hall.

Miles, M. B., & Huberman, A. M. (1994). *An expanded sourcebook: Qualitative data analysis.* Newbury Park, CA: Sage.

Miller, G., & Holstein, J. A. (1993). Constructing social problems: Context and legacy. In G. Miller & J. A. Holstein (Eds.), *Constructionist controversies: Issues in social problems theory* (pp. 3–20). Hawthorne, NY: Aldine de Gruyter.

Miller, S. D., Hubble, M. A., & Duncan, B. S (1996). *Handbook of solution-focused brief therapy.* San Francisco: Jossey-Bass.

Neimeyer, G. J. (Ed.). (1993). *Constructivist assessment: A casebook.* Newbury Park, CA: Sage.

Neimeyer, R. A. (1993a). An appraisal of the constructivist psychotherapies. *Journal of Consulting and Clinical Psychology, 61,* 221– 234.

Neimeyer, R. A. (1993b). Constructivism and cognitive psychotherapies: Some conceptual and strategic contrasts. *Journal of Cognitive Psychotherapy, 7,* 159–172.

Neimeyer, R. A., Baker, K., & Neimeyer, G. J. (1990). The current status of personal construct theory: Some scientometric data. In G. J. Neimeyer & R. A. Neimeyer (Eds.), *Advances in personal construct psychology* (pp. 3–24). Greenwich, CT: JAI.

Neimeyer, R. A., & Mahoney, M. J. (1995). *Constructivism in psychotherapy.* Washington, DC: American Psychological Association.

O'Hanlon, W., & Weiner-Davis, M. (1989). *In search of solutions: A new direction in psychotherapy.* New York: W. W. Norton.

Payne, M. (1991). *Modern social work theory: A critical introduction.* Chicago: Lyceum.

Phillips, D. C. (1990). Postpositivist science: Myths and realities. In E. G. Guba (Ed.), *The paradigm dialog* (pp. 31–45). Newbury Park, CA: Sage.

Pincus, A., & Minahan, A. (1973). *Social work practice: Model and method.* Itasca, IL: F. E. Peacock.

Polkinghorne, D. (1983). *Methodology for the human sciences.* Albany, NY: State University of New York Press.

Polkinghorne, D. (1984). Further extensions of methodological diversity for counseling psychology. *Journal of Counseling Psychology, 31,* 416–429.

Polkinghorne, D. (1991). Two methodological calls for methodological reforms. *Counseling Psychologist, 19,* 103–114.

Pollner, M. (1991). Left of ethnomethodology: The rise and decline of radical reflexivity. *American Sociological Review, 56,* 370–380.

Pollner, M. (1993). The reflectivity of constructionism and the construction of reflexivity. In G. Miller & J. A. Holstein (Eds.), *Constructionist controversies: Issues in social problems theory* (pp. 69–82). Hawthorne, NY: Aldine de Gruyter.

Rafter, N. H. (1992). Some consequences of strict constructionism. *Social Problems, 39,* 38–39.

Real, T. (1990). The therapeutic use of self: Constructionist/systemic therapy. *Family Process, 29,* 255–272.

Richan, W. C., & Mendelsohn, A. R. (1973). *Social work: The unloved profession.* New York: New Viewpoints.

Rosenau, P. M. (1992). *Post-modernism and the social sciences.* Princeton, NJ: Princeton University Press.

Rubin, A., & Babbie, E. (1989). *Research methods for social work.* Pacific Grove, CA: Brooks/Cole.

Russell, R. L. (1991). Narrative in views of humanity, science, and action: Lessons for cognitive therapy. *Journal of Cognitive Psychotherapy, 5,* 241–255.

Saleebey, D. D. (1992). *The strengths perspective in social work practice.* New York: Longman.

Sarup, M. (1993). *An introductory guide to poststructuralism and postmodernism* (2nd ed.). New York: Harvester/Wheatsheaf.

Schutz, A. (1962). *Collected papers I: The problem of social reality.* The Hague, Netherlands: Martinus

Nijhoff.

Sirles, E. A., Lipchik, E., & Kowalski, K. (1993). A consumer's perspective on domestic violence interventions. *Journal of Family Violence, 8,* 267–276.

Smalley, R. (1967). *Theory for social work practice.* New York: Columbia University Press.

Spector, M., & Kituse, J. I. (1974). Social problems. *Social Problems, 21,* 145–158.

Spector, M., & Kituse, J. I. (1977). *Constructing social problems.* Hawthorne, NY: Aldine de Gruyter.

Speed, B. (1991). Reality exists okay? An argument against constructivism and social constructionism. *Family Therapy, 13,* 395–409.

Spence, D. (1982). *Narrative truth and historical truth.* New York: W. W. Norton.

Sprenkle, D. H., & Bischof, G. P. (1994). Contemporary family therapy in the United States. *Family Therapy, 16,* 5–23.

Strong, S. R. (1991). Theory-driven science and naive empiricism in counseling psychology. *Journal of Counseling Psychology, 38,* 204–210.

Van den Broek, P., & Thurlow, R. (1991). The role and structures of personal narratives. *Journal of Cognitive Psychotherapy, 5,* 257–274.

Varela, F. J. (1989). Reflections on the circulation of concepts between the biology of cognition and systemic family therapy. *Family Process, 28,* 15–24.

Wallace, R. A., & Wolf, A. (1991). *Contemporary sociological theory* (3rd ed.). Englewood Cliffs, NJ: Prentice Hall.

Walter, J. L., & Peller, J. E. (1992). *Becoming solution-focused in brief therapy.* New York: Brunner-Mazel.

Watzlawick, P. (1984). *The invented reality.* New York: W. W. Norton.

Webster, D. C., Vaughn, K., & Martinez, R. (1994). Introducing solution-focused approaches to staff in inpatient psychiatric settings. *Archives of Psychiatric Nursing, 8,* 251–261.

Weick, A. (1987). Reconceptualizing the philosophical perspective of social work. *Social Service Review, 61,* 218–230.

White, M. (1988, Winter) The process of questioning: A therapy of literary merit? *Dulwiche Centre Newsletter,* pp. 8–14.

White, M. (1993). Commentary: The histories of the present. In S. Gilligan & R. Price (Eds.), *Therapeutic conversations* (pp. 121–135). New York: W. W. Norton.

White, M. (1994, February). *Narrative therapy.* Workshop presented at the Meeting of the Austin Child Guidance Center, Austin, Texas.

White, M., & Epston, D. (1990). *Narrative means to therapeutic ends.* New York: W. W. Norton.

Witkin, S. L. (1990). The implications of social constructionism for social work education. *Journal of Teaching in Social Work, 4*(2), 37–48.

Witkin, S. L. (1991). Empirical clinical practice: A critical analysis. *Social Work, 36,* 158–163.

Woolfolk, R. L. (1992). Hermeneutics, social constructionism and other items of intellectual fashion: Intimations for clinical science. *Behavior Therapy, 23,* 213–223.

Woolgar, S., & Pawluch, D. (1985). Ontological gerrymandering: The anatomy of social problems explanations. *Social Problems, 32,* 214–227.

# Part 2:

◉ **Assessment in Constructivist Practice** ◉

# 4

## Qualitative Assessment: A Methodological Review

*Cynthia Franklin & Catheleen Jordan*

During the past decade social workers have been encouraged to use assessment methodologies grounded in the empiricist research traditions of the empirical practice model (Rodman, 1987). For example, practitioners are taught to use measurement in assessing their clients (Corcoran & Fischer, 1987; Franklin & Jordan, 1992; Hudson, 1982; Mattaini & Kirk, 1991). Both Rodman (1987) and Scott (1989) criticize empiricist assessment methods and suggest that assessment methodologies grounded in qualitative/naturalistic research are better suited for social work practice. Allen-Meares and Lane (1990) further provided an integrative synopsis of how qualitative and quantitative assessment methods could be combined in social work practice. Little has been written, however, defining and illustrating qualitative assessment methodologies. This chapter defines qualitative assessment methods and summarizes the philosophical and theoretical underpinnings that emanate from constructivist epistemologies. Several qualitative assessment methods used in clinical practice are discussed. Finally, validity and reliability of qualitative assessment data are summarized.

## Description and Definition

Meyer (1993) recently defined assessment as a search for the meaning of a problem: the cognitive process whereby the social worker comes to understand cases in their full complexity. This definition is consistent with the methods of qualitative assessment. Qualitative assessment methods give clinicians access to a client's meaning systems, frame of reference, personal beliefs, cognitive schemas, values, cultural realities, and personal motivations (Gilgun, Daly, & Handel, 1992; Landfield & Epting, 1987; Moon, Dillon, & Sprenkle, 1990; Polkinghorne, 1991). Words, pictures, diagrams, metaphors, and narrative rather than numbers or operationalized concepts are used to tell the client's unique story (Borden, 1992; Guba, 1990; Moon et al., 1990; Neimeyer, 1993; Taylor, 1993). When numbers are used in a qualitative assessment, they do not represent absolute reified phenomena, but are descriptors or anchors along a continuum that represent the client's reality and experience.

Qualitative assessors usually prefer words or narrative symbols over numbers as descriptors of the client. Description, sometimes referred to as "thick description," provides enriching details about the client's experience so clinicians gain a full understanding and appreciation for the complexity of a client's problem (Gilgun et al., 1992). For example, instead of quantifying clients' marital arguments as severe because of a cutoff score on a measure or from tracking the number of weekly arguments spouses had, the clinician uses language to describe one or more of these arguments in a detailed narrative or pictures and expounds upon the impact of the arguments on clients' lives.

## Theoretical and Philosophical Underpinnings

Theoretical models supporting qualitative assessment methods evolved from approaches such as ethnography/ethnomethodology, symbolic interaction, psychoanalytic process, cybernetic systems theories, ecological psychology, and constructivist psychology (Jacob, 1989; Mahoney & Tyler, 1987; Smith, 1989). In particular, clinical approaches such as cognitive constructivism, Adlerian therapy, family therapies (e.g., solution-focused therapy and collaborative language systems), and personal construct therapies develop and use qualitative and constructivist assessment methods (Borgen, 1984; Jacob, 1987; McNamee & Gergen, 1992; Neimeyer, 1993; Polkinghorne, 1984, 1991).

Qualitative methodologies evolved from several disciplines within the social sciences. Lancy (1993) reviewed qualitative methodologies across several disciplines including anthropology, sociology, psychology, and human ethology and drew many comparisons in philosophical orientations and methodologies. Historically, social work practice has been influenced by the qualitative/naturalistic research traditions. Borrowing from the sociological traditions, in particular, early social workers made use of interviews, participant observations, and other field methods in their work. Diverse approaches to practice such as psychoanalytically based casework and the settlement house movement used case studies and other qualitative methods to study and diagnose human problems.

Qualitative methods developed from a relativistic ontology (view of reality) rather than from an empiricist view; that is, realities are considered to be subjective and contextually bound (Mahoney & Lyddon, 1988; Rodman, 1987; Smith, 1989). The epistemologies (theories of knowing) undergirding qualitative methods are constructivist or social constructionist, asserting that humans create and act on their own personal realities, thus precluding objective social and psychological realities (Mahoney & Lyddon, 1988; Saleebey, 1992).

Qualitative assessment methods therefore are holistic, open ended, individualistic, ideographic, and process oriented; they seek to discover subjective human reality. Qualitative assessors do not assume a stable, knowable psychological or social reality of the client that can be assessed. Rather, the way to know a client is to discover the client's own personal constructs, unique world view, and context (Landfield & Epting, 1987; Neimeyer, 1993; Weick, 1987). The assessment methods described in the following sections are grounded in constructivist philosophical traditions and qualitative/naturalistic research.

## Ethnographic Interviewing

Ethnographic interviewing is a nonstructured form of interviewing that encourages practitioners to join with the subjective meanings of clients. To someone watching an ethnographic interview, the practitioner appears empathic, nondirective, and conversational. The tone of the interviewer is tentative, curious, spontaneous, and caring. Conversations are structured to match the language and belief systems of the client. Ethnographic interviews are similar to other forms of clinical interviewing such as approaches stemming from client-centered or humanistic-practice models. These interviewing methods encourage practitioners to follow client responses verbally, reflect responses and feelings, and probe for deeper and more specific meanings (Hepworth & Larsen, 1993). Ethnographic methods purposefully expand this approach to understanding by emphasizing the need to gain entrance into a client's world in such a way that makes it possible to become aware of the client's culture or beliefs.

Interviewing methods used in ethnographic approaches differ, however, from more directive, diagnostic, and investigative interviews such as are found in mental health and child welfare practice. In ethnographic interviewing, the practitioner's goal is to use the conversation as a means to form a dialogue with the person and to understand the situation from the client's view. Some practitioners may see similarities between ethnographic interviewing and the mirroring responses that occur in psychoanalytic interviews. But ethnographic interviewing differs from standard psychoanalytic interviewing in that the practitioner is more collaborative and informal with the client and does not try to maintain an "objective" or formal distance from the client. Theories such as ego psychologies or any other models would not be imposed on the client or assumed to be explanatory of the client's situation. Instead, multiple theories, interpretations, and realities are considered relevant.

The ethnographic interview, a formal discourse between client and social worker, occurs within the context of forming a mutually respectful and cooperative relationship. During face-to-face conversation and mutual observation, the social worker treats the client as an expert and assumes a position of "not knowing" or "one-down" equality or collaboration (Berg, 1989; Crabtree & Miller, 1992; Fetterman, 1989; Taylor & Bogdan, 1984). The following dialogue between clinician and family illustrates an example of the ethnographic interviewing process:

*Clinician: Hello. I am _____. I like to be called ____. What would each of you like for me to call you? [Father says Pete. Stepmother says Gretch. Robert is silent.]*

*Stepmother: He likes to be called Bobby.*

*Clinician: Bobby, is that what you would like to be called?*

*Bobby: Yeah.*

*Clinician: I don't know anything about you and hope that today you will help me begin to understand you and your situation. Will you help me?*

*Pete: Sure.*

*Clinician: Thank you, Pete. What about you, Gretch and Bobby? Will you also help me?*

*Gretch: Yes.*

*Bobby: [Nods and shrugs.]*

*Clinician: Good, I find the families I work with are real experts concerning their situations and with your help we can find solutions. To begin, out of curiosity, I'm wondering, what do you call this place to which you've come today?*

*Pete: Huh? Uh, counselor. You're a counselor.*

*Bobby: Shrink.*

*Gretch: Counselor.*

*Clinician: So, how did you decide to come to a counselor/shrink?*

*Pete: The school told us to come or Bobby couldn't get back in his classes. He got kicked out for getting in a ruckus with another kid.*

*Clinician: You got sent here by the school because of Bobby's ruckus? So you're here to get him back in school?*

*Pete: That's it. Don't know much else because I wasn't there. Bobby, tell her what happened.*

In ethnographic interviewing, as illustrated above, social workers take a client-centered position and echo responses back to clients. The social worker's questions may frame responses in a way that constructs a joint reality. The clinician's question concerning what the family called the social worker's office attempted to develop a mutual understanding. Clients are viewed as "teachers" telling the social worker about their personal experiences. In order to understand the client, the social worker's interpretations are couched within the client's framework or world view.

Ethnographic interviews may be structured, semistructured, or open ended (Berg, 1989), although the latter two approaches are more suitable to the exploratory nature of the ethnographic interview (Fetterman, 1989). In every interview situation, the ethnographic interviewer resembles an anthropologist seeking to discover the culture, meanings, and personal frames of reference of the client. Ethnographic interviewing utilizes various questioning techniques to gather client information (Berg, 1989; Crabtree & Miller, 1992; Fetterman, 1989). (See Table 1 for examples of questioning techniques.)

**TABLE 1.** *Questioning techniques used in ethnographic interviewing.*

*Descriptive*: Broadly open-ended questions. "Grand tour" descriptive questions attempt to elicit a rich story from the client. "Describe your experiences at the high school after you became pregnant." "Tell me about life on the reservation." "Describe your future." "Mini-tour" descriptive questions elicit smaller units of experience. "What did your boyfriend do when he found out you were pregnant? Your teachers? Mother?" "Tell me about your last experience at the sweat lodge."

*Structural questions*: Questions of inclusion that expand the focus of experience. "Have you been married before?" "Tell me what he does when he gets mad."

*Substituting frame questions*: Taking a term or phrase the client uses and inserting it into another question. "Tell me what your mother is like." "She comes across like she is cold and gripey." "What else does she come across like?"

*Contrast questions*: Questions of exclusion that expand experience. "You said that you and Johnny had some good times together in the past. How has that changed now?" "You mentioned seeing a marital therapist in the past. How is your relationship different now?"

*Rating questions*: Asking clients to give differential meaning to their experience. "What is the worst experience you have had since you've been pregnant?" "What is the best thing someone did that really made a difference in your life?"

*Circular questions*: Questions that elicit information about transactions and operations embedded in a system. "How do Mom and Dad solve arguments between them?" "What do you think your brother would say when Dad goes hunting on the weekends?" "What does Mom do?"

# Narrative Assessment Methods

Narrative assessment methods may be defined in two ways. First, narrative methods are textual approaches borrowed from literary fields and adapted to the behavioral sciences. Narratives take into account life stories and the meanings associated with experience. Every person's life is like a text that may be read, and narratives are the structure of conversations about self and others that provide meanings. From this perspective, humans are believed to organize their experiences by narrative structures or the stories by which they explain and ascribe meanings to behaviors (Borden, 1992). Narrative meaning is created by explaining that something is either a part of a whole or is caused by something else (Polkinghorne, 1988). For example, a client may explain that her son commits crimes because he is like his father who is in prison or she may explain his behavior as occurring because she is a bad mother and did not raise him properly.

Either explanation gives structure to the meaning of events and may set in motion other behaviors or events that are consistent with this explanation. For instance, if the mother believes the first explanation, she may perceive her son as hopeless and destined to a life of crime and may not be inclined to act in ways that might prevent this outcome. If the social worker believes the first explanation, he or she may label the son with "antisocial personality disorder" and recommend the son be handled by the juvenile correction system. If the mother believes the second explanation, she may become involved in guilt-ridden responses that repeatedly rescue her son from the consequences of his behavior and inadvertently make his behavior worse. If the social worker believes the second explanation, she may decide the mother is an incompetent parent and recommend the son be removed from the home and sent to a residential treatment center.

Second, narrative assessment methods encompass oral and written dialogue and their expressions, which may be used to describe and analyze a person's experiences. The client usually communicates the narrative orally, although he or she may also do so in writing. The social worker may then make a written report of the information or may communicate it orally at a case conference. Writing the narrative makes it possible for social workers to record and reflect on the client's meanings as well as on their own responses to those private meanings. Written narratives are also used to communicate to others the client's experiences in a manner that provides insight into human behavior and motivations (Richardson, 1990). Both of the above understandings of narratives are used in narrative assessment methods. Two narrative assessment methods are covered below: case studies and self-characterizations.

## Case Studies

A case study systematically organizes and presents information in the form of a narrative summary about an individual case. It is typically undertaken to elucidate a particular clinical entity or problem requiring reflection and/or intervention (Trepper, 1990). Case studies can be completed on individuals, families, groups, or organizations (Feagin, Orum, & Sjoberg, 1991; Yin, 1989). Case studies use multiple sources of information, including interviews, social histories, life histories, and observations (Yin, 1989). Client functioning along certain dimensions is explored. For example, the case study might elucidate the impact of early developmental history on the client's current relationship functioning or discuss the impact of culture on the client's response to treatment. Case studies are also used to discuss treatment effectiveness and outcomes (Trepper, 1990). A practitioner may discuss or write up a case in order to demonstrate how a certain set of interventions leads to the resolution of a client's problems.

Historically, case studies were the preferred method for clinical assessment in various fields, including social work, until the increased focus on empiricism in clinical science held them in disrepute. In recent years, the case study has achieved higher status within clinical practice among researchers and practitioners (Trepper, 1990). For example, proponents of single-case-study designs brought a new empiricism to the case study. At the same time, other qualitative practitioners continued to see the usefulness of case studies and used them in their traditional forms. (See Gilgun [1994] for a detailed analysis of how case studies can be used in social work assessment, intervention, and outcome.) In order to present case studies that are rich in detail and filled with thick description, practitioners must take copious notes of their interviews and observations of the client (Crabtree & Miller, 1992; Yin, 1989). As it is with all qualitative assessment methods, practitioners must make sure they are reporting the empirical processes that emerge from the client case.

Five guidelines for keeping detailed notes for a case study are presented below. First, record key pieces of information while interviewing and observing the client.

This may be in the form of key words or jotting. Use exact phrases and differentiate clinical impressions from what the client said verbatim and empirical observations. Second, limit the amount of time the practitioner comes into contact with the client. For example, if making a home visit, limit it to one to two hours so that stimulus overload does not occur and you can keep track of the information. Third, make notes about the sequence of events and context in which behaviors occur. Fourth, write up detailed case notes that include a narrative account of the interview, observations, and clinical impressions immediately after seeing the client. Finally, write case notes before sharing details of the case or clinical impressions with a colleague or supervisor. Other colleagues may be asked to read the case notes later to provide feedback on the interpretations.

After the case notes are written, the social worker must find a method for reflecting on them and interpreting them into the assessment. The immersion/crystallization analysis method used in the heuristic research paradigm serves as a useful method for examining the case notes in order to identify clinically relevant patterns and themes (Crabtree & Miller, 1992).

The following steps for analyzing case notes may be implemented.

■ As an interpreter and reflector, the social worker would enter (read) the text (case notes) with the intent of empathetically immersing him- or herself until an intuitive insight/interpretation or crystallization of the text emerges.

■ Concerned reflection, intensive inner searching, and the yearning for insight are the modes of investigation and interpretation used in examining the case notes. Clinical intuition is relied upon to gain insights into the clinical themes and patterns present in the case notes.

■ A cycle of empathic immersion in the case notes and crystallization of insights is repeated until an interpretation arrives or a new understanding occurs from the examination of the notes.

■ After an insight or interpretation emerges from immersion in the case notes, the results may be reported as a part of the assessment.

## Self-Characterizations

Narrative methods may make use of written self-descriptions by the client. Journaling and diaries make use of clients' written descriptions of themselves and their problems and are useful in assessing the context, frequency, magnitude, and severity of problems (Jordan & Franklin, 1995). Cognitive–behavior therapists, in particular, use narrative information such as self-monitoring and self-recording to perform a contingency analysis to help identify antecedents (stimulus events) and reinforcers and maladaptive thinking processes that maintain a client's problems. Qualitative practitioners also ask clients to record narrative data about themselves. Self-characterization, for example, is a self-recording method developed within personal construct therapy (Landfield & Epting, 1987; Neimeyer, 1993).

The self-characterization assessment technique asks clients to write a description of themselves as if they were a principal character in a play (Neimeyer, 1993). They are instructed to take the position of an intimate friend or personal and empathetic confidant in writing their description. The purpose is to assess how the client constructs the world in relationship to how he or she must maintain him- or herself in some kind of role. The unique cognitive structures of the client and his or her social roles can then be explored and changed in therapy (Neimeyer, 1993). Self-characterizations were developed for use with individual clients but have been extended for use with families. Feixas, Proctor, and Neimeyer (1993) give the following example of how practitioners may give an instruction to family members in order to gather a "family characterization."

> The couple and family are asked to take about 15 minutes to write a brief character sketch of the family. They are to write it from the perspective of someone who knows the family intimately and sympathetically, perhaps better than anyone else knows the family. It is to be written in the third person. For example, begin by saying, I know the Smith Family. . . . (p. 161)

## Repertory Grids

Repertory grids, described by George Kelly, are the most popular and best researched of the constructivist assessment methods. The grid has appeared in more than 1,000 studies and is considered by some to be the Minnesota Multi-phasic Personality Inventory or Rorschach of constructivist assessment (Neimeyer, 1993). Repertory grids are used as a qualitative assessment tool for assessing personal meanings or constructs. Others have sought to perfect the grid as a quantitative measure by statistically analyzing the patterns within the repertory grid and computerizing the grid (Sewell, Adams-Webber, Mitterer, & Cromwell, 1992).

According to Neimeyer (1993), repertory grids elicit a client's construction of some domain of experience by asking him or her to compare or contrast representatives from that domain (e.g., family members, possible careers) and then to describe systematically each of them on his or her own "repertory" of dimensions of evaluation, or personal constructs. The grid may be administered as a formal interview, written assignment, or on a computer. The following suggestions, adapted from Neimeyer (1993), provide guidelines for developing a repertory grid.

First, practitioners may consider what area of the client's experience he or she wishes to explore in depth. For example, does the social worker want to know about the client's relationship with his or her spouse or partner, parenting skills, family relationships? Any element of experience can be used in the grid method as long as it comes from the same domain of experience. Different domains of experience cannot be mixed because they may not be construed in the same way.

Second, after the elements are chosen, the practitioner may elicit from the client the construct elicitation part of the grid or, more simply put, the items from the client's experience that are represented as a construct or a polar opposite for that realm of experience. Different options can be used for eliciting the constructs. Constructs may be elicited by inviting the client to compare or contrast elements. For example, if the elements on the grid concern intimate relationships, the client might be asked questions such as how his or her father and mother are alike/different. How is he or she different from or similar to a brother/sister? How is a male client's wife different from/similar to his mother? Or the client might be given a set of three elements on the grid and asked to compare two of the elements and contrast them with a third. Based on the answers to these questions, constructs would emerge that would be represented as polar opposites of experience and could be put on the repertory grid as representations of the client's constructs concerning intimate relationships. For example, if a client said that his mother and father differed in that one was lenient and easygoing and the other was strict and harsh, these dimensions would become polar opposites of relationship experiences and would be put on the grid.

In keeping with the qualitative approach to the assessment of meaning, clients' own words and representations should be used in developing the grid. Constructs may be developed by the clinician from the session material. For example, if the social worker took an extensive social and family history from a client, it might be possible to ascertain what some of the client's constructs might be from that material. Standardized constructs might be used to compare one client with a group of clients with similar characteristics. For example, it is believed that clients who have been sexually abused have similar experiences psychologically, and much research literature is available to describe their experiences. It might be possible to describe the relationship experiences of your client from that material. Constructs such as control versus lack of control, trust versus mistrust, manipulation versus honesty might be used as constructs for the intimate relationship experiences of incest victims, for example.

Finally, after eliciting several constructs from the client, possibly as many as 10 to 20, the social worker asks the client to compare, contrast, rank, or rate each element according to the construct dimensions elicited. Results of grid assessments can be interpreted in two ways. At the content level, grids can be analyzed in a qualitative manner by considering the patterns or unique constructions of the elements and constructs on the grid. At a formal level of content analysis, grids can be coded according to themes and/or intrapersonal or interpersonal content. Themes such as fear, forcefulness, violence, and dependency may emerge as clinically relevant material, for example. Level of abstractness suggesting a client's cognitive abilities in construing others may also be considered in the content analysis. Analysis of themes and analysis of how abstract is the content suggested by the client are similar to methods of assessment used in the projective measures. Such methods apprise clinicians of the latent or hidden psychological characteristics of a client's interpersonal experiences.

At the structural level, grids can be analyzed with quantitative measurement methods by concentrating on the degree of differentiation within the client's construct system or among the elements on the grid—specifically, relationships between the constructs and the elements—and on a host of more subtle structural features that can be assessed by computerized grid-scoring programs. Many of these computer programs provide interactive feedback during the grid administration (Neimeyer, 1993). Figure 1 presents an example of a repertory grid constructed on a client. N, a

| Column 1 | Mother | Father | Happy person | Successful person | N (self) | D (son) | M (son) | C (partner) | B (lover) | Therapist | Column 2 |
|---|---|---|---|---|---|---|---|---|---|---|---|
| Someone I love | 1 | 1 | 1 | 1 | 2 | 1 | 1 | 1 | 1 | 1 | Someone I hate |
| Lack sensitivity | 1 | 2 | 1 | 2 | 2 | 2 | 2 | 2 | 2 | 2 | Sensitive |
| Committed to family | 1 | 1 | 1 | 1 | 1 | 1 | 2 | 2 | 2 | 2 | Independent |
| Understanding | 2 | 1 | 1 | 1 | 1 | 2 | 1 | 2 | 1 | 1 | Impatient |
| Bright | 1 | 1 | 1 | 1 | 2 | 1 | 1 | 1 | 1 | 1 | Just average |
| Very inward | 1 | 1 | 2 | 1 | 1 | 1 | 1 | 2 | 2 | 1 | Very outspoken |
| Child-like inside | 2 | 1 | 2 | 1 | 1 | 1 | 1 | 2 | 1 | 2 | Get what you see |
| Communicative | 2 | 2 | 2 | 2 | 2 | 2 | 1 | 1 | 1 | 1 | Aloof |
| Easygoing | 2 | 1 | 1 | 1 | 1 | 1 | 1 | 2 | 1 | 1 | Emotional |
| Unaffectionate | 2 | 2 | 1 | 1 | 2 | 2 | 2 | 1 | 2 | 0 | Likes to touch |

*1 = person is better described by first column; 2 = person is better described by second column; 0 = neither column applies.*

**FIG. 1.** *Repertory grid.*

bisexual, was experiencing anxiety and indecision with regard to her lover, B. N had a heterosexual relationship with C who had reentered her life, creating confusion around her feelings about her sexual orientation. The grid elements include a list of persons at the top and the relationship constructs on the sides. The numbers in the boxes represent N's comparisons of elements and constructs.

## Graphic Methods

Graphic assessment methods are qualitative assessment tools that use pictures, drawings, spatial representatives, or images to assess the client. The ecomap is a classic graphic method used to assess families by providing a pictorial representation of the family from a cross-sectional perspective (Hartman, 1978). Tracy and Whittaker (1990) recently developed a social network map offering a qualitative assessment measure of social support. Readers are referred also to Mattaini (1993) for more detailed coverage of graphic methods. Two diverse graphic methods are summarized here.

The PIE graphic assessment method measures individuals' and family members' psychological commitment to the different roles in their lives (Cowan, 1988). Initially, this method was used to assess spouses' feelings regarding their roles as they made the transition into parenthood, but it may be applied to whole families. The PIE is easy to use. Each family member is given a page with an eight-inch-diameter circle, hence the name PIE. Family members are asked to list the primary roles in their lives: husband, wife, parent, son, friend, student, and so forth. The family members are then asked to divide their PIE to reflect the importance of each role to them. The different sections of the PIE can be measured to determine what percentage of the PIE is allocated to each role. These scores are described as representing the psychological self of each family member.

The Self Concept and Motivation Inventory (SCAMIN) is a graphic method developed for use with small children. Children are shown different drawings of faces: one face with a happy smile, a second with a straight line for a mouth, and a third with a downturned mouth. They are asked to mark the face that best depicts their feelings about certain conditions, for example, how they feel at home (Farrah, Milchus, & Reitz, 1968). This method is good for understanding the feelings of young children and for assessing depression in particular. Some clinicians, however, have adapted the method for work with families by asking family members to draw a face for each family member. Extended family members can also be included. Younger children can be included in this assessment technique by asking them which face belongs to each family member. See Figure 2 for an example of a family SCAMIN drawing done by a female client.

# Participant Observation

Qualitative assessment makes use of specialized forms of observation called nonstructured and participant observations. Clinicians use nonstructured observations to collect client data without a coding scheme. Information is reflexively recorded as it emerges in interactions with the client. Participant observation takes the nonstructured method a step farther by encouraging the practitioner to observe the client in everyday life, even participate with the client in his or her daily routine in order to be as nonintrusive as possible. Participant observations vary along a continuum that encompasses two dimensions—observation and participation. In some situations, the clinician may be more of an observer and less of a participant, as is the case in observing a family argument during a session or visiting a child's school. In other situations, the clinician may become a full participant in the client's daily routine, for example, when working in a group home for the developmentally disabled.

Participant observation originated from social and cultural anthropology. In social work, a recent resurgence of interest in this methodology has come from family therapists and qualitative researchers (Gilgun et al., 1992). Participant observation emphasizes understanding how the activities of groups and interactions of settings give meaning to certain behaviors or beliefs (Jorgensen, 1989). This methodology, of course, requires clinicians to obtain permission from clients to observe them and assumes a prolonged period of observation during which processes and relationships

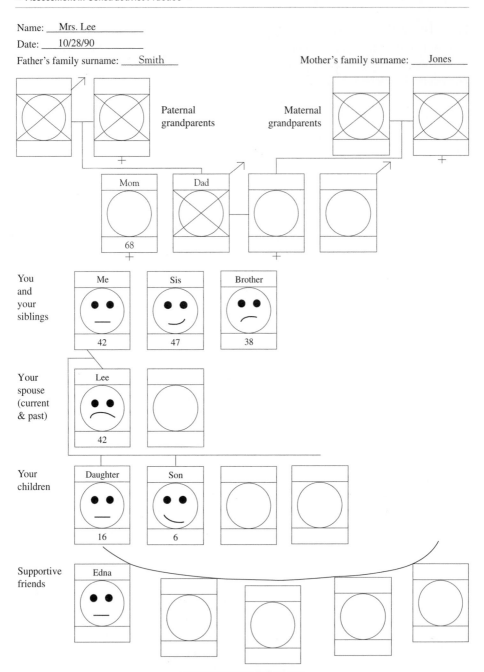

Name: ___Mrs. Lee_____

Date: ___10/28/90_____

Father's family surname: ___Smith___          Mother's family surname: ___Jones___

**FIG. 2.** *Family SCAMIN.*

among people can be studied (Jorgensen, 1989). As an assessment method, participant observation is especially useful in the following situations: (1) little is known about the client, (2) important differences exist between outsider and insider views, as in the case of diverse cultures, (3) phenomena are usually obscured from outsiders, such as occurs in family life, and (4) phenomena are intentionally hidden from public view, such as in the case of illegal behaviors (Crabtree & Miller, 1992; Jorgensen, 1989).

Different types of observations are used in a participant observation. *Descriptive observations* are less systemic; they represent a shotgun approach whereby everything about clients and their situation is observed in order to obtain an overall impression. *Focused observations* are based on the specific interests of the assessor. For example, perhaps the only issue is how the client parents her children, and therefore the social worker wishes only to observe the client in her interactions with her children (during play, dinner, or bedtime).

*Selective observations* enable clinicians to zero in on specific characteristics or attributes, for example, when the social worker's only interest is in assessing how the client disciplines her children. She therefore may observe specific situations in which the parent attempts to discipline the children (Crabtree & Miller, 1992; Jorgensen, 1989).

Clinicians who use unstructured or participant observation use case notes, video-, or audiotapes to keep track of what they are observing. Notes on observations should shed light on these questions: Who is present? What is happening? When does the activity or behavior occur? Where is the activity or behavior happening? Why is the activity or behavior happening? How is the activity or behavior organized? (Crabtree & Miller, 1992).

Recording case notes according to the above format helps clinicians draw upon their observations in formulating a meaningful assessment of the client. Keeping track of the sequence of events and the emotions being expressed during these events may provide the clinician with further insights into the motivations of the client.

## Validity and Reliability of Qualitative Data

Validity and reliability of qualitative assessment data rest on the credibility, thoroughness, completeness, and consistency of the information interpreted within a narrative assessment report and the logical inferences the clinician uses to draw conclusions from this information about the client. Although accuracy of the clinician's report is difficult to ascertain, the validity and reliability of the interpretations made by the clinician may be evaluated by using the criteria listed below (Berg, 1989; Crabtree & Miller, 1992). These criteria help clinicians to differentiate between observations and inference and are similar to empirical assessment principles used in standard clinical practice.

■ Does the information tell a complete and coherent story, and do the conclusions drawn make sense in relationship to the client's story? For example, do big gaps appear in the information or is the information too sketchy or does it skip around too much to make a clear connection with the clinician's interpretations?

■ Are details or information missing that would put the clinician's interpretations in doubt? For example, does the clinician make a diagnosis that is not supported by the data in the report, or does the clinician fail to disqualify a differential diagnosis that is equally as plausible as the one given?

■ Do any contradictions disqualify the clinical impressions, and if so, does the clinician explain them in the interpretations? For example, if the clinician interprets that the client had a warm and secure upbringing but mentions that the family moved frequently as a result of personal and economic hardships, then perhaps this interpretation should be questioned without further explanation to resolve inconsistencies in information.

■ Do the metaphors, pictures, or diagrams used make sense and can themes and patterns in them be interpreted? All diagrams and pictures should be packaged as part of the results of the assessment report to give others an opportunity to evaluate the accuracy of the assessment interpretations. Although more than one clinical interpretation can be drawn from these methods, the clinical themes interpreted and reported by the clinician should be easily discerned from the data.

■ Did the clinician collaborate with the client in the formulation and interpretation of problems? In other words, did the clinician check out his or her interpretations with the client? Qualitative assessment relies on the personal stories of clients and their private meanings. Clinicians should ensure that they are representing the client's life context appropriately and assure the readers of the report that clinicians remained closely connected to the personal accounts of clients without undue interpretations or unsupported inferences. The client's own language should be used throughout the report, and clinicians should explicitly differentiate their interpretations from the client's report of his or her experience. Every interpretation should be backed up with empirical referents to what the client did and said. Every deviation from this format should be logically explained from the clinician's experience or subjective impressions. If the report is not written in this manner, then its conclusions should be questioned.

■ Were multiple methods used to gather the information? Qualitative assessment relies on multiple methods to assure the credibility of data. Triangulation of data-gathering techniques, such as observation or interview methods, or sources of information, such as client and other reports, are used to interpret assessment data. All methods and sources should be compared and contrasted in interpreting results. For example, are the client's interview data consistent with the social worker's clinical interpretations? Did the social worker's observations of the client agree with collateral sources reported? If agreement was lacking, was it logically explained?

■ Has the clinician tried to disqualify his or her own interpretations? In qualitative assessment, clinicians should seek to prove themselves wrong by looking for other explanations for a client's behavior. For example, if the clinician believes a client is depressed, he or she would look for evidence to determine whether his or her judgment about the client's depression would hold up to further exploration and probing.

## Conclusion

Several qualitative techniques are available for clinical assessment. Only five methods were reviewed because discussion of all qualitative assessment methods is beyond the scope of this chapter. We agree with other authors in the field that respect for context and a client's personal reality in qualitative assessment is highly congruent with social work practice methods and values (Gilgun et al., 1992; Rodman, 1987; Scott, 1989; Weick, 1987). Social work practitioners are urged to explore further the applicability of these techniques.

Qualitative methods may have limitations in agency-based or private practice. Foremost is the fact that many of the methods are time consuming and process intensive. Detailed case notes needed for intensive case studies, for example, take a lot of time to produce. Many practice environments do not allow the time to perform participant observations or to develop a graphic method such as a social network map or other qualitative assessment techniques. This is especially true in the managed-care and brief-therapy environments. From their vantage points, qualitative methods may not be as useful as quantitative methods. Quantitative measures also have the advantage of providing numerical data to use with funding sources. In addition, computer technologies are available for use with quantitative methods to score measures, develop narratives, and produce case reports (Franklin, Nowicki, Trapp, Schwab, & Petersen, 1993).

How many practitioners favor or use quantitative measures, however? A recent study in marriage and family therapy, for example, indicated that few practitioners used marital and family measures (Boughner, Hayes, Bubenzer, & West, 1994). If practitioners do not rely heavily on quantitative measures in their assessments, what approaches do they use? Although we can only speculate from our clinical experience, we believe that their methods resemble qualitative approaches such as interviewing and self-characterizations. If given a choice, we also believe that many clinicians would prefer to use abbreviated forms of qualitative assessment over rapid assessment measures. Qualitative methods provide clinicians with a depth of understandings and meanings concerning cognitive and interpersonal processes. These methods have the advantage of linking assessment to direct clinical experiences with clients and to the clinical process used to promote change.

Further attention should be focused on making qualitative assessment methods more practical to use. Practitioners and researchers may enhance the use of qualitative methods by describing how these methods are being used successfully in their practices. We believe, however, that a combination of both qualitative and quantitative methods makes the best assessment protocol and that it is possible to combine methodologies in the development of assessment methods (Jordan & Franklin, 1995). The repertory grid provides an example in point, in that the grid combines a qualitative, narrative assessment of clients with the rigor of a quantitative measurement approach. Practitioners may wish to consider the complementary aspects of both approaches (Allen-Meares & Lane, 1990).

Computer technology may eventually provide solutions to the elongated task of assessing and studying clients through qualitative methods. Voice-activated computers will make it possible for software programs to produce printed narratives from taped or videotaped sessions. Clinicians' notes and observations may also be printed from dictated notes. Qualitative research software programs may make it possible systematically to review the recorded observations in a manner that will enhance clinical judgment. Such technology should be on the market in the next 5 to 10 years. This type of technology will undoubtedly revolutionize the use of qualitative research methodologies in the social sciences. Of course, this does not mean that agencies and individual practitioners will have immediate access to these technological aids. Nevertheless, qualitative technology will have far-reaching applications with regard to narrative approaches to assessment.

# References

Allen-Meares, P., & Lane, B. A. (1990). Social work practice: Integrating qualitative and quantitative data collection techniques. *Social Work, 35*, 452–458.

Berg, B. L. (1989). *Qualitative research methods for the social sciences*. Boston: Allyn and Bacon.

Borden, W. (1992). Narrative perspectives in psychosocial intervention following adverse life events. *Social Work, 37*, 135–141.

Borgen, F. H. (1984). Reaction: Are there necessary linkages between research practices and the philosophy of science? *Journal of Counseling Psychology, 31*, 457–460.

Boughner, S. R., Hayes, S. F., Bubenzer, D. L., & West, J. D. (1994). Use of standardized assessment instruments by marital and family therapists: A survey. *Journal of Marital and Family Therapy, 20*, 69–75.

Corcoran, K., & Fischer, J. (1987). *Measures for clinical practice*. New York: Free Press.

Cowan, C. P. (1988). Working with men becoming fathers: The impact of a couples group intervention. In P. Bornstein & C. P. Cowan (Eds.), *Fatherhood today: Men's changing role in the family* (pp. 276–298). New York: John Wiley.

Crabtree, B. F., & Miller, W. L. (Eds.). (1992). *Doing qualitative research*. Newbury Park, CA: Sage.

Farrah, G. A., Milchus, N. J., & Reitz, W. (1968). *The self-concept and motivation inventory: What face would you wear? SCAMIN manual of direction*. Dearborn Heights, MI: Person-O-Metrics.

Feagin, J. R., Orum, A. M., & Sjoberg, G. (Eds.). (1991). *A case for case study*. Chapel Hill, NC: North Carolina University Press.

Feixas, G., Proctor, H. G., & Neimeyer, G. J. (1993). Convergent lines of assessment: Systemic and constructivist contributions. In G. J. Neimeyer (Ed.), *Constructivist assessment: A case book* (pp. 143–178). Newbury Park, CA: Sage.

Fetterman, D. M. (1989). *Ethnography: Step by step*. Newbury Park, CA: Sage.

Franklin, C., & Jordan, C. (1992). Teaching students to perform assessment. *Journal of Social Work Education, 28*, 222–241.

Franklin, C., Nowicki, J., Trapp, J., Schwab, A. J., & Petersen, J. (1993). A computerized assessment system for brief, crisis-oriented youth services. *Families in Society, 74*, 602–616.

Gilgun, J. F. (1994). A case for case studies in social work research. *Social Work, 39,* 371–380.

Gilgun, J. F., Daly, K., & Handel, G. (Eds.). (1992). *Qualitative methods in family research*. Newbury Park, CA: Sage.

Guba, E. G. (Ed.). (1990). *The paradigm dialog*. Newbury Park, CA: Sage.

Hartman, A. (1978). Diagrammatic assessment of family relationships. *Social Casework, 59*, 465–476.

Hepworth, D. H., & Larsen, J. A. (1993). *Direct social work practice: Theory and skills* (4th ed.). Pacific Grove, CA: Brooks/Cole.

Hudson, W. W. (1982). Scientific imperatives in social work research and practice. *Social Service Review, 56*, 246–258.

Jacob, E. (1987). Qualitative research traditions: A review. *Review of Educational Research, 57*, 1–50.

Jacob, E. (1989). Qualitative research: A defense of traditions. *Review of Educational Research, 59*, 229–235.

Jordan, C., & Franklin, C. (1995). *Clinical assessment: Quantitative and qualitative methods*. Chicago: Lyceum.

Jorgensen, D. L. (1989). *Participant observation: A methodology for human studies.* Newbury Park, CA: Sage.

Lancy, D. F. (1993). *Qualitative research in education: An introduction to the major traditions.* New York: Longman.

Landfield, A. W., & Epting, F. R. (1987). *Personal construct psychology: Clinical and personality assessment.* New York: Human Sciences Press.

Mahoney, M. J., & Lyddon, W. J. (1988). Recent developments in cognitive approaches to counseling and psychotherapy. *Counseling Psychologist, 16,* 190–234.

Mahoney, M. J., & Tyler, J. G. (1987). Psychotherapy and cognitive sciences: An evolving alliance. *Journal of Cognitive Psychotherapy, 1,* 39–56.

Mattaini, M. A. (1993). *More than a thousand words.* Silver Spring, MD: National Association of Social Workers.

Mattaini, M. A., & Kirk, S. (1991). Assessing assessment in social work. *Social Work, 36,* 260–266.

McNamee, S., & Gergen, K. J. (1992). *Therapy as social construction.* Newbury Park, CA: Sage.

Meyer, C. H. (1993). *Assessment in social work.* New York: Columbia University Press.

Moon, S. M., Dillon, D. R., & Sprenkle, D. H. (1990). Family therapy and qualitative research. *Journal of Marital and Family Therapy, 16,* 357–373.

Neimeyer, R. A. (1993). Constructivist approaches to the measurement of meaning. In G. J. Neimeyer (Ed.), *Constructivist assessment* (pp. 58–103). Newbury Park, CA: Sage.

Polkinghorne, D. E. (1984). Further extensions of methodological diversity for counseling psychology. *Journal of Counseling Psychology, 31,* 416–429.

Polkinghorne, D. E. (1988). *Narrative knowing and the human sciences.* Albany, NY: State University of New York.

Polkinghorne, D. E. (1991). Two conflicting calls for methodological reform. *Counseling Psychologist, 19,* 103–114.

Richardson, L. (1990). Narrative and sociology. *Journal of Contemporary Ethnography, 19,* 116–135.

Rodman, M. K. (1987). Naturalistic inquiry: An alternative model for social work assessment. *Social Services Review, 61,* 231–246.

Saleebey, D. (1992). *The strengths perspective in social work practice.* New York: Longman.

Scott, D. (1989). Meaning construction in social work practice. *Social Services Review, 63,* 39–51.

Sewell, K. W., Adams-Webber, J., Mitterer, J., & Cromwell, R. L. (1992). Computerized repertory grids: Review of the literature. *International Journal of Personal Construct Psychology, 5,* 1–23.

Smith, J. K. (1989). The relationship of the investigator to what is investigated. *The nature of social and educational inquiry: Empiricism versus interpretation* (pp. 63–86). Norwood, NJ: Ablex.

Taylor, J. B. (1993). The naturalistic research approach. In R. M. Grinnell, Jr. (Ed.), *Social work research and evaluation* (4th ed., pp. 53–78). Itasca, IL: F. E. Peacock.

Taylor, S. J., & Bogdan, R. (1984). *Introduction to qualitative research: The search for meanings.* New York: John Wiley.

Tracy, E. M., & Whittaker, J. K. (1990). The social network map: Assessing social support in clinical practice. *Families in Society, 71,* 461–470.

Trepper, T. S. (1990). In celebration of the case study. *Journal of Family Psychotherapy, 1,* 5–13.

Weick, A. (1987). Reconceptualizing the philosophical perspective of social work. *Social Services Review, 61,* 218–230.

Yin, R. K. (1989). *Case study research: Design and methods.* Newbury Park, CA: Sage.

# 5

**Intervening in Meaning:**
**Applications of Constructivist Assessment**

*Greg J. Neimeyer, Chad L. Hagans, & Ruth Anderson*

The late 20th century has witnessed the rapid translation of constructivist episte-mology into clinical practice. The congeniality of the human sciences to constructivist ideas is signaled by the rapid incorporation of these concepts in the literature, with the number of allusions to the concept of "construction" more than doubling within less than 20 years (Mahoney, 1996). Nowhere have the seeds of constructivism been more rapidly sown than in the helping professions, where many distinctive therapies have been cultivated within several closely allied fields.

This chapter addresses the translation of these therapeutic traditions into clinical practice and traces how these developments affect the concept of assessment from a constructivist perspective. After characterizing the spectrum of contemporary con-structivist expressions, we identify specific assessment tools that have been spawned by each. A detailed case illustration follows, grounding the broader discussion of con-structivist assessment by bringing its application into relief without sacrificing the background that supports it. The self-confrontation method that is illustrated here reflects themes that occupy prominent positions in various constructivist traditions. For that reason it can be viewed as a microcosm of this expanding field and as a tool that enables integration among these otherwise disparate traditions insofar as it respects the central tenets of each.

## Constructivist Perspectives on Assessment

### An Assessment Overview

The discussion that follows relies on a basic understanding of the premises of constructivism (see Mahoney, 1991; R. A. Neimeyer & Mahoney, 1995) and the implications of these premises for psychological assessment (see G. J. Neimeyer,

1993). It assumes, for example, an understanding of the features of constructivist assessment that would distinguish it from assessment that follows from a more traditional, positivist epistemology. Positivists assume the existence of a real world and the possibility of gaining access to it through ongoing inquiry. Applied to the practice of psychological assessment, this perspective suggests that assessment is a process by which we may gain valid knowledge of real psychological phenomena. Postmodernism, however, calls into question the assumptions implicit in this account. Direct access to "real" phenomena is not possible (Rosenau, 1992), leaving people's beliefs, values, attitudes, and perceptions without direct correspondence to an objective and knowable reality outside themselves.

Rosenau (1992) suggests that the postmodern view of the relationship between subjective and objective reality is commonly associated with one of two epistemological positions. Skeptical postmodernists claim that subjective reality is socially created and bears no relationship to objective reality (e.g., Gergen, 1994). Affirmative postmodernists, on the other hand, hold that we acquire knowledge of the world through our construal of it. Most constructivist approaches to psychotherapy subscribe to the latter position (Efran, Lukens, & Lukens, 1990; Mahoney, 1991; White & Epston, 1990). Further, these approaches view an individual's constructions as responsive to perceived experience. In other words, people revise or replace their constructions of the world on the basis of their experience of it.

This constructivist view of meaning making suggests a unique role for psychological assessment: Assessment is focused on identifying the means by which an individual comes to construe his or her world. Both the constructions and the processes underlying the formulation and revision of those constructions are central to the process of constructivist assessment. Consistent with this understanding, R. A. Neimeyer (1993) identified three possible foci of constructivist assessment: (a) the identification of the client's belief systems (personal constructions), (b) the articulation of the relationships among these beliefs (systems of personal constructions), and (c) the process of construing.

### Conducting Assessment

To accomplish assessment, constructivist approaches may use various formal instruments or informal assessment procedures. These commonly are designed to refine an understanding of what Mahoney (1991) calls the individual's "felt experience" rather than to provide what he wryly dubs "symptomatic snapshots" (p. 294) of their pathology.

The administration of psychological assessment is more generally understood as a mutual, or co-constructive, enterprise, with two experimenters jointly involved in a process of discovery and exploration. This mutual involvement tends to translate into procedures that take the form of interactive interviews that are conducted with, rather than administered to, clients.

For example, in discussing the creation of meaning in incest survivors, Clarke (1993) illustrates a "meaning symbolization" intervention that is designed to clarify the personal meaning of a client's significant emotional experience. In discussing the incestuous relationship with her father, a client reveals that her sister, too, was an incest victim and was impregnated by her father and forced by him to have an abortion. In discussing the powerful and confusing feelings associated with this experience, the following exchange occurred, highlighting the co-constructed nature of their collective meaning making:

*Client: I've often wondered why I feel like crying when I see a laughing, happy child. And I think it's connected here. Because we were so cheated out of that.*

*Therapist: He stole your childhood.*

*Client: Yes, exactly, we were robbed.*

*Therapist: Robbed of happiness, robbed of laughter.*

*Client: Yeah—people often say to me, "smile," 'cause I don't much.*

*Therapist: Your smile was stolen a long time ago. . . . (p. 198)*

In this illustration the therapist imports the metaphoric image of the father as a "thief," an image that resonates with the client and is spontaneously adopted and embellished by her in later dialogue. This kind of exchange illustrates the dialogical embeddedness of meaning symbolization, and represents a form of what Viney (1987) referred to as the Mutual Orientation Model of clinical assessment.

Regardless of the level of involvement of the interviewer in the assessment of clients, constructivists maintain that assessment is not a neutral process, but rather one that is informed by and contingent upon a given (personal, interpersonal, cultural) context. Nor is assessment discrete from intervention for constructivists, with efforts to articulate personal meanings often seeding shifts and changes in those meaning structures. The relationship between assessment and intervention is ambiguous within a constructivist perspective; each serves a vital and inseparable role in the ongoing dialectic of personal revision.

And finally, it follows from this discussion that assessment within this postmodernist paradigm is concerned more with what clients believe and how they come to believe it than with the extent to which these beliefs accurately represent a reality outside themselves. The "paradigmatic utility" (i.e., its viability or usefulness) of a system of constructions, rather than its "bedrock validity" (Mahoney, 1988, p. 5), therefore, is most central to constructivist assessment.

## *Defining Assessment*

In contrast to more enduring and traditional approaches, constructivist assessment is both less and more ambitious. It is less ambitious in that it relinquishes the pursuit of stable traits or factors that underlie or represent psychopathology. Likewise, it abandons the quest for an identification of features that inhere within the individual or family and as such have an existence independent of the context or the interpersonal interactions that support them. It is more ambitious, on the other hand, in that constructivism understands assessment as relationally contingent and embraces the likelihood that the features being "assessed" are themselves born of a larger interpersonal, social, and cultural fabric. Ultimately, a separation between the "assessor" and the "assessee" is as ambiguous as the discrimination between the observer and the observed. As a result, constructivist traditions tend to admit the burden of this ambiguity and to interrogate the nature of what is properly understood as inherently a co-construed process of assessment. A reflexive stance toward assessment is therefore embraced, one that involves all participants in inspecting and reflecting on the "outcomes" of assessment, recognizing these "outcomes" as cross-sectional snapshots of a co-constructed process.

And finally, the criteria for determining the adequacy of constructivist assessment tools follow from its philosophical commitments. Although psychometric properties may be critical to the evaluation of an approach, hermeneutic criteria such as coherence and generativity may figure as prominently. In other words, the criteria for adequacy for a constructivist assessment may be interpretive as well as statistical, as is discussed in greater detail elsewhere (G. J. Neimeyer & R. A. Neimeyer, 1993). Moreover, although they characterize the broad spectrum of approaches in the field, it is nonetheless true that each constructivist expression is distinguished by the particular features that it highlights in the process and outcomes of assessment.

## Constructivist Expressions

Across the long history and broad application of constructivist thinking (see Mahoney, 1991), many assessment tools have been constructed and utilized. To understand constructivist assessment, however, it is necessary to clarify what is essential to it. Foremost among its features are its attention to aspects of meaning, an appreciation of the backdrop(s) that support and sustain this meaning (developmental, personal, interpersonal, cultural), and the contemporary contexts within which this meaning is reconstructed and co-constructed. Considering these features, constructivist assessment can be regarded as the contextually contingent process of reconstructing and articulating meaning. Coordinated within the clinical context, assessment is designed to illuminate those features of meaning that regulate the individual's participation in personal, social, and cultural life. Because this coordination is itself situated within differing clinical traditions, different constructivist expressions tend to support and sustain different methods of assessment. Understanding different methods of constructivist assessment, therefore, relies on understanding the differing traditions themselves.

The broad spectrum of constructivist orientations has been understood in various ways. These include considering the epistemological and ontological commitments that bind and distinguish them (Botella, 1995), the metaphors that guide and direct their operation (R. A. Neimeyer, 1995), and the world views with which they articulate (Lyddon, 1995). Another way of organizing the growing array of constructivist approaches is according to the scope and size of the meaning unit that is most central to their conceptualization. This is especially useful in a clinical context because it carries direct implications for the level of therapeutic assessment (individual, familial, societal). According to this ordering, contemporary constructivist orientations can be distinguished in relation to the sweep or particularity of their primary metric of meaning. This metric can operate primarily at the personal and interpersonal levels, at the family or systemic level, or at the social and cultural level.

**Personal and interpersonal assessment.** The most enduring and arguably most comprehensive constructivist orientation to psychotherapy evolved from Kelly's (1955) personal construct psychology. Kelly's theory is organized around the primacy of individual experience. The most molecular unit of meaning in theory is the "personal construct," which is defined as a perceived basis of discrimination among events in one's experience. In other words, a personal construct is constituted by the way in which an individual views some things as alike and different from others. Judy, a 43-year-old woman seeking marital therapy, described what she viewed as the abusive behavior of her father when she was growing up and of her first husband during their brief marriage. She characterized both of these figures in her life as "threatening, unsafe, and unpredictable," which contrasted with her current husband who was "pretty dull and mostly into himself." This contrast, "threatening, unsafe, and unpredictable" versus "dull and into himself," is a personal construct. It is a dimension of meaning that informs and sustains Judy's contemporary experience of men and of relationships.

According to Kelly's theory, this elemental metric of meaning is largely individual, although it may be forged within and supported by interpersonal relationships. The attention to personal levels of construction has been reflected in the largely individualized ways in which many of the theory's distinctive methods of assessment have been developed, in which an individual is invited to write a short description of him- or herself from a third-person perspective (e.g., the self-characterization sketch; G. J. Neimeyer, 1995). Foremost among these assessment methods is the role-construct repertory test, or reptest, which is designed to articulate an individual's predominant personal constructs and the matrix of meaning that they jointly constitute. The reptest is a method for eliciting a set of personal constructs by asking an individual to compare and contrast significant people in his or her life. The reptest remains the most commonly used method of assessment within the personal construct literature (R. A. Neimeyer, Baker, & G. J. Neimeyer, 1990) and it enjoys a considerable contemporary attention directed at its continued promise and potential pitfalls (Bell, 1990; Yorke, 1989). Chapter 7 presents a detailed discussion of the reptest and an illustration of its use in a clinical context.

A second expression of constructivist therapy that adheres to the personal and interpersonal levels of construction is represented by the developmental approaches. Among the most visible of these is the constructivist developmental theory of Guidano (1995a, 1995b). This approach places primary inflection on the parent–child attachment relationship and the consequent interactional pattern that it supports. According to this approach, the earliest constructions in life are scaffolded by the nature and quality of the primary attachment relationship. A secure attachment relationship provides the child with a stable and secure sense of self from which to launch explorations of the world. Qualifications in the attachment relationship, however, compromise the child's sense of self by introducing insecurity (anxiety or avoidance) into the relational base, jeopardizing the child's active pursuit of novelty and exploration.

Profoundly respectful of the role of primary caregivers in the construction of the self, this developmental approach has given rise to distinctive assessments consistent with this emphasis. The "movieola" technique, a method for assessing and restructuring early developmental constructions (Guidano, 1995b), for example, emphasizes the irreducible selfhood dynamic of what he terms the "I–me" relationship. The "I–me" relationship refers to the distinction between the *experiencing* self and the *explaining* self. The experiencing self is derived most directly from the primary attachment relationship, whereby the child initially learns to experience the world in relation to, or through, that relationship. Later cognitive and emotional development enables a separation between this immediate experience and the explanation or account made of this experience. Because no single account can exhaust the particularities of experience, the explaining self necessarily abstracts only selected elements of events into its ongoing account. The movieola procedure is designed to assess the meanings that clients attribute to their perceived experience and to harvest the multiplicity of alternative accounts that lie dormant beneath the heavy blanket of the dominant account. By returning the client to the elemental features of powerful emotional events, the technique reimmerses him or her in the experience and then systematically facilitates the (re)construction of an explanatory framework to accommodate previously unaccounted-for elements of experience. Changes either in the embedded immediacy of the explaining self or the abstracted scaffolding of the explaining self necessarily carry implications for changes in the other. These twin processes work in tandem, each supporting the process of ongoing self (re)construction.

A broad range of other assessment procedures has evolved from allied developmental-constructivist accounts. Mahoney's (1991) "mirror time" and "streaming" are two tools that share with Guidano's movieola method a respect for developmental processes. Mirror time consists of a series of gently guided discussions with oneself in front of a mirror. The purpose is to establish a self-relationship that permits constructive self-appraisal and confrontation. In "streaming," the client sits in front of a mirror and is invited to "close your eyes for a few seconds and take a deep, relaxing breath. Set your intentions to be self-aware and self-caring. Before you reopen your eyes, invite yourself to also be open to the possibility of seeing or feeling yourself in a new or different way" (Mahoney, 1991, p. 308). The client is then asked to reflect upon whether "there are any differences between the person you see in the mirror and the person you feel yourself to be? What do you (dis)like about yourself?" (p. 308) and so on, gradually encouraging the development of a supportive but confrontive relationship with one's self.

Likewise, "streaming" is a free-associative method for assessing the processes that underlie self-construction. Clients are invited to screen any disclosures that they would care to withhold, but they are nonetheless encouraged to speak whatever is on their mind in a free-form, stream-of-consciousness way. The procedure yields a glimpse into the processes that undergird self-construction, the purpose of which is more exploratory than interpretive. As with other constructivist methods, this assessment tool is designed to provide the person with self-reflexive access to his or her own processes of construction, facilitating an awareness that can trigger construction–system change.

**Systemic assessment.** The growth of constructivist therapies is nowhere clearer than in family therapy (Hoffman, 1992). Advocates of this orientation consider human systems as fundamentally language generating, with meaning being forged through social discourse and action. From this perspective, meaning is inherently systemic; it arises through communicative exchange rather than residing in or emerging from within the individual. Assessment becomes a "co-constructive" negotiation of meaning, and the renegotiation of that meaning is the work of therapy. Members of a "problem-organizing system" (Anderson & Goolishian, 1992), including the therapist, "language" about the problem and the contexts that support it. The therapist functions largely as a conversation manager, assuming a "not knowing" approach (Anderson & Goolishian, 1992). Particular methods, such as circular questioning (Selvini-Palazzoli, Boscolo, Cecchin, & Prata, 1980; Feixas, Procter, & G. J. Neimeyer, 1993), might be used to explore and articulate the assumptions underlying the presenting problem and each family member's view of it.

Proponents of such systemic approaches regard meaning as language based and dialogically sustained. Here language is an elastic concept that stretches beyond the conventional notions of the spoken word. Emotional tonalities, interactional patterns, and symbolic representation complement verbal and paraverbal exchanges as components of the "languaging" process. Therapy involves the emergence of a new account that coheres with the family's current system of constructions yet provides elaborative potential as well. One assessment technique that has evolved from this tradition is the systemic "bow tie" (Procter, 1987).

The "bow tie" technique is a conceptual tool for clarifying partners' positions within a relevant system of construction. Position is defined as the integral stance that each individual takes at two different levels, the levels of construction and action. The level of construction includes the person's construing about the self and others. The level of action refers to the behaviors that follow from these constructions. Because all family members have positions within a system, their behaviors provide evidence that validates or invalidates other members' constructions, resulting in feedback loops that can function to maintain dysfunctional systems of interaction. This technique provides a method for assessing these interlocking constructions and developing a plan for intervening in them.

An illustration of the technique can be seen in my (G. J. Neimeyer) work with Debbie and Al, who came to therapy complaining about dissatisfaction with their marriage. Each blamed the other for their difficulties. To break this gridlock, I suggested that we map out a diagram of their perspectives, teasing apart their thoughts (level of construction) and behaviors (action). At the level of construction, Debbie described her thoughts about Al, whom she regarded as a "self-absorbed do-nothing" who never initiated anything without being hounded to do it. Furthermore, she felt "unloved and taken for granted by him" insofar as she expected that "if someone

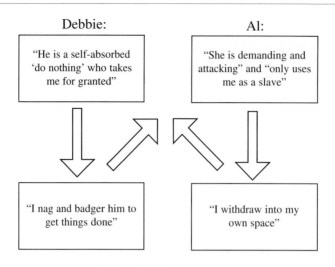

**FIG. 1.** *The bow tie diagram.*

loves you, they do their part to make things work." At the level of action, she frequently "nagged and badgered him to do things" and felt "angry at him for making me the bad guy in the relationship."

For his part, at the level of construction, Al viewed Debbie as someone who "mercilessly hounded" him, refusing to give him "any peace or quiet" and always "demanding and attacking" him. He felt "used" by her insofar as he felt "more like a slave than a partner" in the relationship. At the level of action, Al found himself "retreating into his own space" to avoid confrontation and generally "withdrawing" into his own activities to minimize his engagement with Debbie.

The bow tie diagram depicted in Figure 1 resulted from a process of "zig-zag" questioning (Procter, 1985), alternating between levels of construction and action. By looking at the bow tie diagram, the partners could disengage from blaming each other long enough to focus on the interactional process between them. They could see how their own behaviors cohered with their respective constructions of the situation, and for that reason they could experience some validation that their actions were not unwarranted. More important, they could also see how each of their sets of behaviors provided apparent validation of the (problem-maintaining) constructions of the partner, giving rise to the seamless web of mutual validation that had no clear beginning and no clear end. Tracing over the arrows in the diagram with a pen, I emphasized the interconnectedness of the components of their system, resulting in a horizontal "figure 8" or bow tie. Interestingly, the act of sharing this diagram with Debbie and Al was itself therapeutic. Both partners felt better understood on their own terms and both could see how the other person's behaviors followed from that person's (very different) constructions. The physical diagram then became emblematic of the pattern. Whenever we saw it emerging in subsequent sessions, one of us would note that "that bow tie has sneaked back into the relationship again," raising awareness of the dynamic and typically halting the otherwise escalating argument.

As with other systemic approaches, this constructivist method is designed to assess the interaction between or among members of a system, rather than localizing the assessment within individuals. This approach has the advantage of dislodging participants from the notion of localized blame, transporting issues of responsibility to the systemic level. The problem then can be externalized (White & Epston, 1990), insofar as it resides outside either of them. This, in turn, enables family members to join together to combat a common enemy, rather than directing their enmity inward toward each other. In short, it facilitates the development of a posture whereby partners can be on each other's side rather than "on each other's case."

The bow tie can also provide a potential road map for interventions as well, insofar as it suggests four potential targets for change. These targets correspond to the constructions and actions of both partners. In other words, a change in either partner (Debbie or Al) at either level (construction or action) would help break the chain that otherwise locked them into their conflictual pattern. More detailed illustrations of the bow tie technique can be found in R. A. Neimeyer (1993) and G. J. Neimeyer and R. A. Neimeyer (1994).

**Social and cultural assessment.** The broadest level of construction is represented in the fields of narrative constructivism and social constructionism. These approaches move toward the larger, global processes that inform or undermine local (personal, interpersonal, and systemic) constructions. Adherents of these orientations struggle to preserve the concept of self and its attendant capacity for agency (see Butt, Burr, & Epting, 1997) but generally acknowledge that individuals swim in a sea of culturally determined meanings. They can either succumb to the waters surrounding them or they can buoy themselves through a process of interrogating and deconstructing cultural conventions and constructing more localized, personal accounts that permit novel understandings and actions. Individual construction, then, becomes the engine for overcoming dominant or oppressive cultural narratives.

Among the best known of these therapies is the work of White and Epston (1990), which concerns the development of a narrative means to therapeutic ends. The initial step in liberating clients from oppressive cultural accounts is to help them "externalize" their problem, personifying the symptom as something outside, rather than residing within, the self. The therapist then guides clients through the process of assessing the "real effects" of the problem on their daily lives. Having distanced themselves from the problem, clients are better able to develop alternative accounts and resist efforts to be co-opted back into performing the dominant story that they are trying to revise. Important contributions to this effort can be made by the therapist and the client jointly. For example, identifying "unique outcomes" (i.e., events or experiences that do not fit with the dominant or oppressive narrative) can help articulate "gaps" in the client's current narrative account by identifying those events that do not conform to or are inconsistent with the dominant narrative. Therapeutic progress can be underscored through the use of certificates of accomplishment, between-session letters of acknowledgment, and so forth. Recruiting audiences to support therapeutic gains is another strategy designed to support therapeutic gains.

These and other methods are designed to facilitate a context of change by insinuating themselves between the individual and the oppressive or dominant narrative and supporting the ongoing quest for greater coherence in the developing therapeutic narrative account.

**Respect for meaning making.** Although different constructivist traditions tend to focus on different levels of meaning (personal, interpersonal, systemic, cultural), they share key ingredients. Foremost among these is respect for meaning making. Moreover, although constructivist traditions acknowledge the wide variety of possible forms of symbolized meaning, they tend especially to honor the human penchant for imposing narrative structure on events. Bruner (1990) identifies this penchant as "one of the crowning achievements of human development" (p. 67), and Polkinghorne (1988) adds:

> We live immersed in narrative, recounting and reassessing the meanings of our past actions, anticipating the outcomes of our future projects, situating ourselves at the intersections of several stories not yet completed. We explain our actions in terms of plots, and often no other form of explanation can produce sensible statements. (p. 160)

These key features, the orientation toward meaning making and the role of narrative construction, are evident at every level of constructivist psychotherapy. From the relative individualism implied by Kelly's (1955) self-characterization technique through the systematic orientation of the bow tie method to the cultural contingency of narrative therapy, the notion of human beings as storytellers has potent appeal (Mair, 1988; Sarbin, 1986). And each of these features figures prominently in the self-confrontation method, a recently developed assessment tool that can be used to illustrate the assessment process from a constructivist perspective.

# The Self-Confrontation Method

## *Overview*

Pioneered by Hermans (1976), the self-confrontation method cuts across the molecular–molar dimension of constructivism. Anchored in constructivism by its idiographic emphasis on personal meaning structures, the method invites individuals to articulate units of meaning that thematically represent and inform significant experience. Hermans and Hermans-Jansen (1995) define these subjective units of meaning, or *valuations,* as "anything people identify as . . . relevant meaning unit[s] when telling their life narrative" (p. 15). They further describe these valuations by indicating that

> a valuation is any unit of meaning that has a both positive (pleasant), negative (unpleasant), or ambivalent (both pleasant and unpleasant) value in the eyes of the self-reflecting individual. It can include a broad range of phenomena: a precious memory, a difficult problem, a beloved person, an unreachable goal, the anticipated death of a significant other, and so forth. (p. 15)

As in Guidano's (1995b) movieola technique, "the concept of valuation can be described as an interplay between the I and the Me, the two components of the self

. . . units of meaning that the I as author relates about the Me as actor involved in the interactions with others" (Hermans & Hermans-Jansen, 1995, p. 15).

Examples of valuations include the following: *No matter how hard I tried, I just couldn't perform as well as my peers in school. Taking daily walks with my wife/husband helps keep our relationship a priority. I have a recurrent dream about leaving my wife/husband.* Hermans (1995) postulates that an individual's system of valuations is characterized by two fundamental motives: the striving for self-enhancement (S) and the longing for contact and union with others (O). To support this distinction, Hermans and Hermans-Jansen (1995) illustrate prominent "self–other" themes throughout the history of philosophy and psychology. Included are Empedocles's basic forces of "strife" and "love," Bakan's (1966) "agency" and "communion," Angyal's (1965) "autonomy" and "homonomy," and Klages' (1948) "bindung" and "losung," each of which highlight a "striving toward an independent existence [self-enhancement] and at the same time a tendency to want to participate in something greater [contact and union with others]" (p. 22). According to Hermans and Hermans-Jansen (1995), moreover, the traditional notion of self-esteem "belongs more to the realm of what we have summarized as the S motive than to the realm of the O motive. … It is precisely in the flexible movement between the S and O motive that a more extended and flexible functioning of the self is developed" (p. 25). In addition to the self–other construct, valuations are characterized along a positive (P) and negative (N) dimension: "It is supposed that each valuation is associated with a pattern of positive and negative feelings so that the difference between both types of affect may give information about the extent to which the basic motives are gratified" (Hermans & Hermans-Jansen, 1995, p. 27).

The self-confrontation method is conducted as a semistructured interview that begins by eliciting valuations through a set of questions regarding significant past, present, and future life experiences (see Table 1). Individuals are asked to focus on people, events, or experiences that are particularly important or influential in shaping their lives. After engaging in a narrative account of these events, the individual is asked to formulate finalized responses as sentences, single words, or phrases that provide clearly delineated and condensed valuations (Hermans & Hermans-Jansen, 1995). The therapist should highlight several points when eliciting valuations: (a) the sentence should overtly concern the self; (b) the sentence should be a close approximation of the client's intended meaning; (c) the sentence should contain those aspects of the intended meaning that are felt by the client to be most crucial (for more detailed instructions, see Hermans & Hermans-Jansen, 1995).

Having finalized a set of valuations derived from significant life experience, individuals are asked to classify each valuation in relation to a set of 16 predetermined affect terms (e.g., happiness, intimacy, worry) that index the self–other (S–O) and positive–negative (P–N) dimensions (see Table 3 for a complete list). In developing the affect-term list, Hermans and associates evaluated the internal homogeneity of each of the four affective groups (S, O, P, and N) and found that they achieved alpha coefficients of at least .83 (Hermans & Hermans-Jansen, 1995). In another procedure

**TABLE 1.** *Questions of the self-confrontation method.*

*Set 1: The Past*

These questions are intended to guide you in reviewing one or more aspects of your past life that may have been of great importance to you.

■ Has there been anything of major significance in your past life that still continues to exert a strong influence on you?

■ Was there in the past any person, experience, or circumstance that greatly influenced your life and that appreciably affects your present existence?

*Set 2: The Present*

This set consists of two questions referring to your present life that will lead you, after a certain amount of reflection, to formulate a response.

■ Is there anything in your present existence that is of major importance to you or exerts a significant influence on you?

■ Is there in your present existence any person or circumstance that exerts a significant influence on you?

*Set 3: The Future*

The following questions referring to your future should again guide you to a response. You are free to look as far ahead as you wish.

■ Do you foresee anything that will be of great importance for or exert a major influence on your future life?

■ Do you feel that a certain person or circumstance will exert a significant influence on your future life?

■ Is there any future goal or object that you expect will play an important role in your life?

*Note:* See Hermans & Hermans-Jansen (1995).

---

(Hermans, Hermans-Jansen, & Van Gilst, 1985), 127 valuations from different clients were rated by five independent judges for the extent to which the content reflected self-enhancement or contact and union with others. Interrater reliability of the five judges was .86 (coefficient alpha); and judges' and clients' ratings of the valuations were clearly congruent with respect to the expression of self-enhancement or contact and union with others. The procedure of classifying each valuation in relation to the affect terms results in a matrix of valuations and ratings that can then be reviewed and evaluated, as illustrated in the following case example.

## *Case Example*

**Initial procedure.** Susan, a 25-year-old white female, was a married university student without children at the time she completed the self-confrontation method. The method began as a semistructured interview, during which Susan was oriented to the procedure and presented with the initial question set (see Table 1). She was asked to review this question set and to "phrase the valuations in [her] own terms so that the formulation is as much as possible in agreement with the intended meaning" (Hermans & Oles, 1996). In response, she provided a stream of personal associations in which she seemed to weigh the significance of several life experiences. During her intermittent pauses, the interviewer attempted to reformulate her responses by reflecting on and connecting her various associations. When this process had led to a definitive end, Susan was instructed to formulate a finalized response that themat-

**TABLE 2.** *Susan's valuations.*

1. My father left me when I was nine.
2. When my father left me, I was forced to see the inhumanity in people.
3. After my father left me, I secluded myself in my schoolwork to show other kids that I was better than they at something.
4. After my father left me, I tried to excel in school to show him I was worthy of his approval.
5. My first boyfriend's emotional abuse still has an effect on my marriage.
6. When I finally rebelled against my mother and first boyfriend's manipulation, it made me take control of my life.
7. My performance in school has a great influence on my overall behavior.
8. I have the ability to become really mad at my husband.
9. My family will be of great importance in my future.
10. My level of success in my career will leave me feeling either fulfilled or like a failure.

ically captured the significance of the experience. Illustrated below are Susan's initial response to the question set, her gradual movement toward finalizing a valuation, and summaries of the various directives from the interviewer.

> Susan: (reflecting) I guess my father leaving when I was little had a tremendous effect on my entire childhood. ... I mean, he just left one night while I was sleeping and didn't even say goodbye. ... Then I was forced to realize at an early age that nothing was forever. ... I guess that made me kind of insecure.

> [The interviewer reviews this response, summarizes, and asks the participant if she can now express, in a sentence, its most significant aspects.]

> Susan: (suggests the following formulation) My father left me, and I was forced to see the inhumanity in people.

> [The interviewer inquires whether this formulation adequately covers what she has in mind and if this is indeed the major point she wants to make. The participant confirms that it is, and the interviewer then asks if the same question set evokes other significant experiences.]

The questioning continued, with Susan using the list from Table 1. Although most participants produce between 20 and 40 valuations (Hermans, 1987), the interviewer worked with Susan to produce a smaller set of 10 distinct valuations (see Table 2 for a complete list). Consistent with the notion that a valuation should be a single meaning unit, Susan's first valuation ("My father left me, and I was forced to see the inhumanity in people") was split into separate valuations that she agreed captured distinct experiential themes ("My father left me when I was nine" and "When my father left me, I was forced to see the inhumanity in people"). She was then given the set of 16 affect terms (Table 3) and asked to indicate on a 0–5 scale the extent to which she experienced each affect in relation to each valuation (0 = not at all, 1 = a little bit, 2 = to some extent, 3 = rather much, 4 = much, and 5 = very much). Table 4 (lines 1 through 10) reflects her ratings of the 10 valuations along the 16 affect terms. For example, Susan's ratings for valuation 1 ("My father left me when I was nine" were 0 for joy, 0 for self-esteem, 0 for happiness, 2 for worry, and so forth (see Table 4).

**TABLE 3.** *Affect terms used in the self-confrontation method.*

| | |
|---|---|
| 1. Joy (P) | 9. Unhappiness (N) |
| 2. Self-esteem (S) | 10. Tenderness (O) |
| 3. Happiness (P) | 11. Self-confidence (S) |
| 4. Worry (N) | 12. Intimacy (O) |
| 5. Strength (S) | 13. Despondency (N) |
| 6. Enjoyment (P) | 14. Pride (S) |
| 7. Caring (O) | 15. Disappointment (N) |
| 8. Love (O) | 16. Inner calm (P) |

*Note:* See Hermans & Hermans-Jansen (1995).

In addition to rating each of her 10 valuations in this way, Susan was asked to characterize her present *general feeling* along each of the 16 affect terms in response to the question "How do you generally feel these days?" and to characterize her *ideal feeling* by responding in a similar manner to the question "How would you like to feel?" These questions tap the participant's overall present and ideal affect so that they can be compared with affect evoked by the elicited valuations. The complete matrix of Susan's valuations and these affective ratings are presented in Table 4.

**Modality analysis.** The modality analysis, perhaps the most intriguing component of the self-confrontation method, involves a quantitative manipulation of the valuations and their correlates, producing qualitatively insightful results. The flexibility inherent in the modality analysis allows a wide variety of possible implementations; however, Hermans and Hermans-Jansen's (1995) original format begins with the question "Which valuation represents a relevant starting point for discussion?" (p. 55). With this thought in mind, the therapist and client choose a valuation that seems to have important repercussions for the system as a whole. This decision may be facilitated by examining the correlations between the affective pattern associated with the *general feeling* and any valuation. Strongly positive correlations suggest an appreciable relationship between the affect associated with a valuation and the client's overall affect, signaling the possibility that the valuation(s) may play a pivotal role in relation to his or her present outlook. Having chosen this pivotal valuation(s), the therapist and client may examine it in conjunction with the valuation with which it most strongly correlates (positively or negatively). Finally, the client is invited to concentrate on the common meaning between the two correlated valuations and to provide an interpretation that includes or integrates both of them. The process may be repeated stepwise by strength of correlation until an overarching theme becomes apparent. As Hermans and Hermans-Jansen (1995) note, "The modality analysis takes us to the heart of the self-confrontation method because it is the most direct road to a theme that plays a major role in the ordering of the client's life in a particular period" (p. 58). One can expect the valuation-elicitation segment of the self-confrontation method to require one or two 50-minute therapy sessions and the modality analysis to require another session after the clinician has calculated the correlations between sessions. (For information on a computerized scoring package, see Hermans and Hermans-Jansen, 1995).

**TABLE 4.** *Matrix of valuations X affect: Raw ratings from Susan and sum scores.*

| | 1 (P) Joy | 2 (S) Self | 3 (P) Hap | 4 (N) Wor | 5 (S) Str | 6 (P) Enj | 7 (O) Car | 8 (O) Love | 9 (N) Unh | 10 (O) Tend | 11 (S) Conf | 12 (O) Int | 13 (N) Desp | 14 (S) Pride | 15 (N) Dis | 16 (P) Calm | S | O | P | N |
|---|---|---|---|---|---|---|---|---|---|---|---|---|---|---|---|---|---|---|---|---|
| Valuation[b] | | | | | | | | | | | | | | | | | | Sum Scores[c] | | |
| 1 | 0 | 0 | 0 | 2 | 4 | 0 | 0 | 0 | 5 | 0 | 0 | 0 | 5 | 0 | 5 | 0 | 4 | 0 | 0 | 17 |
| 2 | 0 | 1 | 0 | 4 | 5 | 0 | 2 | 0 | 4 | 0 | 2 | 0 | 5 | 0 | 5 | 0 | 8 | 2 | 0 | 18 |
| 3 | 0 | 2 | 1 | 1 | 5 | 2 | 1 | 0 | 2 | 0 | 3 | 0 | 2 | 1 | 0 | 2 | 11 | 1 | 5 | 5 |
| 4 | 0 | 2 | 0 | 4 | 4 | 0 | 5 | 5 | 1 | 1 | 1 | 4 | 2 | 1 | 1 | 0 | 8 | 15 | 0 | 8 |
| 5 | 0 | 2 | 0 | 1 | 5 | 0 | 0 | 0 | 1 | 0 | 2 | 0 | 2 | 0 | 0 | 0 | 9 | 0 | 0 | 4 |
| 6 | 4 | 5 | 4 | 0 | 5 | 4 | 2 | 0 | 1 | 0 | 5 | 0 | 0 | 5 | 0 | 4 | 20 | 2 | 16 | 1 |
| 7 | 1 | 1 | 0 | 4 | 0 | 0 | 0 | 0 | 4 | 0 | 0 | 0 | 0 | 0 | 1 | 0 | 1 | 0 | 1 | 13 |
| 8 | 0 | 0 | 0 | 5 | 0 | 0 | 0 | 0 | 5 | 0 | 0 | 0 | 5 | 0 | 5 | 0 | 0 | 0 | 0 | 20 |
| 9 | 4 | 4 | 4 | 3 | 3 | 3 | 5 | 5 | 0 | 3 | 2 | 4 | 0 | 5 | 0 | 2 | 14 | 17 | 13 | 3 |
| 10 | 0 | 0 | 0 | 5 | 0 | 0 | 2 | 2 | 0 | 0 | 0 | 0 | 0 | 0 | 0 | 0 | 0 | 4 | 0 | 5 |
| General Feeling | 2 | 1 | 4 | 2 | 1 | 3 | 3 | 2 | 2 | 2 | 2 | 2 | 2 | 2 | 2 | 1 | 7 | 10 | 5 | 10 |
| Ideal Feeling | 4 | 5 | 5 | 0 | 5 | 5 | 4 | 4 | 0 | 4 | 5 | 5 | 0 | 4 | 0 | 5 | 19 | 17 | 19 | 0 |
| MA 1[d] | 0 | 0 | 0 | 5 | 0 | 0 | 0 | 0 | 5 | 0 | 0 | 0 | 5 | 0 | 5 | 0 | 0 | 0 | 0 | 20 |
| MA 2 | 0 | 0 | 0 | 5 | 0 | 0 | 0 | 0 | 5 | 0 | 0 | 0 | 5 | 0 | 5 | 0 | 0 | 0 | 0 | 20 |
| MA 3 | 5 | 5 | 5 | 0 | 5 | 5 | 4 | 4 | 0 | 4 | 5 | 4 | 0 | 5 | 0 | 5 | 20 | 16 | 20 | 0 |
| MA 4 | 0 | 0 | 0 | 5 | 0 | 0 | 0 | 0 | 5 | 0 | 0 | 0 | 5 | 0 | 5 | 0 | 0 | 0 | 0 | 20 |
| MA 5 | 4 | 5 | 3 | 2 | 5 | 4 | 0 | 0 | 2 | 0 | 4 | 0 | 2 | 5 | 0 | 2 | 19 | 0 | 12 | 8 |
| MA 6 | 0 | 0 | 0 | 4 | 0 | 0 | 0 | 0 | 5 | 0 | 0 | 0 | 5 | 0 | 5 | 0 | 0 | 0 | 0 | 19 |

[a]The columns labeled 1 through 16 correspond to the affect terms listed in Table 3.

[b]The rows labeled 1 through 10 correspond to the valuations listed in Table 2.

[c]The letters S, O, P, and N (*S*elf, *O*ther, *P*ositive, and *N*egative) refer to the type of affect indexed by the terms in Table 3. The ratings along each of the four indices are summed to produce sum scores of each type of affect.

[d]The rows labeled MA 1 through MA 6 correspond to the interpretations elicited through the modality analysis (see Table 5).

In Susan's case, valuation 9 ("My family will be of great importance in my future") was most highly, but still only modestly, related to her general feeling ($r = .20$). The valuation with which it most strongly correlated ($r = -.75$) was valuation 8 ("I have the ability to become really mad at my husband"). Susan was asked to concentrate on the common meaning between these valuations (valuations 8 and 9) and to provide an interpretation that helped her integrate or make sense of both of them. In response, she suggested, "I don't envision my future with my family being like my present relationship with my husband."

Our attention then turned to comparing two present-focused valuations that achieved strongly negative correlations on the *idealization index* (a set of correlations between affect associated with each valuation and the *ideal feeling*; see Table 4), indicating the possibility that these valuations were accounting for most of the difference between Susan's general and ideal feeling. Valuation 7 ("My performance in school has a great influence on my overall behavior") and valuation 8 ("I have the ability to become really mad at my husband") were not only negatively correlated with Susan's ideal feeling (valuation 7, $r = -.86$; valuation 8, $r = -.98$), but were themselves strongly correlated ($r = .88$). Susan responded to this comparison with two interpretations: (a) "My performance in school and my husband have a lot of control over my happiness" and (b) "I should have more control over my happiness." Susan was asked to indicate, as with the valuations, the extent to which she experienced each affect in Table 3 in relation to the newly formulated interpretations. And finally, Susan was presented with three additional strongly correlated valuation pairs and likewise asked to provide interpretations. Table 5 depicts these interpretations.

The strong correlations between Susan's ideal feeling and her first interpretation ("I don't envision my future with my family being like my present relationship with my husband," $r = -.98$), and between her ideal feeling and her third interpretation ("I should have more control over my happiness," $r = +.98$) highlight the potential power and utility of this procedure. In contrast with psychotherapeutic procedures in which the therapist is the primary authority on the client's experience, the modality analysis, congruent with its constructivist leanings, empowers the client with the expertise necessary for significant experiential interpretations. Related themes of Susan's past and present experience were brought to light introspectively by her. Blurring the boundary between assessment and intervention, the modality analysis and the thematic insight it facilitates can be used as a point of departure for therapy:

> The client can go home with this theme in mind and try to become more sensitive to the patterns of experiences and interactions in daily life that are closely related to this theme. ... Eventually the client and psychologist arrive at a point where they can translate the guiding theme into concrete behavioral steps to be incorporated into the client's daily life. (Hermans & Hermans-Jansen, 1995, p. 58)

**Reflexive assessment.** Following the completion of the self-confrontation method, the client and therapist can participate in two levels of further analysis. The first analysis engages the client in reflecting on the process and procedures of the method; the second engages the therapist in locating the client's valuations within a broader professional matrix of meaning. As a means of eliciting client reflection on the self-confrontation method, Hermans and Hermans-Jansen (1995) suggest supplying the client with a valuation entitled "my self-confrontation" and asking him or her to rate this experience along the set of 16 affect terms outlined in Table 3. In our case, a more informal post-assessment interview was conducted with Susan to ascertain her thoughts and feelings regarding several facets of the procedure. She responded enthusiastically, indicating her satisfaction with having acquired what she felt to be valuable and profound insights into herself and her world. In affirming the method's meaningfulness, Susan highlighted the ease with which it was completed and the importance of the personal issues it elicited for her. She expressed fascination regarding the way in which seemingly unrelated valuations become connected through the modality analysis into various overarching life themes.

**TABLE 5.** *Susan's modality analysis valuations, correlations, and interpretations.*

| Paired valuations | Correlations | | | Interpretation(s) |
|---|---|---|---|---|
| | General feeling | Ideal feeling | Valuations[a] | |
| 8. I have the ability to become really mad at my husband. | −.05 | −.98 | −.75 | MA 1. I don't envision my future with my family being like my present relationship with my husband. |
| 9. My family will be of great importance in my future. | .20 | .67 | | |
| 7. My performance in school has a great influence on my overall behavior. | −.11 | −.86 | .88 | MA 2. My performance in school and my husband have a lot of control over happiness. |
| 8. I have the ability to become really mad at my husband. | −.05 | −.98 | | MA 3. I should have more control over my happiness. |
| 2. When my father left me, I was forced to see the inhumanity in people. | −.24 | −.78 | .78 | MA 4. I'm easily affected by the way people treat me. |
| 8. I have the ability to become really mad at my husband. | −.05 | −.98 | | |
| 3. After my father left me, I secluded myself in my schoolwork to show other kids that I was better than they at something. | −.34 | .17 | .86 | MA 5. I'm trying to overcome some of the shortcomings from my past. |
| 5. My first boyfriend's emotional abuse still has an effect on my marriage. | −.49 | .01 | | |
| 1. My father left me when I was 9. | −.22 | −.78 | .83 | MA 6. Other people have the ability to make me feel strong emotions. |
| 8. I have the ability to become really mad at my husband. | −.05 | −.98 | | |

*Note:* See Table 4 for Susan's affective ratings of interpretations MA 1 through MA 6.
[a]These refer to the correlations between the paired valuations.

In addition to this reflection, the therapist can conduct a second level of analysis, which involves classifying the client's valuations into six categories representing the extent to which the self-enhancement (S) and union with others (O) motives are realized through positive (P) and negative (N) affect. (See Figure 2 for a model and description of these categories; see Hermans & Hermans-Jansen, 1995, for a complete discussion.)

In Susan's case, for example, valuation 6 was rated like this:

| "When I finally rebelled against my mother and first boyfriend's manipulation, it made me take control of my life." | S | O | P | N |
|---|---|---|---|---|
| | 20 | 2 | 16 | 1 |

Strongly self-enhancing (S) and positive (P) in character, this valuation fits into the category of *autonomy and success* illustrated in Figure 2.

On the other hand, valuation 7 is characterized by negative (N) affect associated with low levels of both self-enhancement (S) and contact and union with others (O) and would be categorized as *powerlessness and isolation:*

| "My performance in school has a great influ- ence on my overall happiness." | S | O | P | N |
|---|---|---|---|---|
| | 1 | 0 | 1 | 13 |

As a gauge of therapeutic change, Hermans (1995) suggested repeating the entire self-confrontation when the client and therapist feel that significant parts of the valuation system have been reconstructed. During successive administrations of the method, clients may maintain, modify, reformulate, or develop new valuations and may substantially modulate the associated affect. For example, one gauge of treatment gains for Susan might be movement toward greater positive self-enhancement, indicated by valuations associated with affect suggesting *autonomy and success.* It is possible that after a therapeutic focus in which school is reframed as a potential source of positive accomplishment for Susan, a second self-confrontation would reveal significant change in this direction.

## Empirical Considerations

Although the self-confrontation method has received widespread attention only recently, several research studies have demonstrated its efficacy. These studies include empirical group research designs as well as clinical case studies.

**Empirical group studies.** Integrating idiographic and nomothetic research methods, the self-confrontation method personalizes the study of values. Hermans and Oles (1994) wanted to assess the degree to which societal values are perceived differently by different individuals. They contextualized the set of questions used in the self-confrontation method (see Table 1) within Spranger's (1924) six types of societal values (aesthetic, economic, political, religious, social, and theoretical), and asked 53 psychology students to articulate their personal experience of these values by providing valuations corresponding to each value area. Drawing from the wide-ranging content and affective modalities of the valuations elicited within these areas, the researchers concluded that "objective" (i.e., societal) values may be more usefully understood through individual interpretations of these values, rather than "conceived of as stable and coherent structures that guide people's actions and form the cultural basis of community" (Hermans & Oles, 1994, p. 575).

Additional work by Hermans and Oles (1996) used the self-confrontation method to study the affective organization of individuals in a value crisis. A value crisis was defined as disorganization of the value system. Disorganization is marked by predominantly negative or ambivalent valuations that correlate highly with an individual's present general feeling as well as an affective discontinuity between valuations referring to past and present experience. To test their position regarding value disor-

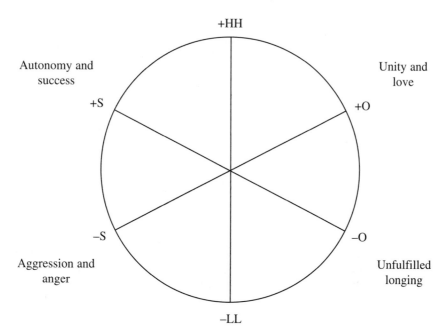

Strength and unity

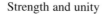

Note: +S = positive self-enhancement; –S = negative self-enhancement; +O = positive contact with others; –O = negative contact with others; +HH = positive combination of high self-enhancement and high contact with others; –LL = negative combination of low self-enhancement and low contact with others (Hermans & Hermans-Jansen, 1995).

**FIG. 2.** *Types of valuation.*

ganization, 48 students were split into three groups—one high, one medium, and one low in value crisis. The results generally supported the hypothesis; when examining the valuations that generalized highly in the system of high-crisis individuals, it was found that these valuations referred to negative affect (high N). A further exploration of valuations in two specific cases revealed negativity (high N) associated with participants' past and present view, but positivity (high P) associated with future anticipation. It was concluded that a value crisis may represent a search for a positive direction in life and that it presents an opportunity for confusion and loss of direction as well as growth and development.

**Clinical case studies.** In recent work by Hermans (1996), the self-confrontation method was used to gauge the progress of a female client whose valuations during her first self-confrontation indicated an overall theme of *unfulfilled longing* (negative, N, affect referring to contact and union, O; see Figure 2), and whose general and ideal feeling were negatively correlated ($r = -.67$). Nine months following the initial self-confrontation, the client's valuations not only represented more positive experiential themes, but referred to affect suggesting *strength and unity* (positive, P, affect referring to a combination of self-enhancement, S, and contact and union, O). Moreover, the relationship between her general and ideal feeling had improved significantly ($r = .96$).

In another recent case study, Hermans (in press) integrated a concept labeled *meaning of life,* which invites reflection on the overall affective quality of an individual's life, into the self-confrontation method. As is done in obtaining the general and ideal feeling, the client was asked to rate along the set of 16 affect terms his answer to the question "How do I experience the meaning of my life?" The results of these ratings were then correlated with the client's valuations. Consistent with the client's problematic struggle to maintain autonomy at the expense of meaningful relationships with others, affect associated with his meaning of life and the valuations with which it positively correlated suggested *aggression and anger* (negative, N, affect referring to self-enhancement, S). Valuations with which the client's meaning of life negatively correlated were those suggesting *unfulfilled longing.* Two and a half years later, the client's third self-confrontation denoted significant change implied by the positive correlation of the *meaning of life* with valuations suggesting *strength and unity,* thereby indicating a positive integration of his wishes for autonomy *and* contact and union with others. Hermans (in press) notes that "the self-confrontation method can be seen as a procedure which contributes to organization and reorganization of the valuation system," and summarizes its value in this way:

> On the basis of the [assessment] and the insights gained ... the person transforms the self-confrontation into action by giving detailed attention to the specific experiences in daily life and taking new initiatives. ... In Investigation 2 psychologist and client explore to what extent these initiatives have led to further development of the valuation system. Altogether, the method aims to combine assessment, change, and evaluation.

**Future concerns.** Because the self-confrontation method has been studied using only small samples of college students and single case studies, research is needed to assess its efficacy in large clinical samples. Specifically, future studies should focus on therapeutic impact and treatment outcome, using traditional measures in conjunction with measures associated with the method itself (i.e., general feeling, level of self-enhancement, and so forth). Research in this area may also suggest clinical populations for which the self-confrontation method is most effective. Because the method uses clients' reported life experience as the springboard for assessment and intervention and requires the cognitive–affective sophistication necessary to perform the modality analysis, it may be best suited for clients who are forthcoming with their life experience and for whom the verbal and cognitive rendering of their life experience is at most moderately challenging.

# Conclusion

Constructivist assessment reflects the commitments of its underlying epistemology. As a co-constructed enterprise, the assessment of meaning is assumed to be a joint venture. Client and therapist are engaged in a mutual effort to explore the frameworks of understanding that inform and guide the client's perspective on the world. Efforts to assess these frameworks are sensitive to the contexts (temporal, interpersonal, cultural) within which they are embedded and they naturally give rise to shifts or changes in these frameworks themselves. In short, constructivist assessment is understood as the contextually contingent process of articulating and (re)constructing meaning. The blurred boundaries between assessment and intervention highlight the interdependence of these tandem processes from a constructivist position. The articulation of the client's framework does more than simply set the stage for subsequent intervention; it actually initiates the ongoing process of intervening in meaning.

The self-confrontation method (Hermans, 1976) illustrated here shares this and other features in common with other methods derived from constructivist traditions. It respects the primacy of personal experience, for example, and honors the perspective that the individual brings to bear on it. It recognizes the linguistic medium and traditions that support the person's constructions and the capacity of those features simultaneously to subjugate and liberate the individual. It honors the transformative capacity of reflection, the ability to reflect upon and transcend current constructions in the service of growth and change. And it acknowledges the provisional, proximal goals of all our outcomes, outcomes that inevitably yield to processes of erosion, revision, and reconstruction over the course of continued living. It follows that the processes of psychotherapeutic assessment and intervention are likewise malleable and friable, themselves contingent mechanisms for articulating meaning and leveraging change. For that reason constructivist traditions tend to honor a diverse array of therapeutic stances and tools, rather than privileging select forms (e.g., statistical) as preferable to others. As Kelly (1969) notes in his reflections on the nature of psychotherapy,

> The relationships between therapist and client and the techniques they employ may be as varied as the whole human repertory of relationships and techniques. It is the orchestration of techniques and the utilization of relationships in the ongoing process of living and profiting from experience that make psychotherapy a contribution to human life (p. 223).

# References

Anderson, H., & Goolishian, H. (1992). The client is the expert: A not-knowing approach to therapy. In S. McNamee & K. J. Gergen (Eds.), *Therapy as social construction* (pp. 25–39). Newbury Park, CA: Sage.

Angyal, A. (1965). *Neurosis and treatment: A holistic theory.* New York: Wiley.

Bakan, D. (1966). *The duality of human existence.* Chicago: Rand-McNally.

Bell, R. C. (1990). Analytic issues in the use of repertory grid technique. In G. J. Neimeyer & R. A. Neimeyer (Eds.), *Advances in personal construct psychology* (Vol. 1, pp. 25–48). Greenwich, CT: JAI Press.

Botella, L. (1995). Personal construct theory, constructivism, and postmodern thought. In R. A. Neimeyer & G. J. Neimeyer (Eds.), *Advances in personal construct psychology* (Vol. 3, pp. 3–36). Greenwich, CT: JAI Press.

Bruner, J. S. (1990). *Acts of meaning.* Cambridge, MA: Harvard University Press.

Butt, T. W., Burr, V., & Epting, F. R. (1997). Core construing: Self discovery or self intervention? In G. J. Neimeyer & R. A. Neimeyer (Eds.), *Advances in personal construct psychology, 4.* Greenwich,

CT: JAI Press.

Clarke, K. M. (1993). Creation of meaning in incest survivors. *Journal of Cognitive Psychotherapy, 7,* 195–203.

Efran, J. S., Lukens, M. D., & Lukens, R. J. (1990). *Language, structure, and change: Frameworks of meaning in psychotherapy.* New York: W. W. Norton.

Feixas, G., Procter, H., & Neimeyer, G. J. (1993). Convergent lines of assessment: Systemic and constructivist contributions. In G. J. Neimeyer (Ed.), *Constructivist assessment: A casebook* (pp. 143–178). Newbury Park, CA: Sage.

Gergen, K. J. (1994). Exploring the postmodern: Perils or potentials? *American Psychologist, 49,* 412–416.

Guidano, V. F. (1995a). Constructivist psychotherapy: A theoretical framework. In R. A. Neimeyer & M. J. Mahoney (Eds.), *Constructivism in psychotherapy* (pp. 93–108). Washington, DC: American Psychological Association.

Guidano, V. F. (1995b). Self-observation in constructivist psychotherapy. In R. A. Neimeyer & M. J. Mahoney (Eds.), *Constructivism in psychotherapy* (pp. 155–168). Washington, DC: American Psychological Association.

Hermans, H. J. M. (1976). *Value areas and their development: Theory and method of self-confrontation.* Amsterdam: Swets & Zeitlinger.

Hermans, H. J. M. (1987). Self as an organized system of valuations: Toward a dialogue with the person. *Journal of Counseling Psychology, 34,* 10–19.

Hermans, H. J. M. (1995). From assessment to change: The personal meaning of clinical problems in the context of the self-narrative. In R. A. Neimeyer & M. J. Mahoney (Eds.), *Constructivism in psychotherapy* (pp. 247–272). Washington, DC: American Psychological Association.

Hermans, H. J. M. (1996). The self-confrontation method: Assessment, change, and evaluation of personal meaning systems. *Revista de Psicopatologia y Psicologia Clinica, 1,* 269–282.

Hermans, H. J. M. (in press). Meaning as an organized process of valuation: A self-confrontational approach. In P. T. P. Wong & P. Fry (Eds.), *Handbook of personal meaning.* Northvale, NJ: Erlbaum.

Hermans, H. J. M., & Hermans-Jansen, E. (1995). *Self-narratives: The construction of meaning in psychotherapy.* New York: Guilford.

Hermans, H. J. M., Hermans-Jansen, E., & Van Gilst, W. (1985). *The basic motives of human existence: Their expression in personal valuation.* Lisse, The Netherlands: Swets & Zeitlinger.

Hermans, H. J. M., & Oles, P. K. (1994). The personal meaning of values in a rapidly changing society. *Journal of Social Psychology, 134,* 569–579.

Hermans, H. J. M., & Oles, P. K. (1996). Value crisis: Affective organization of personal meanings. *Journal of Research in Personality, 30,* 457–482.

Hoffman, L. (1992). A reflexive stance for family therapy. In S. McNamee & K. J. Gergen (Eds.), *Therapy as social construction* (pp. 7–24). Newbury Park, CA: Sage.

Kelly, G. A. (1955). *The psychology of personal constructs.* New York: W. W. Norton.

Kelly, G. A. (1969). The psychotherapeutic relationship. In B. A. Maher (Ed.), *Clinical psychology and personality: The selected papers of George Kelly* (pp. 216–223). New York: Wiley.

Klages, L. (1948). *Charakterkunde* (Characterology). Zurich: Hirzel.

Lyddon, W. J. (1995). Forms and facets of constructivist psychology. In R. A. Neimeyer & M. J. Mahoney (Eds.), *Constructivism in psychotherapy* (pp. 69–92). Washington, DC: American Psychological Association.

Mahoney, M. J. (1988). Constructivism metatheory I: Basic features and historical foundations. *International Journal of Personal Construct Psychology, 1,* 1–35.

Mahoney, M. J. (1991). *Human change processes: The scientific foundations of psychotherapy.* New York: Basic Books.

Mahoney, M. J. (1996). Constructivism and the study of complex self-organization. *Constructive Change, 1,* 3–8.

Mair, M. (1988). Psychology as storytelling. *International Journal of Personal Construct Psychology,*

*1,* 125–137.

Neimeyer, G. J. (Ed.). (1993). *Constructivist assessment: A casebook.* Newbury Park, CA: Sage.

Neimeyer, G. J. (1995). The challenge of change. In R. A. Neimeyer & M. J. Mahoney (Eds.), *Constructivism in psychotherapy* (pp. 111–126). Washington, DC: American Psychological Association.

Neimeyer, G. J., & Neimeyer, R. A. (1993). Defining the boundaries of constructivist assessment. In G. J. Neimeyer (Ed.), *Constructivist assessment: A casebook* (pp. 1–30). Newbury Park, CA: Sage.

Neimeyer, G. J., & Neimeyer, R. A. (1994). Constructivist methods of marital and family therapy: A practical précis. *Journal of Mental Health Counseling, 16,* 85–104.

Neimeyer, R. A. (1993). Constructivist approaches to the measurement of meaning. In G. J. Neimeyer (Ed.), *Constructivist assessment: A casebook* (pp. 58–103). Newbury Park, CA: Sage.

Neimeyer, R. A. (1995). Constructivist psychotherapies: Features, foundations, and future directions. In R. A. Neimeyer & M. J. Mahoney (Eds.), *Constructivism in psychotherapy* (pp. 11–38). Washington, DC: American Psychological Association.

Neimeyer, R. A., & Mahoney, M. J. (Eds.). (1995). *Constructivism in psychotherapy.* Washington, DC: American Psychological Association.

Neimeyer, R. A., Baker, K. D., & Neimeyer, G. J. (1990). The current status of personal construct theory: Some scientometric data. In G. J. Neimeyer & R. A. Neimeyer (Eds.), *Advances in personal construct psychology* (Vol. 1, pp. 3–22). Greenwich, CT: JAI Press.

Polkinghorne, D. (1988). *Narrative knowing and the human sciences.* Albany, NY: State University of New York Press.

Procter, H. (1985). A personal construct approach to family therapy and systems intervention. In E. Button (Ed.), *Personal construct theory and mental health* (pp. 327–350). London: Croom Helm.

Procter, H. (1987). Change in the family construct system. In R. A. Neimeyer & G. J. Neimeyer (Eds.), *Personal construct therapy casebook* (pp. 153–171). New York: Springer.

Rosenau, P. M. (1992). *Post-modernism and the social sciences: Insights, inroads, and intrusions.* Princeton, NJ: Princeton University Press.

Sarbin, T. R. (1986). The narrative as the root metaphor for psychology. In T. R. Sarbin (Ed.), *Narrative psychology: The storied nature of human conduct* (pp. 3–21). New York: Praeger.

Selvini-Palazzoli, M., Boscolo, L., Cecchin, G., & Prata, G. (1980). Hypothesizing–circularity–neutrality. *Family Process, 19,* 3–12.

Spranger, E. (1924). *Psychologie des jugendalters* [The psychology of youth]. Leipzig, Germany: Quelle & Mayer.

Viney, L. (1987). *Interpreting the interpreters.* Malabar, FL: Krieger.

White, M., & Epston, D. (1990). *Narrative means to therapeutic ends.* New York: W. W. Norton.

Yorke, M. (1989). The intolerable wrestle: Words, numbers, and meanings. *International Journal of Personal Construct Psychology, 2,* 65–76.

# Part 3:

◙ **Constructivist Practice With Individuals and Groups** ◙

# 6

## Constructivist Psychotherapy

*Donald K. Granvold*

Cognitivism has achieved widespread acceptance among practitioners and theoreticians across the helping professions. Its impact has been so pervasive that the movement has been called "revolutionary" (Baars, 1986; Dember, 1974; Mahoney, 1977). Cognitive therapy emerged in an era when psychoanalytic theory was predominant and being challenged by behaviorism. Ellis (1962) and A. T. Beck (1976) pioneered the movement at a time when behaviorism was growing and psychoanalytic theory declining. Today, more than 20 varieties of cognitive therapy have been identified (Mahoney, 1991, 1993). Common among all cognitive approaches is the special role cognition fulfills in human functioning and change. Although most cognitivists embrace reciprocal determinism (Bandura, 1978)—that is, the view that cognitions, behavior, personal factors (emotion, motivation, physiology, and physical factors), and social–environmental factors are interactive—cognition and cognitive processes comparatively are weighted heavily as targets of assessment and intervention.

Cognitive methods and modifications of early cognitive therapies as initially practiced have proliferated. This development and maturation, considered the "evolution within the revolution" (Mahoney, 1991; Mahoney & Lyddon, 1988), has produced expanded and detailed conceptualizations of cognitive content, process, and structure and has spawned diverse methods designed to treat specific disorders (A. T. Beck, Freeman, & Associates, 1990; A. T. Beck, Rush, Shaw, & Emery, 1979; Granvold, 1994a; Kingdon & Turkington, 1994; Linehan, 1993; Wilson & Fairburn, 1993). The cognitive treatment "family" has been shaped by various theories and influences and has evolved while remarkable developments were likewise occurring in experimental psychology, the life sciences, and the philosophy of science. (See Mahoney, 1991, for a discussion of these and other contextual developments.)

This chapter considers only a few movements within cognitive treatment that have had evolutionary impact. Many people who embraced cognitive therapy had a background in social learning theory (e.g., Bandura, 1969; Cautela, 1966; D'Zurilla & Goldfried, 1971; Homme, 1965; Meichenbaum, 1977; Rehm, 1977). Their influence can be seen in role playing, behavioral homework assignments, self-control procedures, problem solving, implosion procedures, and attention to "controlling variables" (secondary gains). The name cognitive–behavioral therapies reflects the extensive infusion of behavioral methods in cognitive therapy. The recent name change of Albert Ellis's rational–emotive therapy (RET) to rational–emotive behavior therapy (REBT) acknowledges the behavioral aspects of RET (Corsini, 1995; Ellis, 1995; Franks, 1995; A. A. Lazarus, 1995). The focus on positive emotionality, "hot cognitions" (Safran & Greenberg, 1986), and the use of procedures designed to evoke emotion as part of the change process reflect the influence of Gestalt and other experiential therapies on cognitivists. Emotion, once viewed as a postcognitive phenomenon, is viewed by many contemporary cognitivists as playing an intrinsic role in cognitive and behavioral functioning and in facilitating enduring change (Greenberg & Safran, 1984, 1987; Guidano, 1991; R. S. Lazarus, 1982, 1989; Mahoney, 1991; Safran & Segal, 1990). A profound development has been the emergence of constructivism, a family of theories based on the idea that "humans actively create and construe their personal realities" (Mahoney & Lyddon, 1988, p. 200). This view stands in opposition to the concept of an objective reality that is singular, stable, and knowable through the senses. The constructivist view holds that our understandings "are contextually embedded, interpersonally forged, and necessarily limited" (G. J. Neimeyer & R. A. Neimeyer, 1993, p. 2). Mentation is proactive as opposed to passive and receptive, internally created as opposed to directly representative of an external "reality," and generative, characterized by the living system's capacity to self-organize and determine its own evolution (autopoiesis). (For a detailed description of autopoiesis, see Maturana and Varela, 1980.)

Assumptions about reality, knowledge, and causality supporting traditional cognitive therapy have been formidably challenged by constructivism. This challenge has resulted in the development of alternative definitions of problem and dysfunction, treatment goals, therapist behavior, assessment methods, treatment procedures, outcome research, and other aspects of the human change process. Applying this "new way of conceptualizing" has resulted in the development of constructivist therapy, described by W. T. Anderson (1990) as "not so much a technique as a philosophical context within which therapy is done, and more a product of the zeitgeist than the brainchild of any single theorist" (p. 137). As implied, constructivist approaches to clinical practice comprise a "fuzzy set" and they have been criticized for being "long on theory and short on practice" (Franklin, 1995; R. A. Neimeyer, 1993b; O'Hara & Anderson, 1991).

The remainder of this chapter presents an overview of constructivist metatheory, an elucidation of the conceptual bases and treatment practices of constructivist therapy vis-à-vis traditional cognitive therapy, and an introduction to several constructivist intervention methods.

# Constructivist Metatheory

A metatheory is a group of related theories that share assumptions and assertions. The cardinal assertion of constructivism is that human knowing is proactive and that people are active participants in the creation of their own reality. The philosophical roots of constructivism can be traced to the works of Giovanni Battista Vico, Immanuel Kant, and Hans Vaihinger (Mahoney, Miller, & Arciero, 1995). Despite its historical roots, constructivism has only recently assumed prominence in psychological theory, specifically cognitive theory. Ontologically, constructivism stands in contrast to realism. According to realism, a singular, stable external reality can be known; constructivism asserts that "humans actively create and construe their personal and social realities" (Mahoney, 1988a, p. 364). The implications of realism are that it is possible to achieve a "reality check" and that "truth" exists objectively. R. A. Neimeyer (1993a) notes that, according to this correspondence theory of truth, "the validity of one's belief systems is determined by their degree of 'match' with the real world, or at least with the 'facts' as provided by one's senses" (p. 222). Constructivism rejects validity in favor of *viability*. Here, the viability of any construction (conceptualized personal reality) "is a function of its consequences for the individual or group that provisionally adopts it (cf. von Glasersfeld, 1984) as well as its overall coherence with the larger system of personally or socially held beliefs into which it is incorporated" (R. A. Neimeyer, 1993a, p. 222).

Epistemologically, constructivism is based upon a *motor theory* of the mind in which "the mind appears as an active, constructive system, capable of producing not only its output but also to a large extent the input it receives, including sensations that lie at the base of its own constructions" (Guidano, 1988, p. 309). Knowledge is an evolutionary result and an interactive process. Knowledge development is biased by the self-organizing abilities of human mental processing (Guidano & Liotti, 1983), which represents a shift away from the *sensory theories* that hold that information flows inward through the senses to the mind, where it is maintained. Popper (1972) refers to this view as "the bucket theory of the mind." The constructivist view further holds that a two-level model of knowledge processing exists, consisting of a tacit–explicit duality whereby unconscious processes are accorded a central role in the formulation of cognitive structures necessary for the ordering of everyday experience. Hayek (1978), in referring to the existence of an abstract order, states,

> All the conscious experience that we regard as relatively concrete and primary, in particular all sensations, perceptions, and images, are the product of a superimposition of many "classifications" of the events perceived. ... What I contend, in short, is that the mind must be capable of performing abstract operations in order to be able to perceive particulars, and that this capacity appears long before we can speak of a conscious awareness of particulars. (pp. 36–37)

The process of knowledge development, therefore, relies inherently on a tacit level of functioning and a capacity to generate abstractions.

This two-level model of knowledge processing (central and peripheral), referred to as *nuclear morphogenic structure*, asserts that "central (core, nuclear) processes are

(a) given special 'protection' from challenge (and hence change) and (b) that these central processes constrain the range of particulars that can emerge at a peripheral ('surface structure') level" (Mahoney et al., 1995, p. 107). Deep cognitive structures have abstract ordering capabilities and function at tacit or unconscious levels. These tacit ordering rules govern the individual's conscious processes and constrain the individual's sense of self and the world. The protective function of core processes and the tacit level at which they operate have significant implications for practice. In short, they are difficult to access and, once accessed, they are difficult to change. A further implication is that surface-level change may fail to effect meaningful change in the individual's core ordering processes.

The life-span-development and systems movements have influenced constructivist metatheory (Mahoney & Lyddon, 1988). Interest has focused on processes of attachment and psychosocial development throughout the life cycle (Bowlby, 1969; Guidano, 1987, 1991; Guidano & Liotti, 1983; Parkes, Stevenson-Hinde, & Marris, 1991; Safran & Segal, 1990; Stern, 1985; Young, 1990). The developmental attachment history of the individual shapes self-knowledge, including self-schemas, abstract rules, and expectations for interacting interpersonally and with the environment. Attachment is regarded as "an organizing construct whose value lies in its integrative power" (Guidano, 1988, p. 313). Encompassed in the process of integration are such factors as cognitive growth, emotional differentiation, identification, individuation, self-schemas, and views of the world. The development of self-knowledge inherently involves tacit levels of organization from which explicit structural levels of self and the world are drawn. Drawing from this conceptualization of development, Guidano (1988) states that personal identity

> consists, essentially, in a whole arrangement of beliefs, memories, and thought procedures about the self, producing a coherent self-image and a sense of personal singleness and continuity in time. Although personal identity is fundamentally an inferred theory of oneself, biased by one's own tacit self-knowledge, it represents the basic structure of reference and constant confrontation by which every person becomes able to monitor and evaluate him- or herself in relation to ongoing experience. A structured self-identity, in particular, provides a set of basic expectations that direct the individual's patterns of self-perception and self-evaluation in accordance with the selected self-image. (p. 317)

Sense of self is the product of an open, generative knowledge system in which the individual is simultaneously being and becoming, referred to by Guidano (1995) as the experiencing *I* and explaining *me*. As noted by Maturana (1988), "we human beings live our lives in a curious recursive involvement, between awareness and becoming" (p. 81). R. A. Neimeyer (1995b) further elucidates this point: "One's sense of self is never fully consistent, because experience continues to perturb current patterns of self-explanation, pushing for their progressive refinement across the course of one's life" (p. 21).

Systems theory has made a significant contribution to the contemporary practice of psychotherapy. In the 1960s and 1970s, many social scientists, drawing upon general systems theory (Von Bertalanffy, 1967), applied a systems model to human functioning among individuals, families, groups, communities, and other complex human organizations (R. E. Anderson & Carter, 1974; Hearn, 1969; Olsen, 1968). According to this conception, the human system is viewed as purposive, ever-evolving, steady-state seeking, and self-perpetuating. The system comprises interacting, interdependent subsystems and functions interactively with other systems—living and nonliving. Life is an ongoing recursive process of perturbation and adaptation, disorganization and distress, and emerging complexity and differentiation. The process is one of evolutionary self-organization—a dynamic organization–reorganization activity. Knowledge development, specifically self-knowledge, is assumed to follow this pattern. More complex and integrated levels of self-identity are achieved through the assimilation of perturbations produced by interactions with the world (Mahoney & Lyddon, 1988). Change, development, and the emergence of more viable patterns of interaction are dependent upon this process of system "disturbance."

## Rationalist and Constructivist Cognitive Therapies: Debate or Debacle?

Mahoney (1988a, 1988c, 1991) suggested the existence of a philosophical bifurcation in cognitive therapy: *rationalism* and *constructivism*. He presented these philosophies as being ontologically, epistemologically, and causally dichotomous. Ontologically, rationalists tend to be realists; reality is singular, external, stable, and knowable. Constructivists, as described above, contend that reality is a personal construct and reject the view that it is external and stable. Constructivists "portray the brain as an active sculptor of reality, proactively 'projecting' its tacit 'expectations' onto each next millimoment of experience" (Mahoney & Lyddon, 1988, p. 213). Epistemologically, rationalists believe that knowledge and knowing are authorized or justified through such information channels as "sense experience, empirical data, logic, science, expert authority, revelation, and so on" (Mahoney, 1988a, p. 369). Public verification is sought to establish the rationality of inferences and decisions. Correspondence between mental representations and the external world is considered possible. For constructivists, knowing is a complex, proactive process involving active explorations toward greater awareness and understanding. Abstract or tacit schemata constrain the individual's meaning making of experience without specifying particulars (Hayek, 1978; Mahoney, 1991). Knowledge is considered to be evolutionary rather than certain and subjective as opposed to objective. Constructivists propose that individual and collective knowing processes, rather than being "valid," are viable, that is, flexible, generative, complex, resilient, and of developmentally adaptive consequence. Causal and change processes according to the rationalist perspective tend toward "billiard-ball determinism" (Mahoney, 1988a), in which learning is linear and associationistic. Knowledge is "built" by chaining discrete events. Constructivists contend that causation and change involve modifications in the human knowing system (structural differentiation). Mental representations become more refined and complex as developmental and structural transformations take place.

Mahoney (1977, 1991, 1993; Mahoney & Lyddon, 1988; Mahoney, Lyddon, & Alford, 1989) identified Ellis's RET as epitomizing the rationalist perspective. Ellis vigorously defends RET as not only not philosophically rationalistic but as highly constructivistic. He admits that early RET methods were largely based on the scientific philosophy of logical positivism, with a focus on empirical realities and attention to sensorial data (Ellis, 1993). He identifies current RET practice as including both rationalist and constructivist positions. Ellis (1989, 1990, 1994) specifies many aspects of RET that support his contention that the method is not rationalist and states that actually it may be more constructivist than Mahoney's cognitive developmental therapy.

It may be more viable (constructively speaking) to consider cognitive–behavioral therapies along a rationalist–constructivist continuum than to adhere to a bipolar view. Philosophically, most cognitive–behavior therapists lean strongly toward the constructivist end of the continuum. This may account for Mahoney's comment that virtually every cognitive therapist he knows considers him- or herself a constructivist (Mahoney, 1995a). When it comes to practice, however, many of these same "constructivists" likely use traditional cognitive interventions. Recent research by DiGiuseppe and Linscott (1993) found that although Albert Ellis-trained RET therapists supported more rationalist attitudes than did cognitive–behavioral therapists, in general, RET therapists were as constructivist in attitude as were other cognitive –behavioral therapists. Furthermore, the researchers found evidence to suggest that the preference for disputing underlying schemata or irrational beliefs early in therapy was representative of both rationalist and constructivist philosophies. The authors concluded that "there is yet no evidence that these philosophical differences reflect actual differences in the way therapists conduct therapy" (p. 128).

The boundaries between traditional or orthodox cognitive therapy (represented here as rationalist in leanings) and constructivist therapy are vague. Conflicting perspectives have been proffered without resolution regarding the meaning of the rationalist label applied to traditional cognitive–behavioral therapy. Contrasts in the two approaches to treatment are discussed below. However, they also have features in common as well as comparable intervention techniques. To analogize, the ambiguity of differentiating boundaries, the lack of clarity in our understandings, and ongoing scholarly debate can be represented as "perturbations" of the psychotherapy "systems" under consideration.

## Principles of Therapeutic Change

Intervention in cognitive–behavioral therapy traditionally has emphasized the modification of explicitly held beliefs, information-processing errors, and behavior. The contention is that change in these phenomena may not effect structural change. Watzlawick, Weakland, and Fisch (1974) refer to this "peripheral" level change as *first-order change* or "change without change." *Second-order change* is change that produces a structural change in the system. Liotti (1987) asserts that "peripheral processes can change, within a given range of variability, without any modification of the core processes" (p. 97). He goes on to state that the reverse is not possible; core-process change implies modification of peripheral processes. Environmental contingencies can produce change at the peripheral level, whereas deep structures may not change in response to the environment.

Constructivists (e.g., Guidano, 1987, 1991; Liotti, 1987; Lyddon, 1990; Mahoney, 1991; Watzlawick et al., 1974) believe that core processes or deep structures are highly change resistive. If, however, deep-structure (second-order) change is accomplished, it is believed that peripheral (first-order) change, which has a more pervasive effect on the individual, is produced. Although lower-order functioning (peripheral) can change without change occurring in higher-order functioning, it is *possible* to produce higher-order effects through modification at the lower level. It is well established that behavioral change often evidences corresponding changes in cognitive, emotional, and physical or physiological functioning. Although these may well be considered to be peripheral-level associations, it is plausible that change in peripheral cognitive processing and beliefs that are closely connected to core beliefs produces deep-structure change. When new complaints replace old solutions, however, it can be concluded that first-order change has failed to produce effective or lasting second-order change (Efran & Clarfield, 1993; Watzlawick et al., 1974).

The focus on first-order change by early cognitivists is evident in A. T. Beck and Weishaar's (1986) definition of cognitive therapy as "a collaborative process of empirical investigation, reality testing, and problem solving between the therapist and patient" (p. 43). This definition exposes the realist orientation and the attention to validation and sensory-based knowledge. Any objective to produce a second-order change tended to be sought through the production of first-order change. A. T. Beck, Ellis, Meichenbaum, and others have shifted their emphasis recently to the restructuring or reconstruction of schemas (core ordering processes consisting of beliefs, underlying assumptions, and attitudes) that "both direct and influence our behavior and help to give meaning to our world" (Freeman, 1993, p. 54). Although schematic change has received attention, the treatment approaches of most traditional cognitive–behavioral therapists have included significant concomitant attention to change in behavior, surface cognitions, and information processing. A. T. Beck, for example, in addition to focusing on schemas, seeks changes in mastery and pleasure activities with depressed clients as an important ingredient in the treatment package (A. T. Beck et al., 1979). Thus, although schematic change may be sought, it is not done exclusive of other change. Traditional cognitive–behavioral therapists can be characterized as being attentive to both first- and second-order change, although their intervention plans are not as strongly focused on core meanings and schematic change as are those of their constructivist counterparts.

## Practical Differences Between Traditional Cognitive–Behavioral Therapy and Constructivist Therapy

As noted above, the boundaries separating traditional cognitive from constructivist approaches are not well defined. Some practical distinctions, however, characterize the two practice typologies. Recognizing the "fuzziness" of the boundaries between the approaches, R. A. Neimeyer (1993b) identifies contrasting features as representative of emphasis rather than fundamental difference.

## *Goal of Therapy: Problem or Process?*

Traditional treatment approaches tend to focus on problems. Intervention is designed to reduce or eliminate the presenting problem and its symptomatology and in so doing to isolate for modification:

■ Cognitive dysfunction (irrational beliefs, faulty information processing, misattributions, self-expectancy, maladaptive self-statements)

■ Behavioral excesses or deficiencies

■ Controlling variables (e.g., secondary gains, discriminative stimuli)

■ Social–environmental contextual factors

■ Physical or physiological factors confounding the presenting problem

Problem solving typically is here-and-now oriented as opposed to historically or developmentally focused. Treatment often incorporates educational content to enhance the client's understanding of human behavior, human-change processes, and unique aspects of the presenting problem and its context. Intervention is highly biased toward first-order change. Therapy has a corrective goal.

The constructivist approach tends to emphasize various historical, developmental (e.g., attachment), and self-organizational themes. In this structural and process orientation to change, "the specific cognitive focus involves exploring clients' personal meanings (structural focus) and facilitating the transformation of these meanings (process focus) in the direction of more viable representations of experience" (Lyddon, 1990, p. 124). The shift is away from the presenting "problem" as the target of intervention. In addressing the shortcomings of a problem-focused orientation, Saleebey (1992) aptly states that "naming the poison leads us to the antidote. But in the world of human activity, human nature, and the human condition, such linear thinking ignores the steamy morass of uncertainty and complexity that typify human affairs" (p. 5). The client's presenting problem is considered to be a perturbation and provides an opportunity to explore new meanings. A problem is conceptualized as a discrepancy between a client's current capacity and the developmental challenges being experienced. The focus is shifted away from surface-structure problem resolution to deep-structure change. Client views of self, the world, and their relationship become primary considerations. Treatment is more creative than corrective, with the promotion of meaning making and personal development as the goals of treatment (R. A. Neimeyer, 1995b; R. A. Neimeyer & Harter, 1988).

## *Assessment*

Traditional cognitive assessment relies on client self-report to gain access to such covert content as internal dialogues, automatic thoughts, irrational beliefs, negative attributions, and statements of self-efficacy. Comprehensive assessment strategies include, along with assessment interviews, the use of standardized assessment instruments, in vivo procedures (e.g., daily records of cognitions and corresponding emotions, thought sampling), and video-prompting methods (Granvold, 1995; Granvold & Wodarski, 1994; Merluzzi & Boltwood, 1989; Merluzzi, Glass, & Genest, 1981). These methods seek frequency, intensity, and typology data related to client cognitive content, cognitive process, and associated patterns of emotional expression.

Constructivist assessment may employ paper-and-pencil measures along with interviewing, but the focus is on the implications of a personal representation (construct) among other constructions of self, others, and the world (R. A. Neimeyer, 1993b; G. J. Neimeyer & R. A. Neimeyer, 1993). Repertory grid (Kelly, 1955) is a method frequently used for exposing relationships among constructs. Deeper meanings of peripheral content are sought through the use of such procedures as laddering or downward-arrow methods of vertical exploration toward more central constructs. Narrative methods, including journal writing, stream of consciousness (Mahoney, 1991), and storytelling, provide opportunities for highly unstructured assessment and unharnessed self-exploration. See G. J. Neimeyer (1993), Mahoney (1991), and White and Epston (1990) for information on constructivist assessment.

Both traditional cognitive and constructivist therapists gather global assessment data. Information is gathered on medical and health functioning, financial and fiscal needs, family relationships and social functioning, past treatment experience and its meaning, and client expectations of the therapist and change outcomes desired. When the client presents with an immediate problem or problems of an acute nature, global assessment activity is delayed. Attention is directed to an evaluation of the risk of self-injury, suicide, and aggression toward others, along with an appraisal of the client's coping capacity and strategies, family- and social-support systems, and available resources. If indicated, immediate crisis-intervention measures are taken to alleviate the critical risks evidenced by the client before undertaking further assessment or initiating cognitive–behavioral treatment of peripheral and core structures inherently related to the presenting crisis. (See Dattilio and Freeman, 1994, for information on cognitive–behavioral crisis-intervention strategies for a broad range of clinical problems.)

### *Treatment of Emotion*

Traditional cognitive–behavioral therapists have implemented interventions to control, alter, or terminate emotions such as anxiety, depression, anger, worry, sorrow, sadness, guilt, and the like—emotions regarded as "negative." Emotional expressions have tended to be conceptualized as intrusive, maladaptive, debilitating, and generally unpleasant to experience and negative in effect. Little attention has been focused on the positive potential of emotions aside from the encouragement to "get in touch with your feelings" in order to avoid repression, denial, or displacement. After emotions are exposed, the therapist and client assess them etiologically and functionally and develop cognitive and behavioral strategies to manage or eliminate them. Emotional expressions are considered the problem and faulty cognitions the cause. Cognitive restructuring of the faulty cognitions and changes in behavior are implemented to produce the desired change in emotional responses.

Constructivists consider emotions to be integral to the person–meaning process in which, throughout the life span, the individual continuously evolves through organization–reorganization of self. "Emotions somehow integrate past, present, and anticipated experiences" (Mahoney & Lyddon, 1988) and play a functional and transformational role in personal development. Intense feelings produce affective disequilibrium, a condition that, if sufficiently intense, affords access to core beliefs and state-dependent cognitions (Greenberg & Safran, 1989; Lyddon, 1990). In recognition of this role, constructivists encourage emotions and emotional expressions for the purpose of rendering deep-structure (Guidano, 1987) or second-order change. Efforts to control, diminish, or terminate emotional expressiveness are viewed as counterproductive. Guidano (1991) states,

> while thinking usually changes thoughts, only feeling can change emotions; *that is, only the emergence of new emotional experiences, resulting from the addition of new tonalities of feelings to the unitary configuration of core emotional themes, can affect self-regulation, modify current patterns of self-perception, and thus facilitate a reordering in personal meaning processes (p. 96).*

Clients are encouraged by constructivist therapists to explore, experience, and express an array of emotions through the use of experiential exercises (Mahoney, 1993). Guided discovery, imagery, imaginary dialogues (empty-chair technique), and rituals are representative methods for accessing affective states and promoting emotional arousal.

## Therapist Style of Intervention

Both traditional cognitive–behavioral and constructivist therapists promote a collaborative relationship with the client and both seek an understanding of the idiosyncratic meanings the client brings to therapy regarding him- or herself, the world, and the presenting factors prompting treatment. As noted earlier, however, the inquiry into idiosyncratic meanings is markedly different on the basis of divergent treatment goals. After an understanding of the client's unique views and meanings is achieved and initial assessment procedures have yielded content regarding cognitive, emotional, and behavioral functioning, the traditional cognitive–behavioral therapist proceeds to target cognitions for modification. Typically, the therapist educates the client regarding the role of cognitions and cognitive processes in human function and change (J. S. Beck, 1995; A. T. Beck et al., 1979; Granvold, 1994b). In addition, many traditional cognitive–behavioral therapists address social-learning-theory factors as well (e.g., conditioning, vicarious learning). Drawing from the cognitive–behavioral treatment model, the therapist and client collaboratively identify cognitions for modification—irrational beliefs, automatic thoughts, exaggerated or unrealistic expectations, faulty attributions, information-processing errors (e.g., personalization, dichotomous thinking). The therapist guides the client in forceful disputation of the "faulty thinking." Ellis (1994) identifies emotive and behavioral disputation methods in addition to cognitive challenge. The therapist assumes an active-directive stance and, depending on the unique therapeutic proclivities of the counselor, may be more softly Socratic (e.g., A. T. Beck) or may challengingly attack client cognitions Socratically or disputationally (e.g., Ellis). It should be noted that the questions asked may promote a more rationalist or alternatively constructivist view (Rosen, 1993). "What evidence supports that view?" "How could you test that belief?" These rationalist questions seek to expose distorted, "unrealistic" thinking. Constructivist questions may invite an alternative view or may challenge viability: "In what other ways could you view that?" "What are the consequences for you when you think of it that way?" Rosen (1993) notes that A. T. Beck's Socratic style evidences both types of questions in a manner that "smoothly integrates realism and constructivism without doing violence to either" (p. 407). Despite the inclusion of constructivist philosophy, a more distinct "problem" orientation is evident in the behavior of traditional cognitive–behavioral therapists, a "tighter" application of methodology, and a more directive approach than is typically displayed by constructivist therapists.

Constructivists are less directive in behavior and provide less information to their clients. The constructivist model is looser, and the therapist's behavior is correspondingly more lax. The constructivist seeks client change from within through collaboratively accessing the idiosyncratic meaning system of the client, a process that requires less directiveness. As noted by R. A. Neimeyer (1993c), however, the degree of structure varies among constructivist interventions. The application of more highly structured approaches (e.g., repertory grid technique) obligates the therapist to taking a more active, definitive role, whereas the opposite is true when less structured procedures are implemented (e.g., therapeutic story). Constructivists also place greater emphasis on life-span-development factors, including attachment processes (Guidano & Liotti, 1983; Liotti, 1991; Lyddon, 1993; Mahoney, 1988b; Young, 1990). Hence client developmental history receives more focused attention than typically occurs in traditional cognitive–behavioral treatment. R. A. Neimeyer (1993b) also noted that the constructivist's cognitive style is more metaphoric, approximate, exploratory, and intuitive. He further noted that another distinguishing characteristic of constructivist therapy influencing the style of intervention is its more extensive integration with couples and family systems therapies. He identifies constructivist family therapy as "one of the most vigorous areas of development in constructivist thinking over the last 10 years (Feixas, 1990; Hoffman, 1988; Procter, 1987)" (p. 167).

## Constructivist Interventions

As the literature shows, constructivism is more highly developed philosophically than methodologically. Addressing this issue, Mahoney (1986, 1991) proclaimed that he is opposed to technolatry and the possible "tyranny of technique." Other constructivists share this concern, calling for caution to avoid a proliferation of techniques (Guidano, 1991; Rosen, 1993). Mahoney (1988b) further posited that the reluctance of constructivists to write "cookbooks" on how to help may reflect the recognition that "skillful therapy (like all other complex skills) defies explicit mechanical operationalization" (p. 301). Techniques as tools of practice are not to be given greater credit than they deserve relative to other aspects of practice. Cognitivists ascribe great meaning to client and therapist characteristics and therapeutic-relationship development in producing effective therapeutic outcomes (A. T. Beck et al., 1990; Freeman, Pretzer, Fleming, & Simon, 1990; Guidano, 1991; Mahoney, 1991; Muran & Safran, 1993; R. A. Neimeyer, 1993b; Robins & Hayes, 1995; Rothstein & Robinson, 1991; Safran & Segal, 1990; Young, 1990). The development of a quality therapeutic relationship with such characteristics as acceptance, understanding, trust, and caring is a prime objective of constructivists.

Constructivist treatment methods have evolved in a rather deliberate fashion. The above considerations notwithstanding, it is fitting to note that the abstract nature of change sought calls for more creative than corrective interventions. Hence, the goals of constructivist therapy lend themselves less to narrowly definable techniques than do traditional cognitivist goals. Stated another way, the methods for producing first-order change may be easier to explicate than those for second-order change. The development of constructivist treatment techniques is relatively recent. Comparatively, traditional cognitivism is more methodologically mature in that it has been around longer.

Despite a reluctance to describe techniques and the more obscure nature of deep-structure functioning, constructivists have developed various interventions to promote second-order change or, as Mahoney (1991) states, to encourage psychological development. Intervention options include techniques such as movieola, stream of consciousness, repertory grid, downward arrow, externalizing the problem, symptom prescription, narrative writing, life review, reconstruction (constructivist cognitive restructuring), enactments (role plays, e.g., empty-chair technique), journaling, imagery and guided discovery, mirror exercises, embodiment exercises (promoting sensory and physical awareness), bibliotherapy, and therapeutic ceremonies or rituals. (See Mahoney, 1991, for summaries of selected techniques, including most of those noted above.)

Before proceeding to the application of constructivist techniques to clinical problems, it should be noted that constructivists are not opposed to the treatment of first-order change. Many issues expressed in therapy may be effectively treated through first-order change and, in these situations, the operative cognitive, behavioral, and other factors are targeted for intervention. When a determination is made that the issues confronting the client are not amenable to effective change through the modification of peripheral-level cognitions, core structure meanings (self-schemas, attachment and developmental experiences) become goals of intervention. As a point of comparison, the traditional cognitivist is more likely to begin with first-order change before shifting focus to second-order change, whereas the constructivist's tendency is to target second-order change first and attend to symptomatic complaints at the first-order level when the intensity of the "maladaptive functioning" demands measures that produce more immediate responses. This shift in focus from second-order to first-order change is based on the greater amenability of peripherally held cognitions to change vis-à-vis both the difficulty in accessing core cognitions and the tendency of the individual vigorously to resist change in core meaning structures.

The following sections discuss selected constructivist interventions. The goal of each procedure is to access and stimulate change in core meaning structures, although first-order change may be sought as well. Consistent with Mahoney (1991), the methods that follow abandon an explication of what to look for and what to change in favor of an invitation to the client to explore, examine, appraise, experience, define, and redefine themselves, their life experiences, and their directions in life both inside and outside the session.

## *Journaling*

Journaling has been used by many therapists as a vehicle for self-discovery, emotional stimulation, and greater resolution of current and past experiences (Mahoney, 1991; R. A. Neimeyer, 1993a, 1995a; Progoff, 1975, 1980; Rainer, 1978; White & Epston, 1990). Mahoney (1991) identified the use of separate categories in journaling, including current events, memories, life review, dreams and fantasies, and reflective "notes to myself."

Consider, for example, Joe, a 38-year-old client who was experiencing extreme loss, depression, hurt, and guilt over the recent termination of his 16-year marriage. When he did feel emotionally "up," he reported feelings of guilt because he hadn't "paid proper penitence for divorcing" (his strongly held religious teachings prohibited divorce with few exceptions). Joe reported no suicidal ideation, planning, or death wishes. Journaling was encouraged to address his range of current emotional responses and their corresponding cognitions, behaviors, and situational contexts (including interpersonal, physical, and physiological factors) and to access any beliefs related to his emotions and sense of self. Joe's "negative" emotions were not targeted initially for change despite his scoring in the moderate depression range of the Beck Depression Inventory (A. T. Beck et al., 1979). Rather, he was informed by the therapist that it is normal to experience a range of more or less comfortable emotions during the postdivorce adjustment process and that many people report feeling as if they are on an emotional roller coaster during this time. Content from Joe's journal was discussed at each session. He was guided in an ever developing awareness of the interrelatedness of feelings, cognitions, behavior, physical and physiological factors, interpersonal functioning and environment (e.g., discriminative stimuli, resources), and the powerful role that one's own descriptions of life events have on one's functioning. The influence of personal meanings on feelings as well as actions related to those feelings received particular attention. Joe concluded that a range of emotional responses to the divorce was acceptable to him "within limits" and for a time. In the fourth session, however, he solicited from the therapist a strategy to limit the frequency, intensity, and duration of his array of negative feelings to honor more effectively the limits he set for himself. He was concerned that his job was suffering as a result of his emotional state. Joe's journaling also exposed core schemata of a strongly negative and self-critical nature, content appropriate for direct exploration and restructuring.

## Constructivist Exploration and Restructuring

Therapist and client joined in the construction and reconstruction of meanings considered important in the client's life. The client was guided in this exploration and change through the use of Socratic questioning and occasional information sharing, interpretation (e.g., suggesting connections and relatedness), supportiveness, encouragement (e.g., coping statements), structuring (suggesting and discussing alternative techniques), and challenge (e.g., appraisal, judging, and decision making).

Joe's journaling proved to be an effective means to explore his personal development through the divorce process. The following excerpt presents the restructuring designed to meet Joe's desire to maintain his emotional reactions within self-defined tolerance limits and to promote change in core self-schemas related to the divorce.

*Therapist: How do you feel when you think, "I'm a total failure for getting a divorce and a heathen to boot?" [These statements were taken from Joe's journal entries and expressions in session. The question is an exploration of consequences.]*

*Joe: I feel a lot of self-loathing, depression, hurt, some loss ... sadness, I guess ... sadness.*

*Therapist: Any other feelings?*

*Joe: Yeah, I feel really guilty, guilty, you know, for not honoring my commitment to stay married . . . forever. And disappointment in myself for hurting everyone—Mary [ex-wife], my kids, and my folks. Then there's the church. I feel so bad about that. It's a sin to divorce, you know, a big sin. Guilt, I feel lots of guilt there.*

*Therapist: So you feel many different feelings related to various aspects of the divorce.*

*Joe: Yes.*

*Therapist: What thoughts do you have about these feelings, given that sometimes painful feelings are actually helpful in life?*

*Joe: I understand the idea that feelings help me change—maybe be a better person. But I get so down that I'm just immobilized, mired in my own pitiful existence.*

*Therapist: Are you meaning that you think the intensity of these negative feelings goes past the useful level?*

*Joe: Yes, that's what I think. I know I'm going to feel bad but I'd like to feel less bad.*

*Therapist: Going back to your earlier statements, "I'm a total failure for getting a divorce and a heathen," what other meanings exist for you related to the divorce?*

*Joe: Mary and I drifted apart; we developed very different interests and really did little together. We cared about each other as people, but the spark was gone and neither of us was interested in any further efforts to capture it and change. It was past the point of no return ... for us both, I think.*

*Therapist: Taking the description you just gave of your marriage, what appraisal could you make of the decision to divorce?*

*Joe: That it really wasn't so bad for us as a couple to divorce. It's the effects of it on our kids and all that is hurtful.*

*Therapist: What feelings tend to be related to this meaning?*

*Joe: I feel mostly just disappointment.*

*Therapist: And the depression, hurt, sense of loss, sadness, and guilt … do you feel them to any degree?*

*Joe: Yes, somewhat, but not nearly so intensely as before.*

*Therapist: So the focus on this latter meaning prompts you to feel less intense negative feelings.*

The restructuring of the meaning of Joe's divorce is viable both in terms of its *consequences* for Joe (less intense negative feelings) and its *correspondence* with the social system beliefs. The meaning created by Joe is his own construction; the therapist served as a guide in the process. For homework, Joe and the therapist discussed ways to promote the latter description of his marriage and ultimately the divorce. Joe decided to practice thinking of himself as a failure for divorcing, on a daily basis, followed by a shift to the restructured meaning of the divorce. He abandoned the construct "I am a failure" and adopted the construct "The divorce wasn't so bad for me or Mary. The marriage was pretty empty." He agreed to keep a record of his rehearsals and any spontaneous restructuring he might accomplish.

During the next treatment session, the issue of Joe's negative self-schemas related to the divorce was explored. He had previously referred to himself as a total failure and a heathen. Core beliefs discovered through the exploration revealed the following thoughts: I always screw up. I've always been a big disappointment to my folks. I am a flawed human being. I am a failure. I am bad. Joe had been reared by a critical, highly perfectionistic father who typically pointed out Joe's "failures" while overlooking his accomplishments. For example, as a high school quarterback, Joe threw six touchdown passes in one game. His father's comment to him after the game was "You should have thrown seven TD passes tonight; you missed a wide open receiver in the corner of the end zone in the third quarter." Such focus on negatives had left Joe feeling unworthy, unloved, and defective.

Joe's religious education emphasized the depravity of humans, the likelihood that all people will succumb to temptation and deserve to be punished for it, and that there are no exceptions to God's laws (one of which is "Thou shalt not divorce"). The messages from Joe's father coupled with his religious training produced early maladaptive schemas (EMSs)—"extremely stable and enduring themes that develop during childhood and are elaborated upon throughout an individual's lifetime" (Young, 1990, p. 9). Young notes that most EMSs are unconditional beliefs, self-perpetuating, change resistant, often the core of an individual's self-concept and view of the world, activated by environmental events, closely associated with high levels of affect arousal, and produced by dysfunctional experiences with parents, siblings, or peers early in life. The divorce activated a cluster of EMSs within Joe.

Treatment involved both abstract and concrete methods to promote schematic change (DeRubeis & Feeley, 1990). Deeper meanings were explored as noted above through journaling (which shifted to a life-review focus) and through probing and Socratic questioning (abstract). These procedures produced awareness of the repetitive criticism, devaluation, and rejection Joe experienced primarily from his father (although his mother was not as punitive and openly critical, she failed to protect Joe, according to recollection). Joe learned to judge his self-worth on the basis of his behavior and his behavior was repeatedly criticized.

At this point, intervention shifted from an abstract to a more concrete form. The therapist and Joe discussed the inherent flaws in making self-worth contingent upon behavior given that *all* humans are flawed, fallible, and "screwed up" and are destined to err, perform poorly, and fail in some ways. Joe learned that he was prone to expect criticism and lack of appreciation and that his expectations influenced his perceptions and ways of thinking (e.g., dichotomous thinking, personalization). He was instructed in the meanings, self-applications, and negative consequences of information-processing errors and how they tend to reinforce maladaptive self-schemas. He learned that his schemas reflected strongly held beliefs that he had learned long ago, were highly influential on his emotions and sense of self, had been repeatedly reinforced for years, and were highly resistive to change. The therapist informed Joe that schematic change is slow and demanding. It was important for Joe to understand that change might be slow in order to avoid his becoming discouraged and to establish that repetitive self-challenge and reconstruction of his schemas and the matrix of cognitive functions supporting them are a demanding, laborious process. Statements regarding his abilities encouraged him to achieve change (instillation of self-efficacy), and identification of the tremendous rewards that he would realize through effective change offered him support.

Schematic restructuring or reconstruction was implemented to challenge Joe's maladaptive schemas. Data for restructuring were taken from his journal and from a mood-tracking scale Joe completed three times daily. In each instance, Joe took superficial data inward; that is, he connected thoughts and feeling states with underlying beliefs. He challenged these beliefs on the basis of viability. This activity was possible, in part, because Joe understood the basis of his maladaptive schemas. The therapist, through use of Socratic methods, guided Joe in determining consequences associated with the schemas under consideration and the generation of new "scripts" that, by Joe's definition, produced more adaptive outcomes. Homework assignments involved cognitive restructuring (reframing) and behavioral strategies. For example, Joe engaged in activities in which he was least skilled to test his perfectionistic judgments and "failure" tolerance. These experiences allowed Joe opportunities to restructure his dysfunctional thoughts in vivo.

Treatment outcome was evaluated on two measures along with Joe's subjective reports of change. Joe's Beck Depression Inventory (BDI) score on day one of treatment was 32 (moderate depression). No suicidal ideation was reported. A mood scale was used to track his daily moods. The scale, a 10-point Likert scale (0 = terrible and 9 = very good), produced three ratings daily and gave Joe the freedom to identify all moods and a combination of moods. Joe marked his mood numerically on the scale and identified "thoughts, feelings, or events that might explain my mood" corresponding to the self-rating. Joe's ratings fluctuated significantly, even within a given day. His average after two weeks was 2.6. Joe was seen weekly for 12 weeks, bimonthly for 8 weeks, and at three-week intervals for 4 sessions leading to termination (a total of 20 sessions). At termination, Joe's BDI score was 8 (normal ups and downs) and his daily mood score average for the most recent three weeks was 6.2. Telephone and mail follow-up at six months after termination yielded a subjective report of "moderate" mood fluctuations (predominantly guilt and loss) and a mailed BDI yielded a score of 12 (mild mood disturbance). For a more comprehensive and in-depth exposure to schematic cognitive restructuring, see A. T. Beck et al. (1979); J. S. Beck (1995); Bricker, Young, and Flanagan (1993); Dowd and Pace (1989); Ellis and Dryden (1987); Freeman (1990, 1993); Robins and Hayes (1995); Safran and Segal (1990); Safran, Vallis, Segal, and Shaw (1986); and Young (1990).

## Experiential Techniques

Many experts support the use of experiential techniques such as role playing, psychodrama, behavior rehearsals, imagery and guided discovery, and empty chair (two-chair) for incorporation into cognitive therapy (Bricker et al., 1993; Daldrop, Beutler, Engle, & Greenberg, 1988; Greenberg, Safran, & Rice, 1989; Mahoney, 1991; Safran & Segal, 1990). The purpose of these techniques varies: the stimulation of feelings related to a life event, a preparatory rehearsal of a behavior (e.g., assertive expression), gaining a better understanding of another's thoughts or feelings (e.g., role reversal), and processing negative or ambivalent thoughts or feelings regarding past or contemporary experiences. Greenberg and colleagues (1989) state,

> the goal in experiential therapy is to discover and explore what one is experiencing and use this to inform choice and action. The therapist is reflective or experimental in style, guiding the client's attentional focus and making suggestions to stimulate new experience. The therapist refrains from being an expert on the client's experience and from interpreting the client's reasons for his or her experience or advising him or her on how to solve problems. (pp. 169–170)

Consider Rose, a 42-year-old corporate bookkeeper who repeatedly was sexually abused by her stepfather when she was from five to eight years of age. She presented for treatment unhappy with her marriage and life. She felt she was "merely existing." She believed that her marriage could be satisfying if she could be more emotionally intimate. Rose had three or four truly meaningful relationships with female friends, but her other relationships were superficial. Her treatment goals were to improve her marriage through self-improvement and to develop a greater "feeling for life." Assessment of her developmental history revealed explicit recollections of the sexual abuse, her mother's disbelief of the abuse when Rose reported it to her when it was occurring, and the sense of distrust and abandonment she felt in her relationship with her mother. (Rose had no relationship with her biological father because her mother refused to disclose his identity.)

Rose began keeping a journal to produce effective recall of abuse and her reports of the abuse to her mother. She found "little meaning" in the exercise and read from her diary with flat affect, although she stopped occasionally to express her hatred toward her stepfather and feelings of hurt, resentment, and anger toward her mother for failing to believe her or to protect her. These feelings were also expressed with flat affect. After several sessions, it was apparent that journaling alone was not likely to change her sense of well-being, to produce change in emotional intensity, or to promote effective movement toward greater resolution of abuse. (Absolute resolution is not a viable objective.)

Two-chair dialogue was implemented. Imagining her stepfather sitting opposite her in an empty chair, Rose was asked to express her thoughts and feelings to him. Her initial expressions were vague and showed little or no emotion. Rose was prompted to express her recollections of the abuse vividly and to allow herself to be aroused emotionally. After several iterations during which Rose's emotional level gradually increased, she tearfully and angrily "confronted" her stepfather. This process was applied to Rose's various recollections of the abuse. She also applied the method with respect to her mother. The two-chair technique stimulated heightened awareness of her thoughts and feelings toward both her stepfather and mother in relation to the abuse. Immediately following each performance, the therapist used probing and Socratic questioning to gather Rose's reactions to the experience both cognitively and emotionally and to explore any possible reconstruction of the abusive events and her responses to them. Attention was focused on her current expectations of her stepfather and mother, the likelihood of these expectations being met, and her action plans related to the abuse. This two-chair technique was repeated during 10 of 16 weekly sessions. The variable use of the technique was in response to Rose's occasional lack of interest in experiencing the level of emotional arousal inherent in the successful performance of the method. Rose ultimately reported greater closure with regard to the abuse. She recalled thinking about it less often. When she did think about it, it was less "unsettling." Significantly, Rose felt more intense emotions about various aspects of life, engaged in more frivolity, felt joyful more frequently, and felt more intimate and happier in her marriage.

## Conclusion

Are constructivist psychotherapies efficacious? To date, no major controlled outcome studies support the efficacy of the approaches (Mahoney, 1995b; R. A. Neimeyer, 1993a; R. A. Neimeyer & Mahoney, 1995). Furthermore, the data-collection methods and analytic procedures that characterize most psychotherapy research are being questioned by constructivists (R. A. Neimeyer, 1993a). Although obviously committed to effective outcomes, constructivists focus on treatment process. Adequate research methodologies and instruments have not been developed to meet the challenges of process evaluation. Constructivists tend to avoid being outcome driven, lest process be contaminated. As constructivist methods become further developed and treatment manuals produced, however, outcome studies will likely emerge.

Constructivism represents a growth spurt in the evolution of cognitivism. Negative consequences associated with rapid development have not been avoided by the constructivist movement. It is difficult to argue against the basic philosophy, but the translation of philosophy to practice is a major challenge, representing a "hard sell" for those weaned on social-learning theory and empiricism. The infusion of constructivist methods with more traditional cognitive approaches, however, is highly viable. The boundaries are both fuzzy and dynamic. Rich insights into human change and new practice methods can be anticipated from the ongoing dialogue between cognitive and constructivist psychotherapists.

# References

Anderson, R. E., & Carter, I. E. (1974). *Human behavior in the social environment: A social systems approach.* Chicago: Aldine.

Anderson, W. T. (1990). *Reality isn't what it used to be.* San Francisco: Harper & Row.

Baars, B. J. (1986). *The cognitive revolution in psychology.* New York: Guilford.

Bandura, A. (1969). *Principles of behavior modification.* New York: Holt, Rinehart & Winston.

Bandura, A. (1978). The self systems in reciprocal determinism. *American Psychologist, 33,* 344–358.

Beck, A. T. (1976). *Cognitive therapy and the emotional disorders.* Madison, CT: International Universities Press.

Beck, A. T., Freeman, A., & Associates. (1990). *Cognitive therapy of personality disorders.* New York: Guilford.

Beck, A. T., Rush, A. J., Shaw, B. G., & Emery, G. (1979). *Cognitive therapy of depression.* New York: Guilford.

Beck, A. T., & Weishaar, M. E. (1986). *Cognitive therapy.* Philadelphia: Center for Cognitive Therapy.

Beck, J. S. (1995). *Cognitive therapy: Basics and beyond.* New York: Guilford.

Bowlby, J. (1969). *Attachment and loss: Vol. 1. Attachment.* New York: Basic Books.

Bricker, D., Young, J. E., & Flanagan, C. M. (1993). Schema-focused cognitive therapy: A comprehensive framework for characterological problems. In K. T. Kuehlwein & H. Rosen (Eds.), *Cognitive therapies in action: Evolving innovative practice* (pp. 88–125). San Francisco: Jossey-Bass.

Cautela, J. R. (1966). The treatment of compulsive behavior by covert sensitization. *Psychological Record, 16,* 33–41.

Corsini, R. J. (1995). Putting the "B" in RET: It had to be. *Journal of Rational–Emotive and Cognitive–Behavior Therapy, 13,* 5–7.

Daldrop, R. J., Beutler, L. E., Engle, D., & Greenberg, L. S. (1988). *Focused expressive psychotherapy: Freeing the overcontrolled patient.* New York: Guilford.

Dattilio, F. M., & Freeman, A. (Eds.). (1994). *Cognitive–behavioral strategies in crisis intervention.* New York: Guilford.

Dember, W. N. (1974). Motivation and the cognitive revolution. *American Psychologist, 29,* 161–168.

DeRubeis, R. J., & Feeley, M. (1990). Determinants of change in cognitive therapy for depression. *Cognitive Therapy and Research, 14,* 469–482.

DiGiuseppe, R., & Linscott, J. (1993). Philosophical differences among cognitive behavioral therapists: Rationalism, constructivism, or both? *Journal of Cognitive Psychotherapy, 7,* 117–130.

Dowd, E. T., & Pace, T. M. (1989). The relativity of reality: Second-order change in psychotherapy. In A. Freeman, K. M. Simon, L. E. Beutler, & H. Arkowitz (Eds.), *Comprehensive handbook of cognitive therapy* (pp. 213–226). New York: Plenum.

D'Zurilla, T. J., & Goldfried, M. R. (1971). Problem-solving and behavior modification. *Journal of Abnormal Psychology, 78,* 107–126.

Efran, J. S., & Clarfield, L. E. (1993). Context: The fulcrum of cognitivist psychotherapy. *Journal of Cognitive Psychotherapy, 7,* 173–182.

Ellis, A. (1962). *Reason and emotion in psychotherapy.* New York: Lyle Stuart.

Ellis, A. (1989). Comments on my critics. In M. E. Bernard & R. DiGiuseppe (Eds.), *Inside ratio-*

*nal–emotive therapy* (pp. 199–233). San Diego, CA: Academic Press.

Ellis, A. (1990). Is rational emotive therapy (RET) "rationalist" or "constructivist"? In A. E. Ellis & W. Dryden (Eds.), *The essential Albert Ellis* (pp. 114–141). New York: Springer.

Ellis, A. (1993). Reflections on rational–emotive therapy. *Journal of Consulting and Clinical Psychology, 2,* 199–201.

Ellis, A. (1994). *Reason and emotion in psychotherapy.* New York: Birch Lane Press.

Ellis, A. (1995). Changing rational–emotive therapy (RET) to rational–emotive behavior therapy (REBT). *Journal of Rational–Emotive and Cognitive-Behavior Therapy, 13,* 85–89.

Ellis, A., & Dryden, W. (1987). *The practice of rational emotive therapy.* New York: Springer.

Feixas, G. (1990). Personal construct theory and the systematic therapies: Parallel or convergent trends? *Journal of Marital and Family Therapy, 16,* 1–20.

Franklin, C. (1995). Expanding the vision of the social constructionist debates: Creating relevance for practitioners. *Families in Society, 76,* 395–406.

Franks, C. M. (1995). RET, REBT and Albert Ellis. *Journal of Rational–Emotive and Cognitive–Behavior Therapy, 13,* 91–95.

Freeman, A. (1990). Cognitive therapy. In A. S. Bellack & M. Hersen (Eds.), *Handbook of comparative treatments for adult disorders* (pp. 64–87). New York: Wiley.

Freeman, A. (1993). A psychosocial approach for conceptualizing schematic development for cognitive therapy. In K. T. Kuehlwein & H. Rosen (Eds.), *Cognitive therapies in action: Evolving innovative practice* (pp. 54–87). San Francisco: Jossey-Bass.

Freeman, A., Pretzer, J., Fleming, B., & Simon, K. M. (1990). *Clinical applications of cognitive therapy.* New York: Plenum.

Granvold, D. K. (Ed.). (1994a). *Cognitive and behavioral treatment: Methods and applications.* Pacific Grove, CA: Brooks/Cole.

Granvold, D. K. (1994b). Concepts and methods of cognitive therapy. In D. K. Granvold (Ed.), *Cognitive and behavioral treatment: Methods and applications* (pp. 3–31). Pacific Grove, CA: Brooks/Cole.

Granvold, D. K. (1995). Cognitive treatment. In R. L. Edwards (Ed.), *Encyclopedia of social work* (19th ed., pp. 525–538). Washington, DC: NASW.

Granvold, D. K., & Wodarski, J. S. (1994). Cognitive and behavioral treatment: Clinical issues, transfer of training and relapse prevention. In D. K. Granvold (Ed.), *Cognitive and behavioral treatment: Methods and applications* (pp. 353–375). Pacific Grove, CA: Brooks/Cole.

Greenberg, L. S., & Safran, J. D. (1984). Integrating affect and cognition: A perspective on the process of therapeutic change. *Cognitive Therapy and Research, 8,* 559–578.

Greenberg, L. S., & Safran, J. D. (1987). *Emotion in psychotherapy.* New York: Guilford.

Greenberg, L. S., & Safran, J. D. (1989). Emotion in psychotherapy. *American Psychologist, 44,* 19–29.

Greenberg, L. S., Safran, J., & Rice, L. (1989). Experiential therapy: Its relation to cognitive therapy. In A. Freeman, K. M. Simon, L. E. Beutler, & H. Arkowitz (Eds.), *Comprehensive handbook of cognitive therapy* (pp. 169–187). New York: Plenum.

Guidano, V. F. (1987). *Complexity of the self.* New York: Guilford.

Guidano, V. F. (1988). A systems, process-oriented approach to cognitive therapy. In K. S. Dobson (Ed.), *Handbook of cognitive–behavioral therapies* (pp. 307–354). New York: Guilford.

Guidano, V. F. (1991). *The self in process: Toward a post-rationalist cognitive therapy.* New York: Guilford.

Guidano, V. F. (1995). Self-observation in constructivist psychotherapy. In R. A. Neimeyer & M. J. Mahoney (Eds.), *Constructivism in psychotherapy* (pp. 155–168). Washington, DC: American Psychological Association.

Guidano, V. F., & Liotti, G. (1983). *Cognitive processes and emotional disorders.* New York: Guilford.

Hayek, F. A. (1978). *New studies in philosophy, politics, economics, and the history of ideas.* Chicago: University of Chicago Press.

Hearn, G. (Ed.). (1969). *The general systems approach: Contributions toward an holistic conception of social work.* New York: Council on Social Work Education.

Hoffman, L. (1988). A constructivism position for family therapy. *Irish Journal of Psychology, 9,* 110–129.

Homme, L. E. (1965). Perspectives in psychology: XXIV: Control of coverants, the operants of the mind. *Psychological Record, 15,* 501–511.

Kelly, G. A. (1955). *The psychology of personal constructs.* New York: W. W. Norton.

Kingdon, D. G., & Turkington, D. (1994). *Cognitive–behavioral therapy of schizophrenia.* New York: Guilford.

Lazarus, A. A. (1995). REBT: A sign of evolution or devolution? An historical perspective. *Journal of Rational–Emotive and Cognitive–Behavior Therapy, 13,* 97–100.

Lazarus, R. S. (1982). Thoughts on the relations between emotion and cognition. *American Psychologist, 37,* 1019–1024.

Lazarus, R. S. (1989). Constructs of the mind in mental health and psychotherapy. In A. Freeman, K. M. Simon, L. E. Beutler, & H. Arkowitz (Eds.), *Comprehensive handbook of cognitive therapy* (pp. 99–121). New York: Plenum.

Linehan, M. M. (1993). *Cognitive–behavioral treatment of borderline personality disorder.* New York: Guilford.

Liotti, G. (1987). The resistance to change of cognitive structures: A counterproposal to psychoanalytic metapsychology. *Journal of Cognitive Psychotherapy, 1,* 87–104.

Liotti, G. (1991). Insecure attachment and agoraphobia. In C. M. Parkes, J. Stevenson-Hinde, & P. Marris (Eds.), *Attachment across the life cycle* (pp. 216–233). London: Routledge.

Lyddon, W. J. (1990). First- and second-order change: Implications for rationalist and constructivist cognitive therapies. *Journal of Counseling and Development, 69,* 122–127.

Lyddon, W. J. (1993). Developmental constructivism: An integrative framework for psychotherapy practice. *Journal of Cognitive Psychotherapy, 7,* 217–224.

Mahoney, M. J. (1977). Reflection on the cognitive-learning trend in psychotherapy. *American Psychologist, 32,* 5–13.

Mahoney, M. J. (1986). The tyranny of technique. *Counseling and Values, 30,* 169–174.

Mahoney, M. J. (1988a). The cognitive sciences and psychotherapy: Patterns in a developing relationship. In K. S. Dobson (Ed.), *Handbook of cognitive therapies* (pp. 357–386). New York: Guilford.

Mahoney, M. J. (1988b). Constructive metatheory: II. Implications for psychotherapy. *International Journal of Personal Construct Psychology, 1,* 299–315.

Mahoney, M. J. (1988c). The continuing evolution of cognitive therapies. *Cognitive Behaviorist, 10,* 7–9.

Mahoney, M. J. (1991). *Human change processes: The scientific foundations of psychotherapy.* New York: Basic Books.

Mahoney, M. J. (1993). Introduction to special section: Theoretical developments in the cognitive psychotherapies. *Journal of Consulting and Clinical Psychology, 61,* 187–193.

Mahoney, M. J. (1995a). Continuing evolution of the cognitive sciences and psychotherapies. In R. A. Neimeyer & M. J. Mahoney (Eds.), *Constructivism in psychotherapy* (pp. 39–67). Washington, DC: American Psychological Association.

Mahoney, M. J. (1995b). The cognitive and constructive psychotherapies: Contexts and challenges. In M. J. Mahoney (Ed.), *Cognitive and constructive psychotherapies: Theory, research, and practice* (pp. 195–208). New York: Springer.

Mahoney, M. J., & Lyddon, W. J. (1988). Recent developments in cognitive approaches to counseling and psychotherapy. *Counseling Psychologist, 16,* 190–234.

Mahoney, M. J., Lyddon, W. J., & Alford, D. J. (1989). An evaluation of the rational–emotive theory of psychotherapy. In M. E. Bernard & R. DiGiuseppe (Eds.), *Inside rational–emotive therapy: A critical appraisal of the theory and therapy of Albert Ellis* (pp. 69–94). New York: Academic Press.

Mahoney, M. J., Miller, H. M., & Arciero, G. (1995). Constructive metatheory and the nature of mental representation. In M. J. Mahoney (Ed.), *Cognitive and constructive psychotherapies: Theory, research, and practice* (pp. 103–120). New York: Springer.

Maturana, H. R. (1988). Reality: The search for objectivity, or the quest for a compelling argument. *Irish*

*Journal of Psychology, 9,* 25–82.

Maturana, H. R., & Varela, F. J. (1980). *Autopoiesis and cognition: The realization of the living.* Boston: Reidel.

Meichenbaum, D. (1977). *Cognitive-behavior modification: An integrative approach.* New York: Plenum.

Merluzzi, T. V., & Boltwood, M. D. (1989). Cognitive assessment. In A. Freeman, K. M. Simon, L. E. Beutler, & H. Arkowitz (Eds.), *Comprehensive handbook of cognitive therapy.* New York: Plenum.

Merluzzi, T. V., Glass, C. R., & Genest, M. (Eds.). (1981). *Cognitive assessment.* New York: Guilford.

Muran, J. C., & Safran, J. D. (1993). Emotional and interpersonal considerations in cognitive therapy. In K. T. Kuehlwein & H. Rosen (Eds.), *Cognitive therapies in action: Evolving innovative practice* (pp. 185–212). San Francisco: Jossey-Bass.

Neimeyer, G. J. (Ed.). (1993). *Constructivist assessment: A casebook.* Newbury Park, CA: Sage.

Neimeyer, G. J., & Neimeyer, R. A. (1993). Defining the boundaries of constructivist assessment. In G. J. Neimeyer (Ed.), *Constructivist assessment: A casebook* (pp. 1–30). Newbury Park, CA: Sage.

Neimeyer, R. A. (1993a). An appraisal of constructivist psychotherapies. *Journal of Consulting and Clinical Psychology, 61,* 221–234.

Neimeyer, R. A. (1993b). Constructivism and the cognitive psychotherapies: Some conceptual and strategic contrasts. *Journal of Cognitive Psychotherapy, 7,* 159–171.

Neimeyer, R. A. (1993c). Constructivist psychotherapy. In K. T. Kuehlwein & H. Rosen (Eds.), *Cognitive therapies in action: Evolving innovative practice* (pp. 268–300). San Francisco: Jossey-Bass.

Neimeyer, R. A. (1995a). Client-centered narratives in psychotherapy. In R. A. Neimeyer & M. J. Mahoney (Eds.), *Constructivism in psychotherapy* (pp. 231–246). Washington, DC: American Psychological Association.

Neimeyer, R. A. (1995b). Constructivist psychotherapies: Features, foundations, and future directions. In R. A. Neimeyer & M. J. Mahoney (Eds.), *Constructivism in psychotherapy* (pp. 11–38). Washington, DC: American Psychological Association.

Neimeyer, R. A., & Harter, S. (1988). Facilitating individual change in personal construct theory. In G. Dunnett (Ed.), *Working with people* (pp. 174–185). London: Routledge & Kegan Paul.

Neimeyer, R. A., & Mahoney, M. J. (1995). *Constructivism in psychotherapy.* Washington, DC: American Psychological Association.

O'Hara, M., & Anderson, W. T. (1991, September–October). Welcome to the postmodern world. *Family Therapy Networker, 15,* 18–25.

Olsen, M. (1968). *The process of social organization.* New York: Holt, Rinehart and Winston.

Parkes, C. M., Stevenson-Hinde, J., & Marris, P. (Eds.). (1991). *Attachment across the life cycle.* London: Routledge.

Popper, K. R. (1972). *Objective knowledge: An evolutionary approach.* London: Oxford University Press.

Procter, H. G. (1987). Change in the family construct system. In R. A. Neimeyer & G. J. Neimeyer (Eds.), *Personal construct therapy casebook* (pp. 153–171). New York: Springer.

Progoff, I. (1975). *At a journal workshop.* New York: Dialogue House Library.

Progoff, I. (1980). *The practice of process mediation.* New York: Dialogue House Library.

Rainer, T. (1978). *The new diary: How to use a journal for self-guidance and expanded creativity.* Los Angeles: Jeremy P. Tarcher.

Rehm, L. P. (1977). A self-control model of depression. *Behavior Therapy, 8,* 787–804.

Robins, C. J., & Hayes, A. M. (1995). An appraisal of cognitive therapy. In M. J. Mahoney (Ed.), *Cognitive and constructive psychotherapies: Theory, research, and practice* (pp. 41–65). New York: Springer.

Rosen, H. (1993). Developing themes in the field of cognitive therapy. In K. T. Kuehlwein & H. Rosen (Eds.), *Cognitive therapies in action: Evolving innovative practice* (pp. 403–434). San Francisco: Jossey-Bass.

Rothstein, M. M., & Robinson, P. J. (1991). The therapeutic relationship and resistance to change in cognitive therapy. In T. M. Vallis, J. L. Howes, & P. C. Miller (Eds.), *The challenge of cognitive therapy* (pp. 43–55). New York: Plenum.

Safran, J. D., & Greenberg, L. S. (1986). Hot cognition and psychotherapy process: An information processing/ecological perspective. In P. C. Kendall (Ed.), *Advances in cognitive–behavioral research and therapy* (Vol. 5, pp. 143–177). Orlando, FL: Academic Press.

Safran, J. D., & Segal, Z. V. (1990). *Interpersonal process in cognitive therapy.* New York: Basic Books.

Safran, J. D., Vallis, T. M., Segal, Z. V., & Shaw, B. F. (1986). Assessment of core cognitive processes in cognitive therapy. *Cognitive Therapy and Research, 10,* 509–526.

Saleebey, D. (1992). Introduction: Power in the people. In D. Saleebey (Ed.), *The strengths perspective in social work practice* (pp. 3–17). White Plains, NY: Longman.

Stern, D. N. (1985). *The interpersonal world of the infant.* New York: Basic Books.

Von Bertalanffy, L. (1967). *Robots, men and minds: Psychology in the modern world.* New York: George Braziller.

von Glasersfeld, E. (1984). An introduction to radical constructivism. In P. Watzlawick (Ed.), *The invented reality* (pp. 17–40). New York: W. W. Norton.

Watzlawick, P., Weakland, J. H., & Fisch, R. (1974). *Change: Principles of problem formation and problem resolution.* New York: W. W. Norton.

White, M., & Epston, D. (1990). *Narrative means to therapeutic ends.* New York: W. W. Norton.

Wilson, G. T., & Fairburn, C. (1993). Cognitive treatments of eating disorders. *Journal of Consulting and Clinical Psychology, 61,* 261–269.

Young, J. E. (1990). *Cognitive therapy for personality disorders: A schema-focused approach.* Sarasota, FL: Professional Resource Exchange.

# 7

# Trauma, Healing, and the Narrative Emplotment of Loss

*Robert A. Neimeyer & Alan E. Stewart*

In recent years, constructivist and narrative approaches have begun to challenge the objectivist foundations of clinical practice, placing renewed emphasis on the personal and communal processes of meaning making and their transformation in psychotherapy (Franklin, 1995; Neimeyer & Mahoney, 1995). However, with some notable exceptions, the constructivist paradigm has been better articulated at an epistemological than at a strategic level, contributing to the frequently heard criticism that constructivism is "long on theory and short on practice" (Minuchin, 1991; Neimeyer, 1997).

The goal of this chapter is to help close this gap between theory and practice by considering a form of psychological distress that has become the focus of considerable attention—namely, post-traumatic stress disorder (PTSD)—and by describing a constructivist/narrativist approach to its conceptualization, assessment, and treatment. In so doing, we hope to illustrate the applicability of an abstract framework to a concrete problem and add to the fund of concepts and procedures for understanding and intervening in the "real world" of human suffering.

We will approach this task first by discussing the narrative nature of existence and narrative accounts of problems in living. A narrative conceptualization of post-traumatic stress disorder is presented, and implications of this model for psychotherapy are discussed. The chapter concludes with a case study illustrating this narrative model, together with implications for clinical assessment and psychotherapy.

## The Narrative Nature of Existence

Sarbin (1986) asserted that events in the world, or historical acts, are understood in the context in which they occur. This process of contextualizing historical acts constitutes a narrative. Emplotment, the activity and operation of a narrative, organizes the life events and experiences into a coherent, ever-evolving life story. These stories help a person to understand and respond adaptively to life's occurrences. Some regard narrative to be the basic way in which life experiences are organized meaningfully over time (Atkinson, 1995; Bruner, 1986; Polkinghorne, 1988, 1991; Sarbin, 1986). Russell and Van den Broek (1992) similarly emphasized that people store, organize, and relate to phenomena they encounter through schemata that assume a narrative form. Polkinghorne (1988, 1991) also described how schematic knowing processes help to pull together and configure bits of information. In reviewing the work of the French psychoanalyst Pierre Janet, Van der Kolk and Van der Hart (1991) noted that memories for events in life are stored in a narrative, contextualized form.

We view narratives as being associated with the psychological roles or situated identities we enact in various life contexts. According to this role-theory conceptualization of narratives (McCall & Simmons, 1978), the person who (willingly or unwillingly) assumes a role typically constructs a story that relates it to his or her preexisting sense of self or adopts one of the countless variations of the classical, timeless mythic narratives that organize and attribute significance to life events (Atkinson, 1995). Narratives provide structures of meaning that allow the person to understand both the role and the wider social or cultural plot of which it is a part.

As part of our role-theoretic view, we believe that a self, consisting of the individual's awareness of his or her identity, continuity, and self-images (Chapman, 1985; Guidano, 1995a), emerges as the person repeatedly, progressively, and successively emplots roles through narratives. A person can assume many possible selves (Markus & Nurius, 1986) as that person takes up roles and forms narratives to emplot them. The selves are maintained and supported to the extent that roles remain available and narratives assist the individual in understanding and fulfilling role requirements. Individuals are motivated also to maintain and enhance their idealized self-conceptualizations (McCall & Simmons, 1978). Although some narratives are specific to particular roles in a person's repertoire, a primary narrative coordinates the meaning-making activities of these component selves. The primary narrative corresponds to the "I," or self, as the storyteller. The component narratives emplot the "mes," or selves, as objects in their respective roles (Mancuso & Sarbin, 1983; Mead, 1934).

## Narrative Conceptualizations of Problems in Living

Although narrative descriptions of life and psychotherapy have proven attractive to clinical audiences on both the literal and metaphorical levels (Terrell & Lyddon, 1995; White & Epston, 1990), narrative descriptions of the way problems in living arise and endure are somewhat lacking. For instance, Gustafson (1995) noted that problematic periods in life are characterized by gaps in an individual's life story. White and Epston (1990) describe how problems arise when narratives no longer reflect lived experiences. In such cases, a person "gets lost" using his or her own "road map." Polkinghorne (1991) maintains that narratives "decompose" or "disintegrate" when they become unable to emplot and unify new or forgotten phenomena. This threat to the narrative wholeness of the self-concept results in anxiety as the person is unable to make sense of some event in the world (see Kelly, 1955).

For Wigren (1994), problems ensue when narratives are incomplete, either because a narrative has not been developed or because it has been interrupted or otherwise prevented from operating in its usual way. Thus, psychotherapeutic interventions might benefit from the diagnosis of a narrative's incompleteness. For example, the affectless sexual-abuse survivor may need help dealing with memories of the trauma in an effort to complete the story of the abuse affectively. Subsequent activities in psychotherapy such as storytelling or journal writing could serve the vital intrapersonal function of helping establish a continuity in the client's lived experience (Neimeyer, 1995).

The common feature of these explanations involves the suspension or malfunctioning of the narrative, which leaves the individual unable to finish some event in the past and somewhat inflexible in meaningfully construing ongoing events in the present. These accounts also share the similarity of treating narratives and life stories as *products* of meaning-making processes. However, regarding the trauma victim as suffering simply from a "broken" or "incomplete" story may distract clinicians from focusing upon the distressed *person* who created the narrative or is living with its limitations.

## Challenge of Trauma to Narrative Development

The traumatic experience may manifest itself at a level more basic and deep than that at which narratives operate. Fundamental memory processes of coding, consolidation, and retrieval that constitute the substrates of narratives (Kotre, 1995; Mancuso & Sarbin, 1983; Siegel, 1995) may remain both fragmented and unintegrated with the more factual, declarative, and descriptive accounts of the trauma (Siegel, 1995; Van der Kolk & Van der Hart, 1991). That is, the heightened autonomic arousal and speechless terror of the trauma attach themselves to the memory of the event and in so doing *become* the memory. This sustained level of arousal may also preclude fuller elaborative processing of the trauma as well as the person's development of a narrative account of the trauma.

Memory research consistent with the tradition of Janet emphasizes that both the traumatic event and life thereafter are experienced as painfully fragmented and unorganized, that is, as dissociated or shattered (Siegel, 1995; Van der Hart & Brown, 1992; Van der Kolk & Van der Hart, 1991). Rather than a single self holding traumatic memories at bay or processing them in a fragmented manner, the dissociative perspective suggests the existence of a traumatized self (or selves) that must be integrated with the victim's set of core selves for healing to occur. In summary, the traumatic experience not only disrupts or damages the victim's narrative stream of consciousness, but may also fundamentally challenge the unity of the victim's selfhood. A narrative conceptualization of trauma, therefore, would be incomplete if it did not acknowledge the existence of both multiple selves and corresponding narratives.

# Narrative Conceptualization of Trauma

Consistent with our role-theoretic conceptualization of narratives, a person who experiences a particular event as traumatic (in either the normative or idiopathic sense) develops the role of victim, mourner, injured, maimed, survivor, refugee, and the like in the context of that experience. The person participating in the trauma is assigned one or more of these roles without an opportunity to develop the role in the usual way, that is, successively to generate narratives for the role and plot.

A new narrative (trauma narrative) and self (traumatized self) emerge. The role and narrative create a "traumatic world" for the person. The traumatic self differs from other selves in that it was created with psychological processes that operated very differently from the way they operated when the person was not involved in defending, escaping, surviving, or being victimized. The traumatic self is forged from psychological processes (sensation, perception, and cognition) that were hypervigilantly channeled, operating in primitive (yet adaptive) dichotomous modes, and that involved "hot," survival-based emotions. The traumatic self thereafter operates in a psychologically consistent way with the processes that existed at the time the self was created.

As an essential part of the person, the traumatic self constrains the other possible selves. That is, as long as the traumatic self exists in its original form, the cognitive, perceptual, and emotional processes invoked during its creation place limits on psychological processes available to the premorbid selves (Klion & Pfenninger, 1996). The narrative, meaning-making processes of the former selves become more like those of the traumatic self. Subjectively, a trauma victim may feel as if "I'm not the person I once was."

The traumatized person is not without a narrative as much as he or she is faced with a traumatic narrative that, by definition, is very different from the primary, coordinating story. The traumatic narrative is "written" with symbols and languages very different from the premorbid, primary life text. This narrative may be created with memories of sights, sounds, smells, and feelings experienced during the trauma. It may also specify rules for how to relate to other persons who were encountered during the trauma. This narrative is in part problematic because, unlike all other narratives in the victim's repertoire, the trauma narrative is not elaborated or developed actively and deliberately by the person at the time of the trauma. Facing familiar roles with constrained narratives may create a potent sense of loss of former selves.

A special relationship between the traumatic role and the narrative develops during the experience. Although the traumatic self emerges from the melding of the role and narrative, the traumatic narrative performs a special function that is uncharacteristic of other texts or scripts. In trauma, a very strong feedback loop is formed between the operation of the narrative and the assumption of the traumatic role subsequent to the original trauma. This means that as the traumatic narrative operates, traumatic roles are developed in situations in which the person previously did not create them. The traumatic self experiences these events as if they were the original occasion in which the traumatic role was instantiated.

# Psychotherapy

This conceptualization of traumatic narrative emphasizes two issues in providing psychotherapeutic interventions for trauma victims. First, the conceptualization places primacy upon the victim's selfhood and suggests that basic psychological processes of the person may be temporarily or permanently altered by the traumatic experience. Second, psychotherapy with the traumatized person involves not only diagnosing the way the person's primary narrative is incomplete or damaged, but also involves finding ways to join the traumatic self and associated narrative with the pre-existing selves and primary narrative. Here, the emphasis is not only on ameliorative goals (e.g., the reduction of symptoms) and restorative goals (e.g., the return to pre-morbid functioning), but also on elaborative goals (such as the construction of new, possible selves) (Harter & Neimeyer, 1995). Attention to the traumatic past is supplemented with helping the individual develop beyond the point at which the trauma was encountered.

Regarding general approaches to treatment, a consensus is emerging that psychotherapy of PTSD may be both multimodal and multiphasic (Hyer, 1994). During active phases of treatment, psychotherapy optimally occurs on at least two general levels (Hyer, 1994; Stewart, 1995). The first level involves intense emotional exploration of the sequence of traumatic events and of their impact on the victim's life through the use of techniques such as hypnosis, imagery, awareness of sensorial aspects of the trauma, and so forth. In many respects, work at this level involves the exploration and expression of the victim's traumatic self.

The second tier of treatment involves more reflective and integrative work. Here, the person may move in and out of the trauma experience to weave together initially disparate identities. The activity of experiencing and subsequent reflecting is particularly consistent with Guidano's (1995b) "movieola" technique, in which the client alternates between experiencing some aspect of existence and reflecting on it during the session. Narrative therapy techniques and therapeutic work on narratives may be focused on either or both of these levels.

Various specific narrative approaches to psychotherapy and to the treatment of trauma have been developed by constructivist scholars. Several of these approaches are illustrated in the case study below, which traces the course of a relatively brief therapy for PTSD along narrative lines.

# Reweaving the Trauma Narrative: The Emplotment of Loss

Mark,[1] a 42-year-old-man, was referred to me (the lead author) for therapy by a regional managed-care organization for the treatment of a cluster of personal, occupational, and relational problems following a violent and traumatic assault he had suffered approximately one year earlier. At the time of the attack, he was working for a

---

1. Identifying information has been altered to preserve the client's anonymity.

utility company repairing electrical lines, a job he had held successfully for 14 years. While making a residential call, he was approached by four armed young men who demanded his wallet; when he raised his hands, they pistol whipped him to the ground and proceeded to beat him savagely until he lost consciousness. As a result of the assault, he suffered extensive damage to his abdomen and especially to his head, requiring a total of seven facial and dental reconstructive surgeries to restore a normal appearance. Although surgical interventions were largely successful, subsequent neuropsychological examinations underscored significant continuing decrements in verbal and nonverbal memory functions and problem-solving abilities, which conflicted with the expected recovery curve following head injury of the type that he had suffered. Mark's fragmentary memory of the assault itself and his difficulty in formulating viable responses to interpersonal difficulties were consistent with this evaluation, as described below.

In his own terms, Mark reported feeling "just confused" by his post-assault adjustment. He noted that he was "pissed off all the time" and felt an urge to "hurt people who harass others." This sense of barely suppressed rage in interpersonal situations that he viewed as involving victimization was a primary concern to Mark and those involved with his treatment. The significance of this issue was underscored by his report of an incident in which he "blanked out" and physically accosted a belligerent customer in a drugstore who he perceived was "attacking" a sales clerk. Despite his generally congenial and cooperative demeanor during therapy, Mark noted that he always felt "a fire burning inside" that was easily kindled by encounters with persons he perceived as "predators."

Although Mark's anger and its potential for physical expression clearly commanded therapeutic attention, he also complained about various other symptoms compatible with a PTSD diagnosis that he had experienced during several weeks of inpatient psychiatric treatment for anxiety and depression following his medical stabilization. These symptoms included intrusive recollections of his assault, often accompanied by spontaneous crying and elevated anxiety; marked sleep disturbance; chronic physiological activation (which he described as "shaking inside"); and general avoidance of social situations. Mark also reported difficulty concentrating on reading, television, and other activities for extended periods, in part because of intrusive daydreams regarding the assault and his fantasized revenge against his assailants. Psychological testing confirmed his difficulties with elevated anxiety and depression and uncontrolled anger. Mark's previously troubled marriage had disintegrated into a formal separation under the pressures of his immobilization and unpredictability. Also, he had been placed on indefinite medical leave from his job out of concern for Mark as well as for those with whom he came into contact.

## History of Treatment

Despite a history of periodic panic attacks prior to his assault, Mark's first contact with the mental health system came during his inpatient hospitalization following the trauma. Mark remembered the five-week program with some ambivalence, noting that he earned the reputation for being passive–aggressive as a result of his resentful compliance with staff demands. He was subsequently discharged to the care of a psychiatrist and psychologist who followed him for several more months in outpatient treatment. Mark reported no gains from the antidepressant medication prescribed by the physician, an impression that was corroborated in the psychiatrist's treatment summary. Moreover, the cognitive–behavioral strategies employed by Mark's psychotherapist (e.g., relaxation training, response prevention through avoidance of situations likely to trigger his anger, and rational disputation of his self-defeating thoughts) had produced only transitory symptom relief, contributing to Mark's sense that his "life was closing in," as if he were being "forced to live in a closet." Thus, after a year of marginal therapeutic progress, Mark was referred to me for more specialized outpatient treatment of his post-traumatic adjustment.

As Mark recounted his story in our first session, I was struck by his saying, "I don't know myself anymore; I feel like I'm losing my mind. It's like I've lost who I *was*." As I encouraged him to elaborate on this remark, he stated, "I don't know if I can get back to who I was, but I don't like what I am. It's like I can't remember the piece that has consumed me." This theme of disrupted identity and lost memory had apparently been neglected in previous therapy, which was more focused on symptom relief than on helping Mark reconstitute a viable new sense of self to accommodate the trauma while not confining him to it. I offered Mark an alternative that required greater contact with and temporary immersion in his traumatic experiences. Mark courageously opted for this new alternative.

## *Jigsaw Memories*

The first step in Mark's treatment was to facilitate a deeper exploration of his trauma memories. Constructivist scholars have developed several methods that are useful in this regard. Stewart (1995) helped combat victims contact their traumatic experiences through writing and drawing exercises that require victims to focus on progressively more detailed aspects of the trauma. Similarly, Gonçalves (1995) proposed a five-step process to assist victims in recalling the sensorial, affective, and cognitive aspects of traumas so these aspects may be incorporated into narrative accounts. Gonçalves (1995) first helps clients recall narratives and the events they emplotted. Next, clients focus on the objective aspects of events, then on how they were subjectively experienced. In the fourth step, Gonçalves helps clients find alternative ways in which narratives may emplot experiences and events. Finally, the new narratives are tested in real life. Aspects of these interventions were used in Mark's psychotherapy.

In the first step toward exploring Mark's trauma memories, I metaphorically described his recollection of the assault as a jigsaw puzzle from which some of the pieces seemed to be missing. He felt this was an appropriate image, saying he could recall isolated fragments of the attack and its aftermath, but "the whole picture didn't come together." This suggested a collaboratively designed homework assignment, which consisted of Mark writing these fragmentary memories, sensory details, and the rest on separate index cards and then adding new details as they came to mind. He was asked to reconstitute a more coherent narrative of the attack sequence by arranging the cards in chronological order and by concentrating on any gaps in order to bridge these fragments. Because I anticipated that this immersion in the trauma would likely be distressing to him, we constructed a list of time-out strategies he could use to break the tension associated with the task (in his case, listening to classical music, walking, and so forth).

Mark faithfully tackled the assignment, despite his self-consciousness about his writing—something he had done relatively little of since completing high school 24 years previously. He brought in the completed narrative the following week scrawled in red ink on a series of index cards. It began,

> *Walking toward the pole with the transformer, noticed four men [here he crossed out "men" and substituted "things"] under streetlight. When I got to pole they came running toward me spread out where I couldn't run. They came up to me and put a 9 mm Ruger Automatic to my head. Said what you got, raised my hands, said take it. When they got what they wanted, they hit me in the head with the gun and I went to the ground. He said you motherfucker before he hit me on the ground. Remember flashes of bright light; it was so bright I couldn't see anything. All these guys were kicking me in the head. But one in particular was running back and jumping on my face. I remember feeling intense rage mostly at the one jumping on me. I was thinking how I could hurt him easy if I could get up. I decided it would be worth getting shot just to get one good shot to his nose with the palm of my hand with an upward thrust. I decided I was going to do this no matter what, but every time I raised up I would get knocked back to the ground. I tried many times to do this, I would guess 20 times.*

In discussing his construction of this account in our subsequent session, Mark noted that he "remembered things he couldn't before." As new recollections "came to him every day" he worked on the narrative. In particular, he became aware of sensory details of the attack as well as his efforts to resist his assailants. For example, he described how he "just remembered the heel of the cowboy boot [worn by his most vicious assailant] coming down. The heel is very vivid. . . . I'll never forget it as long as I live." The only feeling he could recall during the attack was rage, though he acknowledged, "I should have been scared."

As we considered the fragmentation of memories associated with the trauma, we gradually broadened the discussion to include the continuing sense of fragmentation in his life. Mark connected this with his subsequent disruption of interpersonal relationships as he not only "holed up inside himself," but experienced others distancing from him in response to his "spaciness" and "craziness." As he noted, this feeling of being a stranger to others as well as to himself was "more a feeling than a thought," but one that had remained virtually unchanged by the passage of time since the assault.

### Biographical Grid

Although Mark acknowledged that "rehashing and figuring out the incident with somebody else almost made him feel good," it was clear that more than a reconstruction of the trauma event itself was necessary to give Mark a greater sense of wholeness and meaning. I therefore introduced a second strategy, the biographical grid

(Neimeyer, 1985a), as a way to assess and focus therapeutic attention on the broader life narrative of which the trauma episode was part. Stewart (1995) used similar methods successfully in therapy with combat veterans. Her approach involved having victims create written character sketches of themselves at various points in their lives, including during and after the combat trauma. These sketches are compared and contrasted as a way to enhance the client's sense of continuity across both time and situations. Sewell (1996) likewise found the grid technique helpful in documenting the isolation of an unelaborated traumatic self among survivors of mass murder.

As a variant of the repertory-grid technique (Fransella & Bannister, 1977; Kelly, 1955; Neimeyer, 1993), the biographical grid is administered in three steps: identification of significant life events or stages, elicitation of life themes or personal meanings, and weaving themes through events.

**Identifying significant life events or stages**. This narrative variation of the grid procedure begins by identifying with the client particular autobiographical memories that anchor his or her sense of identity at various points in the life trajectory. These may include episodic memories (e.g., "when my brother died"), significant ages corresponding to marker events (e.g., at age 18 upon graduation from high school), or even random intervals (e.g., ages in five-year intervals beginning at age 1). This material provides a sampling of a client's different selves before the trauma experience. In addition to sampling anchor events from the individual's past, including the trauma, it is also useful to include the self at present and a projection of a future self (e.g., five years from now) to assess the perceived continuity of these horizons. Finally, the inclusion of an "ideal self" element provides a convenient way to analyze the positivity or negativity of the various situated identities on the grid. Although standardization of these elements may be desirable in research contexts, in clinical settings it is usually more valuable to identify life events or stages that have special relevance for the person whose life narrative is being assessed.

With Mark, I began my inquiry by asking, "From your early childhood, what events stand out for you in shaping your identity in important ways or representing who you were at that time?" Mark immediately responded by recounting an earlier vicarious trauma in his life, which occurred when he was seven years old. At that time his father—who was working in the same capacity with the same electric company for which Mark now worked—was severely injured in an accident that sent potentially lethal levels of voltage coursing through his body. Although he was "not expected to live," Mark's father stubbornly held on and was rushed from the emergency clinic in their small town to an urban medical center several hours away for extended treatment. He ended up being treated in an inpatient facility for nine months, during which time Mark's mother moved to that city to assist in caring for her husband. Mark, left in the custody of a little-known aunt and uncle, had no visits to or from his parents during these months and was "protected" from discussion of his father's "sickness" or mother's whereabouts. Not surprisingly, he resonated to my reflection that it seemed that he was "almost orphaned" by this tragedy, elaborating on his feeling "pretty insecure," to the point of bedwetting, which led to teasing by his cousins.

His sense of himself at age seven, when his father was injured, thus became one of the episodic identities to be used in the grid task.

Other significant anchor points for his construction of self were elicited in this same way. For example, Mark nominated his later childhood and early adolescence, when he played Little League and Pony League baseball, as important in helping him pull out of the loneliness and fearfulness of his early childhood years. With a smile, he also remembered his early childhood at age three or four, when he independently rode his tricycle home from the neighborhood swimming pool. While his "disappearance" terrified his mother at the time, he recalled that they were able to laugh at this display of youthful initiative in later years, giving the memory a positive valence in the present. High school was significant for him because of the constant "bullying" by others he was subjected to as a relatively "scrawny" 17-year-old. He was able to end this persistent abuse by "picking up anything he could find and hitting them with it." Though Mark earned the reputation of "being crazy," he "got his licks in" and the bullying stopped. The parallels between Mark's handling of this high school bullying and his spontaneous response to the assault one year ago were striking and became a theme we returned to in processing the results of the biographical grid in later sessions.

Finally, as we moved into Mark's adult life, he nominated still other episodic memories that varied in their valence. From the "proud moment" at age 26 when his son was born, we moved forward to the attack that precipitated his treatment, adding present-self, future-self, and ideal-self elements as described above. These 10 elements were then chronologically arranged and entered into Mark's biographical grid (see Figure 1).

**Elicitation of life themes or personal meanings.** In narrative terms, the elicitation of critical life events emplots the individual's life story, providing a "landscape of action" in terms of which the person's life story unfolds. In complementary fashion, the elicitation of the personal meanings underpinning these events draws themes from this story, offering a glimpse of the "landscape of consciousness" that gives the person's life story a unique intentionality and significance. The second step in the biographical-grid procedure involves teasing out these themes, revealing the important dimensions of transition or identity constructs that provide scaffolding for the individual's emerging sense of self. These constructions can be literal or metaphoric, cognitive or affective, as long as they represent meaningful dimensions of comparison or contrast that the person uses to organize and explain his or her life trajectory.

To initiate this inquiry, I presented Mark with random sets of three episodic memories from step one written out on three index cards. I then asked him, "How are two of these events or ages alike in some important way and different from the third?[2] For

2. This same "triadic sort" method of construct elicitation has been used and documented for other forms of grid technique, as discussed by Fransella and Bannister (1977), Winter (1992), and others. Although I employed this procedure in the more intimate context of a clinical interview, a host of computer-based grid elicitation and analysis programs could also be employed with the biographical-grid procedure (Bringmann, 1992; Sewell et al., 1992). In fact, I used one such program in generating results to discuss further with Mark.

example, presented with self elements at age seven (when his father was electrocuted), age 26 (when his son was born), and his ideal self, Mark distinguished the latter two elements, which he associated with "liking himself," from the first, which he associated with "hating himself." This theme became the first construct on the grid. Further themes were extracted through the presentation of additional triadic sorts until 10 thematic constructs were elicited. For example, he discriminated between the Little League years and high school, on the one hand, and his assault at age 41, on the other, because at the first two points in time, he was "able to keep what was his," whereas during the attack, he was "violated." Likewise, he differentiated between his present and future self, which he associated with "a fire always there," and his self-image while in Little League, when he was "able to reason." The 10 themes underpinning Mark's significant life events are portrayed in Figure 1.

**Weaving themes through events**. Although a picture of the significant shifts and continuities in the respondent's life experience begins to emerge in the above two steps, the third step in the biographical-grid procedure explicitly invites the person to weave interpretive constructs through autobiographical memories. This may be done qualitatively in the course of the interview (e.g., by asking, "In which of these other times did you experience yourself as violated?"), but it can also be done in more precise, quantitative form. In either case, the aim is to move beyond objective descriptions of life

| | | Elements | | | | | | | | | | Grid type: |
| | | 1 | 2 | 3 | 4 | 5 | 6 | 7 | 8 | 9 | 10 | Scale (–6 to 6) |
|---|---|---|---|---|---|---|---|---|---|---|---|---|
| C1 | like myself | –6 | 2 | –6 | –6 | –5 | –6 | 4 | 6 | 5 | –6 | hate myself |
| C2 | happy | –6 | 6 | –6 | –6 | –4 | –6 | 4 | 5 | 5 | –6 | sad |
| C3 | mad | 6 | –6 | 6 | 6 | 4 | 6 | –6 | –5 | –5 | 6 | relaxed |
| C4 | good family life | –6 | 6 | –6 | –6 | –5 | –5 | –3 | 6 | 5 | –6 | chaotic/dysfunctional |
| C5 | not in control | 4 | –6 | 5 | 6 | 5 | 5 | –6 | –4 | –5 | 6 | in control |
| C6 | violated | 6 | –5 | 6 | 6 | 5 | 5 | –6 | –5 | –5 | 6 | keep what's mine |
| C7 | "life's a bitch" | 6 | –5 | 6 | 6 | 5 | 5 | –6 | –5 | –5 | 6 | "life's great" |
| C8 | funny | –6 | 6 | –5 | –6 | –5 | –6 | 6 | 5 | 5 | –6 | disgusted |
| C9 | don't like people | 6 | –2 | 6 | 6 | 5 | 6 | –6 | –5 | –5 | 6 | love people |
| C10 | able to reason | –4 | 4 | –5 | –5 | –5 | –6 | 6 | 6 | 6 | –6 | fire always there |

E1:  Age 3: Tricycling to pool
E2:  Age 7: Daddy electrocuted
E3: Age 9–12: Little League
E4:  Age 14: Pony League
E5:  Age 17: High school
E6:  Age 26: Son born
E7:  Age 41: When attacked
E8:  Age 42: Me now
E9:  Age 47: Five years in future
E10:  Ideal self

**FIG. 1.** *Biographical grid for Mark.*

events to the construction of their meaning in personal terms. With Mark, I requested actual quantitative ratings of the elements on the thematic constructs, asking, "Where would you place yourself at age four on this 13-point scale that ranges from 'liking yourself' [–6] to 'hating yourself' [+6]?" When Mark was accustomed to performing this task, I allowed him to complete in the office the ratings of each element on each construct, a task that required only a few minutes. With a longer grid procedure, the completion of such ratings could be performed as between-session homework.

## Analysis and Interpretation

Prior to our fourth session, I conducted a formal analysis of Mark's grid, which he had completed the session before. Of the several levels of analysis that are possible for grid data of this type (Neimeyer, 1993), I chose first to examine the overall pattern of ratings of event elements on the thematic dimensions, which ranged from –6 (referring to constructs on the left of the grid in Figure 1) through 0 to +6 (constructs on the right side of the grid). Even at an impressionistic level, it was evident that Mark's ratings were highly polarized, with the modal response being one of the extreme poles of the construct dimension. This style of construing is noteworthy, insofar as it has been associated with more rigidly dichotomized and dysfunctional belief systems (Sewell, 1996). Stated differently, Mark tended to construe his life story in terms of extreme contrasts, with few "shades of gray" in between.

Perhaps the simplest use of the biographical grid in therapy would be to scan the themes associated with particular roles and identities, discussing significant patterns (e.g., Mark's construing of the trauma event, variations in his sense of control over time) as the therapist and client scan the ratings together. Alternatively, the pattern of ratings can be summarized through simple hand calculations or through more complex statistical procedures with the help of software programs.

As an example of hand-calculated analysis of Mark's grid, I constructed a simple "life-ideal profile" of the positivity or negativity of each successive phase of his life. This consisted of summing the absolute values of the differences between each of the first nine elements or selves in Figure 1 and the corresponding ratings for the ideal self. The resulting score for each column (which could range from 0 to 120) was then subtracted from 120 to yield a similarity score, which was then plotted on paper as depicted in Figure 2. This quick plotting technique provided an easily interpreted summary of the peaks and valleys of Mark's life story and served as a useful prompt for further therapeutic discussion.

Finally, to gain a more detailed analysis of his grid, I entered Mark's paper-and-pencil grid into G-Pack, one of several automated scoring programs available for grid data (Bell, 1990; Bringmann, 1992; Sewell, Adams-Webber, Mitterer, & Cromwell, 1992). This software performed a principal-components factor analysis of Mark's significant autobiographical elements in the context of his life themes. Part of G-Pack's output includes a plot of both the elements and themes in the two dimensions obtained by factoring the themes (see Figure 3). Concepts displaying greater similarity are represented by their greater proximity on the plot.

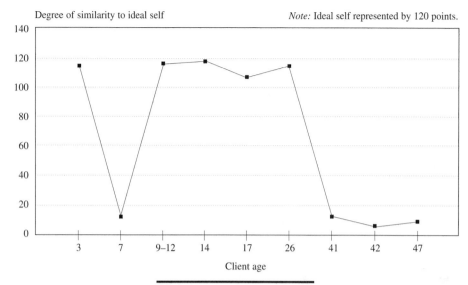

Degree of similarity to ideal self                    *Note:* Ideal self represented by 120 points.

**FIG. 2.** *Life-ideal profile for Mark.*

Several features of this analysis were of clinical interest. First, this formal statistical analysis provided a visual confirmation of the impression of polarization gleaned from a glance at Mark's raw ratings. His construing of his life was organized into two diametrically opposed clusters, one of which consisted of his positively valenced self elements—on the tricycle, when playing baseball, when his son was born, and even in high school when he successfully struck back at bullies. This tight grouping of self-identities closely approximated his ideal and was woven through with constructs implying control, ability to reason, liking himself and others, happiness, and keeping what was his. Somewhat more distantly, they also were associated with better family life and greater relaxation.

In sharp contrast, both his current post-traumatic self and his projected future self were tightly linked, recapitulating in virtually every detail the themes he associated with his experience at age seven in the aftermath of his father's injury. Now, as then, Mark viewed himself as hating others as well as himself, as having lost control, and as disgusted, sad, and violated. Moreover, all three identities were linked to his experiencing a "fire inside," with anger and chaotic dysfunction only slightly farther away. No life events bridged or articulated these two opposing clusters of situated self-identities, suggesting an instability in self-image associated with vulnerability to depression and other forms of distress (Kelly, 1955; Neimeyer, 1985b).

Mark's biographical grid suggested that he had assimilated the experience of his recent assault into the meaning structure associated with an earlier trauma in his life, namely, the multiple losses tied to his father's shock injury. Both left him contemptuous of self and others and both triggered a smoldering rage and impotence associated with a sense of violation. But in neither case could he find ways to accommodate these traumatic selves into the larger texture of his primary narrative, leaving him isolated in a regressive identity that was radically discontinuous with his pretraumatic

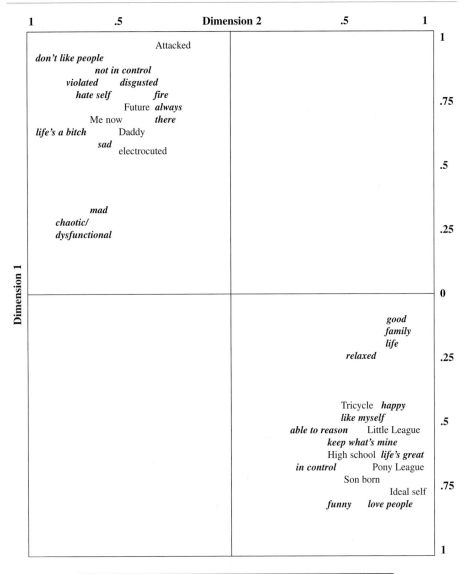

**FIG. 3.** *Principal-components analysis of biographical grid for Mark.*

self. The result was a life story that was painfully incoherent, with no clear way of integrating his experience of loss into the preexisting structure of his life. Although speculative, it is tempting to conjecture that the isolation of his previous traumatic identity in the text of his life posed a vulnerability factor for his later development of PTSD in response to the assault, providing a ready-made but fragmentary template within which to give meaning to his subsequent attack.

Discussion of these patterns with Mark in the next session was powerful for him as well as for me. For example, when I asked him to reflect on the striking parallel between his construction of his life at age seven and following his attack, he replied,

*I never thought about it, but it makes good sense. It's a real eye-opener. It's like I'm at the same place in life as when I was in first grade. Hmm . . . I never put that together before.*

Likewise, when asked to consider the polarization of his situated identities into two nonoverlapping groupings, Mark responded,

*I often thought that there was no in-between; life was either good or it sucks. I kind of always thought this way, even before the attack happened. It just came to me now; I don't think I ever realized it. I just thought everyone was that way.*

The results of Mark's biographical grid were instructive in identifying Mark's resources as well as his liabilities, as was illustrated by his response to a question concerning "what strengths he had at age seven that let him reengage the world at age nine." Mark hesitated for a moment and then noted that he "just made himself do it" because he "was going downhill and had nothing to lose." He went on to observe that he was "procrastinating now, avoiding people because he was so uncomfortable with them." We further considered the facilitative role of organized baseball in "drawing him out of himself" and giving him a safe way to "reconnect with others." Indeed, it was the upward life trajectory established by his Little League and Pony League years that buoyed him into his more turbulent late adolescence and gave him the conviction that he could resist, rather than submit, to the bullying of his high school peers.

## Subsequent Therapy

The remaining nine sessions of therapy with Mark first explored, then enacted, and finally consolidated the potential for reconstruction suggested by discussion of the biographical grid. Mark surprised me in the fifth session by proudly announcing his stiffness from having played a "pick-up game of baseball" in his neighborhood, his first in more than 15 years. With genuine astonishment and excitement, I validated the powerful importance of this "unique outcome," which represented resistance against the oppressive influence of the "dominant narrative" of his identity as a trauma victim (White & Epston, 1990). Consideration of other ways for him to "get back into society" soon followed. For example, we identified a coffee shop in which Mark had once spent time and discussed the "flash points" that would sometimes fuel Mark's "inner fire" when arguments would arise among the "regulars" about urban crime and other social problems reminiscent of his assault. This led to some emotionally intense role plays in my office, the goal of which was to broaden Mark's response repertory for managing potential conflict without resorting to physical aggression. As Mark returned periodically to the themes identified in the biographical grid and experimented with more exploratory behaviors, he reported a gradual reduction in many of the symptoms of PTSD (e.g., hypervigilance, elevated anxiety, rage) that had preoccupied him for the past year.[3]

---

3. In Mark's case, many of these gains were documented with standard symptom inventories to measure depression, anxiety, and interpersonal conflict. A more direct assessment of the reconstruction of his self-identity could also have been provided by a post-therapy administration of the biographical grid, although this was not done in Mark's case.

By session eight, Mark had begun to envision an alternative future, one predicated on his gaining additional training in mechanics at the community-college level. This ability to orient toward a possible future that was different from the traumatic past was itself a remarkable achievement, one that he followed with concrete exploration of job retraining as an alternative to accepting long-term psychiatric disability. Naturally, the road to reconstruction of his primary sense of self was not without obstacles. He occasionally reported "getting sidetracked" by traffic confrontations, abrasive interactions with his in-laws in the course of his divorce, and other events that once again fueled his urge to retaliate against the "attacks" of others. Interestingly, these urges were often accompanied by the feeling that he "was in a trance," suggesting an involuntary reactivation of the dissociative remoteness characteristic of his traumatic self.

Gradually, however, we were able to identify self-monitoring strategies that enabled him to "enter" and "leave" this traumatic self-identity more easily, although this required considerable fortitude for him to develop. For instance, whenever he began to sense the physical symptoms of anxiety (e.g., feeling "jumpy" or "nervous") in social situations, I encouraged him to scan for activation of the themes he associated with the trauma (e.g., fear of violation, loss of control). This helped Mark attribute his arousal to a historical event that was no longer present and to remind himself that the current circumstance was different. In addition to such cognitive interventions, I occasionally found behavioral strategies that helped him stay with uncomfortable situations rather than flee from them. For example, Mark was first acutely vigilant of any prospect of movement behind him, insisting on sitting or standing with his back to the wall, even during our therapy sessions. Initially, Mark would become visibly distraught if I asked him to take a seat with its back to the open room, although he knew that no one was behind him. Gradually, we desensitized him to this fear by progressively moving his chair a few inches at a time from the wall and eventually prompting him to sit in this more open fashion in restaurants and other public places. As Mark acquired new skills for managing conflict verbally rather than physically, he began to reformulate his abstract goals for life, opting to "be *prepared*, rather than always be *safe*." By the tenth session, he was implementing these goals, rebuilding his long-neglected motorcycle, and touring across the state in a journey of self-discovery reminiscent of his youth.

## Discussion and Conclusions

How can we understand Mark's experience of "rebiographing" (Howard, 1991) in the context of psychotherapy? At the most general level, he appeared to have restored his elaborative meaning making about the events surrounding his victimization, literally and figuratively rewriting a coherent story of the assault that encompassed his previously fragmentary recollections of it. As he did so, and subsequently reinstated this powerful but isolated sequence in his life script, he was better able to move from it to more empowering self-identities that engaged the world and other people less stereotypically and more adaptively. Far from being a mystical process, Mark's transition required a clear delineation of his disrupted sense of identity and concerted cognitive and behavioral efforts to achieve a more adequate sense of self that could adaptively confront difficult situations rather than blindly retreat from them or reenact the trauma experience.

At another level, he seemed to have recovered the threads of his more optimistic primary narrative, the one that was instantiated in his earliest childhood, his baseball years, and his young adulthood. In other respects, however, his reconstructed identity did not simply recapitulate the thematic structure of these simpler times. Indeed, for some weeks, he grieved the "loss of innocence about life" that he associated with them. He felt partially compensated for this loss, however, by his enlarged capacity to "be empathic with others who are hurting or crazy" and by his greater ability "to deal with anger openly, rather than passively, the way he used to." As a result, he seemed to have rewritten his life narrative in more fundamental ways, reaching toward a more complex self that accommodated life's tragic as well as comic moments. As we terminated therapy after a few months of contact, Mark had amicably accepted his divorce, strengthened his contact with his 16-year-old son, grown closer to his father, and enrolled in a mechanics program that provided job retraining for subsequent employment. A six-month follow-up with his managed-care company confirmed that he had maintained these gains.

Obviously, the broad range of constructivist psychotherapies (Kuehlwein & Rosen, 1996; Mahoney, 1995; Neimeyer & Mahoney, 1995) is too rich in theory to be conveyed in a discussion of a single disorder and too multifaceted in practice to be illustrated in a single case study. But as a relatively new field of research and practice, the area of trauma and loss invites novel conceptualization to which we have tried to respond by extending a constructivist account of post-traumatic stress and providing a concrete example of its application.

Despite our advocacy of this approach, we are aware of several concrete limitations in using narrative and constructivist methods with trauma victims. First, some clients may be unable fully to engage tasks that involve writing about their traumas or developing character sketches because a certain amount of verbal ability is required. In these cases, alternative means of self-expression such as the use of diagrams, drawings, music, and other art work may be required to help the person bring traumatic experiences into the forum of therapy. Second, clients will differ in the extent to which they can easily complete a technique like the biographical grid; some persons will need guidance throughout this exercise to assure they derive the maximum benefit from it. Finally, we are aware that the narrative model we have found compelling on a heuristic level is only beginning to be evaluated empirically (Hermans, 1995; Martin, 1994; Toukmanian & Rennie, 1992), just as its concrete ramifications for the helping professions require further elaboration and refinement.

# References

Atkinson, R. (1995). *The gift of stories*. Westport, CT: Bergin and Garvey.

Bell, R. C. (1990). Analytic issues in the use of repertory grid technique. In G. J. Neimeyer & R. A. Neimeyer (Eds.), *Advances in personal construct psychology* (pp. 25–48). Greenwich, CT: JAI.

Bringmann, M. W. (1992). Computer-based methods for the analysis and interpretation of personal construct systems. In G. J. Neimeyer & R. A. Neimeyer (Eds.), *Advances in personal construct psychology* (pp. 57–90). Greenwich, CT: JAI.

Bruner, J. (1986). *Actual minds, possible worlds*. Cambridge, MA: Harvard University Press.

Chapman, J. P. (1985). *Dictionary of psychology*. New York: Dell.

Franklin, C. (1995). Expanding the vision of social constructionist debates: Creating relevance for practitioners. *Families in Society, 76,* 395–406.

Fransella, F., & Bannister, D. (1977). *A manual for repertory grid technique*. New York: Academic Press.

Gonçalves, O. (1995). Cognitive narrative psychotherapy: The hermeneutic construction of alternative meanings. In M. J. Mahoney (Ed.), *Cognitive and constructive psychotherapies: Theory, research, and practice* (pp. 139–162). New York: Springer.

Guidano, V. F. (1995a). Constructivist psychotherapy: A theoretical framework. In R. A. Neimeyer & M. J. Mahoney (Eds.), *Constructivism in psychotherapy* (pp. 93–110). Washington, DC: American Psychological Association.

Guidano, V. F. (1995b). Self-observation in constructivist psychotherapy. In R. A. Neimeyer & M. J. Mahoney (Eds.), *Constructivism in psychotherapy* (pp. 155–168). Washington, DC: American Psychological Association.

Gustafson, J. P. (1995). *Dilemmas of brief therapy*. New York: Plenum.

Harter, S. L., & Neimeyer, R. A. (1995). Long-term effects of child sexual abuse: Toward a constructivist theory of trauma and its treatment. In R. A. Neimeyer & G. J. Neimeyer (Eds.), *Advances in personal construct theory: Vol. 4* (pp. 229–270). Greenwich, CT: JAI.

Hermans, H. (1995). *Self-narratives: The construction of meaning in psychotherapy*. New York: Guilford.

Howard, G. S. (1991). Culture tales: A narrative approach to thinking, cross-cultural psychology, and psychotherapy. *American Psychologist, 46,* 187–197.

Hyer, L. (1994). The trauma response: Its complexity and dimensions. In L. Hyer (Ed.), *Trauma victim: Theoretical issues and practical suggestions* (pp. 27–92). Muncie, IN: Accelerated Development.

Kelly G. A. (1955). *The psychology of personal constructs*. New York: W. W. Norton.

Klion, R. E., & Pfenninger, D. T. (1996). Role constriction and Vietnam-era combat veterans. *Journal of Constructivist Psychology, 9,* 127–138.

Kotre, J. (1995). *White gloves: How we create ourselves through memory*. New York: Free Press.

Kuehlwein, K., & Rosen, H. (Eds.). (1996). *Constructing realities: Meaning making perspectives for psychotherapists*. San Francisco: Jossey-Bass.

Mahoney, M. J. (Ed.). (1995). *Cognitive and constructive psychotherapies*. New York: Springer.

Mancuso, J. C., & Sarbin, T. R. (1983). The self-narrative in the enactment of roles. In T. R. Sarbin & K. E. Scheibe (Eds.), *Studies in social identity* (pp. 233–253). New York: Praeger.

Markus, H., & Nurius, P. (1986). Possible selves. *American Psychologist, 41,* 954–969.

Martin, J. (1994). *The construction and understanding of psychotherapeutic change*. New York: Teachers College Press.

McCall, G. J., & Simmons, J. L. (1978). *Identities and interactions* (rev. ed.). New York: Free Press.

Mead, G. H. (1934). *Mind, self and society*. Chicago: University of Chicago Press.

Minuchin, S. (1991, September–October). The seductions of constructivism. *Family Therapy Networker*, pp. 47–50.

Neimeyer, R. A. (1985a). Personal constructs in clinical practice. In P. C. Kendall (Ed.), *Advances in cognitive behavioral research and therapy* (pp. 275–329). San Diego, CA: Academic Press.

Neimeyer, R. A. (1985b). Personal constructs in depression: Research and clinical implications. In E.

Button (Ed.), *Personal construct theory and mental health* (pp. 82–102). London: Croom Helm.

Neimeyer, R. A. (1993). Constructivist approaches to the measurement of meaning. In G. J. Neimeyer (Ed.), *Constructivist assessment: A casebook* (pp. 58–103). Newbury Park: CA: Sage.

Neimeyer, R. A. (1995). Client-generated narratives in psychotherapy. In R. A. Neimeyer & M. J. Mahoney (Eds.), *Constructivism in psychotherapy* (pp. 231–246). Washington, DC: American Psychological Association.

Neimeyer, R. A. (1997). Problems and prospects in constructivist psychotherapy. *Journal of Constructivist Psychology, 10,* 51–74.

Neimeyer, R. A., & Mahoney, M. J. (Eds.). (1995). *Constructivism in psychotherapy.* Washington, DC: American Psychological Association.

Polkinghorne, D. E. (1988). *Narrative knowing and the human sciences.* Albany, NY: State University of New York Press.

Polkinghorne, D. E. (1991). Narrative and self-concept. *Journal of Narrative and Life History, 1,* 135–153.

Russell, R. L., & Van den Broek, P. (1992). Changing narrative schemas in psychotherapy. *Psychotherapy, 29,* 344–354.

Sarbin, T. R. (1986). The narrative as a root metaphor for psychology. In T. R. Sarbin (Ed.), *Narrative psychology: The storied nature of human conduct* (pp. 3–21). New York: Praeger.

Sewell, K. (1996). Constructional risk factors for a post-traumatic stress response following a mass murder. *Journal of Constructivist Psychology, 9,* 97–108.

Sewell, K. W., Adams-Webber, J., Mitterer, J., & Cromwell, R. L. (1992). Computerized repertory grids: Review of the literature. *International Journal of Personal Construct Psychology, 5*(1), 1–24.

Siegel, D. J. (1995). Memory, trauma, and psychotherapy: A cognitive science view. *Journal of Psychotherapy Practice and Research, 4,* 93–122.

Stewart, J. (1995). Reconstruction of the self: Life-span oriented group psychotherapy. *Journal of Constructivist Psychology, 8,* 129–148.

Terrell, C. J., & Lyddon, W. J. (1995). Narrative and psychotherapy. *Journal of Constructivist Psychotherapy, 9,* 27–44.

Toukmanian, S. G., & Rennie, D. L. (1992). *Psychotherapy process research: Paradigmatic and narrative approaches.* Newbury Park, CA: Sage.

Van der Hart, O., & Brown, P. (1992). Abreaction re-evaluated. *Dissociation, 5,* 127–140.

Van der Kolk, B. A., & Van der Hart, O. (1991). The intrusive past: The flexibility of memory and the engraving of trauma. *American Imago, 48,* 425–454.

White, M., & Epston, D. (1990). *Narrative means to therapeutic ends.* New York: W. W. Norton.

Wigren, J. (1994). Narrative completion in the treatment of trauma. *Psychotherapy, 31,* 415–423.

Winter, D. A. (1992). *Personal construct psychology in clinical practice*: London: Routledge.

# 8

## Clinical Observation, Inference, Reasoning, and Judgment in Social Work: An Update

*Paula S. Nurius & John W. Gibson*

Constructivist theory, findings, and practice have stimulated fuller understanding of how individuals search for and construct meanings in their effort to cope and adapt. Professionals in various helping roles, whether direct service practitioner, agency administrator, community organizer, or policy analyst, are increasingly aware of the effects of constructivist thought on their work.

In recent years, we have seen increased attention on reflective practice, on fostering critical thinking and sound reasoning, and on mindful integration of computers and technologies into practice. Many of the contributors in this volume note ways that practitioners can harness the positive potential of constructivism while maintaining safeguards against negative or impeding factors. This chapter is not intended as a comprehensive compendium on constructivist practice but rather as an effort to examine how people attempt to understand themselves and their social worlds and how their efforts likely affect clinical-practice efforts. The goal is to put practitioners in a position to manage the normative aspects of their own constructivism toward the benefit of clients.

Human service practice has never been more turbulent, pressured, and complicated than it is today. Too often, practitioners simply do not have the time, resources, or freedom to undertake the kind of cautious and thorough approach to assessing needs and working toward problem prevention or resolution that is needed. Nevertheless, if we care to improve our practice, we must take into account the context of our own real-life issues.

For additional information on clinical reasoning and its effects on practice, the following books and articles may be helpful.

# Suggested Reading List

Benbenishty, R., & Oyserman, D. (1995). Integrated information systems for human services: A conceptual framework, methodology, and technology. *Computers in Human Services, 12,* 311–325.

Berlin, S. B., & Marsh, J. C. (1993). *Informing practice decisions.* New York: Macmillan.

Brower, A. M., & Nurius, P. S. (1993). *Social cognition and individual change: Current theory and counseling guidelines.* Newbury Park, CA: Sage.

Gambrill, E. (1990). *Critical thinking in clinical practice.* San Francisco: Jossey-Bass.

Gambrill, E. (1997). *Social work practice: A critical thinker's guide.* New York: Oxford University Press.

Gibbs, L., & Gambrill, E. (1996). *Critical thinking for social workers: A workbook.* Thousand Oaks, CA: Pine Forge Press.

Gibson, J. W., & Nurius, P. S. (1992). Procedural knowledge in education for direct practice: Definitions, baselines, and recommendations. *Journal of Teaching in Social Work, 6,* 21–40.

Nurius, P. S. (1995). Critical thinking: A meta-skill for integrating practice and information technology training. *Computers in Human Services, 12,* 109–126.

Nurius, P. S., & Hudson, W. W. (1993). *Human services practice, evaluation and computers: A guide for today and beyond.* Pacific Grove, CA: Brooks/Cole.

# Clinical Observation, Inference, Reasoning, and Judgment in Social Work: An Update

In this article, the authors' principal goal is to provide an update of the professional and empirical literature pertaining to judgment in practice. Specifically, the authors identify and discuss double-edged influences—as assets as well as biasing liabilities—of key subcomponents of clinical observation, inference, reasoning, and judgment. First they review social work's historical concern with clinical judgment and its relation to social work tenets and practice. Then they analyze these assets and liabilities, focusing on the clinical tasks of assessment, diagnosis, and problem formulation. The analysis is structured in terms of the information flow or sequence of activities in clinical observation, inference, reasoning, and judgment—specifically, on attention and perception, interpretation and evaluation, and behavioral confirmation. The term "clinical" is intended to apply to a wide band of treatment-related practice models, settings, and fields.

Consider the following practice scenarios:

■ The child protective service worker determining whether a child should be removed from the home

■ The crisis worker assessing a caller's risk of suicide

■ The discharge planner's efforts to establish the most suitable placement for an acquired immune deficiency syndrome (AIDS) patient

■ The geriatric social worker's assessment to determine whether an elder person can continue to live safely at home

■ The therapist evaluating the mental status of a client and determining an appropriate diagnosis.

These are examples that readily come to mind when social workers speak of the use of judgment in practice. Yet in reality, these are among the more obvious or observable examples of a far more vast and more subtle array of judgments routinely made by practitioners. Clinical judgment and the observational, inferential, and reasoning processes upon which it is based are perhaps practitioners' most fundamental and frequently used processes in clinical activities. Yet, paradoxically, these processes are also among the most vulnerable to unintended biasing influence and to underrecognized fallacies, constituting an insidious Achilles' heel.

## Social Work's Historical Concern With Judgment

The study of clinical judgment is of fundamental importance to social work. Social workers continually draw inferences and exercise judgment as they attend to the constant flow of information about their clients and the clients' environments. Indeed, social work has a long history of concern with and research on clinical judgment and its role in assessment and intervention. As early as 1917, Richmond (1917) raised concerns about the uses of and dilemmas involved with judgment, noting "predispositions," "assumptions," and "habits of thought" as potential sources of bias.

More recently, practice theorists (for example, Bartlett, 1970; Germain & Gitterman, 1980) have identified professional judgment as an integral yet vulnerable part of the common base of social work practice. These theorists have urged more explicit and focused assessment activities and clearer linkages between assessment and intervention planning to strengthen judgment. By and large, however, analysis of underlying cognitive processes has remained at a fairly abstract level.

Clinical perception, judgment, and the effects of bias also have been the source of fairly intense empirical scrutiny in social work (Fanshel, 1958; Shyne, 1959). That increased experience should correspond with increased agreement among judges is one tenet that has received considerable attention. The complexity of the phenomenon of judgment has been illustrated, however, by findings that support different positions; that is, as the experience of clinicians increases, interrater agreement increases (Miller, 1958), remains the same (Briar, 1961), or decreases (Arnhoff, 1954). Complexity has been illustrated more recently through study of the relationship between client and social worker characteristics (for example, race and social class) as these influence clinical judgment (Franklin, 1985), as well as verbal ability of clients (Cousins, Fischer, Glisson, & Kameoka, 1985) and reliance on stereotypes by student practitioners (Kurtz, Johnson, & Rice, 1989).

In training social work students, educators routinely have recognized the tendency toward various biases, and counterbalancing common-sense practice tenets have become a standard part of social work training. One effort to help protect the client from possible social worker biases involves placing priority on the client's wishes. Fortune (1985), for example, noted that "the most important task-centered value is the emphasis on the client's expressed wishes, or the attitude that the client 'knows best' what her problems are and what successful resolutions look like" (p. 2). A host of other tenets and strategies (for example, specification of what professional values social workers should hold, viewing assessment and inference as an ongoing process, the importance of collateral information, and knowledge about cultural and ethnic differences) have arisen in efforts to support and enhance the accuracy of social workers' judgment.

A few systematic efforts to teach social workers to be better, or at least less biased, thinkers and inference makers also have been reported. Miller and Bogal (1977) have trained social work students in the use of logic as a tool for drawing clinical inferences. More recently, the work of Gibbs (1988) in teaching and evaluating critical thinking, identifying common errors in judgment, and creating a standardized measure to assess professional thinking in common clinical settings shows promise in extending social work research and training in the area of clinical judgment and inference.

There has been a tendency to acknowledge the importance of process issues in social work theory and practice, yet little effort has been made to explicitly delineate and dissect the components of this process, especially what has been called clinical judgment. Rather, this component of social work process has been described by such terms as "intuition," "going with one's gut," and "the art of practice." Although this component of social work practice is elusive and difficult to operationalize, the authors maintain that it is important, even essential, to define it more specifically. Further, a growing amount of literature from closely allied fields provides evidence that social workers are vulnerable to common errors of judgment and suggests that efforts to harness, manage, and even transform ways of inferring and making judgments are possible, but that the first requirement is clearer specification of the processes involved.

The nearly exclusive focus to date on outcomes answers some questions, but not those concerning assessment, problem formulation or diagnosis, and early stage clinical judgments. There is a need to more fully differentiate variables involved in effective and ineffective social work practice. In this article, the authors summarize findings regarding "information processing" as such processing bears on clinical assessment and judgment, identifying some common threats to accurate assessment and judgment as well as ways to guard against these threats.

## Dilemmas of Everyday Thinking

The number of judgments and decisions that each social worker makes in his or her daily life as well as professional activities is immense. It is simply not tenable to be continually "on" in a wholly thoughtful or mindful fashion (Langer & Piper, 1987). Even when a decision is personally important, a person rarely has sufficient time, energy, or inclination to consider each option, to weigh every consideration. And even if it were possible, such a strategy would be very costly in terms of time and energy, and thus it would be inefficient and even stifling. Instead, social workers often rely on a number of cost-effective, "quick and dirty" inferential shortcuts to help them sort through and winnow the vast numbers of inputs and outputs.

This reliance on inferential shortcuts is as true of everyday life as it is of the myriad activities involved in clinical practice. The pressures to draw on and subsequently rely on these distilling aids is further amplified in clinical practice—where information typically is clouded or uncertain, time is limited, and the circumstances are far from neutral. Moreover, research on decision making under such conditions of uncertainty and stress reveals that errors of judgment often are not random, but rather reflect systematic bias (Tversky & Kahneman, 1974).

The central point is that biases are inherent in the human cognitive apparatus rather than errors stemming from mere confusion or insufficient information (Kahneman, Slovic, & Tversky, 1982); that is, reliance on potentially biasing aids is essential to manageable reasoning strategies. The authors qualify the term "bias" to emphasize the meaning intended here. Biases and biasing influences are not necessarily problematic or prejudicial in a negative sense. "Biased" essentially means "nonrandom"—a tendency to operate in a particular patterned or directional manner. To contend realistically and effectively with the extraordinary array of information and possible interpretations and reactions that social workers encounter in their social and professional interactions, they simply must rely on some assumptions, rules of thumb, and habits to provide direction. The dilemma lies in the paradoxical danger in clinical practice of being erroneously directed—sometimes with very serious consequences—by the very sources of bias that social workers rely on for effective practice and for the development of expertise.

An emerging paradigm that focuses on these issues and differentiates the various factors and processes governing bias in observation, inference, reasoning, and judgment is that of information processing. Information processing is concerned with how people anticipate, collect, store, modify, retrieve, evaluate, understand, and use both internally generated information and information from the environment (Merluzzi, Rudy, & Glass, 1981). Within this perspective, people are seen not as passive recipients but rather as active seekers, creators, and users of information, influencing their social environments as well as being influenced by them.

Rather than presenting an exhaustive analysis in this article, the authors address the features of information processing that bear most on the clinical tasks so essential and commonly undertaken by social workers: assessment, diagnosis, and problem formulation. As noted above, the authors follow the flow of information-processing activities that generally are entailed in meeting, assessing, and drawing conclusions about clients. The authors realize that this process is not only more complex than they can address fully in this article, but also more intensive than the linear progression that they use to provide structure for their analysis.

## Attention and Perception

As Bruner (1957) noted, there is no such thing as immaculate perception. Social workers, like all people, approach situations with beliefs, values, and theories that generate certain expectations and that are used to filter relevant from irrelevant information and to read or assign meaning held in events and behaviors. These cognitive building blocks thereby play an enormously influential role. They not only produce selective attention to cues and events consistent with expectations, but also fuel active searches for expected input from the social environment and discount or overlook information or possibilities inconsistent with expectations and proclivities (Ingram, 1986).

For example, it is very common in couple and family counseling to observe members stereotyping one another (for example, "He just wants me to be his slave," or "She is constantly after me, nagging me"). They either discount or do not see contradictory evidence, but they vigilantly seek out evidence to make their case (for example, "See what I mean? And she's always like that!"). In a related vein, the phobic or anxious individual will overattend to certain features of a feared situation (the teeth, size, and apparent strength of a dog for the dog-phobic person) and underattend to other features (the social behavior of the dog—licking, rubbing, tail wagging). In similar but perhaps more subtle ways, expectations that the social worker brings will influence the process of assessment and problem formulation.

## *Implicit Personality Theories*

Expectations and subsequent attention and perception are shaped greatly by the manner in which various bits of information (including evaluations, feelings, and personal meaning) have been organized into larger chunks or sets and stored in memory in the form of knowledge structures and by how these structures are used to guide the clinician's information processing. Asch (1946), for example, demonstrated the tendency to unitize attributes and traits into meaningful sets that intuitively seem to go together. These constitute implicit personality theories, which tend to be extraordinarily resistant to change even in the face of evidence contradicting them. For example, when one thinks of a librarian, the descriptors "adventuresome," "sultry," and "zany" do not readily come to mind. Likewise, rightly or not, social workers tend to hold implicit theories organized around social categories (for example, "welfare mothers," "homeless," "old people," "homosexuals," "drug addicts") as well as problem types or diagnostic groups (for example, "passive-aggressive," "histrionic," "adult survivors," "juvenile delinquents," "sex offenders").

## *Knowledge Structures*

Knowledge structures refer to the manner in which clusters of information bits (and associated feelings) are stored so that they can be retrieved easily and used again and again. The various terms used to describe these knowledge structures—for example, "traits," "schemata," "prototypes," "stereotypes," "scripts"—exemplify the various levels of complexity in summarizing bits of information and in shaping subsequent expectations. Attentional and perceptual shortcuts and information sets are necessary, and, by and large, they tend to serve people reasonably well. This is a very normal and even necessary tendency in information processing. Moreover, people have a great intrinsic need for consistency and predictability and consequently construct images of themselves and others that serve to provide a stable and manageable view and understanding of the social world.

The dilemma facing the practitioner is twofold. The practitioner needs these knowledge structures even to begin to make sense out of what otherwise would be a bewildering cacophony of social stimuli. However, the practitioner then must contend with the natural biasing, telescoping, and rigidifying effects that these knowledge structures have on his or her expectations and perceptions.

As educators and professionals, social workers tend to be most concerned about the dilemmas for the novice or beginning clinician. Yet, ironically, it is the longer-term practitioner who is more at risk for these unintended and constraining consequences. That is, when a client or task is novel, practitioners tend to be hypervigilant, to attend closely to their observations, hunches, and decisions. With repeated exposure, experience, and routinization, a more "mindless" state develops, in which clinicians are less conscious of their cognitive processes and constructions and react more automatically (Benner, 1984). The more automatic expectations, attention, and perceptions become, the less likely they are to undergo scrutiny or revision and the more likely the clinician's perceptions—including inferences used to fill in missing information—will seem to him or her to be fact.

## Personal Experiences

A further source of expectations is personal experiences, both past and present. Personal histories predispose people toward certain ways of thinking about how people should behave, what they are conveying through certain actions, and what their meanings and underlying motives are. In his work on ethnographic assessment, Green (1982) noted the idiosyncratic nature of language and the importance of detecting and defining cover terms—terms that literally cover a cluster of ideas, objects, concepts, or relationships that hold particular meaning for the client. Some cover terms are clearly distinctive to a subgroup (for example, adolescents, the drug culture, racial or ethnic minority communities) and alert the social worker to the need for clarification.

What is much less obvious, yet much more insidious, is the assumption that common or familiar terms hold common meanings across practitioners or between practitioners and clients. In fact, terms' intended meanings actually may be quite idiosyncratic. Social workers are all too ready to infer that they know what a client means when the client says he or she is "depressed" or wants more "respect." If clients' attributes or experiences predispose social workers to view them as similar to themselves, then the ongoing risk of social workers using themselves rather than the clients as the principal referents for meaning is exacerbated even further (Loeb & Curtis, 1984). If, for example, a social worker had struggled with and left an abusive relationship, this experience would tend to color his or her perspective—perhaps to search out and read relationship issues in terms of abuse, to assume that his or her own experiences and reactions generalize to others, and to infer emotions, meanings, and theories of causation using his or her own experiences to go beyond the information given.

This concern over social workers' excessive reliance on their own experiences is underscored by the tendency among helping professionals to have personal backgrounds that have sensitized them to the negative effects of social and personal injustices and dysfunction. Indeed, these experiences may be a primary reason or catalyst for joining the profession. These experiences nurture motivation and commitment toward constructive change, which is an essential asset to the profession, yet they also serve to foster needs on the part of the practitioner to seek out and relate to others in terms of selected issues.

The primary observational task in assessment tends to revolve around the problems or concerns that the client brings to treatment. This is understandable. The point is for clients to seek help with problems in living and for social workers to identify clients' needs and to assist them in obtaining needed services. More and more, economics dictate that this process be completed as quickly as possible. Even when social workers consciously assess client strengths or resources, the assessment tends to be in relation to the central issue—the problem or dysfunction. Social workers consequently find that, consistent with their perceived task and role, they enter clinical assessments expecting dysfunction, searching for it, selectively attending to such factors (and consequently attending less to competing indicators), and thereby prone to finding what they are seeking.

# Interpretation and Evaluation

Evidence indicates that conceptualizations, interventions, and evaluations of clients tend to be made very quickly (in some cases in as little as 1 to 3 minutes), suggesting that they are based on a small amount of information and a considerable amount of inference. This tendency holds regardless of experience or theoretical orientation (Gauron & Dickinson, 1969; Sandifer, Hordern, & Green, 1970). These initial impressions then tend to anchor and thereby serve as the basis for subsequent appraisals, inferences, and judgments by the social worker (Nisbett & Ross, 1980; Orcutt, 1964). Thus, both the need for and the potential liabilities of winnowing aids and cognitive shortcuts noted above for attention and perception are equally true for the interpretation and evaluation processes of assessment.

An enormous range of factors potentially influences these processes. The authors address factors that are inherent parts of human cognition and that constitute both assets and potential liabilities for the clinical practitioner. Heuristics are information-processing strategies used to reduce the complexity of judgmental tasks, and they appear to function in a relatively automatic, unconscious fashion. The authors address five heuristics, or shortcut strategies, that hold particular significance for assessment, diagnosis, and problem formulation and that appear to be universal: (1) anchoring, (2) the availability heuristic, (3) the representativeness heuristic, (4) the fundamental attribution error, and (5) the effects of mood on memory and judgment (Hollon & Kriss, 1984; Salovey & Turk, 1988).

## *Anchoring*

"Anchoring" refers to excessive weighing of initial information derived about a client that subsequently serves as a template against which further information is judged. Evidence indicates that judgments tend to be generated early and often on the basis of indirect sources (for example, a colleague's diagnostic comment [Temerlin, 1968]) and on limited direct information (Meehl, 1960). These early impressions tend to be tenacious, even in the presence of new, contradictory information and in the absence of behavioral manifestations after the initial diagnosis or problem formulation has been determined (Ross, Lepper, & Hubbard, 1975).

One of the most famous examples is the Rosenhan (1973) report of voluntarily entering, along with seven friends, a mental health hospital. Each reported their true life histories and emotional states, falsifying only the complaint of hearing voices say "empty," "thud," and "hollow." During their study they exhibited no further symptoms, behaving in their own normative fashions. Anchoring was evident among the mental health staff, who "uncovered" the sources of the pseudopatients' pathologies in their life histories (for example, mixed emotions regarding one's parents); misinterpreted observed behaviors, such as note-taking, as manifestations of the diagnosed problem (for example, schizophrenia); and were reluctant to the point, in some cases, of being unwilling to rescind their diagnoses when the ruse was revealed. In contrast, many of the other hospital patients recognized the normalcy of the pseudopatients, interpreting their note-taking as the work of reporters.

The Rosenhan study (1973) obviously was not a fair test of the effects of anchoring. The hospital staff was deceived, and the expectation of encountering psychological pathology among individuals admitted to a mental health hospital was hardly radical (Spitzer, 1975). Nevertheless, the Rosenhan study vividly illustrates the known effects of labeling—of the pronounced tendency of prior judgments, such as diagnoses, to follow people and to take on a near-fact status.

## Availability Heuristic

The notion of "availability" refers to how readily accessible information (for example, cases, situations) is—that is, how easily it can be recalled or brought to mind. Certain types of information are clearly more accessible than others. Not surprisingly, such information tends to be cases or situations that stand out—that are salient, dramatic, or particularly noteworthy in one way or another. It is not the mundane, average, or typical instances of personal or professional lives that people recall most easily; these tend to blur together. Rather, it is the exceptions—the brilliant highs, the agonizing lows, the vividly distinctive—as well as the freshest or most recent of people's experiences that stand out.

One is said to be employing the availability heuristic when one is estimating the frequency or likelihood of a set of circumstances or an outcome on the basis of the ease with which related information is brought to mind (Tversky & Kahneman, 1973). Almost all social workers have heard in staff meetings, "Oh, I went to a workshop recently and heard about a case just like this," or have seen in intergroup conferences how different specialists search for case evidence with which they are most familiar and concerned (for example, drug or alcohol misuse, schizophrenia, battering, post-traumatic stress symptoms). The potential dilemma is obvious: given the greater distinctiveness of exceptional instances, they will be far more likely to influence estimates and predictions than less distinctive, yet more normative, instances.

This influence becomes very important in risk assessment where the memorable instances are vivid even if atypical and where the consequences of error are serious (Lichtenstein, Slovic, Fischhoff, Layman, & Combs, 1978). Such areas as child, elder, or spouse abuse; suicide; and related safety issues immediately come to mind. Less obvious is the inclination to diagnose on the basis of high-profile characterizations of client groups or syndromes. This is evident, for example, in popularized depictions of adult children of alcoholics. Prevailing profiles of this group have been almost exclusively based on anecdotal case examples, without representative, cross-sectional surveys to ascertain their accuracy or generalizability. Yet, rightly or wrongly, the adult child of an alcoholic has become a salient and ubiquitous image.

Similarly, all social workers have seen how much more compelling and influential a single dramatic case example is relative to statistics characterizing the frequency or probability of a phenomenon, even if the statistics are substantial (Anderson, 1983; Taylor & Thompson, 1982). One highly visible example is that of the tragic and well-publicized abuse case of Hedda Nussbaum and Joel and Lisa Steinberg relative to the reams of less dramatic, yet more representative, evidence and statistics on the problem of domestic violence. For clinical practitioners, the danger is that new information, such as consistent results from credible clinical research, is not likely to be effective in influencing practitioners' thinking relative to their more vivid, yet more idiosyncratic, personal experiences.

## Representativeness Heuristic

The representativeness heuristic involves judgments of how likely it is that a person is a member of a particular category (for example, a diagnostic group) or how likely a given sign (for example, one presented by a drawing or a projective test) or outcome can be explained by a particular set of antecedents (for example, interpretation of family of origin patterns). The degree of representativeness is the degree of similarity or identity that the target is judged as having relative to some preexisting set or hypothesis (Dawes, 1986; Kahneman & Tversky, 1973). For example, Turk and Salovey (1986) described a case conference in which a figure drawn by an adolescent boy with the figure's hands behind its back served as the sole source of evidence for the boy's presumed concern about masturbation. The problem, of course, lies in discerning whether this or alternative interpretations (for example, the boy tired of the drawing task and abbreviated it, or he could not draw hands well so he avoided the attempt) is true and whether, if true, such an occurrence is distinctive or relatively normative (for example, most adolescent boys are not fully comfortable with their sexuality and most are concerned about masturbation).

Similar to the influence of availability, the representativeness heuristic biases a practitioner to underestimate the importance of base-rate or prevalence information, for example, that a given condition occurs relatively rarely. The tendency is to focus instead on single cases that seem "highly representative" (for example, "a typical military type," "a classic case of domineering mother and weak father") and to generalize to the current case from such presumably representative cases. Here again, the effect of expectancies becomes evident not only through the clinician's selectively attending to information that fits with preexisting sets and hypotheses, but also through the clinician's inferring or interpreting its meaning consistent with these, as in the example of the adolescent boy.

Clinicians, like everyone else, tend to draw more confidence from a small body of consistent data that seems to make sense than from a larger body of less consistent information that is therefore harder to get a handle on. Everyone needs and searches for coherence, at times interpreting information to increase its apparent consistency and ignoring or discounting evidence that does not fit our expectancies. Effects of the representativeness heuristic may be exacerbated in circumstances where greater detection of pathology or dysfunction is viewed as a sign of greater skill or status by one's colleagues (Stahler & Rappaport, 1986).

## Fundamental Attribution Error

The "fundamental attribution error" refers to the tendency of actors to focus on situational influences in attributing or explaining causes of behavior, whereas observers tend to attribute causality for the same behavior to stable traits possessed by the actor (Wills, 1978). In the case of assessment and problem formulation, the client is the actor or target and the clinician is the observer. A client in counseling for anger management, for example, may tend to see the problem as stemming from some factor in the environment (for example, stress from the job, the attitude or provocation of others), whereas the therapist is more inclined to see the behavior as a manifestation of underlying characterological factors (for example, personality attributes, coping skill deficits).

This characterological orientation often is confounded by the limited information on which judgments are based. In assessment or diagnostic scenarios, clinicians typically have access to only a small portion of potential information on their clients and the clients' environments. Small samples (of, for example, observed client behaviors, different clients) tend to be less stable and less representative relative to larger samples, rendering it questionable that truly reliable, representative samples of client attributes, behaviors, and circumstances or environments are typically acquired. Yet individuals tend not to be aware of this and are likely to assume and treat even very small samples as equally representative of the larger population (Tversky & Kahneman, 1971). This fact underscores the importance of a clinician's efforts to gauge and strive to increase the reliability of small samples of a client's behavior and to exercise caution in using them in predictions or generalizations.

## Effects of Mood on Memory and Judgment

The ebb and flow of moods within the practitioner are expected and long-attended features of clinical practice. Without such emotional experiences, at times complex and intense, practitioners would be relatively flat, lifeless, and nonempathic—hardly a warm or inviting image. Moreover, feelings experienced by a clinician in the context of practice often have been viewed as important information pertaining to the countertransference process or as reflective of reactions that others in a client's social network likely would experience toward him or her (Kernberg, 1965). What has been far less examined are the potential biasing effects of practitioner moods on the information-processing tasks involved in assessment and problem formulation. Emphasis in this section is on the effects of practitioner mood on attentional focus, memory, and helping responsiveness (Greenberg & Safran, 1989; Salovey & Turk, 1988).

Two effects of mood on attentional focus have been established. The first is that of selectively attending to and reading information that is positive when one is feeling positive and negative when one is feeling negative (Bower, 1981). The second effect of mood is the shift of focus of one's attention to oneself (Salovey & Rodin, 1985). Specifically, when people have affective experiences, they typically become temporarily self-focused. This transitory self-preoccupation is potentially problematic in interpretation and evaluation because of its augmentation of the practitioner's natural tendency to use himself or herself as the referent for the meaning of client experiences, issues, and concerns.

A principal effect of mood on memory involves the tendency to recall information that is consistent with one's present mood (Natale & Hantes, 1982). This suggests that a clinician is inclined not only to look for and see client behaviors congruent with the clinician's current mood, but also to recall and therefore inquire about client issues consistent with the clinician's current mood. Moreover, this predisposition carries the potential of eliciting responses from the clients that are congruent with the clinician's mood as the client responds to the clinician's questions and prompts (Snyder & Thomsen, 1988).

Another relevant feature of mood to clinicians is its influence on their helping responsiveness. For example, when a practitioner feels joyful, the practitioner tends to extend help to others when the joy stems from his or her own experiences, but the practitioner tends to withhold help when the joy stems from the client's experiences (Rosenhan, Salovey, & Hargis, 1981). The reverse is found with sadness, in that practitioner helping is likely when the client feels sad but not when the practitioner feels sad from her or his own experiences (Thompson, Cowan, & Rosenhan, 1980).

Moods also have been related to a variety of variables likely to influence clinician performance—perceived self-efficacy, initiative and risk taking, ability to concentrate and reason, flexibility, and creativity. The experience of mood and its effects is varied and complex. There is still a great deal about its influence on clinical interpretation and evaluation that is unknown.

## Behavioral Confirmation

Over the course of the transactions between client and social worker, a set of factors begins to emerge and to become increasingly influential. These factors involve behavioral confirmation on the part of the client, the role of the practitioner in molding this confirmation, and the influence of this confirmation in shaping future expectations.

The tendency of social workers to rely heavily on assessment strategies oriented toward confirming their hunches or working hypotheses—that is, to pose questions consistent with the working hypothesis while often neglecting alternative hypotheses—is remarkably consistent. It tends to be used across qualitatively different problem areas, even when the expected accuracy of the social worker's hypothesis about the client is low or the hypothesis contains information about contradictory as well as confirming attributes (Synder & Swann, 1978). "Behavioral confirmation" refers to one effect of such strategies—specifically, to a process through which "one individual's preconceived *beliefs* and prior *expectations* about another person channel their interactions in such ways that these initial beliefs (even when they are based on erroneous stereotypes or hypotheses of dubious validity) come to be *confirmed* by the other person's *behavior*" (Snyder & Thomsen, 1988, p. 127). (See also Darley & Fazio, [1980] and Turk & Salovey [1986] for reviews of evidence supporting the phenomenon of behavioral confirmation and its function on self-fulfilling prophecies.)

The distinctive issue here is that a clinician, like anyone else, will treat a client in ways that will incline the client to actually behave in accord with the clinician's general beliefs and expectations (for example, theoretical or therapeutic orientations) as well as with those specific to the client (for example, implicit personality theories or tentative diagnosis). The concern is the impact of the social worker's behavior on the creation of confirmatory data. That is, through the nature of questions posed to the client and the social worker's reactions (particularly given the authoritative expertise presumed of the social worker) to client responses, the clients may be subtly cued to manifest expected symptomatology. This behavioral confirmation by the client serves to confirm the social worker's a priori hypotheses (whether accurate or not), strengthening the social worker's expectancy effects in future interactions with clients (Turk & Speers, 1983), and therein lies the self-perpetuating nature of the process.

For example, in interviewing a new female client, a therapist may have an initial hunch that self-defeating personality attributes are key factors in the client's problems. Questions directed to the client likely would probe for evidence of relevant symptomatology, followed by inquiries related to the presumed causal origins of such a personality type. The therapist may inquire about negative thoughts and feelings that the client has about herself, anxiety about negative evaluation from others, the client's inclination to remain in a job or a relationship she is not happy with, and perhaps strife in the client's childhood relationship with her father.

The client may, understandably, respond only to the questions asked and perhaps articulate and manifest a set of variables fairly typical of a "well-socialized woman" (for example, soft-spoken, tendency to put others' needs before her own, social anxiety in authoritative contexts). The client also may tend to neglect information that the therapist is not pursuing, such as environmental variables, including demoralizing or manipulative treatment by superiors at a job site; conditions of economic hardship or vulnerability; evidence of a lack of sophistication regarding communication or assertiveness skills; or strengths and capabilities in other life domains. In this case, the course of questioning and reinforcement that focuses exclusively on a character-based hypothesis combined with the anxiety-producing nature of the treatment setting and experience for the client may indeed elicit a rather ineffectual, self-denigrating portrayal by the client.

Behavioral confirmation has been demonstrated across a wide variety of beliefs and expectations, for example, conceptions of sex and gender roles; of racial differences; of personalities of physically attractive and unattractive people; and of workers, clients, and students randomly designated as having high potential (Snyder, 1984). Thus, through the mechanism of behavioral confirmation, a social worker's theories of causation, implicit personality theories, and other expectancy sets that constitute the clinician's background, training, and experience will tend to be further strengthened. And, as strengthened, they increasingly will be presumed accurate in work with future clients.

## Conclusion

As Biorck (1977) stated, the

> clinician's art is one of making a tremendous number of clinical judgments each day based on inadequate, often ambiguous data, and under pressure of time and of carrying out this task with the outward appearance of calmness, dedication, and interpersonal warmth. (p. 146)

The elements of the art of practice that the authors have focused on by no means constitute the only important factors. All the precision, accuracy, and mindful vigilance in the world may be for naught if the client's experience of that practice does not include the caring, respect, and goal of self-enhancement and well-being so essential to the social work mission. As caring people, social workers are more than reasoners or information processors, and behind every error or bias there may be a human capacity with significant adaptive advantages.

The authors assume this pluralistic complex of factors to be a given. Their goal has been to isolate one set of factors of critical importance to a problem-solving profession—those of clinical observation, inference, reasoning and judgment—and to thoughtfully weigh their inherent strengths and frailties. The dilemmas that the authors have raised are not easily dealt with and will require continued examination, ingenuity, and perseverance. They also will require an ongoing partnership shared by social work practitioners, researchers, and educators.

# References

Anderson, C. A. (1983). Abstract and concrete data in the perseverance of social theories: When weak data lead to unshakable beliefs. *Journal of Experimental Social Psychology, 19,* 93–108.

Arnhoff, F. N. (1954). Some factors influencing the unreliability of clinical judgments. *Journal of Clinical Psychology, 10,* 272–275.

Asch, S. E. (1946). Forming impressions of personality. *Journal of Abnormal and Social Psychology, 41,* 258–290.

Bartlett, H. (1970). *The common base of social work.* New York: NASW.

Benner, P. (1984). *From novice to expert: Excellence and power in clinical nursing practice.* Menlo Park, CA: Addison-Wesley.

Biorck, G. (1977). The essence of the clinician's art. *Acta Medica Scandinavica, 201,* 145–147.

Briar, S. (1961). Use of theory in studying effects of client social class on students' judgments. *Social Work, 6*(3), 91–97.

Bruner, J. S. (1957). Going beyond the information given. In *Contemporary approaches to cognition: A symposium.* Cambridge, MA: Harvard University Press.

Cousins, P. S., Fischer, J., Glisson, C., & Kameoka, V. (1985). The effects of physical attractiveness and verbal expressiveness on clinical judgments. *Journal of Social Service Research, 8*(4), 59–74.

Darley, J. M., & Fazio, R. (1980). The origin of self-fulfilling prophecies in a social interaction sequence. *American Psychologist, 35,* 867–881.

Dawes, R. M. (1986). Representative thinking in clinical judgment. *Clinical Psychology Review, 6,* 425–441.

Fanshel, D. (1958). A study of caseworkers' perceptions of their clients. *Social Casework, 39,* 543–551.

Fortune, A. E. (1985). *Task-centered practice with families.* New York: Springer.

Franklin, D. L. (1985). Differential clinical assessments: The influence of class and race. *Social Service Review, 59,* 44–61.

Gauron, E. F., & Dickinson, J. K. (1969). The influence of seeing the patient first on diagnostic decision-making in psychiatry. *American Journal of Psychiatry, 126,* 199–205.

Germain, C. B., & Gitterman, A. (1980). *The life model of social work practice.* New York: Columbia University Press.

Gibbs, L. E. (1988). Teaching critical thinking at the university level: A review of some empirical evidence. *Informal Logic, 7,* 137–149.

Green, J. W. (1982). *Cultural awareness in the human services.* Englewood Cliffs, NJ: Prentice-Hall.

Greenberg, L. S., & Safran, J. D. (1989). Emotion in psychotherapy. *American Psychologist, 44,* 19–29.

Hollon, S. D., & Kriss, M. (1984). Cognitive factors in clinical research and practice. *Clinical Psychology Review, 4,* 35–76.

Ingram, R. E. (Ed.). (1986). *Information processing approaches to clinical psychology.* New York: Academic Press.

Kahneman, D., Slovic, P., & Tversky, A. (Eds.). (1982). *Judgment under uncertainty: Heuristics and biases.* New York: Cambridge University Press.

Kahneman, D., & Tversky, A. (1973). On the psychology of prediction. *Psychological Review, 80,* 237–251.

Kernberg, O. (1965). Notes on countertransference. *Journal of the American Psychoanalytic Association, 13,* 38–56.

Kurtz, M. E., Johnson, S. M., & Rice, S. (1989). Student's clinical assessments: Are they affected by stereotyping? *Journal of Social Work Education, 25,* 3–12.

Langer, E. J., & Piper, A. 1. (1987). The prevention of mindlessness. *Journal of Personality and Social Psychology, 53,* 280–287.

Lichtenstein, S., Slovic, P., Fischhoff, B., Layman, M., & Combs, B. (1978). Judged frequency of lethal events. *Journal of Experimental Psychology: Human Learning and Memory, 4,* 551–578.

Loeb, R. G., & Curtis, J. M. (1984). Effect of counselor's self-references on subject's first impressions in an experimental psychological interview. *Psychological Reports, 55,* 803–810.

Meehl, P. E. (1960). The cognitive activity of the clinician. *American Psychologist, 15,* 19–27.

Merluzzi, T. V., Rudy, T. E., & Glass, C. R. (1981). The information-processing paradigm: Implications for clinical science. In T. V. Merluzzi, C. R. Glass, & M. Genest (Eds.), *Cognitive assessment* (pp. 77–124). New York: Guilford.

Miller, R. R. (1958). An experimental study of the observational process in casework. *Social Work, 3,* 96–102.

Miller, S., & Bogal, R. (1977). Logic as a tool for clinical training in social work. *Psychiatric Quarterly, 49,* 18–28.

Natale, M., & Hantas, M. (1982). Effect of temporary mood states on selective memory about the self. *Journal of Personality and Social Psychology, 42,* 927–934.

Nisbett, R., & Ross, L. (1980). *Human inference: Strategies and shortcomings of social judgment.* Englewood Cliffs, NJ: Prentice-Hall.

Orcutt, B. A. (1964). A study of anchoring effects in clinical judgment. *Social Service Review, 38,* 408–417.

Richmond, M. (1917). *Social diagnosis.* New York: Russell Sage Foundation.

Rosenhan, D. L. (1973). On being sane in insane places. *Science, 179,* 250–258.

Rosenhan, D. L., Salovey, P., & Hargis, L. (1981). The joys of helping: Focus of attention mediates the impact of positive affect on altruism. *Journal of Personality and Social Psychology, 40,* 899–905.

Ross, L., Lepper, M. R., & Hubbard, M. (1975). Perseverance in self-perception and social-perception: Biased attribution processes in the debriefing paradigm. *Journal of Personality and Social Psychology, 32,* 880–892.

Salovey, P., & Rodin, J. (1985). Cognitions about the self: Connecting feeling states and social behavior. In P. Shaver (Ed.), *Self, situations, and social behavior* (pp. 143–166). Beverly Hills, CA: Sage.

Salovey, P., & Turk, D. C. (1988). Some effects of mood on clinician's memory. In D. C. Turk & P. Salovey (Eds.), *Reasoning, inference, and judgment in clinical psychology* (pp. 107–123). New York: Free Press.

Sandifer, M. G., Hordern, A., & Green, L. M. (1970). The psychiatric interview: The impact of the first three minutes. *American Journal of Psychiatry, 126,* 968–973.

Shyne, A. W. (1959). *Use of judgments as data in social work research.* New York: NASW.

Snyder, M. (1984). When belief creates reality. In L. Berkowitz (Ed.), *Advances in experimental social psychology* (Vol. 16). New York: Academic Press.

Snyder, M., & Thomsen, C. J. (1988). Interactions between therapists and clients: Hypothesis testing and behavioral confirmation. In D. C. Turk & P. Salovey (Eds.), *Reasoning, inference, and judgment in clinical psychology* (pp. 124–152). New York: Free Press.

Snyder, M., & Swann, W. B. (1978). Behavioral confirmation in social interaction: From social perception to social reality. *Journal of Experimental and Social Psychology, 14,* 148–162.

Spitzer, R. L. (1975). On pseudoscience in science, logic in remission, and psychiatric diagnosis: A critique of Rosenhan's "On being sane in insane places." *Journal of Abnormal Psychiatry, 84,* 442–452.

Stahler, G. J., & Rappaport, H. (1986). Do therapists bias their ratings of patient functioning under peer review? *Community Mental Health Journal, 22,* 265–274.

Taylor, S. E., & Thompson, S. C. (1982). Stalking the elusive "vividness" effect. *Psychological Review, 89,* 155–181.

Temerlin, M. K. (1968). Suggestion effects in psychiatric diagnosis. *Journal of Nervous and Mental Disease, 147,* 349–353.

Thompson, W. C., Cowan, C. L., & Rosenhan, D. L. (1980). Focus of attention mediates the impact of negative affect on altruism. *Journal of Personality and Social Psychology, 38,* 291–300.

Turk, D. C., & Salovey, P. (1986). Clinical information processing: Bias inoculation. In R. E. Ingram (Ed.), *Information processing approaches to clinical psychology* (pp. 306–323). New York: Academic Press.

Turk, D. C., & Speers, M. A. (1983). Cognitive schemata and cognitive-behavioral intervention: Going beyond the information given. In P. C. Kendall (Ed.), *Advances in cognitive–behavioral research and therapy* (Vol. 2, pp. 3–31). New York: Academic Press.

Tversky, A., & Kahneman, D. (1971). Belief in the law of small numbers. *Psychological Bulletin, 76,* 105–110.

Tversky, A., & Kahneman, D. (1973). Availability: A heuristic for judging frequency and probability. *Cognitive Psychology, 5,* 207–232.

Tversky, A., & Kahneman, D. (1974). Judgment under uncertainty: Heuristics and biases. *Science, 183,* 1124–1131.

Wills, T. A. (1978). Helpers' perception of clients. *Psychology Bulletin, 85,* 986–1000.

# 9

# Group Development as Constructed Social Reality Revisited: The Constructivism of Small Groups

*Aaron M. Brower*

Constructivism focuses on how people make meaning in their lives. Nowhere is this phenomenon more clearly seen than in group work, a modality that forces members to develop a shared understanding of the treatment setting (Llewelyn & Dunnett, 1987). Kelly's (1955) theory of personal constructs, focusing as it does on how psychotherapy clients understand their world and how they place themselves and others within it, encourages clients to experiment actively with social interactions in controlled settings, which fits the group modality perfectly. Kelly recognized this application, stating that the client can develop roles and constructs within the group and learn how to apply them to other members and to the interactions within the group. The group "is like having a large well-equipped social laboratory" (Kelly, 1955, p. 1156).

In addressing this topic, one could talk about constructivism *in* small groups, or how constructivist techniques are used by members for individual change. One could also talk about the constructivism *of* small groups, or how constructivist thinking is used to describe group processes. In this chapter, I focus primarily on the latter—how constructivism can be used to describe certain small-group processes important for those who lead groups for client change (see Nye & Brower [1996b] for research on this topic). Several constructivism techniques that have been found to be particularly well suited for group settings are presented.

Use of constructivist techniques in groups requires group members to be in a certain psychological and social "place," whereby members are open to the experience of "hypothesis testing," in Kelly's terms, and have the language to test their constructs in the group. From a constructivist point of view, the group must be brought along as a loose collection of individuals, each of whom has his or her own perceptions and meanings, and developed into a cohesive, coordinated group in which perceptions and meanings are shared.

Group development is often described as a collection of individuals with loose ties to one another who develop into a unified entity with an identity, structure, behavioral norms, and roles for members. The process by which a collection of individuals becomes a group has been described in the literature on stages of group development. Constructivism is a good theoretical perspective from which to reexamine these stages.

Franklin (see Chapter 3) described the differences between *constructivism* and *social constructionism*—differences important for professionals interested in theory development and the application of theory to practice. In reading her chapter, I realized that my own thinking has focused primarily on constructivism—on how people make meaning in their lives through their perceptions, the operation of their cognitive and affective processes, and the mechanics of memory storage and retrieval. Small groups provide an ideal context for comparing how people differ in their use of these mechanical constructivist processes as they make sense of themselves within the small group.

At the same time, small groups can provide an ideal arena for the study of the operations of social constructionism, because a group's development of norms, roles, rules, and beliefs can serve as an analogue to the process that society goes through to develop its own norms, roles, rules, and beliefs. Note that the following list of elements conceptualizing "groupness" are similar to elements that define society (summarized from Hartford, 1963):

■ Acceptance of other members and the development of patterns in interpersonal relations

■ Development of group spirit, bond, identification with the group, cohesion, or "we" feeling

■ Development of group goals and of sufficient commonness of purpose to make some decisions

■ Evolution of group structure, the development of patterns of status and roles, and means of group control

■ Development of continuity through program content and group activity

■ Development of group culture through the creation of group norms, values, and patterns of expected behavior

■ Stable and regular membership

■ Development of relationships with relevant forces or agencies outside the group

The model of group development presented here is a description of how members develop shared and complementary schemas (or cognitive and affective representations) for their group—including perceptions of other members, rules and norms for behavior, and views of themselves in the group. To make the description of this process easier to understand, it is necessary to make some assumptions about an "idealized" group. It will be assumed that the group has a well-defined beginning, whereby all members join at the same time, members feel committed to the group, and the group requires active interactions among the members. The model of development presented is also idealized in that it is described as if it proceeds in a straightforward, linear fashion. In these ways, I join other small-group theorists who use an idealized group form to facilitate their theory building (see Bennis & Shepard, 1956; Lang, 1981; Tuckman

& Jensen, 1977; Wheelan & Hochberger, 1996; Yalom, 1995). Although real groups are often "messier" than an ideal group, the model of development that is presented is nevertheless applicable (see Wheelan & McKeage, 1993).

# A Constructivist Model of Group Development

## *Beginning Anomie*

The constructivist model of group development begins with a description of the group as inherently marked by anomie, or normlessness. The beginning group is similar to Merton's (1957) description of social anomie, which he defines as members in society facing disparities between social goals (or ends) and having the means to achieve them. Due to this disparity, beginning groups lack structures of communication, relationship, power, leadership, norms, and roles. Members lack clear purpose for themselves, and the group lacks a clear goal for itself. Each member attends to cues in the group situation that have salience for him or her and each struggles individually to "make sense" of these cues (Brower, 1989).

This beginning anomie defines a basic assumption of both constructivists and social constructionists—that what is important in a given situation is what the participants read into it rather than what is objectively present. This assumption is stated most succinctly by "radical constructivists" (see Chapter 3); situations in and of themselves impart no meaning to participants; rather, participants imbue situations with meaning through the cues they pick out and respond to and through the messages they interpret from the situations. In fact, as humans we are compelled to make sense of situations; we are "hard wired" to do so (see Chapter 2). When we cannot make sense of a situation, anomie confronts us head-on with the anxiety of being "at sea" or "groundless" (Yalom, 1980).

## *The Initial Schema*

Members are compelled, then, to make sense of the group situation by themselves, on the basis of their own past experiences with groups and other situations that are "group like" (such as classmates or families). Research in the area of social cognition finds that people store and retrieve information in "packets" or organized structures that are called *schemas* (see Brower & Nurius, 1993; Cohen, 1981; Neisser, 1976). Schemas describe the ways in which we have learned to put together the social concepts and rules that we apply to particular situations. Our "group schemas" contain our understanding of the rules and concepts (i.e., norms for behavior, roles, expectations, and so forth) that allow us to make sense of the group situation. This is not a new idea for small-group theorists: Garland, Jones, and Kolodney (1973) argued that group members make the new group understandable and predictable by drawing on past experiences that appear similar to the present situation. Again, this idea, that we make sense of situations on the basis of our own histories of experience, is basic to both constructivists and social constructionists.

But what is important here is that each member accesses his or her *own* schemas to make sense of the group situation, making the group understandable and predictable from his or her point of view. Each member perceives the group differently—reading different cues as important and assigning different meanings to these cues, reading the behaviors of the leaders and other members differently, and having idiosyncratic goals and expectations for what their group experience will bring. At the beginning of the group, then, each member has an understanding of the group that is different from that of other members (see Nye and Simonetta [1996] for research demonstrating how members' initial schemas affect evaluations of their group experiences).

## The First Reality Crisis: Turning to the Leader

The more experience the members have with groups of this sort, the more realistic and elaborate will be their group schemas. But because members need to interact, they are forced to violate one another's schematic realities of the group and therefore confront the anomie inherent in the group situation. One might describe this as a "reality crisis," because a member's sense of the group is challenged by other members whose actions and behaviors are based on a different set of perceptions and beliefs about the group. Members may feel somewhat powerless and confused about the group.

This should not come as a surprise. In new situations, we should expect to feel confused and to turn to designated leaders who can help us through our initial confusion. Even though this situation might be considered a reality crisis, it is a relatively minor crisis in terms of its disruptive power for members. A powerful social rule begins to operate, that is, the leader will explain the rules and provide guidelines. In the language of constructivism, the leader describes the "reality" for the group. We have ample experience with the validity of this rule: The designated leader—in classrooms, families, work groups, and the like—sets the agenda, establishes the rules and behavioral norms, and provides the "vision" to help members come together.

To the extent that the leader provides an adequate vision for members, the level of anxiety caused by anomie is reduced (Bednar & Battersby, 1976; Evensen & Bednar, 1978; Lee & Bednar, 1977; Nye & Forsyth, 1991). A power differential is therefore highlighted in this early group stage, a concept typically described in the group-development literature as the "dependency" or "orientation" phase (see Tuckman & Jensen, 1977; Wheelan, 1994). At this stage, the leader's vision for the group shapes the members' vision. Or in the language of constructivism, at this early stage in the group, the leader's group schemas shape the group members' schemas.

## The Second Reality Crisis: Turning to the Self

This stage is often short-lived in groups. Members usually begin to question the vision of the leader when they become comfortable speaking their minds. Moreover, members' goals and expectations for themselves and for others are almost always more complex than those prescribed by the leader (Nye & Forsyth, 1991). Challenges to the leader and to one another ensue. The group-development literature refers to this phenomenon as the "rebellion" or "storming" stage (Tuckman & Jensen, 1977; Wheelan, 1994). From a constructivist view, this stage can be seen as the point at which the members seriously question the schemas of the leader and of other members and begin to assert their own (Brower, 1986; Wheelan & Johnson, 1996).

This might be seen as a second reality crisis for members in that it often represents a critical point in their decision to stay in the group given the challenges to their construction of group reality. At this point, members face the decision to become a real group with shared understandings of themselves and one another.

Whereas the response to the first reality crisis is well practiced (i.e., look to the leader for direction), the response to this crisis is less so. Members have three options in responding to this reality crisis (see Brower, 1989).

■ *Members can drop out.* Faced with the realization that the group reality does not match their own schemas of the group, members may decide it is not worth the effort and drop out of the group. In a sense, members who choose this option decide to hold onto their own group schemas rather than engage in the development of shared schemas.

■ *Members can "freak out."* Faced with the realization that their schemas do not match the schemas of other members, some members may abandon their own schemas entirely. Leiberman, Yalom, and Miles (1973) describe this phenomenon as a casualty of encounter groups, whereby members who are challenged in the group decompensate and begin to question the reality of everything in their lives. The anomie of the group initiates an avalanche of uncertainty that engulfs them.

■ *Members can negotiate.* Rather than remaining rigidly wedded to their initial group schemas or questioning everything in their lives, members can take a position between these extremes. These members remain grounded in their beliefs about themselves, others, and the world while loosening their adherence to their initial group schemas. They can engage in the situational anomie of the group without becoming engulfed by it. These members will feel anxiety as a result of the group being as yet "unformed" but will feel enough commitment to the group or members to begin to work through their anxiety.

Assuming that this third choice is the most functional for members (in the sense of being the option that enables them to form into a group), then their task becomes determining how to reevaluate their own goals and roles within this group. They ask themselves, "What am *I* doing here and what is it *I* want from this group?" Members begin to see what the group has to offer them and, within this frame, begin to examine what they hope to gain from it and contribute to it.

This "turning to themselves" has been reported in research on personal construct theory (PCT) applications in groups. Johnson and Neimeyer (1996) found that the only group constructs that members are able to describe at this stage are those that are attached to themselves. Members turn to themselves first—literally center themselves first—within their burgeoning group schemas.

### Developing Shared Schemas

Starting with their own role or sense of self within the group, members begin to develop and negotiate other aspects of their shared schemas for the group. This process began with members placing themselves within shared group schemas and developing their sense of self by exhibiting consistent patterns for their own behavior within the group (Patterson, 1996). The next step in the process is to negotiate shared understandings of basic rules or norms for behavior, that is, setting boundaries for membership in the group (Mullen, Rozell, & Anthony, 1996) and determining basic rules for acceptable group behavior, for example, being on time, amount of time each member should talk, acceptable topics for discussion (see Patterson, 1996). Finally members begin to recognize one another's behavior and roles within the group and begin to expect and count on particular members for certain types of contributions (Johnson & Neimeyer, 1996).

From a PCT perspective, after members begin to develop their sense of self, they begin to develop shared group schemas by first establishing the "constructs" (the dimensions of behavior considered important in their judgments of one another) and then establishing the "roles" (how members are perceived by one another). For example, Huici (1980) found that after a two-hour group exposure, group members began to use similar constructs in their descriptions of one another. Moreover, these constructs were highly appropriate to the specific group setting, which was a "t-group" experience: Members' constructs focused on interpersonal characteristics, were not judgmental, and were explicitly interactive. Other research using similar PCT methodologies found that members' perceptions of one another began to coalesce after the first few sessions (Johnson & Neimeyer, 1996; Neimeyer & Merluzzi, 1982). In these studies, members began to exhibit more consensual "role" rating of one another by the sixth and eighth sessions, respectively.

At this stage of group development when members are developing shared schemas, members elicit feedback from and give feedback to one another. Group goals, roles, and structures of power, intimacy, and communication are developed on the basis of observations of behavior within the group and analysis of their shared experiences together. This phenomenon has been described as the "norming" or "trust and structure" phase of group development (Tuckman & Jensen, 1977; Wheelan, 1994).

The development of the components of these shared schemas continues until members' anomie is reduced and the group becomes understandable and predictable for members. At this point, members will have established a shared perception and reality of their group, enabling them to focus more directly on the work before them (i.e., their shared purpose and reason for being together). Interestingly, at this point in the group, members switch from an egocentric to a sociocentric posture, whereby they use cognitive and affective strategies in dealing with the group similar to those they use in dealing with themselves (Forsyth & Kelley, 1996). At this point in the group's development, members can be said to extend their ego boundaries to the boundaries of the group (Nye & Brower, 1996a).

The group is now in position to take advantage of several constructivist interventions that can help individual members in their personal-change process. Throughout the group's remaining life, elements of the shared schemas will continue to be renegotiated as members confront problems and misunderstandings that arise during their time together.

# Clinical Applications and Guidelines

## *Utility of a Constructivism Framework*

In order to use constructivist techniques in groups, the group itself must be at the right "place." Members must have the language, concepts, and awareness of their own perceptions and social meaning-making mechanisms to allow them to talk about and process interventions directed at their constructivist processes. If a group worker uses a constructivist framework to analyze and provide feedback to members' behaviors and interactions, constructivist language and concepts will become part of the group lexicon.

In fact, several practitioners have found that a constructivist framework is extremely useful for helping their group clients make changes in their lives. Neimeyer and Neimeyer (1987) present several examples of the use of PCT in groups (see also Alexander & Follette, 1987; Button, 1987; Llewelyn & Dunnett, 1987; G. J. Neimeyer, 1987). Balgopal and Vassil (1983) present lengthy illustrations of the use of an "ecological" perspective, which Franklin (see Chapter 3) terms social constructionism. Brower (1989) describes how social cognition theory, falling under what Franklin considers constructivism, can be used in a group setting. Each of these practitioners found that the use of a constructivist framework and lexicon helped their clients achieve insights into their interactive patterns and characteristic styles of processing information about themselves and the world. This framework has worked well in groups as diverse as those for general psychotherapy (Balgopal & Vassil, 1983; Brower, 1989), eating disorders (Button, 1987), incest (Alexander & Follette, 1987), and marital couples (G. J. Neimeyer, 1987).

Although it is beyond the scope of this chapter to present an exhaustive examination of the application of constructivism in groups, several implications of the group-development model presented here can be outlined. First, according to the model, two crisis points are associated with members' commitment to the group. By recognizing these points, the leader can provide structure and guidance to modulate the anxiety that these crises generate. With the first crisis, the group needs direct guidance from the leader, such as providing pregroup orientations and presenting clear guidelines for attendance or turn-taking. With the second crisis, the leader's power needs to be redistributed (sharing agenda-setting responsibilities and renegotiating group norms) to the members to facilitate their development of shared group schemas. This initial structure and assistance can be implemented in a manner that is consistent with the group's goals and structure. The initial match between members' initial schemas and the group setting greatly influences whether members stay with the group. Although it is impossible to provide them with a vision of the group that will endure much beyond the initial sessions (given that the group is not really a group until the members make it so), it is desirable to help members access schemas that are compatible with the intended group goals and format. Nye and colleagues (Nye & Forsyth, 1991; Nye & Simonetta, 1996) and Bednar and associates (Bednar & Battersby, 1976; Evensen & Bednar, 1978; Lee & Bednar, 1977) provide guidance in this area. Again, good pregroup orientation meetings and clear guidance in early meetings on group norms and rules are needed to help potential members develop compatible initial group schemas (i.e., compatible expectations of the group and leader).

Second, according to the model, a sense of anomie is inevitable in groups. Merton (1957) suggests that this phenomenon helps create an ideal setting from which life changes can be made. He outlines four ways of adapting to anomie (his definition of anomie consists of disparity between means and ends in society): *innovation*, holding on to the ends while developing new means to achieve them; *ritualization*, holding onto the means while losing sight of the ends; *retreat*, letting go of both the means and ends without substituting others; and *rebellion*, adopting new means and ends in opposition to society. From a group worker's perspective, these styles of adaptation to anomie can be encouraged or manipulated for members, depending on the goals of the group. For example, in many behavioral-change groups, innovation is fostered by highlighting (and therefore solidifying) goals, or ends, for clients while helping them find new ways to achieve them. In social-action groups in which empowerment is desired, active rebellion may be encouraged by helping clients realize alternative social goals and the means to achieve them. By recognizing the anomie inherent in the situation and by working with the processes by which clients adapt to it, the group worker is in position to make optimal use of the group modality.

Third, the language of constructivism and schemas can create a mindset for clients that facilitates change. Constructivist tenets and language state that life is a creative and constructive process as opposed to a corrective process (R. A. Neimeyer, 1993). Clients are therefore helped through constructivist language to recognize that they are doing the best they can, given what they know and perceive. At the same time, they are provided with the language to understand that the truth that they find in their lives is *their* truth and not *the* truth (Brower & Nurius, 1993).

Fourth, different clients exhibit different problems with living associated with different memory storage and retrieval elements (Brower & Nurius, 1993; see Chapter 2). For example, one client might read a situation accurately—that is, perceive the right cues and put them together in a sensible way—yet lack a repertoire of functional responses for the situation. These clients might best be served through skills training that teaches flexibility of response. Another client, however, might respond appropriately but be inflexible in his or her activation of schemas; that is, the client may see all situations as being essentially the same. These clients do not need behavioral skills *per se* but need to be taught ways to read situations and interactions that incorporate social feedback into their constructivist processes (see Brower & Nurius, 1993; Mahoney, 1991).

## Constructivist Techniques

Two constructivist techniques—narratives and role plays—are particularly well suited to a group modality.

## *Narrative*

A lot has been written about the use of narrative in constructivist psychotherapy (R. A. Neimeyer, 1993, 1994). Rather than review this material here, the following discussion focuses on narrative in a group setting.

Narrative theory highlights the ways in which we use stories to make sense of events, to facilitate predictability, to find meaning, and to make choices. Clients are taught that narratives have a beginning (a historical context), a middle (the present situation), and an end (a hoped-for projection of ourselves into the future). Group members can be asked to keep journals in order to develop narratives about their lives outside the group. In this way, the use of narratives in groups becomes a simple analogue to the use of narratives in individual treatment.

I have found it useful for members to develop journal narratives specifically about their group experiences and feelings. When using this technique, I structure time into sessions during which members read portions of their entries to the group. Members begin to develop a story about themselves in the group and about their group as a whole—a narrative that gives their group experience coherence, history, rules, myths, and meaning. This technique creates opportunities during early sessions for discussing miscommunications and experimenting with alternative roles and responses and during later sessions for deepening insight and mutual understanding. I have found that the use of narratives in groups greatly facilitates cohesion and group identity, which from a constructivist point of view stems from the group's explicit development of a shared group narrative.

## *Role Play*

The group modality is an ideal medium for the practice of social roles and social understanding. From a PCT perspective, Llewelyn and Dunnett (1987) and Dunnett and Llewelyn (1988) provide excellent guidelines for role playing in group work. Their work consists of three main steps: (a) helping clients recognize the roles and constructs (schemas) they characteristically use in social interactions through self-reflection and feedback techniques in the group, (b) helping clients experiment with a larger repertoire of roles and constructs in the group, and (c) helping clients extend their experimentation to their outside lives through various group and homework exercises.

In the first step, members are encouraged to play out various interactions with others (initially those outside the group but eventually persons within the group), experimenting with different outcomes, emotions, and responses in order to highlight patterns. In the second step, members learn about their own roles and those of others in the group. Members are encouraged to select members for role plays in order to replicate various situations that they wish to work through (members are selected because their own natural roles and constructs are strategically close to those that the member hopes to practice). In the third step, members again select group members to practice situations and are encouraged to experiment with their new roles, constructs, and responses outside the group. In subsequent sessions, members role play with group members what happened during these outside experiments.

Llewelyn and Dunnett's use of role play uses the social laboratory of groups to its fullest potential. Members are actively encouraged to draw parallels between their feelings, experiences, and behaviors inside and outside the group. Through the creative use of role plays, members use the group's real interactions and experiences as an analogue to experiment with interactions on the outside as well as bring the outside into the group as material for further experimentation.

## Summary and Conclusion

Small groups are an ideal medium for the application of constructivist frameworks and techniques. They provide what Kelly (1955) has called a true "social laboratory" where socially constructed rules, roles, norms, and shared perceptions can emerge.

The model of group development presented here capitalizes on this constructivist perspective. It begins with a description of the group situation as anomic, or lacking external meaning. In the face of this, one enters the group having to rely on one's own group schema—one's best guess, based on prior group experiences, as to what the group means and how to behave. Then, for this group of individuals to become a "real" group, members must develop a shared group schema—a shared understanding of the norms, rules, roles, and meaning of their actions and interactions. The process occurs in stages. Research in the areas of social cognition, schema development, and personal-construct theory describes these stages and the cognitive and affective processes active in each stage.

Using the language of constructivism to make sense of group interactions has been found to be very effective in helping members understand themselves and their group interactions. Moreover, the group worker has a certain leverage over the course of development based on how much and in what ways he or she structures the group experiences for the members. The model of group development described here outlines two specific "crisis points" that can be manipulated by the group worker in order to facilitate specific group and individual change. Finally, the use of narratives and role plays works well in the small group setting. It is my hope that the model of group development examined in this chapter and the discussion of techniques and applications that follow from such an examination will provide a springboard for further developments in the constructivism of *and* in small groups.

## References

Alexander, P. C., & Follette, V. M. (1987). Personal constructs in the group treatment of incest. In R. A. Neimeyer & G. J. Neimeyer (Eds.), *Personal construct therapy casebook* (pp. 211–229). New York: Springer.

Balgopal, D. R., & Vassil, T. V. (1983). *Groups in social work: An ecological perspective*. New York: Macmillan.

Bednar, R. L., & Battersby, C. P. (1976). The effects of specific cognitive structure on early group development. *Journal of Applied Behavioral Science, 12*, 513–522.

Bennis, W. G., & Shepard, H. A. (1956). A theory of group development. *Human Relations, 9,* 415–437.

Brower, A. M. (1986). Behavior changes in psychotherapy groups: A study using an empirically tested statistical model. *Small Group Behavior, 17,* 164–185.

Brower, A. M. (1989). Group development as constructed social reality: A social-cognitive understanding of group formation. *Social Work with Groups, 12*(2), 23–41.

Brower, A. M., & Nurius, P. S. (1993). *Social cognition and individual change.* Newbury Park, CA: Sage.

Button, E. J. (1987). Construing people or weight? An eating disorders group. In R. A. Neimeyer & G. J. Neimeyer (Eds.), *Personal construct therapy casebook* (pp. 230–244). New York: Springer.

Cohen, C. E. (1981). Goals and schemata in person perception: Making sense from the stream of behavior. In N. Cantor & J. F. Kihlstrom (Eds.), *Personality, cognition, and social interaction.* Hillsdale, NJ: Lawrence Erlbaum.

Dunnett, G. N., & Llewelyn, S. P. (1988). Elaborating personal construct theory in a group setting. In G. N. Dunnett (Ed.), *Personal construct psychology in clinical settings.* London: Routledge and Kegan Paul.

Evensen, E. P., & Bednar, R. L. (1978). Effects of specific cognitive and behavioral structure on early group behavior and atmosphere. *Journal of Counseling Psychology, 25,* 66–75.

Forsyth, D. R., & Kelley, K. N. (1996). Heuristic-based biases in estimations of personal contributions to collective endeavors. In J. Nye & A. M. Brower (Eds.), *What's social about social cognition: Research on socially shared cognition in small groups.* Newbury Park, CA: Sage.

Garland, J. A., Jones, H. A., & Kolodney, R. L. (1973). A model for stages of development in social work groups. In S. Bernstein (Ed.), *Explorations in group work* (pp. 17–71). Boston: Milford House.

Hartford, M. E. (1963). *The social group worker and group formation.* Doctoral diss., School of Social Work, University of Chicago.

Huici, C. (1980). Initial disposition and intermember in experimental groups. *Small Group Behavior, 11,* 297–307.

Johnson, M. E., & Neimeyer, R. A. (1996). Perceptual sets and stimulus values: The social relations model in group psychotherapy. In J. Nye & A. M. Brower (Eds.), *What's social about social cognition: Research on socially shared cognition in small groups* (pp. 154–174). Newbury Park, CA: Sage.

Kelly, G. A. (1955). *A theory of personality: The psychology of personal constructs.* New York: W. W. Norton.

Lang, N. C. (1981). Some defining characteristics of the social work group: Unique social form. In S. L. Abels & P. Abels (Eds.), *Social work with groups, proceedings, 1979 symposium* (pp. 18–50). Louisville, KY: Committee for the Advancement of Social Work with Groups.

Lee, F. T., & Bednar, R. L. (1977). The effects of group structure and risk-taking disposition on group behavior, attitudes, and atmosphere. *Journal of Counseling Psychology, 24,* 191–199.

Lieberman, M. A., Yalom, I. D., & Miles, M. B. (1973). *Encounter groups: First facts.* New York: Basic Books.

Llewelyn, S. P., & Dunnett, G. N. (1987). The use of personal construct theory in groups. In R. A. Neimeyer & G. J. Neimeyer (Eds.), *Personal construct therapy casebook* (pp. 245–258). New York: Springer.

Mahoney, M. J. (1991). *Human change processes: The scientific foundations of psychotherapy.* New York: Basic Books.

Merton, R. K. (1957). *Social theory and social structure.* Glencoe, IL: Free Press.

Mullen, B., Rozell, D., & Johnson, C. (1996). The phenomenology of being in a group: Complexity approaches to operationalizing cognitive representation. In J. Nye & A. M. Brower (Eds.), *What's social about social cognition: Research on socially shared cognition in small groups* (pp. 205–229). Newbury Park, CA: Sage.

Neimeyer, G. J. (1987). Marital role reconstruction through couples group therapy. In R. A. Neimeyer & G. J. Neimeyer (Eds.), *Personal construct therapy casebook* (pp. 127–152). New York: Springer.

Neimeyer, G. J., & Merluzzi, T. V. (1982). Group situation and group process: Personal construct theory and group development. *Small Group Behavior, 13,* 150–164.

Neimeyer, R. A. (1993). An appraisal of constructivist psychotherapies. *Journal of Consulting and Clinical Psychology, 61,* 221–234.

Neimeyer, R. A. (1994). The role of client-generated narratives in psychotherapy. *Journal of Constructivist Psychology, 7,* 229–242.

Neimeyer, R. A., & Neimeyer, G. J. (1987). *Personal construct therapy casebook.* New York: Springer.

Neisser, U. (1976). *Cognition and reality: Principles and implications of cognitive psychology.* San Francisco: Freeman.

Nye, J., & Brower, A. M. (1996a). What's social about social cognition research? In J. Nye & A. M. Brower (Eds.), *What's social about social cognition: Research on socially shared cognition in small groups* (pp. 311– 323). Newbury Park, CA: Sage.

Nye, J., & Brower, A. M. (Eds.). (1996b). *What's social about social cognition: Research on socially shared cognition in small groups.* Newbury Park, CA: Sage.

Nye, J., & Forsyth, D. R. (1991). The effects of prototype-based biases on leadership appraisals: A test of leadership categorization theory. *Small Group Research, 22,* 360–379.

Nye, J., & Simonetta, L. G. (1996). Followers' perceptions of group leaders: The impact of recognition-based and inference-based processes. In J. Nye & A. M. Brower (Eds.), *What's social about social cognition: Research on socially shared cognition in small groups* (pp. 124–153). Newbury Park, CA: Sage.

Patterson, M. L. (1996). Social behavior and social cognition: A parallel process approach. In J. Nye & A. M. Brower (Eds.), *What's social about social cognition: Research on socially shared cognition in small groups* (pp. 87–105). Newbury Park, CA: Sage.

Tuckman, B. W., & Jensen, M. A. C. (1977). Stages of small-group development revisited. *Group and Organization Studies, 2,* 419–427.

Wheelan, S. A. (1994). *Group processes: A developmental perspective.* Boston: Allyn and Bacon.

Wheelan, S. A., & Hochberger, J. M. (1996). Validation studies of the group development questionnaire. *Small Group Research, 27*(1), 143–170.

Wheelan, S. A., & Johnson, F. (1996.) The role of informal member leaders in a system containing formal leaders. *Small Group Research, 27*(1), 33–55.

Wheelan, S. A., & McKeage, R. L. (1993). Developmental patterns in small and large groups. *Small Group Research, 24*(1), 60–83.

Yalom, I. D. (1980). *Existential psychotherapy.* New York: Basic Books.

Yalom, I. D. (1995). *The theory and practice of group psychotherapy* (4th ed.). New York: Basic Books.

# Part 4:

## ◘ Constructivist Practice With Families ◘

# 10

## Family-Centered Practice In the Postmodern Era

*Joan Laird*

The 1950s witnessed the birth of the family therapy movement and a growing interest in systemic and cybernetic theories, whereas the 1960s and 1970s ushered in widespread interest in systems and ecological theories as well as renewed interest in the family. The late 1980s and early 1990s have brought yet another major metaperspective for understanding human beings in their social environments. The postmodern movement in its various forms—constructivism, deconstruction, poststructuralism, and social constructionism—is generating new thought and theory in the arts and humanities, the physical and social sciences, and the mental health and social service professions. It has had a profound influence on the family therapy field. Family theorists have both responded and contributed to a dramatic reconceptualization of assessment and intervention in the helping process. These contributions, in turn, are beginning to influence social work practice and education (Laird, 1993b).

It is too early to know how widespread this paradigmatic shift will be or how long its staying power. Nevertheless, it is forcing reexamination of some of social work's long and dearly held assumptions.

In this chapter, I assume that the reader has some familiarity with social constructionist philosophy and ideas. The focus here is on how these ideas are being applied in the field of family therapy and the implications of this body of thought for social work practice. I avoid the terms "theory" or "model," because current definitions of various categories in social work imply preunderstandings or prior maps for practice in ways that do not always fit well with a social constructionist stance. Instead, the material is organized around the questions this new metaperspective raises for social work practice:

- What is the role of knowledge?
- What is the role of values?

- How are problems defined, who is the client, and what constitutes change?
- How is the worker–client relationship conceptualized?
- How are assessment and intervention conceptualized?
- How shall we evaluate our professional stance and our practice?

Although discussion is limited to clinical practice with individuals and families, these considerations have powerful implications for larger-system practice as well.

# The Role of Knowledge

In social constructionist thought, *knowledge* is not some measure of *reality* separate from either the knower or the process of knowing. The processes of human knowing, as Weick (1993) phrases it, "are deeply rooted in and shaped by our culture, conditions, and psyches. Because perception itself is mediated by constellations of factors, the possibility of seeing something 'as it really is is no longer tenable' " (p. 17). Human knowledge is subjective, that is, a matter of interpretation.

> The knower always intimately influences what is known and how it is known. Human beings are pattern-makers because they interpret or attach meaning to what they observe. The phenomenon of human experience suggests that people are active shapers of their reality, not passive observers of events played out on a screen. If, through interpretation, human beings create what they see, then we can no longer claim that truth rests on an absolute standard existing outside ourselves. (Weick, 1993, p. 18)

Although constructivists, cognitive psychologists, and others have been interested in learning how the individual perceives or comes to *know* and describe the outside world, social constructionists have stressed the *intersubjectivity* of knowing. Knowledge becomes a matter of the meanings assigned to experience. Those meanings are negotiated in interaction with others, in relationships, and in social and cultural worlds of meaning. Those larger social discourses, which change over time and differ from culture to culture, provide the reservoirs of meaning and language from which individuals and families fashion their stories. Knowing, then, is narrative.

Reality is never experienced directly but is always filtered through human processes of knowing and creating meaning. It is, as Lily Tomlin so pungently put it, "a collective hunch." Furthermore, our own seeing and knowing of the world cannot be separated from our prior personal and professional stories, that is, from prior texts, prior codes, or "forestructures of understanding" (McNamee & Gergen, 1992, p. 1). We force our current experiences and perceptions into our prior categories for knowing, thus creating what it is we think we see and know. History, from a constructionist's perspective, is always in the making, a more or less changing narrative about the same events, a recasting and reexperiencing whereby events cannot be isolated from the interpreter of these events (Spence, 1982).

We cannot understand knowledge outside its connections with power. Knowledge and power, argued Foucault (1980), are inseparable.

*Power produces knowledge. . . . There is no power relation without the correlative constitution of a field of knowledge, nor any knowledge that does not presuppose and constitute at the same time, power relations. (Foucault, 1979, pp. 27–28)*

In clinical work, the effort is not to search out "truth" or "reality" according to the directions contained in a set of prior theories or bodies of knowledge but to find out how people have made sense of their experiences, how they have interpreted them, and what effects those interpretations have had on their lives. In the therapeutic conversation, knowledge is inductive and cocreated; it emerges from the interactions among the participants. Schön (1983) calls this "knowledge in action," and Geertz (1983) describes it as the making of "local knowledge."

From a constructionist perspective, knowledge and theory cannot be neatly differentiated—both are seen as culturally situated, creative narratives. "Theory is not an external knowledge-packet but a fluid, creative process of constructing new guesses" (Weick, 1993, p. 26). Knowledge and theory, then, are always provisional, always negotiable.

If knowledge is not to be evaluated in terms of how well it matches the outer world in some empirical sense or how it is vested with power and authority, how shall we evaluate our knowledge and theories, what criteria should we use? Weick (1993) suggests we adopt a more egalitarian stance toward knowing, one in which all theories are seen as provisional and the process of knowing is more valued than the content of knowing. Such a stance encourages dialogue and negotiation, conversations in which everyone is "an interpreter, a creator, a seer" (p. 19). Furthermore, it allows us to move beyond the limitations of empiricist science and to listen to and value alternative ways of knowing, that is, knowledge as perceived by the marginalized, the dissidents, and those who do not live their lives by the various canons that assume authority and a special hold on "truth."

## The Role of Values

In the modernist era, with its emphasis on scientific thought, rationality, and the objective and neutral stance of both researcher and practitioner, clinicians were to be aware of but to hold in abeyance their personal values and biases. The modernist practitioner, insofar as was possible, was to assume the stance of the value-free, objective expert (Allen, 1993). Values, with the exception of those that were articulated in professional codes of ethics, were to be carefully screened out. Practitioners were urged to judge their work with clients according to scientific principles and to demonstrate the utility of their theories and their assessment and intervention strategies in measurable ways. Practice, many argued (and continue to argue), could be quantified (see Hudson, 1982).

In social constructionist thought, however, reality is not perceived as a value-free, measurable entity; rather, it is always mediated, indeed constituted, through language and conversation. As social work practitioners and theorists, we, with our clients, participate in the creation of a changing narrative and thus a changing reality. The narrative changes as a result of a conversation in which both the problem and its possible solutions shift and are reframed. Reality is not being tested, measured, or sought; people consider and reconsider reality through their conceptions of and experiences with it. It is not discovered; rather, it is created and recreated.

Values are screened *in*, not out. Our theories are *never* neutral or value-free; indeed, science itself is value-laden. We can never fully distinguish between facts and values, and the values of everyone concerned are relevant to the mutual change endeavor. As researcher or practitioner, we cannot participate without influencing or being influenced by what we are observing. Therefore, our values must be identified, reexamined, made transparent, and brought into the therapeutic conversation. The practitioner's values should not carry more weight than those of the client or other parties involved in the dialogue because we are more "expert" or our values are somehow better or more true.

Various authors have argued that practice is always political and always concerns values. Rhodes (1986), for example, maintains that we must acknowledge the sociopolitical aspects of our professional ethics, and Allen (1993) points out that even our widely accepted social work values of self-determination and respect for the dignity and worth of each individual are uniquely Western and Eurocentric. Some family therapists, notably Waldegrave (1990), have argued for a therapeutic stance in which connectedness and the aims of social justice are valued.

White and Epston (1990), leaning on the work of Foucault (1979, 1980), among others, explored the intricate relationships between knowledge and power, in which certain values are privileged and given the status of "knowledge" or "science," whereas the views and values of others are subjugated. White (1994) articulates the political aspects of therapy, an endeavor in which knowledge and power always play an active role.

As the role of power in the shaping of social discourse became a central quest for the deconstructionist, several thinkers in the family field emphasized exploration of the voices of the subjugated. For example, feminist family therapists, in work not always identified as "constructionist," have nevertheless deconstructed prevailing family theories and models to show their failure to account for the gender and power relationships inherent in assumed "knowledges," in theories of family life, and in the family itself (see Goldner, 1985, 1988; Goodrich, Rampage, Ellman, & Halstead, 1988; Hare-Mustin, 1978, 1987; Laird, 1992). Boyd-Franklin (1989), Falicov (1983), and McGoldrick, Pearce, and Giordano (1982), among others, examined white, Eurocentric biases in dominant family therapy models, and Crawford (1987) and Laird (1993a) looked at culturally biased conceptions of the lesbian family.

## Defining Problems, the Client, and Change

Family clinicians view the family as the most salient context for understanding and changing many individually defined problems. Hartman and Laird (1983), for example, argued that family systems theories inform work with individuals, couples, families, and even larger systems. The central guiding notion is that every human system needs to be understood in its sociocultural context, over time and in space. The family, which provides the major context for individual growth and development and mediates between the individual and society, seemed a fruitful location for understanding and intervening in individual and family problems.

Today, some family theorists suggest that the idea of "family" itself is a widely varying social construction with shifting forms and boundaries and that it may not always be the most salient system in defining problems or in selecting the unit of attention for practice. Anderson and Goolishian (1988, 1992), for example, maintain that problems exist "in language"; that is, a problem is something that a particular group of people has decided to call a problem. Furthermore, the problem-defining system usually assigns a particular cause or locus of blame. The defining group may be one individual, a family, or some larger constellation of people or systems who agree on problem definition. These definitions may be idiosyncratic local narratives or may be supported by larger social discourses. For example, in this society, "diagnostic" discourses, rooted in the medical tradition and elaborately encoded in the DSM series (but also part of popular culture and the lay public's own narratives), most often define problems in terms of individual human defects. These defects are commonly blamed on genetic or other biological roots or on faulty child rearing (particularly mothering). They are rarely understood as products of powerful social forces. In what may be the most far-reaching effort to date to medicalize all of human experience, the latest version of the *Diagnostic and Statistical Manual of Mental Disorders* (American Psychiatric Association, 1994) includes disorders of reading, writing, and arithmetic. In the discussion of these disorders, no mention is made of poverty, racism, sexism, or other social experiences that might shape individual experience.

Similarly, in the family field, problems have been perceived as products of faulty family structure, hierarchy, communication, rule systems, or unresolved intergenerational issues, many of which are attributed to faulty mothering. Many family therapists have argued that everyone in the family must be seen if the therapy is not to be undermined (Napier & Whitaker, 1978). Sometimes the client system might be expanded to include the referring party or another highly involved professional (Selvini-Palazzoli, Boscolo, Cecchin, & Prata, 1980a) or, in the case of Bowen family systems theory (Bowen, 1978; Carter & McGoldrick, 1980, 1988; Framo, 1976; Hartman & Laird, 1983), other family-of-origin members. However, the nuclear or intergenerational family occupied center stage in the various models, which fits society's emphasis on defining family in biological rather than social terms.

The idea that the client system should be defined by prior ideas of structure and process (individual personality, family, group, and so forth) is being challenged by today's constructionist thinkers in the family field, who believe that theory, model, or client should not be defined by the size of a particular system but rather by an exploration of who is "languaging" the situation at hand as a problem and who might best work on *dis-solving* or *restorying* that problem narrative. Change is perceived as having occurred when new narratives or new stories are cocreated in such a way that the problem is dis-solved; that is, it is no longer seen as a problem. A new set of meanings emerges in the therapeutic conversational process.

White and Epston (1990), like Anderson and Goolishian (1988, 1992), argue that problems should not be located inside people or even in the relationships between people. People have problems because they and/or others have or are making sense of (or authoring) their life experiences in ways that inhibit their moving forward and consequently are disempowering. In other words, the experience itself is not the problem, but rather the narrative describing the experience. In these authors' view, people have problems with problems; change occurs when the relationship between the person and "problem" evolves. This approach does not minimize or abrogate responsibility for intervening in the stresses between people and their environments or seeking to undermine oppressive conditions in the real world, although to date little articulation of these issues has appeared in the family constructionist literature.

Calling their work a "therapy of literary merit," White and Epston (1990) conceptualize problems as paralyzing or handicapping narratives, stories for living that limit possibilities. For example, labeling a client as "borderline" often engenders a sense of hopelessness on the part of both client and clinician. White and Epston's notion of "externalizing the problem" aims to free people from self-blaming positions, enabling them to mobilize their lives in ways that undermine the influence of such problem narratives.

For example, in a recent videotape, White (1992b), demonstrated his work with a man with a prior diagnosis of "manic–depressive disorder," searching with him for a more "experience-near" narrative or story that might better fit the man's experiences and meanings and empower him to take more charge of his life. Together they decided that the man was "overenthusiastic" at times, a description that led to their coconstructing actions that might monitor the man's "overenthusiasm" in ways that would put the man, to use his own language, "in the driver's seat." In his well-known encounter with "Sneaky Poo," White (White & Epston, 1990) helped a young boy with a prior diagnosis of encopresis and his parents defeat a "formidable adversary" who was soiling their environment and spoiling their lives. Again, neither the child nor family relationships nor parenting methods were assessed as the problem.

Such an approach does not deny painful life experiences—the events themselves—but rather questions whether the person's storying of those experiences fits the experience as lived, draws on strength and potential, and potentiates change. Thus a woman with a history of sexual abuse, diagnosed as having "borderline personality disorder," might be helped to rework her narrative in such a way that she moves from self-blaming victim to competent and assertive survivor. A man defined as a batterer or abuser may be helped to reexamine his stories and expectations of "manliness" in a way that helps him to perceive his actions differently and to take responsibility for them.

In all of these situations, new narratives are coconstructed in such a way that they are less negatively defining and less distant from the person's or family's lived experience than are most "expert" categorizations. And they are shaped in a therapeutic dialogue in which strengths and competence are highlighted—what White (1989) calls "unique outcomes" and de Shazer (1985) terms "exceptions," that is, times when people are able to overcome the "problem."

In the view of Anderson and Goolishian (1988), then, the individual or the family should not be considered the client, but rather the nexus of people and organizations directly concerned about a particular situation and "in language" about it. Thus, the clinician may wish to see a single individual, an extended family, a father and son, a couple and their closest friends, a girl and her coach and teammates, the tenants of a building, or professionals and patients on a hospital ward. Although the epistemology is somewhat different, these notions are not unfamiliar to social workers who have long advocated for "case to cause" approaches and an "extended action" or "extended client system" stance, whereby the problem is followed wherever it leads (Hartman, 1974), and who understand problems from an ecological perspective (Germain, 1979).

In social constructionist thought, then, "reality" is always filtered through human language—we cannot gain direct access to it. That is not to say that violence, poverty, pain, and mental or emotional anguish are not problems, but rather that they are experienced and *storied* differently. For example, a woman who had an illegal and secret abortion in the 1940s or 1950s, a time when abortion was storied in society as shameful, will have had an experience very different from that of a woman of the 1990s who chooses to have a legal abortion, is offered counseling, and may share her experience with others. People understand and assign different meanings to their pain, poverty, successes, and failures and thus experience the same reality differently.

These ideas challenge the artificial divisions that currently exist among various theories of human behavior as well as the ways that social work education and practice are organized according to theory and system size. Thus, our models, theories, programs, education sequences, professional organizations, and so forth are defined primarily by allegiance to a particular body of theory (e.g., psychodynamic, behavioral, family systems, group dynamics) that is applied to a particular size system. Because social constructionism is part epistemology and part metatheory, that is, a theory about theories, the approaches to practice emerging from this perspective cannot be categorized in the same way. Just as generalist practice ideas emerged during the decades of systems and ecological theories, so may new ideas about how to organize theory, practice, and education emerge as we move toward the millennium. The concept of the individual or the family as the systems of relevance to clinical practice may be called into question.

## Conceptualizing Worker–Client Relationship

In recent years, various authors (Hillman & Ventura, 1993; Lerner, 1986) have argued that the practice of therapy, with its emphasis on "diagnosing" or "assessing" the other, is by its nature disempowering. Gergen and Kaye (1992) suggest that the very structure of the process

> *furnishes the client a lesson in inferiority. The client is indirectly informed that he or she is ignorant, insensitive, woolly-headed, or emotionally incapable of comprehending reality. In contrast, the therapist is positioned as all-knowing and wise—a model to which the client might aspire. The situation is all the more lamentable owing to the fact that in occupying the superior role, the therapist fails to reveal any weaknesses. (p. 171)*

In such situations, the client often leaves therapy with a sense of having had and still having a personal defect that from time to time may require the help of an "expert." One of the central ironies in social work and in other mental health professions is that, on the one hand, we wish to create contexts in which our clients may be empowered and, on the other hand, it is to our professional advantage to define ourselves as "experts" for a population in need of experts. In so doing, a hierarchical relationship is established that fosters a sense of disempowerment in clients.

Until relatively recently, family therapists often viewed themselves as experts on families and as strategists maneuvering in ways that forced families to make shifts, restructure family relationships, or dislodge members from a "stuck" position. Eschewing medical metaphors in favor of mechanistic and militaristic systemic language, family therapists described families and individuals as enmeshed or disengaged, differentiated or fused, homeostatic, faulty feedback systems, and dysfunctional. Family therapists perceived themselves as battling with families to counter or neutralize the family's power or interrupt its "game" in order to stimulate the change process.

To my knowledge, Andersen (1987, 1991), a Norwegian psychiatrist, and Hoffman (1985), an American social worker, were among the first to argue publicly for a new conception of therapeutic power in which the therapist attempted to shed his or her power and retreat from the expert position by voicing his or her own uncertainties. Andersen developed the notion of the "reflecting team," a clinical mode now widely used in the United States. Simultaneously, in the 1980s, Anderson and Goolishian (1988) drew from postmodern theory, anthropology, and the ideas of psychologist Kenneth Gergen (Gergen, 1985; Gergen & Kaye, 1992) to challenge the notion of mental health professional as expert, arguing instead on behalf of a "not-knowing," "de-expertized" position. The "not-knowing" stance of the clinician is certainly controversial. However, it does not imply that clinicians lack important knowledge, but rather describes how clinicians' knowledge and understanding are used in the relationship.

Anderson and Goolishian (1992) and Laird (1989, 1994) conceptualized the role of the therapist as the respectful stranger, not unlike that of an ethnographer visiting a new society to learn about the local culture and mores. This stranger is infinitely curious, searching for multiple views of (rather than the "truth" of) the local culture and, in the case of therapy, multiple descriptions of the problem. As Cecchin (1992) points out, curiosity generates respect and "provides the opportunity for the construction of new forms of action and interpretation" (p. 91).

Such a stance, which moves away from locating causes and assigning blame or defect, invites participation and collaboration. A respectfully curious stance also "de-privileges" (but does not obviate) the therapist's prior texts or preunderstandings.

The clinician, like the ethnographer, attempts to bracket her or his prior knowledge in order to listen without judging or categorizing words and behaviors according to prior sets of diagnoses or other professional maps. Such prior maps tend to lead us to conjure up what we expected to learn and prevent us from hearing the client's narrative. As Allen (1993) points out, "when we already 'know' what is happening, we lose curiosity and respect suffers" (p. 48). Although our preunderstandings and closely held personal and professional knowledges and ethics are not irrelevant, they are not more "true" or privileged than those of clients. To the extent possible and useful, the clinician's thinking is shared, made transparent, and offered tentatively as "ideas" for consideration.

This does not mean that immoral behavior, the misuse of power, or oppression should be approved or validated. In many situations, a worker's first responsibility must be to attend to the safety or protection of one or more individuals. And sometimes the family practitioner represents the authority of a larger system mandated by the community to regulate human behavior and human relationships. In these instances, the worker is guided by concepts of justice and social responsibility. From a constructionist perspective, these larger "authorities" are not viewed as having an edge on truth, but rather as having an edge on defining what shall be considered knowledge or truth for a particular time and place.

Of course, notions of right and wrong change over time. For example, in the emerging social discourse today, forced sex in a marriage may be termed "marital rape." Such an idea was "out of language" and thus did not exist a few years ago. Our individual narratives are shaped within the context of larger social discourses that both constrain and potentiate our narratives of family, community, and the larger society. We think and act within the constraints of these folklores/mythologies/narratives; they define the repertoires of possibilities for storying our own lives.

## Conceptualizing Assessment and Intervention

Assessment of the person-in-situation complex has been the *sine qua non* of social work ever since the publication of Mary Richmond's (1917) *Social Diagnosis*. Authors of social work practice texts such as Hamilton (1951), Hollis (1964), Compton and Galaway (1979), Germain and Gitterman (1980), Hartman and Laird (1983), and Meyer (1993) have placed assessment at the heart of practice. Their emphasis, of course, has varied. Some social work theorists have paid far more attention to assessment of the person, others to the family or group, and others to the environment or to the relationship between person or family and environment. Furthermore, the power of the scientific metaphor and the widespread use of psychodynamic and psychoanalytic theories have fostered an emphasis on locating "causes," usually discovered in the past, and a search for "cures," often through the development of insight. Social workers have been and are educated to pursue careful histories and to make thorough psychosocial assessments. If the assessment is complete, the "whats" and "hows" of intervention should be evident.

For the most part, family-centered theorists (like behaviorists) have been more interested in assessing and intervening in here-and-now patterns of family interactions. Individual problems or symptoms are viewed as adaptations to faulty communication patterns (Satir, 1967), family structures (Minuchin, 1974; Minuchin & Fishman, 1981), organization and hierarchy (Haley, 1976), solutions to problems (de Shazer, 1985; Watzlawick, Weakland, & Fisch, 1974), or rule systems (Papp, 1983; Selvini-Palazzoli, Boscolo, Cecchin, & Prata, 1980b). The exception, of course, is Bowen family systems theory (Bowen, 1978), in which current problems in individual, couple, or family interaction are closely linked to unresolved issues of differentiation from families of origin. Although what is placed in the center of the lens varies, family theorists, drawing on cybernetic and systemic theories, have tended to minimize individual in favor of family assessment.

From a social constructionist perspective, neither the person nor the family is assessed. In fact, assessment as we know it seems to disappear from clinical language altogether. Diagnosis and assessment imply an expert "knower" who interprets the past and present experiences of another—primarily a one-way process in which the professional's experiences and emotions are hidden from view and rarely enter the conversation. This stance places the professional in a "colonizing" position and makes it exceedingly difficult to hear the client's story. Our preunderstandings hamper our ability to listen and crowd out new possibilities for understanding because we become preoccupied with fitting or matching what we hear with the narratives we bring to the encounter. This dilemma is similar to that of the ethnographer, who attempts to enter another's world unfettered by his or her own cultural understandings and biases. In the social constructionist view, *collaboration*, *reflexivity*, and *multiplicity* replace assessment and intervention as key elements in the process.

## *Collaboration*

The therapeutic dialogue (in the worker–client relationship and as it extends into the community in pursuit of social justice) is a collaborative attempt to generate new meanings and new possibilities. These meanings are "local," in the sense that they refer to "the language, the meaning, and the understanding developed between persons in dialogue, rather than broadly held cultural sensibilities" (Anderson & Goolishian, 1992). Global, totalizing knowledges, such as are expressed in various psychological and systemic theories, are eschewed in favor of local meanings and vocabularies.

The client's history is as important for its narrative as it is for its factual truth (Spence, 1982). Instead of trying to recover "what really happened," the worker and client explore clients' perceptions of their life experiences and the impact their beliefs about those experiences have had on their life and problems. The clinician may ask questions such as: Does this set of meanings reflect your experiences as lived? Does the story constrain or open up possibilities for you? Does this story of your life foster self-disparagement? Self-blaming? Hopelessness? Does it diminish opportunities for you to achieve your full potential? Does it prevent you from taking responsibility for your actions? Does it preclude action altogether? Does it isolate you or others from potential resources? How did you learn this way of being a woman? A man? A parent? Are there other possible interpretations for what happened to you?

Although therapists are not responsible for changing the behavior of another or for the clients' insights, they are accountable for the effects of their interactions on clients, for examining their own biases and privileges, for confronting the limits of their own understandings, for making transparent and naming the ideas that influence their work, and for confronting injustices and oppression in the surrounding community (White, 1994).

Waldegrave (1990) and his colleagues in New Zealand have described "just" therapy—a therapy that is culturally sensitive, that views the clinician as a mediator between client and community, and that articulates the various responsibilities of both clinician and client. Closer to home, People's Bridge Action sponsors a project called MOSAIC (Mothers of Survivors Are Interested in Children), in which social constructionist concepts are implemented in work with families. Mothers in the MOSAIC project become peer advocates for new mothers entering the program, accompanying them to school and to court or simply providing a friendly ear. These women tell their stories and reauthor their lives in individual and group therapeutic conversations, write and publish their own newsletter, speak at conferences, make guest appearances in social work and other classes, and have produced an educational film (MOSAIC Project, 1994). Currently, they are working conjointly on a book.

In another example of social constructionism in the community, clinicians at the Family Institute of Cambridge (Roth, Chasin, Chasin, Becker, & Herzig, 1992) sponsor a Public Conversations project, in which people with sharply differing views listen to and develop respect for others' ideas. For example, participants on both sides of the abortion controversy have aired their views in public conversations in an effort to enhance mutual understanding and foster greater tolerance for difference.

## Reflexivity

Narratives, stories, and meanings, then, are intersubjective. They are created and recreated in the conversational spaces among people and are influenced and shaped by the larger social discourse. No story or text is ever fixed, because each listener and each reader bring something new to the encounter. Furthermore, the conversation is reflexive, that is, ideas fold back upon themselves. The editing or reauthoring of our stories is an ongoing process. As Lax (1992) frames it, "It is the act of making oneself an object of one's own observation" (p. 75). In the intersubjective space between client and consultant, stories take on fresh perspectives that allow participants to develop different social performances of those stories.

The circular, systemic questioning ideas inspired by Bateson (1972) and developed in the work of Selvini-Palazzoli and colleagues (1980b) and others pioneered the reflexive process in family interviewing. In its "reflective team" form, the consultant team may offer its reflections, after which the client may reflect on the team's reflections with the clinician. A "consultant" or "reflector" may sit in on the interview and from time to time offer his or her comments, which, in turn, can be discussed. Letters may be sent (White & Epston, 1990) or written reflections brought into the session (Penn & Frankfurt, 1994). Reflections are offered tentatively as ideas and as possibilities for further thought, conversation, or action. They are never critical or negative; rather, they search for strengths and for alternative possibilities in stories and actions. The reflexive interchange renders the conversation less hierarchical, shifting the typical power arrangement between clinician and client.

### Multiplicity

Drawing on Bateson's (1972) notion of both/and rather than either/or and Maturana's (1988) idea that as many possible understandings of a situation exist as there are people to give voice to them, *multiplicity* allows the conversation to be structured in ways that encourage multiple ideas and multiple possibilities. The clinician's job is to create a context in which this can happen. He or she (and other consultants or a reflecting team) may identify with the client's experiences and may share their own stories to the extent that the stories relate to the content of the interview as well as offer ideas or metaphors for change. The clinician offers ideas tentatively and, insofar as possible, in positive ways that connect to client strengths, while making clear that these ideas are based on experience and belief, not on expertise or authority.

The clinician's role is to open up conversational spaces in order to generate new ideas. Andersen (1991) suggests that reflections that are too radical from the client's perspective may paralyze the client, whereas those that are too similar will fail to stimulate change. The length of collaboration is not prescribed and clients who choose not to return are not defined as "resistant." Clients may come for a single consultation or may choose to continue the dialogue for a longer period.

Sometimes, of course, clinicians must insist that certain ideas prevail, because they represent the law, agency policy, or community mores or because someone needs protection from the oppressive ideas and actions of another. Clinicians, as Efran and Clarfield (1992) phrase it, "are not prohibited from having and expressing preferences, hopes, and opinions. They are only enjoined from claiming that these belong to someone else, or derive from a privileged access to an outside objective reality" (p. 205).

## Evaluating Practice

The constructionist practitioner, therefore, cannot claim to be objective or to have special expertise regarding external "reality." Similarly, practice cannot be evaluated through some set of objective criteria that exist separate from dialogue.

Is therapy, then, a contest of values? If, in a social constructionist stance, neither science nor the search for "truth" undergird our efforts, to what are we held accountable? How do we evaluate our work? Are we left with a rampant relativism in which every "truth," every story, every intervention is equal? Clearly we need a new set of criteria for making judgments. But those criteria must account for the fact that we are valuing and meaning-making human beings, that none of us has an edge on the truth, and that our values and meanings are always part of the reality that we are trying to understand.

Measurement, which is so highly valued in the modernist era in general and in social work in particular, in constructionist thought is perceived as a useful metaphor or language, a socially constructed set of symbols that can help us understand phenomena, not as a path to truth. For example, it may be helpful for social workers to document information such as the number of contacts; canceled appointments; individual or family incomes; individual, couple, family, or group rankings on various psychological or social scales; tests indicating progress; and so forth. However, these efforts are not value-free.

Measurement cannot capture a complex and recursive sociopolitical process in which both reality and relationships are constantly being negotiated and recreated. Narrative, ethnographic, and other qualitative research forms encourage deep and detailed descriptions and capture the intricacies of clients' meanings and beliefs as well as the movement of the therapeutic dialogue.

Accountability requires more than documentation of process and/or outcome. It also requires striving for practice that is moral, ethical, responsible, and just, in which the worker struggles to understand whose morality, whose justice, and whose meanings are being endorsed. As family theorist Keeney (1983) suggested, we must move from an ethic of objectivity to an ethic of responsibility. Our obligation, argue Efran and Clarfield (1992), is to be true to ourselves and to invite clients to take responsibility for their beliefs and their actions.

## Toward a Just and Responsible Postmodern Practice

Although social constructionist ideas hold promise for a more democratic and empowering stance in practice and although they seem to open up the possibilities for listening in new ways, some cautions are in order.

First, it is important to maintain a critical and decontructionist stance toward the constructionist metaperspective itself. The temptation to reify "truth," philosophy, and theory is difficult to resist in social work. Constructionist philosophy implies a critical stance that must be willing to turn its gaze upon itself.

Second, the therapeutic encounter always takes place within a political context. To date, few theorists in the family field have examined the relationship between the "local knowledges" generated in the therapeutic conversation and the larger social discourses that penetrate and shape our individual and family narratives (Laird, 1993b; Hare-Mustin, 1994). By extension, the notion of differential power in the ability to voice one's story in private or in public is rarely addressed. These subjugating discourses, in my view, must be brought to the surface when they clearly limit the possibilities for moving forward.

Some scholars, notably Hoffman (1992) and Gergen and Kaye (1992), believe that for the therapist to bring a Marxist or feminist or other political stance to the clinical situation is to promote a biased and potentially oppressive set of assumptions. Such assumptions, they believe, suggest privilege and expertise on the part of the clinician.

My own view is closer to that of White. "Local knowledges" do not spring simply from the local intersubjective experience. Each individual's narratives are influenced by the narratives in the cultural surround, that complex of cultural discourses that have been negotiated over time within relations of knowledge and power (Foucault, 1980) and that are accepted as "truth." Furthermore, not all stories are equal. For example, women's stories, voices, and genres for narrating their own lives have been highly constrained (Laird, 1989), as have the stories of other marginalized groups in our culture—people of color, gays and lesbians, people in poverty. Therapy, for lack of a better term, should be in part a matter of deconstruction, of consciousness-raising, of learning how one's own stories have been constrained or demeaned or depriveleged in varying contexts of knowledge and power. White (1992a) argues that clients need to be helped not only to deconstruct their self-narratives, but also the dominant cultural narratives and the discursive practices that constitute their lives.

The postmodern clinician must be alert to how such dominating discourses are shaped, whose interests they serve and whose they may subjugate, and how they influence the "local stories" in the clinical situation. This does not mean that clinicians deliver their political views as truths, but rather that they remain sensitive to hearing both the larger social messages as well as the underlying messages that cannot be voiced due to lack of power or knowledge. Alertness to the privileging and unjust social discourses that *do* indeed have colonizing effects allows us to open up conversational spaces and to hear the ways that clients may be limiting their own possibilities for growth and change.

Finally, few family-centered constructionist theorists have moved beyond the therapeutic conversation to the larger social realities that surround the individual narrative. In addition to engaging clients in an empowering therapy, we must promote social justice in the world. Minuchin (1991) wonders if postmodern theory is rescuing us from having to face the evils and hopelessness in the world around us, reducing our concerns to the individual "story," whose plot is often dictated by powerful forces outside the interviewing room.

In my view, a social constructionist stance offers possibilities for crossing some of the artificial barriers that exist today between scholars and practitioners in various theoretical camps. Some of the ideas sound familiar—old wine in new bottles (Dean, 1993). Nevertheless, it is wine flavored with new ideas about the process of social work practice and about the role of the social work practitioner and his or her relationship to the client.

# References

Allen, J. (1993). The constructivist paradigm: Values and ethics. In J. Laird (Ed.), *Revisioning social work education: A social constructionist approach* (pp. 31–54). New York: Haworth.

American Psychiatric Association. (1994). *Diagnostic and statistical manual of mental disorders* (4th ed.). Washington, DC: Author.

Andersen, T. (1987). The reflecting team: Dialogue and meta-dialogue in clinical work. *Family Process, 26*, 415–428.

Andersen, T. (Ed.). (1991). *The reflecting team: Dialogues and dialogues about the dialogues.* New York: W. W. Norton.

Anderson, H., & Goolishian, H. (1988). Human systems as linguistic systems: Preliminary and evolving ideas about the implications for clinical theory. *Family Process, 27,* 371–394.

Anderson, H., & Goolishian, H. (1992). The client is the expert: A not-knowing approach to therapy. In S. McNamee & K. J. Gergen (Eds.), *Therapy as social construction* (pp. 25–39). Newbury Park, CA: Sage.

Bateson, G. (1972). *Steps to an ecology of mind.* New York: Ballantine.

Bowen, M. (1978). *Family therapy in clinical practice.* New York: Jason Aronson.

Boyd-Franklin, N. (1989). *Black families in therapy: A multisystems approach.* New York: Guilford.

Carter, B., & McGoldrick, M. (Eds.). (1980). *The family life cycle: A framework for family therapy.* New York: Gardner Press.

Carter, B., & McGoldrick, M. (Eds.). (1988). *The changing family life cycle: A framework for family therapy.* New York: Gardner Press.

Cecchin, G. (1992). Constructing therapeutic possibilities. In S. McNamee & K. J. Gergen (Eds.), *Therapy as social construction* (pp. 86–95). Newbury Park, CA: Sage.

Compton, B., & Galaway, B. (1979). *Social work processes* (rev.). Homewood, IL: Dorsey Press.

Crawford, S. (1987). Lesbian families: Psychosocial stress and the family-building process. In Boston Lesbian Psychologies Collective (Eds.), *Lesbian psychologies: Explorations and challenges* (pp. 195–214). Urbana, IL: University of Illinois Press.

Dean, R. (1993). Constructivism: An approach to clinical practice. *Smith College Studies in Social Work, 63,* 126–146.

de Shazer, S. (1985). *Keys to solution in brief therapy.* New York: W. W. Norton.

Efran, J., & Clarfield, L. (1992). Constructionist therapy: Sense and nonsense. In S. McNamee & K. J. Gergen (Eds.), *Therapy as social construction* (pp. 200–217). Newbury Park, CA: Sage.

Falicov, C. (1983). *Cultural perspectives in family therapy.* Rockville, MD: Aspen Systems Publications.

Foucault, M. (1979). *Discipline and punish.* New York: Vintage.

Foucault, M. (1980). *Power/knowledge.* New York: Pantheon.

Framo, J. (1976). Family of origin as a therapeutic resource for adults in marital and family therapy: You can and should go home again. *Family Process, 15,* 193–210.

Geertz, C. (1983). *Local knowledge.* New York: Basic Books.

Gergen, K. J. (1985). The social constructionist movement in American psychology. *American Psychologist, 40,* 266–275.

Gergen, K. J., & Kaye, J. (1992). Beyond narrative in the negotiation of therapeutic meaning. In S. McNamee & K. J. Gergen (Eds.), *Therapy as social construction* (pp. 166–185). Newbury Park, CA: Sage.

Germain, C. G. (1979). *Social work practice: People and environments.* New York: Columbia University Press.

Germain, C., & Gitterman, A. (1980). *The life model of social work practice.* New York: Columbia University Press.

Goldner, V. (1985). Feminism and family therapy. *Family Process, 24,* 27–31.

Goldner, V. (1988). Generation and gender: Normative and covert hierarchies. *Family Process, 27,* 17–31.

Goodrich, T. J., Rampage, C., Ellman, B., & Halstead, K. (1988). *Feminist family therapy: A casebook.* New York: W. W. Norton.

Haley, J. (1976). *Problem-solving therapy.* San Francisco: Jossey-Bass.

Hamilton, G. (1951). *Theory and practice of social casework* (2nd ed.). New York: Columbia University Press.

Hare-Mustin, R. (1978). A feminist approach to family therapy. *Family Process, 17,* 181–194.

Hare-Mustin, R. (1987). The problem of gender in family therapy theory. *Family Process, 26,* 15–33.

Hare-Mustin, R. (1994). Discourses in the mirrored room: A postmodern analysis of therapy. *Family Process, 33*, 19–35.

Hartman, A. (1974). The generic stance and the family agency. *Social Casework, 55*, 199–208.

Hartman, A., & Laird, J. (1983). *Family-centered social work practice*. New York: Free Press.

Hillman, J., & Venura, M. (1993). *We've had a hundred years of psychotherapy and the world's getting worse*. San Francisco: Harper Collins.

Hoffman, L. (1985). Beyond power and control: Toward a "second order" family systems therapy. *Family Systems Medicine, 3*, 381–396.

Hoffman, L. (1992). A reflexive stance for family therapy. In S. McNamee & K. J. Gergen (Eds.), *Therapy as social construction* (pp. 7–24). Newbury Park, CA: Sage.

Hollis, F. (1964). *Casework: A psychosocial therapy*. New York: Random House.

Hudson, W. H. (1982). Scientific imperatives in social work research and practice. *Social Service Review, 56*, 246–258.

Keeney, B. (1983). *Aesthetics of change*. New York: Guilford.

Laird, J. (1989). Women and stories: Restorying women's self-constructions. In M. McGoldrick, C. Anderson, & F. Walsh (Eds.), *Women in families: A framework for family therapy* (pp. 422–450). New York: W. W. Norton.

Laird, J. (1992). Women's secrets—women's silences. In E. Imber-Black (Ed.), *Secrets in families and in family therapy*. New York: W. W. Norton.

Laird, J. (1993a). Lesbian and gay families. In F. Walsh (Ed.), *Normal family processes* (2nd ed., pp. 282–328). New York: Guilford.

Laird, J. (1993b). *Revisioning social work education: A social constructionist approach*. New York: Haworth.

Laird, J. (1994). "Thick description" revisited: Family therapist as anthropologist-constructivist. In E. Sherman & W. Reid (Eds.), *Qualitative research in social work* (pp. 175–189). New York: Columbia University Press.

Lax, W. (1992). Postmodern thinking in a clinical practice. In S. McNamee & K. J. Gergen (Eds.), *Therapy as social construction* (pp. 69–85). Newbury Park, CA: Sage.

Lerner, M. (1986). *Surplus powerlessness*. Atlantic Highlands, NJ: Humanities Press International.

Maturana, H. (1988). Reality: The search for objectivity or the quest for a compelling argument. *Irish Journal of Psychology, 9*(1), 1–24.

McGoldrick, M., Pearce, J., & Giordano, J. (1982). *Ethnicity and family therapy*. New York: Guilford.

McNamee, S., & Gergen, K. J. (1992). *Therapy as social construction*. Newbury Park, CA: Sage.

Meyer, C. (1993). *Assessment in social work*. New York: Columbia University Press.

Minuchin, S. (1974). *Families and family therapy*. Cambridge, MA: Harvard University Press.

Minuchin, S. (1991). The seductions of constructivism. *Family Therapy Networker, 15*(5), 47–50.

Minuchin, S., & Fishman, H. C. (1981). *Family therapy techniques*. Cambridge, MA: Harvard University Press.

MOSAIC Project. (1994). *Not alone*. (Videotape). Athol, MA: People's Bridge Action.

Napier, A., & Whitaker, C. (1978). *The family crucible*. New York: Harper and Row.

Papp, P. (1983). *The process of change*. New York: Guilford.

Penn, P., & Frankfurt, M. (1994). Creating a participant text: Writing, multiple voices, narrative multiplicity. *Family Process, 33*, 217–231.

Rhodes, M. (1986). *Ethical dilemmas in social work practice*. Boston: Routledge and Kegan Paul.

Richmond, M. (1917). *Social diagnosis*. New York: Russell Sage Foundation.

Roth, S., Chasin, L., Chasin, R., Becker, C., & Herzig, M. (1992). From debate to dialogue: A facilitating role for family therapists in the public forum. *Dulwich Centre Newsletter*, No. 2, 41–48.

Satir, V. (1967). *Conjoint family therapy* (rev. ed.). Palo Alto, CA: Science and Behavior Books.

Schön, D. (1983). *The reflective practitioner*. New York: Basic Books.

Selvini-Palazzoli, M., Boscolo, L., Cecchin, G., & Prata, G. (1980a). The problem of the referring person. *Journal of Marital and Family Therapy, 6*, 3–9.

Selvini-Palazzoli, M., Boscolo, L., Cecchin, G., & Prata, G. (1980b). Hypothesizing—circularity—neutrality: Three guidelines for the conductor of the session. *Family Process, 19,* 3–12.

Spence, D. (1982). *Narrative truth and historical truth.* New York: W. W. Norton.

Waldegrave, C. (1990). Social justice and family therapy. *Dulwich Centre Newsletter,* 5–47.

Watzlawick, P., Weakland, J., & Fisch, R. (1974). *Change: Principles of problem formulation and problem resolution.* New York: W. W. Norton.

Weick, A. (1993). Reconstructing social work education. In J. Laird (Ed.), *Revisioning social work education: A social constructionist approach* (pp. 11–30). New York: Haworth.

White, M. (1989). The process of questioning: A therapy of literary merit. In M. White, *Selected papers* (pp. 37–46). Adelaide, South Australia: Dulwich Centre Publications.

White, M. (1992a). Deconstruction and therapy. In D. Epston & M. White, *Experience, contradiction, narrative and imagination: Selected papers of David Epston and Michael White, 1989–1991* (pp. 109–151). Adelaide, South Australia: Dulwich Centre Publications.

White, M. (1992b, October). *Recent developments in the narrative approach.* Workshop at the American Association of Marriage and Family Therapy, Miami, FL.

White, M. (1994). *The politics of therapy: Putting to rest the illusion of neutrality.* (Mimeographed). Adelaide, South Australia: Dulwich Family Centre.

White, M., & Epston, D. (1990). *Narrative means to therapeutic ends.* New York: W. W. Norton.

# 11

## Solution-Building Conversations: Co-Constructing a Sense of Competence With Clients

*Insoo Kim Berg & Peter De Jong*

Human beings, for the most part, will go to great lengths to understand the significance or meaning of their experiences. If an experience is important to a person, he or she reflects on it, puts impressions into words, and converses about it with others. The desire to find and communicate is the most obvious and unique of all human characteristics (Mead, 1934).

The theoretical perspective of social constructionism—as it relates to the above observation about human beings—maintains that people develop their sense of what is real through conversation with and observation of others (Berger & Luckman, 1966; Garfinkel, 1967; Geertz, 1973; Gergen, 1985; Watzlawick, 1984). It also holds that as people interact with and observe one another, their perceptions and definitions of what is real frequently shift, sometimes dramatically.

Therapeutic approaches generally regarded to be consistent with a social-constructionist view attempt to foster client change by opening up new views of reality. The client's "problem," Hoffman (1985) states, "is the meaning system created by the distress" (p. 387). Change occurs through the client and therapist creating new meanings that relieve the distress and allow the client to lead a more satisfying and productive life.

A social constructionist approach can be taken with clients in several ways (see Andersen, 1987; Anderson & Goolishian, 1992; de Shazer, 1991; Tomm, 1987; White & Epston, 1990). In this chapter, we present the solution-focused approach by summarizing its main assumptions and components, illustrating its interviewing procedures with a case example, demonstrating how ongoing measurements of client progress are integrated into solution-focused conversations, indicating how the effectiveness of the approach is beginning to be researched, and suggesting various links between solution-focused procedures and social constructionism.

# Solution-Focused Basics

Solution-focused therapy was pioneered through the work of de Shazer (1985, 1988, 1991, 1994), Berg (1994), Berg and Miller (1992), and their colleagues (de Shazer et al., 1986) at the Brief Family Therapy Center (BFTC) in Milwaukee, Wisconsin. Its assumptions, structure, and procedures were developed inductively during approximately 20 years of disciplined observation of sessions with clients. Similar to Rappaport (1981), de Shazer and his colleagues (1986) concluded that *solutions* for clients are not scientific puzzles (such as unraveling the meaning of DNA codes) to be solved by practitioners, but rather changes in perceptions, patterns of interacting and living, and meanings that are constructed within the client's frame of reference. In addition, de Shazer and colleagues (1986) assume that clients are competent at conceptualizing an alternative, more satisfying future and at figuring out which of their strengths and resources they can draw on to produce the changes they desire.

The practitioner's role in the solution-focused process is continually to invite clients to explore and define two matters: (a) what it is they want different in their lives (goals) and (b) what strengths and resources they can bring to bear on making these desired differences a reality. The practitioner affirms and amplifies client definitions of goals, past successes, strengths, and resources as they emerge through conversation. Consequently, these conversations focus more on building solutions than on solving problems.

De Jong and Berg (1997) state that "building solutions" involves a different set of stages from those used in problem solving. The well-known stages of problem solving (excluding the relationship-focused stages of engagement and termination) include definition of the problem, intervention with the problem guided by the assessment, and evaluation of the intervention. In contrast, the stages of solution building are a brief description of the concern or problem in the client's words, developing well-formed goals, exploring for exceptions (i.e., successes or times in clients' lives when problems do not happen or are less severe), evaluation of client progress as the client defines it, and end-of-session feedback comprising affirmations of client goals, strengths, and successes and usually a homework "task" based on the client's developing definitions of goals and exceptions.

As De Jong and Miller (1995) point out, solution-focused interviews are unique with regard to the concrete and clearly identifiable questions asked: the miracle question (for amplifying client goals), relationship questions (for drawing out alternative and contextualized client perceptions), exception questions (for uncovering client successes and strengths), scaling questions (for measuring client progress and, in general, helping clients render vague perceptions more concrete and definable), in addition to others. In solution-focused interviewing, careful attention is focused on listening for and exploring the client's words and building the next interview question from the client's latest answer.

The respect shown in solution-focused work for client definitions of reality as well as for the process of building solutions through the co-construction of "new and more useful" meanings (Hoffman, 1992, p. 18) is readily apparent in the transcripts of interviews. The following case example illustrates questioning sequences in purposeful solution-focused conversations. The reader is asked to pay particular attention to any shifts in the client's perceptions and definitions as the therapeutic conversation unfolds.

# Case Example

Lucinda, a 19-year-old African American mother of two children, was referred to the therapist by a social services worker because she complained about feeling "depressed and stressed out." Her two children, who were three and four years of age, had been removed by protective services and placed in a foster home 18 months earlier. At the beginning of their session, the therapist's information was limited to Lucinda's name, age, address, telephone number, and the fact that she had been physically abused by a former partner. In solution-focused work, minimal information is usually sufficient because the practitioner always begins by exploring the client's current constructions and works from there.

The following excerpts are drawn from a single solution-focused session[1]. The solution-focused procedures being used are identified in italics. (The reader who wishes more complete information about these procedures should see Berg [1994], de Shazer [1985, 1988], and De Jong and Berg [1997].)

## *Getting Started*

With belief in client competence and respect for the client's perceptions and frame of reference, the therapist begins by asking Lucinda what she wants from the meeting. Instead of asking "What problem brings you in today?" the therapist assumes that the client is capable of expressing her own construction of a successful outcome for their work together.

*Therapist: O.K., what can I do that would be helpful for you?*

*Lucinda: Well, I've been depressed and stressed out.*

*Therapist: Yeah, I can imagine.*

*Lucinda: I just needed someone to talk to.*

*Therapist: (respecting and exploring the client's words) I can imagine. Is that related to your children not living with you … to your stress and being depressed?*

*Lucinda: Yes.*

*Therapist: Or is there something else?*

*Lucinda: Well, the main reason is 'cause my kids are not with me.*

*Therapist: I also understand that you were living with your children's father.*

---

1. The therapy session described in this article is available on videotape from the BFTC, P. O. Box 13736, Milwaukee, WI 53213. The title of the videotape is "I Love My Kids."

*Lucinda: No.*

*Therapist: Some other person?*

*Lucinda: Uh huh.*

*Therapist: I understand he has been very abusive to you.*

*Lucinda: Yes.*

*Therapist: Is that what happened with the children?*

*Lucinda: Yes, not exactly.*

*Therapist: Not exactly. That was a separate thing—between you and him?*

*Lucinda: Right.*

In this dialogue, the therapist asked Lucinda several questions to which she was able to respond "yes." This was purposive because Lucinda's affect seemed depressed and her manner tentative. This type of questioning lets the client know what the practitioner already knows about the client; it also establishes rapport and a pattern for the session whereby the client gives information to the practitioner.

## *Co-Constructing a Sense of Competence*

In a solution-focused interview, the practitioner helps the client develop two primary constructions: what she would like to have different in her life and past successes and strengths that the client can use to make desired differences happen.

When first asked to identify what they would like to change as a result of therapy, clients usually respond by stating a problem. For example, Lucinda responded by saying that she was "depressed and stressed out." One way to proceed and return to solution-focused work (after the client has had an opportunity to describe the problem) is to listen for client successes in dealing with problems and then begin to explore these in detail as part of the co-construction process. In the next sequence, the therapist casts Lucinda in the role of being expert about her own successes and their meaning. The therapist does not know where the exploration will lead but trusts that Lucinda, like most clients, has competencies that she has used in the past to confront problems. Consequently, the therapist conceives her task in the conversation as continuously inviting Lucinda to develop a keener awareness of the successes, strengths, and resources that she might use to make changes in her life. Cantwell and Holmes (1994) call this approach "leading from one-step behind."

*Therapist: And did I hear you correctly that you got out of that relationship?*

*Lucinda: Yes, I did.*

*Therapist: (indirectly complimenting a possible success) Wow! I wonder how you did that.*

*Lucinda: It was hard to do but …*

*Therapist: (affirming Lucinda's perception) I'm sure it wasn't easy.*

*Lucinda: No, it wasn't.*

*Therapist: (exploring and amplifying the success) So how did you do it?*

*Lucinda: I just stayed away.*

*Therapist: You just stayed away from him? That's all?*

*Lucinda: Uh huh.*

*Therapist: He didn't want to end the relationship?*

*Lucinda: No, and I got a restraining order put on him.*

*Therapist: You did? Was it helpful?*

*Lucinda: For a while it was, but he just kept coming back.*

*Therapist: So he didn't want to break up?*

*Lucinda: Right.*

*Therapist: (trusting client expertise and affirming it) But you knew this was best for you?*

*Lucinda: Right.*

*Therapist: So … he didn't want to, he kept coming back, how does he make this happen?*

*Lucinda: Well, he was threatening me, threatening to kill me and …*

*Therapist: (acknowledging the severity of the situation) Wow.*

*Lucinda: And every time he sees me he jumped on me.*

*Therapist: He jumped on you, right. Even after you broke up?*

*Lucinda: Right.*

*Therapist: (indirectly complimenting) So that's when most women sort of become weak and they take him back. How come you didn't?*

*Lucinda: A couple of times I did because I was scared. And the more I kept going back to him, it got worse and worse. And then he ended up hurting my son.*

*Therapist: Oh! Is that what did it?*

*Lucinda: That's what caused me to get my kids taken.*

*Therapist: Right, I see. So your children have been taken away because of what happened with him.*

*Lucinda: Right.*

*Therapist: (asking for the client's definition of the situation) So … was that helpful to break up with him or was it not helpful to break up with him?*

*Lucinda: (in a stronger voice) Yeah, it was helpful. Because I feel that another man don't have no right putting his hand on nobody else's child.*

*Therapist: (respecting and affirming the client's definition) Right.*

*Lucinda: And that child, you know, I feel that if that child didn't do nothing to him, he ain't got no business putting his hand on him.*

*Therapist: Wow. You are very clear about that.*

*Lucinda: Yes. He broke my baby's leg!*

*Therapist: (complimenting strengths) Uh huh. Right. But some women, even though he did that, some women would either get scared of him or, you know, somehow think that he's gonna change and take him back.*

*Lucinda: No. My kids come first.*

*Therapist: For you?*

*Lucinda: Right ... my kids come first.*

*Therapist: Really?*

*Lucinda: And I shouldn't have to keep taking that abuse. And my kids don't have to take it.*

*Therapist: (inviting Lucinda to sharpen her construction of competence and strength) How did you know this? That your kids "didn't have to take it" and you shouldn't "have to take it?" How did you know this?*

*Lucinda: Because if I had stayed with him it would have ended up worse than what it was. Either me or my kids would have been somewhere dead or ...*

*Therapist: Wow.*

*Lucinda: It wasn't worth it.*

*Therapist: Really? So, I mean, you knew it, you were very clear about this—that this is not worth it? No man is worth it.*

*Lucinda: Right, it wasn't. You know it wasn't worth it—beat up, walking around with black eyes and my kids screaming and hollering, seeing their mother be beat on—it wasn't worth it.*

*Therapist: (genuinely impressed and complimenting) It wasn't worth it. Wow. I'm amazed by this. (continuing to foster the construction of a sense of competence) How did you do this? I mean ...*

*Lucinda: I just stayed away from him, you know. I was scared of him but, you know, my father always told me, "Be strong," and that's what I did.*

*Therapist: Really? That's what you did.*

*Lucinda: I stayed strong. And every time I saw him, I didn't run. You know, I let him make all the threats he wanted. I didn't run. Wasn't no need for no running. 'Cause you know you can't run forever.*

*Therapist: That is true. Wow. So lots of things happened to you, right? More than most women will go through in their lifetime.*

*Lucinda: Some women, as you said before ... they'll stay with their person, but ain't no way that I can stay with a man that's going to constantly keep beating on me, 'cause I don't like to be beat.*

*Therapist: Of course not.*

## Co-Constructing a Sense of What the Client Wants

In solution-focused interviewing, neither the practitioner nor the client usually knows before the interview precisely what the client might want to change in his or her life (goals). Also, neither knows the role the practitioner might play in helping the client to make these changes. Consequently, interviewers usually work back and forth between a client's emerging constructions of competence and what the client might want different in his or her life. Clearly, the successes and strengths of most interest and use to the client will be those related, in the client's mind, to what he or she might want different in his or her life.

At this point, the therapist was becoming impressed with the steps Lucinda had already taken and thus turned to some constructionist work around goals:

*Therapist: So it's two years since you've seen him. And you want your children back. But in order to get your children back, you had to do this. Social service said you had to get Marvin out of your life.*

*Lucinda: Right*

*Therapist: And you have done that.*

*Lucinda: Yes, I have.*

*Therapist: (changing focus to goal exploration) And what's the next piece you have to do?*

*Lucinda: Get my kids back. My kids is very important to me.*

*Therapist: Right. O.K. Where do I come in on all this? How can I help? 'Cause, you know, it sounds like … you were able to get Marvin out of your life—even though that was very tough. And I wonder how I can help you with your depression and your stress.*

*Lucinda: You know, I have a lot of things on my mind. Sometimes I be scared.*

*Therapist: Of?*

*Lucinda: I be scared to walk out of my own house.*

*Therapist: Because of Marvin?*

*Lucinda: Right.*

*Therapist: So you are still afraid of him? O.K. And you don't want to be scared anymore? Is that what you mean?*

*Lucinda: Right*

*Therapist: What else? How do you want things to be different?*

*Lucinda: I just want my kids back.*

*Therapist: You "want your kids back." Right. What do you have to do so that … what do they tell you that you have to do?*

*Lucinda: I had to go to a meeting or meetings. At the meetings.we talk about abusive relationships and stuff like that.*

*Therapist: Uh huh.*

*Lucinda: And that's it.*

*Therapist: (exploring whether Lucinda perceives attending the meetings as beneficial) That's it. How helpful is going to that meeting?*

*Lucinda: It's O.K. We have it every Tuesday and Thursday.*

*Therapist: Uh huh.*

*Lucinda: And it's helping me a lot.*

*Therapist: What about the meeting is helpful?*

*Lucinda: You know, they take a lot of things off my mind. We talk about the abusive relationships and how abusive men are and stuff like that.*

*Therapist: Does it help you keep Marvin away from your life?*

*Lucinda: Yeah, it relieves me, you know.*

*Therapist: It does?*

*Lucinda: It takes it off my mind and stuff.*

*Therapist: (exploring other successes) So that's been helpful. What else has been helpful?*

*Lucinda: My father. You know, he talks to me and stuff. He told me, "Don't be scared. Just leave it in the Lord's hands."*

*Therapist: Yeah.*

*Lucinda: And, you know, he'll make a way for that person just to leave me alone. Not physically or mentally, but he'll just make a way for that man to leave me alone. And that way every time he sees me he won't harm me or hurt me. He'll say, "Hi, how I'm doing," and keep on going.*

*Therapist: (exploring resources in Lucinda's environment) Yeah, I see. So your father gives this kind of advice to you. It sounds like he's very helpful to you.*

*Lucinda: Yes.*

*Therapist: What else has been helpful?*

*Lucinda: Social workers. They give me advice. And, you know, they always, 'cause I always talk about my kids and they always tell me don't say I ain't gonna get my kids back, 'cause they'll be home real soon.*

*Therapist: And that's helpful—to hear that, that they're gonna be home soon?*

*Lucinda: Right. And they told me the next time I get involved with a man, sit back and watch how that man treat his mother, and then I know how he would treat me.*

*Therapist: Right. So is that what you're going to do next time?*

*Lucinda: Uh huh.*

*Therapist: So you remember a lot of things, it sounds like?*

*Lucinda: Yes.*

*Therapist: (returning to goal formulation) Good. I want to come back to this. What can I do that would be helpful? It sounds like you do know, you're doing lots of things, you have done lots of things.*

*Lucinda: Just help me see it through. Give me some advice.*

*Therapist: On?*

*Lucinda: Help me be strong.*

*Therapist: Be strong. Sounds like you already are, though.*

*Lucinda: I think I am.*

*Therapist: I mean, if you could stand up to Marvin.*

*Lucinda: It was something hard to do.*

As is often the case, clients' goals are vague and involve someone else doing something differently in order to make their lives more satisfying—a common way in which clients express a sense of powerlessness to practitioners. In response, a solution-focused approach asks interviewers to begin to develop a goal-formulation conversation with clients, inviting them to co-construct a vision of an alternative future that *concretely identifies what will be present in a more satisfying future* and that focuses on what clients might do differently to make that future happen. The therapist opens the following conversation with "the miracle question" and then uses several other questions to assist the client to amplify the vision:

*Therapist: Oh, I'm sure it was very hard. I'm sure it wasn't easy. But somehow you managed to get Marvin out of your life. And that's no small accomplishment. Wow. You said you don't want to be depressed anymore, and you don't want to be stressed anymore. Let me come back to this. I'm going to ask you a very strange question—I have a lot of these strange questions; maybe you never heard them before (speaking slowly and pausing frequently in order to allow the client to absorb the parts of the miracle question). Let's say after you and I talk and whatever you do for the rest of the day and you go to bed tonight and when you are sleeping a miracle happens. And the miracle is the problem that brought you here today to talk to me—about how you want your children back and how you want to be stronger. And all these things happened because of this miracle. All the problems that are related to your children, related to Marvin ... are solved. But this happens when you're sleeping tonight, so you don't know that miracle actually happened. The problem that brought you here is gone, it's solved, it's all taken care of. So when you wake up tomorrow morning, how will you find out ... what will make you say, "Wow, maybe something happened in the middle of the night when I was sleeping; maybe there was a miracle"? How will you be able to say or tell that tomorrow morning?*

*Lucinda: How would I be able to tell that?*

*Therapist: Yeah.*

*Lucinda: To be honest, I wouldn't know. If a miracle were to happen to me, I wouldn't know how I'd tell it, I'd just be excited.*

*Therapist: (exploring the client's construction by repeating and exploring her words/categories) You'd be excited?*

*Lucinda: I'd be excited.*

*Therapist: O.K. That makes sense.*

*Lucinda: So I couldn't tell you how I would be able to tell. I'd just be excited, happy.*

*Therapist: (inviting the client once again to construct a definition of something concrete and small that would be present when her "miracle" happened) O.K., so when you open your eyes, when you're sort of coming out of your sleep in the morning, waking up from a deep sleep, what would be the first thing that will make you think, "Wow, something must have happened when I was sleeping"?*

*Lucinda: If a miracle was to happen to me and I woke up, and if it do happen, I hope the miracle would be that my kids would be there when it happened.*

*Therapist: Ah. So your kids would be in the same place with you, same house with you. That will make you very excited.*

*Lucinda:* Yes.

*Therapist:* (affirming Lucinda's definition) Good. So suppose that happened.

*Lucinda:* (starting to smile and in a stronger voice) I'd be excited. I'd jump for joy!

*Therapist:* Jump for joy. Great. So suppose you're jumping for joy, you are very happy. That means you are very cheerful, right?

*Lucinda:* Uh huh.

*Therapist:* You move, you'd get up, right?

*Lucinda:* Right.

*Therapist:* (starting to invite the client to focus on concrete things that she would do) You'd be excited to get up in the morning and do things.

*Lucinda:* Yes.

*Therapist:* (inviting Lucinda to expand her miracle picture by asking for her perceptions of how the children would be different when the miracle happens) What would your children be like?

*Lucinda:* They'd be happy to see me.

*Therapist:* They'll be happy to see you. O.K.

*Lucinda:* They won't have to worry about nobody else raising them. They know who their mother is.

*Therapist:* Yeah, I understand they're in a foster home.

*Lucinda:* Right. And they wouldn't have to worry about no strange person, you know, telling them what to do and stuff like that.

*Therapist:* Right, O.K. And so they will be happy and you will be happy. You'll be excited and they'll be excited to be back with Mama.

*Lucinda:* Yeah, and no strange person laying next to them.

*Therapist:* O.K., so there will be no strange person laying next to them.

*Lucinda:* It'll be their mother.

*Therapist:* (returning the focus to what will be present and what Lucinda will do concretely) Right, it'll be you. What would you do then? What would be the first thing you would do in the morning when this all happened?

*Lucinda:* I'd grab my kids, give them a hug, tell them I love them. Tell them how much I love them. And how glad, you know, how glad I am to have them back home with me.

*Therapist:* And what would they be like?

*Lucinda:* They'd be happy.

*Therapist:* They'd be happy, too.

*Lucinda:* Big smile on their face.

*Therapist:* And you want to see that.

*Lucinda:* Yeah.

*Therapist:* I suppose they want to see you smile too, right? They want their mama to be happy.

*Lucinda: Yes.*

*Therapist: What else will be different when this actually, you know, suppose this actually happened?*

*Lucinda: If it happened, things would change for me. I won't be depressed anymore. I won't have to worry about being stressed out anymore 'cause my kids ain't there with me.*

*Therapist: Right. (asking for what will be present—not absent) What would you be like instead?*

*Lucinda: I'd feel like a mother should feel.*

*Therapist: (exploring the client's meanings, not assuming how a mother should feel) What's that?*

*Lucinda: 'Cause, you know, without your kids, it's a hurting feeling when your kids get taken from you. You know, it hurts.*

*Therapist: Sure.*

*Lucinda: And I'd just be one happy parent. You know, one happy mother.*

*Therapist: And so, when you are not depressed anymore you'll be happier, you'll be a happy mother. What else?*

*Lucinda: I'd be thankful.*

*Therapist: Oh, you'd be thankful. To whom?*

*Lucinda: That I have my kids back. You know, I won't have to worry about going through that ... or sitting there worrying about when I'm going to get my kids back, when are these people going to give me my kids back. And is my kids going to stay gone forever, and all that. ...*

*Therapist: Oh, so all that will be gone from your head?*

*Lucinda: Right.*

The therapist understood at this point that Lucinda's miracle picture involved mainly the return of her children. The therapist also understood (as did Lucinda perhaps more fully) that Lucinda's stress and depression had a lot to do with her children's absence.

The therapist continued to invite Lucinda to expand her emerging construction of her "miracle picture." She asked Lucinda what she would do with her children that would tell her children that she was happy to have them home. Lucinda responded with several ideas about positive parenting, which the therapist took as strengths, asking, "Where did you learn to be such a good, loving mother?" Lucinda then continued to sharpen her perceptions about the strengths that she could draw upon to make her miracle picture a reality, telling the therapist how she had cared for her younger siblings from the time that she was eight years old and presenting concrete parenting techniques and general advice that she had received from her father.

At this point, Lucinda made an observation that is typical of many clients with whom we have worked.

*Lucinda: (her voice now much stronger) I've been through a lot.*

*Therapist: (truly impressed and indirectly complimenting) Sounds like it. But you also learned a lot. Wow. Amazing. So, you know, I'm amazed by this again. Year and a half, this year and a half, two years with Marvin and with your having your children taken away. That has not been easy.*

Lucinda: *And then, you know, well, I got in a relationship with him after my little sister was buried. So I guess that's what made it worse.*

Therapist: *Your sister was buried?*

Lucinda: *My 13-year-old sister. She died of asthma.*

Therapist: *Wow. So I guess you're right, you have been through a lot. So in the middle of all this, how did you learn to be so strong?*

Lucinda: *I got a best friend, you know, somebody that's been there for me, somebody that I ain't got to worry about her turning her back on me. And when I have problems I know who I can go talk to. You know, somebody who's just going to be there for me.*

Therapist: *(affirming her resource) And you had a friend like that?*

Lucinda: *Right, she's still my friend.*

Therapist: *And you also said your father was very helpful?*

Lucinda: *Right, you know, they was there. They was by my side. You know, they was in my corner.*

Therapist: *They were in your corner. And that helped?*

Lucinda: *Uh huh.*

Therapist: *(inviting Lucinda to think about the meaning she attaches to her supports) So knowing that they were in your corner with you, what about that was helpful?*

Lucinda: *They just helped me, they helped me focus, keep my mind off a lot of things. Just told me, "Don't worry about it. Be strong." Told me I was going to get my kids back real soon.*

Therapist: *Reminding you that you were going to get your kids back, that was helpful, you say?*

Lucinda: *Yeah.*

Therapist: *(inviting Lucinda to identify her strengths and successes) Was there anything that you did that was helpful?*

Lucinda: *I went to see my kids all the time. I had them every weekend and stuff like that. You know, I was always there for them.*

Therapist: *Oh, right, so you stayed in touch with them.*

Lucinda: *Let them know who their mother is, you know. So when I do get them back, they won't think I'm some stranger or nothing like that.*

Therapist: *Right. So you made sure that they knew that you're their mother.*

Lucinda: *Right.*

Therapist: *Good. What else did you do to help yourself to stay strong?*

Lucinda: *I stayed in the meetings.*

Therapist: *You stayed in the meetings. O.K.*

*Lucinda: And I was always with my social worker. You know, something that would keep my mind off of everything. I moved around a lot.*

*Therapist: So try to keep busy and ...*

*Lucinda: Right, and just keep my mind off a lot of stuff.*

*Therapist: Keep your mind off a lot. So let me come back to this, how did you overcome this fear of going outside and fear that maybe Marvin is, you know, might be jumping on you and stuff like that? How did you learn to overcome that?*

*Lucinda: Well, like I said before, you know, you got to be strong. And my father always told me to put it in God's hands. He told me I'm one of God's childs; I can't be harmed.*

*Therapist: Really.*

*Lucinda: And I took his word for it.*

*Therapist: When you heard this from your father, you put that into practice?*

*Lucinda: Right*

*Therapist: You knew how to make it work for you?*

*Lucinda: Right.*

# Scaling: Measuring Client Constructions of Competence

Several authors (Rappaport, 1990; Riessman, 1993; Saleebey, 1992) observed that professionals must find new ways to measure client progress in individual treatment sessions as well as client outcomes in more formal studies of treatment effectiveness. More specifically, these authors emphasize that measurement must respect and incorporate the categories and meanings of clients. In solution-focused interviewing, scaling questions are used extensively to analyze client "meanings" (Berg & de Shazer, 1993). In the following dialogue, the therapist invents a scaling question to measure Lucinda's perception of her own progress:

*Therapist: Let me ask you this, let's say on a scale of 1 to 10, 10 stands for how you will be when you finally get your children back, and 1 is what you were like when your children were taken away from you. Remember those days? How bad you felt?*

*Lucinda: Yeah.*

*Therapist: Where would you say things are today?*

*Lucinda: I'd say between 8 and 9.*

*Therapist: Between 8 and 9? Whoa! (reinforcing client's perception of competency) How'd you do that? I mean, that's a lot of improvement. Isn't it? (therapist using her note pad as though it were a scale from 1 through 10) I mean, how you felt from here to all the way up here?*

*Lucinda: Yep. I see it. I see my kids coming back home any day now.*

*Therapist: Oh, you can see it.*

*Lucinda: And I can feel it. (in a confident, strong voice) I know it.*

*Therapist: I see. Wow. That's a lot of improvement. (relationship scaling-question) What about your father? If I were to ask your father, where he thinks Lucinda is between 1 and 10, if 1 was what he saw you were like when your children were first taken away? He knows you very well, right?*

*Lucinda: He might say 10.*

*Therapist: He might say 10. So he also agrees with you that you've come a long way.*

*Lucinda: I see it, you know, 'cause my grandmother, she's a, you know, she's a Christian lady. And she told me, she said she see it and she can feel it, my kids will be home soon. I call my grandmother all the time and that's all I talk about—my kids. She pray with me over the phone.*

*Therapist: She does? So your grandmother also sees, she can feel that the children are coming home.*

*Lucinda: My kids is coming home.*

*Therapist: (affirming and complimenting the supports in Lucinda's environment) So you believe her. You are surrounded by some good people.*

*Lucinda: Yeah.*

*Therapist: O.K. In your mind, then, what needs to happen? Your dad, your father thinks that you already are at 10. But in your mind, what needs to happen so that you can be up to 10?*

*Lucinda: Continue seeing my kids. Paying them visits. Gettin' them on the weekends and continue my meetings. And they'll be there.*

*Therapist: Great. I think I explained to you I'm going to take some time out and think about what you said to me … is there anything you want to ask me?*

*Lucinda: Not really, no.*

After 45 minutes of conversation, the therapist took a break to think about what Lucinda had said and to formulate her end-of-session feedback. The feedback consisted of an affirmation of Lucinda's goal, several compliments that affirmed Lucinda's strengths and resources, and a related task. As she made observations about Lucinda's constructions, the therapist was careful to use Lucinda's words:

*Therapist: Well, Lucinda (pause), it seems to me that it's reasonable and natural for you to be depressed …*

*Lucinda: Yes.*

*Therapist: … and stressed out, under the circumstances.*

*Lucinda: Yes.*

*Therapist: So, I mean, it makes sense to me that you would be … depressed, because, as you were saying, your children are everything to you. (implicitly affirming Lucinda's goal) And everything has been taken away from you. So it's perfectly understandable. What's amazing about you, however, is that you have been through a lot in your life.*

*Lucinda: Yes, I have.*

*Therapist: You have been through a lot. A lot's happened to you. And you also say you learn things from that.*

*Lucinda: Yes, you learn from your mistakes.*

*Therapist: (complimenting) But what's amazing about you is that at your age, you're only 19 ...*

*Lucinda: Yes.*

*Therapist: ... and you have used what you have learned. You have used what happened to you in your life. You have learned and you have used it to make yourself a better person. And that's really absolutely amazing to me. For someone as young as you are. And so, I guess, for someone your age you are very wise already.*

*Lucinda: (smiling, straightening, and with a confident voice) Yes, I am. Because, you know, some young parents, they get their kids taken and don't even want them back. But me, I think the world of my kids. You know, 'cause that's all I got.*

*Therapist: (affirming her goal) Yeah.*

*Lucinda: And that's what slowed me down. You know, I had my first when I was 15. You know, maybe God, you know, the Lord thought that was best, maybe He thought it would slow me down, and it did, you know. My first child slowed me down.*

*Therapist: So again you learned from that.*

*Lucinda: And like I said, everybody makes mistakes. And I don't think there's any person out there that can tell me they ain't never made no mistakes. 'Cause everybody make mistakes.*

*Therapist: Absolutely. And you learned that too. And then you use what you learned.*

*Lucinda: Right. So from now on I have to think before I act.*

*Therapist: Right. (complimenting) And the other thing is this—I'm amazed by how you've been able to break off this relationship from Marvin ... you were able to stand up and ...*

*Lucinda: I wanted to let him know.*

*Therapist: Let him know?*

*Lucinda: You know, you caused me to get my kids taken from me and ain't no way that ... you know, excuse my language, but ain't no way in hell that I would be able to take, accept that man back in my life or my kids' life after what he done took me through, took my kids through.*

*Therapist: Right. Well, I think that you are almost there—to 10. As your father says and as your grandmother says and as your social worker says—you are almost there. And I tend to agree with that. You are almost there. And soon you are ready to be at 10. You have come a long way from 1 all the way up to 8 or 9. It wasn't easy, but ...*

*Lucinda: No it wasn't. It was hard.*

*Therapist: ... but you really worked hard to be at that. (suggesting a "task" based on the constructions that emerged in the interview) And so, I guess, obviously you need to keep doing it because you know how to do it and you've done it. (putting the client in charge of termination) And I don't see any.... You know, at this point, I'm not sure if we need to get together again, even. What do you think?*

*Lucinda: I don't think so. Hopefully things will go right for me.*

*Therapist: Right. Sounds like it will. Sure sounds like it will.*

*Lucinda: I hope so.*

*Therapist: Yeah. Sounds like it will. And it sounds also like you are determined to make it go all right for you and your children.*

*Lucinda: Right. I just got to put my foot down. And stay strong.*

*Therapist: That's right. O.K. Well, thank you for coming. Good luck to you.*

*Lucinda: Thank you.*

## Case Summary

This case illustrates how client perceptions and definitions can shift during a purposeful, solution-focused conversation. Lucinda's initial perception was that she was "depressed and stressed out." Early in the session, she was passive, answering the therapist's questions with a simple yes or no. As the therapist respectfully and persistently asked questions and made reality-based observations that implied that Lucinda was a sensible, caring, and competent person, Lucinda was able to expand her repertoire of strengths and resources and what she wanted to happen in her future. By the end of the session, having co-constructed with the therapist a clearer sense of what she wanted and how to make it a reality, Lucinda decided that she did not need to return. As she put it: "I just got to put my foot down. And stay strong." Presumably, she did just that; Lucinda never called for another appointment, and her children were returned to her.

# Outcome Evaluation

Solution-focused therapy has been around for only the past 15 years. Therefore, outcome research is scarce (see Adams, Piercy, & Jurich, 1991). Another outcome study at the BFTC in Milwaukee has been completed (De Jong & Berg, 1997) that includes data on 275 clients who came for services between November 1992 and August 1993. Outcomes were measured while clients were in therapy and through telephone contacts at seven to nine months after therapy. Because the study was conducted according to a single-group design and no control or comparison groups were employed, the findings must be understood within the context of these limitations. Highlights of the findings and comparisons with other studies are presented below.

## Practice Evaluation and Intermediate Outcomes

In solution-focused work, practitioners regularly ask clients the following scaling question: "On a scale of 1 to 10, in which 10 means the problem(s) with which you came to therapy is solved and 1 is 'the worst it has ever been,' where is it now on that scale?" This question is useful in developing a sense of client progress.

This scaling question also approximates the single-system design for measuring progress under social constructionist and strengths-based principles. The question approximates the single-system design by estimating the state of the client's problem at three points in time—when it was the "worst ever" (the baseline), in the future when the problem is solved, and "now." Further measurement occurs when the question is asked in later sessions. The question also respects constructionist and strengths-based principles by accessing client constructions about progress and how it occurred. For example, when a client says that "things are about a 5 right now," the practitioner follows up with questions such as "A 5! What have you been doing differently this week to help you climb to a 5?"

As part of the recent outcome study at BFTC, 10 therapists asked clients this scaling question at each session, then recorded their progress score in the session notes in each client's file. The therapists did this for 81% of all sessions. By subtracting progress scores for clients' first sessions from those for their final sessions, we obtained one measurement of outcome—an "intermediate outcome"—that measures outcome over the course of therapy. (Clients had to attend therapy for at least two sessions to obtain a score on intermediate outcome; 76% of the clients came for two or more sessions.) A zero or negative score on intermediate outcome indicated no progress or a worsening of the client's problems; positive scores indicated progress.

Theoretically, a client's score on intermediate outcome could range from –10 to 10. In actuality scores ranged from –3 to 8. Intermediate-outcome scores were collapsed and labeled as follows: –3 through 0 = "no progress"; 1 through 3 = "moderate progress"; and 4 through 8 = "significant progress." Twenty-six percent of valid cases showed no progress over the course of therapy, 49% showed moderate progress, and 25% significant progress.

Fifty-seven percent of the 275 clients in this study were African American, 5% Latino, 3% American Indian, and 36% White. At the time of their first visit, 43% of clients were employed and 57% were not. Sixty percent were female and 40% male. De Jong and Berg (1997) report no differences in intermediate outcomes by categories of diversity; that is, African American clients, Latinos, Whites, employed, unemployed, men, and women all showed similar rates of progress.[2]

Solution-focused practice is conducted in the same way regardless of the client's presenting complaint or problem. Unlike most other forms of practice, solution-focused therapy does not assume a necessary connection between a client's problem and its solution. Consequently, notions of assessment and related interventions play a smaller role. De Jong and Berg (1997) also present analysis of intermediate outcomes by type of client problem. This analysis was conducted by operationalizing type of problem as the practitioner's *Diagnostic and Statistical Manual of Mental Disorders* (DSM-IV) (American Psychiatric Association, 1994) diagnosis and by using the client's own estimate of the problem. In both instances, no difference was found in intermediate outcomes by different types of client problems. The outcomes proved to be essentially the same for cases involving depression, suicidal thoughts, job-related problems, family violence, sexual abuse, and self-esteem problems as well as the seven DSM-IV diagnoses on which we had sufficient data for analysis.

---

2. Pearson chi-square tests were calculated for several client characteristics in relation to outcomes in this study. Statements of "difference" or "no difference" are based on the results of running this test of significance.

## *Outcomes at Follow-up*

Outcomes were also measured at seven to nine months after clients had participated in their last therapy session. After receiving a letter alerting them to the follow-up, clients were contacted by telephone and asked several questions about the usefulness of their sessions at BFTC. Responses were obtained from 50% of the original 275 clients. Clients were asked whether their treatment goal was met; in those cases in which clients said it was not met, clients were asked whether any progress had been made toward the goal. This line of questioning resulted in three categories of response: "treatment goal met," "some progress toward treatment goal," and "no progress toward treatment goal."

Using this measure of outcome, the BFTC study found a 77% "success rate," with 45% of contacted clients saying that their treatment goal was met and another 32% indicating some progress toward their treatment goal. The average number of sessions for these clients was 3.0. The study also found no differences in success rates by categories of diversity. Success rates also did not vary significantly by type of problem or DSM-IV diagnosis.

## *Comparisons With Other Studies*

A similar outcome study was conducted at BFTC (Kiser, 1988; Kiser & Nunnally, 1990). Kiser's study involved contacting 164 clients at 6, 12, and 18 months after termination of therapy. Kiser relied on a question to measure outcomes similar to the one cited above because he wanted to make comparisons with the results of a study at the Mental Research Institute (MRI) in Palo Alto, California, that had measured outcomes in a similar manner (Weakland, Fisch, Watzlawick, & Bodin, 1974). Kiser found highly successful outcomes. De Shazer (1991) gives this summary of Kiser's result:

> We found an 80.4% success rate (65.6% of the clients met their goal while 14.7% made significant improvement) within an average of 4.6 sessions. When contacted at 18 months, the success rate had increased to 86%.

This rate of success is higher and required fewer sessions than that reported for the MRI study, which reported a success rate of 72% over 97 cases, with 40% of clients experiencing "complete relief of the presenting complaint" and 32% making significant improvement. The average number of sessions for the MRI clients was 7.

In summary, available outcome data on solution-focused practice suggest that it is an effective way to work with clients. Although both studies at BFTC were conducted without control or comparison groups, their "success rates" compare favorably with the average success rates reported in Lambert and Bergin's (1994) meta-analysis of outcome research on the range of practice approaches in use today. Lambert and Bergin, who report primarily on outcome studies using experimental designs with controls, indicated that on average 66% of clients who received some form of therapy showed improvement. (They also indicate that 34% of persons in the control groups improved without therapy.) The success rates in the BFTC studies compare favorably with these percentages. Although this is a promising comparison indicating that clients receiving solution-focused therapy report change rates at percentages comparable with change rates in other more rigorously tested populations, the effectiveness of solution-focused therapy remains to be demonstrated using controlled experimental designs to establish the internal validity and efficacy of the treatment. We hope that the study reported here will prompt further evaluations of this kind.

## Linking Solution-Focused Procedures and Social Constructionism

Social constructionism is a metatheory about people's interpretations of the world and their experiences. As such, it encompasses other theories about how and why people have particular cultural, social, and personal meanings. Hoffman (1990) states, "Social construction theory is really a lens *about* lenses" (p. 4).

Metatheory is far removed from the realities of work with clients. Solution-focused procedures arose out of many years of treating clients, observing outcomes, and thinking critically about treatment procedures; they were not deduced from existing theory. However, social constructionism theory and solution-focused procedures are connected.

**Belief in the social construction of reality.** Hoffman (1990) states that many therapies otherwise thought to be in tension with one another can stand together under the broad umbrella of social constructionism. This can be the case "as long as their practitioners agree that all therapy takes the form of conversations between people and that the findings of these conversations have no other 'reality' than those bestowed by mutual consent" (p. 4). The case illustration and comments indicate that solution-focused therapy belongs under this umbrella.

**Language as the medium through which personal meanings are expressed and constructed.** Stagoll describes social constructionism as asserting,

> There is no access to any absolute reality or foundation outside of language: language does not merely mirror reality, but it is our major means of constructing what we perceive as "reality." ... Reality consists of interpretations which arise from dialogue between interacting participants. (quoted in Cantwell and Holmes [1994, p. 18])

The relationship of language to the client's construction of meaning is complex and deserves ongoing study. De Shazer (1991, 1994) articulates the role that language plays in solution-focused therapy.

**Client change through the discovery of new meanings.** Social constructionism maintains that clients change by developing new meaning constructions. Different therapies use various procedures to foster new, more useful constructions. Anderson and Goolishian (1992) use a posture of "not knowing" or "genuine curiosity" about the client's constructions. Andersen (1987) uses the "reflecting team." Epston and White (1990) describe procedures that "externalize the problem." In contrast, this chapter shows how new meanings arise out of solution-focused conversations initiated by a therapist asking the miracle question, exception questions, and scaling questions.

**The client as expert, the practitioner as "leading from one step behind."** Gergen (1985) points out that social constructionism challenges many of the assumptions of "the traditional Western conception of objective, individualistic, historical knowledge" (pp. 271–272), a conception highly influential among social scientists and therapists. A fully developed metatheory of knowledge more consistent with social constructionist assumptions has not yet been developed. However, upon completion, it surely will involve an emphasis on *contextualized knowledge*—knowledge about people that is relative to time, place, and individual. Bloor (1983) offers a promising beginning toward such a theory based on the work of Wittgenstein.

At the level of therapy, respect for contextualized knowledge means encouraging the client to be the expert about his or her own meanings. Because only clients possess knowledge about the details of their current perceptions, definitions of reality, and past experiences, the therapist's task is to ask questions that elicit these perceptions and definitions. In solution-focused therapy, the therapist invites the client to be the expert by listening for, repeating, and exploring the meaning of the client's key words and by building the next therapeutic question from the client's latest answer. In these conversations, the client is invited to act as "knower"; the therapist keeps the conversation going by "leading from one step behind" (Cantwell & Holmes, 1994, p. 20).

**Taking a collaborative stance.** Social constructionists, in part because of their misgivings about scientifically acquired knowledge, are skeptical about practitioners having *a priori* expertise sufficient to categorize and solve client problems objectively. Instead, they maintain that client constructions about problems and solutions are essential to effective therapy and that the therapist's role is one of collaborating with clients. Goolishian and Anderson (1991) state that therapy informed by social constructionist thinking becomes

> *a collaborative and egalitarian process as opposed to a hierarchical and expert process. The therapist's expertise is to be "in" conversation with the expertise of the client. The therapist now becomes the learner to be informed, rather than a technical expert who knows.*

Solution-focused therapy shares this commitment to collaboration. In the interview presented earlier, the therapist collaborated with Lucinda's expertise by asking questions that consistently put the therapist in a "not knowing" position (Anderson & Goolishian, 1992) and by affirming and complimenting Lucinda's view of her life.

**Use of reflexivity.** Lax (1992) defines reflexivity as "the act of making oneself an object of one's own observation" (p. 75). Social constructionists point out that reflexivity is closely tied to people's tendency to reshape and expand their meanings. By virtue of their capacities to abstract and use language, clients, for example, can climb outside themselves and reflect on how they are functioning in their particular life contexts, how they are perceived by others, how they might act differently, and so forth. Such reflexivity can open up new meanings and increase the possibility of client change.

Different therapies attempt to stimulate client reflexivity in different ways. Andersen (1987, 1991) introduced the idea of a reflecting team, whereby clients are invited to hear the reflections of a team of practitioners about their own case. In contrast, solution-focused therapy uses "relationship questions." For example, the therapist invited Lucinda to draw on her capacity for reflexivity by asking, "If I were to ask your father where he thinks you are between one and ten, where would he say you are?" Lucinda then described her improvement as she perceived her father saw her, a second lens through which to view herself.

**Emphasis on client strengths.** Franklin (see Chapter 3) points out that Saleebey uses social constructionism in the "strengths model"—a model that asserts that clients and their environments possess strengths and resources that practitioners and clients can cooperatively explore and apply to problems. The strengths model is social constructionist in its insistence that problems are social and that individual constructions can be reframed in ways beneficial to human well-being:

> *Rather than accepting our self-imposed definitions of human problems, we can radically shift our perspective from the negative to the positive pole. Instead of asking questions that direct our attention to the deficiencies and limitations in human situations, we can choose to ask questions with positive loading. For example, instead of asking, "What's wrong with this individual?" we can ask, "What are the strengths that have helped this person survive? What are her aspirations, talents, and abilities?" (Saleebey, 1992, p. 22)*

In Lucinda's case, the therapist invited Lucinda to move from the negative pole to the positive pole. Solution-focused procedures used to open up and amplify client strengths and successes include the miracle question, exception questions, coping questions, "what's better" questions, in-session compliments, and end-of-session feedback composed of compliments and tasks drawn from emerging client definitions of competence. De Shazer (1994) states that solution-focused therapy as a whole represents a shift from "problem talk" to "solution talk."

**Solutions are co-constructed.** We have come full circle. We began this chapter by stating that social constructionism is rooted in the idea that peoples' meanings are formed in interaction with and through conversation with others. That is, new and more useful meanings are "co-constructed" or, as Weick (1993) states, "The act of dialogue is the vehicle through which meaning gets made" (p. 25). De Shazer (1994) similarly perceives solution-focused therapy as a process of co-construction. Drawing from the ideas of Russian literary critic Mikhail Bakhtin, he states:

> *Bakhtin's perspective leads to the idea that the relations between therapist and client continue to alter in the very process of the conversation. There is no ready-made meaning that is transferred or handed over from one to the other. Rather, meaning develops or takes form in the process of interacting. A message is not transmitted from one to the other but "constructed between them, like an ideological bridge; it is constructed in the process of their interaction." (Bakhtin, 1928, quoted in Todorov) (de Shazer, 1994, p. 52)*

# References

Adams, J. F., Piercy, F. P., & Jurich, J. A. (1991). Effects of solution-focused therapy's "formula first session task" on compliance and outcome in family therapy. *Journal of Marital and Family Therapy, 17,* 277–290.

American Psychiatric Association. (1994). *Diagnostic and statistical manual of mental disorders* (4th ed.). Washington, DC: Author.

Andersen, T. (1987). The reflecting team: Dialogue and meta-dialogue in clinical work. *Family Process, 26,* 415–428.

Andersen, T. (Ed.). (1991). *The reflecting team: Dialogues and dialogues about the dialogues.* New York: W. W. Norton.

Anderson, H., & Goolishian, H. (1992). The client is the expert: A not-knowing approach to therapy. In S. McNamee & K. J. Gergen, *Therapy as social construction* (pp. 25–39). Newbury Park, CA: Sage.

Berg, I. K. (1994). *Family based services: A solution-focused approach.* New York: W. W. Norton.

Berg, I. K., & de Shazer, S. (1993). Making numbers talk: Language in therapy. In S. Friedman (Ed.), *The new language of change: Constructive collaboration in psychotherapy.* New York: Guilford.

Berg, I. K., & Miller, S. D. (1992). *Working with the problem drinker: A solution-focused approach.* New York: W. W. Norton.

Berger, P., & Luckmann, T. (1966). *The social construction of reality: A treatise in the sociology of knowledge.* Garden City, NY: Anchor.

Bloor, D. (1983). *Wittgenstein: A social theory of knowledge.* New York: Columbia University Press.

Cantwell, P., & Holmes, S. (1994). Social construction: A paradigm shift for systemic therapy and training. *Australian and New Zealand Journal of Family Therapy, 15,* 17–26.

De Jong, P., & Berg, I. K. (1997). *Interviewing for solutions.* Pacific Grove, CA: Brooks/Cole.

De Jong, P., & Miller, S. (1995). How to interview for client strengths. *Social Work, 40,* 729–736.

de Shazer, S. (1985). *Keys to solution in brief therapy.* New York: W. W. Norton.

de Shazer, S. (1988). *Clues: Investigating solutions in brief therapy.* New York: W. W. Norton.

de Shazer, S. (1991). *Putting difference to work.* New York: W. W. Norton.

de Shazer, S. (1994). *Words were originally magic.* New York: W. W. Norton.

de Shazer, S., Berg, I. K., Lipchik, E., Nunnally, E., Molnar, A., Gingerich, W., & Weiner-Davis, M. (1986). Brief therapy: Focused solution development. *Family Process, 25,* 207–221.

Garfinkel, H. (1967). *Studies in ethnomethodology.* Englewood Cliffs, NJ: Prentice-Hall.

Geertz, C. (1973). *The interpretation of cultures.* New York: Basic Books.

Gergen, K. J. (1985). The social constructionist movement in American psychology. *American Psychologist, 40,* 266–275.

Goolishian, H. A., & Anderson, H. (1991). An essay on changing theory and changing ethics: Some historical and post structural views. *American Family Therapy Association Newsletter,* No. 46, 6–10.

Hoffman, L. (1985). Beyond power and control: Toward a "second order" family systems therapy. *Family Systems Medicine, 3,* 381–395.

Hoffman, L. (1990). Constructing realities: An art of lenses. *Family Process, 29,* 1–12.

Hoffman, L. (1992). A reflexive stance for family therapy. In S. McNamee & K. J. Gergen (Eds.), *Therapy as social construction* (pp. 7–24). Newbury Park, CA: Sage.

Kiser, D. (1988). *A follow-up study conducted at the Brief Family Therapy Center.* Unpublished manuscript. Milwaukee, WI: Brief Family Therapy Center.

Kiser, D., & Nunnally, E. (1990). *The relationship between treatment length and goal achievement in solution-focused therapy.* Unpublished manuscript. Milwaukee, WI: Brief Family Therapy Center.

Lambert, M. J., & Bergin, A. E. (1994). The effectiveness of psychotherapy. In A. E. Bergin & S. L. Garfield (Eds.), *Handbook of psychotherapy and behavior change* (4th ed., pp. 143–189). New York: John Wiley.

Lax, W. D. (1992). Postmodern thinking in clinical practice. In S. McNamee & K. J. Gergen (Eds.), *Therapy as social construction* (pp. 69–85). Newbury Park, CA: Sage.

Mead, G. H. (1934). *Mind, self and society*. Chicago: University of Chicago Press.

Rappaport, J. (1981). In praise of paradox: A social policy of empowerment over prevention. *American Journal of Community Psychology, 9,* 1–25.

Rappaport, J. (1990). Research methods and the empowerment social agenda. In P. Tolan, C. Keys, F. Chertak, & L. Jason (Eds.) *Researching community psychology* (pp. 51–63). Washington, DC: American Psychological Association.

Riessman, C. K. (1993). Teaching research: Beyond the storybook image of positivist science. In J. Laird (Ed.), *Revisioning social work education: A social constructionist approach* (pp. 281–303). New York: Haworth.

Saleebey, D. (Ed.). (1992). *The strengths perspective in social work practice*. New York: Longman.

Tomm, K. (1987). Interventive interviewing: Part II. Reflexive questioning as a means to enable self-healing. *Family Process, 26,* 167–184.

Watzlawick, P. (Ed.). (1984). *The invented reality*. New York: W. W. Norton.

Weakland, J. H., Fisch, R., Watzlawick, P., & Bodin, A. (1974). Brief therapy: Focused problem resolution. *Family Process, 13,* 141–168.

Weick, A. (1993). Reconstructing social work education. In J. Laird (Ed.), *Revisioning social work education: A social constructionist approach* (pp. 11–30). New York: Haworth.

White, M., & Epston, D. (1990). *Narrative means to therapeutic ends*. New York: W. W. Norton.

# 12

# Social Constructionism in Action: Using Reflecting Teams in Family Practice

*Joan L. Biever & Cynthia Franklin*

Social constructionist family therapies that focus on deconstructing meanings and providing new explanations as a basis for behavior change have their roots in previous therapeutic approaches such as constructivist systemic approaches, cognitive therapies, and existential therapies (Kelly, 1996). Social constructionism provides a set of practice methods that are dialogic and highly cognitive–phenomenological in their approach to assessing and intervening with people. This chapter focuses on the application of social constructionism to clinical practice through the use of reflecting teams. The relationship between the practice methods of reflecting teams and the theory of social constructionism is discussed. The processes involved in reflecting-team practice are also defined and described. Research on reflecting-team therapies is reviewed, along with the limitations of using this approach. Finally, reflecting-team practice is illustrated with a case transcript and follow-up interview from an African American family that participated in the therapy.

## Social Constructionism—A Postmodern Approach

Postmodern ideas are becoming increasing influential in social work and allied disciplines (Gorman, 1993; Kelly, 1994, 1995; Pozatek, 1994; Saleebey, 1994; Sands & Nuccio, 1992; Scott, 1989; Van den Bergh, 1995). Postmodernism refers to a movement in our culture away from the belief in and search for fundamental truths. Some describe this movement as the result of an evolving and increasingly complex view of the world: "Postmodern Mind is one [that] has come to question whether [reality] is ordered in a way in which man's reason can lay bare" (Smith, 1989, p. 7). Postmodernism has been described as "a linguistic theory that proposes that the social world cannot be treated as an objective system" (Pardeck, Murphy, & Jung, 1994, p. 343).

Within clinical practice, two social science theories have been repeatedly discussed as postmodern metatheories for practice: cognitive constructivism and social constructionism (R. A. Neimeyer & Mahoney, 1995). Both cognitive constructivism and social constructionism share the belief that reality is actively constructed through sociocultural and psychological processes. Therapies derived from both metatheories focus on changing meanings and understandings as important to the process of changing behaviors (see Chapter 1; Chapter 3; Chapter 10; Franklin & Jordan, 1996; Kelly, 1996; Laird, 1993, 1994; G. J. Neimeyer, 1995; R. A. Neimeyer & Mahoney, 1995). Cognitive constructivists, however, focus more on individual cognitive processes involved in constructing reality and changes that occur within an individual, whereas social constructionists focus on the construction of reality as an interactive process and change as occurring within social contexts, such as the family. See Chapter 3 for further distinctions of therapies from varying constructive perspectives.

Social constructionism suggests that our reality results from our linguistic distinctions formed in our interactions with others (Gergen, 1985). Understandings, meanings, and subsequent labels that individuals attach to any given behavior, interaction, or event serve as a basis for structuring beliefs concerning reality, and such understandings are determined by social and cultural contexts (Berger & Luckmann, 1966). These social and linguistic operations result in embedded beliefs and consequent reactions on the part of individuals and groups. Although it is not the intent of this chapter fully to explicate social constructionist theory and its clinical practice applications (see Chapter 3; Anderson & Goolishian, 1988; Biever, Gardner, & Bobele, in press; Gergen, 1985; McNamee & Gergen, 1992, for a more comprehensive treatment), the following ideas derived from social constructionism have influenced the thinking and interventions of most therapists practicing from social constructionist perspectives.

▪ Meanings are developed through social interaction and social consensus. It is important for therapists to entertain the idea that many possible understandings, descriptions, and conversations may be helpful to clients (Anderson & Goolishian, 1988; Gergen, 1985; Hoffman, 1990). That is, all ideas are potentially useful.

▪ Generally speaking, all understandings are socially and linguistically negotiated and related to the context within which they are embedded, especially the current conversation. Gergen (1985) asserts that many kinds of knowledge are the result of things that people do together, which suggests that knowledge is a cooperative, active, here-and-now enterprise.

▪ Narratives and meanings are always changing in relation to the social contexts in which stories are developed and told. Thus, "problems" evolve in the contexts of the narratives people tell themselves about their own and others' lives.

▪ To the extent that we can expand narratives (and therefore meanings), we can expand the possibilities for novel actions. In addition, therapists need to consider the social, political, cultural, and economic contexts in which narratives occur because not all narratives are equally possible in all contexts (Hoffman, 1990).

▪ Psychological theories are merely agreed-upon understandings or stories that have proven useful in one or more contexts (Howard, 1991). No account or interpretation of reality can be proven more accurate than any other interpretation. Instead, the focus is on how and when a theory is useful rather than on trying to prove or disprove theoretical ideas.

It's difficult to describe specific methods and techniques of social constructionist family therapies, because these approaches to therapy were developed by various individuals and groups: Goolishian and Anderson in Texas, White in Australia, Epston in New Zealand, Andersen in Norway, and Hoffman in Massachusetts. Further, as noted by de Shazer (1993), for every theoretical idea are a multitude of clinical practices or techniques to express it. Indeed, Anderson and Goolishian (1988) argue against deliberate interventions, and White and Epston (1990) argue that constructionism may become endangered if the theory is not translated into practices.

## Social Constructionist Therapeutic Orientation

Therapy from the social constructionist perspective represents a collaborative effort between clients and therapists. Therapists are not viewed as being in a privileged position with regard to knowledge and understandings. Rather, clients are viewed as having expertise regarding their experience, memories, responses, and goals. The expertise of therapists lies in their ability to create therapeutic contexts in which alternative understandings, shifts in cognitive meanings, and consequent behaviors can be generated.

Therapy generally begins with exploring the client's understanding of and explanations (personal theories) about the problems or concerns that brought them to therapy. Rather than exploring how the client's problems and life situation match the therapist's theories about the nature of psychological problems, diagnostic categories, and change, the therapist focuses on the client's subjective views regarding the origins of the difficulties. Clients' explanations are valued because they are potentially useful in understanding the meaning of the concerns and how those concerns are communicated and subsequently maintained within a social context. The therapist then proceeds to "deconstruct" these understandings. Through the deconstruction process, (a) the client's ideas are questioned, (b) the origins of the client's beliefs are traced, (c) underlying assumptions of the client's explanations and beliefs are unmasked, and (d) alternative explanations are suggested. Thus, the cognitive–phenomenological orientation of the social constructionist therapies becomes apparent. During the course of therapy, therapists facilitate the expansion of descriptions and understandings regarding the presenting concerns. As part of therapy, therapists present alternative understandings through the use of Socratic questions, reflections, inquiring probes, and new descriptions that are presented tentatively as possibly helpful ideas. Clients interpret these questions and descriptions and use them in their own change processes.

Social constructionist therapies do not emphasize theoretically (or politically) correct explanations or ideas for interpreting problems and concerns of clients. However, some ideas are believed to be more pertinent to client's concerns than are others. Ideas and beliefs that come from the dominant culture, however, and are seen as oppressive influences or constraining choices are often a focus of deconstruction by the therapist. For example, if a single mother believes that she is a "bad mother" because she got a divorce and can no longer provide as well for her children, her interpretation may be viewed as a constraining belief, the roots of which can be traced to society's view of divorced women. Thus, social constructionist therapists take the position that a client internalizes these dominant societal discourses and is constrained by them in terms of their self-concept and behaviors. To continue the example of the divorced mother, it may be noticed during therapy that the woman's children also join in on this constraining discourse by stating that they are "no longer a family." A social constructionist therapist in that situation would attempt to deconstruct these constraining ideas and introduce points of contrast in the form of alternative explanations that might point out parental and family strengths.

Social constructionists view deconstructing understanding and knowledge as a process that is never complete and constantly changing. Anderson and Goolishian (1992) caution therapists not to assume too quickly that they understand clients. When therapists "understand" clients, the possibilities for deconstruction and for expanding and creating meanings are reduced. Therapists who work from the social constructionist perspective value diversity as well as multiple perspectives and ideas. One method for supporting multiple perspectives is the adoption of a *both–and* stance in place of an *either–or* stance. The both–and stance removes therapists from judging who is right in disagreements. The focus is on how a belief came into being rather than on which belief is correct or best. Exploring intents or underlying meanings provides a way out of either–or standoffs. When therapists take this stance, even logically inconsistent ideas can coexist.

Social constructionist therapies often focus on stories or narratives. For instance, Hoffman (1990) described problems as stories people tell themselves. Generally, social constructionist family therapists believe that viewing the presenting problem as a "story" presupposes that it is possible—perhaps inevitable—that the story will change with each telling. Changing the story changes the meanings attached to events, behaviors, and interactions. However, the manner in which stories are used in therapy differs among postmodern therapists. For instance, White (1993) and White and Epston (1990) focus on the ways in which clients' stories are restrained by dominant narratives such as those coming from the sociopolitical contexts of the broader society. Cultural narratives, for example, that support patriarchy or oppressive stories that develop out of abusive situations are frequently considered. In contrast, Sluzki (1992) discusses how narratives can be transformed by focusing on the structure of stories. Therapists may facilitate the transformation of client stories by attending to the following dimensions: time, space, causality, interactions, values, and the telling of the story. Sluzki describes a continuum for each of these dimensions along which stories may shift. Where clients fall on the continuum is not important; the job of therapists is to help clients shift their position. Finally, in the collaborative-languaging approach developed by Anderson and Goolishian (1988, 1992), the focus is on developing stories rather than on providing frameworks for changing stories. Therapy is seen as an opportunity for clients to explore various stories while discouraging commitment to any particular story as the "truth" (Gergen & Kaye, 1992).

# Reflecting Teams and Social Constructionism

Reflecting-team therapy has its origins in social constructionism and postmodern family perspectives (Biever & Gardner, 1995). Reflecting is perhaps the most novel technique that has evolved from social constructionist family therapies. In this approach, the client meets with the therapist while a team of therapists, usually three to five members, observes behind a one-way mirror or screen. After a designated amount of time, the reflecting-team members offer their perceptions about the client and the situation for approximately 10 minutes. After observing the team, the client comments on the team's reflections.

The term reflecting was first used by Andersen (1987, 1991). Andersen and his associates developed the term from the Norwegian *refleksjon* and offered this practical definition: "something heard is taken in and thought about before a response is given" (Andersen, 1991, p. 12). According to this approach, by expanding the client's meanings and realities through the presentation of multiple explanations from a reflecting-team group, it is possible to construct new meanings that may help clients resolve their presenting problem. Andersen (1987) believes that the client's shift from being the "talk participant" to the "observer participant" is an effective intervention. That shift helps clients gain a metaperspective on the presenting issues (Young et al., 1989).

Hoffman (1992) describes reflecting as indicating "a preference for a mutually influenced process between consultant and inquirer as opposed to one that is hierarchical and unidirectional" (p. 17). Finally, Griffith and Griffith (1994) describe reflecting as

> a listening position. In its most fundamental aspect, it is a place in a conversation where one can listen to others talk without feeling compelled to respond or can listen freely to one's inner talk without feeling compelled to relegate it to total secrecy or total exposure. (p. 160)

In the course of time, the idea of reflecting has been expanded and is now used to describe a process (reflecting conversations) and a stance (reflecting position) that can be used by therapists regardless of whether they work in teams, co-therapy, or alone. Reflecting is talking about the content and process of the therapy session without talking directly to clients. Andersen (1992) describes the reflecting process as consisting of inner and outer conversations that allow therapists and clients to shift back and forth between talking and listening. He further states, "These two different positions in relation to the same issues seem to provide two different perspectives, and these two perspectives of the same will most probably create new perspectives" (p. 62). Reflecting helps clients step into a metacognitive position as they listen to several therapists have a conversation about them. From this metaposition, clients may become more open to new explanations and interpretations of their problem.

# Reflecting-Team Practice

Originally, reflecting was developed as an alternative (Andersen, 1987) to the family therapy, Milan-style team structure. In the Milan structure a team of therapists behind a one-way mirror discuss the case without the involvement of the clients and provide feedback and directives to the family after their discussions. In contrast, the reflecting approach allows the clients to listen to the team discuss their understandings and ideas rather than wait for feedback or messages from the team to be delivered by the therapists. Thus, reflecting teams give clients direct access to the teams' ideas, rather than funneling teams' ideas through the therapists working directly with the clients.

Postmodern family practice approaches such as the reflecting team engenders a therapeutic technique that emphasizes the clinical usefulness of multiple descriptions, explanations, and meanings. Such methods have been discussed as being especially sensitive to diversity in that they embrace multiple realities and emphasize the social and cultural origins of human behavior. For instance, reflecting teams are a natural application of the idea of multiple perspectives as reflecting-team discussions include the views and perspectives of various team members. Andersen (1991) suggests that reflecting-team members keep two questions in mind: "How else can this situation/behavior/pattern be described?" and "How else can this situation/behavior/pattern be explained?" Team members then discuss their ideas and highlight the differences and similarities with regard to how they understood the comments of clients and therapists and how they would describe and explain the situations discussed in therapy. Reflecting-team discussions also illustrate the ways in which people make different meanings from one another and how different meanings can be explored and generated through conversation. This happens both through reflecting-team discussions and during post-reflecting-team discussions between therapists and clients. This conversation, again, highlights similarities and differences of meanings and descriptions and provides a means for changing or expanding descriptions and meanings.

Finally, the notion that all ideas are potentially useful and that clients are the best judges of what will be useful for them is also put into practice on the reflecting team. The reflecting-team process encourages members to share their ideas, all of which are viewed as potentially useful. The team does not attempt to come to a consensus regarding what ideas are more accurate or useful. The potential usefulness of ideas is left for clients and therapists to discuss and clients ultimately to determine.

## *Expanding the Use of Reflecting Conversations*

Reflecting has been expanded for use by therapists who work alone or in co-therapy teams. For instance, Madigan (1993) describes the use of "listening therapists" who are situated in the room along with the therapist conducting a session and who periodically offer reflections concerning the content and process of the therapy session. Therapists who work alone may incorporate reflecting by taking brief breaks as "thinking time." Therapists leave the room or simply ask for a few minutes to reflect on the session up to that point. Clients may be invited to do the same. Therapists and clients then share their reflections.

As noted above, the reflecting process was conceived originally as part of a team process (Andersen, 1987). However, since the introduction of reflecting teams, various uses of the reflecting process have been discussed. Andersen (1995) suggests the following methods for incorporating reflecting processes into the therapeutic process. Therapists can reflect (a) with teams either in the same room or behind a one-way mirror, (b) with an observing colleague at various times throughout the session, (c) with one member of the family while others listen, then with the remaining family members while the first person listens, or (d) by asking clients about their thoughts on how they think others would think or talk about an issue. Andersen also notes that reflecting can be applied in contexts other than therapy, such as supervision groups, staff meetings, management or other types of training groups, and qualitative research. In each of these contexts, the groups can be divided so part of the group listens and then reflects on a discussion or interview.

## How to Conduct Reflecting Teams

As discussed above, reflecting teams may watch from behind a one-way mirror or be seated in the therapy room. The physical limitations of the facility most often dictate the physical arrangements. When the reflecting team is seated in the therapy room, members reflect only when invited to do so by the therapist–client system. Reflecting-team members talk only with one another and not with the family. Thus, clients listen to ideas of team members without having to formulate responses. Regardless of the context, reflecting conversations have common elements that distinguish them from other types of therapeutic or everyday conversations.

As outlined by Andersen and others (Andersen, 1987, 1991, 1995; Biever & Gardner, 1995; Freedman & Combs, 1996; Griffith & Griffith, 1994; Lax, 1995) reflections are based on what has been discussed in the interview and offer alternative ideas, descriptions, and understandings. Negative connotations and evaluative statements are avoided. Wangberg (1991) suggests that therapists differentiate reflecting comments from other therapeutic exchanges by looking at the floor or window while reflecting.

Andersen (1995) further cautioned against offering statements, opinions, or meanings, because clients may understand such offerings as something that should be done. Thus, alternative descriptions and meanings should be stated tentatively, and the team should offer multiple alternatives. Reflections focus on strengths and generally have an optimistic tone. Reflecting-team members avoid either–or positions. Lax (1995) notes that a both–and position can be facilitated by indicating that potentially polarizing comments "are in *addition to*, not *opposed to*" (p. 162, italics in original) ideas expressed by other team members. Directives and tasks are not assigned during reflecting conversations. However, ideas about possible tasks may be discussed in a tentative manner as one possibility for a course of action to follow. Lax (1995) suggested that reflecting comments not be restricted to family members, that is, that reflecting comments and questions be directed to the therapists as well to family members.

# Research on Reflecting Teams

Reflecting teams have become popular in family therapy practice, training, and supervision (Andersen, 1991; Biever & Gardner, 1995; Friedman, 1995; Jenkins, 1996). Despite their increasing popularity in clinical practice, little research on the process or outcomes of reflecting teams has been done. Most studies have focused on the process of reflecting teams instead of the outcomes or effectiveness of the approach. Constructionist practitioners seem to prefer qualitative methods such as case studies, ethnography, and discourse analysis (see Chapter 4) in their investigations of the process of reflecting teams. Research has yielded promising findings regarding the usefulness of the approach. Clients generally report favorable perceptions of the reflecting-team process. In addition, changes in meanings, perceptions, and affective tone of clients have been observed by therapist-researchers and confirmed through client self-reports.

Using a case study, Andersen (1995) discussed the immediate differences observed after a reflecting team was implemented into a therapy session. The family's attitudes toward the future were reported to be "very different" from what members' attitudes were prior to the reflections. Griffith and colleagues (1992) used the Structural Analysis of Social Behavior (SASB) to compare family interactions before and after a reflecting-team intervention. They found that communications following a session using reflecting teams showed significant changes in family conversations and an increased significance in codes for trusting, relying, comforting, and nurturing.

In the most comprehensive study conducted on reflecting teams, Sells, Smith, Yoshioka, and Robbin (1994) used qualitative methods—specifically, ethnographic interviewing—to study the reflecting-team process and to further understanding concerning the client's perceptions of the effectiveness of reflecting-team therapy. Recurring themes from the clients' feedback indicated the value of the multiple perspectives. Further research is needed to replicate these findings and to examine whether changes in the presenting problems accompany the positive perceptions of the clients regarding the reflecting team and the changes in their psychological functioning that have been observed.

# Limitations of Reflecting Teams

The researcher facing postmodern therapies is presented with several problems concerning the best way to establish the validity of these therapies. Yet, without establishing the validity of postmodern methods, it is impossible in current practice environments that emphasize accountability for social constructionist approaches to establish themselves as effective methods of treatment. A pragmatic concern arises in communicating with colleagues and managed care organizations, whose language and understandings may be very different from those of the postmodern therapist. Issues of diagnosis, treatment planning, and outcomes are often described in terms that are less useful to the postmodern therapist. Despite these challenges, several features of social constructionist approaches like reflecting teams make them viable in social work practice.

One feature is that social constructionist approaches use a strengths orientation. They utilize resources of the client and social system to find agreeable solutions. Thus, therapy using a client-centered approach is likely to lead to high ratings in the area of consumer satisfaction, which is important for managed behavioral health care organizations and other funders of clinical services.

Second, social constructionist approaches also usually focus on the here and now in the stories that clients bring to therapy. They move quickly to change these narratives and to help clients to get "unstuck" so that they can move on with their lives. This qualifies postmodern perspectives as a brief-therapy approach.

Third, postmodern perspectives use social supports and other social resources in resolving problems. Postmodern therapists influence the social networks that surround families and their problem stories. From this vantage point, the move beyond the therapy room into the natural environments in which people live is a method of dis-solving problems and finding solutions. This type of approach has a high level of success in decreasing relapse patterns, which is important to the cost-containment efforts of managed care.

The contextual approach of the social constructionist therapies also makes them excellent therapies for use within the person–environment approach in social work practice. Social constructionist therapies are a natural match for social work because they subscribe to the idea that everyone, including the larger community, involved in defining the problem should be included in a narrative dialogue aimed at dis-solving the problem. The team approach can work well in bringing different minds and perspectives together to offer new ways to solve problems. Reflecting is an important process because it puts all participants into a metaposition that may create an openness to change and allow for consensus building and mutual problem solving.

The idea of therapists, or clients for that matter, working in teams to solve problems may be foreign to some managed care companies that may view such practice as not being cost effective. As noted by Biever and colleagues (in press), however, the teams may offer an important solution for training in managed care settings. It is important to managed care companies, for example, always to have a licensed therapist who can see the clients. This presents a challenge with regard to how to offer practice experience to interns and other students in training. Teams made up of interns and students can help resolve this dilemma. Also, as mentioned previously, it is not necessary for a team to be present for the therapist to use the reflecting approach. Therapists can use themselves and their clients to maintain the reflexive stance necessary to conduct this type of therapy.

Some alternative ways of using reflecting conversations may prove both helpful and cost effective. Using family members or other social- or community-systems members (extended family, friends, case workers) as reflecting-team members has the added advantage of creating a linked dialogue between systems for the purpose of generating alternative perspectives and solutions. The therapist may also construct multifamily groups or other groups to provide a social-support system that reflects on group members' problems. Another approach may be to use groups of colleagues as part of staff development or peer supervision.

## Case Example

The following case example illustrates the use of reflecting teams at the Community Counseling Service, a training clinic in San Antonio, Texas. This clinic is operated by the Department of Psychology at Our Lady of the Lake University and serves both university and community clients. In this setting, reflecting teams typically consist of two to four graduate students and a faculty member who serves as a clinical supervisor. Teams are incorporated into each therapy session and serve as a training model. In the initial session, therapists explain that a team is behind the one-way mirror and that the team will offer ideas at some point in the session. Clients are given the option as to whether they wish to listen in on this discussion. Almost all clients choose to listen to the discussion, if not in the first session, then in the second and subsequent sessions. Reflecting conversations typically begin with team members giving a brief introduction followed by comments regarding the observed strengths of the family and changes that have been made. This "joining phase" is followed by reflections that offer alternative explanations and descriptions. Comments and ideas are phrased tentatively and as possibilities. Team members link their comments to one another with transitional statements even when offering ideas that have little in common with the previous ideas. The intent is for team members to have a conversation with one another, not simply offer disconnected ideas.

The names and identifying information and events in this case example have been altered to protect the confidentiality of the clients. The Joneses, an African American family who self-referred to the Community Counseling Service, consist of Robert and Carol Jones and their daughters, Kim, age 35, and Roberta, age 15. Mr. and Mrs. Jones have been married for 30 years. Kim is the biological child of Mrs. Jones and adopted child of Mr. Jones. Roberta was adopted by the Joneses and is the biological child of a distant relative of Mrs. Jones. Kim returned to her parents' home about the time of the birth of her six-year-old son and resided with them until shortly before the family requested therapy. Mr. and Mrs. Jones work in civil-service jobs. Kim is employed as a manager in a retail business, and Roberta is a sophomore at a special-interest high school for gifted and talented students.

Therapy was initiated by Mr. and Mrs. Jones and lasted for eight sessions. The sessions were not held in consecutive weeks; in the latter part of therapy they were spaced several weeks apart. The family's presenting problem was described as concern for the welfare of their daughter Roberta, who had recently started skipping school, disobeying her parent's rules, staying out late at night, and becoming sexually involved with adult men. The most recent precipitating incident happened the week that the family entered therapy and led the parents to call for help. Roberta left school and stayed out all night in a hotel with an older boy. Her parents did not know where she was for almost 24 hours, which resulted in a police investigation. She was found by the police and returned to her parents.

Mr. and Mrs. Jones attended therapy alone for the first session, feeling they needed some advice as parents. Both daughters attended the second session. The remaining seven sessions were attended by family members who were available; for example, Robert missed one session because he was ill. Reflecting teams were incorporated into each of the therapy sessions. The following edited excerpts illustrate the reflecting-team process and several points throughout the therapy process.

### Session One

The session focused on obtaining descriptions of the problem and eliciting goals from the parents. The identified problem was Roberta's behavior: She was failing in school and "acting the teenage part" by sneaking out at night and becoming sexually involved with older boys. The parents also identified "communication problems," specifically that Robert rarely talked to the girls except when he was angry. Carol was described as the bridge between her husband and daughters. Despite these problems, Carol noted, "We do love one another. It's not that we don't love. We just . . . I'd say we just don't have enough communication." Both parents indicated they would do "whatever it takes" to get the problems straightened out. Robert described the recent family problems as his biggest challenge since his fight with cancer. He noted that he was successful in fighting for his health and that he would fight just as hard for the health of his family.

**Reflecting process.** The reflecting team focused initially on the love and commitment demonstrated by the parents as a way of joining with the family and highlighting their strengths:

> *Team member 1: I am struck by the commitment that this couple has made to their family. (The member added a tentative explanation for some change that occurred between the telephone call and the first session and a tentative suggestion of a metaphor that could lead to further change.)*

> *Team member 2: ... and they want all of the family to be together. After hearing Carol say that things got a little better between Robert and Kim after the phone call, I'm wondering if Kim sensed the shift that her parents made to make some changes and that might have changed her attitude or something. I can't help but think things can get even better for this family, because of the willingness and commitment of the parents.*

> *Team member 3: I just wonder ... and I might be completely wrong on this, I'd really like to know from her, that when they talked about her being the bridge, I wonder if she's a little weary of that? You know? Because when you're a bridge, people walk all over you.*

> *Team member 2: To get from one side to the next.*

> *Team member 3: Yeah, not that she's not willing to do it, but I wonder if it is making her very tired.*

The following comments linked past successes to possible ways to deal with the current problems and complimented the family on their demonstrated strengths:

*Team member 2: Yet she will do whatever it takes … Robert, too. I was struck by Robert's openness and willingness to take advice. It's like since his cancer, he's more willing to make some moves and listen to people. (Noting that both Carol and Robert are committed to change.) And maybe this is making a difference with his daughters, too. Maybe they are more willing to be open … after all that they have been through.*

*Team member 4: Yeah, some families might have fallen apart after the incident with Roberta, that one incident could literally tear a family apart.*

*Team member 2: A family that didn't have the kinds of ties.*

*Team member 4: But this family didn't fall apart. They grew together.*

Finally, the team proposed that the family could find ways of changing both on their own and through counseling.

*Team member 2: They pulled together. They came here. They're looking for some answers. They've already gotten some things working for themselves … but they've come here as well.*

Carol and Robert responded positively to the comments of the reflecting team. However, they began to wonder if they had presented themselves in too positive of a light, for example, would the team have different ideas about them after listening to the girls? They then requested the therapists and team to "tell us where we went wrong … or if we went wrong. Or if I'm wrong. I would just like to know what caused her to rebel in school. I push education,. …" This was understood as a message to the team not to be overly optimistic and to pay attention to the struggles of the parents.

## *Session Two*

During the second session the girls were seen without the parents. They agreed that the main problems in the family were the way their dad did (or didn't) talk to them and their mother's tendency to "hold on" too tight. Roberta commented that her friends' families seemed happier than her family.

**Reflecting process.** The reflecting team chose Roberta's comment as a place to begin to search for alternative descriptions.

*Team member 1: Roberta talked about how some of her friends' families were nothing like hers, and I thought, I wonder what she thinks about the cause of why her family is different? What are some of the things that they do differently?*

*Team member 2: I wonder what other kids looking at Roberta and her family would say.*

The team then offered an explanation for the parents' request for therapy:

*Team member 3: I wonder what she thinks about her parents' feeling so strongly about coming to counseling. … There is lots of care … desire to get things worked out.*

*Team member 4: The parents have tried trying to control Roberta … bars on the windows and all that. They seemed bound and determined to control her … but sounds like maybe her parents are … like they got to the point where they're thinking, well, we can't control her by intimidation and force.*

*Team member 2: So counseling may be another way of learning to work with Roberta rather than trying to control her.*

*Team member 4: Yeah, 'cause the more they try to control her, the more I think they're going to fail.*

Finally, an alternative explanation for Roberta's behavior was offered:

*Team member 3: Yeah, maybe Roberta finally convinced them of that!*

After the reflecting team finished, Roberta joked with the therapists about her unwillingness to let her parents control her life.

## *Session Four*

This session began with the family members joking and laughing with one another, a marked change from their earlier demeanor. The discussion focused on Robert and Roberta's improving relationship. Carol was feeling somewhat left out. Carol and Robert also shared the circumstances of Roberta's adoption, which they felt explained Carol's pattern of being protective of Roberta.

**Reflecting Process.** The reflecting team started with their observations on visible changes in the family.

*Team member 1: It's nice seeing Roberta. She has a whole new look tonight, smiling and talking to us. As soon as she walked in the room, I noticed it.*

*Team member 2: Yeah, and she's bringing up her grades.*

*Team member 3: Working on her grades and getting a scholarship.*

*Team member 2: Sort of an unexpected gift, huh?*

The team expressed curiosity about changes that the mother may have noticed and whether these changes were meaningful to her:

*Team member 3: Yeah, really. And, I guess along with that, one of the things I was wondering ... was how ... how does Carol see it? Does she see improvement? I'm wondering what she has noticed.*

*Team member 4: I'm thinking along those same lines, how much change has Carol seen and how will she know when she can let up on the need to protect, defend, nurture, and take care of Roberta?*

An alternative description of the mother's "controlling" behavior was offered:

*Team member 1: When I heard the story about Roberta's childhood, or infancy, really, one thing that became clear to me is why Carol might feel so strongly that she has to keep Roberta close to her and keep her safe from harm and on the right track. That's what she had to do, that history sort of influences what kind of patterns get set up today. I'm wondering if Carol will know when she's done her job well and maybe she can trust Roberta to carry on the hopes and dreams and all that she wanted for that little girl she rescued. Carol and Robert have already given Roberta so much.*

*Team member 3: She's had a different kind of life, different kinds of opportunities. And it may be that she's nearing the time when she can kind of find her way more on her own, or ... just come back every once in a while for support, rather than needing full-time protecting.*

The team suggested possible means for changing one of the identified problems:

*Team member 2: Another thing, I was thinking about Carol feeling like she had to chase down Robert and Roberta. ... It must be hard to always be the one pursuing. ... I wonder how else she can interact with them that is different from chasing. Is there a way to invite them into conversation?*

*Team member 4: Or maybe Robert and Roberta could do something to invite Carol into conversation, maybe join her when she's doing her chores.*

*Team member 1: Or what other kinds of stuff do they like to do? Sometimes it's easier to talk when you're doing something, not just sitting and staring at each other.*

The rest of the session focused on activities they could do together and that would give them a chance to talk to one another as well.

## Session Eight

This session focused on all the changes that had been made and on their plans for vacation, which involved driving long distances.

**Reflecting Process.** The reflecting team comments focused on the love and commitment that had always been present and the changes that had been made.

*Team member 1: When I heard Roberta talking about not wanting to disappoint her family, that she has hopes just like her mom, I thought back to the first session, when Carol talked about the love that was present in the family.*

*Team member 2: It's like they've taken some bad circumstances, some really traumatic circumstances, and each one not only dealt with it personally, but they dealt with it as a family.*

*Team member 3: The whole family has come together. ... They're talking better than they did before Roberta snuck out. ... I wonder where they will go now, what kind of changes will be next?*

A possible explanation for change was offered:

*Team member 4: It seems like Roberta has figured some things out and her parents have figured some things out. Maybe they discovered the trust and confidence they were looking for.*

*Team member 2: The test will be if they figure out how to communicate during their three-day drive!*

The rest of the session focused on plans for the trip and how they were going to maintain the changes they had made. The final session took place about six weeks later. The vacation had gone very well, and the new school year had gotten off to a good start for Roberta.

## Interview on Experiences With Reflecting Teams

As part of a research project, the Joneses were interviewed about their experiences in therapy. The following comments were excerpted from that interview. The family commented first on the explanations and descriptions provided by the team:

*Robert: I thought they analyzed pretty good from what information that they had.*

*Carol: We thought it would just be the two therapists, but then when they said the team was back there analyzing what we said, I didn't mind that.*

*Robert: I think they do a good job back there. I really do. Piecing it all together, coming up with different ways of looking at what happened.*

The family credited the team with shifting their focus from blaming individuals to working together as a family:

*Robert: Well, the good part is that ... it was ... a case that they were really interested in and ... they would like to pursue it further if they could.*

*Interviewer: Oh?*

*Robert: Not in those particular words, but that's what I got out of it. The definition I put to what they were saying is that it was a case that they were interested in, and we were not here ... not to pursue a divorce or get problems solved between a husband and a wife, but the whole family to solve a problem. We're looking at it in a different way.*

*Interviewer: Can you say more about that?*

*Robert: We're looking about it as a group problem instead of individual problems.*

*Interviewer: Mm-hmmm. And whose problem did you think it was?*

*Robert: It stems from ... each one of us had our own individual problems within ourselves.*

*Roberta: When I heard my dad say that it's not just mine, it's not my fault or whatever, it's everybody's having their own. And we're here to get help as a whole and not as individuals. So I kind of eased down, well, I relaxed a little bit. And I just listened to everybody to see what's going on.*

The family thought about what the team said after they got home as illustrated below:

*Interviewer: Well, I'm curious to know ... where did you get this idea that it was a group, you know, problem, instead of ... an individual problem?*

*Robert: I listened to what they said and ... and then I went home and analyzed what they said and put it all together. And from what they were saying, it was giving not one individual advice, but they're giving the family advice.*

*Interviewer: O.K.*

*Robert: So I figured this was a group problem instead of an ... individual problem. ... The individual was the one that accumulated most of the problem, but what it all boils down to everybody had a problem within themselves and when we came in here and they start to analyze the two together, then they come and told us what each one had done. And I figured it was a group problem.*

The family liked the multiple ideas discussed by the team as illustrated by the comments below:

*Interviewer: How would the therapy be different without a team?*

*Robert: I can't answer that. Because I depend on ... at the end of the session, I depend on their reaction to what I have said all night. I look forward to it.*

*Carol: They give you points I wouldn't ordinarily think of. … They tell you what they have heard over the session.*

*Robert: And … the suggestions that they make, if we put it into practice, … might work for us, might not work for us, I'm saying. But they put it out there and it's up to us to put it in into practice.*

*Carol: They put a lot of ideas out. … And you can analyze it and put it into practice. Without the team I think we would have longer sessions … it would take a longer period of time to find solutions to our problems.*

*Interviewer: O.K.*

*Carol: They provide a lot of the information that we need. They give us ideas and without them we wouldn't have ideas to take. We'd have to think of them ourselves. And we'd have to probably work our mind more, because they give us a lot of helpful hints and a lot of helpful hints to act upon.*

*Interviewer: So, if the team weren't there, you would have to come to therapy for a longer period of time.*

*Robert: It would cost more money!*

Despite being behind a one-way mirror, the team was able to communicate their interest and caring to the family:

*Interviewer: What else do you all think is helpful about the reflecting team?*

*Carol: Their friendliness toward us and our problems. They are interested in … in the situation and how we present it each session.*

*Robert: Their interest and their level of concern. They know we've got a problem and how to solve it … is complicated.*

*Carol: During the therapy sessions they don't … act like they are strangers. They try to put themselves in our place. And they think … what they would do in our place, how they would solve it, and then they bring the information back to us to see if it would help us, help our family also.*

The family was contacted approximately one year after the last session. At that time, Carol reported that Roberta was a senior and doing better in school but that she continued to be a challenge to her parents. She then added, "The communication is still there, it is still good."

## Conclusion

Reflecting teams are only one way to conduct social constructionist therapy, but both the reflecting conversations and stance represent an important contribution. The reflecting conversation is a good example of how the dialogic process elicits changes in meanings in clients for the expressed purpose of helping them find solutions to their problems. Taking a reflecting stance provides a basis for gaining metacognitive awareness and further allows a shift in social contexts and meanings. The reflecting process assumes that complex problems are embedded in unique social contexts that are perspectival and subject to multiple explanations. Finally, the positive presentation of problems through reflexive language and the offering of multiple perspectives and explanations concerning client problems help clients create new meanings and find new ways of acting.

# References

Andersen, T. (1987). The reflecting team: Dialogue and meta-dialogue in clinical work. *Family Process, 26,* 415–428.

Andersen, T. (1991). *The reflecting team: Dialogues and dialogues about the dialogues.* New York: W. W. Norton.

Andersen, T. (1992). Reflections on reflecting with families. In S. McNamee & K. J. Gergen (Eds.), *Therapy as social construction* (pp. 54–68). Newbury Park, CA: Sage.

Andersen, T. (1995). Reflecting processes: Acts of informing and forming. In S. Friedman (Ed.), *The reflecting team in action: Collaborative practice in family therapy* (pp. 11–37). New York: Guilford.

Anderson, H., & Goolishian, H. (1988). Human systems as linguistic systems: Preliminary and evolving ideas about the implications for clinical theory. *Family Process, 27,* 3–12.

Anderson, H., & Goolishian, H. (1992). The client is the expert: A not-knowing approach to therapy. In S. McNamee & K. J. Gergen (Eds.), *Therapy as social construction* (pp. 25–39). Newbury Park, CA: Sage.

Berger, P., & Luckmann, T. (1966). *The social construction of reality.* Garden City, NY: Doubleday.

Biever, J. L., & Gardner, G. T. (1995). The use of reflecting teams in social constructionist training. *Journal of Systemic Therapies, 14*(3), 47–56.

Biever, J. L., Gardner, G. T., & Bobele, M. (in press). New postmodern perspectives for brief therapy: Social construction and narrative family practice. In C. Franklin & C. Jordan (Eds.), *Family practice: Brief systems methods for social work.* Pacific Grove, CA: Brooks/Cole.

de Shazer, S. (1993). de Shazer and White: Vive la différence. In S. Gilligan & R. Price (Eds.), *Therapeutic conversations* (pp. 112–120). New York: W. W. Norton.

Franklin, C., & Jordan, C. (1996) Does constructivist theory offer anything new to social work practice? In B. A. Thyer (Ed.), *Controversial issues in social work practice* (pp. 16–28). Boston: Allyn and Bacon.

Freedman, J., & Combs, G. (1996). *Narrative therapy: The social construction of preferred realities.* New York: W. W. Norton.

Friedman, S. (1995). *The reflecting team in action: Collaborative practice in family therapy.* New York: Guilford.

Gergen, K. J. (1985). The social constructionist movement in modern psychology. *American Psychologist, 40,* 266–275.

Gergen, K. J., & Kaye, J. (1992). Beyond narrative in the negotiation of meaning. In S. McNamee & K. J. Gergen (Eds.), *Therapy as social construction* (pp. 25–39). Newbury Park, CA: Sage.

Gorman, J. (1993). Postmodernism and the conduct of inquiry in social work. *Affilia, 8,* 247–264.

Griffith, J. L., & Griffith, M. E. (1994). *The body speaks: Therapeutic dialogues for mind–body problems.* New York: Basic Books.

Griffith, J. L., Griffith, M. E., Krejnas, N., McClain, M., Mittal, D., Rains, J., & Tingle, C. (1992). Reflecting team consultations and their impact upon family therapy for somatic symptoms as coded by structural analysis of social behavior (SASB). *Family Systems Medicine, 10,* 53–58.

Hoffman, L. (1990). Constructing realities: An art of lenses. *Family Process, 29,* 1–12.

Hoffman, L. (1992). A reflexive stance for family therapy. In S. McNamee & K. J. Gergen (Eds.), *Therapy as social construction* (pp. 7–24). Newbury Park, CA: Sage.

Howard, G. S. (1991). Culture tales: A narrative approach to thinking, cross-cultural psychology, and psychotherapy. *American Psychologist, 46,* 187–197.

Jenkins, D. (1996). A reflecting team approach to family therapy: A Delphi study. *Journal of Marital and Family Therapy, 22,* 219–238.

Kelly, P. (1994). Integrating systemic and postsystemic approaches in social work with refugee families. *Families in Society, 75,* 541–549.

Kelly, P. (1995). Integrating narrative approaches into clinical curriculum: Addressing diversity through understanding. *Journal of Social Work Education, 31,* 347–357.

Kelly, P. (1996). Narrative theory and social work treatment. In F. J. Turner (Ed.), *Social work treatment* (4th ed., pp. 461–479). New York: Free Press.

Laird, J. (1993). Family-centered practice: Cultural and constructionist reflections. *Journal of Teaching in Social Work, 8,* 77–110.

Laird, J. (1994). Thick description revisited: Family therapist as anthropologist–constructivist. In E. Sherman & W. J. Reid (Eds.), *Qualitative research in social work* (pp. 175–189). New York: Columbia University Press.

Lax, W. D. (1995). Offering reflections: Some theoretical and practical considerations. In S. Friedman (Ed.), *The reflecting team in action: Collaborative practice in family therapy* (pp. 145–166). New York: Guilford.

Madigan, S. P. (1993). Questions about questions: Situating the therapist's curiosity in front of the family. In S. Gilligan & R. Price (Eds.), *Therapeutic conversations* (pp. 219–230). New York: W. W. Norton.

McNamee, S., & Gergen, K. J. (Eds.). (1992). *Therapy as social construction.* Newbury Park, CA: Sage.

Neimeyer, G. J. (1995). The challenge of change. In R. A. Neimeyer & M. J. Mahoney (Eds.), *Constructivism in psychotherapy* (pp. 129–148). Washington, DC: American Psychological Association.

Neimeyer, R. A., & Mahoney, M. J. (Eds.). (1995). *Constructivism in psychotherapy.* Washington, DC: American Psychological Association.

Pardeck, J. T., Murphy, J. W., & Jung, M. C. (1994). Some implications of postmodernism for social work practice. *Social Work, 39,* 343–345.

Pozatek, E. (1994). The problem of certainty: Clinical social work in the postmodern era. *Social Work, 39,* 396–403.

Saleebey, D. (1994). Culture, theory, and narrative: The intersection of meanings in practice. *Social Work, 39,* 351–356.

Sands, R., & Nuccio, K. (1992). Postmodern feminist theory and social work. *Social Work, 37,* 489–494.

Scott, D. (1989). Meaning construction and social work practice. *Social Service Review, 63,* 39–51.

Sells, S. P., Smith, T. E., Yoshioka, M., & Robbin, J. (1994). An ethnography of couple and therapist experiences in reflecting team practice. *Journal of Marital and Family Therapy, 20,* 247–266.

Sluzki, C. E. (1992). Transformations: A blueprint for narrative changes in therapy. *Family Process, 31,* 217–230.

Smith, H. (1989). *Beyond the postmodern mind.* New York: Quest.

Van den Bergh, N. (Ed.). (1995). *Feminist visions in the 21st century.* Washington, DC: NASW Press.

Wangberg, F. (1991). Self-reflection: Turning the mirror inward. *Journal of Strategic and Systemic Therapies, 10*(4), 19–29.

White, M. (1993). Deconstruction and therapy. In S. Gilligan & R. Price (Eds.), *Therapeutic conversations* (pp. 22–61). New York: W. W. Norton.

White, M., & Epston, D. (1990). *Narrative means to therapeutic ends.* New York: W. W. Norton.

Young, J., Perlesz, R., Paterson, R., O'Hanlon, B., Newbold, A., Chaplin, R., & Bridge, S. (1989). The reflecting team process in training. *Journal of Family Therapy, 10,* 69–74.

# Part 5:

Constructivist Practice With
Communities and Organizations

# 13

# Toward a Social Constructionist Method for Community Practice

*Lorraine M. Gutiérrez & Charles Lord*

Social constructionist social work practice focuses on the role of narrative and meaning in the helping process. It originates from theory and practice that identified ways in which individuals and collectivities are active agents in constructing their social reality (Berger & Luckmann, 1967; see Chapter 3). It views individuals as active participants in their own process of change (Greene, Jones, Frappier, Klein, & Culton, 1996).

This perspective has been most influential in the area of direct practice (see Chapter 3). The practice of family therapy, with its focus on the ways in which families define and frame their perceptions of themselves and the world, has made significant contributions to this field. Narrative models for practice, which most commonly involve individuals, also emerged from a social constructionist perspective (Rees, 1998). However, little direct connection has been made between social constructionist practice and work on community change.

With increased focus on the prevention of mental illness, child abuse, and other social problems through community-based education and development, attention focused on community practice is also increasing. The increased focus on community methods is particularly significant in light of current and emerging efforts to transfer the administration of federal programs to local control. This new interest in community focuses on the degree to which existing models of community practice adequately address community needs. For example, how does living in an increasingly multicultural society affect our understanding of communities and methods for working with them? Social constructionist practice, which pays close attention to meaning, can inform existing practice methods, particularly in the ways in which we identify communities and mobilize them to work toward common goals.

In this chapter we explore the interconnections between social constructionist theory and social work practice in communities. Because this area is underdeveloped, our primary focus is on the integration of current knowledge arising from community practice methods, social constructionist theory, and social science research. Rather than presenting a series of well-documented and researched studies, we share our practice experiences and explore how these methods might be evaluated more effectively. We discuss social constructionism, briefly review community practice methods, and present practice examples that use social constructionist theory and methods. We view this chapter as an early contribution to the discussion of the connection between community work and social constructionism.

## Social Constructionism and Social Work

Berger and Luckmann's (1967) *The Social Construction of Reality* is the starting point for many contemporary genealogies of constructionism. Identifying this source, however, obscures the varied and complex intellectual traditions that have voiced their frustrations with a naive positivist and dualistic perspective. For instance, Marxist cultural assertions that social being determines consciousness (Williams, 1977), pragmatist's efforts to locate meaning in the practical consequences of an idea (Rorty, 1982), and symbolic interactionists' more fluid concept of the self (Mead, 1934) have also contributed to our thinking about social constructionism. Although we take issue with the notion that Berger and Luckmann's work represents an unprecedented turnabout in social theory, the title alludes to a significant phenomenological dimension that has in large part been responsible for the benefits, as well as the pitfalls, of such an approach.

Before exploring this dimension more closely, we begin by establishing some of the more familiar assumptions that are believed to define a social constructionist approach: (a) realities exist as mental constructs and are relative to those who hold them; (b) knowledge and the knower are part of the same subjective entity; and, therefore, (c) findings are a result of the identification, comparison, and description of the various constructions that exist (Guba, 1990). We can begin to see from this short list that the attention to *experience* or *phenomenology* derives not only from a radical empiricism but also from attempts to define a different way to think about the world.

In social constructionism, the analyst strives to understand how life experience is constitutive of particular *self–other* interactions that ultimately create particular "life-worlds" (Shotter, 1993). This latter term is used in place of popular cognitive-like terms that focus on concepts such as "world view" in order to highlight the experiential dimension of social constructionism. A constructionist perspective defines itself against traditions that strive to reduce reality to models, schemas, and knowledge. It reflects the understanding that individuals are more than vessels of knowledge or that *knowing-in-the-world* is superior to *being-in-the-world*.

Social constructionism in its various versions has always shown a marked dissatisfaction with descriptions that distinguish between inner and outer worlds or with perspectives based on a doctrinaire objectivism or a romantic subjectivism. Historically, those who occupy the middle ground between these two extremes have focused on the contingent flow of communicative interactions between individuals—that is, how speakers and listeners create and maintain between themselves an extensive contextual background of relations both living and lived that sustain the relationship being constructed at that moment (Shotter, 1993). This approach represents a return to focusing on language. Not in its general, systematic, or grammatical dimension, but as *talk*, particular utterances in specific contexts. Language in this sense does not merely convey information; in fact that dimension of language may in the final analysis be the least significant. Rather, language is believed thoroughly to *mediate everything* that is known. The focus on language is more on its formative and pragmatic dimensions; it becomes constitutive of a dialectical process between the creators of reality and reality itself.

Phenomenology, in its attempt to be a scientific study of experience, has sought throughout its various movements to describe human consciousness in its lived immediacy. Its method is to *bracket* all assumptions in order to understand the essences of things (Jackson, 1996). Indeed, in its more doctrinal iterations, phenomenology strives to understand or get beneath the notion of identity between words and the world. This attention to *experience* has also generated an almost heretical attention to language. Language in this context is thus understood to lend a "first form" to what are otherwise only vaguely or partially ordered feelings and activities (Jackson, 1996).

Attention to "talk" counters the tendency of theory to subordinate actions that occur in real time and history to a slice of time. Complementary uses of language in a *lifeworld* focus attention on either *dialogue* or *narrative* (Jackson, 1996). Dialogue can be understood as more than its commonsensical definition might suggest—as a text or a social interaction across which multiple voices contend with one another (Shotter, 1993). Narrative is understood in this context to play a crucial role in constituting and organizing an individual's experience (Jackson, 1996). In this sense, narrative becomes a way of *being* just as much as it is a way of *saying*.

A social construction of reality depends upon a diverse set of intellectual inspirations. Yet in practice several key conceptual moves have become synonymous with this approach. Berger and Luckmann (1966) define these as (a) objectification, (b) externalization, and (c) internalization. Each of these processes represents a moment within a continuous loop when individuals partake in the construction of reality. The process is essentially experiential, founded upon a transformation in the character of human activity and interaction into something that is embodied by a quality of objectivity.

This perspective suggests a couple of basic questions about the nature of the analytical enterprise itself: (a) how do we interact in worlds that *theoretically* have been defined as distinct and separate entities, and (b) how do we move routinely among realities in our daily lives? We not only constitute and reconstitute our social worlds but we are made and remade in the process.

From a social scientific perspective, social constructionism has ultimately led to a radical reconceptualization of the relationship between structure and agency. Rather than assuming the traditional view in which actions are treated as a reflection of mental structure, the notion of *dialogue* in particular helps us arrive at a view that structures *emerge* from situated action—actions, words, and discourses situated within a social, historical, and a political moment (Tedlock & Mannheim, 1995). From a social work perspective we can begin to transcend an approach to social problems that views deviance as the disruption of the status quo. This may in turn open up dialogue on the nature of social work's problems and interrogate the assumptive and inherited quality with which problems are presented to us. Such an approach asks us to analyze critically how we understand our society, our profession, and the ways in which we work. In this way, social constructionism challenges our past and current perspectives on social work practice.

## Current Perspectives on Community Practice

Community organization can be understood as the practice of purposive social and community change. The overarching goal of community organization is the creation of social environments that support human growth and social justice by influencing policies, program development, or local governance (Weil, 1996). Community change tactics can range from short and focused activities, such as public hearings, to long and sustained projects, such as the development of alternative services (Kettner, Daley, & Nichols, 1984; Mondros & Wilson, 1994). Although the target of change is the community, the forum for this change can be with individuals, families, groups, or organizations. For example, efforts to reduce violence in the community may begin with a series of dialogues and small-group meetings that result in the development of a social-action organization (Lewis & Ford, 1990). This social-action organization can then work to influence policy affecting economic and social institutions.

Understanding social justice is at the heart of community-organization practice. Social justice refers to equity, equality, and fairness in the distribution of societal resources (Crouse, 1996). It includes a focus on the structures and outcomes of social processes and how they contribute to equality, places an explicit value on achieving social equity through democratic processes, and assumes that our role is to develop policy and practice that contribute to these goals (Crouse, 1996; Van Soest, 1994). Social justice plays close attention to the creation of spaces within which oppressed groups can achieve collective autonomy and empowerment (Crouse, 1996). Although community organizers may work toward local or short-term goals, the overall vision focuses on social justice and a reduction of social inequality. This often requires transformation of power relations between more powerful and less powerful groups.

Theories of community practice in social work have focused primarily on models of practice (Rothman, 1995), levels of conflict (Warren, 1971), or the primary practice methods used (Mondros & Wilson, 1994; Netting, Kettner, & McMurty, 1993). Rothman's tripartite approach has been particularly influential. This approach defines three ideal types of practice: locality development, social action, and social planning. Each type of practice is distinguished by its goals, assumptions, methods, roles, and other attributes. For example, the goal of locality development is to develop community capacity by involving a broad cross section of citizens to define and solve their own problems. A common strategy for locality development involves increasing communication among community members through developing collaborative projects. Rothman (1995) describes each strategy as being particularly appropriate for specific goals and community conditions. For example, locality development is most effective with a homogeneous community or in a community with general agreement about the problem and desired outcomes (Rothman, 1995).

Rather than looking at models, Warren (1971) analyzes community organization in relation to conditions in the community and the use of collaborative, campaign, or contest strategies. Collaborative strategies assume a preexisting situation of consensus; after facts have been gathered, a solution can be easily selected and implemented. Campaign strategies assume lack of agreement on issues that can be remedied through education and persuasion. Contest strategies assume that consensus cannot be achieved and that change efforts must be pursued without community collaboration. These strategies involve advancing one side of the argument to bring out the conflict inherent in the situation.

Warren (1971) suggests that collaborative or campaign strategies are often used in organizations that cannot risk conflict. Contest strategies tend to be used by groups outside the organization to be changed. Like Rothman, Warren suggests that a specific model of practice could include a combination of these strategies and that the goal of the intervention, as well as community perceptions of the problems, should guide the intervention selected (Warren, 1971).

Recent work in community-organization practice has attempted to bring together these divergent models while grounding them in the activities of social work practitioners (Mondros & Wilson, 1994). These newer models pay particular attention to emerging social issues as well as issues of gender, sexual orientation, and racial and ethnic diversity (Rivera & Erlich, 1992; Weil, 1996). They are grounded in historical, contemporary, and emerging issues. For example, they include perspectives for organizing neighborhoods and other geographic communities as well as "virtual" communities or communities of identity. They also reflect the dual focus on social and economic development that exists in current feminist, urban, and multicultural practice (Bradshaw, Soifer, & Gutiérrez, 1993; Hyde, 1989; Medoff & Sklar, 1994; Rivera & Erlich, 1992).

Most methods for community practice are built upon a planned social-change process (Netting et al., 1993). This process identifies specific steps that individuals and groups can use to make change in large social systems, including identifying and analyzing the *change opportunity*—a problem or condition in a community that should be changed—and then developing and implementing change strategies. Identifying and analyzing change strategies involves the participation of multiple actors in the community and the development of an *action system* to be involved in the change process. Activities can involve focus groups, meetings with key informants, accessing census or other administrative data, force field analysis, and observations of community conditions (Homan, 1996). The process includes gathering objective data about the change opportunity as well as the perceptions and feelings of community residents.

The knowledge gathered is then used to select, implement, and evaluate a change strategy with the participation of the *action system*. This phase of the process involves the selection and implementation of one or more of the strategies for community organization discussed previously. Typically, this phase also involves multiple strategies and the mixing and phasing of different models for community practice (Bradshaw et al., 1993; Homan, 1996). The evaluation of the change strategy is ongoing and includes both informal meetings to gather impressions and reactions to activities as well as objective measures of community-change outcomes.

# Social Constructionism in Community Organization Practice

Social constructionism can inform and challenge our current understanding of community practice. Although a social constructionist method for community organization does not exist, the theory and methods of social constructionism have relevance for community practice, and its theoretical assumptions are often implicit in community-organization methods. Although community-organization practice is concerned with changing material reality and working toward social justice, many of its methods for engaging people in change focus on affecting individual perceptions of the social world. In this section we discuss ways in which a social constructionist understanding can be brought into community practice in different phases.

## *Identifying Community Assets and Strengths*

Analyzing a change opportunity involves understanding the issues and the community. Traditionally, this process has been described as needs assessment and problem identification. Current work in community organization is examining the assumptions behind the needs-assessment focus, with its implication that community conditions reflect a lack of capacity that must be remedied by outside intervention (Delgado, 1996; Kretzmann & McKnight, 1993). Instead, community organizers are encouraged to shift their perspective from needs and problems to the strengths and capacities that exist in all communities. This paradigm shift pays explicit attention to the significance of language and its meanings in shaping how we work with communities (Hardcastle, Wenocur, & Powers, 1997; Kretzmann & McKnight, 1993).

Focusing on capacities and strengths can lead to empowering strategies for community practice (Delgado, 1996; Hardcastle et al., 1997). This process requires active partnership between community organizers and community residents. Change strategies build from client strengths, which means first identifying areas of positive functioning, then using those areas to improve community conditions (Hardcastle et al., 1997; Kretzmann & McKnight, 1993; Solomon, 1976). Building from strengths means recognizing and validating skills, capacities, and institutions that have been unnoticed and unrewarded. The community organizer must recognize that many communities have been involved in a process of struggle against oppressive structures for a long time and that this involvement has required considerable strength.

The work of Core Cities Neighborhood, Inc. (CCN), in Detroit is a good example of an organization performing this kind of work (Pham, Kinsler, Smith, Fuqua, & Davis, 1996).[1] Founded in the 1980s, CNN is located in an economically depressed, predominantly African American community in Detroit. The neighborhood was hit hard by the loss of manufacturing jobs and the movement of many middle-class families to the suburbs.

Staff and volunteers at CCN have used a strengths perspective to create and implement community programs. The problems of under- and unemployment, crime, and failing public institutions in the community are readily apparent. The strengths, abilities, and assets within the community are less apparent. To identify these underlying strengths, CCN underwent an "asset mapping" approach (Kretzmann & McKnight, 1993), which systematically identifies the multiple assets in a community. The approach focuses on both formal and informal resources. For example, an asset map identifies the formal organizations that provide educational programs, such as public schools, as well as the informal organizations that provide education, such as older people who may be available to teach gardening or home repair. At CCN, this process involved the deployment of community volunteers who went door to door to identify the skills and abilities of neighborhood residents. These findings were then plotted onto an asset map to identify the location of resources in this community.

The asset-mapping process resulted in the creation of programs and projects within the community. For example, various older people with sewing ability were identified. These individuals were invited to join a sewing circle that creates quilts and other crafts that could be sold to generate income for the organization. In turn, these older individuals were provided with a social activity to bring them together and make their talents visible to the community at large. Other projects involving citizen assets include a landscaping business with contracts with the city to mow vacant lots, a housing restoration program, and a CB crime-prevention team. These innovative programs have improved the physical and social fabric of the community by moving from a "problem" to a "possibilities" paradigm.

## *Framing Issues for Action*

Despite differences in typology, most models for community-organization practice face challenges with regard to ways to engage and mobilize individuals in community-change efforts. This requires change strategies that encourage individuals to act toward a collective good. Social constructionist theory and methods can assist in translating the personal into the political.

The community-organization literature identifies "issues" as the primary means for engaging communities in change efforts. By identifying change opportunities as issues, organizers play a strategic role in framing the work that needs to be done (Homan, 1996; Kettner et al., 1984). The development of issues throughout a com-

---

1. For more information about this organization, contact Core Cities Neighborhood, Inc., 3301 23rd St., Detroit, MI 48208.

munity-change effort is ongoing. Initially, issues may be identified to mobilize and recruit individuals into a change effort. After they are involved, community members may redefine these issues to focus on a desired outcome. Underlying these issues may be other fundamental issues that are identified as contributing to multiple problems in a community (Homan, 1996). Throughout this process, the social construction of reality is negotiated, renegotiated, and reinterpreted by citizens and community organizers.

Research on social cognition suggests that the perception of issues can have a profound effect on this process (Brewer & Kramer, 1985; Tajfel, 1981; Turner & Oakes, 1986; Zavalloni, 1975). One's perceptions of the legitimacy and stability of an existing social structure have a strong effect on one's propensity to engage in social action. If the structure is perceived as being stable and strong, individuals are more apt to accommodate the structure; if the system is perceived to be illegitimate, unstable, or weak, then efforts to initiate change are more likely to occur.

Emerging research on the relationship between narrative and social action identifies ways in which these perceptions can be generated and reinforced through social interaction (Kling, 1996). Narratives refer to the stories individuals tell themselves and one another in an effort to interpret their world. Community organizations, the media, and other social institutions can influence these narratives by providing interpretive frames for understanding social and personal conditions. Involvement in community action takes place when individuals accept the narratives of organizations to being relevant to their personal life (Kling, 1996).

In translating this theory into action, community issues that question the legitimacy or stability of current conditions are effective in mobilizing communities as well as in framing issues in a way that is personally relevant to individuals. For example, a program for low-income families in a suburban area faced the challenge of developing support for the families it served. Because of the affluence of residents in the county at large and stereotypes about low-income people, many community residents believed that homeless families were coming to the agency from a nearby urban center. This view of poverty and the community at large interfered with the organization's ability to generate support. To raise funds for a shelter for homeless families, organizers questioned the legitimacy of these assumptions in two ways. Organizational data established that most recipients of help had been citizens of the county, including residents of its most affluent cities. These data were then reinforced and represented by the testimony and narratives of community residents who had personally experienced poverty in order to redefine the issue as helping displaced *neighbors* through donation, volunteerism, and financial support. The similarities between recipients of services and more affluent community residents were reinforced. Reframing the issue by legitimizing claims for community support and encouraging identification with those receiving services helped engage the support of the local city government, churches, and voluntary organizations. This attention to language and narrative led to methods that were more effective than previous efforts that focused on sympathy for the client population.

## *Change Through Education*

During the past two decades, Paulo Freire's work in the area of adult education has had considerable influence on the study and practice of community organization. Although Freire does not label his educational work as community organizing, many community organizers have drawn from the concepts and techniques that he has developed (Burghardt, 1982; Kieffer, 1984; Rose & Black, 1985; Wallerstein, 1992). Among all strategies for community change, popular education is most deeply rooted in concepts of social constructionism because of its attention to ways in which language and dialogue contribute to human agency.

Freire developed the process of *conscientization* as an alternative means for teaching literacy skills to poor persons in Latin America. He argued that traditional literacy training techniques, which he labeled as "banking education," treated knowledge as a commodity, the learner as a passive recipient of information, and the instructor as all knowing. Banking education incorporated the poor into a system that in itself was responsible for their dependency without giving them the skills to become active participants in their world. Freire (1970) based his work on the following idea:

> *Becoming literate, then, means far more than learning to uncode the written representation of a sound system. It is truly an act of knowing [author's emphasis] through which a person is able to look critically at the culture which has shaped him, and to move toward reflection and positive action upon his world. (p. 205)*

Freire, therefore, developed a form of pedagogy that involved learners in acting and analyzing their world, with the goal of assisting them to view themselves as subjects, rather than objects, of society. In becoming subjects, they begin to believe in their ability to change their world. This transformative process is crucial to social change (Freire, 1970, 1973).

Freire developed various processes and techniques for engaging individuals in the process of conscientization. Intervention is based on a process of authentic dialogue between teachers and students regarding issues of common concern. The goal of this dialogue is to develop critical consciousness—an understanding of the social and economic context of everyday life. This dialogue is facilitated by *codifications*, that is, vignettes that act as the focus for discussion and allow group participants to gain distance from the issues that concern them. The analysis of a series of codifications is presented as a dialectical process that leads to the development of critical consciousness. The development of critical consciousness, in turn, leads to actions that transform the social environment. With the development of actions, group participants are encouraged to engage in praxis—the analysis of their actions. The process of praxis leads to deeper levels of critical consciousness. This process can be repeated indefinitely as group participants become more active in transforming their world (Freire, 1970, 1973).

How have these methods been used in contemporary community-organization practice in the United States? They have been used with many groups, including low-income elderly (Minkler & Cox, 1980), multiethnic adolescents (Wallerstein & Bernstein, 1988), and homeless individuals (Yeich & Levine, 1992). These projects are characterized by attention to community building and support, the creation of peer education and leadership development efforts, a cycle of listening and problem-posing dialogue, and action in the world.

## Implications for Community Practice

Although the social constructionist movement in social work practice has not directly affected intervention at the community level, this review of the literature suggests that social constructionist ideas have influenced community-organization practice methods. Popular education's focus on meaning, dialogue, and action indicates a direct connection between the theoretical base of social constructionism and community change. Similarly, social constructionist ideas are evident in methods for community practice that focus on identifying issues that can be used to mobilize communities (Homan, 1996). Such methods emphasize the importance of identifying issues that are salient, comprehensible, and personally involving (Homan, 1996). In selecting issues for mobilization, community organizers bring the assumptions of social constructionist theory into action.

These areas of similarity and convergence should not obscure a critical area of conflict, perhaps contradiction, inherent in social constructionist practice. Community organizers, with their focus on social justice and material conditions, would take exception to a radical constructivist perspective that suggests that our primary focus should be on cognitive processes. The notion that perceptions supersede reality can conflict with efforts to intervene in concrete social conditions. For example, the asset-based approach to community planning (Kretzmann & McKnight, 1993) has been criticized by some because of its predominant focus on community strengths and lack of recognition of the conditions that threaten communities. Therefore, community organizers need to maintain a balance between social constructionist theory and the dynamics within a particular community.

This discussion on practice emphasizes models of practice over methods of practice. It suggests that a closer look at the interpersonal dynamics of community practice, such as modes of communication, interpersonal perceptions, and individual identities, can help us to improve our practice skills and teaching methods. This focus on practice methods for entering and defining communities, identifying issues, mobilizing support, and building leadership can deepen and enrich our understanding of community-practice methods. Social constructionist theory is one tool for building our knowledge about effective community work.

## References

Berger, P., & Luckmann, T. (1966). *The social construction of reality: A treatise on the sociology of knowledge.* Harmondsworth, Middlesex, England: Penguin.

Bradshaw, C., Soifer, S., & Gutiérrez, L. (1993). Toward a hybrid model for effective organizing in communities of color. *Journal of Community Practice, 1,* 25–42.

Brewer, M., & Kramer, R. (1985). Psychology of intergroup attitudes and behavior. *Annual Review of*

*Psychology, 36,* 219–243.

Burghardt, S. (1982) *The other side of organizing.* Cambridge, MA: Schenkman.

Crouse, K. (1996, September). *The limits of community and identity politics.* Paper presented at the (Re)Defining Community/(Re)Examining Society Conference, Flint, MI.

Delgado, M. (1996). Puerto Rican food establishments as social service organizations: Results of an asset assessment. *Journal of Community Practice, 3*(2), 57–77.

Freire, P. (1970). *Pedagogy of the oppressed.* New York: Seabury.

Freire, P. (1973). *Education for critical consciousness.* New York: Seabury.

Greene, G., Jones, D., Frappier, C., Klein, M., & Culton, B. (1996). School social workers as family therapists: A dialectical-systemic-constructivist model. *Social Work and Education, 18,* 222–236.

Guba, E. (1990). *The paradigm dialogue.* London: Sage.

Hardcastle, D., Wenocur, S., & Powers, P. (1997). *Community practice: Theories and skills for social workers.* New York: Oxford University Press.

Homan, M. (1996). *Promoting community change: Making it happen in the real world.* Pacific Grove, CA: Brooks/Cole.

Hyde, C. (1989). A feminist model for macro practice: Promises and problems. *Administration in Social Work, 13,* 145–181.

Jackson, M. (1996). *Things as they are: New directions in phenomenological anthropology.* Blooming-ton, IN: Indiana University Press.

Kettner, P., Daley, J., & Nichols, A. (1984). *Initiating change in organizations and communities: A macro practice model.* Pacific Grove, CA: Brooks/Cole.

Kieffer, C. (1984). Citizen empowerment: A developmental perspective. In J. Rappaport, C. Swift, & R. Hess (Eds.). *Studies in empowerment: Steps toward understanding and action* (pp. 9–36). New York: Haworth.

Kling, J. (1996, September). *Narratives of possibility: Social movements, collective stories and the uncertain future of organized practice.* Paper presented at the (Re)Defining Commu-nity/(Re)Examining Society Conference, Flint, MI.

Kretzmann, J., & McKnight, J. (1993). *Building communities from the inside out: A path toward find-ing and mobilizing a community's assets.* Evanston, IL: Northwestern University Press.

Lewis, E., & Ford, B. (1990). The Network Utilization Project: Incorporating traditional strengths of African-American families into group work practice. *Social Work With Groups, 13*(4), 7–22.

Mead, G. (1934). *Mind, self and society.* Chicago: University of Chicago Press.

Medoff, P., & Sklar, H. (1994). *Streets of hope: The fall and rise of an urban neighborhood.* Boston: South End Press.

Minkler, M., & Cox, K. (1980). Creating critical consciousness in health: Applications of Freire's phi-losophy and methods to the health care setting. *International Journal of Health Service, 10,* 311–322.

Mondros, J., & Wilson, S. (1994). *Organizing for power and empowerment.* New York: Columbia Uni-versity Press.

Netting, E., Kettner, P., & McMurty, S. (1993). *Social work macro practice.* New York: Longman.

Pham, A., Kinsler, C., Smith, D., Fuqua, D., & Davis, K. (1996). *An assessment of a grass-roots orga-nization: Core City Neighborhoods, Inc.* Department of Psychology, University of Michigan, Ann Arbor, MI.

Rees, S. (1998). Empowerment of youth. In L. Gutiérrez, R. Parsons, & E. Cox (Eds.), *Empowerment in social work practice: A sourcebook* (pp. 186–194). Pacific Grove, CA: Brooks/Cole.

Rivera, F., & Erlich, J. (1992). *Community organizing in a diverse society.* Boston: Allyn & Bacon.

Rorty, R. (1982). *Consequences of pragmatism.* Minneapolis: University of Minnesota Press.

Rose, S., & Black, B. (1985). *Advocacy and empowerment: Mental health care in the community.* Boston: Routledge & Kegan Paul.

Rothman, J. (1995). Approaches to community intervention. In J. Rothman, J. Erlich, & J. Tropman (Eds.), *Strategies of community intervention* (pp. 26–63). Itasca, IL: F. E. Peacock.

Shotter, J. (1993). *Cultural politics of everyday life: Social constructionism and knowing of the third world.* Toronto: University of Toronto Press.

Solomon, B. (1976). *Black empowerment.* New York: Columbia University Press.

Tajfel, H. (1981). *Human groups and social categories.* Cambridge, England: Cambridge University Press.

Tedlock, D., & Mannheim, B. (1995). *The dialogic emergence of culture.* Urbana, IL: University of Illinois Press.

Turner, J., & Oakes, P. (1986). The significance of the social identity concept for social psychology with reference to individualism, interactionism, and social influence. *British Journal of Social Psychology, 25,* 237–252.

Van Soest, D. (1994). Peace and social justice. In R. Edwards (Ed.), *Encyclopedia of social work* (19th ed.). Washington, DC: NASW Press.

Wallerstein, N. (1992). Powerless, empowerment and health: Implications for health promotion programs. *American Journal of Health Promotion, 6,* 197–205.

Wallerstein, N., & Bernstein, E. (1988). Empowerment education: Freire's ideas adapted to health education. *Health Education Quarterly, 15,* 379–394.

Warren, R. (1971). *Truth, love, and social change and other essays on community change.* Chicago: Rand McNally.

Weil, M. (1996). Model development in community practice: An historical perspective. *Journal of Community Practice, 3*(3–4), 5–67.

Williams, R. (1977). *Marxism and literature.* Oxford, England: Oxford University Press.

Yeich, S., & Levine, R. (1992). Participatory research's contribution to a conceptualization of empowerment. *Journal of Applied Social Psychology, 22,* 1894–1908.

Zavalloni, M. (1975). Social identity and the recoding of reality. *International Journal of Psychology, 10,* 200–217.

# 14

## Constructing the Community: The Emergent Uses of Social Constructionism in Economically Distressed Communities

*Dennis Saleebey*

Many observers, writers, pundits, and theorists have suggested that society has come to the edge of an immense chasm and that we are teetering there morally, spiritually, politically, and socially. Marin (1996), however, puts it slightly differently:

> *America is a huge and relatively young nation. We are an immigrant society with permeable borders and a population in constant flux. We draw our moral and cultural notions from many conflicting ethnic traditions, and these in turn are beset by astonishingly rapid rates of technological, economic, and cultural change and by a popular culture more powerful in its effects than our formal institutions are. ...*
>
> *To this heady mix one must add one final element: our passion for freedom. Our freedom is obviously spotty, uneven, and marred by inequities, but in cultural terms alone we insist upon levels of choice and self-creation that far exceed what is to be found in other societies. (pp. 42–43)*

This freedom, however ambivalent we may feel about it, brings in its wake a carnival of differing points of view, ideologies, practices, and groups. Some of these are menacing, some merely benighted, some probably essential to our well-being as a society, and some seeming to harbor dissension and conflict. Marin (1996) states,

> *If you do not understand that whatever their differences, the woman who wants an abortion on demand and the patriot who wants an Uzi in his hands are cut from the same American cloth, then you do not understand either the nation or the intractability that we face. (p. 43)*

Liberty raises two important challenges. First, the notion that we can reinvent ourselves, collectively and individually, is particularly American. In American hands, social constructionism, an intellectual offshoot of various academic contrivances of self and other (e.g., symbolic interactionism) that is grounded in various European philosophic traditions (Nietzsche, Wittgenstein, and Vygotsky), as well as the deconstructivist school of French literary criticism (Derrida and Lyotard, principally), has developed an embryonic but fervent kind of energy behind it (Gergen, 1991).[1] This energy, in some ways, reveals our cultural obsession with the continuous remaking of society and self. Like most obsessions, ours has an underside: We want some ideas, values, institutions, and inventions to stay just as they are (conservatism). Second, given our hunger for the ideal of individual liberty, the idea of community seems wistful and plaintive. Nonetheless, a tide of interest in rediscovering and redefining, perhaps reinventing, community is rising around the world (Freire, 1996; McKnight, 1995). Some see this as an urge of the postmodern condition (Gitlin, 1989). Others see this impulse as a way out from the dominator/patriarchal view of social relations (Eisler, 1987). But there are barriers to the rediscovery of community. Certainly, the natural, geographic definitions of communities have disappeared in many areas of the country. Given the counterweights of antic individualism and the responsibilities and antinomies of a free society, building a sense of community in a particular locality, let alone constructing the idea conceptually, may seem foolhardy. But efforts are under way. And much of the effort, although not necessarily identified as such, is impelled by an appreciation for constructionist tenets.

## Social Constructionism and Community: Preliminary Thoughts

In this postmodern world, the definitions of almost every human experience, institution, and conception are up for grabs. Ideas about community are no exception. While many of us wring our intellectual and moral hands about whether community is disappearing, communities are being constructed, symbolically as well as factually, throughout the world. In the Western world, and in the United States in particular, individualism as the central tenet of social being endures. However, increasingly, groups and institutions are recognizing the moral, spiritual, and social perils of reliance on unbridled individualism as a figurative and linguistic fulcrum for our political, social, and economic pursuits. As Sagoff (1997) states, "Well-being depends upon health, membership in a community in which one feels secure, friends, faith, family, love, and virtues that money cannot buy" (p. 95).

A social constructionist understanding requires that we recognize the centrality of meaning making in human affairs. The question of the reality of the external world notwithstanding, human beings, individually and collectively, historically and contemporaneously, create meaning—a sense of the world, constructions of the exterior and interior contexts of life—to provide support, accessibility, predictability, rationale, interest, and explanation. Bruner (1986) writes of two incommensurable views of the world—argument and story. Argument is meant to convince us of the truth. The

---

1. Others should be acknowledged here: Berger and Luckmann's (1966) seminal work, George Henry Gadamer, Richard Rorty, and, in social work, among others, Ann Hartman, Joan Laird, Ann Weick, Howard Goldstein, and Edmund Sherman.

scientific enterprise is founded on such a way of knowing. Story convinces us of the lifelikeness of particular human conditions, moments, relations, and possibilities. Stories are constructions that provide a sense of place, purpose, exposition, and relevance. On a daily basis, most of us traffic in stories and narratives as we seek understanding and comforts, guideposts and directions, significance and substance. This is the essence of meaning making. All of us are, in this sense, theorists, folk psychologists trying to put a symbolic wrap around our lives.

In a short story by John Barth (1995), the narrator states,

> It has occurred to Ms. Mimi Adler, whom I like a lot, to wonder whether people reflexively think of their lives as stories because from birth to death they are exposed to so many narratives of every sort, or whether, contrariwise, our notion of what a "story" is, in every age and culture, reflects an innately dramatistic sense of life: a feature of biological evolution of the human brain and of human consciousness, which appears to be essentially of a scenario-making character.
>
> In the face of so much wretchedness and gravity, what justification have Mimi and I for entertaining such chicken-or-egg questions as whether people's lives or stories have, so to speak, ontological primacy?
>
> That question, believe me, we take as seriously as the question that it questions. (p. 96)

Upper-class daintiness notwithstanding, the role of language and story, narrative and myth, text and discourse is clearly of interest to Mimi, the narrator, and social constructionists. Meaning, regarding both the canonical and the exceptional circumstance, is conveyed through story and textual means. This clearly implicates the role of language as a kind of pretext and forestructure (an a priori conceptual or axiological device) through which the world is apprehended and filtered or received (Aptheker, 1989; Bruner, 1990; Gergen, 1991; Rosaldo, 1989). The constructionist relies heavily on the storied narrative. The view of conversation or discourse is largely ontological and subjunctive: How can I act in this world, what shall I be or become, what can we make of this moment together, how shall I construe my past, what will guide me in my world at this moment?

Social constructionism suggests, then, that no inviolable and universal processes of mind and relationship, no singular truths, exist. Rather, we have creations, conventions, and interpretations of groups of people socially, historically, and morally situated in specific social worlds. In Nietzsche's (1990) words:

> What, therefore, is truth? A mobile army of metaphors, metonymies, anthropomorphisms; . . . which after long use seem firm, canonical, and obligatory to a people: truths are illusions of which one has forgotten they are illusions. (p. 84)

The idea that we might discover and identify universal autonomous processes is itself a fabrication, elaborate and compelling to be sure, but nonetheless a linguistic and symbolic artifice. It is also important to acknowledge that individuals rarely create meaning on their own. Rather, meaning is derived from cultural, familial, historical, and interpersonal sources and thus is often public and shared. The search for meaning is driven by the need to know, to find regularity in one's world, to explain oneself to others, and to make the world habitable. A constructionist takes the position "that there is a publicly interpretable congruence between saying, doing, and the circumstances in which the saying and doing occur" (Bruner, 1990, p. 19).

In terms of community, the first social constructionist principle is that meaning evolves and pronounces itself in a forum that is public and communal rather than capricious and private. The second principle is that in a constructionist appraisal we must understand the varied definitions of communities—from those of the theoretical high ground to those emanating from the life world of "locals"—as artifacts of history, relationships, and a political and economic context. Because the specific concern of this chapter is socially dominated, geographically segregated, and economically depressed communities (public housing, in particular), one of our concerns is to examine a major issue for policy, programs, and practice: whose construction prevails and with what consequences? The third principle, which is related to the first two, is that for professionals, politicians, and planners to appreciate another community, they must understand the local constructions and stories that breathe life into that community and give it its unique flavor, tempo, and substance, its distinctive institutional and associational life.

Today, policies and programs for particular kinds of communities such as public housing are spoken in the language of individualism and intervention (interdiction of problems). We think of these inner-city[2] communities as being populated by individuals and families with various needs and problems, many of which are overwhelming and dangerous. The "sociology of virtue" (Dionne, 1996) recently revived by conservative politicians directs our attention to the moral fallibility of individuals in the inner city as reflected by teenage pregnancy, drug addiction, drug dealing, gang membership, welfare dependency, and family dissolution. Our policies and programs suppose that cadres of professionals are able to intervene to meet needs and to prevent problems or that individuals can be exhorted or threatened into moral reputability (which usually means getting a job and off the taxpayer's back). These individualistic and pessimistic constructions of poor communities effectively ensure that the community will continue to be disabled (Kretzmann & McKnight, 1993; McKnight, 1995). These narratives do three things: First, they ignore or suppress the variety of indigenous stories, conventions, and narratives that sustain the lives of most of the law-abiding citizens who live there. Second, they assure that these communities will continue to be "clients" of professional services and rehabilitative social policies because the mantle thrown over the corpus of the community uses the language of services and clients. One problem "solved" begets another (the side-effect phenomenon), or another politically or professionally fashionable clinical approach spurs another round of interventions. Third, these narratives fail to capture the internal energies, assets, and symbolic and behavioral configurations of daily life that might be parlayed into a vibrant, nurturing environment.

---

2. The construct "inner city" is interesting. When it is used, it certainly does not refer to, for example, the recently gentrified cores of large urban areas. We "know" what it means in that it is a creation of sociologists, and lately of politicians, who talk about race and class in code when they refer to the inner city.

*Creative neighborhood leaders across the country have begun to recognize this hard truth, and have shifted their practices accordingly. They are discovering that effective community development efforts are based on an understanding, or map [read: construction], of the community's assets, capacities, and abilities. For it is clear that even the poorest neighborhood is a place where individuals and organizations have resources upon which to rebuild. (Kretzmann & McKnight, 1993, p. 5)*

Even liberal and radical thinkers and practitioners of community work tend to employ conventions that are problem focused. They typically write plot lines and characterizations that focus on oppression, marginalization, victimization, and segregation. Although some of these constructions, from the more conservative to the more liberal, have some currency, even among the indigenous populations to which they refer, they still represent the accepted wisdom. This "wisdom" assumes the following: these communities are rife with problems or deficits to be overcome; individuals are the key to understanding and solving the problems or assessing and meeting the needs; solutions to problems must come from outside the community; indigenous knowledge is a barrier; assessment of the life of the community can be made in quantitative terms (usually demographic or financial); and, most important, professionals (and politicians) know best. This, in a word, is the helper or physician story that has so dominated the Western conception of professions (Bledstein, 1978).

Like negative constructions of the self that occur with labels of mental illness such as "schizophrenic" (Estroff, 1989), disparaging labels applied to communities can have a negative effect on the ethos, singularity, and spirit of community members. Of course, to deny the conflicts, tensions, and terrors that may exist in, for example, a public-housing community is to overlook or discount elements of the life and discourse of residents. But to deny other constructions and elements of the relational and conversational life of residents and to apply only official versions of the narrative or interactional plot and characterizations of residents is to deny the rich and nurturing relationships that sustain community members in the face of adversities.

Given this brief introduction, the themes to be pursued throughout this chapter are as follows:

■ If one believes that conceptions of the self are linguistic and symbolic creations, one must believe the same with regard to conceptions of community.

■ Tension usually exists between the external constructions of communities (those originating outside the community) and internal, indigenous ones. The politics of the employment of external constructions are particularly fateful for the well-being and life chances of economically and socially vulnerable and segregated communities such as public housing projects.[3]

■ External constructions ordinarily are unremittingly invalidating and repudiating.

---

3. The construction "project" surely does not invite visions of communities, neighborhoods, and citizenship. Rather, it seems to suggest a scheme developed with a purpose in mind: perhaps to contain problems or to remove blight or, more positively, to provide shelter for poor people. A skeptic might wonder if the residents themselves are not thought of, at one level, as projects for moral and civil rehabilitation.

■ External constructions can be absorbed into the individual entities that make up the community as well as the communal identity (far too many public-housing residents, for example, believe the characterizations generated by a fearful and unsympathetic community).

■ The external constructions of the community are typically assembled with a rationalist, positivist, technical, interventionist lexicon and diction, all of which obscure the indigenous narratives, visions, and assets.

■ The identity of any community is more than the summation of the constructions of the individuals who are part of the community; the community itself is a subject of discourse and characterization.

■ The focus of the constructionist view of community work is to discover the assets and competencies, the ethos and identity, the stories and myths, and the tools and rituals of the community. This approach attempts to refashion stories of community problems that need to be repaired into an awareness of strengths and possibilities that exist within and around the community.

■ The constructionist view that reality is relational is important to this work; acknowledging and promoting connection, participation, collaboration, conviviality, mentoring, and mutuality are the cornerstones of theory and practice (Bellah, Madsen, Sullivan, Swidler, & Tipton, 1991; Freire, 1996; Gergen, 1991; Kretzmann & McKnight, 1993; McKnight, 1995; Mills, 1995; Saleebey, 1997; Shaw, 1996).

An intriguing element of the conversation between Mimi and the narrator is the reference to the wretchedness and gravity of the daily world (Barth, 1995). Whereas their concerns are more precious in posing questions in the face of war, genocide, brutality, and poverty, my focus is on the extent to which any approach gets one close enough to the life experience of people to allow one to do some good.

## Social Work and Communities

Social work, like many other helping professions, has gradually developed an intense preoccupation with the individual—the individual's flaws as well as possibilities. Although the family has assumed more importance in theory and practice in recent years, the individual nevertheless reigns. Social workers talk of the person–environment relationship, but clearly the *person* carries more heft than the environment. Furthermore, defining the transactions between the person and the environment are intellectually and practically difficult (Brower, 1988; Morrell, 1987; Wakefield, 1996). Some have called for the profession to return to work in the community (McKnight, 1995; Mondros & Wilson, 1994). However, social work's constructions of the community lack the interest, complexity, and elegance of conceptions of the self and the family. Nonetheless, if ideas about community, particular communities, and kinds of communities are as much social and relational constructions as are constructions of other social phenomena such as personal traits, personality characteristics, and the like, then it is important for social work to strengthen its fabrications of community. The profession seems to be somewhat reluctant to invigorate conceptions of community and to promote community work. In the end, it would require a different approach to social work practice, conceivably even greater circumspection regarding practice protocols that are centered on the individual or a loosening of the ties to psychotherapy as the central social work enterprise. Luckily, interest in programs and practices focused on community development and the creation of indigenous community services is rekindling (Weil, 1996). Likewise, some of the newer family approaches based on constructionist tenets are more aware of the effects of context on discourse and meaning making (see Chapter 3; Freedman & Combs, 1996). Although some change has been spurred by the social work profession, community leaders, educators, and community psychologists are also refocusing their attention on community.

## Community Development in Economically Distressed Communities

Economically distressed and socially isolated communities, as we have said, are often viewed as being problem saturated, —overwhelmed with problems, deficits, and aberrations. Most policies, program initiatives, and legislation are modernist, based on the conceit of being rational, materialist, pragmatic, functionalist, progressive, individualist, effective, and efficient. The effect of these constructions is the depiction of these communities and their residents in negative and discouraging language filled with the imagery and symbols of danger, disorganization, dysfunction, and disreputability. These negative images and story lines tend to focus on the individual or the family, thus portraying these communities as being permeated with criminals and socially repugnant residents. Programs are cropping up around the country that are based on different constructions of depressed and compromised communities. These constructions typically do not advertise themselves in the language of constructionism, but each presents a radically different story about the community and its residents. The following descriptions are more a matter of convenience than definition.

### The Association-Based Community

Most communities, even distressed communities, are composed of associations—local collectivities established through the consent of participating residents that provide a place for people to pursue their interests and concerns using the natural tools and resources in their environment and to promote the stories and visions of their community. Associations are often interdependent and tend to proliferate until everyone—even the most fallible and disreputable—finds his or her place in the community. Associations help give voice to everyone and are responsive to the problems and needs, as well as hopes, of residents. Associations can be cultural and ethnic; they may focus on common interests (hobbies); they might be formed through churches or community-based businesses (e.g., an aerobics class in someone's house). What they have in common is their capacity for inclusion, celebration, problem solving, creativity, and the recounting and restoration of residents' wisdom, lore, narrative, ritual, and story.

In a public-housing community in which most residents were African American, many single mothers, and most unemployed or underemployed, a Bible study group started by one resident became a de facto association of young mothers learning about child rearing and supporting each other under the wise guidance of an 85-year-old woman who had raised 11 children. Individuals in this group learned to appreciate their ability to survive and to understand their "Africanicity" (Billingsley, 1992) as a moral anchor tying them to their religious and spiritual roots. In the same community, a youth association, which met after school, began to attract parents as children invented activities, for example, a celebration of Black History Month that tickled the interest and involvement of some parents. In both these examples, rituals, celebration, and language formed the basis for connecting, caring, and "restorying."[4] As McKnight (1995) states,

> In summary, the community of associations provides a social tool in which consent is the primary motivation, interdependence creates wholistic [sic] environments, people of all capacities and fallibilities are incorporated, quick responses are possible, creativity is multiplied rather than channeled, individualized responses are characteristic, care is able to replace service, and citizenship is possible. (p. 167)

Belief in the capacity of communities and their associations requires that we hear the stories and honor the folklore and local constructions of the residents.

## Community of Assets and Resources

Similar to the way the community of associations trumps the construction that economically distressed communities need the authority and skills of professional associations and institutions, the assets-based community undermines the canonical story that these communities are bereft of resources, capabilities, and strengths. Clearly, distressed communities need resources from the outside world. However, resources can be much more effectively employed if the community is mobilized and able to combine them with their own competencies and resources. The assets-based approach proceeds from three principles:

■ This approach must begin with an accounting and a mapping of the *assets and capacities* of the community, its residents, families, and associations and not with an assessment of what is missing and what is wrong. The primary concern is with the human, physical, and social capital available and already employed in the community. This provides an immediate and handy symbolization and model of the "new" reality, that is, this community, defined in terms of having few assets and little spirit, actually has plenty of both.

■ This approach is *internally focused* in that it begins from within the community, capitalizing on the relationships, resources, visions, agenda, and interests of its residents and associations. A major resource to be employed is the stories, recollections, narratives, and myths of the residents. These inform us about the moral, social, and psychological riches available in the community.

---

4. I don't know with whom this felicitous term originated, but I first heard it from Joan Laird of Smith College.

■ The process is clearly *relationship driven*. Relationships are established and reestablished because they are the medium through which the bounty of the community is exchanged and multiplied and through which the narrative riches are spread (Kretzmann & McKnight, 1993).

Two elements of this construction of community are particularly important to those who work in community development or community building. First, it is important to acknowledge that everyone has gifts to share with the community. The word gift implies more than assets by indicating its celebratory and good-will elements. Kretzmann and McKnight (1993) state,

> *Every living person has some gift or capacity of value to others. A strong community is a place that recognizes those gifts and ensures that they are given. A weak community is a place where lots of people can't give their gifts and express their capacities. (p. 27)*

Second, a strong community has a place for everyone, from the strong and resolute to the vulnerable and disreputable. The Foundation for Community Encouragement puts it this way: "A true community is inclusive, and its greatest enemy is exclusivity. Groups who exclude others because of religious, ethnic, or more subtle differences are not communities" (cited in Shaffer & Anundsen, 1993, p. 12). Because our traditional constructions of communities in distress and their residents focus on problems and needs, we do not see the capacities and "gifts" that a teenage mother, a disabled person, an elder, a gang member, or a person with mental illness might contribute to the community's coffers.

Mills's (1995) programs in various distressed communities have been remarkably successful. The programs are based on trust in the capacity of people to right themselves. In a project involving 142 families and their 604 children in public housing, for example, drug trafficking diminished by 65%, delinquency by 75%, and parent–child conflict by 87% after three years. Such programs are based on a psychology of health, that is, the innate resilience and wisdom of individuals living in stressful environments. The goal of these programs is "to reconnect people to the health in themselves and then direct them in ways to bring forth the health in others. The result is a change in people and communities which builds up from within rather than being imposed from without" (Benard, 1994, p. 22). Such change is developed through rapport, respect, and reciprocity. As Mills states,

> *Rapport is just getting to know people as a friend. ... Because people's innate mental health is buoyant ... [we] can say it's more likely that it will come back under these conditions, with these types of relationships, in this kind of setting where people are relaxed, having fun, enjoying themselves, and not feeling pressured. (Benard, 1996, p. 16)*

Again, such programs represent a dramatic restorying of the inner-city plot line.

A gang member in a public-housing community empathizes with younger kids and has a facility for getting their attention and making them laugh. He takes on the role of protector for some of these kids so that, for example, their vegetable garden isn't destroyed or overrun or their playground area isn't trashed. Seniors provide tax-preparation assistance for low-income elderly persons at local libraries (see Kretzmann & McKnight, 1993). A resident of public housing uses his long-dormant writing skills to put together a manifesto and procedural manual for the Resident Management Corporation, a document that strengthens the credibility and power of the group with the local housing authority. In each of these instances, a professional or student operating from a strengths/assets perspective facilitated these resources and processes in the community. These are simple examples of assets and resources being put to work. To focus on assets and solutions is to practice at the community level what constructionist therapists call "externalization"—placing problems outside one's identity and infusing possibilities for change in their place.

## *Community of Connection and Relationship*

Ernesto Cortés, an organizer from the Industrial Areas Foundation, helped the residents of San Antonio's *colonias* mobilize their energies and resources to fight the city's real-estate-development policies, which had led to continual flooding and water contamination in the Hispanic communities. Prior to his involvement approximately 20 years ago, the residents were hesitant to speak out or to organize against these policies. Cortés helped them form Communities Organized for Public Service (COPS). He promoted the political power of relationship and connection, out of which grows resolve and from which emerges leadership in heretofore silent communities.

> But if politics is going to be meaningful, there has to be a dimension of transformation that takes place—and that's only going to occur to the extent that people begin to understand what we mean by this kind of power called relational power. Which is not only acting on but allowing other people to act on you. ...
>
> You begin to share your interest, your story, with other people and allow them to act on you, to challenge you, and then you begin to reweave your story. So it becomes connected to other people's stories ... in public political conversation. (Crimmins, 1995, p. 39)

The Western Regional Center's (Benard, 1994) efforts to prevent and ameliorate adolescent drug abuse and its associated difficulties (truancy, violence, crime) takes a community approach that uses three basic elements. The first element is *caring and connection.* When young people have someone on whom they can rely, who steadfastly supports them, and who genuinely cares about them regardless of their circumstances, they do better. As Tito, a former gangbanger, says, "Kids can walk around trouble, if there is someplace to walk to, and someone to walk with" (McLaughlin, Irby, & Langman, 1994, p. 219).

The second element is *high expectations.* Schools, parents, associations, peers, and professionals who have high expectations of youth in school, at home, and in the community together with a belief in youth will not fail to provide a cognitive, motivational, and interpersonal foundation upon which young people can build their lives. In California, for example, the establishment of a college core curriculum in a disadvantaged, inner-city community resulted in more than 65% of its graduates going on to college (compared with 15% before the program began). One student said a major factor in his decision was "having one person who believed that I could do it!" (California Department of Education, 1990).

The third element is *meaningful participation in the moral and civic life of the community and school.* Too many youth have too little to do in their communities. Providing young people with opportunities to become involved in the intellectual, social, and political life of the school and community does not require special programs as much as it

> requires adults to let go of the role of "sage on the stage" [and] become the "guide on the side," to see youth as a valuable resource, to willingly share power with youth, to create a system based on reciprocity and collaboration rather than on control and competition; in other words, to create a democratic community. (Benard, 1994, p. 16)

Low-income youth receive on-the-job training from professionals in housing rehabilitation principally for homeless youth (some of these trainees are homeless). Sometimes they live in the houses they reconstruct. Most important, however, 65% of them go on to find construction jobs. Some of the youth are appointed to the advisory council of Youth in Action and become directly involved in decisions about the program (Kretzmann & McKnight, 1993). The program flourishes, in part, because of the participation of these youth. A young Vietnamese man living in a public housing community offers to be an interpreter for the Vietnamese on the Resident Management Corporation Board (composed of six African Americans, six Vietnamese, and one Anglo American). As a result of his intelligence and humor and the encouragement of established leaders, he is elected to the board and becomes an influential member who is especially adept in helping to smooth relationships among the various cultural groups.

Although it is clear that each of these approaches has a "forestructure" by which they construe and construct the communities of their interest, in each case these depart dramatically from the conventions of definition that surround the kinds of communities described above. Likewise, they are benign, ameliorative, and healing in their practices and use language that is uplifting and that contains calls to a better future and quality of life. It is also true that they rely, in one way or another, on the indigenous meanings that abound in these communities and their residents. They incorporate elements of building community as outlined by Gardner (1994), including inclusiveness (diversity), participation, affirmation, caring and trust, and a developmental perspective. Finally, and most important, they utilize the narrative therapy device of externalization, that is, discovering, honoring, and putting to work the means and resources individuals and families employ in order to resist and survive the ordeals of their daily life, the debilitating policies and programs of external agencies, and the hostilities of surrounding communities.

## Distressed Communities, Enterprise, Investment, and Education: Turning the Tables

From 1989 to 1996, the School of Social Welfare at the University of Kansas sponsored a program in public-housing communities in the area. The program, KU Outreach, was designed to help residents build the kind of community and neighborhood that they wanted on their terms. It was also based philosophically on the idea that all the residents and families had strengths and capacities that could be used to their own as well as the community's advantage. The program incorporated the following three elements:

**Case management and direct services.** These are basic services. Many individuals and families, under the pressures of poverty, under- and unemployment, child-rearing responsibilities, policies of the local housing authority, and problems in self-care, are at risk. We helped them manage their crises, meet their needs, and obtain the external resources they needed to cope. But beyond that, we helped them identify and elaborate on their own resources, strengths, capacities, and assets.

**Technical assistance.** The Department of Housing and Urban Development (HUD), under Secretary Kemp's leadership, proposed that resources and money from HUD should be directed at helping residents move toward managing their own properties, perhaps eventually owning them. Although the latter was unlikely to happen, the former was a good idea. However, like people in most communities, the residents had not learned to manage and govern their community and neighborhood. KU Outreach assisted the Resident Management Corporation Board (a group of residents elected by other residents to oversee the management of the physical, social, and, in a limited fashion, fiscal capital of the community) by providing supportive, educational, and technical assistance.

**Community development.** Assets, strengths, and needs assessments guided our efforts to help residents and leaders identify residents who would offer their talents and gifts to the community. The experience of successful programs around the country indicated that a community under siege by drug dealers, occasionally gangs, and the insensitive, marginalizing policies at the federal and local government levels had to employ the competencies and human capital of residents in order to build a communal life for itself. Gradually, we discovered that one of the best ways to ascertain the resources and strengths of residents was through stories, many of which were tales of travail and triumph (Saleebey, 1997). Through stories, residents and workers were able to identify hopes and visions, capacities and resources in the community as well as discover leaders.

One outcome was the establishment of a minigrants program. A panel of residents and staff (staff consisted primarily of MSW students) reviewed applications completed by residents for grants of up to $200 for projects that would enhance an element of local community life. These grants allowed residents to have a stake in the community, to realize some of their talents and interests, and to normalize their life somewhat. People were encouraged to share their stories and their interests, many of which stood in stark contrast to the stereotypical tales about public housing residents. As we became aware of the importance of story and narrative in the life of the community, residents and service providers initiated other events and celebrations—a street fair, a Kwanzaa celebration, communal Thanksgiving, talent shows—to build a sense of community and to provide a mechanism for sharing stories, as suggested by the earlier quote by Cortés.

Our experience taught us that our cultural constructions of the poor—about their lack of motivation and intelligence, poor work habits, inability to manage money, and commitment to bettering themselves—are bankrupt and stultify policy and program development at all levels of society. People in poverty have as many difficult personal, interpersonal, and familial situations and as many contentious, depressed, and angry people as does any community. Clearly, some of these problems can be laid at the door of poverty, stress, racism, and segregation. But the compelling stories are tales of courage, hope, redemption, and possibility.

A doctoral student, with help from residents and MSW interns, did a study of the strengths of 12 residents who had lived in the community for five years or longer (O'Brien, 1995). The basic question was what stories of survival and renewal, difficulty and trouble, triumph and possibility were told in the community? A story that was shared by many of the residents was that of resilience. One resident stated,

> It also depends on you, too. Now, if you just want to sit and do nothing and not go anywhere in life ... if you have a negative attitude of not doing anything with yourself, then life is going to be hard. ... But if you want to survive and struggle and do better, it will be hard, but it won't be that hard, so terrible, you can always see a way around things. (p. 171)

Another common story revolved around dreams. For example, Jasmine wanted a better life for her two children and herself. A leader in the community, she told us about her dream to own a bed-and-breakfast establishment some day. She eventually moved out of public housing and found a good-paying job with a local government agency. Who's to say that she won't one day own a bed and breakfast? Allying with the dreams, hopes, strengths, and resiliencies of residents was, in its own way, a constructionist project. People discovered and rediscovered narratives of possibility and hope.

In the long run, such stories and others like them from around the country should become part of our policy narratives. We need to turn the tables. An investor and entrepreneur once said that the rich do not necessarily know anymore about money than anybody else, including the poor. We just hardly ever see their mistakes and ignorance.

## *Community Investment Project*

The Community Investment Project, a derivative of the KU Outreach program described above and created to establish a partnership among the Kansas University School of Social Welfare, a large metropolitan family service agency, and the community in which it will be run, is a set of programs designed to strengthen the economic, human, and physical capital of distressed communities. The programs that make up its core are developed from similar successful programs in other communities around the country. In a sense, the Community Investment Project invests in the citizenship of people who exist on the margins of democratic participation—citizens without portfolios. Distressed communities provide "surfaces of emergence" (Foucault, 1972) that condense and contain "problem spaces" (e.g., a public-housing community) over and about which civic and later professional apparatus codify, rationalize, theorize, administer, regulate, punish, scrutinize, police, and sequester. The codifications and theories as well as some of the control activities are frequently provided by professions, including social work. Rose (1996) states,

> It was the normativity of the apparatus itself—the norms and standards of the institution[s] [governments and professions], their limits and thresholds of tolerance, their rules and their systems of judgment—that conferred visibility on certain features [such as family disorganization or teenage parenting] and illuminated the topography of the domains that psychology [and, I would add, social work] would render intelligible. (p. 115)

Turning the tables means that the codifications and designations of problem spaces are refashioned so that containment and scrutiny are replaced with participation and involvement. On a more practical level, the emergent diction at HUD since Jack Kemp's administration and especially under the leadership of Henry Cisneros and now Andrew Cuomo has focused on enterprise, investment, citizenship, and participation. Policies conceived and written with such language are much more common than they were 10 years ago. This shift in language and emphasis is extremely important. Such changes are not generally considered in constructionist terms, but changes in rhetoric bring with them inevitable changes in the quality and direction of policy, practical discourse, and programs. This language has been central to the American experience but unavailable to the poor and disenfranchised except to remind them that "they have failed even though anything was possible."

**Family asset building.** The distribution of assets in this country is more skewed even than the distribution of income (Page-Adams, 1996). The top 20% of citizens holds approximately 45% of national income but almost 75% of the nation's assets (Sherraden, 1991). This inequity did not happen by accident. Federal tax policy is heavily weighted toward providing asset protection and accumulation for people who are not poor. Whether in the form of capital gains, home mortgage deductions, or tax deferments for retirement pension accounts and annuities, laws and policies encourage the accretion of assets (Page-Adams, 1996). By and large these protections are not available to the poor. Furthermore, welfare policy traditionally has been based upon limiting the assets (means testing) of those who would be eligible for welfare benefits. The stereotypical response to this is that the poor visited their problems upon themselves and that they don't have the tools, motivation, or interest in participating in the moral, civic, and economic life of the community.

Assets building for the poor is increasingly seen as an avenue out of poverty and a key to the gate leading to full participation in the civic life of the community. Saving and investing is a much surer route out of poverty than is income transfer. As Sherraden (1994) points out, asset holding has desirable effects on attitudes and behaviors, including family stability, social status, political and social participation, community involvement, pride, and sense of accomplishment. Currently, many communities have assets-based programs. New welfare initiatives in many states have prompted proposals and legislation to lift asset limits on recipients of welfare benefits (Edwards & Sherraden, 1995). Some of the most successful economic and social development policies in the history of the United States were assets based—the Homestead Act and the G.I. Bill, for example (Page-Adams, 1996). Finally, assets-based programs normalize and externalize the moral, personal and cultural resources of many poor people.

The Family Asset Building (FAB) program, recently funded, is designed to help people accumulate assets that can be used for education, self-employment, or home ownership. This program helps people secure their family's economic future, build economic literacy, and learn effective investment strategies. The monthly savings of families that participate is matched at a ratio of 4:1 by corporate and nonprofit sponsors (increments of $10, starting with $25). Participants join an investment club that meets at least monthly with an expert (a sponsor) to learn about investment strategies, management of money and credit, and to track the growth of their investment. A sponsor invests their money for them, but participants never lose their own contributions. In addition, the match money and subsequent investment earning must be used for education, self-employment, and/or home purchase. It is anticipated that these clubs will also function as "narrative circles" in which new constructions about self, family, and community can be developed and nurtured. As one resident stated, "Hey, this is our own individual 401K" (D. Page-Adams, personal communication, April 30, 1997).

**Microenterprise ownership.** Self-employment through the development of a small, usually home-based, community enterprise is a new approach to combating poverty and unemployment. As Banerjee (1996) states, it is a

> *tiny business, owned and operated by low-income individuals with a very small loan from an outside source, that may employ up to five individuals. Examples of micro-enterprises operating in the U.S. are flower shops, designer dress shops, beauty salons, catering businesses, [the] selling of items like hot butter cookies, ethnic jewelry, clothes, music and books, housecleaning or janitorial services, recycling, word processing, and so forth. (p. 2)*

A 1994 survey found more than 200 public and private microenterprise programs in the United States (Banerjee, 1996).

The program begins with small, low-interest loans to people who want to start a business with which they have some familiarity. Five individuals form a "peer lending group" and six groups form a "center." Group membership and involvement are essential to the success of the program in terms of durability of the enterprise and repayment of the loan. If a group member defaults on repayment of the loan, the other members of the group become ineligible for a loan. Thus, the group provides support, guidance, and peer pressure. As part of the program, business training and appropriate skills development are provided for those who request it. Some individuals and groups require only a loan, others a loan and technical training (business start-up, maintaining a ledger, and the like), and skills development (e.g., customer relations, management, and administrative skills).

Like the FAB program, microenterprise programs have demonstrated success. Bornstein (1996) reported that the Women's Self-Employment Project, the first private-sector microenterprise initiative, funded by the Shorebank Corporation in Chicago's South Side, has extended nearly $1 million in loans to more than 300 small businesses and provided business counseling to more than 5,000 women. The repayment rate for the loans is greater than 90%. Evans (1996) reported that during a three-year period, for all the microenterprise efforts in the country, 25% of the participants are no longer in poverty, 80% of the businesses are still thriving, 60% of the participants' net worth increased, and two thirds of the businesses pay at least six dollars an hour to their employees. Like the FAB program, the microenterprise program is recently funded and provides a forum for the development of narrative circles that highlight success, achievement, and possibility.

**The Saturday Academy.** The Saturday Academy[5] is a genuine academy, not a remedial or tutoring curriculum for children and youth who are not doing well in school. This program is designed to help parents and their children become prepared for full participatory citizenship: the job market, higher education, community involvement, and social productivity. One goal is that each family that participates will develop a stronger appreciation of their own resources and knowledge, cultural and ethnic lore, and practices. The children in this program may be "at risk" or not doing well, but participation of their parents is mandatory.

The day begins with breakfast with parents, children, and staff; acknowledgment of the importance of what they are doing; and a review of the day's activities. Children receive a curriculum (part of which is determined by the community) consisting of computer literacy, communication skills, science and math, arts and performance, cultural and ethnic appreciations, and understanding money. Each course is grounded in the life experience of the family. For example, science activities would take into account the local geography—how to make the environment safe, secure, and "green."

Parents also enroll in some of the class sessions, according to their interests, but much of their involvement occurs in discussion groups that focus on daily issues and concerns that parents wish to manage, life hopes and dreams they want to realize, and learning skills and tools to make their lives more manageable and satisfying.

Children and parents take field trips together to places that they may not generally have access to: from shopping malls to museums, rural areas to other parts of the city, government offices to the local police department, blues festivals to symphonies.

From a constructionist view, an important part of the curriculum is each family's development of three portfolios: a portfolio of financial goals and achievements (it is likely that some of these families will be involved in the FAB or microenterprise program), an album of artistic creations, and a portfolio celebrating family roots, stories, and ethnic heritage. These portfolios signify and speak to the family's accomplishments and learning. They ground the family's narratives in themes of accomplishment and achievement.

Saturday academies have been successful throughout the country (Aetna Foundation, 1996) in reducing dropout rates, increasing graduation rates, helping students move on to higher education, increasing employment rates, and solidifying family rela-

---

5. The term was coined by Lou Beasley, former dean of the School of Social Work at Atlanta's Clark University, who began one of the first academies in the United States in the early 1990s.

tionships. These successes have occurred in communities that have experienced difficulty in these areas. Our program will be evaluated in the summer of 1998.

Clearly, these three programs value local knowledge and meaning constructions, discover and encourage the strengths and resources of families and the community, and normalize the lives and dreams of people who have been marginalized. In other words, such programs represent constructionist work of the highest order.

## *Evaluation*

Basically, two strategies of evaluation exist. The first is individual and familial and has been employed with great success by KU Outreach and other strengths-based programs (Rapp & Wintersteen, 1989). The second is an emerging kind of "fourth-generation program evaluation" (Guba & Lincoln, 1989) that also borrows from empowerment evaluation as developed in community psychology (Fetterman, 1994). Both strategies involve the stakeholders and participants from beginning to end. The purpose of the research is to bring improvements or desired changes to the individual and communal lives of the stakeholders.

The individual and familial strengths-based evaluation is founded on a simple premise: Elicit the consumers' hopes, dreams, and objectives in various domains of their lives (financial, spiritual, interpersonal, medical, domestic and interpersonal, etc.); identify resources and possibilities; account for resources that have been used in the past; set specific, doable, and concrete goals (find a job-training program, learn to use the transportation system) that will eventually bring the individual closer to the larger objective; and lay out the tasks, resources, and responsibilities that are required to achieve each goal and ultimately the larger objective (see Kisthardt, 1992). The relevance of the work is understood as the percentage of goals achieved in movement toward one or more objectives. Preliminary results from KU Outreach and other strengths-based projects suggest that a great many goals are achieved.

The program evaluation designed for the Community Investment Project begins with a partnership between the staff of the project and the residents of the community and their leaders. That partnership is embodied in a Developmental Evaluation Advisory Board (DEAB) composed of representatives of staff and residents. The purpose of the DEAB is to (a) set a research and evaluation agenda; (b) develop a mutually crafted understanding of the uses to which the research agenda, if accomplished, could be put on behalf of the community; (c) develop a research design, methodology, and instruments that are consistent with the values and interests of the community and are replete with indigenous understandings; (d) monitor continuously the unfolding of the process and achievement of program and community goals as well as the research agenda; (e) recreate through dialogue and shared interpretations elements of the evaluation and research program as required or agreed upon; (f) evaluate, through conjoint interpretation and dialogue, the "findings"—that is, construct them; and (g) get the word out to individuals, associations, institutions, and organizations that are critical to helping convert the findings into a noticeable reality for residents. (The latter three items are consistent with constructionist appreciations and principles.) Stakeholder research is based on education, illumination, advocacy, outreach, collaboration, and negotiation (what does this mean and what should we do?). Finally, it is a device of empowerment:

> *Empowerment means the sharing of power tools and the sharing of leadership. Empowered people make organizational [community] contributions because their empowerment continuously leads them to "figuring out about the place" to productive "sensemaking." ... Fourth generation evaluation is a means to empowerment, both because of its process aspects and because it shares information (which is itself power). (Guba & Lincoln, 1989, p. 227)*

The DEAB is being developed along dimensions suggested by fourth-generation evaluation, which, among other things, requires following the identification of stakeholders, the creation of hermeneutic circles designed to promote within-group constructions, credibility checks, resolution of issues and settling of claims, and negotiating the final construction and use of data (Guba & Lincoln, 1989).

## Conclusion

In working with people who are dispossessed, discounted, and segregated, it becomes immediately clear that their stories, linguistic devices, myths, and rituals are either dismissed or subjugated by the larger mainstream society. Knowledge and power, as many have pointed out, are inseparable. The knowledge of those with power rules in the halls of social institutions—from Congress to the housing authority—and thus becomes the lingua franca by which oppressed communities and individuals are understood, usually to their great disadvantage. To a lesser extent this is true of professional theories and conventions. Social workers and others interested in liberating oppressed people and communities need to raise these subjugated knowledges and let them inform and challenge social agencies, government entities, surrounding communities, local businesses, news media, and schools. Freire (1996) has insisted for years that liberators (which he thinks social workers ought to be) should (a) promote the "conscientization" or full moral and practical awareness of the oppressive effects of dominative knowledge and institutionalized power, (b) promote the resurrection of local knowledge and its generative themes, and (c) ally themselves with the hopes of the oppressed. Local knowledge in the form of stories, narratives, and instrumental themes must be externalized and brought to bear on the life of the community itself and the surrounding influential institutions and organizations whose ideologies affect the life chances of marginalized peoples.

Stephen Jay Gould (1996), commenting on Darwin's wonder at the variety of life forms spawned by evolution, quotes him thus:

> *Whilst this planet has gone cycling on according to the fixed law of gravity, from so simple a beginning endless forms most beautiful and most wonderful have been, and are being, evolved. ... There is grandeur in this view of life. (p. 230)*

Social constructionism celebrates this grandeur.

# References

Aetna Foundation. (1996). *Annual report.* Hartford, CT: Author.

Aptheker, B. (1989). *Tapestries of life.* Amherst, MA: University of Massachusetts Press.

Banerjee, M. (1996). Micro-enterprise ownership program. *Community Investment Project Proposal.* Lawrence, KS: School of Social Welfare, University of Kansas.

Barth, J. (1995, March). Stories of our lives. *Atlantic Monthly, 96–110.*

Bellah, R. N., Madsen, R., Sullivan, W. M., Swidler, A., & Tipton, S. M. (1991). *The good society.* New York: Random House.

Benard, B. (1994, December). *Applications of resilience.* Paper presented at the Role of Resilience in Drug Abuse, Alcohol Abuse, and Mental Illness Conference. Washington, DC: National Institute on Drug Abuse.

Benard, B. (1996, Summer). Roger Mills: A community psychologist discovers health realization (an interview with Bonnie Benard). *Resiliency in Action, 1,* 15–18.

Berger, P., & Luckmann, T. (1966). *The social construction of reality.* Garden City, NY: Doubleday.

Billingsley, A. (1992). *Climbing Jacob's ladder: The enduring legacy of African-American families.* New York: Simon & Schuster.

Bledstein, B. (1978). *The culture of professionalism.* New York: W. W. Norton.

Bornstein, D. (1996). *The price of a dream: The story of the Grameen Bank and the idea that is helping the poor change their lives.* New York: Simon & Schuster.

Brower, A. (1988). Can the ecological model guide social work practice? *Social Service Review, 62,* 411–429.

Bruner, J. (1986). *Actual minds, possible worlds.* Cambridge, MA: Harvard University Press.

Bruner, J. (1990). *Acts of meaning.* Cambridge, MA: Harvard University Press.

California Department of Education. (1990). *Enhancing opportunities for higher education among under-represented students.* Sacramento, CA: Author.

Crimmins, J. C. (1995). *The American promise: Adventures in grass-roots democracy.* San Francisco: KQED Books.

Dionne, E. J., Jr. (1996). *They only look dead: Why progressives will dominate the next political era.* New York: Simon & Schuster.

Edwards, K., & Sherraden, M. (1995). *Individual development accounts: Assets-based policy innovation.* St. Louis, MO: Center for Social Development, Washington University.

Eisler, R. (1987). *The chalice and the blade.* San Francisco: Harper.

Estroff, S. (1989). Self, identity, and subjective experiences of schizophrenia: In search of the subject. *Hospital and Community Psychiatry, 15,* 189–196.

Evans, C. (1996, March 29). *Poverty alleviation through micro-enterprise development.* Luncheon address at the Second Golden Door Knob Meeting of the First Step Fund. Kansas City, MO.

Fetterman, D. M. (1994). Empowerment evaluation. *Evaluation Practice, 15,* 1–15.

Foucault, M. (1972). *The archeology of knowledge.* New York: Random House.

Freedman, J., & Combs, G. (1996). *Narrative therapy: The social construction of preferred realities.* New York: W. W. Norton.

Freire, P. (1996). *Pedagogy of hope.* New York: Continuum.

Gardner, J. W. (1994). *Building community for leadership studies program.* Washington, DC: Independent Sector.

Gergen, K. J. (1991). *The saturated self: Dilemmas of identity in contemporary life.* New York: Basic Books.

Gitlin, T. (1989, July–August). Post-modernism explained at last. *Utne Reader, 34,* 52–61.

Gould, S. J. (1996). *Full house: The spread of excellence from Plato to Darwin.* New York: Harmony Books.

Guba, E. G., & Lincoln, Y. S. (1989). *Fourth generation evaluation.* Newbury Park, CA: Sage.

Kisthardt, W. (1992). A strengths model of case management. In D. Saleebey (Ed.), *The strengths perspective in social work practice* (pp. 70–71). New York: Longman.

Kretzmann, J. P., & McKnight, J. (1993). *Building communities from the inside out: A path toward finding and mobilizing a community's assets.* Chicago: ACTA Publications.

Marin, P. (1996, December). An American yearning: Seeking cures for freedom's terrors. *Harper's,* 35–43.

McKnight, J. (1995). *The careless society: Community and its counterfeits.* New York: Basic Books.

McLaughlin, M. W., Irby, M. A., & Langman, J. (1994). *Urban sanctuaries: Neighborhood organizations in the lives of inner city youth.* San Francisco: Jossey-Bass.

Mills, R. C. (1995). *Realizing mental health: Toward a new psychology of resiliency.* New York: Sulzburger and Graham.

Mondros, J. B., & Wilson, S. M. (1994). *Organizing for power and empowerment.* New York: Columbia University Press.

Morrell, C. (1987). Cause *is* function: Toward a feminist model of integration for social work. *Social Service Review, 61,* 144–155.

Nietzsche, F. (1990). On truth and lies in a non-moral sense. In F. Nietzsche, *Philosophy and truth: Selections from Nietzsche's notebooks from the early 1870s.* (D. Brazeale, ed. and trans.). Atlantic Highlands, NJ: Humanities Press International.

O'Brien, P. (1995, Summer). From surviving to thriving: The complex experience of living in public housing. *Affilia, 10,* 155–178.

Page-Adams, D. (1996). Family assets building. *Community Investment Project Proposal.* Lawrence, KS: School of Social Welfare, University of Kansas.

Rapp, C. A., & Wintersteen, R. (1989). The strengths model of case management: Results from twelve demonstrations. *Journal of Psychosocial Rehabilitation, 13,* 23–32.

Rosaldo, R. (1989). *Culture and truth: The remaking of social analysis.* Boston: Beacon Press.

Rose, N. (1996). Power and subjectivity: Critical history and psychology. In C. F. Graumann & K. J. Gergen (Eds.), *Historical dimensions of psychological discourse* (pp. 103–124). Cambridge, England: Cambridge University Press.

Sagoff, M. (1997, June). Do we consume too much? *Atlantic Monthly, 279,* 80–96.

Saleebey, D. (1997). Community development, group empowerment, and individual resilience. In D. Saleebey (Ed.), *The strengths perspective in social work practice* (2nd ed., pp. 199–216). New York: Longman.

Shaffer, C. R., & Anundsen, K. (1993). *Creating community anywhere: Finding support and connection in a fragmented world.* New York: Putnam.

Shaw, A. (1996). *Social constructionism and the inner city.* http://el.www.media.mit.edu/people/acs/introduction.html.

Sherraden, M. (1991). *Assets and the poor: A new American welfare policy.* Armonk, NY: M. E. Sharpe.

Sherraden, M. (1994). *Organizing and developing a community reinvestment corporation and individual development account in St. Louis.* St. Louis, MO: Center for Social Development, Washington University.

Wakefield, J. C. (1996). Does social work need the eco-systems perspective? Part II. Does the perspective save social work from incoherence? *Social Service Review, 70,* 183–213.

Weil, M. O. (1996). Community building: Building community practice. *Social Work, 41,* 481–499.

# 15

## Constructing and Deconstructing Organizations: An Empowerment Perspective

*Wes Shera*

As we approach the new millennium, organizations, private and public, are struggling to cope with an ever accelerating pace of change. Change in how an organization functions, who its members and leaders are, what form it takes, how it allocates resources, and how it responds to environmental demands significantly affects our personal world of work (Huber, Sutcliffe, Miller, & Glick, 1993). Today's turbulent times are not a transition into a new era; rather the turbulent times *are* the new era (Huber & Glick, 1993). Social work, both as a profession and as an educational enterprise, is caught squarely in the middle of this maelstrom. The confusing array of federal and state mandates, numerous demands for accountability, and an increasingly complex environment often adversely affect the operation of human service agencies. The effects of these conditions include a sense of powerlessness by workers (Pinderhughes, 1983), fragmentation of services, inappropriate care of clients, and problems in recruiting and retaining qualified staff (Kahn & Kamerman, 1990).

In recent years, we have seen an enormous increase in the restructuring, downsizing, and privatization of human service organizations (Berger, 1993). Much of this organizational transformation has involved replacing public service administration with a private-sector management culture (Harrow & Willcocks, 1992). Managed care in the United States and the development of "social markets" in the United Kingdom are examples of the efforts to use market mechanisms in the delivery of public services (Shera, 1996). Much of this activity is driven by governments' desire to reduce deficits, which typically results in overall reductions in the allocation of resources to the human service sector.

Although the need to improve the performance of human service agencies is great, a single-minded focus on market approaches will not achieve this objective (Corcoran & Vandiver, 1996; Harrow & Willcocks, 1992). While recognizing the limitations of a "market model" approach to providing services, it is critical to seek out other approaches to achieving organizational effectiveness. Recent developments in the areas of empowerment practice in social work and constructionism perspectives in understanding organizational life may provide some useful insights for developing new directions.

## Social Constructionism

The constructionist paradigm comfortably embodies self-determination, dignity of the individual, empowerment, and social justice as basic social work values (Allen, 1993). Franklin, in her discussion of social constructionist research and practice, describes three types of social constructionist research (see Chapter 3). These include the external epistemological subjectivist view that one should not make assumptions about objective reality; the objectivist position, which presupposes an objective order that is perceived and defined differentially; and the contextual position, which assumes that attending to social conditions helps locate a problem within its social context. Some authors have argued that the subjectivist view leads to hopeless relativism (Best, 1989). From a social work practice perspective, it can lead to continuing analysis without guidance for appropriate intervention. The objectivist type of social constructionism is much more helpful and is congruent with the postpositivist paradigm's emphasis on multiplism (Cook, 1985) and systemic perspectivism (Ball, 1977). This approach validates multiple realities that are in constant flux and encourages us to look for meaning behind the data. It presupposes a determinate, objective order in which people differentially perceive, define, and make claims about objective conditions (Pollner, 1993). Contextual analysis is critical to social work practice in general and certainly to those who seek to improve the functioning of human service organizations. Contextual constructionists study claims making within the context of culture and social structure (Best, 1993). Much of the social constructionist literature in social work focuses on the application of this approach in clinical practice. This chapter focuses on its utility in understanding and intervening in organizations. In so doing, it draws on the objectivist and contextual forms of social constructionism and uses an empowerment practice framework as the unifying theme.

## Empowerment

Schulz, Israel, Zimmerman, and Checkoway (1995) describe empowerment as a construct that occurs at three levels: *individual,* which relates to psychological and behavioral variables; *organizational,* which relates to resource mobilization and participatory opportunities; and *community,* which relates to sociopolitical structure and social change. This multilevel construct suggests that empowerment both affects and is affected by empowerment at other levels.

Concepts relating to organizational empowerment are prevalent in the management, organizational, and business literature (Bass, 1990; Belasco, 1990; Block, 1987;

Boyadjis, 1990; Conger, 1989; Conger & Kanungo, 1988; Eden, 1986; Evered & Selman, 1989; Macher, 1988; McKenna, 1990; Messmer, 1990; Pollack, 1989; Stein & Kanter, 1980; Their, 1989; Thomas & Velthouse, 1990; Topaz, 1989–1990). This literature suggests that empowering practices within organizations lead to increased employee satisfaction, management and leadership satisfaction, morale, motivation, organizational functioning, productivity, and consumer satisfaction.

Lacking in the psychology and social work literature is the application of the concept of empowerment to employees and organizations, particularly human service agencies. Although the human service field is beginning to tap into management strategies used in the business sector (Ginsberg, 1988; Hodge, 1986; Rapp & Poertner, 1992), such as those described in Peters and Waterman's (1982) *In Search of Excellence*, systematic attempts to implement the concept of empowerment within organizations has been minimal (Cox & Joseph, 1998; Gutierrez, GlenMaye, & DeLois, 1995).

### *Intersection of Constructionism and Empowerment*

The threads that weave together the constructionist and empowerment approaches are their commitment to process and a common value base. Values and ethics are central concerns in both constructionist and empowerment perspectives. The active role of social context and practitioner values is acknowledged (Allen, 1993).

In models of therapy that reflect a constructionist paradigm, significant efforts are invested to empower clients by creating a respectful, egalitarian climate. The hallmarks of such a process are mindfulness, respect, and empowerment (Allen, 1993). Both empowerment and constructionist approaches at various levels of practice promote the integration of the personal and the political. Interventions that target social-justice issues are ultimately supportive of the social work value of empowerment.

### *Empowerment at the Organizational Level*

Empowerment at the organizational level is defined as a process of enhancing self-efficacy among organizational members by identifying conditions that foster powerlessness and removing them both formally through organizational practices and informally by means of techniques that provide efficacy information (Conger & Kanungo, 1988). Because of the bureaucratic, top-down nature of most organizations, employees have a greater tendency to become vulnerable as a result of lack of communication; lose control in a patriarchal organizational culture; and become helpless, a situation in which employees subscribe to the bureaucratic norms in order to survive. Vulnerability, loss of control, and a sense of helplessness, similar to conditions faced by clients, foster powerlessness. The task of removing these and other conditions, then, becomes a major focus in the process of developing a more empowered organization.

## Lessons Learned

In an effort to inform constructionist practice at the organizational level, we conducted an exhaustive review of the literature on organizational empowerment. This knowledge base draws upon a wide variety of literature from rigorous research to practice wisdom. The review focused primarily on relevant literature in the past 10 years. Empirical literature in this area is minimal because further conceptual and psychometric development is needed. The lessons derived from this review are the themes that emerged from the analysis. The intent, in keeping with a social constructionist perspective, is not for the practitioner to apply these lessons indiscriminately but rather to assess their transferability in a given context. It should also be noted that this is not in any way a final set of principles but rather an ongoing learning process. The major lessons that we derived from this search include the following:

■ *Establish a clear vision.* Empowering agencies have a common vision (Topaz, 1989–1990). Agency norms and values are clearly communicated (Gross & Shichman, 1987). Values rather than rules dominate (Peters, 1990). An empowering executive is a person who facilitates the creation of a vision, then inspires colleagues to join in its achievement (Belasco, 1990).

■ *Services should be client-driven.* Keep clients (customers) in mind at all times throughout the process, not only in terms of their needs and interests but in terms of actively obtaining client-generated information and evaluation (Gowdy & Rapp, 1989; Rapp & Poertner, 1988, 1992). Any process taking place in human service agencies that is not client centered will be counterproductive in the long run.

■ *Process is important.* Recognize the important benefits that the process of empowering has on people regardless of outcome (Culbert & McDonough, 1986; Peters, 1990; Weil, 1988). If empowerment efforts are made, those efforts in and of themselves will be found to be empowering and empowerment will be more easily and naturally attained.

■ *Structure can facilitate empowerment.* An empowering process must take place on a parallel, nonhierarchical level with power being shared (Block, 1987; Elden, 1986; Hollander & Offerman, 1990; Penzer, Eisman, & Gates, 1990; Peters, 1990; Stein & Kanter, 1980). Organizational relationships are based on a partnership (May & Kruger, 1988; Von der Embse, 1989), which often involves changing the existing organizational chart (Block, 1990).

■ *Democratic procedures are important.* Democratic activities, in which participative decision making, goal setting, and planning and democratic dialogue are the process norm, should take place (Bahr, 1987; Bass, 1990; Gustavsen & Engelstad, 1986; Nelson & Taylor, 1990; Penzer et al., 1990; Rodriguez, 1988; Takanaka, 1985–1986).

■ *Individuals are important.* The way clients and staff are treated by the organization will largely determine the success or failure of a given effort (Hodge, 1986). In empowering agencies, managers show concern and respect for people as individuals (Wallace, 1988). Employees are encouraged to discuss how they feel (Block, 1990). Emphasis is on individual empowerment and autonomy at all levels (Cherniss, 1980; Elden, 1986; Weil, 1988), including secretarial and support staff (Tissue, 1988). Empowering agencies emphasize performance, not credentials (Von der Embse, 1989). Personal uniqueness and diversity are respected (Griggs & Louw, 1995;

Gutierrez, 1992), as are people's interests and different work styles and methods (Von der Embse, 1989). People generally are allowed to do their best work in their own way (Topaz, 1989–1990).

■ *Empowerment is a learning process.* The empowerment process is viewed as a learning process and the organization as a learning environment (Gowdy & Rapp, 1989). All organizational members should be allowed, expected, and willing to make mistakes (Hollander & Offerman, 1990; Topaz, 1989–1990) and encouraged to engage in self-study and self-observation (Bonifant, 1986; Eden, 1986; Elden, 1986). Because the agency is a learning and therefore changing environment, ambiguity should be tolerated (Block, 1990; Bonifant, 1986; Eden, 1986; Elden, 1986; Peters, 1990; Rodriguez, 1988). All organizational events and circumstances should be viewed as opportunities to experience mastery (May & Kruger, 1988). MacLeod (1986) describes experiential learning by employees as being empowering. Elden (1986) states that the process of inquiry, learning, and self-study empowers because it allows for the exploration of new possibilities and explanations for current circumstances.

■ *Conflict is viewed as constructive.* Emphasis is on effective problem-solving and conflict-resolution behaviors and practices from a nonhierarchical and democratic stance (Bolin, 1989; Gowdy & Rapp, 1989; Hirsch & David, 1983; Stein & Kanter, 1980; Zimmerman & Rappaport, 1988). Conflict is viewed as natural, constructive, and part of the empowerment strategy (Elden, 1986; Rodriguez, 1988). Conflict stimulates productive effort and creative outcomes (Goddard, 1986). Conflict should be handled assertively. Passive behavior is discouraged and confronted (Block, 1987), as is passive–aggressive behavior. Confrontations require honest desires for solutions, with an awareness of each party's emotional involvement (Macher, 1988).

■ *Expect positive outcomes.* Positive outcomes are expected and communicated throughout the process. Expectations and confidence levels should be raised (Bass, 1990; Boyadjis, 1990; Collins, Ross, & Ross, 1989; Conger & Kanungo, 1988; Eden, 1986).

■ *Emphasize personal strengths.* Emphasis is on personal strengths as opposed to deficits (Bass, 1990; Hodge, 1986). The organization believes in the abilities of employees and makes that belief explicit (Conger, 1989). Empowering managers promote individual abilities and encourage members to grow (Boyadjis, 1990).

■ *Supportive environment is critical.* The empowerment process takes place in a positive, supportive environment with a warm socioemotional climate, group cohesion, integrity, and trust (Block, 1990; Conger, 1989; Culbert & McDonough, 1986; Evered & Selman, 1989; Hirsch & David, 1983; Jayaratne, Himle, & Chess, 1988; May & Kruger, 1988). When managers create "hassle-free" working conditions, staff can succeed and commitment can be maximized (Haggerty, 1987).

■ *Teamwork is essential.* Empowering agencies promote teamwork (Von der Embse, 1989). Teamwork rather than competition is essential (Goddard, 1986) or, as Peters (1990) states, "the team comes before the star."

■ *Communication is the key.* Communication is direct (Block, 1990) and honest. Important information is channeled appropriately (Ofner, 1985). Information that employees help generate is shared (Crosby, 1986). Managers share information in an accurate and timely manner (Hodge, 1986; Topaz, 1989–1990).

■ *Leadership is critical.* Genuine leadership in managerial roles gives an agency a sense of empowerment (Bennis, 1987). Leadership on nonmanagerial levels is based on tasks and expertise related to that task (Weil, 1988). Bennis (1987) describes the results of empowering leadership: People feel significant and part of the community, learning and competence become important, and work becomes exciting.

## Translating Lessons Into Action

These lessons can be used to construct a wide range of strategies for empowerment within organizations. Strategies can be grouped around organizational structure, interpersonal relationships, and technology (Shera & Page, 1995).

An agency structure that facilitates empowerment is one in which leadership and responsibilities are shared, communication and interaction patterns are based on principles of empowerment, and organizational changes originate from both lower and upper levels of the organization. Examples of empowerment through organizational structure include peer supervision (Richard & Rodway, 1992), team approaches to problem solving and decision making (Plunkett & Fornier, 1991), periodic reanalysis of roles and responsibility (Weil, 1988), and alterations in job design (Cherniss, 1980).

An empowerment perspective assumes that workers, when given opportunity, support, and assistance, will improve their performance. Examples of empowerment through relationship strategies include institutionalized value examinations (Coye, 1986), sensitivity training, discussion of positive client outcomes (Gowdy & Rapp, 1989), rewards (Conger & Kanungo, 1988), promotion of agency culture (Rapp & Poertner, 1992), development of employee skills (Gross & Shichman, 1987), and mutual feedback systems (Evered & Selman, 1989).

Technology, both hard and soft, can contribute significantly toward achieving excellence in service delivery. Examples of soft technology include service technologies that empower, such as Rapp and Poertner's (1992) client-centered model of administration, Saleebey's (1997) strengths-assessment model, and client-driven models of case management (Roberts-DeGennaro, 1987; Rose, 1991). Computer programs and educational technologies can also empower agencies and workers. Computers, for example, can generate information relevant to client tracking, case-load management, and financial monitoring (Hudson, 1990). Educational technology can enhance the role of the agency as a learning environment for workers and clients.

Agencies that value and implement strategies of empowerment are seeing the positive results of their efforts (Gutierrez et al., 1995). Organizations can observe higher levels of commitment (Stein & Kanter, 1980; Weil, 1988), autonomy (Elden, 1986; Penzer, 1991), morale (McNeely, 1988; Penzer, 1991; Rodriguez, 1988), communication (Stein & Kanter, 1980), and motivation (Cherniss, 1980). Workers experience greater learning, higher raises, and more promotions (Stein & Kanter, 1980);

greater job satisfaction (Cherniss, 1980; Rodriguez, 1988); a greater sense of community (Bennis, 1987); and a higher level of trust and goal attainment (Swift & Levin, 1987). This success in turn encourages agencies that are considering changing their traditional approaches.

## Best Practices in Downsizing

Many of these empowerment strategies can be used in downsizing to maintain organizational effectiveness. The empirical literature in this area, although scant, identifies three strategies for downsizing: Work-force reduction focuses on reducing the number of employees in the workplace; organization redesign eliminates or modifies structures and functions; and systemic change focuses on changing the organization's culture and the attitudes and values of its work force (Cameron, Freeman, & Mishra, 1993).

Just as we have identified lessons or "best practices" in designing empowering organizational contexts, so must we identify what works best in organizational downsizing. Research in this area identifies the importance of both an overall orientation toward downsizing and specific activities that achieve this end. Downsizing is more effective when it is seen as every employee's responsibility, motivated by improvement, approached proactively as an opportunity, reflects innovation, and assigns high value to human resources (Cameron et al., 1993). Specific best practices include:

- Preparation and extensive analysis
- Employee involvement and participation
- Sharing of information about costs
- Improvements in information systems
- Use of multiple downsizing strategies
- Consistency of downsizing strategy with organizational culture and vision
- Active, aggressive, accessible leadership
- Focus on process improvements
- Simplification of structure, processes, products, technology
- Advanced training of all employees (Cameron et al., 1993)

Most of these best practices are similar to or at least resonate with the lessons derived from the literature on organizational empowerment.

The task for the constructionist practitioner is to assess what strategies for empowerment or downsizing are transferable to the particular context of a given organization. This task involves selective application of previous practice wisdom and research, modification of existing alternatives, or development of innovative approaches. From a constructionist perspective, this process involves taking best-practice information derived from an objectivist perspective and modifying or "sculpting" it to be congruent with the organizational context. This may also include, in the absence of transferable best practices, the development or emergence of innovative solutions. This process has been described by K. Weick (1993), who contends that the organizational design should be an improvisational rather than a fixed design process. Improvisation is about process and designs that are continually reconstructed.

*Design, viewed from the perspective of improvisation, is more emergent, more continuous, more filled with surprise, more difficult to control, more tied to the content of action, and more affected by what people pay attention to than are the designs implied by architecture. Even though improvisation may involve more uncertainty, it does not thereby become any less effective. Emergent, continuous designing is sensitive to small changes in local conditions, which means the design is continuously updated as people and conditions change. (K. Weick, 1993, p. 350)*

Good organizational designs, then, incorporate practice wisdom, intuition, experimentation, and debate, features prominent in improvisation. The way out of turbulence may lie in continuous improvisation in response to continuous change in local conditions (K. Weick, 1993). Starbuck and Nystrom (1981) maintain that a well-designed organization is not a stable solution to achieve, but a developmental process to keep alive.

## Implications for Constructionist Practice in Organizations

Constructionist practitioners who are involved in organizational change need a wide range of skills. A knowledge of strategies of empowerment, although a useful foundation, needs to be complemented with a thorough understanding of organizational change and analytic and interactional skills (A. Weick, 1993).

To engage in successful organizational change, social workers should be familiar with the concepts of planned change, including ways of assessing the economic, political, and organizational forces in the environment and the multiple interests of colleagues, and have the ability to analyze the internal forces for change within the organization (Fisher & Karger, 1997). Additionally, skills in planned change include preparing the organization for change as well as initiating and institutionalizing change (Brager & Holloway, 1978).

Although very little has been written about constructionist practice at the level of the organization, many of the analytical and methodological tools used in constructionist clinical practice can be employed at that level. In the assessment phase one needs to go beyond the traditional frameworks for analyzing organizations (Hasenfeld, 1984). Using concepts such as power, narrative, and discourse, the practitioner conducts an assessment that reveals the organization's history, cycles (Tichy, 1980), and strengths (Saleebey, 1997).

In establishing a foundation for successful change, the practitioner emphasizes collaboration or change as a co-evolutionary process in which the worker tries to shed power and foster a spirit of partnership in pursuit of change (Laird, 1993). The intent is to mobilize members of an organization by creating an empowering context in which change can occur (Berger, 1993; Cox & Joseph, 1998). This process is very similar to that which is undertaken in clinical practice to establish working or therapeutic alliances. Through dialogue, co-learning, and the generation of multiple ideas, new formulations regarding appropriate organizational interventions are developed. It's important to emphasize that developing new formulations does not mean throwing out all other theories and practices (Dean, 1993). Best practices, efficacy information, and lessons learned are all evaluated in terms of their applicability, utility, and transferability to and resonance with (Maruyama, 1974) the focus of the change effort being undertaken. Although the constructionist practitioner may have greater knowledge of possibilities for change, organizational members have the lived experience essential to assessing the transferability of this knowledge. Solutions, then, are derived through a process of co-construction.

## Conclusion

Throughout the various phases of organizational change, one can readily envision the application of constructionism's core concepts. These core concepts include a belief in the social construction of reality, the importance of language in the construction of meaning, change through the discovery of new meanings, expertise as multidimensional, the centrality of collaborative processes, the use of reflexivity, an emphasis on strengths, and the co-construction of solutions (see Chapter 11).

Many of the concepts emerging from the empowerment-practice literature in social work are congruent with the growing literature on constructionist practice in social work. These two paradigms are intimately connected through a common value base. Their integration provides us with new insights for promoting effective practice at multiple levels of intervention.

## References

Allen, J. A. (1993). The constructivist paradigm: Values and ethics. *Journal of Teaching in Social Work, 8,* 31–54.

Bahr, M. (1987). Participative decision-making—CWA's approach. *Quality Circles Journal ,10*(2), 4–6.

Ball, R. A. (1977). Equitable evaluation through investigative sociology. *Sociological Focus, 10*(1), 1–14.

Bass, B . (1990). From transactional to transformational leadership: Learning to share the vision. *Organizational Dynamics, 18*(3), 19–31.

Belasco, J. A. (1990). *Teaching the elephant to dance: The manager's guide to empowering change.* New York: Penguin.

Bennis, W. (1987). Four competencies of great leaders. *Executive Excellence, 4*(12), 14.

Berger, C. (1993). *Restructuring and resizing: Strategies for social work and other human services administrators in health care.* Chicago: American Hospital Association.

Best, J. (1989). Afterword. In J. Best (Ed.), *Images of issues* (pp. 243–253). Hawthorne, NY: Aldine de Gruyter.

Best, J. (1993). But seriously folks: The limitations of the strict constructivist interpretation of social problems. In J. A. Holstein & G. Miller (Eds.), *Reconsidering social constructionism: Debates in social problems theory* (pp. 129–147). New York: Aldine de Gruyter.

Block, P . (1987). Empowering employees. *Training and Development Journal, 41*(4), 34–39.

Block, P. (1990). How to be the new kind of manager. *Working Woman, 15*(7), 51–52, 54.

Bolin, F. (1989). Empowering leadership. *Teacher's College Record, 91*(1), 81–96.

Bonifant, L. (1986). The 423 minute manager. *Personnel Administrator, 31*(7), 22–28.

Boyadjis, G. (1990). Empowerment managers promote employee growth. *Healthcare Financial Management, 44*(3), 58–62.

Brager, G., & Holloway, S. (1978). *Changing human service organizations: Policy and practice.* New

York: Free Press.

Cameron, K., Freeman, S., & Mishra, A. (1993). Downsizing and redesigning organizations. In G. Huber & W. Glick (Eds.), *Organizational change and redesign* (pp. 19–65). New York: Oxford University Press.

Cherniss, G. (1980). Human service programs as work organizations: Using organizational design to improve staff motivation and effectiveness. In R. Price & P. Politser (Eds.), *Evaluation and action in the social environment* (pp. 125–153). New York: Academic Press.

Collins, D., Ross, R., & Ross, T. L. (1989). Who wants participative management: The managerial perspective. *Group and Organizational Studies, 14,* 422–445.

Conger, J. (1989). Leadership: The art of empowering others. *Academy of Management Executive, 3*(1), 17–24.

Conger, J. A., & Kanungo, R. N. (1988). The empowerment process: Integrating theory and practice. *Academy of Management Review, 13,* 471–482.

Cook, T. D. (1985). Postpositivist critical multiplism. In R. L. Shotland & M. Mark (Eds.), *Social science and social policy* (pp. 21–62). Beverly Hills, CA: Sage.

Corcoran, K., & Vandiver, V. (1996) *Maneuvering the maze of managed care: Skills for mental health practitioners.* New York: Free Press.

Cox, E. O., & Joseph, B. (1998). Social service delivery and empowerment: The administrator's role. In L. Gutierrez, R. Parsons, & E. O. Cox (Eds.), *Empowerment in social work practice: A sourcebook* (pp. 167–186). Pacific Grove, CA: Brooks/Cole.

Coye, R. (1986). Individual values and business ethics. *Journal of Business Ethics, 5,* 45–49.

Crosby, B. (1986). Employee involvement: Why it fails, what it takes to succeed. *Personnel Administrator, 31*(2), 95–96, 98–106.

Culbert, S., & McDonough, J. (1986). The politics of trust and organization empowerment. *Public Administration Quarterly, 10,* 171–188.

Dean, R. G. (1993). Teaching a constructivist approach to clinical practice. *Journal of Teaching in Social Work, 8,* 55–75.

Eden, D. (1986). OD and self-fulfilling prophecy: Boosting productivity by raising expectations. *Journal of Applied Behavioral Science, 22,* 1–13.

Elden, M. (1986). Sociotechnical systems ideas as public policy in Norway: Empowering participation through worker-managed change. *Journal of Applied Behavioral Science, 22,* 239–255.

Evered, R., & Selman, J. (1989). Coaching and the art of management. *Organizational Dynamics, 18*(2), 16–31.

Fisher, R., & Karger, H. J. (1997). Empowering the social service workplace: Democracy and organizational change. In R. Fisher & H. J. Karger (Eds.), *Social work and community in a private world* (pp. 149–173). New York: Longman.

Ginsberg, L. H. (1988). Applying modern management concepts to social work. In P. Keys & L. Ginsberg (Eds.), *New management in human services* (pp. 30–45). Silver Spring, MD: NASW.

Goddard, R. (1986). The healthy side of conflict. *Management World, 15*(5), 8–11.

Gowdy, E., & Rapp, C. (1989). Managerial behavior: The common denominator of effective community-based programs. *Psychosocial Rehabilitation Journal, 13*(2), 31–51.

Griggs, L. B., & Louw, L. (1995). *Valuing diversity: New tools for a new reality.* New York: McGraw-Hill.

Gross, W., & Shichman, S. (1987). How to grow an organizational culture. *Personnel, 64*(9), 52–56.

Gustavsen, B., & Engelstad, P. H. (1986). The design of conferences and the evolving role of democratic dialogue in changing working life. *Human Relations, 39,* 101–115.

Gutierrez, L. (1992). Empowering ethnic minorities in the twenty-first century: The role of human service organizations. In Y. Hasenfeld (Ed.), *Human services as complex organizations* (pp. 320–338). Beverly Hills, CA: Sage.

Gutierrez, L., GlenMaye, L., & DeLois K. (1995). The organizational context of empowerment practice: Implications for social work practice. *Social Work, 40,* 249–258.

Haggerty, A. G. (1987). IMCA meeting: Commitment boosts bottom line tally. *National Underwriter,*

*91*(6), 25, 27.

Harrow, J., & Willcocks, L. (1992). Management, innovation and organizational learning. In L. Willcocks & J. Harrow (Eds.), *Rediscovering public services management* (pp. 50–83). London: McGraw-Hill.

Hasenfeld, Y. (1984). Analyzing the human service agency. In F. Cox, J. Erlich, J. Rothman, & J. Tropman (Eds.), *Tactics and techniques of community practice* (pp.14–26). Itasca, IL: F. E. Peacock.

Hirsch, B., & David, T. (1983). Social networks and work/nonwork life: Action-research with nurse managers. *American Journal of Community Psychology, 11,* 493–507.

Hodge, M. (1986). Supervising case managers. *Psychosocial Rehabilitation Journal, 12*(4), 51–59.

Hollander, E., & Offerman, L. (1990). Power and leadership in organizations. *American Psychologist, 45,* 172–189.

Huber, G., & Glick, W. (1993). Sources and forms of organizational change. In G. Huber & W. Glick (Eds.), *Organizational change and redesign* (pp. 3–15). New York: Oxford University Press.

Huber, G., Sutcliffe, K., Miller, C., & Glick, W. (1993). Understanding and predicting organizational change. In G. Huber & W. Glick (Eds.), *Organizational change and redesign* (pp. 215–265). New York: Oxford University Press.

Hudson, W. (1990). *Computer assisted social services.* Beverly Hills, CA: Sage.

Jayaratne, S., Himle, D., & Chess, W. (1988). Dealing with work stress and strain: Is the perception of support more important than its use? *Journal of Applied Behavioral Science, 24*(2), 191–202.

Kahn, A., & Kamerman, S. (1990). Do the public social services have a future? *Families in Society, 71,* 165–171.

Laird, J. (1993). Family-centered practice: Cultural and constructionist reflections. *Journal of Teaching in Social Work, 8,* 77–109.

Macher, K. (1988). Empowerment and the bureaucracy. *Training and Development Journal, 42*(9), 41–45.

MacLeod, J. (1986). Self empowerment training programs for employees. *Employment Relations Today, 13*(1), 33–36.

Maruyama, M. (1974). Endogenous research vs "experts" from outside. *Futures, 6,* 389–394.

May, G., & Kruger, M. (1988). The manager within. *Personnel Journal, 67*(2), 57–65.

McKenna, J. F. (1990). Smart scarecrows: The wizardry of empowerment. *Industry Week, 239*(14), 8–9, 12, 16, 21.

McNeely, R. L. (1988). Five morale enhancing innovations for human services setting. *Social Casework, 69,* 204–213.

Messmer, M. (1990). How to put employee empowerment into practice. *Woman CPA, 52*(3), 25.

Nelson, M., & Taylor, N. (1990, September). Conceptual tools to make participation work for you. *Journal for Quality and Participation, 13,* 64–69.

Ofner, A. (1985). Middle management: The neglected resource. *Personnel Journal, 64*(12), 14–16.

Penzer, E. (1991, May). The power of empowerment. *Incentive, 165,* 97–99.

Penzer, E., Eisman, R., & Gates, M. (1990, January). Winning companies: Performance through people. *Incentive, 164,* 16–22.

Peters, T. (1990). The best new managers will listen, motivate, support: Isn't that just like a woman? *Working Woman, 15*(9), 142–143, 216–217.

Peters, T. J., & Waterman, R. H. (1982). *In search of excellence.* New York: Harper and Row.

Pinderhughes, E. B. (1983). Empowerment for our clients and for ourselves. *Social Casework, 64,* 331–338.

Plunkett, L. C., & Fornier, R. (1991). *Participative management: Implementing empowerment.* New York: John Wiley.

Pollack, S. (1989, December). Four keys for empowerment. *Journal for Quality and Participation, 12,* 88–91.

Pollner, M. (1993). The reflexivity of constructionism and the construction of reflexivity. In J. A. Holstein & G. Miller (Eds.), *Reconsidering social constructionism: Debates in social problems theory* (pp. 199–212). New York: Aldine de Gruyter.

Rapp, C., & Poertner, J. (1988). Moving clients center stage through the use of client outcomes. *Administration in Social Work, 11*(3–4), 39–100.

Rapp, C. A., & Poertner, J. (1992). *Social administration: A client-centered approach.* New York: Longman.

Richard, R., & Rodway, M. (1992). The peer consultation group: A problem-solving perspective. *Clinical Supervisor, 10,* 83–100.

Roberts-DeGennaro, M. (1987). Developing case management as a practice model. *Social Casework, 68,* 466–470.

Rodriguez, N. M. (1988). A successful feminist shelter: A case study of the family crisis shelter in Hawaii. *Journal of Applied Behavioral Science, 24,* 235–250.

Rose, S. (1991). Strategies of mental health programming: A client-driven model of case management. In C. Hudson & A. Cox (Eds.), *Dimensions of state mental health policy* (pp. 138–154). New York: Praeger.

Saleebey, D. (Ed.). (1997). *The strengths perspective in social work practice* (2nd ed.). New York: Longman.

Schulz, A. J., Israel, B. A., Zimmerman, M. A., & Checkoway, B. N. (1995). Empowerment as a multi-level construct: Perceived control at the individual, organizational and community levels. *Health Education Research, 10,* 309–327.

Shera, W. (1996). Managed care and people with severe mental illness: Challenges and opportunities for social work. *Health and Social Work, 21,* 196–201.

Shera, W., & Page, J. (1995). Creating more effective human service organizations through strategies of empowerment. *Administration in Social Work, 19*(4), 1–15.

Starbuck, W. H., & Nystrom, P. C. (1981). Why the world needs organizational design. *Journal of General Management, 6,* 3–17.

Stein, B., & Kanter, R. M. (1980). Building the parallel organization: Creating mechanisms for permanent quality of work life. *Journal of Applied Behavioral Science, 16,* 371–388.

Swift, C., & Levin, G. (1987). Empowerment: An emerging mental health technology. *Journal of Primary Prevention, 8*(1–2), 71–94.

Takanaka, A. (1985–1986). Some thoughts on Japanese management centering on personnel and labor management: The reality and the future. *International Studies of Management Organization, 15*(3–4), 17–68.

Their, M. (1989, February). Have you been empowered? *Journal for Quality and Participation, 12,* 10–11.

Thomas, K., & Velthouse, B. (1990). Cognitive elements of empowerment: An "interpretive model" of intrinsic task motivation. *Academy of Management Review, 15,* 666–681.

Tichy, N. (1980). Problem cycles in organizations and the management of change. In J. R. Kimberly & R. H. Miles (Eds.), *The organizational life cycle* (pp. 164–183). San Francisco: Jossey-Bass.

Tissue, G. (1988). Empowering the secretarial workforce. *Personnel, 65*(3), 50–54.

Topaz, L. (1989–1990). Empowerment—human resource management in the 90's. *Management Quarterly, 30*(4), 3–8.

Von der Embse, T. J. (1989). Transforming power into empowerment. *Manage, 41*(3), 25–28.

Wallace, J. D. (1988). Excellence: Craze or commitment? *Personnel Administrator, 33,* 14–16.

Weick, A. (1993). Reconstructing social work education. *Journal of Teaching in Social Work, 8,* 11–30.

Weick, K. (1993). Organizational redesign as improvisation. In G. Huber & W. Glick (Eds.), *Organizational change and redesign* (pp. 346–379). New York: Oxford University Press.

Weil, M. (1988). Creating an alternative work culture in a public service setting. *Administration in Social Work, 12*(2), 69–82.

Zimmerman, M., & Rappaport, J. (1988). Citizen participation, perceived control, and psychological empowerment. *American Journal of Community Psychology, 16,* 725–750.

# 16

**Co-Constructing Your Business Relationships**

*Tracy Todd*

In public-sector behavioral health care, many states have been granted a "super-waiver," which gives the state direct control of the funding available to clinical service delivery. As a result, states are adopting a managed care model for publicly funded mental health services. In the private sector, managed care has penetrated nearly every market and continues to grow in the mental health services. Whatever managed care model is implemented, its focus is to create a service-delivery system that is held accountable for the services provided. This sense of accountability is a major paradigm shift for nearly all clinical delivery systems. A significant consequence of heightened accountability is that organizations must maintain a productive working relationship with the agency monitoring the care delivery.

Relationships, for the most part, deepen when the involved parties' expectations are met. And the more closely their expectations are realized, the better the relationship. The impact of these working relationships is far reaching and may not be fully appreciated by many agencies and individuals. For example, in a traditional service-delivery design, a community-based service center that exceeded its budget would typically be granted money by the state and continue to operate as usual. The service center would, at year's end, request more money for the next year with the hope of meeting its budget. The state would also try to allocate more money for mental health service delivery in the public sector. The following year this process would typically be repeated. Now, however, service centers are allocated a set amount of money and compete with other centers in how well they manage the money and services. A center that does not meet its goals may not receive funding the following year. To remain viable, private and public agencies must compete or merge with other agencies that provide similar services. Under this scenario, agencies must focus on how to meet the needs of payers, stay competitive with regard to costs, and demonstrate value and effectiveness.

These variables are not new to the field, but their priority relative to one another has shifted. To remain viable in such a market, individuals and agencies need particular skills. Constructivism can help. Although applying an esoteric philosophical construct to the business sector may seem incongruous, in actuality constructivism has always been practiced there. Consider the relationship between a potential buyer of a house and a real estate agent. The buyer contacts an agent, and they meet to discuss what kind of house the buyer desires. The agent listens carefully to the buyer's description, paying attention to variables (cost, location, school system, number of bedrooms, etc.) and their priority level. As the agent takes the potential buyer on a tour of homes, he or she pays close attention to how the buyer responds to the houses they visit. Does the buyer like hardwood floors better than carpet, gas or electric range, or a fenced yard? As the agent learns what the buyer wants and the buyer learns what is available in his or her price range, they begin to construct a reality about what can be purchased. They begin to narrow the selections. They co-construct a reality that informs them of the house that eventually can be purchased.

A real estate agent must be competent in co-constructing the house that suits the buyer. A good agent is likely to stay in business and thrive. The same principle applies to clinical service delivery. Therapists must expand their ability to practice constructivism beyond microsystems (client and client families) and apply it to macrosystems (economics and global market trends) in order to stay in business and thrive.

The focus of this chapter is on applying constructivism to the macrosystem relationship between service-delivery sectors and the marketplace. The skills discussed emphasize the parallel process between what is done in the clinical arena and in developing a healthy, viable working relationship with the marketplace. Most individuals have the skills necessary for working with microsystems and simply need to learn to generalize those skills to the macrosystem work.

## Clinical Analogy

Co-constructing the therapeutic process involves relationship building, identification of goals, development of strategies to obtain those goals, implementation of tasks, and measurement of goal achievement. Berg and De Jong (see Chapter 11) state that to start a solution-building conversation, the therapist must ask the client what he or she wants from the meeting. This helps the client and therapist begin to co-create a therapy process that is respectful of the client's belief system and that attempts to meet the client's needs. Haley (1976) states, "If therapy is to end properly, it must begin properly by negotiating a solvable problem."

Solution-oriented conversations attempt to create a sense of competency so that clients can begin to feel hopeful about achieving their goals (Cade & O'Hanlon, 1993; Chapter 11). Competency is created by assisting clients in the co-creation of goals that are doable in the present, action-oriented, and measurable (Berg & Miller, 1992; Walter & Peller, 1992). As these goals are co-constructed, therapists and clients dialogue about possible solution-development strategies. In the course of time, clients inform therapists about the status of their goal achievement. If clients are achieving their goals, therapy can either end or a new therapeutic contract can be established. If clients are not achieving their goals, new strategies must be considered, taking care not to blame clients (de Shazer, 1985; O'Hanlon & Weiner-Davis, 1989; Walter & Peller, 1992). New strategies need to be co-constructed until goals are achieved. This oversimplified description of conducting therapy from a solution-oriented, co-constructed process is similar to the process that occurs with macrosystem economics.

## *Market Relations*

The term "market" is defined as all potential sources involving the buying and selling of goods or services (Random House College Dictionary, 1979). The market in behavioral health care includes sources such as managed-care organizations, preferred-provider panels, community mental health centers, state block grants, and social service agencies. Our first step is to assess what the market expects so we can establish a productive working relationship and meet market needs. Similarly, in a clinical setting we attempt initially to assess clients' problems and to establish a working relationship with the client. In conducting an assessment, we may use paper-and-pencil tools, interviews (which may be done by someone other than the therapist), and collaborative information gained by talking to others involved with the client. During this assessment we try to obtain a clinical picture of our client. While conducting the interview we attempt to join with our client and build rapport so that a positive working relationship can occur.

In the business environment, a similar process occurs. First, we identify potential clients, try to assess their needs, and then begin to build a positive working relationship. For example, an agency might identify that a funding source has few services for hospital diversion. This funding source could be a local mental health center, a managed-care organization, a geriatric facility, or even a psychiatric hospital. You would approach this source and do an assessment. Such questions as "Do you need a mobile crisis unit?" "Does your crisis team do extensive follow up?" "How do you measure effectiveness of the crisis team?" would help identify what is needed by the funding source. The next step is to try to build a positive working relationship with this entity. Will they give you a small portion of business to test out your services and allow you to begin to build trust? What do they need from you in order to feel confident in your service?

By assessing the problem and building rapport (trust), one begins to co-create a business relationship. This relationship is based on another agency's perceived needs and a collaborative working relationship. When delivering clinical services, one considers such factors as race, religion, cultural mores, educational levels, and belief systems. Such considerations are also needed with the behavioral health care marketplace. Provider saturation, levels of accountability, general behavioral health trends, managed mental health care, primary-care physicians, probation officers, employee assistance programs (EAPs) must be weighed.

The political and economic climate are important variables that must be weighed for, especially in the public sector. Constructivism takes into account in which a relationship is forged (ethnicity, religion). Likewise, in the business sector of clinical service delivery, the political situation and the distribution of power must be considered. Political parties holding office create favorable or unfavorable market conditions with regard to the distribution of federal and state money. These factors must be considered when trying to co-create business relationships with funding sources. A funding source may be significantly influenced by the political climate, which needs to be accounted for in the joining phase of a business relationship. Clinicians have many strategies with which to deal with a power issue in a clinical setting. One strategy is to take a "one down" position and allow the client to lead until the clinical situation can be turned in a productive direction. Similarly, when developing a business relationship, one may need to give the funding source the lead. Too often, agencies and individuals become agitated with the power dynamics and terminate the relationship or alienate the funding source. Taking a subordinate position with a funding source allows one to become educated; the clinical injunction "do no harm" is appropriate in dealing with such business relationships.

## Learn the Language

A rule of thumb in co-constructing a therapeutic relationship is always to use the client's language (de Shazer, 1985; O'Hanlon & Weiner-Davis, 1989). The same is true in establishing a relationship with a potential revenue stream. Too often, such language intimidates therapists. Some terms necessary for understanding the market are explained.

**Exploitation.** Random House College Dictionary (1979, p. 466) defines exploitation as "utilization for profit." In discovering a new referral stream that few have accessed, your task would be to exploit (use) the referral stream to make a profit. A private practitioner might develop a relationship with a church that has money for counseling services. The practitioner might offer services to church members at a discount. In effect, this practitioner is exploiting a market.

**Revenue source.** A revenue source is the funding entity. For example, a community mental health center may have a state contract or a grant awarded by the federal government as a major funding source. In private practice, a funding source could be a managed care organization, insurance company, or an EAP.

**Referral source.** A referral source is where the referral originated. Be careful not to [confu]se referral sources with a revenue source. For example, a primary-care physi[cian's off]ice may be a very good referral. However, that office does not pay for the [services (]revenue source). In public agencies, referral sources can be the police [department], a detoxification program, probation officers, a victim's advocate pro[gram, and t]he like.

**[Diversif]ying revenue sources.** Having multiple payers helps businesses experi[ence less ne]gative effects if a revenue source loses funding. For example, a public [mental health] agency may receive 70% of its funding from state grants. If the state [cuts funding,] the agency may be negatively affected because so much funding is

**Diversifying referral sources.** Diversifying referral sources means having multiple referral sources. Each business must determine its comfort level with regard to diversity. Some businesses may be comfortable with fewer than five referral sources; others may not.

**Profit margins.** The amount (percentage or dollar) over the actual costs of services or products represents the profit margin. Profit margins should be calculated in all projections involving services or products. For example, if your agency decides to develop a revenue stream from educational seminars, you might calculate the following:

*Expenses*

| | |
|---|---|
| Presenter's fee | $ 50.00 |
| Newspaper advertisement | $125.00 |
| Room rental | $ 50.00 |
| Materials/handouts | $ 20.00 |
| Labor for set up of presentation | $ 48.00 |
| Total | $293.00 |

| | |
|---|---|
| Profit margin of 15% | $ 43.95 ($293.00 * 15%) |

| | |
|---|---|
| Total | $336.95 ($43.95 + $293.00) |

*Income*

| | |
|---|---|
| Fee for seminar | $ 15.00 |
| Fee x 23 registrants | $345.00 |

In this scenario, the goal of achieving a profit of 15% was achieved. However, for every registrant under the projected number of registrants needed (23), the profit margin would diminish.

**Stockpiling.** Stockpiling means delaying the development of new products, services, or information that have the potential to create profit (Johansson, McHugh, Pendlebury, & Wheeler, 1993). For example, one would likely maintain a mailing list of all former clients desiring notification of future seminars. Such a list can generate business as well as new referrals. Stockpiling the names and addresses of these former clients helps generate income in the future.

**Information purchasing.** Information purchasing refers to the buying of strategies or ideas that may enhance practice. The purchase of this book is an information purchase. Gathering and manipulating information can give a business a great advantage over its competitors. Clinicians need to be aggressive in purchasing information so they can stay ahead of other businesses that provide clinical services. Other examples of information purchasing include software programs that provide clinical guidelines for behavioral health care issues, names and addresses of major businesses within a geographic location, or consultant services for information on industry trends.

## Identifying Goals

Identifying goals to meet market needs is a key task. Agencies need to assess their market's needs and expectations. One way to construct goals is to conduct an interview with a potential referral or revenue source. Meet with key decision makers and find out what they want from your services. During this process, both parties will begin to shape and construct goals that are specific and identifiable. The market expects quality services. Your customers have goals related to quality and cost-effective care. Creating mutually compatible co-constructed goals can help you secure a contract from a revenue source.

## Business Strategies

Similar to creating strategies to assist clients, therapists need to create interventions that help the referral sources and themselves. Such interventions may include marketing, research studies, or streamlining access to services. Remember, strategies produce change. Using effective strategies can create a win–win situation for the market and your business. For example, an outpatient center that is part of a large community mental health center is engaged in managing its own care. You want to increase your revenue, decrease individual client contacts, and improve quality of care to crisis clients. The strategy your team chooses is to conduct two crisis groups per week (Wednesday evening and Saturday morning). Crisis clients are referred to these groups, and the clinician in charge of the group implements crisis stabilization and triage. The suggestion you make to the community mental health center is to test this strategy during a course of four months and compare costs and outcomes with another outpatient center within the system that uses a different method in managing crises. This strategy will help the larger system (community mental health center) by attempting to improve quality and outcomes while decreasing costs. At the same time, you gain referrals and possibly recognition as an outpatient center that is setting measurement standards. Finally, clients potentially can experience better service delivery because access to care has improved.

## Implementation

Implementation is a critical step in developing a co-constructed strategy for the business–market relationship. As therapists, we have worked with clients who discuss strategies and interventions but do not complete them. We might assume that the client is not willing to follow the strategy or that the client is not ready for achieving therapeutic gains.

Consider the following two factors when implementing business strategies. First, is the market responding to your strategies? If the answer is yes, good. If it is no, what needs to change in order for the market to respond? Clinicians and agencies may not always be able to influence this variable. However, it is critically important that as a treatment agency you adapt and create new strategies. For example, assume that your group practice receives many referrals from an EAP of a large company near your office. The EAP loses that contract, which has a negative effect on your business.

What new strategies do you need to put into place? Did the company sign a with a different EAP from which you can gain referrals? Does the original EA smaller contracts to which you can market your services? What insurance or ma care vendor does the large company use? Can you gain referrals from that venc

The second factor to consider during implementation involves the executic the strategy. Many agencies have great ideas about how to stimulate revenue but to follow through with the plan. They talk as though they are determined to ma changes, but their actions prove otherwise. DiClemente (1991) discussed stages change as they apply to individuals: precontemplator, contemplator, determinec action, maintenance, relapse. These stages are useful in examining an agency's moti-vational level.

*Precontemplators* are individuals who do not recognize change is needed. They construct realities that represent rebellion and reluctance to change. A drunken driver arrested for driving while intoxicated who believes that the police officer was harassing him because his car's tail light was burned out is a good example of a precontemplator. These individuals blame external events for their situation and do not take responsibil-ity for their actions. *Contemplators* recognize that change is needed but are ambivalent about implementation and follow through. The *determined* stage of change occurs when persons recognize that change is needed and are determined to try any strategy. Crisis clients best represent this stage; these clients will follow directives closely in order to alleviate the crisis situation. The *action* stage is represented by persons who have a plan of change and are implementing the strategies. The primary characteristic of this stage is having an effective strategy so that motivation can be maintained. During the *main-tenance* stage one maintains the strategies that have been implemented, making modi-fications if they are necessary, recognizing what strategies are effective, and maintain-ing motivation. The *relapse* stage occurs during a time of setbacks and lack of effective strategies. The primary focus here is to return to a level of motivation that is productive (determined, action) and not to discontinue formulating strategies.

In implementing a plan, it is vital to consider your agency's motivational level. DiClemente (1991) described the action phase of change as involving a public com-mitment to action and the creation of external monitors of activity. Administrators need to assess whether they are ready for such a commitment or whether the agency needs preparation for this type of commitment. Often, determined agencies fail to commit human or financial resources to make the necessary changes or they focus superficial attention to an issue resulting from a crisis. Leaders need the support of the board of directors and other significant persons in an organization. I have heard directors of large mental health organizations comment on the need for changes and the conse-quences of not making those changes, then not do anything to initiate change. After one commits to change, it is important to create a timeline for the project, including due dates, who will be accountable for the project, and who will direct the project.

In today's behavioral health care market, many clinicians and administrators are cautious about making changes because they want guarantees that the change will be successful. These clinicians and agencies are stuck in the contemplation or deter-

...sk is necessary if one is to stay competitive. An agency's
...nced by leadership, feasibility studies, and consultants.

### ...ent

...nuously assess their progress with clients. We must do the same
...n the market and making changes in the agency. Mental health pro-
...o be sophisticated in monitoring their business in relation to market
...ctations (Todd, 1994). Strategy management allows a business to adapt
...uctuations and to create or adjust strategies and interventions. Large
...health care corporations, such as community mental health centers, need
...strategies and processes that allow for quick adaptability so that they may
...financially viable in a highly volatile marketplace.

### ...mary

As this synopsis of the conceptual ideas behind the therapist–market relationship
indicates, it and the client–therapist relationship are parallel processes. Many ideas,
strategies, and skills used in providing clinical service are applicable in trying to construct collaborative business relationships within the marketplace.

## Practice Implications

### Learn About the Market

Therapists need to learn how to conduct a market and needs analysis. An incor-
rect assumption about what the market needs, or what you would like the market to
need, can lead to a frustrating experience. Think of those rare clients whose therapeutic needs you may not have truly heard. The therapeutic process with them was
most likely frustrating and difficult.

One way to learn about your local market is to conduct a zip-code analysis.
List out the zip codes of all your clients in the past 12 to 18 months. Then do a zip-
code analysis of the therapists serving the same zip codes. Do you find any client
population being underserved or any client population projected to need service?
Some populations projected to need services include HIV/AIDS, behavioral medicine, partners of sexual-abuse survivors, work-related problems, medical rehabilitation, chronic pain, infertility, and therapy with the geriatric population (Merit lists
13 clinical specialties, 1995; Niche marketing, 1996). You want to learn which clinical populations are overserved and which ones are sources of potential growth for
your agency.

After assessing the populations being served, identify the payers of services and
the services they are reimbursing. Perhaps you discover that workers-compensation
assessment and treatment is underserved and money is available to pay for such services in your area. Given such a scenario, you might pursue a contractual relationship
with the programs and co-construct a service-delivery plan that accomplishes their
goals. It's important to assess how other providers are serving this population. Per-

haps they are leaving out a component of care that you feel is vital to the success of the program and the clients served. Your strategy might include this component.

Every market has some basic expectations: measurement of outcomes and client satisfaction, ability to deliver a few specialty services, integrated service-delivery systems for billing and appointment setting, the ability to deliver wellness and prevention programs, and so forth. Agencies need to be cognizant of these expectations when they join with a revenue source.

## Changes for Therapists

Those providing clinical services need to become computer literate. Weil and Rosen (1994) reported that only 5% of psychotherapists could use a computer beyond basic word processing. Psychotherapists need to be able to access information and data. A zip-code search is easy to do with a computer program. Providing clinical services requires data management. Therapists need to learn how to use computer software to analyze information. Also, clinicians need to become more cognizant of and comfortable with buying information. Clients in therapy are buying information from therapists or when they attend seminars. Therapists need to do the same with experts in the field who have information they lack. It's also important for psychotherapists to become self-reliant in obtaining information. Companies sell information systems related to monitoring quality, determining clinical costs, reporting outcome data, and developing sound treatment plans. Most of these companies have web sites from which you can access information and resources (see Appendix A).

## Setting Goals

Similar to setting goals with clients, therapists and revenue sources have expectations and goals of each other. A revenue source may expect you to decrease costs, improve quality, measure effectiveness, and improve accessibility to services. How will they measure and evaluate your agency on these dimensions?

Businesses desiring to increase revenues need to set goals. Some goals that agencies consider include increased non-managed care revenues, increased cash-pay clients, more referrals from primary-care physicians (family physicians and internists), better return rate on satisfaction surveys, and less time between initial telephone call and first appointment.

Total quality management is overused and misused. However, it is important to define what "quality" means to your organization and how you measure it. Quality is a dynamic process that must be continuously stimulated through new and innovative goals. These goals, if you have assessed the market carefully, should fit or closely parallel goals of your referral and revenue sources.

For example, in a public agency providing services to the indigent, the time between initial contact and first appointment is an average of 13 days. For crisis- or urgent-care clients, the average is less than two days. Thus the incentive is for clients to have crises, which in turn creates a culture of crisis intervention. For example, a revenue source may feel that quality care requires that urgent care clients must be seen within 24 hours and nonemergent clients must be seen within five business days. These new goals are set for your agency and you are given three months to achieve this goal. Your agency must then create strategies and monitoring systems that hold the agency and staff accountable. Within two months, your agency achieves this goal. As a secondary gain, the number of crisis calls decreases.

On the surface, this example may appear trite. However, many changes, goals, and total quality management strategies are evident:

■ First, someone recognized the need for a revenue source. How did this happen? Who initiated this assessment?

■ Second, the agency needed to be in the determined and action stages of change. How does one create an agency culture that is determined and action oriented?

■ Third, a strategy was needed to meet the goal. Who created the strategy? How was the strategy modified? How did the agency get staff involved in helping to create these strategies?

■ Fourth, an information management system needed to be put in place to measure the effectiveness of the strategy. What kind of system was created? Were all staff able to work within the system? How was motivation kept in determined and action stages?

Constructivism plays a vital role in moving an organization toward change and total quality management. Lamb and Lamson (1996) state, "It is only when staff begin to feel that the process is about real quality for real customers that they will fully commit to the improvement effort" (p. 36). The agency and revenue source, supervisors and supervisees, and staff in general need to construct a reality that increases motivation and cooperation to obtain the desired goals. If a workable co-created reality is not achieved in any of these relationships, the strategies and goals are less likely to succeed.

Behavioral health care professionals need to move beyond the belief that therapy cannot be made into a science. Although the process of therapy may always elude our complete understanding, we can measure our progress. For instance, a family enters therapy because a child is having five temper tantrums per day. If while in therapy the child goes without a temper tantrum for four months, that is support that therapy has had a positive impact. Too often psychotherapists forget the basic research premise of obtaining baseline data, conducting intervention, and measuring the difference between baseline and outcome.

Behavioral health care specialists also need to become more accountable in achieving goals related to all aspects of business, including quality. Most businesses create annual business reports that demonstrate profit-and-loss statements, gains made during the year, projections for the upcoming year, and areas that will be developed. This task involves keeping data, having a management-information system, and being able to create and use spreadsheets for statistical analyses. Private practitioners need to create management-information systems that assist in monitoring the goals of the business (clinical, financial, and business development). Administrators of public service agencies need to pay attention to constructing a culture that encourages staff to work toward these goals and to hold one another accountable for their achievements. Lamb and Lamson (1996) report that approximately 75% of quality-improvement efforts fail and that the failures can typically be attributed to the lack of leadership and the inability of an organization's culture to make a paradigm shift to a quality focus.

## Strategic Development

Developing a business strategy is similar to developing treatment strategies. It is important to assess strategies according to what creates the greatest potential for success and how to find the best personnel to maximize this potential.

Many therapists need to take a hard look at their practice and peer affiliation. Historically, groups of therapists would come together to decrease costs on office space and general overhead. Now these therapists are creating formal business operations. These colleagues may be great friends and supporters, but are they good business people? Will they help their agency succeed? Do they share a vision and mission?

The actual business plan is another factor in creating successful strategies. Developing any new product or service moves through three phases. Phase one is the research, development, and start-up phase. Allocating time and money is important in this phase. Patience is necessary. Many therapists want instant success in their new project or relationship with a revenue source. However, focusing on overnight success is an obstacle to delivering quality services (Capezio & Morehouse, 1993). Such an approach seduces agencies into taking shortcuts in their services, thereby creating lesser quality service. Phase two is the growth phase, which includes the implementation of strategies and monitoring of goals (e.g., moving from 5 to 10 referrals from primary-care physicians per month). Phase three is maturation. During this phase one monitors the competition and one's performance. Reaching a goal is much different from maintaining a goal. Other agencies will engage in market analysis, examine your services, and determine if they can deliver better services.

Probably the most difficult change for many therapists in today's market concerns their collegial affiliations. Every clinician and agency needs to ask the difficult question "Who will help us succeed or fail?" Interdependent relationships with other professionals are critical to success. Historically, overhead was the only shared business endeavor. Today, therapists' profit-and-loss margin, potential contract development, and marketing are dependent on one another's performance. This change can be potentially painful and hurtful, but it can also maximize a psychotherapist's longevity. Similarly, public agencies may need to assess potential alliances with other organizations. Alliances should heighten the potential for success and decrease the risk of failure. For example, collaborating with a university in setting up and implementing a research model for clinical services could help a community mental health center demonstrate positive outcomes and maintain a total quality management perspective.

Therapists also need to develop and write a business plan. This task can be very challenging and time consuming. Business plans help organizations meet market demands and remain current in health care trends. Therapists need to predict and control costs so that they can take risks (Managed care insider, 1996). With a business plan, therapists begin to deal with variables such as realizing a return on investment, achieving goals to keep the organization profitable, and defining risks and opportunities.

## *Implementation*

Who implements and functions as the decision maker for a business plan? Answering this question is critically important in implementing a project. Too often, agencies want to make sure that all clinicians react positively to their decisions. This cannot happen. Some decisions will upset some people. The objective of implementing a plan is to stay in business, not necessarily to make everyone happy. Some therapists become trapped in processing the strategy and never engage the plan. It's frustrating to work with clients who overanalyze their situation and do not make changes. The same is true in implementing a business plan.

Dealing with risk is the greatest change facing therapists in the marketplace. Therapists need to understand and become more comfortable taking necessary risks. Taking the time to create sound business plans and strategies, continuously obtaining information about market trends, and using consultants for feedback about proposed strategies help reduce risk. Therapists also need to become more comfortable making decisions. Discussing strategies is important, but eventually someone has to make the critical decision. The market does not wait for agencies to make decisions.

## *Strategy Management*

Clinicians and administrators can feel overwhelmed when they begin to consider macrosystem strategies. However, unlike clinical research, which is frought with potential contaminants, measuring the impact of co-constructing a relationship with a revenue or referral source is quite easy. Depending on the goals set with a revenue or referral source, a few standard variables are used to measure outcomes.

**Revenue.** Revenue is a simple variable to measure. If your goal was to increase a revenue source by 5% this year and you made $25,000 from that revenue source last year, did you achieve the goal of increasing revenue by $1,250?

**Number of referrals.** If your goal was to decrease the number of referrals of a lesser paying contract from 50 to 40 and increase the referrals of a higher paying contract from 20 to 30, did you achieve that goal?

**Repeat Customers.** Repeat customers come in two forms. First, referral sources should be repeat customers. Of 24 primary-care physicians, 18 (75%) used your services, and 7 of the 18 sent you more than one referral. Is that ratio acceptable?

Clients are also repeat customers. You opened 125 cases this year; how many were repeat customers? What percentage would you like to be repeat customers or become referral sources for you? Therapists have been reluctant to perceive former clients as repeat customers because of negative feelings about recidivism. However, assume you saw someone with regard to parenting issues of an eight-year-old and treatment was successful. These clients also have a 14-year-old. Would a parenting seminar on adolescent behavior interest these parents? Would you be likely to send them a notice about this seminar?

**Percentage distribution among referral sources.** This variable is vitally important to measure because it helps you picture your agency. Discovering trends helps you discover the areas where the agency and the market do not fit together.

**TABLE 1.** *Feel Good Therapy revenue distribution.*

| Revenue source | Year one (%) | Year two (%) | Year three (%) |
|---|---|---|---|
| MCO X | 35 | 25 | 14 |
| MCO Y | 15 | 11 | 9 |
| MCO Z | 12 | 7 | 9 |
| PPO A | 5 | 8 | 8 |
| PPO B | 8 | 12 | 13 |
| Cash pay | 10 | 14 | 20 |
| Seminars | 5 | 9 | 10 |
| Consultations | 10 | 14 | 17 |
| Total | 100 | 100 | 100 |

For example, data indicate that during a three-year period the Feel Good Therapy Center's revenue distribution experienced the following changes: (a) a decrease in managed care revenues; (b) an increased income from cash-pay clients, seminars, and consultations; and (c) generally stable PPO revenues (see Table 1). The center must make decisions regarding these trends and what they would like to do about them.

**Satisfaction with services.** Measuring satisfaction with services is very important in co-constructing a profitable business relationship. Consider the following factors when developing a satisfaction survey. First, what variables do you want to measure? These are some examples of satisfaction survey questions that are important to ask: Would you use this agency's services again? Would you refer others to this agency? Did you find the services helpful? What level of improvement (1 = none, 5 = great) have you noticed? Second, you may want to incorporate variables that referral and revenue sources desire. Some managed care organizations (MCOs) want to know how difficult it was to get an appointment with your agency or whether a client was satisfied with the time it took to get an appointment. It's important to gather this information during the "learning about your customer" phase so that you can co-construct a satisfaction survey that is mutually beneficial.

Some companies specialize in creating satisfaction surveys. However, it's important to remember that they may create a survey that does not evaluate what a local MCO is interested in. Make sure that you can use the data to improve your services and that the data can be reported to your contracted MCOs in a useable format.

Appendix B provides an example of how to use a satisfaction survey. A couple of years ago our agency was receiving satisfaction surveys that indicated clients were frustrated playing "telephone tag" when trying to schedule an appointment (see question 1). We developed a plan that would allow us to hire a part-time receptionist, which in turn improved customer service in scheduling initial appointments. Additionally, our volume increased because clients were able to schedule appointments immediately rather than wait for a therapist to return their call.

Another area of satisfaction that many agencies overlook is their contractor's satisfaction with services. Managed care organizations often incorporate this satisfaction measurement into an annual provider profile or report card. You should learn what variables the MCO evaluates to rate your organization, collecting these data so that you know beforehand the results of your evaluation.

**Cost per unit of service delivery.** The cost per unit of service delivery enables an agency to compare itself with other agencies as well as the expectations of the revenue source. Furthermore, it helps in making decisions regarding case-rate contracts or clients who want to pay cash for services. For example, you decide to help families that have a member diagnosed with attention deficit hyperactivity disorder (ADHD). Your format for treatment is assessment, education, treatment, and follow-up. The assessment costs $65, the education is $70 for a four-hour educational seminar, treatment is $50 per session for an average of five sessions, with one follow-up session two months after the final session for $50. Total cost of this service is $435. Is this cost efficient? How does this cost compare with the costs of others who treat ADHD?

**Outcome measurement.** Thompson and Lyons (1996) discuss the importance of breaking from traditional academic measurements that use control groups and complex statistical compilations, arguing that it's important to use data measurements that measure variables in practice and the degree of change in the course of time. Additionally, it's important to measure similar variables between practice agencies and across geographic locations. The difference lies in what is being measured. In traditional academic settings, the measurement focuses typically on explaining and predicting. Benchmark-data measurement focuses on the degree of change in treatment.

Implementation of an outcomes-management system needs careful consideration (Berman & Hurt, 1996; Zieman & Kramer, 1996). Zieman and Kramer (1996) discuss steps in implementing an outcomes program, concluding that the data collected need to be useful for all payers so quality improvement can be achieved. Berman and Hurt (1996) state, "Clinicians must take on added responsibility for collecting outcomes data, yet may perceive the process as having little relevance to direct patient care" (p. 39).

To create an effective outcome-management system, special consideration should be given to whether the data-collection system is modifiable, the purpose of having outcome measurements, and the ease with which the data can be collected. Any outcome-management system implemented in an agency needs to be easily modifiable. Agencies and payers must continuously try to improve the quality of services. Continuous improvement means that the outcome-measurement process is dynamic, not static. If a process is implemented that cannot be altered, then new variables to measure may be lost because the system determines what gets measured, not what needs to be measured. The second area of consideration is the purpose of the data. Shern and Flynn (1996) state that one principle of outcome assessment is that assessment should be appropriate for the question being dealt with. Some agencies or practices assume the approach of "get as much as we can, then we will figure out what to use." Although this approach to generating outcomes may seem safe and reasonable, it creates unnecessary work for those who collect and process the data. Data that are not processed are useless. Each variable should have a purpose that serves the agency. Vieweg, Graber, Wilson, and Cho (1997) state, "Measuring anything well is better than measuring nothing. Measuring anything poorly is not better than measuring nothing at all" (p. 33). Finally, if the data are difficult to collect, those who collect data will avoid the process. Typically, clinicians collect data because they are in frequent contact with clients. Can the data-collection procedure be streamlined so that it does not intrude on the often overwhelming responsibilities of the clinician? For example, can the client use a touch-screen computer program to enter symptom level prior to starting the session? Berman and Hurt (1996) state that a rule of thumb in helping staff accept such change is ensuring that the process, not the client, is being studied.

**Change for therapists.** Therapists need to dust off their old research methods and statistics books to become involved in outcome measurements. They need to create or purchase computer programs such as databases and spreadsheets that capture relevant data. See Appendix C for a list of measurement tools.

Data are used for two purposes. First, the data highlight areas of development for an agency. These data are important for holding everyone accountable for quality services. Data are also used in marketing. Agencies need to have data about their performance. Service-delivery dollars are granted to agencies that demonstrate efficient and effective services with a high degree of client satisfaction. Without such data, both public and private agencies are not able to market themselves to third-party payers. Because the dollar distribution will continue to be increasingly competitive, the better the data that are collected and reported the better the marketing opportunities that will open up.

# Strengths and Weaknesses of Adapting a Co-Created Marketplace Philosophy

## Strengths

**Accountability.** Accountability is essential in maintaining a clinical practice. Even clinicians who are developing the cash-pay client will find it increasingly difficult to compete for referrals if they do not have a system that integrates accountability.

Accountability helps businesses maintain a competitive edge in marketing, referral, and revenue-source development. The advantages include having sophisticated data that can be used in marketing plans, understanding the agency's strengths and areas of needed improvement, and being more confident that services are quality services.

**Career development.** This co-constructed model of business development allows both veterans and young professionals of behavioral health care more career opportunities. Limiting behavioral health care to the delivery of clinical services is misleading. Opportunities await clinicians in research, marketing, strategic planning, software development, and business consulting. These new career spin-offs of behavioral health care are particularly advantageous to young professionals entering the field. These professionals can be assets to an organization if they have good data-collection or -presentation skills. These young professionals are valuable employees if they know how to build a statistical program to measure effectiveness or understand marketing strategies than can help secure additional revenue sources. However, they need to have training in these areas before they enter the job market.

The behavioral health care field consists of more than therapists and middle managers. Therapists need to be able to assert themselves in the areas of research, administration, program development, and planning. Clinical skills are no more or less important than these other skill areas. For example, I recently had a student who was also very good at building web sites for the Internet. This student was beginning to work with the university and agencies in assisting them with programmed learning formats so that the web sites could be used for self-help purposes. His knowledge about behavioral health care and computers gave him an advantage over many others.

**Financial viability.** Financial viability is probably the most significant advantage of a co-constructed model. We cannot practice our trade if we cannot stay in business. Given that the field is saturated with behavioral health care specialists and universities continue to graduate students at high rates, competition in the field will only increase. A co-constructed business–market relationship assists in the development of financial viability.

**Additional training.** Traditionally, clinicians could be good therapists, find a referral source, do their job, and sustain their professional life. Under this scenario, the therapist's job was to provide therapy. But providing therapy is no longer a necessary and sufficient condition. Clinicians must demonstrate that they have skills in addition to being a good therapist. Good therapists are easy to find in an oversaturated, hypercompetitive field. But good therapists with business planning, computer programming, or research skills are not as easy to find. To remain viable in a highly competitive field, both the experienced clinician and new professional will need to receive additional training. Such training may be in research design and benchmark-data collection, marketing, or writing business plans.

## Weaknesses

**Increased cost.** Implementing a business model can be expensive. Therapists are typically reluctant to invest in research and development of projects. Some projects may require hiring a consultant to examine the feasibility of developing a particular revenue source, hiring a computer consultant to design and implement a management-information system, or simply using a consultant to examine current marketing strategies. These projects are not profitable immediately and may not be profitable at all. However, without them the business may fail. If a new tool becomes available that has the potential to increase profits, the business should seriously consider purchasing the tool. The business may need to secure a small business loan in order to purchase the tool, with a plan on how the tool can pay for itself over the years. Today's office needs to have a facsimile machine, computer, research tools (paper-and-pencil assessment tools), and a copy machine. The agency may need to invest in a statistical package, a server to allow for integration of services, a separate telephone line for Internet and server applications, and self-help computer programs. These tools are no longer supplements to clinical services, but rather essential tools that are critical for survival.

**Increased practice size.** To maintain viability, clinicians need to pool their talents and financial resources. Group practice is a major adaptation for many clinicians.

Some clinicians are difficult to work with in a team-business approach because they have been working independently for such a long period.

**Few trainers.** Many clinical trainers are available, but few professionals have experience in both the clinical and business worlds to help train today's professionals and students.

Universities need to adapt accordingly. Professors who see five or six clients per week while teaching at the university may be less qualified to teach students about running a successful business in clinical service delivery than is someone who is in the throes of practice management. To adapt and preserve our professional status in the community, universities must prepare students to enter this new generation of service delivery. Regardless of our role in the service-delivery continuum, we will need new knowledge and skills that allow us to interact with the business community.

# Application

## *Business Profile*

You are a co-owner of ASCJ Problem-Solving Center. Your business has been successful adapting to the managed care market because your treatment philosophy is consistent with that of managed care; that is, treatment should be goal directed, have measurable outcomes, and achieve a high degree of satisfaction from clients and payers. However, in the past 18 months, your referrals have been declining from two sources and no one seems to know why. Also, you are becoming frustrated with one managed care organization and want to expand your referral base from other sources. What steps should you take?

First, you need an objective picture of your organization. According to your revenue-distribution profile (see Table 2), revenue from MCO X has decreased by 11% in four years, MCO Y has decreased by 4%, cash-pay has increased 12%, consultation has decreased by 4%, and PPO A has increased by 7%. Are these changes favorable?

Your agency's goal was to decrease MCO X by 10% because this MCO was too demanding and paid too little. You accomplished this goal. However, you enjoyed working with MCO Y and were attempting to grow the revenue source. Your organization had moved steadily toward this goal until 1995 (+7%), but 1996 saw an 11% drop in revenue. What happened? Also, you wanted to increase the PPO A revenue, as it is a very user-friendly system, but the same dynamic occurred: You increased

**TABLE 2.** *Percentage of revenue distribution for ASCJ Problem-Solving Center.*

| Revenue | 1993 (%) | 1994 (%) | 1995 (%) | 1996 (%) |
|---|---|---|---|---|
| MCO X | 48 | 45 | 39 | 37 |
| MCO Y | 28 | 30 | 35 | 24 |
| Cash pay | 3 | 7 | 2 | 15 |
| Consultation | 11 | 5 | 3 | 7 |
| PPO A | 10 | 13 | 21 | 17 |
| Total | 100 | 100 | 100 | 100 |

business generally, but experienced a 4% drop in revenue between 1995 and 1996. How do you interpret these fluctuations? Do these reductions mean that your agency is not meeting market needs?

### Learn About Your Market

What do MCO Y and PPO A expect from your agency? How do you gain such information? You and your partners decide to hire a health care strategist to develop a strategic plan that will help you meet the market needs of these two revenue sources. This plan will cost $5,000. At $60 per session and four sessions per client ($240 per referral), you will need 21 new referrals to pay for the investment. You and your partners agree that the cost–benefit analysis presents a reasonable risk and hire the strategist. The health care strategist files a report outlining current market expectations, the changes ASCJ Problem-Solving Center will need to make, and a strategy for making such changes (see Appendix D).

### Goal Setting

The ASCJ Problem-Solving Center now recognizes the needs of the market and must begin to co-construct a relationship that will benefit the agency and exploit the market. Realizing that this plan will not bear a return on the investment for possibly 18 months, you and your partners need to set specific goals for getting this plan accomplished. The health care strategist outlined some general goals. You must break these into achievable and observable goals. Also, are staff equally motivated to accomplish these goals?

You decide that you want to be more aggressive in implementing these strategies. In order to be more aggressive, staff need to be given authority to make decisions and implement strategies swiftly. This style of running the business is related directly to the trust and teamwork among the owners.

### Strategy Management

Evaluating benchmarks every two or three months is necessary in that you have set an aggressive plan to make changes in co-constructing a relationship with the clinical services market. Additionally, the ASCJ Problem-Solving Center will need to assess its practice profile every six months to measure whether this strategy is working. You might find that when you implement your server system, you are able to gain referrals from unanticipated referral and revenue sources. Also, you will need to measure the impact of your strategy on your finances in order to assess the return on the investment.

## Conclusions

A few leaders in the behavioral heath care field have always been aware and knowledgeable about the need for good business practices in the delivery of clinical services. These administrators worked hard to secure funding from targeted sources. Whether an administrator of a community mental health center trying to secure state and federal grants, or the director of an EAP trying to sell services to a corporation, these individuals applied sound business principles in their work. They dealt with political and power issues, built and nurtured collaborative relationships with funding sources, and set financial goals for their organization. However, in many organizations, clinicians, intake workers, program planners, and others did not understand how revenue sources were developed and maintained. Today, however, everyone must play an integral role in maintaining the viability of an organization. From data collection to accountability for services to marketing, team effort is needed to create and maintain a vital behavioral health care business.

Constructivism plays an integral role in creating this team effort—from defining quality to encouraging employees to create a culture of accountability to developing business relationships and working with the market. As the field continues to mature, the ability to construct productive working relationships in the business sector will be vital to an agency's success.

The changes occurring in the field are not limited to specific clinical delivery systems. For profits, not for profits, community agencies, social service sectors, child-placement agencies, and private companies will be affected by the changes. Clinical service delivery systems must adapt to the changes and begin training personnel to work toward agencies' goals.

The process of co-constructing relationships with the marketplace is similar to co-constructing therapeutic relationships. Clinicians have experience with and knowledge about this process and need to use it to strengthen their position in the behavioral health care marketplace.

# References

Berg, I., & Miller, S. (1992). *Working with the problem drinker: A solution-focused approach.* New York: W. W. Norton.

Berman, W. H., & Hurt, S. W. (1996). Talking the talk, walking the walk: Implementing an outcomes information system. *Behavioral Healthcare Tomorrow, 5*(3), 39–43.

Cade, B., & O'Hanlon, W. H. (1993). *A brief guide to brief therapy.* New York: W. W. Norton.

Capezio, P., & Morehouse, D. (1993). *Taking the mystery out of TQM: A practical guide to total quality management.* Hawthorne, NJ: Career Press.

de Shazer, S. (1985). *Keys to solution in brief therapy.* New York: W. W. Norton.

DiClemente, C. C. (1991). Motivational interviewing and the stages of change. In W. H. Miller & S. Rollnick (Eds.), *Motivational interviewing: Preparing people to change addictive behavior* (pp. 191–202). New York: Guilford.

Haley, J. (1976). *Problem-solving therapy: New strategies for effective family therapy.* San Francisco: Jossey-Bass.

Johansson, H. J., McHugh, P., Pendlebury, A. J., & Wheeler, W. A. (1993). *Business process reengineering: Breakpoint strategies for market dominance.* New York: Wiley.

Lamb, R., & Lamson, G. (1996). Overcoming barriers to comprehensive quality improvement. *Behavioral Healthcare Tomorrow, 5*(3), 33–37.

Managed care insider warns about healthcare market: The new wave. (1996, December). *Family Therapy News,* pp. 7, 30.

Merit lists 13 clinical specialties; recruits elite provider core for referrals. (1995, November). *Practice*

*Strategies, 1*(10), 1, 7.

Niche marketing: Finding profitable practice niches. (1996, May). *Psychotherapy Finances, 22*(5), 1–3.

O'Hanlon, W. H., & Weiner-Davis, M. (1989). *In search of solutions: A new direction in psychotherapy.* New York: W. W. Norton.

*Random House college dictionary.* (1979). New York: Random House.

Shern, D., & Flynn, L. (1996). The outcomes roundtable: Developing, evaluating, and disseminating outcomes monitoring technology. *Behavioral Healthcare Tomorrow, 5*(3), 25–30.

Thompson, B. J., & Lyons, J. (1996). Lessons from the front: Implementing outcomes projects. *Behavioral Healthcare Tomorrow, 5*(5), 85–87.

Todd, T. (1994). *Surviving and prospering in the managed mental health care marketplace.* Sarasota, FL: Professional Resource Press.

Vieweg, B., Graber, P., Wilson, R., & Cho, D. (1997). Missouri's statewide outcomes study: Lessons and surprises from the public sector. *Behavioral Healthcare Tomorrow, 6*(2), 31–34.

Walter, J., & Peller, J. (1992). *Becoming solution-focused in brief therapy.* New York: Bruner/Mazel.

Weil, M., & Rosen, L. (1994). The "psychology" of technology. *Behavioral Healthcare Tomorrow 3*(3), 37–39.

Zieman, G., & Kramer, T. (1996). Implementing a practice-based outcomes program. *Behavioral Healthcare Tomorrow, 5*(3), 65–67.

# Appendix A

## *Companies That Focus on Outcome Measurements or Management Information*

*Data management services*
Compass Information Services
1060 First Ave, #4120
King of Prussia, PA 19406
610-992-7069

*Data collection systems and tools*
DeltaMetrics
800-238-2433

*Management information systems*
CMHC Systems
570 Metro Place North
Dublin, OH 43017
800-434-CMHC
http://mis.cmhc.com

*Data management system for outcome measurements OQ45.2 and YOQ*
Algorithms for Behavioral Care
800-357-1200
http://www.regimen.com

*Software applications for practice management*
UniCare
1010 High House Road, #301
Cary, NC 27513
941-467-9295

*Evaluation of health care services*
Performance Based Outcomes
http://consultnews.com

*Software systems*
Echo Management Group
800-635-8209
http://www.echoman.com

*Integrated clinical information system*
PsychServ
419-531-4442
http://www.psychserv.com

*Interactive assistance in clinical decision making*
Quality First
800-241-9611

*Informational technologies for managing behavioral health care*
Medipay
800-842-1973
email: medipay@medipay.com

# Appendix B

## *Follow-up Questionnaire Used by Brief Therapy Institute of Denver*

Circle one number

| | | | | |
|---|---|---|---|---|
| 1. Did you have difficulty getting an initial appointment with this clinic or therapist? | 1 Great difficulty | 2 Moderate difficulty | 3 Little difficulty | 4 No difficulty |

If you experienced difficulty, what was the problem? _____

_____

_____

| | | | | |
|---|---|---|---|---|
| 2. How convenient is the location of this clinic/therapist? | 1 Not at all | 2 Somewhat | 3 Pretty | 4 Very |
| 3. How did you find the offices of this clinic to be? | 1 Very uncomfortable | 2 Somewhat uncomfortable | 3 Mostly comfortable | 4 Very comfortable |
| 4. How satisfied were you with the therapy you received? | 1 Not satisfied | 2 Somewhat | 3 Satisfied | 4 Very satisfied |
| 5. Please rate the effectiveness of your treatment providers. | 1 Not effective | 2 Somewhat | 3 Effective | 4 Very effective |
| 6. Comparing your situation to before treatment, how would you describe it now? | 1 Worse | 2 Same | 3 Moderately improved | 4 Very improved |
| 7. How much have you accomplished in treatment? | 1 Very little | 2 Some | 3 Satisfactory | 4 A lot |
| 8. How hard are you working in therapy? | 1 Very little | 2 Some | 3 Satisfactory | 4 A lot |
| 9. Have the services you received helped you to deal more effectively with your problems? | 1 No, made things worse | 2 No | 3 Yes | 4 Yes, they helped greatly |
| 10. Do you feel that the clinic/therapist kept your problems confidential? | 1 No, they did not | 2 It appears they didn't | 3 Yes, they have | 4 Yes, they have clearly |

11. My last counseling session was _____ weeks or days ago, or the date _____

12. For how many sessions did you see a therapist? _____

13. How many days did it take for you to get your initial appointment? _____

14. Has there been a change in any of the following? (Please circle all that apply to you.)

| | | | |
|---|---|---|---|
| Medical problems | Improved | Same | Worsened |
| Work/school problems | Improved | Same | Worsened |
| Alcohol or drug use | Improved | Same | Worsened |

| Out-of-control behavior | Improved | Same | Worsened |
| Personal relationships | Improved | Same | Worsened |
| Overall functioning | Improved | Same | Worsened |

15. Do you have any comments or suggestions that may help improve the quality of care delivered in this clinic?

_____

_____


# Appendix C

## *Outcome Measurement Tools*

*An extensive reference guide to the listing of outcome tools*
Behavioral Healthcare Outcomes
National Community Mental Healthcare Council
12300 Twinbrook Parkway, #320
Rockville, MD 20852
301-984-6200

*System inventory for use by clinician or client*
Behavior and Symptom Identification Scale (Basis-32)
Evaluative Services Unit
McLean Hospital
115 Mill Street
Belmont, MA 02178-9106
617-855-2425

*Symptom inventory for adults*
Ask for the YOQ for children OQ45.2
American Professional Credentialing
10421 Stevenson Rd., Box 346
Stevenson, MD 21153-0346
410-329-3777

*Health status survey*
SF-36
Medical Outcomes Trust
P.O. Box 1917
Boston, MA 02205-8516
617-426-4046

*Substance abuse survey*
Substance Use Disorder Diagnosis Schedule (SUDDS)
New Standards, Inc.
1080 Montreal Ave., #300
St. Paul, MN 55116
612-690-1002

*Satisfaction survey with variables that can be compared to national norms*
MHCA Satisfaction System
800-447-3068

# Appendix D

*Needs Analysis Report for the ASCJ Problem-Solving Center*

## Question: What needs to be done to increase revenue from MCO Y and PPO A?

### *MCO Y*

Following an investigation into what MCO Y expects from its providers, the provider-relations director reported two major changes. First, MCO Y began experimenting with provider groups that have computer capabilities to allow for integration of services; that is, MCO Y was using agencies that could interface electronically with them for appointment setting and billing. One goal was to have clients make only one telephone call before getting an appointment. When potential clients called MCO Y, the intake specialist would access an electronic server and immediately set the appointment for the client and therapist, thereby decreasing the need for the client to leave a message on voice mail. Previously, it sometimes took hours or days before an appointment was set with the therapist. With a server system, clients' appointments were set immediately, thereby increasing accessibility.

The second change was also part of the integrated delivery system. MCO Y has moved to electronic billing from agencies and is striving for a paperless billing system. In 1996, MCO Y experimented with agencies that worked under one tax identification number and could electronically bill the MCO. This integration of services had an impact on ASCJ Problem-Solving Center's revenue in that MCO Y favored those groups with the capability to engage in the pilot project.

### *PPO A*

Regarding PPO A, the ASCJ Problem-Solving Center could do little to keep from losing this business. Four major employers near the ASCJ Problem-Solving Center changed mental health benefits. This change in benefits decreased the number of employees accessing care from the ASCJ Problem-Solving Center.

## Strategies

The ASCJ Problem-Solving Center has done an exceptional job in meeting market demands of accountability. The center has implemented rigorous data-collection systems that will benefit the agency in the long term. Especially important are the satisfaction-survey results and the outcome measurements currently in place. Nearly all referral and revenue sources will desire these data-collection variables.

### *MCO Y*

In developing these data-collection systems, the agency may have overlooked some opportunities in helping MCOs improve accessibility of care to their client populations. Because the center already has the computer sophistication to generate data, developing a server system seems a wise move. A server system will allow a more integrated service-delivery system with MCOs as they need these systems.

### *PPO A*

The ASCJ Problem-Solving Center made the mistake of relying on random referrals from the PPO. When the major employers changed the benefit plans, subjecting the center to economic changes beyond its control, the center lost revenue.

A strategy for the next 18 months is to investigate the primary-care physicians who are also part of this PPO and located within a three-mile radius of the center. Targeting these primary-care offices as potential referral sources is critical for referral development. Also, the major employers switched their benefits to PPO B and a staff model HMO. Your group may need to work at getting into the PPO B panel. By focusing on integrated billing, you have excellent potential for acceptance.

# Strategic Planning for the Next 18 Months

## *MCO Y*

*First 6 months*
1. Investigate and implement a server system that will set appointments by an MCO or office manager for all clinicians involved with the ASCJ Problem-Solving Center.
2. Investigate converting to electronic billing to streamline the billing process.
3. Meet with the provider-relations director of MCO Y and educate this person about your plan for a new computer system that will allow you to integrate appointment setting with them.

*Months 6–12*
1. Meet with the provider-relations director of MCO Y and devise a plan about how you can enter into any pilot projects and begin receiving referrals with this system.
2. Meet with other MCOs you want to do business with and educate them about your new integrated system capabilities for appointment setting.
3. Have an integrated billing system ready so you can capitalize on any requests to implement such a system.

*Months 12–18*
1. Implement the integrated appointment-setting system.
2. Implement the integrated billing system with companies wanting to engage in such a system.
3. Educate all MCOs that these systems are now in place.

## *PPO A*

*First 6 months*
1. Compile a list of all primary-care physicians in three-mile radius.
2. Compile a list of all primary-care physicians of the clients you have seen in the past 12 months, noting those physicians with whom you have had a positive working relationship.
3. Develop a marketing brochure specifically for the primary-care physicians.

*Months 6–12*
1. Begin to market the primary-care physicians you have worked with productively.

*Months 12–18*
1. Contact primary-care physicians with whom you have not worked (cold call).
2. Track the primary-care physicians you marketed to in months 6–12 for referrals. Follow up as is needed.

# Summary

The ASCJ Problem-Solving Center has an excellent opportunity to meet its goals and recover business from the desired referral sources. Making these changes (integrated billing and appointment setting, primary-care-physician-referral development) will position the center for short- and long-term business viability.

The center has the computer sophistication to begin working with an integrated delivery system. This adaptation not only will increase its potential to regain business lost, but will also make it attractive to other MCOs looking for such a system. The emphasis on primary-care physician-referral development will add stability to the practice because it will assist in bypassing toll-free telephone-referral systems, create diverse referral streams, and most likely create a higher level of quality in service delivery as a result of coordinated care.

# 17

# A Technically Eclectic Blend of Paradigms and Epistemologies for Multicultural Clinical Relevance

*Roberto Cortéz González*

*Keep in mind that negative connotation, or the invalidation, of any major participant (including one's colleagues) is destructive to the process of opening space for conversation. (Anderson & Goolishian, 1991, p. 7)*

*An important question for the future [given social constructionism's intertextual relationship to a number of intellectual traditions] concerns the desirability of domain sanctity, that is, the value of clear differentiations between one conceptual orientation and another. ... Depending on pragmatic considerations, there are times when generic purity may be usefully sacrificed for alternative ends, and a ... mixing of [related genres, with little concern for purity] may be counted as desirable. (K. J. Gergen, 1994b, p. 69)*

*In terms of [social constructionist] therapy practice, we must consistently ask ourselves whether or not we believe that we offer truth to our clients and we must guard against the seduction of certainty. We must consider whether or not we are behaving in a manner that is consistent with what it is we say we believe and avoid portraying ourselves as experts. We must also avoid pathologizing language and must be sensitive to the impact of discourse at many levels. ... We must consider what we are communicating, both by what we say and by what we don't say, what we do and what we don't do. (Becvar & Becvar, 1996, p. 95)*

These three quotations signify my current *location of study* for a technically eclectic blend of *paradigms* and *epistemologies* for multicultural clinical practice. Richardson (1993) discusses location of study as a point of view that roots knowledge in subjective reality. Rosenau (1992) refers to it as *situated knowledge*. *Paradigm* refers to "a central overall way of regarding phenomena [and] may dictate what type of explanation will be found acceptable" (Flew, 1984, p. 261). As explained by Arndt (1985), a paradigm outlines appropriate domains for (a) a field of inquiry, (b) its research agenda and methodology, and (c) how research results are to be interpreted. With multicultural clients, I find it increasingly effective to work with their multiple explanations for construing both their intrapersonal and interactional processes. In my current situated knowledge, I find it clinically pragmatic to intermingle postmodern epistemologies. *Epistemology* refers to "the nature and derivation of knowledge, the scope of knowledge, and the reliability of claims to knowledge" (Flew, 1984, p. 109). Epistemology is the theory of knowledge or the study of beliefs about knowledge (Peterson, 1970). It concerns itself with views of how people come to know about their world and with the standards used to judge knowledge as informative (Dervin, 1994).

My location of study, or working model for clinical practice, takes a pragmatic approach that strives to honor and respect multicultural clients' multiple perspectives, regardless of whether these perspectives fit a romantic, modernist, or postmodernist intellectual tradition. Romantics place primary emphasis on the soul and believe that meaning resides in the individual (K. J. Gergen, 1991b, 1994b; Savickas, 1993). Modernists emphasize objective knowledge and stable predispositions revealed by the scientific method and believe that meaning resides in the world. Postmodernists emphasize subjective knowledge and contextual ways of being, with meaning residing in the language used to interpret and inscribe various life situations.

It would be inaccurate to refer to this blending of paradigms as an integrated framework, which connotes "a kind of scaffold or structure for organizing knowledge, questions, and so forth. . . . It is useful for organizing 'knowledge out there' and implies an independence or disconnection between the knower and the known" (Richardson, 1993, p. 427). In contrast with such a framework, a location of study is the perspective of the knower in relation to what is known; admittedly, one's situated knowledge is affected by the location of the knower (Richardson, 1993).

*Both* the process *and* the content of my clinical work parallel the technical eclecticism of Lazarus (1992), whose multimodal therapy derives techniques from several theoretical approaches, even though these theories have incompatible underlying assumptions. Use of various techniques does not mean that one subscribes fully to the theories upon which these counseling tools were based originally. Rather, the techniques are used according to client needs, and theoretical integration is minimal. In a similar fashion, the therapeutic interventions that I use are drawn from diverse paradigms—romantic, modernist, postmodernist—even though, fundamentally, these paradigms are epistemologically incompatible. My clinical judgments are based in part on how my clients guide me, according to the features and themes of their lived experiences, or "culture tales" (Howard, 1991). Accordingly, I strive to respond in a systematic manner by using the paradigmatic dialect(s) most meaningful for clients and that facilitate change for them. How clients self-define what brought them to therapy and the therapeutic changes that clients make by developing new meanings in their lives will reflect clients' *contextualized knowledge* (K. J. Gergen, 1985) relative to their own time and place. I begin by exploring clients' current constructions of reality and work from there. Multiculturalism as a philosophical orientation also contributes to what I refer to as responding systematically. For another example of the use of a multimodal perspective in therapy, see Baillie and Corrie (1996).

# Multiculturalism in Clinical Practice

## *Definition of Multiculturalism*

For the purposes of this chapter, multicultural clinical practice is defined in two different ways. First, the definition of culture offered by Pedersen (1990) to enhance a multicultural perspective in therapy includes demographic variables (age, sex, place of residence), ethnographic variables (nationality, ethnicity, language, religion), status variables (social, educational, and economic), and affiliations (formal and informal). Every clinical encounter becomes multicultural when clinician and client differ according to such variables. Culture is broadly defined in that it is extremely unlikely that a clinician and client will match up exactly on these variables.

The second definition of multicultural clinical practice reflects the multicultural counseling and therapy (MCT) of Sue, Ivey, and Pedersen (1996). First, MCT is a metatheory, or "theory of theories" (Sue et al., 1996, p. 12), that forms a means of understanding the numerous helping approaches that humankind has developed. Both theories of counseling and therapy developed in the Western world and those helping models that are indigenous to non-Western cultures are judged neither right nor wrong, good nor bad. Instead, each theory is seen as representing a different world view. Second, the totality of experience (individual, group, and universal) and contexts (individual, family, and cultural milieu) must be the focus of treatment. Third, the development of a cultural identity is a major determinant of clinician and client attitudes toward self, others of the same group, others of a different group, and the dominant group. The dynamics of dominant–subordinate relationships among culturally different groups also influence clinician–client attitudes. Fourth, MCT is most effective when the clinician uses modalities and defines goals consistent with the life experiences and cultural values of the client. Fifth, MCT theory emphasizes multiple helping roles—the one-to-one encounter aimed at remediation in the individual, larger social units, systems intervention, and prevention—developed by various culturally different groups and societies. Sixth, MCT theory emphasizes the importance of expanding personal, family, group, and organizational consciousness into self-in-relation, family-in-relation, and organization-in-relation; the resulting therapy is ultimately contextual in orientation as well as allows for the use of traditional methods of healing from various cultures. For the numerous corollaries that accompany these six basic propositions of MCT and its clinical application, see Sue et al. (1996).

## *Critique of Multiculturalism*

These definitions of multiculturalism have both limitations and strengths. For example, a clear distinction between culture and ethnicity is lacking in Pedersen's definition. He also neglects to mention sexual orientation and members of disabled communities as variables in his broad definition of culture. Others have raised concerns that multiculturalism confounds race with culture (Helms & Richardson, 1997). As a metatheory, MCT "is far removed from the realities of work with clients" (see Chapter 11, p. 253). My own multicultural clinical work extends beyond what MCT theory has initially articulated in at least one way. I use a multi-disciplinary approach, incorporating counseling psychology, marriage and family therapy, group therapy, and career development, among other disciplines. Multicultural counseling and therapy theory is just beginning to do this.

On the other hand, a major strength is that Pedersen (1990) differentiates between "multicultural counseling" and "the multicultural perspective," the latter phrase being relatively new (Baruth & Manning, 1991). Multicultural counseling refers to a specialized aspect or subfield, whereas the multicultural perspective expands beyond all previously used terms (e.g., minority-group counseling, pluralistic counseling, cross-cultural counseling) and represents *a philosophical orientation* that encompasses the entire field of clinical practice. Another strength of these definitions of multiculturalism is that their contextual ways of being are shared by postmodernism. To say that a definition has a contextual way of being is similar to an idea current in social psychology that situationalism, rather than dispositionalism (i.e., traits), predominantly influences people's behavior (Ross & Nisbett, 1991). Therefore, the identity and existence of every sociocultural environment depend on the meaning that human beings give to it, and humans, in turn, are changed by the sociocultural environment (Pedersen, 1991).

Ontologically, my clients are *pluralistic* in terms of their beliefs about the nature of reality, human beings, and existence (Dervin, 1994; Gonçalves, 1995a; Peterson, 1970). *Pluralism* has been defined as conditions that produce sustained ethnic differentiation and continued heterogeneity in society (Abramson, 1980). Pluralism affirms distinctive attachments and *world views* among individuals and groups. "A *world view* can be thought of as the frame of reference through which one experiences life. It is the foundation for values, beliefs, attitudes, [and] relations" (italics added; Fouad & Bingham, 1995, p. 335).

## Blending Paradigms: Romantic, Modern, and Postmodern

To open and maintain a space for conversation (Anderson & Goolishian, 1991) with multicultural clients, I find it clinically pragmatic to blend paradigms. In that all human constructs are fallible, I find it difficult to accept that one paradigm is ultimately and always more useful or effective than another. If a client presents his or her issues in modernist terms, then a modernist approach in therapy work is likely to be most effective. This approach is consistent with a multicultural perspective in that it recognizes the importance of clients' values and goals (Pedersen, 1990; Sue, 1992).

**Romanticism.** K. J. Gergen (1991b, 1994b) discusses the Romantic age of the late 18th century and early 19th century, a period when "many romantics considered the central inhabitant of the deep interior to be the soul" (K. J. Gergen, 1991b, p. 20). As summarized by Savickas (1993), during the Romantic age (a) meaning resided in the person, (b) internal feelings were valued and creativity was conceptualized as a reflection of our divine origins, and (c) individual effort and self-expression defined success.

**Modernism.** The modern age, the late 19th century and early 20th century, valued systematic observation and reasoning, a throwback to the Enlightenment era of the late 17th and early 18th centuries. Reason prevailed over emotion (K. J. Gergen, 1991b). Experimentation flourished in the sciences, the arts, urban planning, and public administration, among other diverse disciplines. *Positivism* and *empiricism* were hallmark features of the modern age. *Positivism* contends that "all genuine knowledge is contained within the boundaries of science . . . the systematic study of human nature and human needs would provide . . . a truly scientific basis for the reorganization of society" (Flew, 1984, p. 283). *Empiricism* views valid knowledge as "that which is derived from observation and experiment" (Burr, 1995, p. 184). During the modern age, (a) meaning resided in the world (Savickas, 1993), (b) facts were valued (Savickas, 1993), and (c) from a psychological standpoint, the human essence was revealed as rational (K. J. Gergen, 1991b). Humans were conceptualized as being consistent or stable over time. An individual's essence could be identified like a fingerprint or a birthmark.

**Postmodernism.** O'Hara and Anderson (1991) contend that "without quite noticing it" (p. 20), we have moved into a postmodern world. The cumulative effects of pluralism, democracy, religious freedom, consumerism, mobility, and the rise of the information age are reflected in an emerging social consciousness made up of many beliefs, multiple realities, and a profusion of world views. The absolute truth of modernism has yielded to "social constructions of reality" (O'Hara & Anderson, 1991, p. 22). Likewise, K. J. Gergen (1991b) asserts that the technological advances of the late 20th century—computers, electronic mail, satellites, faxes—mark an accelerating social connectedness that is leading to a state of "multiphrenia," whereby the individual is split into multiple self-investments. The coherent and unified sense of self inherent in modernist conceptualizations is giving way to "ever shifting, concatenating, and contentious currents of being" (K. J. Gergen, 1991b, p. 80). Thus, postmodernism rejects notions that hold that (a) an ultimate truth exists, (b) the world as we see it is the result of hidden structures, and (c) the world can be understood in terms of the so-called universal Grand Narrative of the 20th century (Burr, 1995). Savickas (1993) defines the Grand Narrative as society advancing "toward the better or new with the gradual yet steady progress of reason and freedom and the forward march of human productive capacities" (p. 211). Postmodernism replaces the search for absolute truth with a celebration of equally valid perspectives (Burr, 1995).

## Intermingling Postmodern Epistemologies

Broadly speaking, a constructivist epistemology views humans as "active agents who, individually or collectively, co-constitute the meaning of their experiential world" (R. A. Neimeyer, 1993a, p. 222). Constructivists assert that humans actively construct their personal realities and create their own representational models of the world (Meichenbaum & Fong, 1993). Social constructionists assert that humans develop meanings and understandings of the world through social interaction (K. J. Gergen,

1985). Franklin (Chapter 3) also provides helpful delineations between constructivists and social constructionists.

K. J. Gergen (1985, 1994b) attempts to keep social constructionism as he develops it separate from constructivism. He notes two points of convergence between these conceptual orientations: (a) an emphasis on the constructed nature of knowledge, which challenges the foundationalist (i.e., the pregiven principles) of empirical science, and (b) a challenge to the view of the individual mind as a reflection of an independently knowable world. Yet, K. J. Gergen (1994b) states that, for the social constructionist, neither "mind" nor "world" is granted ontological status, that both are merely social constructs of fundamental categories of being and existence, which therefore removes the grounding assumptions of constructivism. "For the [social] constructionist, terms for both world and mind are constituents of discursive practices; they are integers within language and thus themselves socially contested and negotiated" (K. J. Gergen, 1994b, p. 68). He also takes issue with constructivist epistemology remaining grounded within the tradition of Western individualism and with knowledge claims primarily as intrinsic processes within the individual. K. J. Gergen (1991b) envisions an "erasure" of the individual self and replaces it with a *"populating of the self"* reflecting the infusion of partial identities through the *"technologies of social saturation"* (p. 49; italics in the original). For K. J. Gergen (1994b), social constructionism traces the sources of human action to relationships and the understanding of "individual functioning" to communal interchange. Rather than allowing private experience, which is cherished by many people, K. J. Gergen (1994b) adopts a social constructionist standpoint and attends to *"discourse about experience"* (p. 71; italics in the original). *Discourse* refers to "a system of statements, practices, and institutional structures that share common values" (Hare-Mustin, 1994, p. 19). In social constructionist discourse, the paramount question would remain one of social consequence.

## *Critiques of Postmodernism*

Social constructionism has generated several recent exchanges (e.g., Denner, 1995; Fisher, 1995a, 1995b; Freeman, 1995; Harré, 1995; Hermans, 1995; K. J. Gergen, 1994a, 1995; M. Gergen, 1995; Mente, 1995; Richardson, 1993; Russell & Gaubatz, 1995; Savickas, 1994; Shotter, 1995; M. B. Smith, 1994, 1995; Tinsley, 1994) and critiques (e.g., Efran & Clarfield, 1992; Mascolo & Dalto, 1995; R. A. Neimeyer, Neimeyer, Lyddon, & Hoshmand, 1994). For instance, Fisher (1995b) states,

> *My general concern is that social constructionists overemphasize social context and eclipse individual rights and existence as selves and persons. If moral rules are normative and based on local moral practices only (K. J. Gergen, 1985), then tyrannical norms can result in social agreements that define away or suspend human rights. (p. 344)*

Others have asserted that, unchecked, socially constructed realities can discount the personal experiences of survivors of sexual abuse (Bass & Davis, 1988) and of adolescent females (Gilligan & Noel, 1995; Pipher, 1994; Taylor, Gilligan, & Sullivan, 1995). In more general terms,

*The more I am exposed to readings on postmodernism, to other self-identified postmodern practitioners, and to lower-income and culturally diverse clients, the more I prefer using* both *constructivism* and *social constructionism in my therapy and supervision work. Constructivism allows for a retention of personal responsibility that can balance social constructionism from deteriorating into political manipulation and/or oppressive conspiracies of silence. (González, 1997, p. 379)*

In alcohol- and drug-abuse counseling circles, the phrases "talking the talk" and "walking the walk" are often used. Similarly, I am not convinced that social constructionist therapists "walk the walk" in terms of (a) refraining from denigrating those not of their ideological clique, (b) living outside the therapy room in a manner consistent with what social constructionists say they believe, and (c) explicitly and continually acknowledging that not everyone lives in a postmodern world.

Held (1990) takes issue with the intellectual integrity of multiple realities, stating, "The view that we cannot, under any circumstances, know an independent reality is itself, paradoxically, a reality claim" (p. 181). Coyne (1985) writes of external forces that affect clients' lives that cannot be ignored, such as social conditions that perpetuate the disenfranchisement of African Americans in the United States (Hacker, 1992). Minuchin (1991) warns of postmodern therapists who deny the legitimacy of their own clinical expertise to avoid the appearance of control, thereby anointing themselves as the new crew of experts. He cautions against practitioners who risk becoming clinically irrelevant by getting too wrapped up in abstractions about the subjectivity of all truths. Nonpracticing theoreticians can add to such irrelevance. Efran, Lukens, and Lukens (1988) warn against postmodernism's trifling with language and meanings. Coale (1992) states, "The emphasis on language as *the* mechanism for changing meaning is a contradiction of the constructivist position that all reality is nonobjective and, therefore, that there is room for many ways of understanding and doing anything" (p. 23; italics in the original). She does not view language as being any less instrumental than are behavioral interventions, adding that, in many circumstances, nonverbal interventions (such as art therapy) can be more effective than language in facilitating change. Persons with sensory impairments (i.e., blindness or deafness) may have mechanisms other than language to obtain meaning.

Multiculturally speaking, "what a person says can either be enhanced or negated by his/her nonverbals" (Sue & Sue, 1990, p. 52). Nonverbal communication can be extremely powerful because it tends to be least under conscious control. Often, gestures and facial expressions reveal more than words can ever say. H. Smith (1989), in *Beyond the Post-modern Mind,* discusses how it took confrontations between cultures to bring home the fact that people see the world differently, but that the pendulum has swung too far in the direction of multiplicity. "Multiple views, yes; multiple realities, no. . . . Even if reality were no more than the sum of all . . . multiple realities . . . that sum would stand as the inclusive reality which would not itself be multiple" (pp. 224–235). All movements, whether political or intellectual, have their developmental phases. The postmodern movement, which is both political and intellectual, faces the challenge of transcending the "absolute relativism" of some of its more extreme adherents.

## Forms of Constructivism

Constructivist practitioners are likely to have different forms of constructivism that have contributed to the evolution of their clinical practice. During my doctoral training, I had a strong cognitive–behavioral and social learning foundation, the latter of which Lyddon (1995) has typified as *efficient constructivism.* In postdoctoral supervision, I was exposed to narrative approaches and systems theory, which Lyddon (1995) typified as *formal constructivism* and *final constructivism,* respectively.

**Efficient constructivism.** Efficient constructivism presumes that an ontological reality exists independently of the knower. This form of constructivism has a modernist basis. The world is objectively detected rather than subjectively created. Environmental inputs are interpreted and stored as meaningful information. The knower acts on such information if it is useful. As exemplified by social learning theory, the environment functions as an antecedent variable that linearly directs the knowledge structures that humans must come to know. Information is preformed in external reality (i.e., social and environmental sources of information). From a therapeutic perspective, inaccurate and distorted information processing is at the root of many emotional and behavioral problems. Behaviors are shaped by and may be modified by natural or programmed reinforcers or punishments (Bandura, 1977, 1985; Krumboltz, 1979).

**Formal constructivism.** Formal constructivist theories "assume that reality, rather than being static and categorically knowable, is instead active, ongoing, and socially constituted" (Lyddon, 1995, p. 76). Human activity is situated within an historical event alive in its present context of meanings and relationships. As exemplified by social constructionism, the approach to human knowing emphasizes the inseparable connection among psychological (personally constructed), contextual (socially constructed), and temporal dimensions of experience. From a therapeutic perspective, narrative approaches concern themselves with the stories people create and tell to make sense of their world and are proposed as a viable alternative to the positivist paradigm (Sarbin, 1986). The literary qualities of therapeutic discourses are emphasized. Shared language and meaning systems that develop, persist, and evolve in the course of time constrain constructions of understanding (Lyddon, 1995). Narrative approaches are one of several social constructionist therapies. Corey (1996) provides an excellent introduction to these various approaches. Becvar and Becvar (1996) would serve as a useful follow-up to Corey.

**Final constructivism.** Final constructivism views knowledge as dynamic and directional (Lyddon, 1995). As time passes, knowledge structures are believed to undergo qualitative shifts or transformations in organization toward increased complexity and abstraction. As exemplified by systems perspectives, the dynamic changes that a system may undergo in adapting to both internal and external sources of stress may be one of two types: equilibrium and dissipative change. Equilibrium change refers to a dynamically maintained (ordered) change that preserves the basic structure of a system. Dissipative change refers to a nonlinear transformation in system structures and a qualitative reformulation of the system and its capacities. From a therapeutic perspective, family systems approaches attend to equilibrium change as the essential structuring factor that maintains current communication patterns and power relations among family members. System perturbations, such as increases in family conflict and stress, may lead to dissipative change and a new and potentially more viable family organization and state of equilibrium change.

Although constructivist theories differ in their assumptions about the nature of change and causation, Lyddon (1995) does not preclude the possibility that various forms of constructivism may reflect viable accounts of different aspects of human knowing. This conjecture allies itself to the possibility that a more integrative model of constructivist psychology may be developed.

## Evolutionary Status of Constructivism in Clinical Practice

With regard to constructivist and social constructionist concepts and practice issues, several points stand out. First, when Feixas (1990) claims a privileged position for George Kelly's personal construct theory in the constructivist integration of psychotherapy, opposition is likely to be provoked from practitioners of other theoretical backgrounds. Second, Lyddon (1995) believes that some constructivists are likely to be uncomfortable with the distinctions he draws among the various forms of constructivist psychology, akin to Phillips (1995), who points out the mutual distrust among various constructivists in the broad fields of educational theory and research. Third, none of the existing approaches to constructivist psychotherapy integration has demonstrated its inherent superiority (R. A. Neimeyer, 1993b). Fourth, several authors admit that the efficacy of constructivist therapeutic approaches has not yet been established. For example, Gonçalves (1995b) states, "We are still a long way from an acceptable understanding of the effective ingredients of our clinical practices" (p. 159). Likewise, Guidano (1995), states that the portrait of how people develop and how a constructivist psychotherapist might conceptualize and facilitate such development "is preliminary and conjectural" (p. 104). Furthermore, R. A. Neimeyer (1995a) concludes, "at present, we lack . . . a complete set of tools for helping clients accomplish the aims that their stories might or could embody" (p. 241). These statements and others indicate that constructivism is a work in progress. Fifth, blending paradigms and intermingling epistemologies does not parallel constructivist evolution. For example, constructivist theory does not advocate the integration of multicultural clients' Romantic conceptualizations of experience, much less their non-Western world view. Multicultural clients do not need another therapeutic approach foreign to their cultural background foisted upon them by the dominant culture. In the 21st century, knowledge of the dynamics of power and powerlessness will become increasingly applicable to clinical work with diverse populations and to practitioners themselves (Pinderhughes, 1995).

Other authors postulate that an Anglocentric and androcentric postmodernism will not occur easily. For example, Laird (1991) discusses feminism as applied to postmodern therapy. She also addresses lesbian and gay issues in postmodern clinical practice (Laird, 1993). Richardson (1993) takes vocational psychologists to task for their emphasis on "career counseling" for predominantly college-educated white-collar professionals and little counseling for minority and working-class individuals. She advocates a view of "work in people's lives in which work is considered to be a central activity that is not tied or solely located in the occupational structure" (p. 427), because an exclusive focus on careers both "ignores and marginalizes work done outside this structure" (p. 427). Savickas (1993, 1995) also explores how postmodernism can transform career counseling and vocational psychology.

I situate myself as a *moderate* postmodernist, in contrast with *extreme* postmodernism, which "goes to the very core of what constitutes social science and radically dismisses it" (Rosenau, 1992, p. 4). Extreme postmodernism deconstructs modernity. *Deconstruction* refers to "a postmodern method of analysis. Its goal is to undo all constructions. Deconstruction tears a text apart, reveals its contradictions and assumptions; its intent, however, is not to improve, revise, or offer a better version of the text" (Rosenau, 1992, p. xi). In effect, extreme postmodernism has engendered controversies that have deconstructed the deconstructionists.

Hollinger (1994) makes good practice sense: "Coming to terms with postmodernism does not mean throwing out everything in the classic body of writings, but finding new ways to make old and new ideas work together in specific contexts" (p. 186). The clients with whom I work have assorted—and often incompatible—ways of knowing and existing. Moderate postmodernism allows me to assume Romantic and modernist paradigms as well as non-Western modes of therapy. Bauman (1993) states, "A sufficient residue of modern sentiments has been imparted to all of us by training" (pp. 33–34) and remains with us in our everyday life. The multicultural perspective's emphasis on recognizing that the differences within a racial or ethnic group are often greater than differences between groups (Pedersen, 1990; Sue, 1992) also coincides with a moderate postmodern location. This location also allows for race, culture, ethnicity, gender, demographics, and socioeconomic status as irreducible categories of human existence that more extreme formulations of postmodernism attempt to deconstruct. Objective social and political structures of oppression exist outside the realities created—or glossed over—by language (González, 1997). At times, these realities are perpetuated by socially constructed, dominant discourses that serve as smoke screens to disguise inequities (Hare-Mustin, 1994) or by indirect talk—coded, politically laden, and sarcastic language—that aims to silence others (Capper, 1995). Hence, constructivist approaches to teacher education examine race, culture, language diversity (Cochran-Smith, 1995), and socioeconomic status (DeJong & Groomes, 1996) in order to construct pedagogies that take these variables into account in locally appropriate ways. In a similar fashion, I strive to incorporate these considerations into practice.

## *Linkages Among Issues and Epistemological Approaches*

Ultimately, clients are the final judge in determining what works best for them. Of course, clients who enter therapy feeling at their wit's end are hardly in the mood to hear that they know what is best for themselves or that the competencies they seek already lie within them. Effective clinical practice consists of a technical eclecticism whereby the practitioner uses different paradigms to intervene in clients' lives. Romantic-based interventions are appropriate for issues about morality, the existence of the soul, and self-identification of deep feelings that arise. Modernist-based interventions work well with clients who require immediate symptom relief or quick reestablishment of emotional equilibrium and whose core assumptions about reality, self, and world require only minor adjustments (Lyddon, 1990). Modernist objectivity and linear causality are also vital for clinicians who serve as expert witnesses in court. Postmodernist-based interventions are helpful with clients whose developmental life challenges are such that their core assumptions about reality, self, and world are no longer functional (Lyddon, 1990). Given that multicultural clinical practice emphasizes equally the personal and social experiences of both clinician and client (Axelson, 1993), multicultural interactions in therapy are endowed potentially with moderate postmodern discourse. Some clients will enter therapy with an individualistic perspective, other clients will be comfortable with a communal perspective, and yet other clients will respond well to a perspective based on context. Moreover, clients may have multiple perspectives (i.e., rational objectivist when it comes to finances, postmodern regarding their wide range of friends). Multicultural clinical relevance entails, at the very least, tolerance for these inherently contradictory, yet human, ways of being in the world.

# Implications for Multicultural Clinical Practice

## Geographic, Institutional, and Clinical Context

**Geographic context.** A brief digression is warranted to explain how my location of study is influenced powerfully by the area where I live, the university and college where I work, and the clinical setting where I serve clients. El Paso, Texas, and its *un*identical twin city, Juárez, Chihuahua, México, constitute "the most heavily populated metropolitan area on any international border *in the entire world*" (Draper, 1995, p. 121; italics in the original). Given my situated knowledge, when I read that modernism is rapidly waning (Srivastva, Fry, & Cooperrider, 1990) or dead (Hoffman, 1991), such pronouncements appear premature at best and insensitive at worst. In El Paso County, approximately 72,750 people reside in *colonias* that lack clean drinking water and adequate sewage systems (Self, 1995); the city of El Paso contains the third most poverty-stricken census tract in the United States (Leticia Paéz, personal communication, November 1, 1995). The North American Free Trade Agreement (effective January 1, 1994) and the devaluation of the Mexican peso (December 1994) injured El Paso's economy. The impoverished outskirts of Juárez are clearly seen across the Rio Grande (known as the *Río Bravo* to the *Méxicanos*). The overwhelming majority of Juárez public schools are not equipped with the educational technology to produce K. J. Gergen's (1991b, 1994b) social saturation. Pockets of postmodernism exist, as do pockets of appalling premodern poverty. Postmodern clinical conceptualizations may not always be appropriate when one is working with clients who live in poverty. Such conceptualizations are as likely to be practitioner driven as any a priori assumptions made by a modernist practitioner. Client-driven conceptualizations, on the other hand, vary, and technical eclecticism is a useful response in such instances.

**Institutional context.** The University of Texas at El Paso (UTEP) College of Education, like other UTEP colleges, has a strong commitment to field-based education. The College of Nursing and Health Sciences at UTEP, in partnership with the Texas Tech University Health Sciences Center at El Paso, Texas Tech University School of Medicine, and the County of El Paso, has four multidisciplinary clinics to meet the needs of the largely disenfranchised, rural, and underserved population in the area. In a paradigm shift from a traditional, illness-based approach to community health, clients are seen within the context of their communities to ensure that all aspects of their well-being are considered in treatment (Castiglia, 1996). This emphasis upon clients' contextualized knowledge has led to an opportunity to incorporate postmodern psychotherapeutic approaches into the multidisciplinary services that are offered. Without a client-driven philosophy, it would not have been possible to use a technically eclectic blend of paradigms. Institutional environments play a major role in the implementation and maintenance of any postmodern clinical work with multicultural clients.

**Clinical context.** Currently, I supervise counseling interns at one of the clinics, where I also serve my own client case load. Counseling services are offered at no charge as a public service. A strictly enforced attendance and appointment-cancellation policy minimizes the problem of no-shows and premature terminations as well as keeps the waiting list short. Many so-called nontraditional clients use the counseling services. Clients range from 4 to 82 years of age. More than 50% are monolingual Spanish speaking. Individuals, couples, and families are seen. Socioeconomic levels range from public-assisted fixed-income to professional class. Some clients live in *colonias*. All clinical forms are in Spanish and English; intake forms do not ask for places of birth or citizenship status. The field-based orientation of UTEP's College of Education has facilitated attempts to turn abstract postmodern concepts and ideas into practical, hands-on applications. These clinical opportunities are not possible without institutional support.

**Measurement of clinical process and outcome.** The relevance, appropriateness, and effectiveness of the practice principles described here are supported through both traditional quantitative and qualitative research methods and assessment procedures.

Both formative and summative evaluations are being conducted. Formative evaluation refers to ongoing evaluation that occurs during the course of a program. A mainstay of my current formative evaluation is the Working Alliance Inventory (WAI) (Horvath & Greenberg, 1989, 1994; Horvath & Symonds, 1991). The WAI, administered after the third session, is a 36-item self-report measure that consists of three subscales to assess bond, task, and goal dimensions of the alliance. A Spanish-language version is being pilot tested as part of the program evaluation. This instrument is a useful gauge of client well-being, given the nontraditional backgrounds of most of the clients and the minimal experience of the interns. A systematic clinical response is facilitated for clients who wish to comment on aspects of bond, task, or goal dimensions. A recent addition to the evaluation process is an adaptation of questions drawn from Berg and De Jong (Chapter 11, p. 250): "On a scale of 1 to 10, on which 10 means the problem(s) with which you came to therapy is solved and 1 is 'the worst it has ever been,' where is it now on that scale?" This question measures constructions of client meanings, especially clients' sense of competence or strengths.

Summative evaluation refers to the final evaluation that occurs at the end of a program. Currently, I use the Client Satisfaction Questionnaire (Roberts, Attkisson, & Mendias, 1984; Roberts, Attkisson, & Stegner, 1983), an eight-item measure of general satisfaction with services that is available in English and Spanish and has established reliability and validity. The questionnaire has two open-ended questions about what clients like most about the clinic and what they would change about the clinic. In addition to being appropriate for a bilingual clientele, these formative and summative measures provide the accountability required internally. Furthermore, these measures, especially the tailor-made piloted translations, meet the criteria for the substantial redefinition and innovation that characterize clinical practice from a moderate postmodern perspective. The next step is to incorporate—not substitute—more sophisticated constructivist measures compatible with moderate postmodernism. A related issue is the extent to which constructivistic measures are an acceptable means of accountability to both internal and external funding sources, especially given the fact that from some social constructionist perspectives, assessment procedures are disappearing altogether (see Chapter 10). In the following section, the implications for multicultural relevance are drawn from composites of various clients.

## *Romantic Paradigms*

Many clients incorporate moral or spiritual dimensions into their lives. For example, in some families dealing with the pregnancy of an unwed teenage daughter, although premarital sex may be viewed as immoral, abortion is not considered an alternative because these families believe that the unborn child already possesses a soul. The more pressing concerns include (a) prenatal care, (b) the family's and the teenage daughter's emotional adjustment to the unplanned pregnancy, (c) the possibility of adoption, (d) the possibility of marriage, (e) plans for child care while the new mother finishes her high school education and perhaps receives vocational training, and (f) the supportive role, if any, to be played by the infant's father. Although these concerns lend themselves to postmodern-influenced deliberations, which allow for the expansion of multiple possibilities for clients, family members whose Christian spirituality is based on a Romantic paradigm do not question the existence of the fetus's soul.

K. J. Gergen (1994b) states, "While romanticism ceases to play a commanding role in the intellectual world, it is probably the central means by which persons currently justify their moral positions in daily life" (p. 95). Perhaps Romanticism has lost "its grasp on the intellectual imagination" (p. 97), but it is alive and well in the discourses of many of my multicultural clients. If the world views and values of these clients are to be honored in therapy, then dialog based on a Romantic paradigm is appropriate to use.

In another example, a man was referred for counseling after he found one of his grown sons unconscious from an apparent drug overdose. The father summoned emergency medical technicians, but his son was pronounced dead at the scene. Because the body was still warm, the father insisted that the emergency medical technicians not immediately remove it in a body bag. The father knew his son was a drug user. Because his son had died from a drug overdose, the father believed that his soul would need a few hours to depart from the body. The father believed that the soul would have fled the body quickly if the death had occurred under natural, non-drug-induced circumstances. After the funeral, the father's grief and anguish became unbearable. He sought an appointment with a physician who, in turn, referred him for counseling.

In therapy, the clinician supported and respected the moral position of the father in delaying by a few hours the placement of his dead child into a body bag. The father's spiritual beliefs, especially his convictions regarding the soul's existence and nature, deserved respect. To help the father deal with his grief, the clinician affirmed the father's moral convictions. Postmodern conceptualizations of the father's world view as existing only in the realm of discourse (K. J. Gergen, 1994b) would have been irrelevant and disrespectful. He probably would not have tolerated K. J. Gergen's statement that social constructionism is ontologically mute and neither affirms nor denies foundational descriptions about the world "out there" as opposed to "in here" (K. J. Gergen, 1994b, p. 72). The issue here is whether therapists clearly explain to their clients that they will approach therapy from multiple perspectives and whether clients are well enough acquainted with postmodern concepts to provide informed consent for the therapist to use such approaches. With little or no understanding of postmodernism, how can a client know what he or she is getting into with a postmodern practitioner? Unless the therapist and client are equally familiar with postmodern clinical approaches, then a power differential exists in favor of the therapist. In such instances, clinicians may be oblivious to clients' experiences and thus to the unexamined effects of the clinician's dominant role in the relationship (Freire, 1993).

Family survivors of persons who have committed suicide may wonder if that family member's soul has also gone to hell. From a postmodern perspective, a clinician can dialogue with family members about their individual beliefs about what has happened to their loved one's soul. Some survivors may petition special saints or may voice prayers to redeem the soul of the deceased. With such clients, postmodern-flavored deliberations go only so far. For many clients, the existence of a soul is an absolute truth, not "true in a new, provisional, postmodern way" (O'Hara & Anderson, 1991, p. 22).

Many of my clinical supervisees lack training in theology or pastoral counseling and thus are reluctant to broach spiritual or religious matters. A simple way to broach the subject is to say, "Tell me about your God." Another technique is to ask clients, "What have others said to you, or taught you, about life after death?" Depending on the client's responses, the practitioner can then ask, "From all the things you have heard and been told, what do you believe for yourself?" See Kudlac (1991) for a discussion of a postmodern approach to spirituality in therapy.

Whenever I teach academic courses in social and cultural aspects of counseling, I provide several optional, self-selected activities to help students learn, according to their preferred style, a technique compatible with constructivist educational principles. For example,

> *Attend a service in a house of worship of a religion with which you are not now nor ever have been familiar. Write a brief essay detailing your experience. Suggested items to mention include (a) your internal dialogue as you arrived, (b) music, (c) liturgy, (d) sermon, (e) communion (if any), and (f) things you might have been told about that particular religion while you were growing up that did not appear to be true. You are welcome to include additional items.*

This self-selected activity invites and challenges students to expand their world views in a sensitive area. The task arouses students to think about diverse expressions of faith. The exercise helps students overcome their reticence and awkwardness regarding religious and spiritual issues, which in turn helps them relax and be open in conversing about such subjects with clients.

To the extent that postmodern paradigms deconstruct or extinguish the validity of Romantic realities (K. J. Gergen, 1991b), these paradigms are irrelevant and not respectful in work with diverse populations. Although multicultural clients may not explicitly identify clinical issues as being rooted in the Romantic intellectual tradition, clients' dialogue and preoccupations with, for example, morality, the existence of the soul, or internal feelings reveal the paradigm from which their world view branches. Although postmodern-influenced dialogue may form part of the stories that unfold in therapy sessions, current scholarship of social constructionism and constructivist psychotherapy does not give due credence to those times when the Romantic paradigm is a primary concern for clients.

## *Modernist Paradigm*

If multicultural clients' life circumstances or dialogue suggest their belief that language is an instrument for bearing truth, a reflection of an independent reality, or a means for conveying rational thought, then the clinician should recognize and uphold the integrity of these clients' world views. Many of my multicultural clients are referred from elementary, middle, and high schools. These institutions have standards for conduct and academic performance that students are required to meet. Sometimes, my clinical work takes on a modernist accent, as when I coach young clients and their parents about independent (political) realities regarding schools' expectations for appropriate behavior and tolerance for misbehavior. Many young clients are not aware during their first appointment that they are walking on thin ice and on the verge of being placed in an alternative school or being referred to juvenile court. Although I strive to make it clear to these young people and their parents that the young person is not in trouble with me and that it is not my job to "get on their case," I also attempt to convey the seriousness of their current situation. Many likable, intelligent youth miscalculate and do not understand that they are about to step over the line. When matter-of-fact (not matter-of-interpretation), nonscolding language is used to bear the truth about what will likely happen to them if they do not change their behavior, some young people will change their behavior.

From a modernist standpoint, I agree with Fisher (1995b) and Mascolo and Dalto (1995), who see the need to maintain a sense of personal agency in constructivist models of human functioning. O'Hara and Anderson (1991) admit that although "it is useful to look at the contemporary world as 'postmodern,' … this doesn't mean we have left the modern era behind. It is all around us, and within us" (p. 23). Clinically, to the extent that postmodern paradigms tend to extinguish modernist world views (K. J. Gergen, 1991b), such paradigms are irrelevant for multicultural clients. Many low-income, immigrant clients hope to attain the so-called American dream, an aspiration that contains many elements of a modernist perspective. It is not my place to disabuse these clients of such a notion.

Recent experience has taught me that the legal system is linear in nature: (1) What would a client do if "A" happened? (2) How would situation "B" cause a client to behave? (3) What was the probability of "C" occurring if a client was mandated to ___? The judge, the jury, the client's attorney, and the client him- or herself sometimes need the clinician to serve as expert. Despite postmodern proclamations that the client is the expert (Anderson & Goolishian, 1992) or that experts no longer exist (Savickas, 1993), it will be a long time, if ever, before postmodern paradigms significantly permeate the legal system.

Assuming an expert approach can be vital for clients whose competence to stand trial becomes a question to which a clinical practitioner must respond. Likewise, during a trial, the legal definition of sanity or insanity of the defendant may rely in part on expert testimony. Other instances in which expertise is necessary include (a) making diagnoses for clients who need Supplemental Security Income benefits, (b) providing an informed clinical opinion at school-based hearings that determine whether a student client will be placed in or removed from special education classes or other academic and social services, (c) interpreting a child's assessment results for parents who may not understand why their child was tested and what the results mean, and (d) recommending child-custody arrangements in divorce cases. Such modernist stances make normative assumptions about what is and is not "healthy behavior," an approach that is inherently inconsistent with the multicultural perspective's emphasis on understanding each client's cultural values and beliefs (González, 1997).

## Moderate Postmodernism

The modernist scientific method validates knowledge in reference to theory. In contrast, the postmodern perspectivistic method legitimates knowledge by its usefulness and viability in diverse interpretive communities. Whereas modern questions ask, "Is it true?" "Is it accurate?" postmodern questions ask, "How is it true?" "For whom is it useful?" "Why did he or she say that?" "Could it be otherwise?" "What perspective is most useful in this particular context?" (Savickas, 1993, 1995).

In my clinical practice, I use a postmodern approach to organizational consultation known as appreciative inquiry (Barrett & Cooperrider, 1990; Cooperrider, 1990; Cooperrider & Srivastva, 1987), which moves from "telling it like it is" to "telling it as it may become" (Srivastva et al., 1990). The therapeutic mood is one of "an invitation to see anew, . . . to create scenarios for future action" (Barrett & Cooperrider, 1990, p. 224), whereby anticipatory realities become a guiding image for the future (Cooperrider, 1990). These realities parallel Gonçalves's (1995a) projecting narratives and Tomm's (1985) circular questions between the present and the future. The tone set by appreciative inquiry is appealing in that it diffuses defensive perceptions in a congenial manner.

Home visits and consultations with school personnel provide two sources for conceptualizing clients' situations in multiple ways. Obtaining a sense of where clients live provides ecological data about clients' most intimate ways of being. Exchanging points of view with teachers, principals, and other school administrators may generate shifts in meaning and perspective that can release some young clients from being labeled as troublemakers and behavioral problems. Statements such as "I know what I saw [the student] do" or "[The student] comes from the type of family in which this sort of thing always happens" are not unusual. From a moderate postmodern location, dialogue can evolve during visits and consultations to engender "mutual expertise" (González, 1997) among all participants. In such situations, participants may arrive at partial truths regarding a young client's behavior, motivations, and character. With this approach, adult authorities are less likely to categorize young clients. The young person might be asked, "If this trouble in school continues, what do you think will happen?" Such a question can help an adolescent examine the long-term consequences of his or her behavior. Related questions include, "How will you know when you don't need to come to therapy anymore?" "What is your behavior going to look like when you won't have to come here anymore?" "Who is going to notice these changes first? Who will notice them the most?" Focusing on anticipatory realities, both with the young person and with adults involved in the conversation, can instill hope as well as generate shifts in perception.

Metcalf (1995) offers a wealth of guidelines, questions, strategies, and exercises for helping counselors work with students, parents, teachers, and administrators. Her approach focuses emphasis on exceptions to problems and less emphasis on problems. Solution-focused brief therapy encourages practitioners to view problem students differently. Metcalf encourages students to be responsible for their own change and to resist blaming others. In my own clinical practice, I temper Metcalf's techniques to fit the drastic variations in the socioeducational backgrounds and ways of knowing among my clients and my own moderate postmodernism.

Promoting the notion of mutual expertise facilitates discussions among family members by encouraging them to exchange their views and opinions. Guidano's (1995) movieola technique, in a modified version, is another useful tool. One begins with an event or a series of events that are analyzed in detail. Using cinematographic language, the therapist reconstructs with the client a succession of scenes in the event. The client is trained to "zoom in" on a single scene, focus on particular aspects, and then "zoom out" and reinsert the enriched scene into the therapeutic narrative. With this technique, the immediate experiencing of the event (which occurs when zooming in) interfaces with the symbolic explanation of the event (which occurs after zooming out). This technique enables clients to see themselves from at least two points of view: the subjective viewpoint when they zoom in and the objective viewpoint after they zoom out. Clients are then able emotionally to restructure the situation. The self-referencing or self-observation that occurs provides the raw materials necessary to reconstruct events of therapeutic interest.

Some survivors of drive-by shootings and bystanders to such episodes do not talk about the incident among themselves until they are in the therapy room together. When invited to use the modified movieola technique, bystanders "zoom in" and describe the scene differently from the way survivors describe it. For example, a bystander might mention how quickly the blood from the gunshot wound of the survivor coagulated. The bystander notes how blood from a gunshot wound quickly becomes sticky and gooey, unlike the watery blood seen in the movies. Also, in real life, blood smells. Bystanders might "zoom in" to another scene and recall how the survivors continued to move around on all fours on the front porch, despite multiple gunshot wounds. Survivors may not remember the arrival of emergency medical technicians, which bystanders may recall vividly. Survivors may then inscribe the scenes they remember as happening in slow motion without sound. Survivors might describe the monotonous boredom of hospitalization. The conversation may turn to the relatives and friends of those who died in the shooting. I might ask, "If I, who did not know the persons killed, feel the poignancy of the loss, then how must you, as survivors and bystanders, feel?" In such a situation, each participant becomes a "scriptwriter." We marvel at the different camera angles from which each person records the event and the multiple interpretations that are generated. As therapy progresses, new interpretations of the event are engendered.

When an event is shared by family members or friends, multiple meanings and understandings may be generated. The therapist's job is to create a space, a safe harbor, where clients can exchange views through shared language and meaning systems that evolve in the course of time. In my experience, it helps if I inform clients beforehand that (a) I do not expect to hear the same version of events from each person; (b) it is not my job to take sides; (c) each person will have my undivided attention when speaking; (d) it would be best if no one were penalized later for saying something that others don't want to be revealed in my presence; (e) they should not be surprised by a frank, whole-hearted exchange with me; and (f) we are likely to learn from one another. Listening and being heard are intensely relational acts (Gilligan & Noel, 1995). Family members who perceive they have been listened to and heard are less likely to insist on their version of the truth. I strive to demystify the therapy process, especially when I am conversing in a postmodern dialect, systematically inscribing what we do as it unfolds: What other words can be used to describe the same events? How else could events be interpreted? How many other versions are likely? Unlikely? When will family members know that what I do with them is something they can do at home without me?

In general, working in multidisciplinary settings, which includes professionals who adhere to a medical model, is compatible with a moderate postmodern approach.

All views *are* indeed valuable, even if I don't agree with them. The clinician needs to be flexible and capable of thinking and working with multiple perspectives. Many practitioners today must work within host settings and interact with people from a range of other disciplines and schools of thought. Moderate postmodernism does not reject positivistic paradigms. The infusion of other professions and paradigms is preferable to an inbred environment in which only one paradigm prevails.

Young clients diagnosed with attention-deficit disorder (ADD) are an excellent example of how social constructions of reality can get out of hand if left unchecked. Like many others, I believe that ADD is overdiagnosed and used at times to medicate and tranquilize a young person with whom teachers or parents do not know how to deal. Recognition of adults with ADD is recent and not widespread (Nadeau, 1995). Whether in children or adults, consulting with organizations and other systems that insist on dealing with diagnoses as if such labels had an objective, independent existence requires a pragmatic response. With ADD in children, for example, I find it fruitful to listen to family members' personal and socially constructed responses to such a diagnosis. Circular questioning techniques (Penn, 1982; Tomm, 1985, 1987) are helpful. The child's understanding of what the diagnosis means and his or her personal narrative in response to being diagnosed and the reactions of family members and classmates are crucial. Diagnosis and assessment are tools of the trade, even though these tools have been abused when practiced on ethnic and racial minorities (see Jones & Thorne, 1987). In my clinical practice, I attend to emergent themes that arise while focusing intuitively on what which remains unsaid. Reconstituting with the clients what is said and unsaid into a viable, alternative interpretation is the goal in therapy. I once viewed myself as an *affirmative* postmodernist in orientation (González, 1997). In contrast with *skeptical* orientations, inspired by European philosophies that offer a pessimistic assessment of the postmodern age as one of fragmentation, disintegration, malaise, and meaninglessness, affirmative orientations, which are indigenous to Anglo–North American culture, offer a more hopeful, optimistic view of the postmodern age (Rosenau, 1992). Now, given my concern for paradigmatic and epistemological imperialists who would attempt to colonize and impose their intellectual versions of human functioning on less sophisticated populations, I assert that to the extent that affirmative postmodernism is an Anglocentric paradigm, it may be of little use to diverse groups in the United States and elsewhere. Furthermore, to the extent that postmodernism is a reaction to the Enlightenment era that preceded Romanticism and was revived under modernism, it may have little applicability to Spanish-speaking peoples. The Enlightenment scarcely penetrated beyond the academic circles of Spain and its American colonies (Fuentes, 1992; Gay, 1966), chiefly because of obstruction by the Inquisition. In addition, the modern world criticized by postmodernists was never the modern world of the overwhelming majority of Spanish-speaking peoples (Johnson, 1991). Russell and Gaubatz (1995) point out that postmodern discourse is rarely heard among low-income peoples. Thus, given that postmodernism can hardly be talked about as if it were a single symbolic monolith (Russell & Gaubatz, 1995), the multiple perspectives that I employ in clinical practice encompass a variety of "historically and culturally bounded … provisional metaphors" (R. A. Neimeyer, 1995b, p. 16) contingent upon where clients place themselves in their discourse. In present-day southwestern United States, millions of *mestizos*—so-called Hispanics descended from a mingling of peoples (European and indigenous), cultures (Spanish and indigenous), and religions (Roman Catholic and indigenous)—do not experience the duality of bilingual and bicultural (sometimes multicultural) life as contradictory (United States Catholic Conference, 1991). Native Americans, also, can be both Christians and members of their tribes and feel complete in mind, body, and soul (United States Catholic Conference, 1991). The Southwest is but one geographic area where local narratives are manifested in more than one language and cultural tradition.

## Issues for Further Reflection

The technical eclecticism I espouse here is complex yet systematic in nature. Systematic eclecticism's strength is its selection of interventions on the basis of careful client assessment; its weakness lies in its awkward use of techniques derived from incompatible models (R. A. Neimeyer, 1993b). Incompatible paradigms and epistemologies are more likely to be an issue for psychotherapy scholars than for clinical practitioners (R. A. Neimeyer, 1993b) and their multicultural clients. The aim here is to transcend integrative models of constructivist psychotherapy that fail to capture and encompass the myriad ways in which people know and exist. To that end, I let my clients guide me in terms of the paradigms that have the most meaning for them.

The principle of systematically responding to clients in their own paradigmatic dialect(s) is widely generalizable. However, the proportion of time spent conversing with clients in romantic, modern, or postmodern dialects will vary. Respecting and honoring all dialects is a second principle with broad generalizability. Environments in which only one paradigm prevails are likely to become stale. Politicized environments that approve of postmodernism only can result in rigidity and inflexibility.

The strengths and weaknesses of multicultural counseling and therapy have been discussed elsewhere (Sue et al., 1996). My appraisal of the limitations and possibilities of applying postmodern approaches to multicultural clinical practice (González, 1997) assumes a critical position (Ruggiero, 1990). As a "theory of theories" that is contextual in orientation, multicultural therapy theory appears initially to be congenial to postmodernism. However, postmodernism's relevance to multicultural practice needs to be investigated further. Benhabib (1992), for instance, refers to multiculturalism, feminism, and postmodernism as paradigms that have arisen out of the decline of modernist epistemology. She appraises the compatibility of the metaphilosophical premises of postmodernism with the narrative content of feminism, not just as a theoretical position but as a theory of women's struggle for emancipation. She states that the Enlightenment and modernist principles to which postmodernists are to bid farewell are by no means obvious. Using the phrase "strong version of postmodernism" (p. 213), she asserts that a strong postmodern style undermines feminist commitment to women's agency and sense of selfhood and to the reappropriation of women's own history in the name of an emancipated future. She contends that feminist theory can ally itself with the strong version of postmodernism only at the risk of incoherence and self-contradictoriness. She concludes that postmodernism and feminism are not conceptual and political allies—a verdict that merits careful consideration in terms of postmodernism's relevance to multicultural practice.

Three other issues arise when considering the conceptual and political alliance of postmodernism and multiculturalism. First, the application of a "postmodern only" movement can be as offensive to some ethnic and racial minorities as is the "English only" movement, with its tone of implied superiority over ethnic-minority populations. A postmodern-only movement might resemble psychoanalysis at the turn of the century, which served an elite leisure class. Second, an ethnic- and racial-minority person may not want her or his individual self populated with too many selves that reflect distasteful and undesirable aspects of the dominant culture. Third, computer-literacy education in the schools and the question of who benefits from the technology of social saturation that helps create a postmodern world will require further attention. For example, Young (1989) states that African Americans are more spectators than participants in the technological renaissance in the United States. Despite scientific breakthroughs and technological advances, the conditions of life confronting African Americans are dominated predominantly by poverty, underemployment, few educational opportunities, discrimination, and covert or overt acts of racism. Access to the postmodern world differs between the "haves" and the "have-nots" (Poole, 1996).

I have grave concerns about postmodernism being part of a hidden agenda in therapy to be insinuated into dialogue with unsuspecting and unaware clients (see Reichelt & Sveaass, 1994). If a postmodern paradigm is foisted onto multicultural clients without their informed consent, which I suspect happens more often than not, then co-creations of reality are not happening. In such instances, clinicians may manipulate naive clients' realities under the guise of co-construction. A clearly discernable demarcation zone is needed, a system of checks and balances whereby "conversational artistry" is held accountable when it degenerates into "con artistry" (Efran & Fauber, 1995). Whenever I give K. J. Gergen's (1991a) article "The Saturated Family" to students or clients, they generally relate to the existence he describes. This article may be a useful and practical way to introduce clients to the rationale behind some postmodern clinical interventions. Yet, I believe that if many students and clients read further into the social constructionist literature they would, ironically, not relate to social constructionism's notions about relatedness. The bottom line is that the objective world view is that with which most people have grown up and it grounds their daily life (Efran & Fauber, 1995; O'Hara & Anderson, 1991).

Therapeutic contracts (Huber, 1994) that contain explanations of the postmodern clinical process are an ethical consideration. However, some may counter by saying that nondisclosure is an ethical consideration only insofar as one chooses to define it as such. Integrity is at stake here. It is useful to remember Sue and Sue's (1990) point that for many racial- and ethic-minority persons, the fine words of persons from the dominant culture lose their validity unless supported by actions.

Efran and Fauber (1995) state that preliminary encounters with postmodernism are often jarring for modernist-based practitioners and laypersons. Such an unsettling and disruptive process can "turn off" those who, as Rosenau (1992) states, sense that postmodernism may have something valuable to offer but who also do not want to become casualties of postmodernism's excesses. Furthermore, aspects of postmodernism can oppress and marginalize as much as any modernist world view ever did, especially those clients who speak in other paradigmatic dialects. Thus I am concerned about the hegemonic growth of postmodernism as the latest paradigmatic and epistemological empire. What remains to be seen is a comprehensive constructivist therapy that incorporates (a) multiple disciplines and (b) the various, incompatible, and contradictory ways of knowing and existing that human beings bring to therapy. Until that time, provisions need to be made for the "mutual expertise" of clinician and client working together to honor what works best for the client.

# References

Abramson, H. J. (1980). Assimilation and pluralism. In S. Thernstrom (Ed.), *The Harvard encyclopedia of American ethnic groups* (pp. 150–160). Cambridge, MA: Harvard University Press.

Anderson, H. D., & Goolishian, H. A. (1991, January). *New directions in systemic therapy: A language systems approach.* Symposium presented at the Texas Association of Marriage and Family Therapy, Dallas, TX.

Anderson, H. D., & Goolishian, H. A. (1992). The client is the expert: A not-knowing approach to therapy. In S. McNamee & K. J. Gergen (Eds.), *Therapy as social construction* (pp. 23–39). London: Sage.

Arndt, J. (1985). On making marketing science more scientific: Role of orientations, paradigms, metaphors, and puzzle solving. *Journal of Marketing, 49*(3), 11–23.

Axelson, J. A. (1993). *Counseling and development in a multicultural society.* Pacific Grove, CA: Brooks/Cole.

Baillie, A., & Corrie, S. (1996). The construction of clients' experience of psychotherapy through narrative, practical action and the multiple streams of consciousness. *Human Relations, 49,* 295–311.

Bandura, A. (1977). *Social learning theory.* Englewood Cliffs, NJ: Prentice-Hall.

Bandura, A. (1985). *Social foundations of thought and action: Asocial cognitive theory.* Englewood Cliffs, NJ: Prentice-Hall.

Barrett, F. J., & Cooperrider, D. L. (1990). Generative metaphor intervention: A new approach for working with systems divided by conflict and caught in defensive perception. *Journal of Applied Behavioral Science, 26,* 219–239.

Baruth, L. G., & Manning, M. L. (1991). *Multicultural counseling and psychotherapy: A lifespan perspective.* New York: Merrill.

Bass, E., & Davis, L. (1988). *The courage to heal: A guide for women survivors of child sexual abuse.* New York: Harper & Row.

Bauman, Z. (1993). *Postmodern ethics.* Cambridge, MA: Blackwell Publishers.

Becvar, D. S., & Becvar, R. J. (1996). *Family therapy: A systemic integration* (3rd ed.). Boston: Allyn & Bacon.

Benhabib, S. (1992). *Situating the self: Gender, community and postmodernism in contemporary ethics.* New York: Routledge.

Burr, V. (1995). *An introduction to social constructionism.* New York: Routledge.

Capper, C. A. (1995, October). *Discourses of dysfunction: Being silenced and silencing.* Paper presented at the University Council for Educational Administration Annual Convention, Salt Lake City, UT.

Castiglia, P. T. (1996). Multidisciplinary care and education. In R. W. Richards (Ed.), *Building partner-*

ships: Educating health professionals for the communities they serve (pp. 157–171). San Francisco: Jossey-Bass.

Coale, H. W. (1992). The constructivist emphasis on language: A critical conversation. *Journal of Strategic and Systemic Therapies, 11,* 12–26.

Cochran-Smith, M. (1995). Color blindness and basket making are not the answers: Confronting the dilemmas of race, culture, and language diversity in teacher education. *American Educational Research Journal, 32,* 493–522.

Cooperrider, D. L. (1990). Positive image, positive action: The affirmative basis of organizing. In S. Srivastva, D. L. Cooperrider, & Associates (Eds.), *Appreciative management and leadership: The power of positive thought and action in organizations* (pp. 91–125). San Francisco: Jossey-Bass.

Cooperrider, D. L., & Srivastva, S. (1987). Appreciative inquiry in organizational life. In W. A. Passmore & R. W. Woodman (Eds.), *Research in organizational change and development* (Vol. 1, pp. 129–169). Greenwich, CT: JAI Press.

Corey, G. (1996). *Theory and practice of counseling and psychotherapy* (5th ed.). Pacific Grove, CA: Brooks/Cole.

Coyne, J. C. (1985). Toward a theory of frames and reframing: The social nature of frames. *Journal of Marital and Family Therapy, 11,* 337–344.

DeJong, L., & Groomes, F. J. (1996). A constructivist teacher education program that incorporates community service to prepare students to work with children living in poverty. *Action in Teacher Education, 18*(2), 86–95.

Denner, B. (1995). Stalked by the postmodern beast. *American Psychologist, 50,* 390–391.

Dervin, B. (1994). Information–democracy: An examination of underlying assumptions. *Journal of the American Society for Information Science, 45,* 369–385.

Draper, R. (1995, December). Carrillo's crossing. *Texas Monthly,* 118–121, 139–142, 143–144.

Efran, J. S., & Clarfield, L. E. (1992). Constructionist therapy: Sense and nonsense. In S. McNamee & K. J. Gergen (Eds.), *Therapy as social construction* (pp. 200–217). London: Sage.

Efran, J. S., & Fauber, R. L. (1995). Radical constructivism: Questions and answers. In R. A. Neimeyer & M. J. Mahoney (Eds.), *Constructivism in psychotherapy* (pp. 275–304). Washington, DC: American Psychological Association.

Efran, J. S., Lukens, R. J., & Lukens, M. D. (1988). Constructivism: What's in it for you? *Family Therapy Networker, 12*(5), 27–35.

Feixas, G. (1990). Approaching the individual, approaching the system: A constructivist model for integrative psychotherapy. *Journal of Family Psychology, 4,* 4–35.

Fisher, H. (1995a). Empty sets or empty self: A response to comments on "Whose right is it to define the self?" *Theory and Psychology, 5,* 391–400.

Fisher, H. (1995b). Whose right is it to define the self? *Theory and Psychology, 5,* 323–352.

Flew, A. (1984). *A dictionary of philosophy* (2nd ed., rev.). New York: St. Martin's Press.

Fouad, N. A., & Bingham, R. P. (1995). Career counseling with racial and ethnic minorities. In W. B. Walsh & S. H. Osipow (Eds.), Handbook of vocational psychology (2nd ed., pp. 331–365). Mahwah, NJ: Lawrence Erlbaum.

Freeman, M. (1995). Groping in the light. *Theory and Psychology, 5,* 353–360.

Freire, P. (1993). *Pedagogy of the oppressed.* New York: Continuum.

Fuentes, C. (1992). *The buried mirror: Reflections on Spain and the New World.* Boston: Houghton Mifflin.

Gay, P. (1966). *Age of Enlightenment.* New York: Time, Inc.

Gergen, K. J. (1985). The social constructionist movement in modern psychology. *American Psychologist, 40,* 266–275.

Gergen, K. J. (1991a). The saturated family. *Family Therapy Networker, 15*(5), 27–35.

Gergen, K. J. (1991b). *The saturated self: Dilemmas of identity in contemporary life.* New York: Basic Books.

Gergen, K. J. (1994a). Exploring the postmodern: Perils or potentials? *American Psychologist, 49,* 412–416.

Gergen, K. J. (1994b). *Realities and relationships: Soundings in social construction.* Cambridge, MA: Harvard University Press.

Gergen, K. J. (1995). Postmodern psychology: Resonance and reflection. *American Psychologist, 50,* 394.

Gergen, M. (1995). Postmodern, post-Cartesian positionings on the subject of psychology. *Theory and Psychology, 5,* 361–368.

Gilligan, C., & Noel, N. (1995, April). *Cartography of a lost time: Women, girls, and relationships.* Workshop sponsored by the Austin Women's Psychotherapy Project, Austin, TX.

Gonçalves, Ó. F. (1995a). Cognitive narrative psychotherapy: The hermeneutic construction of alternative meanings. In M. J. Mahoney (Ed.), *Cognitive and constructive psychotherapies: Theory, research, and practice* (pp. 139–162). New York: Springer.

Gonçalves, Ó. F. (1995b). Hermeneutics, constructivism, and cognitive-behavioral therapies: From the object to the project. In R. A. Neimeyer & M. J. Mahoney (Eds.), *Constructivism in psychotherapy* (pp. 195–230). Washington, DC: American Psychological Association.

González, R. C. (1997). Postmodern supervision: A multicultural perspective. In J. Pope-Davis & H. L. K. Coleman (Eds.), *Multicultural counseling competencies: Assessment, education and training, and supervision* (pp. 350–386). Thousand Oaks, CA: Sage.

Guidano, V. F. (1995). Constructivist psychotherapy: A theoretical framework. In R. A. Neimeyer & M. J. Mahoney (Eds.), *Constructivism in psychotherapy* (pp. 93–108). Washington, DC: American Psychological Association.

Hacker, A. (1992). *Two nations: Black and White, separate, hostile, unequal.* New York: Charles Scribner's Sons.

Hare-Mustin, R. T. (1994). Discourses in the mirrored room: A postmodern analysis of therapy. *Family Process, 33,* 19–35.

Harré, R. (1995). The necessity of personhood as embodied being. *Theory and Psychology, 5,* 369–373.

Held, B. S. (1990). What's in a name? Some confusions and concerns about constructivism. *Journal of Marital and Family Therapy, 16,* 179–186.

Helms, J. E., & Richardson, T. Q. (1997). How "multiculturalism" obscures race and culture as differential aspects of counseling competency. In D. B. Pope-Davis & H. L. K. Coleman (Eds.), *Multicultural counseling competencies: Assessment, education and training, and supervision* (pp. 60–79). Thousand Oaks, CA: Sage.

Hermans, H. J. M. (1995). The limitations of logic in defining the self. *Theory and Psychology, 5,* 375–382.

Hoffmann, L. (1991). A reflexive stance for family therapy. *Journal of Strategic and Systemic Therapies, 10,* 4–17.

Hollinger, R. (1994). *Postmodernism and the social sciences: A thematic approach.* Thousand Oaks, Ca: Sage.

Horvath, A. O., & Greenberg, L. S. (1989). Development and validation of the Working Alliance Inventory. *Journal of Counseling Psychology, 36,* 223–233.

Horvath, A. O., & Greenberg, L. S. (1994). *The Working Alliance: Theory, research, and practice.* New York: John Wiley.

Horvath, A. O., & Symonds, B. D. (1991). Relation between the Working Alliance and outcome in psychotherapy: A meta-analysis. *Journal of Counseling Psychology, 38,* 139–149.

Howard, G. S. (1991). Culture tales: A narrative approach to thinking, cross-cultural psychology, and psychotherapy. *American Psychologist, 46,* 187–197.

Huber, C. H. (1994). *Ethical, legal, and professional issues in the practice of marriage and family therapy* (2nd ed.). New York: Merrill.

Johnson, P. (1991). *The birth of the modern: World society 1815–1830.* New York: Harper Collins.

Jones, E. E., & Thorne, A. (1987). Rediscovery of the subject: Intercultural approaches to clinical assessment. *Journal of Consulting and Clinical Psychology, 55,* 488–495.

Krumboltz, J. D. (1979). A social learning theory of career decision making. In A. M. Mitchell, G. B. Jones, & J. D. Krumboltz (Eds.), *Social learning and career decision making* (pp. 19–49).

Cranston, RI: Carroll Press.

Kudlac, K. E. (1991). Including God in the conversation: The influence of religious beliefs on the problem-organized system. *Family Therapy, 18,* 277–285.

Laird, J. (1991). Women and stories: Restorying women's self-constructions. In M. McGoldrick, C. M. Anderson, & F. Walsh (Eds.), *Women in families: A framework for family therapy* (pp. 427–450). New York: W. W. Norton.

Laird, J. (1993). Lesbian and gay families. In F. Walsh (Ed.), *Normal family processes* (2nd ed., pp. 427–450). New York: W. W. Norton.

Lazarus, A. A. (1992). Multimodal therapy: Technical eclecticism with minimal integration. In J. C. Norcross & M. R. Goldfried (Eds.), *Handbook of psychotherapy integration* (pp. 231–263). New York: Basic Books.

Lyddon, W. J. (1990). First- and second-order change: Implications for rationalist and constructivist cognitive therapies. *Journal of Counseling and Development, 69,* 122–127.

Lyddon, W. J. (1995). Forms and facets of constructivist psychology. In R. A. Neimeyer & M. J. Mahoney (Eds.), *Constructivism in psychotherapy* (pp. 69–92). Washington, DC: American Psychological Association.

Mascolo, M. F., & Dalto, C. A. (1995). Self and modernity on trial: A reply to Gergen's *Saturated Self. Journal of Constructivist Psychology, 8,* 175–191.

Meichenbaum, D., & Fong, G. T. (1993). How individuals control their own minds: A constructive narrative perspective. In D. M. Wegner & J. W. Pennebaker (Eds.), *Handbook of mental control* (pp. 473–490). Englewood Cliffs, NJ: Prentice-Hall.

Mente, D. (1995). Whose truth? Whose goodness? Whose beauty? *American Psychologist, 50,* 391.

Metcalf, L. (1995). *Counseling toward solutions: A practical solution-focused program for working with students, teachers, and parents.* West Nyack, NY: Center for Applied Research in Education.

Minuchin, S. (1991). The seductions of constructivism. *Family Therapy Networker, 15*(5), 47–50.

Nadeau, K. G. (1995). ADD in the workplace: Career consultation and counseling for the adult with ADD. In K. G. Nadeau (Ed.), *A comprehensive guide to attention deficit disorder in adults* (pp. 308–344). New York: Brunner/Mazel.

Neimeyer, R. A. (1993a). An appraisal of constructivist psychotherapies. *Journal of Consulting and Clinical Psychology, 61,* 221–234.

Neimeyer, R. A. (1993b). Constructivism and the problem of psychotherapy integration. *Journal of Psychotherapy Integration, 3,* 133–157.

Neimeyer, R. A. (1995a). Client-generated narratives in psychotherapy. In R. A. Neimeyer & M. J. Mahoney (Eds.), *Constructivism in psychotherapy* (pp. 231–246). Washington, DC: American Psychotherapy Association.

Neimeyer, R. A. (1995b). Constructivist psychotherapies: Features, foundations, and future directions. In R. A. Neimeyer & M. J. Mahoney (Eds.), *Constructivism in psychotherapy* (pp. 11–38). Washington, DC: American Psychotherapy Association.

Neimeyer, R. A., Neimeyer, G. J., Lyddon, W. J., & Hoshmand, L. S. (1994). The reality of social construction. *Contemporary Psychology, 39,* 458–463.

O'Hara, M., & Anderson, W. T. (1991). Welcome to the postmodern world. *Family Therapy Networker, 15*(5), 19–25.

Pedersen, P. (1990). The multicultural perspective as a fourth force in counseling. *Journal of Mental Health Counseling, 12,* 92–95.

Pedersen, P. B. (1991). Multiculturalism as a generic approach to counseling. *Journal of Counseling and Development, 70,* 6–12.

Penn, P. (1982). Circular questioning. *Family Process, 21,* 267–280.

Peterson, J. A. (1970). *Counseling and values.* Scranton, PA: International Textbook.

Phillips, D. C. (1995). The good, the bad, and the ugly: The many faces of constructivism. *Educational Researcher, 24*(7), 5–12.

Pinderhughes, E. (1995). Empowering diverse populations: Family practice in the 21st century. *Families in Society, 76,* 131–140.

Pipher, M. (1994). *Reviving Ophelia: Saving the selves of adolescent girls.* New York: G. P. Putnam's Sons.

Poole, G. A. (1996, March 7). Revolution of computers in schools has two faces: Students in private schools have advantages over kids in public schools when it comes to technology. *El Paso Herald Post,* pp. C5, C6.

Reichelt, S., & Sveaass, N. (1994). Therapy with refugee families: What is a "good" conversation? *Family Process, 33,* 247–262.

Richardson, M. S. (1993). Work in people's lives: A location for counseling psychologists. *Journal of Counseling Psychology, 40,* 425–433.

Roberts, R. E., Attkisson, C. C., & Mendias, R. M. (1984). Assessing the Client Satisfaction Questionnaire in English and in Spanish. *Hispanic Journal of Behavioral Sciences, 6,* 385–395.

Roberts, R. E., Attkisson, C. C., & Stegner, B. L. (1983). A client satisfaction scale suitable for use with Hispanics? *Hispanic Journal of Behavioral Sciences, 5,* 461–476.

Rosenau, P. M. (1992). *Post-modernism and the social sciences: Insights, inroads, and intrusions.* Princeton, NJ: Princeton University Press.

Ross, L., & Nisbett, R. E. (1991). *The person and the situation: Perspectives of social psychology.* New York: McGraw-Hill.

Ruggiero, V. R. (1990). *Beyond feelings: A guide to critical thinking* (3rd ed.). Mountain View, CA: Mayfield.

Russell, R. L., & Gaubatz, M. D. (1995). Contested affinities: Reaction to Gergen's (1994) and Smith's (1994) postmodernisms. *American Psychologist, 50,* 389–390.

Sarbin, T. R. (Ed.). (1986). *Narrative psychology: The storied nature of human conduct.* New York: Praeger.

Savickas, M. L. (1993). Career counseling in the postmodern era. *Journal of Cognitive Psychotherapy: An International Quarterly, 7,* 205–215.

Savickas, M. L. (1994). Vocational psychology in the postmodern era: Comment on Richardson (1993). *Journal of Counseling Psychology, 41,* 105–107.

Savickas, M. L. (1995). Current theoretical issues in vocational psychology: Paradigms, theories, and research practices. In W. B. Walsh & S. H. Osipow (Eds.), *Handbook of vocational psychology* (2nd ed., pp. 1–34). Mahwah, NJ: Lawrence Erlbaum.

Self, B. (1995, October 22). *Colonias* cost taxpayers $500 million. *El Paso Times,* 1A, 14A.

Shotter, J. (1995). A "show" of agency is enough. *Theory and Psychology, 5,* 383–390.

Smith, H. (1989). *Beyond the post-modern mind.* Wheaton, IL: Theosophical Publishing Company.

Smith, M. B. (1994). Selfhood at risk: Postmodern perils and the periods of postmodernism. *American Psychologist, 49,* 405–411.

Smith, M. B. (1995). About postmodernism: Reply to Gergen and others. *American Psychologist, 50,* 393–394.

Srivastva, S., Fry, R. E., & Cooperrider, D. L. (1990). Introduction: The call for executive appreciation. In S. Srivastva, D. L. Cooperrider, & Associates (Eds.), *Appreciative management and leadership: The power of positive thought and action in organizations* (pp. 1–33). San Francisco: Jossey-Bass.

Sue, D. W. (1992). The road less traveled. *American Counselor, 1*(1), 6–10, 12–14.

Sue, D. W., Ivey, A., & Pedersen, P. B. (1996). *A theory of multicultural counseling and therapy.* Pacific Grove, CA: Brooks/Cole.

Sue, D. W., & Sue, D. (1990). *Counseling the culturally different: Theory and practice* (2nd ed.). New York: John Wiley.

Taylor, J. M., Gilligan, C., & Sullivan, A. M. (1995). *Between voice and silence: Women and girls, race and relationships.* Cambridge, MA: Harvard University Press.

Tinsley, H. E. A. (1994). Construct your reality and show us its benefits: Comment on Richardson (1993). *Journal of Counseling Psychology, 41,* 108–111.

Tomm, K. (1985). Circular interviewing: A multifaceted clinical tool. In D. Campbell & R. Draper (Eds.), *Applications of systemic family therapy: The Milan approach* (Vol. 3, pp. 33–45). Orlando, FL: Grune & Stratton.

Tomm, K. (1987). Interventive interviewing: Part II. Reflexive questioning as a means to enable self-healing. *Family Process, 26,* 167–183.

United States Catholic Conference (Producer). (1991). *On fire with faith* [videotape]. Washington, DC: Office for Publishing and Promotion Services, United States Catholic Conference.

Young, C. (1989). Psychodynamics of coping and survival of the African American female in a changing world. *Journal of Black Studies, 20,* 208–223.

# Part 6:

◉ **Integrative Practice Theory** ◉

# 18

## The Social-Cognitive Construction of Psychotherapeutic Change: Theory, Practice, and Research

*Jack Martin*

Social constructionism and cognitive constructivism are different psychological and philosophical positions. Social constructionism emphasizes the social, public origins and nature of mind as a product of socially embedded ways of talking and acting. Cognitive constructivism emphasizes the creative capacity of individuals to develop conceptions of themselves and their worlds that form the underlying basis for their actions and experiences. Both constructionism and constructivism share postmodern tenets regarding the untenability of modernist conceptions of objective, empirical, logical, rational knowledge. Radical forms of social constructionism attempt to deconstruct and dismiss conceptions of human subjects as creators of meaning and to replace them with language systems, viewing individuals as vehicles through which these systems speak or write (Derrida, 1973, 1978).

In this chapter, I attempt to reconcile claims concerning the social, linguistic origins of mind with claims concerning the developmentally emergent, creative capacity of individual minds to construct meaning. Much of the discussion bears some affinity to classic symbolic interactionism, particularly as formulated by Mead (1934), Vygotsky (1986), and Kelly (1955). However, the present account also reflects recent theoretical and empirical work of my own (Martin, 1994; Martin & Sugarman, in press). In the following sections, I initially sketch a general view of psychological development that attempts to merge important ideas from both social constructionism and cognitive constructivism. I then offer a theoretical perspective on psychotherapeutic change that assumes this more general conception of psychological development. Following this theoretical rationale, I present a template for psychotherapeutic practice consistent with both the general psychological and specific psychotherapeutic perspectives discussed. Research support for these theoretical and practical ideas is presented, and evaluation procedures that psychotherapists might use to assess the impact of their interventions are suggested.

# Psychological Development: From Social Constructionism to Cognitive Constructivism

A brief presentation of the general theory of psychological development, within which the more specific theory of psychotherapeutic change is housed, may be accomplished through a consideration of four basic propositions. The first principle concerns the existential assumptions of the developmental theory. Here, it is assumed that at birth human individuals are thrown into preexisting physical and sociocultural worlds, equipped only with primitive biological capacities to move, experience, perceive, and remember. The building blocks of all individual psychological development are located in this basic condition and in these rudimentary capacities to move about in the physical and sociocultural worlds we inhabit, to perceive and experience something of what these movements make possible, and to remember some of these perceptions and experiences.

A second proposition concerns the gradual acquisition of a prereflective consciousness. Compelled to act by their basic existential condition, humans gradually internalize sociocultural forms and interrelational practices, the most important of these being conversational practices. In this way, individuals are shaped by the forms, concepts, and practices of the societies and cultures they inhabit. All of this occurs prior to acquiring a sense of self through which they might reflect consciously on such sociocultural conventions and their participation in them.

The third core proposition concerns the gradual emergence of personal theories of world and self that alter the nature of individual consciousness. The gradual appropriation of sociocultural forms and practices as psychological tools allows humans to acquire theories of self through which they organize and understand their own experience in and knowledge of the physical and sociocultural worlds. With the acquisition of such personal theories, individuals take on sophisticated capabilities of reflective memory and imagination through which they are able to revisit and reconsider the past and to project themselves into the future. Such reflectivity becomes the standard mode of operating within constraints imposed by past and present physical and sociocultural realities. The reflective consciousness associated with such capabilities allows individuals to entertain possibilities that transcend these constraints.

Thus, human capabilities of reflective memory and imagination allow individuals to develop psychologically in ways that potentially might transcend their past and present experiences in their societies and cultures. Because of reflective forms of consciousness focused on personal theories of self, individual psychology is not determined entirely by its largely sociocultural origins. At this point in human psychological development, the heavy influence of societies and cultures is joined by influential, constructive capacities for individual creativity. When this happens, the nature of human psychology shifts from one largely determined by external forms and practices to one capable of moving beyond such influences.

Sophisticated, complex, reflective capabilities for memory and imagination tied to theories of self permit transcendence beyond participations and experiences of the past and present and enable a genuinely reflexive and intentional consciousness to emerge. By exercising this transcendent potential, individuals are able to imagine and engage in actions that are not entirely determined by their physical and sociocultural worlds and that can affect and sometimes alter these worlds. The fourth proposition in the developmental theory under consideration concerns the ability of humans to engage in purposeful activity designed to alter their life circumstances and sociocultural contexts. With this ability, humans are unique in their capacity for personal and sociocultural innovation and change. In this way, individual psychology typified by theories of self and reflective consciousness is seen to arise from human experience in the physical and sociocultural worlds, but after it has emerged it cannot be reduced to these same experiences.

The preceding view of human psychological development bridges traditional views of social constructionism and cognitive constructivism. This bridge preserves social constructionist explanations of the origins of human psychology while recognizing the strengths of cognitive constructivism with respect to understanding change and creative innovation that go beyond sociocultural constraints.

## A Theory of Psychotherapeutic Change

Within the general theory of psychological development just sketched, psychotherapy may be understood as a set of conversations and relational activities designed to help individuals alter their theories of self and world to permit more effective goal attainment, problem resolution, or personal coping. In psychotherapy, therapists and clients work to elaborate clients' personal theories through a constructive analysis and interpretation of past and current experience and understanding. Revisions of clients' personal theories (of self, others, and circumstances) are conjointly constructed through psychotherapeutic conversation and activities. These revised theories, as mediated by clients' memories of therapy sessions and imaginative extensions to these memories, permit clients to contribute to their everyday extratherapeutic contexts and circumstances in ways that alter these contexts and circumstances and clients' experiences in them. Ultimately, clients who have benefited from psychotherapeutic conversations and practices are potentially capable of contributing to the personal, interpersonal, social, and cultural contexts in which they exist in ways that alter these contexts.

In the same way in which individual psychology develops from participation and experience in sociocultural settings yet is necessarily underdetermined by such exposure, possibilities for psychotherapeutic change are constructed yet are not entirely constrained in the social context of psychotherapy. As reflective agents possessing the capabilities of memory and imagination, clients inevitably adapt what they take from psychotherapy to their unique life circumstances and their understanding and interpretation of those circumstances and of themselves. Thus, the following template for psychotherapeutic practice avoids making highly prescriptive suggestions about precisely what kinds of psychotherapeutic interventions will lead to exactly what kinds of client-change outcomes. Clients' capacities for cognitive constructivism permit them to understand and act upon psychotherapeutic interventions in ways that never can be entirely predetermined or constrained by the specific nature of these interventions. Consequently, in the following discussion, psychotherapeutic practice is described in more general phases of therapeutic activity, phases in which the kinds of theoretical propositions and principles articulated thus far may be located.

# A Template for Psychotherapeutic Practice

The template for psychotherapeutic practice that follows is consistent with the foregoing theoretical formulations but stops short of prescribing specific psychotherapeutic interventions. Instead, it describes a process of psychotherapeutic change that might be used as a framework within which individual psychotherapists might fit their own preferred intervention strategies in ways consistent with the overall purposes and processes described in each of four phases of psychotherapy: (a) articulation, (b) elaboration, (c) revision, and (d) instantiation.

## *Articulation*

Clients enter psychotherapy as a result of angst associated with difficulties in coping with current life circumstances. In the initial conversations, the client's presenting concerns are revealed, and the therapist and client agree to direct their activities toward particular ends, to divide their labor and responsibility in particular ways, and ideally to respect and trust each other. As the client responds to the initial questions and invitations of the psychotherapist and begins to tell his or her story, the seeds of a solid working relationship between therapist and client are sown. Effective psychotherapy cannot take place in the absence of such a therapeutic relationship.

As conversational partners discussing intimate, personal material, therapists and clients must be able to work together respectfully and cooperatively. Such a working relationship cannot be accomplished unless the goals and tasks of the cooperative enterprise are acceptable and viable to both. Further, the client and therapist must care about these goals and tasks and trust each other to expend effort in advancing them. Through this shared commitment, respectfully and thoughtfully initiated, emerges a genuine sense of mutual caring and respect. In this way, the affective aspects of the relationship between therapist and client cannot be separated from the nature of the activity in which they are engaged. During the client's initial articulation of concerns, problems, and issues, the therapist and client establish viable, acceptable goals for their work together; their initial attempts to work toward these goals draw them closer together. In this way, their conversations and associated activities early in psychotherapy set the stage for the intensive, collaborative elaboration and revision of clients' personal theories that follows.

## *Elaboration*

After the therapeutic relationship is in place and initial concerns and goals have been broached, the subsequent therapeutic conversation may be seen as a joint social construction or narrative of the client's current and past experiences, difficulties, understandings, imaginings, and hopes. A wide variety of discourse vehicles (including storytelling, analogy, metaphor, imagery, and argument) is available for use in this shared effort to portray the client's experiential world. Meanings, attitudes, beliefs, values, and desires are articulated and explored. Both conversationalists offer interpretations that reflect their ongoing and emergent perceptions and understandings. Depending on the form of psychotherapy, relational activities accompanying the therapeutic conversation may be replete with role plays, experiential exercises, emotionally heightened reminiscences, rational analyses, systematic observation, and other social and interpersonal variations. Such activities enhance the conceptual richness of the therapeutic exchange.

The basic therapeutic task is the social and public elaboration, through the co-constructed therapeutic conversation, of the client's concerns and related theories and knowledge. The various discourse devices are employed in a joint effort to portray the client's experiential world as fully as possible. Personal meanings, attitudes, values, beliefs, desires, and habitual actions are explored and articulated, even though they heretofore may have been held in mind tacitly, nonverbally, or subconsciously. As Paivio (1986) demonstrated, vivid, concrete, imagery-laden language typical of the figurative, experiential language employed in psychotherapy can enable the verbalization and conscious awareness of material previously stored only in nonverbal, imaginal representations. The retrieval and verbalization of such material, including clients' memories of past and current extratherapeutic experiences, invariably enter into the therapeutic elaboration of clients' personal theories and stories. Some approaches to psychotherapy emphasize the recollection and examination of personal memories from childhood and adolescence, whereas others emphasize the recollection and examination of relatively current experiences and situations. Regardless of which approach is taken, the therapeutic discussion and elaboration of such memories provide important content for the therapeutic elaboration of clients' concerns and difficulties. As this elaboration advances, interpretations of the client's experiential narrative are forwarded by both therapist and client in ways that recognize patterns of perception, understanding, and action that make explicit the client's relevant personal theories of self and circumstances.

## *Revision*

As the therapeutic conversation unfolds, parts of it become available to the client as content and forms for thought and as psychological tools (of understanding, of possible strategic action, and of reflection) with which to think and act. The outward, conversational, interpsychological relations contained in the therapeutic interactions become available for the client's construction of intrapsychological mental functions. Thus, the process of social construction in psychotherapy is one in which therapists assist clients to change by elaborating social conversations that are meaningful and understandable within the context of socially constructed theories that are available for clients' internalization.

In the course of time, therapists gradually and incrementally introduce into the therapeutic discourse discordant elements that elaborate clients' theories in the public, social arena of psychotherapy in ways not previously available to clients. Some of these discordant elaborations might include the noting of inconsistencies in clients' current theories and understandings, examples of alternative ways of acting on understandings, and observations of clients' nonverbal, affective reactions not immediately available to clients' awareness. Various factors might enhance clients' attention to and subsequent recollections of such discordant elements, including therapeutic dialogue rich in concreteness, vividness, specific illustration, and metaphor. In particular, it may be essential for clients to perceive both the relevance and inconsistency of these conversational elements to their current personal theories. In other words, therapeutic conversations containing seeds for the functional revision of clients' personal theories are more likely to be internalized and recalled by clients if these conversations are perceived as relevant (helpful, interesting, and so forth) yet somehow different from clients' existing construal of themselves and their concerns. Psychotherapists may need considerable artistry and skill to monitor clients' current and evolving understandings so that the therapists' own contributions to the therapeutic conversation gradually and incrementally extend, without exceeding, the clients' awareness and understanding of their currently active personal theories.

## *Instantiation*

In the course of time, clients' appropriation and recollection of therapeutic conversations containing the potentially change-inducing, discordant elements discussed above can act as catalysts to more extensive revision and restructuring of clients' personal theories that might support more adaptive patterns of behavior in relevant contexts outside of therapy. Clients' recollections and understandings of such therapeutic conversations may be activated by cues in their daily life. Once activated, these therapeutically enhanced understandings and the revised personal theories with which they are associated may be used as bases for revised patterns of emotional, perceptual, cognitive, and physical responses to life situations.

In short, that which clients internalize from therapeutic conversations and relational practices may help them amend and revise their existing understandings, frameworks, practices, strategies, and eventually their actions and behaviors. The extent of such change undoubtedly depends on factors particular to clients and their situations. Real life experiences that serve to accommodate change may be initiated in therapy through the use of homework assignments, planned extratherapeutic exercises, preparatory fantasy dialogues, and role plays. These and other methods anticipate and help prepare clients for transferring their therapeutically elaborated and revised theories and insights to their life in appropriate ways.

## *Caveat*

In offering this template for how psychotherapeutic change might be achieved, I do not believe that it is possible to specify a priori what specific change methods or strategies are likely to be effective in instances of psychotherapy. Rather, the selection and employment of methods and strategies should be left to the artistry of the psychotherapist. The foregoing template for therapeutic practice is a heuristically useful framework for conceptualizing phases of therapeutic work. It is intended as a general guide to psychotherapists, not as a rigid prescription. The case illustrations that follow indicate more clearly how this template for psychotherapeutic practice can serve as a heuristically useful guide to the practice of psychotherapy.

# Case Illustrations

## *Case Illustration One*

How clients in psychotherapy internalize therapeutic conversations and how such internalizations can become functional psychological tools for clients are illustrated in the following case study (Martin, 1987). The client was a 35-year-old woman who suffered verbal and physical abuse from a man with whom she lived. Immediately following each of eight sessions of therapy, the woman was asked to free associate to her own name and to her partner's name brief phrases describing her problems and possible solutions to her problems. All of the client's associative responses were recorded on gummed labels—one response to each label. These labels then were returned to the client so that she could organize them on a sheet of laminated paper to indicate relationships among the words or phrases contained on the labels by placing related labels close to one another or by using marking pencils to draw connecting lines between labels or by both methods.

The client's responses to the free association and conceptual-mapping tasks clearly revealed her internalization of therapeutic conversations during the eight therapy sessions. Following the first session of therapy (the initiation of the therapeutic phase of articulation—see above), her conceptual map of her problems consisted of a centrally located, self-referencing label ("me") connected directly to surrounding labels indicative of negative affect ("hopeless," "trapped," "afraid," "ashamed," "can't do anything right") and connected indirectly to clusters of labels representing her partner, her children, and her parents as well as her relationships with them. The labels offered no indication of understanding of or insight into her problems or of possible strategies that might be engaged to address her problems. Following eight sessions of psychotherapy, this client produced a conceptual map of her problems that contained clear indications of both enhanced understanding and possible strategies of responding. In this last map, a centrally located, self-referencing label was connected directly to a cluster of labels representing her unwilling participation in a cycle of family violence in which her partner was represented as a dangerous batterer in need of help. Another cluster of labels, emanating directly from the central self-referencing label, identified strategic options available through a local women's center and through the supportive intervention of her extended family. Affective labels in this map referred to anger and worry but also to hope.

Results obtained on the conceptual-mapping task employed in this case study, when set against transcriptions and tape recordings of the therapy sessions themselves, indicate a clear relationship between salient conversational themes during the course of therapy and the client's free-associative, conceptual-mapping responses following the therapy sessions. The therapeutic intervention, particularly during phases of elaboration and revision (see above), focused primarily on clarifying and elaborating the client's affective reactions, providing information about relationship violence and men who batter women, and exploring options that would remove the client from her currently dysfunctional life circumstances. In this case, the conceptual-mapping responses of the client were interpreted as evidence of her internalization of these therapeutic conversations into her personal theory regarding her problems and possible solutions to them. The eventual ability of this client (in the instantiation phase of psychotherapy) to extricate herself from the abusive relationship she had endured for so many years and to make more favorable arrangements for herself and her children probably was facilitated by this internalization process.

## Case Illustration Two

To illustrate in detail some of the processes of therapeutic change that occur during the elaboration and revision phases of psychotherapy, the following presents an actual therapeutic conversation taken from the sixth session of psychotherapy devoted to assisting a man in his thirties to understand and improve his intimate relationships with women.[1] The psychotherapist, a middle-aged man, employed a combination of experiential, cognitive, and analytic therapeutic interventions. By the sixth session, initial elaboration of the client's current theory of his difficulties had been attempted. On the basis of this therapeutic work, it appeared that the client believed he was extremely "open" in his relationships with the women he dated, as he believed he was with his now-estranged first wife. He thought his difficulties in forming satisfying, lasting relationships with these women resulted from their unwillingness to reciprocate his emotional and intellectual "openness." However, his inability to understand why such reciprocation was not forthcoming left him feeling frustrated and angry.

In the fourth and fifth sessions of psychotherapy (each session lasting approximately 50 minutes, with sessions spaced approximately one week apart), the client illustrated the foregoing theory by describing a series of recent interactions with women and past interactions with his former wife. At the therapist's urging, he attempted to articulate his experiences and reactions to these interactions in a supplement to the third-person accounts he had been providing thus far and in support of his theory regarding his relationship difficulties. Only when the client was asked to "reenter specific, recollected scenes" could he begin to verbalize his own experiential reactions to them. These reactions consisted of mounting frustration and anger at his inability to extract, and at his partner's seeming inability to furnish, details of her own experiential reactions to him and to their activities together. The intensity of these emotions clearly surprised the client.

---

1. This case illustration is reprinted with permission from Martin, J. (1994). *The construction and understanding of psychotherapeutic change: Conversations, memories, and theories.* New York: Teachers College Press.

In the sixth session, the therapist and client began to explore contributions to the client's current manner of relating to women that might arise from his past and current experiences in his family of origin. In the following excerpt from this session, the therapist made purposeful use of concrete, figurative language in an effort to help the client probe his emotional experiences when interacting with his parents. After this session, the client recalled part of this therapeutic conversation (C5 to C11) as especially memorable.

*Client: My mother is a very, very caring person, and in that way I love my mother a lot. Very emotionally strong, although she thinks she's not. She can put up with a lot more than Dad can. He just pulls away and denies any emotional component. [C1]*

*Therapist: He deflects it. [T1]*

*Client: Onto my sister a lot. Whoever the hell he can who's handy. He gets quite upset when you talk about his emotions. You're not supposed to have any. As a kid, he used to talk about being rational all the time. Rational was the best way. You can't give in to your emotions or weaknesses. I remember all that and now it's coming back. It's crap, all of it. [C2]*

*Therapist: As I sit here, I think of you as carrying a big emotional burden. [T2]*

*Client: Hmm. For whom? And why? [C3]*

*Therapist: I don't know. It's just an image I have of you carrying a lot of weight. Maybe some of his weight that he won't carry. [T4: In a postsession interview, the therapist identified this comment as the start of what he considered to be an important section of the therapy session. At this point, he began to employ concrete, figurative language in a purposeful effort to facilitate the client's experiential elaboration of his "story."]*

*Client: Hmm. Like a sponge, taking all the deflections. I let it go right through me instead of bouncing back. And really, it's not my place, any of that. If that's true. [C5: The client recalled this comment as the beginning of a memorable event in this therapy session.]*

*Therapist: Yes, if that's true. Turn inside and focus on how it feels when you're at home. Your dad starts doing his thing. Your mom does her thing in response to him. And you're in the middle. How does that feel? [T5]*

*Client: It feels like I have a knot in my stomach. It feels unnatural. It doesn't feel like I can be myself in that setting. A stranger in a strange land with my own parents. Like I'm being something that I have to be. And playing a role that is necessary in that situation. [C6]*

*Therapist: That knot in your stomach. It gnaws? It weighs you down? [T6]*

*Client: It keeps me down. It holds me back. It prevents me from probably being who I am. Saying exactly what I feel. [C7]*

*Therapist: It's a restraining knot. [T7]*

*Client: Yeah. It's holding me back from, I don't know, possibly hurting somebody by being brutally frank about what I'm seeing, what I'm experiencing. [C8]*

*Therapist: You are restrained with your parents and you're weighted down inside yourself. [T8]*

*Client: Hmm. It's almost like a control element for them. They can restrain me, hold me back. [C9]*

*Therapist: Whatever happens, perhaps you and they, in combination, hold you back. But the end result is that you feel burdened. [Pause] The knot not only restrains, but it also gnaws. [T9]*

*Client: Yeah. Yeah. I'm sure there is a lot of that. About my sister and not being able to tell them about that—her being gay, even though they suspect. And a lot of my dad's emotional crap that gnaws at me. My mother's incessant need to try and make up for 20 years of my childhood that are dead now, that are gone and can't be made up for. That gnaws at me. When will this end? She, we persevered and got through her mental illness, the hellish times until I was—what the hell was I? I guess I was 20 when she stopped having the real severe problems. We went through it. It's done. I don't want to have to relive it, and she constantly wants to relive this crap again. It's not so bad now. It's been getting better, I have to agree, as time goes on, but there's still a lot of crap. There's a lot of concealed stuff that I don't think should be concealed. I tend to be probably a little too honest sometimes, and people get hurt. And that's the one thing I don't like about me is that I can be too honest sometimes. And in this context, with you, I think that's what I'm being. And if I went home and was as honest as I am with you, I would probably "dissemble" the entire family. [C10: The client moves from obvious anger to sadness—moist eyes—to brief, sarcastic laughter.]*

*Therapist: If you gave up all the psychological weight you carry for everybody, all the secrets, it would destroy your family. Intolerable. [T10]*

*Client: Yeah! Yeah! [C11: This ends one of two therapeutic events recalled by the client as especially important in the sixth session of therapy.]*

The client's recollection of the foregoing therapeutic conversation during the sixth session of psychotherapy subsequently mediated an important revision to his personal theory about his relationship difficulties. In sessions seven and eight, the client and therapist elaborated the client's theory by linking his now-verbalized experiences in his family of origin to his current experiences with women. In these jointly constructed conversations, the client began to view himself as someone who was most comfortable when he was in receipt of others' "secrets" and whose intimate, interpersonal interactions were aimed at securing such knowledge from his partners. What the client understood to be his "openness" in such situations was an openness to the intimate expressions of others rather than an openness to expressing his own emotions ("secrets"). This was especially true with respect to any expression of what he referred to as "softer, less masculine" emotions like love, caring, and needing, the expression of which he believed would leave him vulnerable to women who possessed knowledge of these "secrets." When his attempts to extract his partner's secrets were unsuccessful, he became worried that his own feelings of love and attraction might not be reciprocated. This worry inevitably led him to "cover up his own secrets" and to become upset and angry that his feelings for his partner might be too one-sided. Knowledge of this pattern of intimate interactions was new to the client.

Eventually, the client became sufficiently convinced of this new theory of his relationship difficulties that he was able to take it outside the therapeutic conversation (i.e., to internalize it through episodic recall). At the therapist's urging, the client began to discuss his "softer" feelings with his current partner before requesting similar disclosures from her. Fortunately, his current partner, although somewhat put off by the client's previous attempts to "extract her secrets," really did seem to care deeply about the relationship and welcomed his expressions of love, caring, and vulnerability. Thus, toward the end of therapy, the client's recollections of previous therapeutic conversations that elaborated on his personal theory regarding his relationships with women seemed to enable dramatic revisions to this theory. These revisions enabled him to engage in new forms of behavior outside therapy. Clearly, the client's actual and vicarious past and current experiences outside therapy, together with his therapeutic experiences, allowed him to construct a new theory of himself in intimate relationships with women.

The mediational role played by the client's episodic memories of past, extratherapeutic conversations and experiences (in both the therapeutic elaboration and the extratherapeutic revision of his theory of intimate relationships) is readily apparent in this case reconstruction. The therapist's use of expressive, figurative language (together with other therapeutic vehicles such as experiential support, encouragement, interpretation, and challenge) seemed to highlight important parts of the therapeutic conversation and to help the client revise his personal theory.

# Research and Evaluation

## *Formal Research Studies*

From 1988 to 1996, several colleagues and I conducted a series of research studies aimed at demonstrating several change mechanisms and processes postulated in the foregoing account of the social–cognitive construction of psychotherapeutic change. Martin and Stelmaczonek (1988) conducted two methodologically pluralistic studies employing methods of exploratory research and discourse analysis in combination with those of more traditional hypothesis-testing psychological research. The first exploratory study addressed three questions: (a) What kinds of events during psychotherapy do clients and psychotherapists identify as important? (b) Does the nature of such events change in the course of therapy? (c) Do therapists and clients identify the same events as important? Therapists and clients were interviewed by a research assistant immediately following the completion of each of eight psychotherapy sessions and asked to identify "the most important things that happened during the session." Both therapists and clients most frequently recalled as important six categories of therapeutic events. Four types of events related to the therapeutic task of *enhancing clients' personal awareness.* The remaining two types of events related to the therapeutic task of *revising personal theories.* These results were interpreted to demonstrate a therapeutic process that involved the promotion of clients' awareness and articulation of their personal theories and their subsequent elaboration and revision of those theories through psychotherapeutic intervention.

The second study reported by Martin and Stelmaczonek (1988) employed a similar methodology but tested an apriori hypothesis to the effect that discourse during psychotherapeutic events recalled as important by clients would differ from discourse in temporally proximate control events in ways consistent with results from experimental cognitive psychological research on determinants of memorability. To test this hypothesis, discourse during "recalled important" and control events was transcribed and coded for such characteristics as "depth of meaning," "elaboration of meaning through use of figurative language," "clarity," and "conclusion orientation." Results of inferential statistical comparisons revealed that client-recalled important therapeutic events were reliably characterized by significantly more of these discourse characteristics. The events that clients recalled as important were ones commonly associated with the elaboration and revision phases of psychotherapy in which therapists and clients attended to the meanings of clients' experiences, elaborated on these meanings through the use of figurative language, and attempted to draw conclusions concerning clients' experiences.

The second part of this second study by Martin and Stelmaczonek (1988) provided information concerning clients' ability to recall, at a six-month follow-up, events they had identified as important immediately following the psychotherapy sessions studied. The procedure employed was to cue clients' recall (after a six-month period) by having them view a one-minute videotaped segment from the start of each of the therapy sessions in which they previously had participated. In 73% of the cases tested, clients recalled accurately the events they previously had identified as important. The accuracy with which such therapeutic memories were maintained constituted a surprising, unexpected demonstration of persistence, especially when related to the inaccuracy and decay evident in subjects' memories of tasks undertaken in the laboratories of experimental cognitive psychologists. This result hinted at the possibility that memories of material endowed with personal meaning and significance may be much more enduring and influential than are memories of more detached material relatively devoid of such significance and meaning.

The results of these studies were interpreted to lend support for the emerging theory that psychotherapy worked by embedding in the minds of clients relatively lasting episodic memories of therapeutic interactions that could be used as bases for reconstructing clients' personal theories and eventually altering real-life behaviors and experiences during the instantiation phase of psychotherapeutic intervention. A subsequent study by Martin, Paivio, and Labadie (1990) verified results obtained from the hypothesis-testing portion of the second Martin and Stelmaczonek (1988) study. Once again, client-recalled events from psychotherapy sessions in which clients had participated differed from control events from those same therapy sessions in terms of such discourse characteristics as "depth of meaning," "elaboration of meaning through the use of figurative language," and "conclusion orientation."

Of potentially significant clinical and theoretical relevance in the Martin et al. (1990) study, the therapists' contributions to the discourse during client-recalled important therapeutic events contributed most to the differences between these events and the control events. The implication of this result was that therapists could influence clients' recall of therapeutic content and discourse through the nature and manner of their contributions to psychotherapy conversations and activities. This finding encouraged our growing conviction that psychotherapeutic conversations are appropriated by clients as a basis for personal theoretical and behavioral change, that clients' experiential or episodic memories mediate this process of internalization, and that psychotherapists intentionally can influence clients' recollection of therapeutic events through their own conversation and activity. This finding also brought to mind previously unreported findings from this and earlier studies (see Martin, 1994) concerning a relatively common error in client recollections of therapeutic events; that is, it wasn't unusual for clients in these studies to attribute to themselves contributions to therapeutic discourse that actually were made by therapists. The possibility that therapists might intentionally be able to influence client recollections of therapeutic interventions as part of the revision phase of psychotherapeutic intervention began to loom large.

A subsequent study by Martin, Cummings, and Hallberg (1992) attempted to test directly therapists' influence on clients' recollection of therapeutic events through the intentional use of figurative language. Therapists in this study attempted to use therapeutic metaphors when they judged that such intervention might promote therapeutic work and was appropriate to the current therapeutic context. Immediately after therapy sessions were completed, therapists and clients were asked to recall therapeutic events they found to be most memorable and to give reasons for the memorability of these events. Participants also rated each session in terms of its helpfulness and effectiveness.

Specific hypotheses were that clients (a) would tend to recall events associated with therapists' intentional use of therapeutic metaphors and (b) would rate sessions in which they experienced therapists' intentional metaphoric interventions higher than sessions in which they experienced no intentional metaphoric interventions. The rationale for the second hypothesis was the assumption that clients tend to recall therapeutic events when they have succeeded in deriving meaning from them. Thus, sessions during which therapists' intentional metaphoric interventions were experienced might contain more personally meaningful associations than sessions during which therapists' intentional metaphoric interventions were not experienced. Such meaningful consideration and recollection would seem to contribute to clients' perceptions that sessions were effective and helpful.

Results showed that clients recalled therapists' intentional use of metaphor in approximately two-thirds of the sessions in which therapists intentionally employed metaphors. Metaphors that were recalled tended to be developed collaboratively through the active participation of both therapist and client. With respect to clinical impact, clients rated sessions during which they recalled therapists' intentional metaphors as significantly more helpful than sessions during which they did not recall therapists' intentional metaphors.

Martin and colleagues' (1992) study was interpreted as verification of therapists' ability to contribute intentionally to therapeutic discourse in ways that influenced clients' internalization and recollection of specific therapeutic content. Accordingly, results of this study were seen as confirmation of the central proposition that psychotherapeutic discourse can be intentionally constructed in the social, public domain of psychotherapy (especially during the revision phase of psychotherapeutic intervention) with generally predictable effects on the personal, private constructions (memories and theories) of clients.

A study by Buirs and Martin (1997) provides evidence of the dual legacy of experiential constraints and possibilities on clients' ability to use psychotherapeutic interactions as a basis for personal change. The question guiding this research concerned the extent to which the conversational construction of possible selves during psychotherapy is constrained by past and present extratherapeutic social, interpersonal experiences of clients. Six clients (all substance abusers) expressed, explored, and attempted to synthesize their feelings and experiences during two role plays in which they imagined two future scenarios. In one scenario, the negative possible-self role play, the clients imagined that their problems with substance abuse remained unchanged. In the other scenario, the positive possible-self role play, they imagined that these problems had been overcome. All six clients were more likely to express directly feelings and experiences in the negative possible-self role play than in the positive possible-self role play.

Such a result is consistent with a strong social constructionist view that locates the origins of current psychological experience in one's history of experience in relevant social contexts. The fact that all six clients were active substance abusers probably made it easier for them to enact the negative possible-self role plays with greater expressions of feeling and experience than they displayed during the less familiar, positive possible-self role plays. Nonetheless, indications were dramatic and, we believe, reliable that clients' participation in the less familiar positive possible-self role plays enabled them to synthesize newly realized or more fully recognized feelings and experiences more readily than they did in the negative possible-self role plays. I believe that this second result provides some confirmation of the possibility that psychotherapeutic constructions might be internalized by clients as sources of revision to their existing theoretical and experimental beliefs and practices, supplementing and augmenting emergent capabilities of active functional memory and imagination. My faith in this interpretation is strengthened further by the many examples of clients' recollection and apparent internalization of psychotherapeutic discourse and experience in the earlier studies summarized above.

Taken together, the reported studies demonstrate many aspects of the view of psychological development and psychotherapeutic change presented here (see Martin, 1994; Martin & Sugarman, in press). Such demonstrations support the theoretical view of psychotherapy as a unique form of social conversation and interpersonal activity that attempts to help clients alter their personal theories through a process of internalizing therapeutic discourse. Buirs and Martin's (1997) study reminds us that such possibilities for change are always constrained by relevant past and present sociocultural experiences of clients.

## *Informal Assessment of Therapeutic Change*

A less formal aspect of empirical evaluation related to the theory of psychotherapeutic change discussed here concerns the manner in which clinicians might assess and evaluate their interventions in relation to the theory and practice guidelines presented. Practitioners who have used these ideas in their therapeutic practices have tended to adopt and adapt several of the procedures in the foregoing discussion. In particular, methods of free association and conceptual mapping described in the first case example have proven especially useful as a means of monitoring and encouraging the kind of conjoint therapeutic conversations and activities the theory assumes. These same methods can be used as assessment procedures to help both therapists and clients gauge the kind and extent of conceptual change to clients' personal theories as a consequence of their participation in psychotherapeutic interventions.

Other clinical assessment procedures similar to some of the procedures followed in the discussed research include the tape recording of sessions for subsequent listening or viewing by both client and therapist as a means of understanding important themes and conversational elements in therapeutic conversations that, if internalized, might assist clients in resolving and coping with their difficulties. The kinds of memory probes administered by researchers in these studies also have proven to be helpful therapeutic devices when used by therapists to probe clients' recollections of important events and insights from therapy sessions, both immediately following such sessions and prior to the commencement of subsequent sessions. Both tape recordings and memory probes are also useful in conducting follow-up assessments of clients' conceptual, theoretical learning from psychotherapeutic interventions and their use of such learning in extratherapeutic contexts. One way to encourage clients to attend to their extratherapeutic use of understandings and strategies extracted from psychotherapeutic conversations is to encourage clients to keep journals in which they enter and describe instances in their daily lives in which they have recalled and attempted to employ such understandings and strategies.

As with specific therapeutic interventions, the theory of psychotherapeutic change presented is not restricted to particular kinds of clinical assessment procedures but should be used as a guiding framework within which therapists and clients are encouraged to adapt and create both traditional and innovative methods of gauging, monitoring, and evaluating client change as a consequence of clients' participation in psychotherapy. More generally, the ongoing attempt to evaluate therapeutic progress in the context of psychological counseling and therapy should be viewed as an integral part of the therapeutic conversation and intervention. Cooperative attempts by therapists and clients to monitor and evaluate both short-term and long-term effects of their therapeutic work on clients' progress and change can contribute directly to clients' elaboration and revision of their personal theories and to the instantiation of such changes in their lives.

## Conclusions

In this chapter, I presented a theory of psychotherapeutic change grounded in a more general theory of psychological development that incorporates social constructionist thought but still leaves room for the psychological phenomena of agency, intentionality, self, and creativity frequently associated with more cognitive constructivist accounts. Within this theoretical formulation, psychotherapy is seen as a unique form of social conversation and interpersonal activity that attempts to help clients to alter personal theories to permit more effective goal attainment, problem resolution, or personal coping. Psychotherapists work collaboratively with clients to negotiate general therapeutic phases of articulation, elaboration, revision, and instantiation of clients' theories in ways that achieve desired therapeutic ends.

Much of the material in this chapter has benefited from consideration of related theoretical and practical work in psychotherapy by individuals who have adopted one or more constructivistic metaphors. Following Neimeyer (1995), most such metaphors can be subsumed under one or more of five types: (a) therapy as personal science, (b) therapy as the development of self, (c) therapy as conceptual revision, (d) therapy as a kind of narrative reconstruction, and (e) therapy as conversational elaboration. Scholars and practitioners of psychotherapy who have contributed to our understanding of therapeutic change in ways broadly consistent with the foregoing metaphors include Feixas (1990), Guidano (1987, 1991), Howard (1991), Liotti (1986), Lyddon (1995), Mahoney (1980, 1990), Markus and Nurius (1986), Neimeyer and Neimeyer (1987), Penn (1985), Polkinghorne (1988), Procter (1987), and White and Epston (1990). Although the ideas presented here are somewhat unique in combining both constructionist and constructivist metaphors, they clearly have been influenced by the work of these and many other individuals striving to understand the dynamics of human change in the context of psychotherapy.

A great challenge to scholars and practitioners adopting constructionist and constructivist theories and strategies for understanding and conducting psychotherapy is to balance the undeniable potential of clients for constructive change through their reflective capacities as creative agents with the equally undeniable constraints that social circumstances force upon us. By placing undue emphasis on the former, we run the risk of underestimating the constraints of the latter and setting clients up for inevitable disappointment and possible failure. By focusing unduly on the latter, we run the risk of discouraging clients and unnecessarily restricting their capabilities for creative innovation and change. At one extreme are those who favor strongly social constructionistic accounts as a basis for widespread sociocultural change. At the other extreme are those who adopt radically constructivistic viewpoints and place almost total responsibility on individuals to reconstruct the difficult circumstances in which they find themselves. I strongly suspect that discussion relating to these positions will continue to be one of the great conversations of our time. I hope that the kind of synthesis of constructionist and constructivist ideas with which I have been concerned in this chapter may contribute in some measure to a productive, coherent fusion of these quite different viewpoints.

In closing, I realize that the approach to psychotherapeutic practice advocated here may strike some readers as insufficiently specific in a prescriptive sense. As I stated previously, the theory and research discussed are concerned with establishing and describing constructive dynamics and phases of therapeutic change processes and not with establishing the specific effects of particular therapeutic methods. I believe that it simply is not possible, given the highly contextualized nature of human experience and action, to offer instrumental prescriptions for psychotherapeutic practice that assume predictable reactions to particular therapeutic methods across diverse clients and circumstances. To those practitioners who find my descriptions of psychotherapeutic change insufficiently specific to be helpful, I extend the hope that they might be able to create specific, workable ways of employing the templates and understandings offered here in ways that are sensitive to their therapeutic contexts and to the clients with whom they work.

# References

Buirs, R., & Martin, J. (1997). The therapeutic construction of possible selves: Imagination and its constraints. *Journal of Constructivist Psychology, 10*, 153–166.

Derrida, J. (1973). *Speech and phenomena* (D. B. Allison, Trans.). Evanston, IL: Northwestern University Press.

Derrida, J. (1978). *Writing and difference*. (A. Bass, Trans.). Chicago: University of Chicago Press.

Feixas, G. (1990). Personal construct theory and the systemic therapies: Parallel or convergent trends? *Journal of Marital and Family Therapy, 16*, 1–20.

Guidano, V. F. (1987). *Complexity of the self*. New York: Guilford.

Guidano, V. F. (1991). *The self in process*. New York: Guilford.

Howard, G. S. (1991). Culture tales: A narrative approach to thinking, cross-cultural psychology, and psychotherapy. *American Psychologist, 46*, 187–197.

Kelly, G. (1955). *A theory of personality: The psychology of personal constructs*. New York: W. W. Norton.

Liotti, G. (1986). Structural cognitive therapy. In W. Dryden & W. Golden (Eds.), *Cognitive–behavioural approaches to psychotherapy* (pp. 2–128). London: Harper & Row.

Lyddon, W. J. (1995). Forms and facets of constructivist psychology. In R. A. Neimeyer & M. J. Mahoney (Eds.), *Constructivism in psychotherapy* (pp. 69–92). Washington, DC: American Psychological Association.

Mahoney, M. J. (1980). Psychotherapy and the structure of personal revolutions. In M. J. Mahoney (Ed.), *Psychotherapy process* (pp. 157–180). New York: Plenum.

Mahoney, M. J. (1990). *Human change processes*. New York: Basic Books.

Markus, H., & Nurius, P. (1986). Possible selves. *American Psychologist, 41*, 954–969.

Martin, J. (1987). *Cognitive–instructional counseling*. London, ON: Althouse Press.

Martin, J. (1994). *The construction and understanding of psychotherapeutic change: Conversations, memories, and theories*. New York: Teachers College Press.

Martin, J., Cummings, A. L., & Hallberg, E. T. (1992). Therapists' intentional use of metaphor: Memorability, clinical impact, and possible epistemic/motivational functions. *Journal of Consulting and Clinical Psychology, 60*, 143–145.

Martin, J., Paivio, S., & Labadie, D. (1990). Memory-enhancing characteristics of client-recalled important events in cognitive and experiential therapy: Integrating cognitive experimental and therapeutic psychology. *Counselling Psychology Quarterly, 3*, 239–256.

Martin, J., & Stelmaczonek, K. (1988). Participants' identification and recall of important events in counseling. *Journal of Counseling Psychology, 35*, 385–390.

Martin, J., & Sugarman, J. (in press). *The psychology of human possibility and constraint: Bridging social constructionism and cognitive constructivism*. Albany, NY: SUNY Press.

Mead, G. H. (1934). *Mind, self and society*. Chicago: University of Chicago Press.

Neimeyer, R. A. (1995). Constructivist psychotherapies: Features, foundations, and future directions. In R. A. Neimeyer & M. J. Mahoney (Eds.), *Constructivism in psychotherapy* (pp. 11–38). Washington, DC: American Psychological Association.

Neimeyer, R. A., & Neimeyer, G. J. (Eds.). (1987). *Personal construct therapy casebook*. New York:

Springer.

Paivio, A. (1986). *Mental representations: A dual coding approach.* New York: Oxford University Press.

Penn, D. (1985). Feed-forward: Future questions, future maps. *Family Process, 24,* 299–310.

Polkinghorne, D. (1988). *Narrative knowing and the human sciences.* Albany, NY: SUNY Press.

Procter, H. G. (1987). Change in the family construct system. In R. A. Neimeyer & G. J. Neimeyer (Eds.), *Personal construct therapy casebook* (pp. 153–171). New York: Springer.

Vygotsky, L. S. (1986). *Thought and language* (A. Kozulin, Trans.). Cambridge, MA: MIT Press.

White, M., & Epston, D. (1990). *Narrative means to therapeutic ends.* New York: W. W. Norton.

# 19

## Constructivism and the Environment: A Cognitive–Integrative Perspective For Social Work Practice

*Sharon B. Berlin*

For the past several years, I have been working to develop a perspective on social work clinical practice that focuses on the centrality of thinking processes in human functioning—a perspective that recognizes the experience-shaping influences of how one thinks as well as the particular situations and life conditions that one thinks about. My intent has been to move outward from a cognitive base in order to build a framework for practice that acknowledges multiple sources of human problems and multiple avenues for their remediation. The motivation for this work stems in part from my belief that as direct-service practitioners we need a flexible and encompassing theoretical system that helps us think about and work with a wide range of problems—problems that are sometimes clear-cut, often complicated, and usually made up of varying mixtures of personal, interpersonal, and social ingredients.

The cognitive–integrative (C–I) perspective described here is based on the notion that humans are fundamentally *meaning makers*. In our daily lives, we constantly attempt to make sense of and adapt to the events going on around us and within us to do whatever seems in the best interest of our goals and enhances our feelings of security and predictability. We anticipate, arrange, and add to the informational cues generated by interpersonal and other environmental sources and by our own feelings, thoughts, actions, and physiological states. We assume, we expect, we infer—sometimes mindfully or reflectively and often automatically.

This search for meaning is not just a matter of passively picking up, classifying, and storing sensations from the external world. Rather, what we know is a result of our active attempts to respond to environmental challenges. We generate knowledge through active exploration, involving motor activities (moving around, taking different vantage points, trying things out); sensory activities (recognizing sensory regularities); and cognitive activities (making hypotheses about the world and matching our experiences to these expectations) (Guidano, 1995). By anticipating and organizing the cues that we encounter, we not only respond to our environment, but shape the situations to which we respond.

Although we participate actively in constructing our personal realities, we are hardly the sole authors. First, the meanings we assign cannot be independent of the symbols and rules of our culture. Second, environmental events that affect survival, such as cues signaling physical danger or opportunities for bonding, afford similar meanings across cultures. Finally, the families, communities, and opportunity structures into which we are born tell us and show us what things mean and in the process shape our frameworks for understanding. Indeed, physical realities, social structures, and the interpersonal responses of others are ongoing sources of meaning throughout our lives.

In short, the core assumption undergirding the C–I perspective is that all of the important meanings of our lives—who we are, where we stand in relation to others, our prospects and options—are a function of the nature of the information that we encounter and our own patterns or systems for organizing these cues. It follows, then, that in our efforts to help clients change the meanings of their lives, we can differentially focus our attempts on altering the nature of the information available to them (cues stemming from interpersonal interactions, socioenvironmental conditions, and their own specific assessments, emotions, body states, and motor responses) and/or their patterns for formulating meanings.

Although this perspective is intentionally cognitive, it can be distinguished from other cognitive therapies by virtue of three characteristics: (a) an emphasis on social sources of meaning, (b) the integration of several therapeutic approaches for altering the nature of incoming cues, and (c) reliance on memory models for understanding how our minds work to find and protect what is familiar and to develop increased complexity through encounters with discrepancies.

Through its emphasis on the role of social conditions in shaping individual realities and the role of individuals in shaping their social situations, the C–I perspective adheres to ecological principles and metaphors that are central to social work. In addition, it remains faithful to a pragmatic, client-centered, problem-solving approach characteristic of social work practice. Even though the C–I approach builds from a social work perspective and integrates social work strategies, it is distinguishable from prevailing social work intervention systems. For example, on an ideological dimension, the C–I perspective views the person primarily as a *thinker*, as a seeker and creator of meaning. This is in contrast to assumptions that people are fundamentally *doers* and problem-solving actions are the most effective and efficient way to solve difficulties (Epstein, 1992; Reid, 1992); that people are fundamentally *embedded in social systems* and personal change will both require and cause change within one's immediate social system (Germain & Gitterman, 1980); or that people are fundamentally *social creatures* who grow and change in the context of interpersonal relationships (Elson, 1986).

The C–I perspective is consistent with a constructivist metatheory of human knowing, but it also assumes a reality independent of our personal constructions of meaning. On the overall spectrum of constructivist positions, it lies somewhere between critical constructivism (Mahoney, 1991) and modest realism (Held, 1995).

# Memory and Construction of Meaning

If meaning making is a critical adaptive activity, then the literature on memory as generated by the study of social cognition is a critical source for understanding these meaning-making processes. How we draw upon memory patterns of past experiences to classify the present and to imagine the ways that we and our circumstances might be different in the future guides the daily course of our lives. In these terms, we have clear reason for considering what our clients remember about themselves and their options and how they can build on what they know to find and create a more compatible, choice-enhancing reality. Although various memory processes have clear implications for clinical understanding and intervention, this discussion focuses primarily on schematic processes for ordering our experiences.

## *Schematic Ordering Processes*

Because we begin life with a common evolutionary heritage and often grow up and live in similar cultural and physical environments, these organizing processes often generate shared meanings. At the same time, given our individual histories, we often understand similar events differently. For example, given a short deadline, a lot of work to accomplish, and an uncertain outcome, I might fall to pieces and you might relish the challenge. Given a teenager in a family in the full flower of rebelliousness, one parent might delight in the young person's "spunk" while the other parent feels compelled to nip "crime" in the bud. Faced with a mountain of laundry and a sink full of dirty dishes, Ms. X throws herself into a frenzy of work and Ms. Y sinks into bed. We understand things differently. We impose different interpretive patterns (different mental models or different schemata) on similar events. In part, we construct our own experiences.

We enter the world predisposed to search for regularities in our experiences. As these similarities accumulate during the course of our interpersonal encounters, they form the core of a memory system for recognizing ourselves and our place in the world.

*"Poor Judy, she's such a big girl. ... Hard to believe that she is the youngest. Isn't it a shame that Judy has her father's body type?" "Yes, Judy takes after me, we're both on the chunky side." "Judy, stop picking on me. ... It's no fair, you're so big!" "Don't worry about leftovers. Judy will eat them."*

As a result of repeated similar experiences, we learn what to expect, what to do, how to relate to others, and how to understand our own needs and resources. We store these recurring events and situations in memory. As we draw on these memories to understand new events, they become progressively more elaborate and abstract until they operate more as abstract theories or patterns for pulling together information than as memories of specific events or experience. Teasedale and Barnard (1993) explain these organizing systems or schemas in terms of implicit procedural memories of "what goes with what," or as memories for what information bits fit together to make up a meaningful pattern.

Locking my keys in the car on a gray and frigid Chicago day introduces and generates an array of sensory (gray, freezing, windy), verbal (I'll be late, I'll be mugged, how could I be so stupid?), and body-state (frowning, sighing, tensing, shivering) cues that evoke a memory pattern or theme—perhaps the "I am pathetic and can't manage my life" theme. In effect, I "remember" (not consciously) that personal blunders go together with miserable climatic conditions to make up some part of a familiar pattern of self-recrimination and feeling shut down and deenergized. Although our schemas tend to operate automatically apart from our intentions and awareness, by paying attention to our own recurring subjective states we can gauge the themes of meaning that they generate.

Once our memories for cognitive, emotional, and motor patterns have reached this automatic or procedural stage, they are very hard to change. Procedural memories are often described as hierarchies of "condition–action" or "if–then" rules (in constructivist terms, core-ordering rules) that are connected in memory either because they are innate or because of innumerable co-occurrences (Anderson, 1983; Chapter 2). In other words, the more we organize information according to a particular pattern, the more abstract, compact, and automatic that pattern becomes. Once the condition is met, the action (the unfolding of the pattern) follows immediately and without awareness of having thought about anything or applied any organizing schema: "It *is* hopeless." "You *are* a jerk." "I *know exactly* what happened." Subjectively, we believe that we have apprehended the "true" reality. Even in cases in which we are able to see the role we play in forming our own realities, it is often very difficult to get around these proceduralized schematic patterns to make our realities come out any differently. When we try to develop a different pattern of understanding, it often feels like an effortful truth-stretching endeavor. I may say to myself, "This isn't a crisis; so what if I'm late?" but it still *feels* like a crisis. In many instances, we are able to describe an alternative pattern for organizing information. We can put together the concepts about how to think or respond differently but lack the procedural knowledge that instantaneously and automatically pulls together the concepts plus sensory cues plus body-state signals to give us the whole multiinformed feeling of reality.

### Practice Strategies

This difficulty in getting beyond the automatic patterns of memories that are familiar but not adaptive constitutes the main focus of most cognitive practice models. As suggested earlier, schematic patterns can be derailed at two major points. First, it makes sense to change the incoming flow of informational cues that join together to make up a pattern. Several theorists address varying facets of this strategy. Teasedale and Barnard (1993) focus on the change potential of altering the flow of body-state cues, for example, changing one's facial expression from a frown to a half smile in order to feed back a message of relative equanimity instead of discouragement or engaging in vigorous exercise to generate feelings of energy and liveliness. In a classic article, Greenberg and Safran (1981) highlighted the value of reallocating attention to alternative sensory cues in circumventing unwanted patterns, for example, focusing attention on how tired the kids look versus the grating sounds of their whining. We know from Bandura's (1986) work on self-efficacy that problem-solving actions can generate powerful cues for activating the sense of oneself as capable—as a person who can cope with a problem versus a person who is abjectly helpless. Much of the traditional cognitive-therapy literature addresses techniques for helping people change propositional (word-based) appraisals in order to introduce a difference in the mix of activated cues, for example, "This isn't a life-or-death situation; it's just a frustrating situation."

Similarly, it can be useful to search one's memory for feeling elements that can be recruited into an altered pattern, for example, memories of feeling "psyched up" or optimistic or able. Altering the stream of information from life conditions—the daily hassles, intrusive events, and chronic struggles regarding issues such as money, housing, health care, day care, neighborhood crime, and so forth—can also change existing patterns and help develop an alternative framework for understanding problematic situations and events.

It is one thing to block temporarily the flow of information that activates a pattern, but it is another, usually more difficult, enterprise to generate an alternative pattern that seems equally real. Nonetheless, the second main point for intervention is at the level of the schema itself. With this focus, the intent is to replace the maladaptive pattern of organizing informational cues with a more flexible, option-creating alternative. Because it is rarely feasible to go back to ground zero to build up new patterns of procedural knowledge through countless, painstaking repetitions, the pragmatic strategy is to build from what we already know by generalizing from existing procedural knowledge and at the same time introducing critical bits of new information into these old patterns. As suggested by Teasedale and Barnard (1993), one way to introduce new information into familiar core patterns is to alter the values of components in the pattern. For example, in the case of a worried and insecure parent, knowledge that virtually all of the other children in the second grade also have head lice can help transform "I am a horrible parent" feelings into a "such are the trials and tribulations of parenthood" realization. Similarly, substituting the notion that an aversive experience will go away for the feeling that it will last forever could work to block a familiar "depressed and pathetic" schema and replace it with a "having a bad day but rolling with the punches" approach. A similar approach is to change a larger subpattern of elements that are nested into a familiar frame:

> At the schematic model level, elements related to "While I may not be very good at things and often fail, on this occasion I did actually succeed" may enable the evidence of successful achievement to be bound in with the remaining elements to create a modified schematic model. (Teasedale & Barnard, 1993, p. 72)

In this example, the elements "I may not be very good . . . and often fail" serve as discriminating markers. In other words, they are recognizable parts of a familiar pattern and can activate the pattern despite evidence indicating "I did actually succeed." With the pattern activated and the discrepancies linked in, the pattern is different; one has a different sense of self and circumstances. The key therapeutic maneuver is to introduce deviations from the dominating schema that are "true enough" or "nonthreatening enough" to be accepted but nevertheless critically different.

Another strategy for building alternatives without running headlong into existing patterns is to focus on creating and enhancing memories for positive possibilities: "Sure, this is the way things are now and this is the way you see yourself now, but what if . . . ?" The subset of memories that represent possibilities that we are able to imagine for ourselves—our hopes, potentials, desires, plans, and goals—are among our most malleable self-conceptions. With attention, elaboration, and practice, they can develop into alternative schematic structures (Markus & Nurius, 1986). Although our visions of possibility are derived from the kinds of hopes and goals that our past experiences allow us, in some ways these possible selves transcend our past and current selves. They allow us to work on ourselves with at least some freedom from current constraints, while simultaneously making an independent contribution to our adjustment and sense of well-being in the here and now (Markus, Cross, & Wurf, 1990).

The more we reflect on and respond emotionally to the attractive details of specific possibilities, the more elaborate, vivid, compelling, and accessible these conceptions of possibility become. And so we might say to a client, "Well, think a little more about it. What would be good about taking charge in your family (or taking the LPN course or being more assertive with your co-workers)?" The practitioner might offer paraphrases and responses to clients' accounts that add visual and emotional vividness. "Right. I can almost see you at graduation, walking across the stage to get your diploma, with your family wildly clapping and cheering."

In addition to helping clients strengthen the pull of their positive goals via anticipation, by assisting them to plan strategies for achieving their goals and to conduct mental and behavioral simulations of both the outcome and necessary subtasks along the way, practitioners can also help clients gain the expertise to do what is needed. As they imagine and practice the thoughts, emotions, images, motor behaviors, and likely social interactions that make up the desired outcome, clients begin to create the memory pathways that eventually will generate the actual outcomes.

> O.K., let's fill this out a little bit. You kind of like the idea of being on your own, living in your own apartment, fixing things up just the way you want them. Tell me more about this little nest you want to make for yourself. It sounds good—cozy, inviting, just the kind of place you'd like to come home to after a hard day. Can you see that—coming in the door and immediately feeling that you are home, comfortable, safe, relaxed? So how about finding the place, looking at "for rent" ads, calling landlords, tromping around the city looking for places? Can you imagine doing it? Shall we work out the plan?

Another strategy is to encourage clients to organize these details in story form (Bruner, 1990). By creating a narrative of how things might happen, clients fill in the temporal links and causal sequences that can "make the hypothetical come true" (Fiske, 1993).

*Tell me the story again, the story of a woman who is determined to take care of herself. And this time, add the part about how she does it even when she is lonely and feeling blue.*

Overall, increasing evidence suggests that the larger our repertoires of self-schemas—our memory patterns for organizing our sense of self—the larger the range of options we have to draw upon in locating adaptive responses to life circumstances (Nurius & Berlin, 1993; Stein & Markus, 1994). To the extent that we are able to think about ourselves as having a wide variety of traits, roles, abilities, and possibilities, we increase our potential for generating flexible responses to events and situations (Stein, 1994). In contrast to the widespread view that the various facets of self should be well-integrated in order to provide a sense of personal coherence, new research findings suggest that independent patterns for understanding ourselves allow us to compartmentalize problems. Think for a moment about the client who defines herself as a student. If this student role is her primary source of identity, when she encounters disappointment as a student, she is likely to feel as if her whole self has been negatively affected. Similarly, if she sees herself as a student, a teaching assistant, and an aspiring researcher and all of these attributes are interconnected in her student schema, these identity aspects are also vulnerable to disappointment. On the other hand, by understanding herself on multiple dimensions that operate as separate or at least semiseparate interests, commitments, and talents (e.g., student, avid gardener, Sunday school teacher, softball player, great friend), a downturn in one area of her life is less likely to wash over her entire being. She can still see herself as viable in other areas. In other words, if our various self-schemas are not closely interconnected, we should be able to access some parts of ourselves that are not impaired by current difficulties (Stein & Markus, 1994). Thus clients can be helped to expand the ways that they experience themselves and to separate out the parts of the self that are strong and worthy.

## Integrating Theories and Therapeutic Models

The integrative character of the C–I practice perspective occurs in two major ways. First, the theoretical framework is an amalgam of ideas taken from various sources, including social cognition, cognitive developmental psychology, cognitive conceptions of personality, social learning theory, personal construct theory, theories of emotion, object relations theories, constructivist views on human change processes, cognitive psychotherapies, and social work perspectives on problem solving and on the nature of person–environment interactions. Second, given the wide range of potential change targets that are addressed, the C–I perspective draws intervention guidance from several approaches (e.g., interpersonal, narrative, experiential, behavioral, psychodynamic, social environmental), each of which is designed to focus on a particular information domain.

Rather than simply throwing together bits and pieces from other models, the C–I perspective fits several approaches into one unifying framework by suggesting that they serve the common goal of introducing new data that can be synthesized into new meanings. Multiple intervention models are used differentially to generate the cues that can open up new perspectives and options for the client. For example, the C–I framework suggests that when clients' difficulties seem to be a function of oppressive social circumstances, social work knowledge can be used to intervene with the immediate social environment. Similarly, if the delimiting information results from family disorganization and demanding interpersonal relationships, then family systems approaches are a good resource for determining how to craft intervention specifically aimed at these relationships and conditions.

## Social Sources of Meaning and Constructive Models of Change

Like other cognitive and constructive therapies, the C–I perspective acknowledges that we superimpose our predictions and assumptions onto the events and encounters in our lives. We interpret them, add to them, and sometimes precipitate them. But what about the events themselves? Are they essentially void of information until the active, inquiring mind shapes them into meaning? The C–I perspective assumes that meaning exists independent of our own constructive activities.

We live our lives within a system of socially constructed institutions, rules, and relationships that in some sense provide us with a set of prestructured meanings—a social reality that we can conform to, rebel against, or understand in our idiosyncratic ways but that we cannot completely escape or ignore. Our early social experiences form the foundation of our developing mental structures. Regardless of the self-definitions we incorporate in childhood, our evolving sense of ourselves and our prospects can be made better or worse as a result of the ongoing conditions of our lives. And although these ongoing conditions may also be shaped to some degree by our personal interpretations, in many instances the influences of social structures, physical conditions, or chance events on personal meanings seem more powerful.

No one travels through life unscathed, but the mix of positive and negative events and conditions that people encounter varies. These events and conditions are not completely the result of our own doing and are not always responsive to our efforts to change them. In fact, person–environment interactions are often characterized by a power imbalance. For example, we can be more assertive with the receptionist in the emergency room and perhaps be seen ahead of someone else, but we are powerless to change the fact that the emergency room is understaffed and long waits are inevitable. We can attempt to calm ourselves, adjust our expectations, and thus reduce the stress of waiting, but we nevertheless must wait. We can be more frugal with our AFDC check, but regardless of how we cut back on expenses or how we work to minimize the effect of poverty on our self-esteem, we still may not have enough money to pay for child care.

Thus, despite our cognitive constructions, we do not always have, indeed, we rarely have, ultimate control over the outcomes of events in our lives. At the same time, we always have some influence based on our resources and the self- and social definitions that we and those we interact with employ. As practitioners, instead of focusing virtually all our interventive efforts on helping individuals alter the ways in which they organize their experiences (as most cognitive and constructive therapies seem to do), we should also invest creative energy in understanding the nature and meaning of incoming environmental cues. We will not always know how to or have the power to change the social conditions that affect clients' lives, but at least we will not imply to the client that "it's all in your mind."

In many respects, these ideas conform to the position of critical constructivism. Unlike more radical constructivist views that assert that all experience of order is self-generated, critical constructivists acknowledge that the events and conditions of the external world constrain our cognitive formulations to the extent that only a range of interpretation will fit external reality or be viable (see Chapter 1; Mahoney, 1991). The key issue, then, is not the ultimate validity of what we believe (which is probably unknowable), but rather whether our personal constructions are pragmatically useful in charting and maintaining an adaptive course. This acknowledgment—that at least on some level the environment matters—makes it worth our while to explore the ways in which constructive approaches to individual change might enlarge our understanding of clients' dilemmas and help us do better social work. Even though critical constructivists affirm a relationship of reciprocal influence between the person and his or her social and physical environments, this recognition rarely takes a prominent place in actual practice. For the most part, cognitive and constructive therapies seem to focus a lot of attention on the nature of individuals' core ordering processes and relatively little attention on the nature of the information—especially information about social conditions—that they are trying to order.

## Empirical and Practical Warrant

Postmodernism confronts us with multiple realities, social and personal constructions of meaning, and the upending of timeless truth. So given this relativity, how do we know what approaches are worth trying in our attempts to help clients? Consistent with the times, it seems reasonable to search for multiple sources of information about the effects of our work.

### *Is Our Work Useful to the Client?*

In terms of the C–I perspective, the first consideration is the extent to which this approach is useful in opening up new options and possibilities for clients. In other words, do they see it more as a generative resource or as a hindrance? It is one (presumably good) thing if a worker is able to use this perspective to expand his or her understanding of the client's problems and to generate interventions that are productive, but it is even better if the client can also use the perspective as a resource for developing a useful way to think about and approach his or her ongoing life struggles. Like all theoretical frameworks, the C–I approach is most useful when it makes sense to the client. The framework that we employ to organize our work needs to be flexible enough to be understandable to the client on some level and to support what he or she already knows about creating change. Although the C–I perspective is meant to be flexible, it is safe to say that its range of application is not limitless. Not every worker or client will find it useful.

In this regard, the C–I perspective is clearly most appropriate for informing interventions regarding problems that are most directly addressed at the person level. Beyond that, it fits best with problems that are at least partly influenced by the person's patterns for organizing meaning and with people who can eventually see the role that their own patterns of understanding play in influencing problems and solutions and who find that understanding useful. The main strength of the C–I perspective lies in the guidance it gives to sorting through problems perpetuated by complicated person–environment interactions. Commonly, these are interactions in which difficult life circumstances activate narrow, outmoded, and limiting patterns for organizing information, which in turn perpetuate, if not exacerbate, the difficulties. As an adjunct to other services or approaches and at a more general level, the utility of the C–I approach is much broader. For example, in many situations work is focused primarily on teaching/learning behavioral skills or on attaining social resources. Nevertheless, the practitioner also relies on C–I guidelines to help the client transpose improvements into more stable self-conceptions. Moreover, at a metatheoretical level, this framework can help us understand a broad range of person–environment interactions. Regardless of the kind of social work we are doing, it is potentially illuminating to consider the reality-creating exchanges of information that occur between a person and the array of people who make up family, neighborhood, community, and institutional or cultural environments.

## *Do Systematic Observations Support the C–I's Efficacy?*

Repeated systematic observations showing patterns of change or relationships between interventions and outcomes provide another way to assess the utility of the C–I perspective. Controlled studies do not and are not meant to pin down unswerving, universal truth. By clearly describing the clients who make up study samples, specifying interventions and indicators of change, recognizing that outcomes may have alternative explanations and trying to account for at least some of them, and giving credence to findings that have been replicated, systematic investigations give us the means to gauge the limitations of our studies.

Various studies show that cognitive strategies are helpful in resolving various mental health problems, particularly problems of depression and anxiety (Robins & Hayes, 1995). More directly, the C–I perspective has received modest empirical support from tests of early iterations of the model. These studies suggest that attending to multiple sources of information as well as schematic models for organizing meanings helps reduce excessive self-criticism and mild to moderate depression among women (Berlin, 1980, 1985), that teaching women the principles of cognitive coping adds to the longevity of their treatment gains (Berlin, 1985), and that women who are subject to the most distressing social circumstances make the least progress in an approximation of C–I therapy (Berlin, Mann, & Grossman, 1991).

Many more empirical questions should be asked. Critical among these is the question of the *relative* benefits of social and cognitive interventions. If a client's difficulties seem largely supported by miserable social conditions, does adding cognitive interventions to a social intervention program provide additional benefits? For example, do they help clients incorporate new experiences into their patterns for organizing their sense of self?

## Strengths and Limitations

A main strength of the C–I perspective is the potential depth and breadth of its focus. At a fundamental level, it addresses how experiences are organized via memory. In addition, it provides guidance regarding how to insert new information into old patterns. By borrowing strategies and techniques from other intervention models, the C–I approach also focuses on creating new information (e.g., new skills, relationship patterns, social resources, motivations, emotions). Given this scope, the C–I perspective can be used to address a range of problems at varying levels of complexity. An additional strength is its recognition that circumstances—social structures, relationships, and chance events—also contribute to meaning. Although critical constructivists are likely to accept this notion, most constructive and cognitive therapies do little to operationalize it by developing and targeting interventions to alter social circumstances.

In considering how to avoid, replace, or buffer the negative messages that stem from demeaning, disorganized, and dangerous life conditions, the C–I perspective draws on the best of social work practice knowledge but adds little new knowledge to social intervention technology. The C–I perspective relies on social work models for guidance about how to generate resources, make good referrals, link people to social supports, involve clients in organized efforts toward neighborhood or community improvement, and advocate on behalf of clients. To this body of knowledge, the C–I perspective adds strategies to assist clients in noticing, using, and finding meaning in new opportunities. At a time when opportunities and resources for poor and working-class people are dwindling, social workers have become increasingly aware of the limitations of tools for reversing such trends and for buffering their effects.

## Summary

As the influence of postmodern ideologies of constructivism and social constructionism continues to spread and draw our attention to the relativity of reality, we need to avoid assuming that individuals are at complete liberty to model and remodel their life experience. Although as practitioners we want to help our clients find more adaptive interpretations of debilitating life situations, it is important to recognize with them that real obstacles and constraints exist.

Taking a critical constructivist perspective, the C–I approach to social work direct practice views people as actively exploring, anticipating, assuming, and interacting in order to formulate meaning. To create meaning, we rely on memory frameworks for organizing available cues. In large part, we develop these frameworks, or schematic models, through social learning. Experience shapes cognitive schemas and cognitive schemas shape experience to the extent that it is often difficult, if not impossible, to separate the part of our experience that is the result of our systems for understanding from that which is imposed by external situations. Nonetheless, the C–I perspective assumes that external social and physical reality contributes to our experiences and constrains the range of viable meanings that we can construct. In short, the meanings that we formulate are a function both of the nature of the information that is available to us and of the frameworks we have developed to anticipate and organize it.

The C–I perspective looks to other intervention models for guidance about how to alter various kinds of personal, interpersonal, and social information. At the same time, it also draws from the study of social cognition—how people think about themselves and their social interactions—for knowledge regarding memory processes involved in developing and altering patterns of thinking. Although some of our memory patterns for organizing information about ourselves are inherited, for the most part these patterns or schematic models are based on numerous repetitions of similar interpersonal exchanges and feelings. When our memories of patterns reach the automatic or procedural stage and constituent bits of information are picked up by the sensory-perceptual system, the thinking–feeling–acting patterns operate automatically—even when they are not adaptive. Finding ways to build on or reduce the influence of these maladaptive patterns is a major challenge.

In general, interventions to alter meanings should be differentially focused on generating information that contradicts restrictive ways of understanding and opens new options and/or on altering how information is organized and understood. Decisions about focus are based on explorations of the client's goals and strengths and on an analysis of the contributors to his or her current difficulty. For example, are the maladaptive meanings primarily a function of missing skills, interpersonal impasses, blocked feelings, or missing goods and services and can they be altered by addressing one or some of these sources of information? Alternatively, are the person's schematic patterns for organizing information so fixed or unidimensional—or tied into a feedback cycle of generating information that reactivates the problematical pattern—that meaningful change requires a shift at the schematic level? Although meaning-making systems and information provide two major foci for intervention, as we fit this model to the nuances of preferences and problems expressed by our clients, these points of attention combine in various ways.

Understanding how memory processes operate suggests several avenues for helping people create, pay attention to, and use the informational cues that can give rise to more adaptive meanings, even if they don't quite fit with their expectations and assumptions. This chapter briefly outlined a few strategies to illustrate how one might go about the process of introducing different sensory, body-state, thought, or social cues into existing schematic patterns. In assisting the evolution of meaning, difference needs to be introduced in ways that build on what the client already knows and that are acceptable to existing patterns, while simultaneously altering them.

The C–I framework modifies traditional cognitive approaches by expanding their scope and utility. Notwithstanding its potential for addressing a range of problems at varying levels of complexity, it remains an individual-centered approach. Although it adds to social work intervention knowledge regarding helping clients attend to and use different kinds of information, it adds little to one's knowledge about how to generate alternative social information that conveys to clients that life conditions are better now.

# References

Anderson, J. R. (1983). *The architecture of cognition*. Cambridge, MA: Harvard University Press.

Bandura, A. (1986). *Social foundations of thought and action: A social cognitive theory*. Englewood Cliffs, NJ: Prentice-Hall.

Berlin, S. B. (1980). Cognitive–behavioral intervention for problems of self-criticism among women. *Social Work Research and Abstracts, 16*(4), 19–28.

Berlin, S. B. (1985). The effect of relapse prevention on the durability of self-criticism problem change. *Social Work Research and Abstracts, 21*(1), 21–33.

Berlin, S. B., Mann, K. B., & Grossman, S. F. (1991). Task-analysis of cognitive therapy for depression. *Social Work Research and Abstracts, 27*(2), 3–11.

Bruner, J. (1990). *Acts of meaning*. Cambridge, MA: Harvard University Press.

Elson, M. (1986). *Self-psychology in clinical social work*. New York: W. W. Norton.

Epstein, L. (1992). *Brief treatment and a new look at the task-centered approach*. New York: Macmillan.

Fiske, S. T. (1993). Social cognition and social perception. In L. W. Porter & M. R. Rosenzweig (Eds.), *Annual review of psychology* (Vol. 44, pp. 155–194). Palo Alto, CA: Annual Reviews.

Germain, C. B., & Gitterman, A. (1980). *The life model of social work practice*. New York: Columbia University Press.

Greenberg, L. S., & Safran, J. D. (1981). Encoding and cognitive therapy: Changing what clients attend to. *Psychotherapy: Theory, Research, and Practice, 18*, 163–168.

Guidano, V. F. (1995). A constructivist outline of human knowing processes. In M. J. Mahoney (Ed.), *Cognitive and constructive psychotherapies: Theory, research, and practice* (pp. 89–102). New York: Springer.

Held, B. S. (1995). *Back to reality: A critique of postmodern theory in psychotherapy*. New York: W. W. Norton.

Mahoney, M. J. (1991). *Human change processes: The scientific foundation of psychotherapy*. New York: Basic Books.

Markus, H., Cross, S., & Wurf, E. (1990). The role of the self-system in competence. In R. J. Steinberg & J. Kolligan, Jr. (Eds.), *Competence considered*. New Haven, CT: Yale University Press.

Markus, H., & Nurius, P. S. (1986). Possible selves. *American Psychologist, 41*, 954–969.

Nurius, P. S., & Berlin, S. B. (1993). Treatment of negative self-concept and depression. In D. K. Granvold (Ed.), *Cognitive and behavioral treatment: Methods and applications* (pp. 247–271). Pacific Grove, CA: Brooks/Cole.

Reid, W. J. (1992). *Task strategies: An empirical approach to clinical social work*. New York: Columbia University Press.

Robins, C. J., & Hayes, A. M. (1995). An appraisal of cognitive therapy. In M. J. Mahoney (Ed.), *Cognitive and constructive psychotherapies: Theory, research, and practice* (pp. 41–66). New York: Springer.

Stein, K. F. (1994). Complexity of the self-schema and responses to disconforming feedback. *Cognitive Therapy and Research, 18*, 161–178.

Stein, K. F., & Markus, H. R. (1994). The organization of the self: An alternative focus for psychopathology and behavior change. *Journal of Psychotherapy Integration, 4*, 317–353.

Teasedale, J. D., & Barnard, P. J. (1993). *Affect, cognition, and change: Re-modeling depressive thought*. East Sussex, England: Lawrence Erlbaum.

# Afterword

## Progress in Constructivist Practice: A Concluding Note

*Paula S. Nurius and Cynthia Franklin*

This volume traces developments and distinctions in constructivist and constructionist theory as well as examines a broad array of practice applications across multiple levels—individuals, families, groups, organizations, and communities. The application of constructivist and social constructionist theory to communities and organizational practice represents a particularly exciting effort.

This collection strives to reflect contemporary practice in its complexity, addressing, for example, issues in the context of managed care, practical constraints affecting organizations and systems of care, and practice under the pressures of accountability and few resources. This volume brings together several proponents of constructive theory from social work and allied disciplines such as psychology and family therapy. Constructivism in practice is an interesting phenomenon in that it is emerging as a popular metaframework and metaphor for clinical practice during a time when we see important paradigmatic shifts and challenges in the social sciences and services and, simultaneously, in practice communities facing demands for specificity and accountability. This juxtaposition of restraints from managed behavioral health care organizations and other funders to demonstrate and use empirically based practice methods accentuates the need to move from abstract discussions to specific practice contexts, from bifurcations to creative synthesis.

Debates and discussions about constructivism are evident in diverse literatures of therapy: family therapy, mental health counseling, social work, and counseling psychology (Anderson & Goolishian, 1988; Cushman, 1990; Ellis, 1996; Guterman, 1994; Harrison, Hudson, & Thyer, 1992; Held, 1995; Hoffman, 1990; Martin, Cummings, & Hallberg, 1992; Martin, Pavio, & Labadie, 1990; Polkinghorne, 1994; Witkin, 1991). Some authors contrast newer constructivist psychotherapeutic approaches with prior approaches by using abstract language such as postmodernist versus modernist, constructivist versus rationalist, and empirical practice versus heuristics.

This move toward constructive metatheory is particularly noteworthy in the cognitive–behavioral therapies, which are well positioned to integrate constructivist practice theory with their historical emphasis on defining and researching the effectiveness of practice methods. As the chapters in this volume demonstrate, many proponents of cognitive theory and therapy focus on or incorporate the newer practice methods drawn from constructivist thought.

This volume starts the process of defining constructive methods and discussing their research basis. We find it interesting, however, that at a time when practitioners could benefit financially from emphasizing more prescriptive "tried and true" approaches, theorists and practitioners from different camps have nearly in unison become intensely interested in process-oriented, constructive, and reflexive approaches to conceptualizing practice. It makes us ask why people from different backgrounds and perspectives become enamored with constructivism and social constructionism. A preoccupation with social constructionism and constructivism may reflect, as has been suggested by Hoffman (1995), a return to the client-centered perspectives of the former humanistic psychologies. Or, as discussed in this volume by Franklin (Chapter 3), it may reflect a move toward diverse belief systems and a need for practitioners to update models to meet the demands of new epistemologies and a new philosophy of science. Or perhaps it goes further and relates to cultural revolutions and fundamental change in our perspectives of ourselves and the world (Anderson, 1990; Cushman, 1995; Gergen, 1991). Of course, if the latter is the case, will these cultural changes finally overtake and also change the business practices of therapy?

Constructive theory has gained recognition for different reasons among diverse groups. In social work, for example, use of social constructionism reflects a focus on the application of more diverse research methods (e.g., interpretive paradigms), a reemphasis on client strengths and empowerment, and a continuing search for a theoretical base for social work practice that meets the demands of complexity of our person-in-environment perspectives as well as matches the values base of our social action and sociopolitical orientation to practice. Some social work authors interpret information from the tenets of the psychological sciences as a venue for introducing new perspectives using constructive theory as part of the repertoire of social work practice (Berlin, 1996; Brower & Nurius, 1993; Nurius, in press; Nurius & Berlin, 1995). In family therapy, newer social constructionist perspectives represent a move away from machine models and an acceptance of a more client-centered, reflexive, and cultural basis for family processes and change.

In cognitive–behavioral traditions within psychology, constructive theory represents an evolution in psychological theory in which theorists such as Guidano (1991), Mahoney (1991), Mahoney and Lyddon (1988), Martin (1994), and Meichenbaum (1993) have interpreted newer perspectives from basic research within psychology. For at least some, the response to this information was enthusiastic, and theorists and practitioners moved toward developing practice models and methods that matched this information. We are not very far along in that process, however. These constructive practice methods are on the fringe in the same way cognitive–behavioral therapies whose perspectives also emerged from experimental psychology and basic science were on the fringe (Franklin & Jordan, 1996). Others within psychology are attempting to advance constructive theory in the traditions of Adler (1959) and Kelly (1955).

Different practice fields (e.g., social work, family therapy, cognitive therapy) also utilize constructive theories, although from different orientations. Cognitive therapy relies on the experimental research traditions and advances in systems theory. Family therapy relies on the humanities, postmodern philosophers, deconstructionism, and sociology and social psychology writers such as Gergen to ground their constructionist practices. Social work, on the other hand, uses a more eclectic approach and relates the development of constructive theory and methods to the debates about research methods and philosophy of science issues. Each field brings unique strengths and con-